East-West
Business Transactions

edited by
Robert Starr

The Praeger Special Studies program—
utilizing the most modern and efficient book
production techniques and a selective
worldwide distribution network—makes
available to the academic, government, and
business communities significant, timely
research in U.S. and international economic, social, and political development.

East-West Business Transactions

PRAEGER SPECIAL STUDIES IN INTERNATIONAL ECONOMICS AND DEVELOPMENT

Praeger Publishers   New York   Washington   London

Library of Congress Cataloging in Publication Data

Starr, Robert.
    East-West business transactions.

    (Praeger special studies in international economics
and development)
    Bibliography: p.
    1. Commercial policy. 2. Foreign trade regula-
tion. 3. East-West trade (1945-   ) I. Title.
HF1411.S796   382'.09171'301717   73-21469
ISBN 0-275-28870-6

PRAEGER PUBLISHERS
111 Fourth Avenue, New York, N.Y. 10003, U.S.A.
5, Cromwell Place, London SW7 2JL, England

Published in the United States of America in 1974
by Praeger Publishers, Inc.

Many persons have kindly offered assistance or advice in connection with the preparation of this study, including W. E. Butler, London; E. J. Cohn, London; Sumio Iijima, Tokyo; P. Kahn, Dijon; D. Lasok, Exeter; Noritaka Moriuchi, Tokyo; J. Sereghyova, Prague; Zh. Stalev, Sofia; B. Vukmir, Zagreb; J. P. Waehler, Hamburg; and W. J. Wagner, Detroit.

Heartfelt appreciation is expressed to J. D. M. Lew, and C. A. Rathkopf, Jr, who provided supporting assistance in many ways.

Without wishing to neglect the contributions of others, I owe special thanks to my colleagues in the Law Office Frank Boas, who uncomplainingly allowed the book to intrude upon their lives, and especially to Anne Björck for her patient labors—notably in transforming seemingly endless drafts of often illegible script.

Finally, I wish to thank the contributing authors, without whom the undertaking of the book would have remained an unfulfilled aspiration.

R.S.

CONTENTS

ix

The strategic controls and other restrictions on East-West trade established by the United States and other Western nations have been liberalized to permit relatively free trade with communist nations in most goods and technologies. Yet, some Western companies appear reluctant even to explore trade opportunities with state-planned systems. They may be put off by a variety of factors—for example, lack of adequate data on countries with state-planned economies and foreign trade opportunities in those countries; the need to deal with state monopolies over foreign trade and difficulties in identifying "ultimate users"; restrictions on entry, travel, and maintenance of offices and facilities in some countries; concern about protection of industrial property rights; and reports of difficulties other firms have encountered in obtaining full payment in hard currency.

Such concerns are frequently unjustified and may be overcome by the persevering businessman. Acceptable contract clauses can usually be obtained through resolute, if protracted, negotiations.

Although East-West trade relations have entered an era of dynamic expansion, there is a remarkable paucity of legal materials available on the subject and great uncertainty as to the detailed legal ground rules for doing business with state trading nations—particularly for entering into the more sophisticated legal relationships that extend beyond the simple sale or purchase of goods and services, such as agreements involving technology transfers, long-term agreements for scientific, technical, and industrial cooperation, and even investment joint ventures in certain Eastern European countries. It is hoped that this book will shed light on some of the legal problems that arise in these various areas.

Since the field of East-West trade and investment is a rapidly evolving one, any attempt at this stage to draw up a definitive, encyclopedic catalogue of its legal aspects would be hazardous and of questionable value. If the present book is of assistance to those concerned with the legal aspects of East-West trade and offers guidance for further study and research, it will have fulfilled its objectives.

The contributing authors to the present study are from a number of different countries, both East and West, and their chapters reflect both similarities and differences of style and treatment, and to some extent divergent perspectives of those in market-economy and state-planned systems. If East-West trade and investment is to reach full potential, it will be necessary to understand such divergencies, to

xiii

transcend ideology and to accommodate the essential interests on both sides.

There is no point in pretending that differences do not exist. Although the editor has not sought to "homogenize" the various contributions to this study—for this would have constituted unnecessary and excessive zeal—the reader will observe a common plan and thread to the over-all study, and will come upon frequent references to complementary discussion in other chapters.

Part I is designed to provide a comparative analysis of the regulatory framework for East-West transactions that has been established by representative market economy countries with a particularly active role in East-West trade—the United States, Japan, and two members of the European Community (the Federal Republic of Germany, an original member, and the United Kingdom, a member since January 1973). There is a separate chapter on the European Community. Each of the "country profiles" in Part I contains discussion of national export regulations, credit programs and restrictions, import controls, and other pertinent aspects of the regulatory framework for the conduct of the respective national trade with the USSR, Eastern Europe, and China. The chapter on the European Community indicates the areas in which Community law and programs have supplanted national ones in this regard.

Part II begins with an analysis of the role of the Council for Mutual Economic Assistance (Comecon), since the activities of Comecon are of increasing importance to trade between its members and third countries. Subsequent chapters in Part II contain "country profiles" of the foreign trade regimes in each of the member countries of Comecon. Also included in Part II are separate chapters on the foreign trade regimes of Yugoslavia (whose economy has departed furthest from the planned features of the other countries covered by this study) and China.

The Chapters in Part II contain discussion of the political and constitutional principles underlying each country's foreign trade; the principal organizational features of its foreign trade regime and the role of foreign trade planning; procedures and practices with respect to such matters as access to the local market by foreign businessmen, establishing local offices, and engaging the services of local agents; foreign-trade contracting and scope for freedom of contract; protections accorded to industrial property rights, and rules and practices with respect to transfer of technology by licensing; policies regarding the conclusion of industrial cooperation agreements with Western firms; and foreign trade dispute settlement machinery' and practices. In the case of three countries (Yugoslavia, Hungary, and Romania) the discussion includes an examination of recent legislation and practices with respect to the establishment in these countries of equity-type joint ventures between local and foreign capital in productive enterprises.

The chapters in Part III examine certain functional aspects of East-West transactions of current and general interest. There are comparative analyses of protection of industrial property rights, and of the scope for equity-type investments in joint ventures in Eastern countries, and an inquiry into the role of arbitration in settling East-West trade disputes.

Of course, each of the authors has stressed matters of particular interest, and the reader will find that some topics are considered in far greater depth than others. The subject matter of this volume is so broad that it would have taken many volumes to assure truly exhaustive analysis of the many issues covered here. Indeed, publishing considerations forced the editor to eliminate several additional chapters planned for inclusion in this volume, to restrict the discussion in a number of the chapters included here, and to defer consideration of plans for a companion volume of source materials.

It is hoped, nonetheless, that the reader will find the present volume helpful, for the questions raised and the assistance it may provide for further research, rather than for definitive treatment of all issues.

Finally, it should be noted that although the editor has offered comment and suggestions to the contributing authors, the authors are solely responsible for their respective contributions.

London, England

Robert Starr

I

REGULATION OF EAST-WEST BUSINESS TRANSACTIONS BY MARKET-ECONOMY COUNTRIES

THE UNITED STATES
Thomas W. Hoya

In few areas of U.S. foreign economic policy has recent change been as rapid as in the regulation of East-West trade. From the end of World War II to 1969 the regulation was strict, as the U. S. Government sought to deny Cold War adversaries any significant economic benefit from trading with the United States. Then in 1969 a period of progressive relaxation of this regulation began. Congress passed the moderately liberal Export Administration Act of 1969, and the Nixon Administration ended the trade blockade of the People's Republic of China in 1971 and signed a trade agreement with the Soviet Union in 1972.

The regulatory picture that has emerged combines elements of continued strict control with new more moderate provisions.[1] In their most severe form, the controls include an embargo on trade with Cuba, North Korea, and North Vietnam. For the European communist countries and the People's Republic of China, U.S. exports are regulated mainly through export licensing and restrictions on the extension of credit. Imports from these nonembargoed countries are limited chiefly through the denial of most-favored-nation treatment (MFN) to most of them.

Thomas W. Hoya is acting deputy chief counsel, Office of Foreign Direct Investments, U.S. Department of Commerce, Washington, D.C. The views expressed here are the author's and do not necessarily reflect those of any government agency. The author expresses appreciation to the Columbia Journal of Transnational Law for permission to draw upon his article "The Changing U.S. Regulation of East-West Trade," which appeared in 12 Colum. J. Transnat'l L. 1-38 (1973).

THE EMBARGO

After Chinese troops entered the Korean War in 1950, the Truman Administration issued the Foreign Assets Control Regulations to prohibit unlicensed commercial and financial transactions with the People's Republic of China and North Korea.[2] In 1964, the Johnson Administration extended the scope of these Regulations to include North Vietnam.[3] Similar regulations, the Cuban Assets Control Regulations, were issued by the Kennedy Administration in 1963 to apply to Cuba.[4] Issuance of each of these embargo regulations was based on the authority given the president by the Trading with the Enemy Act of 1917, as amended.[5] Commercial and financial transactions with these four communist countries have been almost completely eliminated by the regulations, since almost no such transactions have been licensed.[6]

In June 1971, however, the Nixon Administration ended the embargo for the People's Republic of China.[7] U.S. trade with this country is now subject primarily to the export, credit, and import restrictions described below that apply to U.S. trade with the European communist countries.[8]

EXPORT REGULATION: LICENSING AND CREDIT RESTRICTIONS; AGRICULTURAL, SHIPPING, INVESTMENT, AND OTHER PROGRAMS

For U.S. exports to communist countries other than North Korea, North Vietnam, and Cuba, the basic regulations are export licensing and credit restrictions. Through export licensing, presently authorized by the Export Administration Act of 1969,[9] the U.S. government directly prohibits the export of many products to communist countries. Through credit restriction, financing by the Export-Import Bank is frequently barred and credit extension by private American parties is often limited in transactions involving communist countries.

Export Licensing[10]

The extensive U.S. World War II controls over exports were continued from year to year[11] until enactment of the Export Control Act of 1949.[12] This act became the basis for postwar control of exports and remained in force for 20 years.[13] It was finally replaced by the somewhat more liberal Export Administration Act of 1969.[14]

Essentially, under both the Export Control Act and the Export Administration Act, every export of goods or technical data from the United States to any country of the world (generally excepting

Canada) requires an export license.[15] Under the present act this export control is to be used (1) to protect the national security; (2) to further U.S. foreign policy and fulfill America's international responsibilities; and (3) to protect the domestic economy from shortages and from the inflationary impact of abnormal foreign demand.[16] The national security purpose far outweighs the other two in the administration of export licensing.

The availability of an export license for a particular export depends principally on the type of goods or data to be exported and on the country of destination. Many types of goods and technical data may be exported to Eastern Europe, the Soviet Union, and now the People's Republic of China under a general authorization to export known as a "General License." For an export made under a General License, the exporter need not apply for or obtain a formal document from the government. When, however, an export cannot be made under a General License, because of the strategic nature of the goods or data involved or because of the country of destination, the exporter must apply for and obtain a formal document called a "Validated License."

In order to determine whether a given export may be shipped under a General License or whether it requires a Validated License, and, if the latter, whether a Validated License will be issued, different communist countries are treated differently. To implement the Export Administration Act, the government divides the world into seven country groups. North Vietnam, North Korea, and Cuba constitute one country group, which is subject to an almost total embargo under the act in an overlapping with the Foreign Assets Control Regulations and with the Cuban Assets Control Regulations. (These Assets Control Regulations prohibit unlicensed exports from the United States to these three countries but license generally any such export if it is licensed under the Export Administration Act.[17] Such licenses under the act are rarely issued.) The People's Republic of China, the Soviet Union,[18] most of the European communist countries, and Mongolia make up another country group, to which many nonstrategic exports are permitted under the act. Poland has received favored treatment since 1957. It alone constitutes a separate country group and is accorded more liberal treatment than the other communist countries, with the exception of Romania and Yugoslavia. Romania, as a result of favorable reclassifications in 1964 and 1971, constitutes another separate country group and is given even more liberal treatment. Yugoslavia, the most liberally treated, has since 1948 been classed generally as a noncommunist country. It is in a country group that includes most countries of Western Europe, Africa, and noncommunist Asia and that is mainly subject to restrictions only to prevent diversion of exports to unauthorized destinations.[19]

5

In determining how a commodity should be regulated under the export controls, the U.S. Government generally considers the following factors regarding the commodity:

Its essential features (distinguishing physical or operating characteristics; variations between types, models, grades, and so on; and the technical and strategic significances of these differences).
Its civilian uses.
Its military or military-support uses.
Its end-use pattern in the United States.
Its technological state of development. (Whether it involves a new product and represents the current state of the art. Whether it contains advanced technology that can feasibly be extracted.)
Its availability abroad. (Whether the same or a comparable commodity is available from other noncommunist countries and where and by whom. Whether the foreign product is manufactured abroad with U.S.-origin technology or components.)[20]

For any denial of strategic exports to communist countries to be effective, it must, of course, be implemented by the other Western industrialized nations in concert with the United States. To this end, a multilateral organization was formed in 1949 known as Cocom, which today includes all the NATO countries, except Iceland, plus Japan. The Cocom countries agree to embargo the export of certain strategic items to the European and Asian communist countries except Yugoslavia. (The United States has unsuccessfully tried to have Cuba added to the embargoed countries.) The designated items are a minimum; any Cocom country can unilaterally embargo additional items if it chooses. The Cocom arrangement has never been formalized in a treaty, and participation in it is voluntary.[21]

The U.S. Government has maintained a unilateral embargo list longer than the Cocom list. Under the Export Control Act[22] and its successor, the Export Administration Act,[23] the president is given exceedingly wide discretion to control exports as he chooses. In adopting the Export Administration Act of 1969, Congress did make modest changes from the earlier act to indicate a desire for some relaxation of the U.S. controls.[24] During 1970-71 the Nixon Administration did ease licensing requirements for over 1,700 commodities,[25] and as of May 1973 the number of commodities unilaterally controlled by the United States in excess of the Cocom list was down to 73.[26]

That in past years the U.S. list has been longer than the Cocom list has had a distinct effect on East-West trade. As of the end of 1973, the excess in the U.S. list is so small that this differential probably no longer has a significant effect on trade. But before 1973, the differential was an important reason why American participation in

6

East-West trade was so much less than that of other Organization for Economic Cooperation and Development (OECD) countries. It was a factor leading many American companies to conduct their East-West trade through foreign subsidiaries, which could sometimes obtain from their host government an export license that would be denied to the American parent. Probably another effect of the longer U.S. embargo list was on the types of goods traded. The proportion of finished industrial products—the kind of products chiefly on the embargo list—in American exports to communist countries was less than in American exports worldwide. For OECD exports, on the other hand, the proportion of finished industrial products in exports to communist countries was higher than in OECD exports worldwide.[27] In addition to the strict U.S. export controls, another important factor that limited American participation in East-West trade, that encouraged American companies to conduct this trade through foreign subsidiaries, and that reduced the proportion of finished industrial products in American exports was, of course, the stringent U.S. credit regulation, discussed below.

The U.S. export controls, and especially the excess over the Cocom list, have, however, been a particular subject of controversy. To a large extent this controversy has moderated, of course, now that the U.S. differential has become so much smaller than it was. There is general agreement that the American national interest requires some government control of exports to communist countries and that the government should enforce at least the Cocom embargo list.* But it has been urged that going beyond the Cocom list does not make sense, both because that list represents the reasoned consensus of concerned allies as to what items are strategic and also because items not on the list will be shipped in East-West trade from other Cocom countries even if the United States bars them. The reply supporting a longer U.S. embargo list claims that the United States, as by far the strongest country in the free world, has a responsibility in maintaining free world security that goes beyond the responsibility of its Cocom allies.[29] Furthermore, it is said that in certain important technological areas, American capacity is uniquely advanced, so that a U.S. embargo is an effective East-West trade embargo.[30]

_____

*Such government controls can even further East-West trade in some instances. For example, an American company might hesitate to decide on its own that certain technology could be exported without injuring the national security. The U.S. Government, on the other hand, might be more willing to reach such a decision, so that placing on the government the responsibility for such decision-making may enable transactions to be consummated from which American companies would otherwise hold back.[28]

Credit Controls

The Export-Import Bank is currently prohibited by law from participating in transactions with any communist country unless the president determines such participation to be in the U.S. national interest. To date, the president has made such a determination for only the Soviet Union, Poland, Romania, and Yugoslavia. Congress has subjected the bank to a prohibition of this type since 1963.

From 1968 until August 1971, pursuant to a more severe congressional prohibition, the Export-Import Bank was able to finance exports only to Yugoslavia among the communist countries. This prohibition was not subject to exception by presidential determination. It applied to any country whose government supplied goods or assistance to a country engaged in armed conflict with U.S. armed forces.[31] In practice, because of the Vietnam war, this prohibition meant all communist countries except Yugoslavia. Congressional repeal of this prohibition in August 1971[32] made relevant the original congressional prohibition against Export-Import Bank participation in transactions involving communist countries.[33] This latter prohibition—on the books in similar form since 1963[34] and currently in effect—is unlike the one that was repealed in one important respect. It may be waived by the president for transactions he determines to be in the national interest. The 1971 congressional repeal of the prohibition not subject to such presidential exception was, therefore, a significant liberalization.

The authority for Export-Import Bank financing of exports to Yugoslavia is a presidential determination made in 1968 shortly after congressional passage of the version of the waivable prohibition currently in effect.[35] Since congressional repeal in August 1971 of the nonwaivable prohibition that effectively applied to all of the other communist countries, a presidential determination under the current waivable prohibition has been made for Romania in November 1971,[36] the Soviet Union in October 1972,[37] and Poland in November 1972.[38] During the 1963-68 period, when earlier versions of the current waivable prohibition were in effect, presidential determinations were made with respect to the Soviet Union and several East European countries, but, except for Yugoslavia, only for restricted classes of American exports to each.

In addition to the restrictions on the Export-Import Bank, extension of credit in East-West trade by American private parties is also subject to restraints. As a reaction to substantial defaults by European countries on bonds sold in the United States during World War I and the 1920s, Congress enacted the Johnson Debt Default Act of 1934.[39] The Johnson Act prohibits private individuals and firms in the United States from making "any loan to" or purchasing or selling "the bonds, securities, or other obligations of any foreign government

8

... in default ... [on] obligations ... to the United States."[40] The original act exempts any U.S. Government corporation,[41] and post-World War II congressional enactments exempt any foreign government that is a member of both the International Monetary Fund and the World Bank[42] and any transaction in which the Export-Import Bank participates.[43]

Foreign governments in default on obligations to the United States within the meaning of the Johnson Act apparently include the governments of the Soviet Union and all the East European countries except for Bulgaria and Albania.[44] Yugoslavia and Romania, however, are members of both the International Monetary Fund and the World Bank, and the Export-Import Bank can participate in transactions involving the Soviet Union and Poland (as well as Yugoslavia and Romania). Therefore, the prohibition of the Johnson Act evidently applies to all the European communist countries with the exception of Bulgaria, Albania, Yugoslavia, and Romania and, when the Export-Import Bank participates in the transaction, the Soviet Union and Poland.

The prohibition of the act has, however, been interpreted not to cover an extension of normal commercial credit as part of a specific export transaction. Instead the ban of the act has been construed to be directed at purely financial general purpose loans to the relevant countries.[45] In actual practice, whether the act applies to a given transaction is not always clear. This uncertainty sometimes has an inhibiting effect on East-West trade.

Taken together, the Johnson Act and, more importantly, the restrictions on the Export-Import Bank have constituted a severe impediment to U.S. participation in East-West trade. Much of the growing export business done by Western Europe and Japan with Eastern Europe and the Soviet Union is based on credit extended to the buyer. These communist countries are chronically short of hard currency with which to make their desired purchases. They are also increasing their purchases of major capital equipment normally sold on deferred payment terms.

Consequently, Western Europe and Japan compete vigorously for this East-West trade on the basis of the credit terms offered. Long-term private funds supported by government guarantees have become an important selling feature. Credit extended by Western Europe to Eastern Europe and the Soviet Union now runs from 8 to 10 years.[46] The Bern Union, which includes a majority of the Western export credit institutions, sought to limit such credit extension to five years. The Bern Union limitation has, however, proved ineffective to restrain credit competition in East-West trade. American exporters, because of the Johnson Act and the restrictions on the Export-Import Bank, have been uniquely and seriously handicapped in this competition.[47]

Agricultural and Shipping Programs

The U.S. Government promotes the export of agricultural products principally through three programs: the Commodity Credit Corporation's Export Payment Programs, the Commodity Credit Corporation's Export Credit Sales Program (GSM-4), and the Title I, Public Law 480 Programs. The Export Payment Programs and the Export Credit Sales Program assist exports to communist countries on the same basis as exports to any other foreign country.[48] The Public Law 480 Programs, which provide long-term government financing of sales to "friendly countries,"[49] have certain prohibitions against sales to communist countries.[50] American agricultural products can, of course, be exported without assistance from any of these programs.[51]

Under the Export Payment Programs, when the domestic price of a certain agricultural commodity is higher than the world market price, the government may pay the difference to a U.S. exporter to enable the exporter to sell abroad at competitive world prices. Under the Export Credit Sales Program, the government extends credit up to three years to U.S. exporters to assist them in selling American agricultural commodities.[52]

Under the Public Law 480 Programs, agricultural commodities are sold to friendly foreign countries on long-term credit up to 20 years for dollars and for foreign convertible currencies.[53] "Friendly countries," for the purpose of foreign currency sales, exclude "any country . . . dominated by a Communist government."[54] For both foreign currency and dollar sales, they exclude "any country . . . dominated . . . by a . . . government . . . controlling a world Communist movement" and any country whose ships or aircraft engage in trade with Cuba or North Vietnam.[55] Credit sales for dollars may be made to a communist country if it is determined by the president to be a "friendly country" under the definition of the preceding sentence.[56] No dollar credit sale to a communist country has been made under such a determination since 1966. (In 1956 and 1961, a determination was made that Poland was a "friendly country.")

In the field of agriculture, the U.S. system readily produces surpluses, and communist countries periodically develop serious import needs. The severe restrictions on the availability of the Public Law 480 Programs are not a significant barrier to U.S. agricultural exports in East-West trade because of the availability of the Export Payment and Export Credit Sales Programs. What was a serious legal barrier to these exports—the U.S. flag shipping requirements—has been sharply altered, as described immediately below. With the support of the Export Payment and Export Credit Sales Programs, current prospects for U.S. agricultural exports to communist countries are now good.[57]

During the 1963-64 negotiations for the large 1964 U.S. wheat sale to the Soviet Union, American maritime union pressure forced President John F. Kennedy to adopt by executive action a requirement in aid of U.S. shipping, which stood until 1971. At least 50 percent of all wheat and cereal grains exported to the Soviet Union, and at least 50 percent of all wheat exported to Eastern Europe (except Poland, Romania, and Yugoslavia) and to Mongolia, was required to be shipped in U.S. flag ocean carriers.[58] In June 1971, President Nixon terminated this 50 percent shipping requirement at the same time that he ended the embargo on trade with the People's Republic of China.[59] This shipping requirement had inhibited U.S. wheat and cereal grain sales, because the cost of shipping in U.S. vessels was substantially higher than in foreign vessels.[60] Elimination of the requirement did stimulate U.S. wheat and cereal grain exports.[61]

The shipping situation for both agricultural and nonagricultural goods has now been significantly facilitated further by a U.S.-Soviet maritime agreement signed in October 1972. The agreement contemplates that each country's vessels will carry one-third of the trade between them and that one-third will go to third-country vessels. The higher cost of U.S. shipping for bulk cargoes is accommodated through minimum rates set in the agreement for U.S. vessels and, as an additional accommodation for agricultural bulk cargoes, through a U.S. Government subsidy for U.S. vessels. Forty ports in each country are opened by the agreement to vessels of the other country. The agreement runs through 1975.[62] The American maritime unions reportedly concurred in the agreement in the belief that it would mean more jobs for union members.[63]

Aid and Investment Programs

Foreign aid to communist countries is prohibited expressly by some legislation[64] and implicitly by other legislation.[65] Although it is unlikely for political reasons that the United States would make a direct foreign aid grant to a communist country, it is necessary for any government program assisting commercial foreign trade transactions to avoid these prohibitions.

Direct investment by a U.S. person in a communist country, like direct investment by a U.S. person in any foreign country, is restricted by the Foreign Direct Investment Program.[66] The objective of this program is to improve the U.S. balance of payments position. The program was begun in 1968, and the Nixon Administration intends to terminate it by the end of 1974.[67] The regulations administered by the program divide the whole world (except Canada) into three schedules. All of the communist countries except Yugoslavia have been placed, along with most of the West European countries, in the schedule subject to the most restrictive direct investment limits.68 Yugoslavia has been placed along with most of the developing countries in the schedule with the least restrictive limits.69 The effect of this schedular division is to ease regulation of U.S. direct investment in Yugoslavia and to impose tighter controls over U.S. direct investment in the other communist countries.

U.S. investment in both Yugoslavia and Romania is affirmatively encouraged by authorization of the Overseas Private Investment Corporation (OPIC) to provide its investment incentives for such investment. OPIC offers U.S. private investors in some 90 developing countries insurance against expropriation, inconvertibility of local currency holdings, and war damage. OPIC also guarantees loans made by U.S. lending institutions to private investors and provides U.S. dollar and local currency loans and preinvestment assistance. In February 1972, Congress enacted the Foreign Assistanct Act of 1971, which authorized OPIC investment incentives for Yugoslavia and Romania if the president determined availability of the incentives to be "important to the national interest."70 President Nixon made such a determination in March 1972.71

IMPORT RESTRICTIONS

The denial of MFN treatment is by far the most important restriction on imports from communist countries. All import restrictions, however, affect U.S. exports in East-West trade as well as imports. Import restrictions limit communist capacity to purchase U.S. goods by reducing the dollars these countries can earn through selling their goods in the United States. The limitation is effective because communist countries not only try generally to balance their foreign trade on a bilateral basis but also have chronic shortages of hard currency.

Tariffs—Denial of MFN

Only Yugoslavia and Poland among the communist countries receive MFN for their imports into the United States.72 Under legislation enacted first in 1951,73 products from other communist countries pay duty at the rates prescribed in the Smoot-Hawley Tariff Act of 1930,74 unaffected by the significant reductions in these rates that have been made under the trade agreements program beginning in 1934.75 The American-Soviet Trade Agreement signed in October 1972 accords MFN to Soviet products,76 but this MFN will be without effect until Congress enacts legislation authorizing it. Congress has debated such legislation during much of 1973 without as of the end of 1973 reaching a final decision on the matter.

12

In 1966 President Johnson sent to Congress the East-West Trade Relations Act of 1966, which would have authorized the president to negotiate commercial agreements extending MFN to individual European communist countries.[77] Congress, however, rejected that bill.[78]

Denial of MFN to most communist countries means their products are generally subject to tariffs several times higher than competing foreign goods. In addition, denial of MFN is perhaps the U.S. restriction on East-West trade most resented by communist countries, which contend that MFN should be extended automatically between nations trading with each other in good faith.

Other Regulations of Imports

Dumping of goods by communist countries is potentially a serious problem because state-trading economies are not restricted in their exporting by normal commercial considerations of profitability. The Antidumping Act of 1921,[79] which was passed to protect against dumping from Western Europe, can be hard to apply to imports from a communist country because of the difficulty of determining prices and costs there.[80] A new solution was developed in the American-Soviet Trade Agreement. This agreement authorizes either country to take appropriate measures to prevent imports in the bilateral trade that "cause, threaten or contribute to disruption of its domestic market."[81] To date, dumping of goods in the United States by any communist country has not been a significant problem.[82]

For one line of communist imports the United States has a flat prohibition. The importation of certain fur skins from the Soviet Union and the People's Republic of China is prohibited,[83] an instance of U.S. special-interest legislation.[84]

On the other hand, the U.S.-Soviet maritime agreement signed in October 1972[85] should facilitate the import of Soviet goods. The main purpose of this agreement was, of course, to facilitate U.S. agricultural exports.[86]

U.S.-SOVIET AND U.S.-POLISH TRADE AGREEMENTS

In October 1972 the Nixon Administration signed a trade agreement with the Soviet Union extending MFN to Soviet products, and President Nixon authorized the Export-Import Bank to finance exports to the Soviet Union. In return, the Soviet Union agreed to settle its World War II Lend-Lease debt. If, however, Congress fails to enact legislation authorizing the MFN, the trade agreement will not go into effect, and the amount of the Lend-Lease settlement will be greatly reduced. Other matters besides MFN that are covered in the trade agreement are market disruption, the establishment of trade offices by each side in the country of the other, and arbitration.[87] Essentially completing the U.S.-Soviet trade package is the maritime agreement described above[88] that was also signed in October 1972. The U.S. trade accord with Poland, a matter of much lesser significance, was reached in November 1972.

Settlement of the Soviet Union's Lend-Lease debt put an end to disagreement over the debt that had gone on since the end of World War II. Until resumed in 1972, negotiations had last broken off in 1960, with the Soviet Union offering $300 million and the United States asking $800 million.[89] The settlement finally reached provides for Soviet payment of at least $722 million over a period ending in the year 2001, provided that the Soviet Union actually receives MFN from the United States. Absent receipt of such MFN, the Soviet Union is obligated to pay only $48 million.[90] Partly in return for the Soviet debt settlement, President Nixon authorized the Export-Import Bank to finance exports to the Soviet Union.[91]

In the trade agreement each side promises to extend MFN to products of the other.[92] The trade agreement is to run for three years,[93] and the three years will not start to run unless and until Congress enacts legislation authorizing U.S. extension of such MFN.[94] As part of the Nixon Administration's Trade Reform Act of 1973 submitted to Congress in April 1973, the Administration included a provision authorizing the extension of MFN to communist countries.[95] As of the end of 1973, Congress has not made a final disposition of the proposed act, and the communist MFN provision has become embroiled in serious controversy over Soviet emigration policy.

Extension of MFN by the Soviet Union involves problems for the United States of a different order. There is no question about the authority of the Soviet Government to extend the MFN; the question is as to its value. A state-trading country receiving MFN from a market-economy country obtains the same advantages as another market-economy country receiving that MFN. But a market-economy country's receipt of MFN from a state-trading country can lack significant value. In the case of tariffs, the traditional subject matter of MFN, the state-trading government essentially both pays the duty through the state importing corporation and also collects it through the state customs bureau. Hence any reduction in tariffs from MFN does not ordinarily make goods from a market economy any more salable in the state-trading country.

(The gain from the lowered price to the state trading government ultimately financing the purchase is exactly offset by the loss to the government from the reduced tariff collection. By contrast, in a market economy country, exports becoming salable at a lower price by virtue of MFN's reducing the applicable tariff do become more attractive for purchase. The market economy enterprises making the purchases benefit fully from the lowered price beca se these enterprises have no connection with the governmental tariff collections.)

Market-economy countries have devised several kinds of quid pro quo to receive from a state-trading country in return for giving it MFN.[96] In the American-Soviet trade arrangement, in a broad sense, MFN was one of a list of items including Nixon's authorization of the Export-Import Bank that the U.S. side gave in return for receiving a list of items, including Soviet settlement of the Lend-Lease debt. In a narrower sense the U.S. side received, in the trade agreement and accompanying letters, provisions more directly related to MFN.

The basic problem for a market economy in exchanging MFN with a state-trading economy lies in assuring the market economy's exporters a reasonable chance to sell to the state-trading economy. As a partial solution to this problem, the trade agreement provides that "The [Soviet] Government . . . expects that . . . [Soviet] foreign trade organizations . . . will place substantial orders in the United States."[97] In addition, with respect to American imports from the Soviet Union, the trade agreement authorizes either side to take appropriate measures to prevent disruption of its domestic market by imports from the other.[98] This provision is really of value only to the U.S. side. The Soviet Union, as a state-trading country, can prevent disruption of its domestic market simply through its administrative control of what its foreign trade corporations import.

During the congressional debate on the Nixon Administration's Trade Reform Act of 1973, Senator Henry Jackson and others have advocated linking MFN for communist countries with a policy goal desired by the United States although unrelated to trade. They have urged that a grant of MFN to any communist country be conditioned on that country's maintaining a free emigration policy.[99] The condition would apply to all communist countries[100] but is aimed principally at the Soviet Union and has been stimulated mainly by the unsuccessful attempts of many Soviet Jews to emigrate to Israel. As mentioned above, Congress has, as of the end of 1973, reached no final decision on whether or how to authorize MFN for communist countries.

The American-Soviet Trade Agreement treats important matters other than those that went into the bargaining on MFN. The establishment of trade offices by each side in the country of the other is the subject of an exchange of provisions. In past years, U.S. firms doing business with the Soviet Union have often thought it desirable to have an office there but have encountered difficulty obtaining the requisite permission. A letter from the Soviet Foreign Trade Mininster that accompanies the trade agreement assures U.S. firms of MFN "in all matters relating to accreditation and business facilitation."[101] Of particular interest to the Soviet Union, the trade agreement provides for the establishment of a government-sponsored trade office by each side in the capital of the other.[102] Members of each office will have diplomatic immunity[103] but, contrary to the arrangement the Soviet

Union desired and actually has with many other countries,[104] will not be allowed to conduct trade.[105] Soviet trade with the United States will continue to be conducted, as it has been in the past, by Soviet foreign trade corporations, which are expressly barred by the trade agreement from claiming immunity with respect to commercial transactions.[106]

Arbitration of commercial disputes is another point on which the trade agreement departs from the arrangement the Soviet Union prefers and actually has with many other countries. Soviet policy frequently has supported arbitration in the country of the defendant. Westerners have sometimes had reservations about this arrangement because such arbitration in the Soviet Union must be held before the Soviet Foreign Trade Arbitration Commission, which has only Soviet nationals as arbitrators. To solve this problem, the trade agreement "encourages" arbitration in a third country under the Arbitration Rules of the Economic Commission for Europe, a United Nations agency.[107]

The U.S.-Polish trade accord of November 1972 involves several measures including, perhaps most prominently, authorization by President Nixon of Export-Import Bank participation in trade with Poland.[108] Letters from the Polish trade minister assure U.S. firms of MFN in obtaining offices in Poland[109] and "encourage" third-country arbitration for the settlement of commercial disputes.[110] MFN for Polish imports into the United States was not an issue because Polish products have received such MFN since 1960.[111]

SUMMARY

As of the end of 1973, 1969 stands as the year in which the direction of U.S. East-West trade policy was turned around. The strict pre-1969 policy began in earnest with congressional enactment of the Export Control Act of 1949,[112] which continued the extensive World War II controls over exports.[113] Presidentially ordered embargoes of trade went into effect for the People's Republic of China and North Korea in 1950,[114] for Cuba in 1963,[115] and for North Vietnam in 1964.[116] Congress denied MFN to imports from most communist countries in 1951[117] and restricted Export-Import Bank financing of East-West trade in 1963[118] and 1968.[119]

Then in 1969, on the 20th anniversary of the Export Control Act of 1949, Congress replaced it with the moderately more liberal Export Administration Act of 1969.[120] In 1971 the Nixon Administration ended the trade blockade of the People's Republic of China.[121] Congress in 1971 repealed the flat prohibition on Export-Import Bank participation in transactions with any communist country except Yugoslavia,[122] and in that and the following year Nixon authorized

Bank financing of exports to Romania,[123] the Soviet Union,[124] and Poland.[125] In 1972 the Nixon Administration negotiated a trade agreement with the Soviet Union.[126]

Whether this liberalizing trend begun in 1969 will continue depends next on Congress's response to Nixon's request for MFN for communist countries in addition to Yugoslavia and Poland.[127] Regardless of this congressional decision on MFN, the president at present has the authority to authorize Export-Import Bank participation in transactions involving communist countries besides those four for whom the president has already authorized such participation.[128] A further feature of bank participation in a transaction is that the Johnson Act prohibition does not apply to such a transaction.[129] With respect to the important matter of administering export licensing, the president has been given exceedingly wide discretion under the Export Administration Act of 1969.[130] Here the likelihood is for a continuation of the present situation: a U.S. unilateral embargo list longer than the Cocom list, but not so much longer that it significantly handicaps U.S. as against other Western exporters.

Congress, in addition to rejecting President Nixon's request for MFN for communist countries, could, of course, reduce his present authority in other areas. The most probable target here would be the president's authority to authorize Export-Import Bank financing in East-West trade.[131]

But for the moment, the change in policy direction begun in 1969 has made a real difference. The U.S. regulation of East-West trade is now clearly the most liberal it has been since the end of World War II.

NOTES

1. In preparing the account of U.S. regulation that follows in the text, the author was aided by an excellent analysis of the subject written by Andreas F. Lowenfeld, Professor of Law, New York University School of Law, with the assistance of John B. Rehm. Their analysis was a working paper for a study published by the Committee for Economic Development (CED) under the title A New Trade Policy Toward Communist Countries (1972).

2. 31 C.F.R. Part 500 (1973). The 1950 issuance, 15 Fed. Reg. 9040, was as an incident of the national emergency declared by President Truman in December 1950, Pres. Proc. 2914, 3 C.F.R. 99 (Comp. 1949-53), 15 Fed. Reg. 9029. See Sommerfield, "Treasury East-West Trade Control Regulations" 2 (rev. 1967), on file at the Office of Foreign Assets Control, U.S. Treasury Department; an earlier edition of this article, "Treasury Regulations Affecting Trade with the Sino-Soviet Bloc and Cuba," appears in 19 Bus. Lawyer 861 (1964).

3. 29 Fed. Reg. 6010 (1964). In 1966 the "National Liberation Front of South Viet-Nam," the Viet Cong, and "The Liberation Red Cross" were stated to be "specially designated nationals" of North Vietnam, 31 Fed. Reg. 8586 (1966).

4. 28 Fed. Reg. 6974 (1963) codified at 31 C.F.R. Part 515 (1973). The Cuban Assets Control Regulations replaced the Cuban Import Regulations, 31 C.F.R. 515.101 (1973), which had been issued in 1962 and which had prohibited the import into the United States of goods of Cuban origin and of goods made in third countries with Cuban components, 27 Fed. Reg. 1085 (1962). See Sommerfield, supra note 2, at 11.

5. Ch. 106, Sec. 5(b), 40 Stat. 415, as amended, 12 U.S.C. sec. 95(a) (1970) and also 50 U.S.C. App. sec. 5(b) (1970). Each of these embargo regulations is administered by the Office of Foreign Assets Control, U.S. Treasury Department.

6. See Sommerfield, supra note 2 at 2-13. The prohibitions of the Foreign Assets Control Regulations, but not those of the Cuban Assets Control Regulations, extend also to foreign firms that are owned or controlled by Americans. 31 C.F.R. 500.329-330 (1973); 31 C.F.R. 515.329-30, .541 (1973). See Sommerfield, supra note 2 at 9-12. In December 1969 this provision of the Foreign Assets Control Regulations was relaxed with respect to the People's Republic of China, 34 Fed. Reg. 20191 (1969) codified at 31 C.F.R. 500.541 (1973), as one of the steps that led to the ending of the embargo on trade with the People's Republic of China. See note 7 and accompanying text infra.

7. The Foreign Assets Control Regulations were amended to authorize the import into the United States of goods from the People's Republic of China. 36 Fed. Reg. 11441 (1971) codified at 31 C.F.R. 500.547 (1973). Before June 1971 the Foreign Assets Control Regulations had prohibited unlicensed exports from the United States to the People's Republic of China but had licensed generally any such export directly from the United States if it was licensed under the U.S. export control legislation. 31 C.F.R. 533 (1973). (For this legislation, see section of this chapter entitled "Export Licensing," infra.) Consequently, in June 1971, this export section of the Foreign Assets Control Regulations was left unchanged; but the export licensing regulations, under which previously practically no exports had been licensed (Sommerfield, supra note 2, at 8), were now amended to license a wide range of exports to the People's Republic of China. 36 Fed. Reg. 11808 (1971), U.S. Department of Commerce, Export Control Bull. No. 46 (June 11, 1971). See also 37 Fed. Reg. 5623 (1972). Despite the ending of the trade blockade, the Foreign Assets Control Regulations continue to block certain assets in the United States of the People's Republic of China and to prohibit the bunkering by U.S.

oil companies abroad of Chinese vessels bound to or from North Korea, North Vietnam, or Cuba.

8. One difference is that the European communist countries are not subject to the blocked asset and bunkering restrictions, mentioned at the end of note 7 above, that apply to the People's Republic of China.

9. 50 U.S.C. App. secs. 2401-2413 (1970), as amended (Supp. II, 1973).

10. Comprehensive accounts of U.S. export licensing are contained in Berman and Garson, "United States Export Controls—Past, Present, and Future," 67 Colum. L. Rev. 791 (1967); and in McQuade, "U.S. Trade with Eastern Europe: Its Prospects and Parameters," 3 Law and Pol. Int'l Bus. 42, 69-100 (1971), hereinafter cited as McQuade.

11. Act of July 2, 1940, sec. 6, ch. 508, 54 Stat. 714, as amended, as extended to June 30, 1946, by the Act of June 30, 1945, ch. 205, 59 Stat. 270; to June 30, 1947, by the Act of May 23, 1946, ch. 269, 60 Stat. 215; to July 15, 1947, by the Act of June 30, 1947, ch. 184, 61 Stat. 214; to Feb. 29, 1948, by the Act of July 15, 1947, ch. 248, sec. 4, 61 Stat, 323; and to Feb. 28, 1949, by the Act of Dec. 30, 1947, ch. 526, sec. 3, 61 Stat. 946. See Berman and Garson, note 10 supra at 791-92 and nn. 1-2; and Herman, "East-West Trade: An Overview of Legislation, Policy Trends, and Issues Involved" (Library of Congress Legislative Reference Service) 1-3 (1968).

12. Ch. 11, 63 Stat. 7.

13. Ch. 11, 63 Stat. 7, as amended, codified at 50 U.S.C. App. secs. 2021-2032, as amended, Supp. V (1970).

14. Pub. L. No. 91-184, 83 Stat. 841, codified at 50 U.S.C. App. secs. 2401-2413 (1970), as amended, Supp. II (1973).

15. The government's basic export control program—formerly authorized by the Export Control Act and now by the Export Administration Act—is implemented by the Export Control Regulations, 15 C.F.R. Parts 368-399 (1973). The program is administered by the Commerce Department through its Office of Export Administration. There are, in addition, export controls over various specialized goods and data administered by other government offices. These specialized goods and data, and the controlling government office, include arms, ammunition, implements of war, and related technical data, Office of Munitions Control, State Department, pursuant to the Mutual Security Act of 1954, sec. 414, as amended 22 U.S.C. sec. 1934 (1970)—see also 22 C.F.R. secs. 121-28 (1973); nuclear source materials, facilities, and related technology, Atomic Energy Commission, pursuant to the Atomic Energy Act of 1954, as amended 42 U.S.C. secs. 2011-2282 (1970)—see also 10 C.F.R. pts. 30-73 (1973); gold, Treasury Department, pursuant to the Gold Reserve Act of 1934, 31 U.S.C. secs. 440-46 (1970), 12 U.S.C. sec. 95(a) (1970); narcotic drugs and marijuana, Justice Department, pursuant to the Controlled Substances Import

and Export Act, 21 U.S.C. secs. 951-966 (1970); certain agricultural commodities, Agriculture Department, pursuant to 7 U.S.C. secs. 516, 581-99 (1970); vessels, Maritime Administration, pursuant to the Shipping Act of 1916, 46 U.S.C. sec. 808, 835 (1970); natural gas and electric energy, Federal Power Commission, pursuant to the Natural Gas Act of 1938, 15 U.S.C. sec. 717b (1970), and the Federal Power Act, 16 U.S.C. sec. 824a (e) (1970); and certain internationally determined strategic commodities, Office of Foreign Assets Control, Treasury Department, pursuant to the Transaction Control Regulations, 31 C.F.R. Part 505 (1973), issued under sec. 5(b) of the Trading with the Enemy Act of 1917, as amended, 12 U.S.C. sec. 95(a) (1970) and also 50 U.S.C. App. sec. 5(b) (1970) (see also note 6 supra and Sommerfield, note 2 supra). See also 15 C.F.R. sec. 370.10 (1973); McQuade, supra note 10, at 73 and nn. 114-117, and Berman and Garson, supra note 10 at 793 and nn. 9-10.

16. 50 U.S.C. App. sec. 2402 (2) (1970).

17. 31 C.F.R. 500.533 (1973); 31 C.F.R. 515.533 (1973).

18. The Administration stated that U.S. export controls were not discussed in the negotiations for the 1972 American-Soviet Trade Agreement. 67 Dep't State Bull. 592 (1972); also in U.S. Department of Commerce, U.S.-Soviet Commercial Agreements 1972—Texts, Summaries, and Supporting Paper 75 (1973), hereinafter cited as Commercial Agreements.

19. 15 C.F.R. Part 370, Supp. No. 1 (1973).

20. 15 C.F.R. sec. 370.1(b) (1) (1973). See also Office of Export Control, U.S. Dep't of Commerce, "A Summary of U.S. Export Control Regulations," at iv, cols. 1-2 (rev. Feb. 18, 1971); McQuade, supra note 10 at 88.

21. McQuade, supra note 10 at 71-73. Congress, to create an incentive for other countries to participate in the embargo, passed the Mutual Defense Assistance Control Act of 1951 (the "Battle Act"). This act provides for the termination of U.S. aid to any country exporting certain strategic goods to nations threatening American security, including the Soviet Union and nations under its domination. Ch. 575, 65 Stat. 645, codified, as amended, 22 U.S.C. secs. 1611-13d (1970). Since most U.S. foreign aid to countries that might export strategic goods to communist countries has already ended for other reasons, however, the Battle Act sanction has lost significant meaning.

22. 50 U.S.C. App. secs. 2021-2032, as amended, Supp. V, 1970.

23. 50 U.S.C. App secs. 2401-2413 (1970), as amended, Supp. II, 1973.

24. McQuade, supra note 10, at 83-100; Berman, "The Export Administration Act of 1969: Analysis and Appraisal," Am. Rev. East-West Trade, Jan. 1970, at 19. In 1971 Congress, in extending the 1969 act to 1974, introduced more changes indicating a desire for further relaxation. Equal Export Opportunity Act, Pub. L. No. 92-412, title

I, secs. 101-106, 86 Stat. 644 (1972), amending 50 U.S.C. App. secs.
2401-2413 (1970), codified at 50 U.S.C. App. secs. 2401 (3), 2402 (6),
2403 (b), (e), 2404 (c), 2413 (Supp. II, 1973).

25. U.S. Dep't of Commerce, "Export Control—99th Quarterly
Report, 1st Quarter 1972," at 15 (1972).

26. U.S. Dep't of Commerce, "Special Report—Export Control,
by the Secretary of Commerce to the President, the Senate, and the
House of Representatives, May 29, 1973" at 3 (1973).

27. The proportion of finished industrial products in U.S. exports
to communist countries has been running generally under half, whereas
in American exports worldwide it has been about two-thirds. U.S.
Bureau of the Census, Highlights of the U.S. Export and Import Trade,
Report FT 990 (U.S. Gov't Printing Office, Washington, D.C.) for
December 1972 (dated 1973) at 54-59, for December 1971 (dated 1972)
at 54-59, for December 1970 (dated 1971) at 50-55, for December 1969
(dated 1970) at 50-55, for December 1968 (dated 1969) at 20-25, and
for December 1967 (dated 1968) at 20-25. For OECD exports to communist countries, this proportion has been about four-fifths, whereas
in OECD exports worldwide it has been about three-fourths. Organisation for Economic Co-operation and Development, Trade by Commodities—Analytical Abstracts, Series B, Jan.-Dec. 1969, at 18-19
(1970) and Jan.-Dec. 1970, at 18-19 (1971). The statistics on the basis
of which the proportions stated in this note were computed did not
include, in American exports to communist countries, exports to
Yugoslavia and Cuba, and, in OECD exports to communist countries,
exports to Yugoslavia, Cuba, and Outer Mongolia. For purposes of
these note computations, in the Standard International Trade Classification Revised (SITC), finished industrial products have been considered
to include chemicals, manufactured goods classified chiefly by material,
machinery and transport equipment, and miscellaneous manufactured
articles. Finished industrial products have been considered not to
include food and live animals; beverages and tobacco; crude materials,
except fuels—inedible; mineral fuels, lubricants, and related materials;
animal and vegetable oils, fats, and waxes; and commodities and
transactions not classified according to kind.

28. McQuade, supra note 10, at 71.

29. See, e.g., Scott, Book Review, 4 N.Y.U.J. Int'l L. and Politics
144, 145-46 (1971).

30. McQuade, supra note 10, at 91-93.

31. Export-Import Bank Act of 1945 sec. 2(b) (3), Pub. L. No.
90-267, sec. 1(c), 82 Stat. 47 (1968), as amended 12 U.S.C. sec. 635(b)
(3) (1970), as amended, Supp, II (1973).

32. Export Expansion Finance Act of 1971 sec. (b) (5), Pub. L.
No. 92-126, 85 Stat. 345 (1971), amending Export-Import Bank Act of
1945 sec. (2) (b) (3), 12 U.S.C. sec. 635(b) (3) (1970), codified at 12
U.S.C. sec. 635(b) (3) (1970), as amended, Supp. II (1973). The repeal-

ing measure substituted another provision that bans bank participation principally in exports to a country engaged in armed conflict with U.S. armed forces or in exports to be used by such a country.

33. Export-Import Bank Act of 1945 sec. 2(b) (2), 12 U.S.C. sec. 635(b) (2) (1970), as amended, Supp. II (1973).

34. Foreign Assistance and Related Agencies Appropriation Act, 1965, Title III, Pub. L. No. 88-634, 78 Stat. 1015 (1964).

35. Letter from President Johnson to President of the Senate Humphrey and Speaker of the House McCormack, May 7, 1968, on file at the Export-Import Bank.

36. Presidential Determination, Nov. 22, 1971; letter from President Nixon to President of the Senate Agnew, Nov. 22, 1971; letter from President Nixon to Speaker of the House Albert, Nov. 22, 1971. The Presidential Determination and both letters are on file at the Export-Import Bank.

37. Presidential Determination, Oct. 18, 1972, on file at the Export-Import Bank.

38. Presidential Determination, Nov. 8, 1972; letter from President Nixon to President of the Senate Agnew and Speaker of the House Albert, Nov. 8, 1972. The Presidential Determination and the letter are on file at the Export-Import Bank.

39. Ch. 112, 48 Stat. 574 (1934), as amended, 18 U.S.C. sec. 955 (1970). The Nixon Administration's Trade Reform Act of 1973 proposes repeal of the Johnson Act. H.R. 6767, 93d Cong., 1st Sess., sec. 706(g) 1973). As of the end of 1973, Congress has not made a final disposition of this Administration bill; but the House of Representatives passed the bill on December 11, 1973 without including any repeal of the Johnson Act. H.R. 10710, 93d Cong. 1st Sess.

40. 18 U.S.C. sec. 955 (1970).

41. Ch. 112, 48 Stat. 574 (1934), as amended, 18 U.S.C. sec. 955 (1970).

42. Bretton Woods Agreement Act, Ch. 339, sec. 9, 59 Stat. 516 (1945), as amended, 18 U.S.C. sec. 955 (1970).

43. Export-Import Bank Act of 1945, Ch. 341, sec. 11, 59 Stat. 529, as amended, 12 U.S.C. sec. 635 h (1970).

44. See Statement of Ass't Attorney General Weisl, Hearings on East-West Trade Before the Subcomm. on Europe of the House Comm. on Foreign Affairs, 90th Cong., 2d Sess., at 197, 209 (1968). But see, as to East Germany, McQuade, supra note 10, at 65 n. 83. Actually it is presently unclear whether East Germany has a debt default within the meaning of the Johnson Act. It is, however, evidently clear that the Johnson Act continues to apply to the Soviet Union notwithstanding the October 1972 American-Soviet settlement of the Soviet Union's Lend-Lease debt from World War II. Starr, "A New Legal Framework for Trade Between the United States and the Soviet Union: the 1972 US-USSR Trade Agreement." 67 Am. J. Int'l L.

63, 81 (1973). For a description of the 1972 American-Soviet debt settlement, see the text accompanying notes 89-90 infra.

45. 37 Op. Att'y Gen. 505 (1934); 42 Op. Att'y Gen. 15 (1963); 42 Op. Att'y Gen. 27 (1967). It is not clear whether the act's prohibition would apply to investment by the American party in a coproduction or joint venture arrangement.

46. Address by Harold B. Scott, Deputy Ass't Secretary for Domestic and Int'l Business and Director, Bureau of Int'l Commerce, U.S. Dep't of Commerce, before the Int'l Center of New England, in Boston, Feb. 4, 1971; S. Pisar, Coexistence and Commerce 107-114 (1970).

47. Pisar, supra note 46 at 107-114.

48. A large portion of the sale of agricultural products to the Soviet Union mentioned in note 61 infra was made under the Export Credit Sales Program.

49. Agricultural Trade Development and Assistance Act of 1954, as amended, 7 U.S.C. sec. 1701, 1703(d) (1970).

50. Id. sec. 1703(d), (j).

51. For example, the approximately $18 million sale of corn to the People's Republic of China that was announced by President Nixon in October 1972 was reportedly made without assistance from any of these programs. New York Times, Oct. 28, 1972, at 1, col. 6.

52. Export Marketing Service, U.S. Dep't. of Agriculture, "The Export Marketing Service and Its Program" (1970).

53. Agricultural Trade Development and Assistance Act of 1954, as amended, 7 U.S.C. secs. 1691, 1701-1710 (1970).

54. Id. sec. 1703(d).

55. Id.

56. Id. sec. 1703(d), (j).

57. See, e.g., note 61 infra.

58. Export Control Reg., 15 C.F.R. sec. 376.3 (1971). For a discussion of the history and administration of this shipping requirement, see Bilder, "East-West Trade Boycotts: A Study in Private, Labor Union, State, and Local Interference with Foreign Policy," 118 U. Pa. L. Rev. 841, 873-78 (1970), and McQuade, supra note 10, at 66-69, 77.

59. 36 Fed. Reg. 11811 (1971); New York Times, June 11, 1971, at 1, col. 8. This executive action by President Nixon did not affect the congressionally mandated requirement that at least 50 percent of cargoes procured, furnished, or financed by the United States be shipped in U.S. flag commercial vessels. The Merchant Marine Act of 1936, as amended, 46 U.S.C. sec. 1241(b) (1970). See also McQuade, supra note 10, at 66 n. 90. This legislative 50 percent requirement does not inhibit U.S. agricultural exports to communist countries because, although it applies to exports under the Public Law 480 Pro-

grams, it does not apply to exports under the Export Payment and Export Credit Sales Programs. The executive requirement adopted by President Kennedy and rescinded by President Nixon applied to all the designated wheat and cereal grain exports to the designated communist countries, whether or not made under any of the Public Law 480, Export Payment, or Export Credit Sales Programs.

60. See, for example, New York Times, June 11, 1971, at 1, col. 8.

61. In November 1971 the Nixon Administration announced the commercial sale of nearly $136 million of feed grain to the Soviet Union and said that the key to the sale was removal of the shipping requirement. New York Times, Nov. 6, 1971, at 1, cols. 6-7. In July 1972 the Nixon Administration announced the commercial sale of at least $750 million of wheat, corn, and other grains to the Soviet Union over a three-year period. The deal was said to be the largest grain transaction in history between two nations. Id., July 9, 1972, at 1, cols. 7-8. In August 1972 the U.S. Agriculture Department estimated that the Soviet purchases of U.S. farm products would total $1 billion over the next 12 months, with about half the purchases being for wheat. Id., Aug. 10, 1972, at 1, col. 8.

62. Agreement with the Government of the Union of Soviet Socialist Republics Regarding Certain Maritime Matters, Oct. 14, 1972. Commercial Agreements, supra note 18, at 33.

63. New York Times, Oct. 15, 1972, sec. 1, at 1, col. 1.

64. Foreign Assistance Act of 1961, as amended 22 U.S.C. sec. 2370(f) (1970).

65. Mutual Defense Assistance Control Act of 1951, 22 U.S.C. sec. 1611 et seq. (1970); Foreign Assistance Act of 1961, as amended 22 U.S.C. sec. 2370(n) (1970). See note following 22 U.S.C. sec. 2370 (1970).

66. 15 C.F.R. secs. 1000.101-1000.1407 (1973).

67. New York Times, Feb. 13, 1973, at 1, col. 8.

68. Office of Foreign Direct Investments, U.S. Dep't of Commerce, "1973 Foreign Direct Investment Program" 22-23 (1973).

69. Id.

70. Pub. L. No. 92-226, sec. 104(g) (Feb. 7, 1972), amending the Foreign Assistance Act of 1961, part I, chap. 2, title IV, sec. 239, 22 U.S.C. sec. 2199 (1970).

71. Overseas Private Investment Corporation, Release TS/167 (Mar. 21, 1972).

72. Foreign Assistance Act of 1963, Pub. L. No. 88-205, sec. 402(b), 77 Stat. 390, amending the Trade Expansion Act of 1962, Pub. L. No. 87-794, sec. 231, 76 Stat. 876-77, codified at 19 U.S.C. sec. 1861(b) (1970); Pres. Memo of Mar. 26, 1964, 29 Fed. Reg. 4851 (1964). MFN was never withdrawn from Yugoslavia; it was withdrawn from Poland in 1951 and restored in 1960. For the history of MFN treatment

for Yugoslavia, Poland, and the other communist countries, see Bilder, supra note 58, at 847 n.25, 854 nn.46-47; Berman, "The Legal Framework of Trade Between Planned and Market Economies: The Soviet-American Example," 24 Law and Contemp. Prob. 482, 505-06 and 506 n. 64 (1959).

73. Trade Agreements Extension Act of 1951, ch. 141, sec. 5, 65 Stat. 73; Pres. Proc. 2935, 16 Fed. Reg. 7635, 7637 (1951).

74. Ch. 497, 46 Stat. 590, codified in 19 U.S.C. (1970), as amended, Supp. II (1973).

75. Trade Expansion Act of 1962, Pub. L. No. 87-794, sec. 231, 76 Stat. 876-77 (1962), codified at 19 U.S.C. sec 1861(a) (1970).

76. Agreement with the Government of the Union of Soviet Socialist Republics Regarding Trade, Art. 1, Oct. 18, 1972 (hereinafter cited as U.S.-U.S.S.R. Trade Agreement) 67 Dep't State Bull. 595 (1972); also in Commercial Agreements, supra note 18, at 88.

77. This proposed act was published in 54 Dep't State Bull. No. 1405, 838, 843-44 (May 30, 1966), and in Dep't of State, The Battle Act Report 1966, 19th Rep. to Congress 36.

78. For a brief history of the bill, see Bilder, supra note 58, at 856-57.

79. Ch. 14, title II, 42 Stat. 11, as amended, 19 U.S.C. secs. 160-73 (1970).

80. Feller, "The Antidumping Act and the Future of East-West Trade," 66 Mich. L. Rev. 115 (1967); Berman, supra note 72, at 506-07; S. Pisar, Coexistence and Commerce 232-35 (1970). For a particularly comprehensive account of the problem, together with a thoughtful proposed solution, see Anthony, "The American Response to Dumping from Capitalist and Socialist Economies—Substantive Premises, and Restructured Procedures After the 1967 GATT Code," 54 Cornell L. Rev. 159 (1969).

81. U.S.-U.S.S.R. Trade Agreement, supra note 76, Art. 3 and Annex 1, 67 Dep't State Bull. 596, 598 (1972); also in Commercial Agreements, supra note 18, at 89, 92.

82. Feller, supra note 80, at 132-33; Berman, supra note 72, at 506-07; S. Pisar, Coexistence and Commerce 232-35 (1970). Other U.S. legislation that could create special problems when applied to imports from communist countries because of their particular cost-price system are the provisions in the Tariff Act of 1930 for countervailing duties, ch. 497, title III, sec. 303, 46 Stat. 687, codified at 19 U.S.C. sec. 1303 (1970), see also 19 C.F.R. 16.24 (1973), and for equalization duties, ch. 497, title III, sec. 336, 46 Stat. 701, as amended, 19 U.S.C. sec. 1336 (1970). Feller, supra note 80, at 133-36; Berman, supra note 72, at 506-08. To date there have not been serious problems here.

83. Tariff Schedules of the United States, Schedule 1, part 5, subpart B headnote 4, 19 U.S.C. sec. 1202 (1970), originally enacted as Trade Agreements Extension Act of 1951, ch. 141, sec. 11, 65 Stat. 75, codified at 19 U.S.C. sec. 1367 (1958), and implemented by Pres. Proc. 2935, 16 Fed. Reg. 7635, 7637 (1951). The Nixon Administration's Trade Reform Act of 1973 proposes repeal of this prohibition. H.R. 6767, 93d Cong., 1st Sess., sec. 706(f) (1973). As of the end of 1973, Congress has not made a final disposition of the Administration bill; but the House of Representatives passed the bill on December 11, 1973 without including any repeal of this prohibition. H.R. 10710, 93d Cong., 1st Sess.

84. Berman, supra note 72, at 509.

85. Agreement with the Government of the Union of Soviet Socialist Republics Regarding Certain Maritime Matters, Oct. 14, 1972. Commercial Agreements, supra note 18, at 33.

86. See text accompanying notes 57-63 supra.

87. The Administration stated that U.S. export controls were not discussed in the negotiations for the trade agreement. 67 Dep't State Bull. 592 (1972); also in Commercial Agreements, supra note 18, at 75.

88. See text paragraph accompanying notes 62-63 supra.

89. New York Times, Oct. 19, 1972, at 1, col. 1.

90. Agreement with the Government of the Union of Soviet Socialist Republics Regarding Settlement of Lend Lease, Reciprocal Aid and Claims, Art. 4, Oct. 18, 1972. 67 Dep't State Bull. 604 (1972); also in Commercial Agreements, supra note 18, at 106.

91. See note 37 supra. See also section of this chapter entitled "Credit Controls," first three paragraphs, supra.

92. U.S.-U.S.S.R. Trade Agreement, Art. 1, supra note 76, 67 Dep't State Bull. 595 (1972); also in Commercial Agreements, supra note 18, at 88. See also section of this chapter entitled "Tariff—Denial of MFN," supra.

93. Id. Art. 9, para. 1.

94. 67 Dep't State Bull. 593 (1972); also in Commercial Agreements, supra note 18, at 76.

95. H.R. 6767, 93d Cong., 1st Sess. secs. 501-06 (1973).

96. One possibility is a commitment by the state-trading country to purchase a specified minimum quantity of goods from the market-economy country. American-Soviet trade agreements were concluded on this basis in 1935 and 1937. Commercial Relations Agreement with the U.S.S.R., July 13, 1935, 49 Stat. 3805 (1935-36), E.A.S. No. 81; Commercial Relations Agreement with the U.S.S.R., Aug. 4, 1937, 50 Stat. 1619 (1937), E.A.S. No. 105. The 1937 agreement was subsequently extended for one-year periods: Aug. 5, 1938, 53 Stat. 1947 (1939), E.A.S. No. 132; Aug. 2, 1939, 53 Stat. 2404 (1939), E.A.S. No. 151; Aug. 6, 1940, 54 Stat. 2366 (1939-1941), E.A.S. No. 179; Aug. 2, 1941, 55 Stat. 1316 (1941-1942), E.A.S. No. 215; July 31, 1942, 56 Stat. 1575 (1942), E.A.S. No. 265.

Another alternative is the "commercial considerations" clause, by which the state trading country promises to determine its foreign trade solely on the basis of commercial and financial considerations. Such a provision is included in the General Agreement on Tariffs and Trade (GATT) but has the drawback that it is normally impossible to determine whether the state trading country is actually abiding by it.

In 1967 Poland was accepted as a contracting party to the GATT by promising to buy from all the other GATT countries together a total of goods each year equal to the total of such purchases by Poland during the previous year plus at least 7 percent. In 1971 Romania was accepted as a contracting party to the GATT by expressing its firm intention to increase its annual imports from all the other GATT countries together at a rate not less than the rate provided in Romania's five-year plan for the increase in Romania's total imports. GATT, Press Release 1091, Oct. 18, 1971. The growth of total imports provided in Romania's current five-year plan is between 7 and 8 percent per year. In September 1973 Hungary was accepted as a contracting party to the GATT. Apparently the chief adjustment made to accommodate Hungary's being a centrally planned economy was a provision for periodic consultations between Hungary and the other GATT contracting parties to examine Hungary's actual importing and exporting. See GATT doc. L/3908, Aug. 14, 1973.

Poland, Romania, and Hungary are the only three centrally planned economies to have applied to become and become contracting parties to the GATT. Czechoslovakia and Yugoslavia are also contracting parties; but Czechoslovakia became a contracting party in 1947 before it was a centrally planned economy, and Yugoslavia, which applied in 1958 and became a contracting party in 1965, demonstrated to GATT that it had adopted many market economy principles.

97. U.S.-U.S.S.R. Trade Agreement, supra note 76, Art. 2, para. 4, 67 Dep't State Bull. 596 (1972); also in Commercial Agreements, supra note 18, at 89. As a practical matter in American-Soviet trade, there is little likelihood that the United States will run a deficit during the three-year period of the Trade Agreement. Economic reality suggests that the difficulty in the bilateral trade will be the reverse: that the Soviet Union even with MFN will be unable to sell enough on the competitive American market to finance all that it would like to buy from the United States.

See also Hoya, "The Legal Framework of Soviet Foreign Trade," 56 Minn. L. Rev. 1, 23-28 (1971).

98. U.S.-U.S.S.R. Trade Agreement, Art. 3, supra note 76, 67 Dep't State Bull. 596 (1972); also in Commercial Agreements, supra note 18, at 89. See also text paragraph accompanying notes 79-82 supra.

99. See, e.g., the Jackson Amendment, 93d Cong., 1st Sess., 119 Cong. Rec. 6920-21 (1973), and H.R. 10710, 93d Cong., 1st Sess. secs. 401-407 (1973). The House of Representatives passed H.R. 10710 on December 11, 1973.

100. The Jackson Amendment, note 99 supra, would apply to all communist countries; but H.R. 10710 secs. 401-407, note 99 supra, would apply only to communist countries not receiving MFN as of the date of the bill's enactment, that is, it would not apply to Yugoslavia and Poland.

101. Letter from U.S.S.R. Minister of Foreign Trade Patolichev to U.S. Secretary of Commerce Peterson, quoted in a letter, dated Oct. 18, 1972, from U.S. Secretary of Commerce Peterson to U.S.S.R. Minister of Foreign Trade Patolichev. 67 Dep't State Bull. 600 (1972); also in Commercial Agreements, supra note 18, at 96.

102. U.S.-U.S.S.R. Trade Agreement, Art. 5 and Annexes 2 and 3, supra note 76, 67 Dep't State Bull. 596, 598, 599 (1972); also in Commercial Agreements, supra note 18, at 89, 92, 93.

103. Id. Annex 3, Art. 2, para. 3. 67 Dep't State Bull. 599 (1972); also in Commercial Agreements, supra note 18, at 93.

104 Hazard, "State Trading in History and Theory," 24 Law and Contemp. Prob. 243, 248 (1959).

105. U.S.-U.S.S.R. Trade Agreement, Art. 5, para. 3, supra note 76, 67 Dep't State Bull. 596 (1972); also in Commercial Agreements, supra note 18, at 90.

106. Id. Art. 6, par. 2, 67 Dep't State Bull. 597 (1972); also in Commercial Agreements, supra note 18, at 90.

107. Id. Art. 7, 67 Dep't State Bull. 597 (1972); also in Commercial Agreements, supra note 18, at 90. Another provision in the trade agreement of some significance requires "[a] ll currency payments" to be made in a "freely convertible currency." Id. Art. 4, 67 Dep't State Bull. 596 (1972); also in Commercial Agreements, supra note 18, at 89. Since this provision applies only to "currency payments," it apparently does not preclude barter or other transactions in which compensation is to be paid in a form other than "currency." Soviet trade agreements with market economy countries frequently contain a provision like that in the American agreement requiring currency payments to be made in a convertible currency. Starr, supra note 44, at 71-72.

108. See note 38, supra. See also section of this chapter entitled "Credit Controls," first three paragraphs, supra.

109. Letter from Polish Trade Minister Olechowski to U.S. Secretary of Commerce Peterson, Nov. 8, 1972, on file at the U.S. Dep't of Commerce.

110. Letter from Polish Trade Minister Olechowski to U.S. Secretary of Commerce Peterson, Nov. 8, 1972, on file at the U.S. Dep't of Commerce (not the same letter as the one cited in note 109, supra).

111. See section of this chapter entitled "Tariffs—Denial of MFN," supra.

112. Ch. 11, 63 Stat. 7, as amended, codified at 50 U.S.C. App. secs. 2021-2032, as amended, Supp. V (1970).

113. See references cited in note 11 supra.

114. 15 Fed. Reg. 9040 (1950), codified at 31 C.F.R. Part 500 (1971).

115. 28 Fed. Reg. 6974 (1963), codified at 31 C.F.R. Part 515 (1971).

116. 29 Fed. Reg. 6010 (1964), codified at 31 C.F.R. Part 500 (1971).

117. Trade Agreements Extension Act of 1951, ch. 141, sec. 5, 65 Stat. 73; Pres. Proc. 2935, 16 Fed. Reg. 7635, 7637 (1951).

118. Foreign Assistance and Related Agencies Appropriation Act, 1965, Title III, Pub. L. No. 88-634 (1964), 78 Stat. 1015 (1964); Export-Import Bank Act of 1945 sec. 2(b) (2), 12 U.S.C. sec. 635(b)(3) (1970), as amended, Supp. II (1973).

119. Export-Import Bank Act of 1945 sec 2(b) (3), Pub. L. No. 90-267 sec. 1(c), 82 Stat. 47 (1968), as amended 12 U.S.C. sec. 635(b)(3) (1970), as amended, Supp. II (1973).

120. Pub. L. No. 91-184, 83 Stat. 841, codified at 50 U.S.C. App. secs. 2401-2413 (1970), as amended, Supp. II (1973).

121. 36 Fed. Reg. 11441 (1971), codified at 31 C.F.R. 500.547 (1972); 36 Fed. Reg. 11808 (1971), U.S. Dep't of Commerce, Export Control Bull. No. 46 (June 11, 1971).

122. Export Expansion Finance Act of 1971 secs. (b) (5), Pub. L. No. 92-126, 85 Stat. 345 (1971), amending Export-Import Bank Act of 1945 sec. (2) (b) (3), 12 U.S.C. 635(b) (3) (1970), as amended, Supp. II (1973).

123. See note 36, supra.

124. Presidential Determination, Oct. 18, 1972, on file at the Export-Import Bank. See note 37, supra.

125. See note 38, supra.

126. U.S.-U.S.S.R. Trade Agreement, supra note 76, 67 Dep't State Bull. 595 (1972); also in Commercial Agreements, supra note 18, at 88.

127. H.R. 6767, 93d Cong., 1st. Sess. secs. 501-06 (1973).

128. Export-Import Bank Act of 1945 sec. 2(b) (2), 12 U.S.C. sec. 635(b) (2) (1970), as amended, Supp. II (1973). The fourth communist country for which such bank participation is authorized, along with the three mentioned in the preceding paragraph of text, is Yugoslavia, for which such participation was authorized in 1968. See note 35 supra.

129. Export-Import Bank Act of 1945, Ch. 341, sec. 11, 59 Stat. 529, as amended, 12 U.S.C. sec. 635h (1970).

130. 50 U.S.C. App. secs. 2401-2413 (1970), as amended, Supp. II (1973).

131. See the Jackson Amendment, 93d Cong., 1st Sess., 119 Cong. Rec. 6920-21 (1973), and H.R. 10710, 93d Cong., 1st Sess. secs. 401-407. The House of Representatives passed H.R. 10710 on December 11, 1973.

Since World War II, Japan has acceded to the terms of a variety
of multilateral treaties and agreements affecting her foreign trade,
including the General Agreement on Tariffs and Trade (GATT), the
Convention on Nomenclature for the Classification of Goods in Customs
Tariffs, the Convention Establishing a Customs Cooperation Council,
the Articles of Agreement of the International Monetary Fund, the
Convention on the Organization for Economic Cooperation and Development, and Cocom.[1] Japan has also entered into numerous bilateral
treaties and conventions concerning commerce and taxation with
countries in North America, Western Europe, the Near and Middle
East, Asia, Latin America, Africa, and Oceania.[2] In addition, during
the same period Japan has become a party to bilateral treaties and
agreements concerning commerce with the USSR[3] and most countries
in Eastern Europe.[4] Although normal diplomatic relations between
Japan and the People's Republic of China (PRC) were not restored
until September of 1972, since 1960 and 1962 the countries have engaged
in, respectively, so-called friendship trade and memorandum trade
and the latter's precursor, so-called "L-T trade";[5] it is anticipated
that Japan and the PRC will enter into a trade treaty in 1974 providing
for reciprocal most favored nation (MFN) treatment in tariffs and
customs clearance and annual consultations.*

---

*After the completion of this chapter, an intergovernmental trade
agreement was concluded in Peking between China and Japan on January 6, 1974. It is valid for three years and is automatically to be
renewed unless either side objects. In addition to provisions on most-
favored-nation treatment and annual consultations, the agreement
contains clauses on settlement of trade accounts in both currencies;

Japan is the PRC's principal trading partner. Trade between Japan and the PRC, USSR, and Eastern Europe grows annually. And the Japanese press, echoing business and governmental leaders and private and quasi-public organizations for the promotion of trade with the PRC and USSR,[6] has been replete with reports of the prospects of increased commercial intercourse with the PRC in the wake of restoration of normal diplomatic relations and Japanese participation in the exploitation of Siberian natural resources. The fact remains, however, that trade with so-called communist countries remains a relatively negligible constituent of Japan's total foreign trade.[7]

Thus, for example, Japan's imports from and exports to Eastern Europe (excluding the USSR) constitute less than 1 percent of her total import and export trade.[8] Japan's import and export trade with, respectively, Southeast Asia and Latin America is greater than her combined import and export trade with both the PRC and the USSR; similarly, Japan's exports to Africa exceed her combined exports to the PRC and USSR, while her imports from Africa exceed her imports from either the PRC or USSR (although not aggregate imports from both countries).[9] In 1972 Japan's exports to the PRC and USSR were, respectively, $609.3 million and $504.4 million, while imports were, respectively, $490.9 million and $592.3 million; in the same year, Japan's exports to Western Europe and the United States were, respectively, $4.754 billion and $8.856 billion, while imports from these areas were, respectively, $2.479 billion and $5.848 billion.[10]

Economic and political realities, not the existence or absence of a trade treaty, determine commercial opportunities. The fact that Japan has been a party to trade treaties and agreements with countries in Eastern Europe for more than 10 years has not significantly enhanced the volume of her trade with those countries. In like respect, the absence of a formal trade treaty with the PRC (and the requirement that Japanese enterprises comply with the four principles stipulated by Premier Chou En-lai in 1970)[11] did not prevent the annual increase of Japanese exports to and imports from the PRC. In any event, the prospective trader with Japan will in practice be more concerned in most instances with the labyrinth of domestic legislation and regulations governing Japan's external trade than the sparse abstractions of most treaties and agreements concerning commerce (generally in contradistinction to taxation). For example, the fact that a substantial legal question existed in the 1960s and early 1970s

----

for arbitration of disputes; on promotion of technical exchanges and holding of trade fairs in each country; and on exchange of news correspondents. The Japanese text of the agreement was published in Nihon-Keizai Shinbun, January 6, 1974, at 2.

as to whether the administration of Japanese foreign investment controls was violative of bilateral and multilateral treaty obligations proved as a general proposition wholly irrelevant to foreign investors.[12]

In the absence of overriding provisions of multilateral or bilateral engagements, trade and other commercial transactions between residents of Japan and nonresidents,[13] including the import and export of goods, outward direct investment by residents of Japan, certain types of direct inward investment in Japan by nonresidents and certain types of service, licensing and technical assistance arrangements, are principally governed by the Foreign Exchange Law. Enacted in 1949, this law states as its raison d'etre,

> the control of foreign exchange, foreign trade and other
> foreign transactions, necessary for the proper development
> of foreign trade and for the safeguarding of the balance of
> international payments and the stability of the currency,
> as well as the most effective use of foreign currency funds,
> for the sake of the rehabilitation and the expansion of the
> national economy.[14]

As a matter of drafting methodology, the Foreign Exchange Law seeks to accomplish its objectives by the simple expedient of prohibiting, in the absence of express exemption by the statute itself or a subordinate regulation, the performance of or the conclusion of agreements concerning a comprehensive range of generically characterized transactions between residents of Japan and nonresidents—for example, payments, loans, guarantees, the acquisition of interests in securities and real property, the rendering of services, and the import and export of precious metals.[15] "Exemption" commonly takes the form of a requirement of prior governmental authorization (license).

CONTROLS OVER OUTWARD DIRECT EQUITY INVESTMENT AND THE EXPORT OF TECHNOLOGY AND GOODS

Outward Direct Equity Investment

Outward direct equity investment, both portfolio and nonportfolio, by residents of Japan is subject to the requirement of prior governmental license.[16] Since the late 1960s, controls over outward direct equity investment have been substantially relaxed, and in many instances licenses are now issued on a so-called automatic basis.

Export of Technology

There are no governmental controls over the export of technology by a resident of Japan (unaccompanied by outward direct investment), unless (1) the export is effected pursuant to a cross-licensing arrangement;[17] or (2) the exporter will not receive "adequate" consideration for the export (except in those cases where no or inadequate consideration is customary in light of "social custom" or "business practice");[18] or (3) consideration for the export is not to be received in accordance with a "standard method of settlement," viz., in the case of receipt of payment in connection with invisible transactions, failure to receive the entire consideration in foreign exchange or its equivalent[19] within one year prior or six months subsequent to the export.[20]

Export of Goods

General. The Foreign Exchange Law posits the general principle that "the export of goods from Japan will be permitted with the minimum restrictions thereon consistent with the purposes of this Law."[21] The statute proceeds to identify four constituents of export transactions, each amplified by cabinet order, the presence of any one of which may serve to invoke the requirement of prior governmental license: (1) the nature of the goods; (2) the destination of the export; (3) the nature of the contract; and (4) payment terms.[22] This requirement is to be administered, however, "within the limit necessary for the maintenance of the balance of international payments and sound development of international trade and the national economy."[23]

Requirement of prior governmental license. Prior governmental license is required in respect of the following export transactions, stipulated by the Export Trade Control Order: (1) the export of over 200 categories of goods (as a general proposition strategic goods, including Cocom items,[24] goods required to meet domestic demand, goods subject to United Nations embargo, goods the export of which may elicit the imposition of import controls by the jurisdiction of destination, and conventional contraband) to one, a combination, or all of four areas;[25] (2) the export of any goods to Iran, Iraq, Nigeria, and Southern Rhodesia;[26] (3) the export of goods pursuant to a "processing deal," that is, the export of goods processed in Japan from imported raw materials or a "consignment sales" contract for consignment to a party situated in foreign country for sale there;[27] and (4) the export of goods not in consonance with a standard method of settlement, viz., failure to receive the entire consideration in foreign exchange or its equivalent within prescribed temporal periods and in accordance with one of several methods—for example, to obtain an irrevocable letter of credit prior to export declaration and certification by an authorized foreign exchange bank and to receive payment thereunder by means of drafts payable within five months after sight or within six months after shipment.[28]

The Minister of International Trade and Industry (MITI) enjoys discretion to deny, or stipulate conditions to, requisite export licenses "when he deems it necessary for the maintenance of the balance of international payments and sound development of the international or the national economy."[29]

Requirement of export declaration and certification. With the exception of the export of goods not requiring payment—for example, gifts—or involving settlement in ordinary yen currency, all exporters must make an export declaration to an authorized foreign exchange bank for certification, evidencing (1) compliance with a standard method of settlement or (2) license in respect of a nonstandard method of settlement or a processing deal or consignment contract.[30]

Exceptions to the requirement of prior license and export declaration and certification. Unless the export goods are within one of 18 categories—including, for example, war vehicles and parts—neither prior license nor export declaration and certification are required in the following cases: (1) goods temporarily landed in Japan, but excluding the export of goods transported under bills of lading or similar instruments designating Japan as their destination and certain goods to specified countries, such as lithium ore to A area;[31] (2) certain goods generally for private or public, noncommercial use;[32] and (3) subject to notification to customs, generally, personal and household effects and professional instruments removed by an individual departing from Japan and by certain categories of persons.[33]

Customs confirmation. In accordance with instructions from MITI, customs must confirm that a prospective exporter has obtained any requisite license and certification.[34]

Collection of export proceeds. An exporter is required to collect payment in full for the goods "promptly" after export in accordance with the method of payment certified by an authorized foreign exchange bank (excepting those cases in which a nonstandard method of settlement has been authorized).[35] An exporter is further required to collect payment in full within three months after (1) notice that a draft has been dishonored by the drawee for "bona fide" and "inevitable" cause or (2) in the event of a price increase, the day following the effective date of the increase.[36] If the exporter is unable to collect payment in full for bona fide and inevitable cause within the three-month period, an extension or authorization of noncollection must be obtained from the MITI;[37] in turn, in granting such authorization, the minister must verify, with the prior concurrence of the minister of Finance (MOF), that the failure to collect export proceeds involves neither "flight of capital" nor an attempt to evade law.[38]

Review of export matters. The MITI is empowered to require reports from all persons who obtained license or certification or who have either manufactured or exported the goods in question.[39]

Exports infringing foreign copyrights and industrial property rights. The Export Trade Control Order requires an exporter to secure prior governmental license for the export of goods that would infringe copyrights or industrial property rights or would cause confusion regarding origin in the jurisdiction of destination.[40] In turn, a ministerial Notification Concerning Items Infringing Patents, Etc. in Countries of Destination identifies 20 such infringing items in four broad categories: patents, design rights, trademarks, and copyrights.[41]

Unfair and orderly exports. The Export and Import Trading Law has as its purposes the prevention of "unfair export trade," viz., the export of goods that may infringe on copyrights or industrial property rights in the jurisdiction of destination, bear a false indication or origin, fail conspicuously to satisfy the requirements of contract, or are contrary to "fair commercial practice in international trade" and the maintenance of orderly exports and imports.[42] To this end, the statute permits exporters (and importers) to enter into agreements concerning price, quantity, quality, design, or "any other matter" with respect to the export of the goods in question; agreements of this character must be filed with the MITI not less than 10 days prior to their conclusion.[43] Relatedly, the Export and Import Trading Law permits exporters (and importers) to create associations and trade federations, that is, juridical entities, concerned with, inter alia, prevention of unfair export practices, publicity, export financing and cultivation of foreign markets, and, subject to authorization by MITI, establishment among their members of price, quantity, quality, design, and other standards governing exports and domestic transactions in the goods to be exported. The statute empowers MITI to require, inter alia, prior approval of exports by parties to an industry agreement or members of an export association or trade federation in the interests of "sound development of export trade."[44] The Export and Import Trading Law provides express (albeit qualified) exemptions from the application of the Law Concerning Prohibition of Private Monopoly and Methods of Preserving Fair Trade[45] and contemplates consultation between MITI and the Fair Trade Commission, the governmental agency responsible for administering Japanese antimonopoly controls.[46]

Export incentives. A variety of export incentives are provided by Japanese law, including, for example, special deductions from receipts for the transfer or supply of technology and services to foreign entities allowed as an exception to the Corporation Tax Law,[47] financing extended by the Export-Import Bank of Japan,[48] and insurance available under the Export Insurance Law[49] in respect of the risk of loss from foreign exchange rate fluctuations and "other risks inherent in export trade and other foreign transactions" not within the scope of ordinary insurance.[50] The availability as a practical matter of these incentives—during a period like 1972 and 1973 when Japanese industry associations reportedly took measures at their own initiative and the Japanese Government reportedly sought by formal controls and administrative guidance to inhibit exports—is of course another question. In addition to incentives accorded individual enterprises, the Japan External Trade Recovery Organization (JETRO) was established under the supervision of the MITI for the purpose of promoting in general Japanese foreign trade.[51]

CONTROLS OVER THE IMPORT OF TECHNOLOGY AND GOODS

Import of Technology

The Law Concerning Foreign Investment[52] requires prior governmental authorization (validation) of the conclusion or amendment by a "foreign investor"[53] and a party in Japan of an "A-class technological assistance contract" or the amendment or renewal of a "B-class technological assistance contract" rendering it an A-class agreement.[54] An A-class technological assistance contract concerns the transfer by a foreign investor to a party in Japan of "rights relating to technology, such as industrial property rights and licenses thereof, assistance in techniques of factory management, and others designated by the competent Minister" and possesses a term or period of payment in excess of one year;[55] a B-class technological assistance contract, the conclusion or amendment of which is subject to prior governmental license pursuant to the Foreign Exchange Law, possesses a term and period of payment of one year or less.[56]

In 1968, the Japanese Government adopted a program for the liberalization of the induction of foreign technology (as a practical matter, unaccompanied by inward direct investment).[57] The 1968 program established three basic formulas for liberalization: (1) "automatic" validation or license—that is, approval by the Bank of Japan pursuant to a delegation of authority by the competent ministers,[58] of, respectively, A- and B-class technological assistance contracts contemplating payment of fixed aggregate consideration in an amount equivalent to U.S. $50,000 or less (including certain gratuitous transactions), unless the contract constitutes either a cross-licensing arrangement or an agreement between a foreign investor and its subsidiary or branch office in Japan;[59] (2) "basic delegation" of authority to the Bank of Japan to process applications for validation and license in respect of, respectively, A-class and B-class technological assistance contracts contemplating the payment of consideration in excess of the equivalent of U.S. $50,000 unless the competent minister or ministers elect to intervene in the screening process within one month after the date of application due to apprehension that the contract could have a "serious adverse effect on the Japanese economy";[60] and (3) "nonliberalized" technology subject to case-by-case screening procedures, originally comprising seven categories of foreign technology but now applicable until July 1, 1974 only to certain types of computer technology.[61]

Import of Goods

General. As noted above, the Foreign Exchange Law governs the import of goods into, as well as the export of goods from, Japan. The Import Trade Control Order[62] provides generally that the import of goods into Japan is subject to the requirement of prior license by an authorized foreign exchange bank in accordance with procedures established by MITI;[63] in addition, ministerial license must be obtained pursuant to other provisions of the order, which require discrete prior authorization by the MITI of specified transactions, depending upon the character and quantity of the goods, the character of the contract, the nature of payment terms, or the origin of the goods, either in lieu of, or as a condition precedent to issuance of, the license by an authorized foreign exchange bank.[64] In turn, a ministerial ordinance establishes a dual licensing procedure: (1) the nonliberalized import quota system applicable to goods identified by the MITI by means of public notice, the import of which requires issuance to the prospective importer on an ad hoc basis of an import quota certificate as a condition precedent to the issuance of an import license; and (2) the automatic approval system, generally governing goods not subject to the import quota system (or other requirements of prior license by the MITI), merely requiring pro forma license by an authorized foreign exchange bank.[65]

Requirement of MITI license. In addition to imports requiring the issuance of import quota certificates—that is, goods subject to the import quota system—the following import transactions are subject to the requirement of prior license by MITI in lieu of license by an authorized foreign exchange bank: (1) if the importer will not pay the full value of the imported goods;[66] (2) if payment is to be effected in ordinary yen currency (in contradistinction to foreign currency or free yen, freely convertible into foreign exchange);[67] and (3) if the import is pursuant to a processing deal contract (with the exception of transactions authorized under the Export Trade Control Order).[68]

In contrast, the following import transactions invoke the requirement of prior license by the MITI as a condition precedent to issuance of a license by an authorized foreign exchange bank: (1) if the import is pursuant to a consignment sales contract (limited to consignments by foreign to Japanese parties and excluding consignments entailing payment of the sales proceeds within four months after customs clearance);[69] (2) if the imported goods originate in one of several countries or "shipment areas" stipulated by the MITI;[70] and (3) if the import is not effected in consonance with a standard method of settlement.[71]

In the event that an import transaction invokes the requirement of prior license by the MITI, the minister is accorded broad discretion

> when he deems it necessary for the healthy development
> of foreign trade and the national economy, [to] provide
> for conditions as to delivery time, currency of settlement,
> etc., origin of goods, shipment area, or other matters
> pertaining to import. . . .[72]

Exceptions to the requirement of prior license. Exceptions to the requirement of prior license by an authorized foreign exchange bank of the MITI parallel the exceptions to the requirement of prior license and export declaration and certification applicable to export transactions, that is, generally, the import of goods for private or public, noncommercial use, personal and household effects, and goods temporarily landed in Japan.[73]

Deposits. The MITI is empowered to require persons who have obtained requisite import licenses to effect deposits, calculated as a percentage of the value of the goods to be imported, with authorized foreign exchange banks.[74]

Customs clearance. At the time of clearance of imported goods under the Customs Law, customs must verify the sufficiency of import licenses or the propriety of their omission.[75]

Duties. Importers are required to make both import and duty declarations.[76] Duties are levied on imported goods, generally on an ad valorem basis (including shipping, freight, and insurance costs) and in certain instances on a specific duty basis, pursuant to the Customs Law, the Customs Tariff Law,[77] and special legislation, such as the Temporary Customs Tariff Measures Law.[78] As indicated at the outset, Japan is a party to the GATT and as of June 1973 had subjected to concession or agreement rates approximately 2,288 items.[79] In addition to a statutory basis for extension by Japan of beneficial treaty rates to nontreaty nations,[80] Japan has granted by bilateral agreement MFN treatment to countries that are not members of the GATT, such as the USSR.[81]

Retaliatory duties. The Customs Tariff Law contemplates the levy of additional duties in the following cases: (1) the jurisdiction of cultivation or manufacture does not accord Japanese goods MFN treatment;[82] (2) the goods are exported from or shipped through a jurisdiction that does not accord MFN treatment to Japanese vessels or aircraft or goods exported from or shipped through Japan;[83] (3) the jurisdiction of production or export provides direct or indirect subsidies and the import causes or threatens to cause material injury to, or to inhibit the development of, domestic industry;[84] (4) the goods are "dumped," causing or threatening to cause material injury to, or to inhibit the development of, domestic industry;[85] and (5) an emergency occurs in which the import of goods in increased quantities causes or threatens to cause serious injury to extant domestic industry.[86]

Collection of claimable assets in connection with import transactions. In a manner mirroring provisions of the Export Trade Control Order relative to collection of export proceeds, the Import Trade Control Order requires any person who has acquired claimable assets in connection with an import transaction—such as an agency fee or penalties—to collect the claim at maturity;[87] if the MITI seeks to authorize noncollection, the absence of "flight of capital" and an attempt to evade law must be verified.[88]

Review of import matters. Again in a manner similar to the Export Trade Control Order, the Import Trade Control Order empowers the MITI to require reports from persons who have imported or are importing goods and to review the extent to which the transactions comply with the terms of import documentation and law.[89]

Infringing imports. The act of import of goods into Japan constitutes a use of Japanese industrial property rights and copyrights to which the goods are subject.[90] In August 1972, the Japanese Customs authorities substantially circumscribed the utility of customs procedures available to the owners of registered Japanese trademarks to prohibit parallel imports (although the rights of licensees appear unimpaired).[91] It is uncertain the extent to which this shift in administrative policy may in the future affect the rights of owners of registered Japanese patents, utility models, design rights, and copyrights; it also is uncertain the extent to which the registrant may be able to rely on the provisions of the Copyright Law or the industrial property right statutes (other than the Trademark Law)[92] themselves to prohibit parallel imports, notwithstanding the amelioration of customs controls.

Orderly imports. As indicated above, the Export and Import Trading Law permits importers to enter into agreements and to organize associations and federations for the purpose of regulating import transactions.[93] As in the case of exports, MITI is empowered

to require, among other things, prior approval of imports by parties
to an industry import agreement or members of an import association
or trade federation in the interests of "sound development of import
trade."94

PROGNOSIS

Barring major political or economic change, trade between
Japan and the PRC, the USSR, and Eastern Europe will continue to
grow, although trade with Eastern Europe (excluding the USSR) will
most likely remain a negligible percentage of Japan's total foreign
trade. Intensification of commercial relations is dictated by a variety
of related factors including the assumption by Japan of a diplomatic
stance increasingly independent of U.S. foreign policy (facilitated by
the "Nixon shokkus" and rapprochement between the United States
and the PRC and the USSR), the acute sense of vulnerability experienced
as a result of the energy crisis, an external trade policy directed to
the acquisition and diversification of raw material and energy sources,
and the physical proximity to Japan of the PRC and the USSR. Depending in part upon the volume of Japan's imports of raw materials and
fuels pursuant to joint development projects with the USSR and the
PRC's agricultural capacity, fuel resources, and rate of industrial
growth, it is likely that Japan's trade with the PRC will quite rapidly
outstrip her trade with the USSR.

Notwithstanding the continued growth of trade between Japan and
the PRC, the USSR, and Eastern Europe, and the profound psychological
impact on the Japanese of restoration of relations with the PRC, Japan
will remain economically dependent upon the United States as a market,
as a source of raw materials, and, increasingly, as a base for manufacturing operations. This dependence will only be reinforced by the
abrupt decline in 1973 of Japan's foreign exchange reserves (leading
in turn to the application with renewed vigor of the foreign exchange
and related controls governing external trade discussed herein), the
increased costs attendant upon the spiraling price of fuels, and a
consequent major export promotion effort. Like Joyce's Daedalus,
the extent of Japan's historical economic involvement with the United
States may be a nightmare from which she is trying to awake, but
Japan is habituated to trade with the United States and the United
States provides the only world market capable of absorbing such a
substantial portion of Japan's industrial output. In short, Japan's
stake in the U.S. economy—both as a market and source of supply
and manufacture—is simply too substantial to permit significant
attenuation of the relationship of dependence.

Some observers appear mesmerized by the mere fact of open diplomatic and economic intercourse between Japan (and the United States) and the PRC and the USSR. And, indeed, after so many years of minimal dealings and rigid, sharply delineated international relations, such contact is a striking element on the world landscape. But an analysis that would suggest that Japan's trade with either the PRC or USSR will approach in the foreseeable future the scale and significance of Japan's trade with the West—even assuming equanimity on the part of the PRC and the USSR to the prospect of deep and continued Japanese participation in their natural resources—is chimerical.

NOTES

1. See Teikoku Chiho Gyosei Gakkai, Genko Nihon Holi (hereinafter cited as Current Laws); English language lists appear in the Japan Branch of the International Law Association, The Japanese Annual of International Law.

2. For example, Treaty of Friendship, Commerce and Navigation between the United States and Japan, April 2, 1953, 4 U.S.T. and O.I.A. 2063, T.I.A.S. No. 2863; Arrangements with Japan on Trade in Cotton Textiles, January 28, 1972, 23 U.S.T. and O.I.A. 27, T.I.A.S. No. 7271; Convention Between the United States and Japan for the Avoidance of Double Taxation and the Prevention of Fiscal Evasion with Respect to Taxes on Income, March 8, 1971, U.S.T. and O.I.A. 967, T.I.A.S. No. 7385.

3. Protocol Concerning the Development of Trade and the Mutual Granting of Most Favored Nation Treatment, October 19, 1956, cited in 1 the Japan Branch of International Law Association, op. cit., supra note 1, 88; Treaty Between Japan and the USSR Concerning Commerce, December 6, 1957, 93 Current Laws 608-12; Agreement Between Japan and the USSR Concerning Trade and Payment (Ministry of Foreign Affairs Notification No. 201, 1971), id. at 604-75. The conclusion of treaties requires ratification by the Japanese Diet. In contrast, agreements assume the form of Ministry of Foreign Affairs notifications; a limited number of agreements are reproduced in Current Laws.

4. Treaty Between Japan and Poland Concerning Commerce, April 26, 1958, id. at 608-12; Treaty Between Japan and Yugoslavia Concerning Commerce and Navigation, February 28, 1959, id. at 608-40; Treaty Between Japan and Czechoslovakia Concerning Commerce, December 15, 1959, id. at 605; Treaty Between Japan and Romania Concerning Commerce and Navigation, September 1, 1969, id. at 608-54; Treaty Between Japan and Bulgaria Concerning Commerce and Navigation, February 28, 1970, id. at 608 ff; Agreement

Between Japan and Bulgaria Concerning Trade and Payment (Notification no. 56, 1967), id. at 607. Japan has trade agreements, but not treaties, with Hungary and East Germany.

5. For a historical analysis of trade relations between Japan and the PRC since World War II, see Shao-chuan Leng, "Sino-Japanese Trade," 5 Law and Policy in Int'l Bus. 780 (1973); A. Young, "Japan's Trade with China: Impact of the Nixon Visit," 9 Journal of the American Chamber of Commerce in Japan 37 (1972), reprinted from Royal Institute of International Affairs, 28 The World Today 342 (1972); Japan External Trade Organization, How to Approach the China Market (1972).

6. For example, Japan Council for the Promotion of International Trade, China-Asia Trade Structure Research Center, Japan Chamber of Commerce, Federation of Economic Organizations, Japan-Soviet Joint Economic Committee, Japan-Soviet Union Society, Japan-Soviet Trade Association, and the Organization for Trade Between Japan and the Soviet Union and East Europe. Counterpart organizations and committees exist for the promotion of trade with Poland, East Germany, Hungary, Bulgaria, Czechoslovakia, Romania, and Yugoslavia. See Y. Terada, "The System of Trade Between Japan and the East European Countries, Including the Soviet Union," 37 Law and Contemp. Prob. 429, 437-441 (1972).

7. See figures cited in Oriental Economist, Japan Economic Yearbook 1973 76 and 293 (1973); the Japan Economic Journal (Nihon Keizai Shimbun), Industrial Review of Japan 1974 at 8; Terada, op. cit., at 429-431.

8. Oriental Economist, op. cit. supra note 7 at 76 (approximations on a customs clearance basis).

9. Ibid.

10. Ibid.

11. See Leng, op. cit. supra note 5 at 794 and 796; and Young, op. cit. supra note 5 at 37.

12. See for example, S. Michida, "Capital Liberalization as a Treaty Question and Offensive and Defensive Strategies Concerning Foreign Capital," 2 Law in Japan: An Annual 1 (R. Rabinowitz transl., 1968); Y. Fujita, "Does Japan's Restriction on Foreign Capital Violate Her Treaties—In Response to Michida Article," 3 id. at 162 (1969); Compare Organization for Economic Cooperation and Development (Committee for Invisible Transactions), Liberalisation of International Capital Movements—Japan (1968).

13. See Foreign Exchange and Foreign Trade Control Law (Law No. 228, 1949, as amended)—hereinafter cited Foreign Exchange Law—Arts. 5 and 6, paras. 1(5) and (6). English-language translations of the Foreign Exchange Law and the principal Japanese statutes and subordinate cabinet orders and ministerial ordinances, regulations

and notifications appear in Eibun Horeisha Law Bulletin Series (hereinafter cited EHS); these translations are periodically updated.

14. Foreign Exchange Law Art. 1 in V EHS No. 5010 (with modification).

15. Foreign Exchange Law Arts. 27-32, 36-40, 42-45.

16. Foreign Exchange Law Arts. 32-35, para. 1(1); Cabinet Order Concerning Control of Foreign Exchange Art. 14, para. 1; Ministerial Ordinance Concerning Control of Invisible Transactions (Ministry of Finance Ordinance No. 58, 1963, as amended), hereinafter cited as Ministerial Ordinance Concerning Control of Invisible Transactions, attached list No. 24; Kura-Tame No. 4639, 1968, as amended.

17. Foreign Investment Council Report Concerning Liberalization of Induction of Technology (May 6, 1968), hereinafter cited as Foreign Investment Council Report Concerning Liberalization of Induction of Technology.

18. Cabinet Order Concerning Control of Foreign Exchange Art. 18, paras. 2(2), 3, and 4; Ministerial Ordinance Concerning Control of Invisible Transactions attached list No. IV, 2(C), (F) and (G); Ministerial Ordinance Concerning Control of Invisible Transactions Relating to Foreign Trade attached list No. IX (V) and (VI), attached list No. X (IV) and (V), and attached list No. XII.

19. That is, ordinary domestic yen accompanied by a certificate of foreign currency conversion or "free yen" freely convertible into foreign exchange. Cabinet Order Concerning Exchange Non-Resident Free Yen Account (Cabinet Order No. 157, 1960, as amended).

20. Ministerial Ordinance Concerning Standard Method of Settlement (Ministry of International Trade and Industry Ordinance No. 62, 1962, as amended), hereinafter cited as Ministerial Ordinance Concerning Standard Method of Settlement, attached list No. III.

21. Art. 47 in V EHS No. 5010.

22. Art. 48, para. 1.

23. Art. 48, para. 2 in V EHS No. 5010; Export Trade Control Order art. 1, para. 6.

24. See 1969 Peking Shanghai Japan Industry Exposition v. Japan, Tokyo District Court, July 8, 1969, 20 Administrative Cases 842, holding that denial by MITI on political rather than economic grounds of export licenses in respect of 19 items on the Cocom list was an improper exercise of ministerial discretion beyond the ambit of the Export Trade Control Order Art. 1, para. 6; nevertheless, the court further held that the plaintiff was not entitled to damages for official negligence in denying the requisite licenses because MITI could not be deemed to have acted without care. The decision is discussed in T. Doi, 3 Kokusai Torihiki Hanrei Shu 419 (1971).

25. Of particular relevance here is the "A area," comprising 66 countries including the principal European and Central European

countries, the USSR, the PRC, and North America. Art. 1, para. 1, item (1), and attachment No. I. Export licenses generally have a term of three months from the data of issuance. Export Trade Control Order Art. 8.

26. Art. 1, para. 1, item (1)-2 and attachment No. I-2.

27. Art. 1, para. 1, item (2).

28. Art. 1, para. 1, item (3); Ministerial Ordinance Concerning Standard Method of Settlement attached list No. I. MITI must obtain prior concurrence of MOF in granting licenses pursuant to Export Trade Control Order Art. 1, para. 1, item (3). Art. 1, para. 3.

29. Export Trade Control Order Art. 1, para. 6 in V EHS No. 5060; 1969 Peking Shanghai Japan Industry Exposition v. Japan, supra at note 24.

30. Export Trade Control Order Art. 3; Export Trade Control Regulation Art. 4.

31. Export Trade Control Order Art. 4(1).

32. Export Trade Control Order Art. 4(2) and attachment No. II.

33. Export Trade Control Order Art. 4(3) and attachment No. IV.

34. Export Trade Control Order Art. 5; Export Trade Control Regulation Art. 6. The Export Trade Control Order also provides for delegation by the MITI to Customs of specified authority. Art. 11; Customs Law (Law No. 61, 1959, as amended)—hereinafter cited Customs Law—Arts. 67 and 70.

35. Export Trade Control Order Art. 6, para. 1.

36. Export Trade Control Order Art. 6, para. 2; Export Trade Control Regulation Art. 5, para. 1.

37. Export Trade Control Order Art. 6, para. 3; Export Trade Control Regulation Art. 5, para. 2.

38. Export Trade Control Order Art. 6, para. 4.

39. Export Trade Control Order Arts. 7 and 10; Export Trade Control Regulation Art. 7. The collection of reports may be "entrusted" to the Bank of Japan, Export Trade Control Order Art. 11-2.

40. Export Trade Control Order Art. 1, para. 1, item (1) and attachment No. I, item 211; Ministry of International Trade and Industry Notification No. 342. See Export and Import Trading Law (Law No. 299, 1952, as amended)—hereinafter cited Export and Import Trading Law—Arts. 2(1) and (2) defining "unfair export trading" to include the export of goods "which may infringe industrial property rights or copyrights protected by the laws and orders of the country of destination" or which bear a false indication of origin. In V EHS No. 5560.

41. Ministry of International Trade and Industry Notification No. 342 sec. III(10).

42. Arts. 1 and 2 in V EHS No. 5560.

43. Export and Import Trading Law Art. 5.

44. Export and Import Trading Law Arts. 8-19, 20-27, 27-(2)-27-(16), 28, 29-31 in V EHS No. 5560.

45. Law No. 54, 1947, as amended, hereinafter cited as Antimonopoly Law. In fact, the Antimonopoly Law Art. 8, para. 2 requires filing by trade associations with the Fair Trade Commission of reports within 30 days after their establishment. While the Antimonopoly Law Art. 22 exempts from the scope of its application, inter alia, acts of entrepreneurs or trade associations performed in accordance with the terms of special legislation identified by the Law Concerning Exemptions from the Application of the Antimonopoly Law (Law No. 138, 1947, as amended), that statute omits reference to the Export and Import Trading Law.

46. Export and Import Trading Law Arts. 33-34; see Foreign Exchange Law Art. 65, providing that none of its provisions "shall be construed to repeal, modify or affect the application of [the Antimonopoly Law] . . . or the power of the Fair Trade Commission to take action thereunder in any particular situation." In V EHS No. 5010.

47. Law No. 34, 1965, as amended; Special Taxation Measures Law (Law No. 26, 1957, as amended) Arts. 1, 46-2, and 58.

48. See Export-Import Bank of Japan Law (Law No. 268, 1950, as amended).

49. Law No. 67, 1950, as amended—hereinafter cited as Export Insurance Law—in V EHS No. 5600.

50. Export Insurance Law Art. 1.

51. Japan External Trade Recovery Organization Law (Law No. 95, 1958, as amended).

52. Law No. 163, 1950, as amended, hereinafter cited as Foreign Investment Law.

53. See Foreign Investment Law Art. 3, para. 1(1), and Regulation for Enforcement of the Foreign Investment Law (Foreign Investment Commission Regulation No. 2, 1950, as amended).

54. Foreign Investment Law Art. 10. Very limited exceptions to the requirement are provided in Cabinet Order Concerning Exceptions, Etc. to Standards of Validation Based on the Foreign Investment Law (Cabinet Order No. 221, 1952, as amended)—hereinafter cited as Cabinet Order Concerning Exceptions—Art. 3-2.

55. Foreign Investment Law Art. 3, para. 1(3) in V EHS No. 5410 and Art. 10; Designation of Technological Assistance (Foreign Investment Council Notification No. 5, 1950).

56. Foreign Exchange Law Art. 42; Cabinet Order Concerning Control of Foreign Exchange Arts. 16 and 17, para. 1, item (4); Ministerial Ordinance Concerning Control of Invisible Transactions attached list No. IV(1); Ministerial Ordinance Concerning Control of Invisible Transactions Relating to Foreign Trade attached list Nos. IX(II) and X(I) and (II). On its face, Foreign Investment Law Art. 10

would appear to apply to outward licensing by Japanese licensors in favor of foreign licensees as well as the converse; nevertheless, as a matter of administrative interpretation, outward licensing is excluded from the scope of the article and, hence, from the requirement of validation.

Foreign Exchange Law Art. 42 requires prior governmental license of the conclusion by an exchange resident and an exchange nonresident of a contract for services. The term "services" is not defined by statute. Cabinet Order Concerning Control of Foreign Exchange Art. 16 provides elaboration of the term as including, inter alia, "technical assistance." A so-called remark of indeterminate legal purport, appended to Ministerial Ordinance Concerning Control of Invisible Transaction attached list No. IV, defines "technological assistance" as comprehending

> the guidance of technology pertaining to enterprises such as manufacturing, agricultural-forestry, fishing, construc-tion industries, etc. which is executed by the method of dispatching engineers or supplying technical data, etc. . . .

In V EHS No. 5211. Uncertainty regarding the concept of a contract for services involving the rendition of technological assistance, subject to the requirement of prior license under the Foreign Exchange Law, is compounded by the fact that the Foreign Investment Law requires prior validation of an amendment or renewal of a B-class technological assistance contract making it A-class, without expressly defining the term B-class technological assistance contract. Such an agreement is simply a technological assistance contract other than an A-class technological assistance contract. In short, it possesses a term and period of payment of one year or less and therefore is a contract for services within the ambit of the Foreign Exchange Law rather than the Foreign Investment Law.

57. On June 10, 1968, the cabinet adopted the Foreign Investment Council Report Concerning Liberalization of Induction of Technology.

58. See for example, Ministerial Ordinance Designating Scope of Business to Be Handled by the Bank of Japan in Accordance with the Provisions of the Foreign Investment Law (Ministries of Finance, Welfare, Agriculture and Forestry, International Trade and Industry, Transportation, Postal Services, and Construction Joint Ordinance No. 2, 1967, as amended), hereinafter cited as Joint Ordinance No. 2.

59. Foreign Investment Council Report Concerning Liberalization of Induction of Technology part I; Ministerial Ordinance Concerning Control of Invisible Transactions attached list No. IV (1); Ministerial Ordinance Concerning Control of Invisible Transactions Relating to Foreign Trade attached list No. IX(II)(2).

60. Ibid.

61. Foreign Investment Council Report Concerning Liberalization of Induction of Technology part IV; Ministries of Finance, Welfare, Agriculture and Forestry, International Trade and Industry, Transportation, Postal Services, and Construction Joint Ordinance No. 3, 1972, amending Joint Ordinance No. 2; Ministry of Finance Ordinance No. 60 of 1972, amending Ministerial Ordinance Concerning Control of Invisible Transactions; Ministry of International Trade and Industry Ordinance No. 76, 1972, amending Ministerial Ordinance Concerning Control of Invisible Transactions Relating to Foreign Trade.

62. Cabinet Order Concerning Control of Import Trade (Cabinet Order No. 414, 1949, as amended)—hereinafter cites as Import Trade Control Order.

63. Art. 4.

64. Arts. 3, 8, 9, and 10. Import licenses issued by authorized foreign exchange banks have a term of six months. Import Trade Control Order Art. 7. Import licenses issued by the MITI under Import Trade Control Order Art. 8 generally possess terms of four months; their duration may vary in the event that the MITI "deems its necessary." Import Trade Control Order Art. 8, paras. 2 and 3.

65. Notification of Matters Concerning Import (Ministry of International Trade and Industry Notification No. 170, 1966, as amended). All items subject to the automatic import quota system, the import of which was in principle automatically authorized, were deleted as of February 1, 1972 by Ministry of International Trade and Industry Notification No. 44.

66. Import Trade Control Order Art. 8, para. 1, item (1).

67. Import Trade Control Order Art. 8, para. 1, item (1)-2.

68. Import Trade Control Order Art. 8, paras. 1, item (2) and 4.

69. Import Trade Control Order Art. 10, para. 1, item (1); Regulation for Control of Import Trade (Ministry of International Trade and Industry Ordinance No. 77, 1949, as amended) Art. 6-2; see Cases in Which a Consignee of a Person Who Has Obtained an Import Quota May Obtain License for the Import Without a Permission of MITI (Ministry of International Trade and Industry Notification No. 172, 1964).

70. Import Trade Control Order Art. 10, para. 1, item (2).

71. Import Trade Control Order art. 10, para. 1, item (3); Ministerial Ordinance Concerning Standard Method of Settlement attached list No. II; see Import Trade Control Order Art. 12, requiring prior concurrence of the MOF in the event that the MITI proposes to stipulate a standard method of settlement. Partial or complete payment for imported goods prior to receipt of the goods or shipping documents is permitted in several very limited instances—for example, books, periodicals, and live animals. Ministerial Ordinance Concerning Standard Method of Settlement attached list No. II(1) (B).

72. Import Trade Control Order Art. 11 in V EHS No. 5090.

73. Import Trade Control Order Art. 14 and annexes Nos. I and II.

74. Import Trade Control Order Art. 13, para. 2. No such deposits have been required since May 18, 1972.

75. Import Trade Control Order Art. 16. Import Trade Control Order Art. 18 provides for other specific delegation of authority to Customs—for example, approval of extension by an authorized foreign exchange bank of the duration of an import license for not more than one month.

76. Customs Law Arts. 7 and 67; Customs Law Enforcement Order (Cabinet Order No. 150, 1954, as amended) Arts. 4-4-4.

77. Law No. 54, 1910, as amended, hereinafter cited as Customs Tariff Law; Customs Tariff Enforcement Order (Cabinet Order No. 155, 1954, as amended).

78. Law No. 36, 1960, as amended; Temporary Customs Tariff Measures Law Enforcement Order (Cabinet Order No. 69, 1960, as amended).

79. Director International Affairs Division, Tariff and Customs Bureau, Ministry of Finance, "Japanese Tariff Structure," 10 Journal of the American Chamber of Commerce in Japan 61 (June 5, 1973).

80. Customs Tariff Law Art. 5; Cabinet Order Concerning Application of Beneficial Duties Under Article 5 of the Customs Tariff Law (Cabinet Order No. 237, 1955, as amended).

81. Protocol with the Union of Soviet Socialist Republics Concerning the Development of Trade and the Mutual Granting of Most Favored Nation Treatment, October 19, 1956.

82. Art. 6.

83. Art. 7.

84. Art. 8.

85. Art. 9; Cabinet Order Concerning Anti-Dumping Duties (Cabinet Order No. 233, 1968); see Antimonopoly Law Arts. 19 and 20; Fair Trade Commission Notification No. 11, 1953 (General Designation of Unfair Business Practices).

86. Art. 9-2; Cabinet Order Concerning Emergency Duties (Cabinet Order No. 161, 1961).

87. Art. 15, para. 1.

88. Import Trade Control Order Art. 15, para. 2.

89. Arts. 17 and 17-2. In turn, this authority is delegated to the Bank of Japan. Import Trade Control Order Art. 18-2(2) and (3).

90. Patent Law (Law No. 121, 1959, as amended) Arts. 2, paras. 3 and 100; Utility Model Law (Law No. 123, 1959, as amended) Arts. 2, paras. 3 and 27; Design Law (Law No. 125, 1959, as amended) Arts. 2, paras. 3 and 37; Trademark Law (Law No. 127, 1959, as amended)— hereinafter cited Trademark Law—Arts. 2, para. 3, items (2) and (36); Copyright Law (Law No. 48, 1970) Art. 113, para. 1, item (1).

91. Customs Tariff Law Art. 21, para. 1, item (4); <u>Kura-Kan</u> No. 1443 (August 25, 1972); see Koseitorihiki 7-8 (No. 267, January 1973).

92. It would appear from the reasoning in N.M.C.K.K. v. Shiro Trading Co., Ltd., Osaka District Court, February 27, 1970, 2 Intangible Property Right Court Decisions 71, that neither the owner of a Japanese trademark registration nor an exclusive distributor of imported goods bearing the mark can on the basis of the Trademark Law prevent parallel imports; in contrast, in the case of an exclusive license of a Japanese trademark registration in connection with manufacture, it would further appear that either the licensor or exclusive licensee could rely on the statute to prevent such imports.

93. Arts. 7-(2), 19-(2) - 27(16).

94. Export and Import Trading Law Art. 30 in V EHS No. 5560.

THE EUROPEAN COMMUNITY

R. C. Fischer

The European Community (EC) was created by France; the Federal Republic of Germany, Italy, Belgium, the Netherlands, and Luxembourg (the latter three already united in the Benelux economic union), first as a sectoral economic integration in the European Coal and Steel Community (ECSC) and then extended to an over-all economic union, the European Economic Community (EEC), with special complementary provisions for nuclear energy, the European Atomic Energy Community (Euratom and EAEC). Since 1 January 1973, Denmark, Ireland, and the United Kingdom have been members of the EC.

(Legally speaking there are still three Communities: the ECSC, the EEC, and Euratom. The first was established by the Treaty of Paris of 18 April 1951, the other two by the Treaties of Rome of 3 March 1957. Since the treaties of 8 April 1965 on the merger of certain institutions and of 22 April 1970 on the amendment of certain budgetary provisions, the three Communities now have common institutions and a common budget but still retain their specific policy objectives and instruments. The accession was realized through several instruments of 22 January 1972 including the "Act Concerning the Conditions of Accession and the Adjustments to the Treaties," hereafter referred to as the "Act of Accession.")

The rules evolved by the Community with respect to East-West trade provide the framework for coordinating action by its member states and the Community itself. The existing Community rules will,

―――――――――

The opinions expressed in this contribution are those of the author and do not necessarily reflect the views of the institution to the staff of which the author belongs. The discussion herein reflects the legal situation existing as of the end of 1973.

however, be supplanted and supplemented by others in the course of the further development of the still unachieved economic union.

As an economic union, the Community is necessarily concerned with all economic relations between its member states and the outside world. Among the external economic policies having a special impact on East-West trade, the most important one is the common commercial policy, which deals with all commercial relations (that is, the exchange of goods and services) with third countries. In the other areas of the economic union, the conduct of the external economic relations is only gradually coordinated and taken over by the Community: It is only by implementing its internal policies with respect to a certain matter that the Community acquires the power to deal with that matter in respect to third countries, either autonomously or by agreement with those countries.[1] A special case is the association agreements that the Community may conclude with third countries or international organizations and that may encompass not only commercial relations but also all other matters within the scope of the economic union (Article 238 EEC). Moreover, whenever action by the Community with respect to external economic relations proves necessary to attain one of the objectives of the Community and the treaty has not provided the necessary powers, such powers may be created by unanimous decisions of the Council of Ministers on a proposal from the commission and after consulting the European Parliament (Art. 235 EEC). Finally, in all other matters that are as yet beyond the external powers of the Community but are nevertheless of particular interest to the common market, member states should facilitate the achievement of the tasks of the Community (Art. 5 EEC); in international organizations of an economic character they should proceed by common action, the scope and implementation of which may be determined by the Community (Art. 116 EEC).

Internal or general economic policies that may also affect East-West trade include the common agricultural, transport, cartel, and state aid policies, as well as industrial and monetary policies (the latter two are at present still in the stage of a gradual coordination of national policies). In all these matters, the action of the Community is subject to the general limitations that result from the fact that some matters (for example, defense, external and internal security, public health and morality, and cultural affairs) remain wholly and others (such as nationalization and public services) partly within the responsibility of member states (compare Arts. 36, 37, 90, 222, 223 to 225, EEC).

The present survey must be confined to the commercial policy. It should, however, be noted that certain other policies may also substantially affect the conditions of East-West trade. Thus, the cartel legislation of the Community applies to trade restrictions on imports from third countries, whenever these practices also affect trade between member states, even if the participating enterprises are not established within the Community and even if the latter include state agencies, as may be the case in state-trading countries (Arts. 85 to 90 EEC; compare Arts. 65 and 66 EEC).[2] Similarly, the rules on state aids apply to aids by member states to enterprises outside the Community if such aids affect trade between member states (Arts. 92 to 94 EEC).

SCOPE OF THE COMMON COMMERCIAL POLICY (CCP)

The scope of the Common Commercial Policy (CCP) is not defined by the EEC treaty. The criterion for delimiting the CCP is the specific effect (whether intentional or unintentional) of a government measure on the exchange of goods or services between the Community and third countries. The CCP covers all governmental measures that specifically apply to imports from or exports to third countries, including tariffs, quantitative restrictions, and all other charges and measures having equivalent effect (including state monopolies and restrictions on the payment for imports or exports or on the transfer of such payments); protective measures against dumping, subsidies, and cartels; export aids (compare the illustrative, but not exhaustive list of Art. 113 EEC and Arts. 111 and 112 EEC).

The CCP can also regulate the application to imports or exports of general internal regulations affecting the exchange of goods and services, for example, by granting nondiscriminatory or MFN treatment for imports or exports with respect to internal turnover taxes. Moreover, the CCP is not confined to the traditional tools of trade policy, such as tariffs and quotas but extends also to the more sophisticated instruments that have been developed recently—in the fields of export credit and economic cooperation, for example—and that are increasingly applied, especially in the commercial relations with the state-trading countries in Eastern Europe. Finally, the CCP encompasses not only autonomous measures of commercial policy but also the negotiation and conclusion of bilateral or multilateral agreements concerning commercial relations with third countries.

The CCP is based on uniform principles (Art. 113 [1] EEC). As a common policy, it is conceived and carried out by the institutions of the Community and is not a mere coordination of national policies, as the treaty provides for in certain other fields. The Community, acting through its own institutions, has the exclusive power not only to define the principles but also to apply the instruments of the CCP.

The Council of Ministers, acting by qualified majority vote on proposals from the Commission, defines and implements the CCP. Certain powers may be delegated to the commission. A special procedure is provided for the negotiation and conclusion of commercial agreements (Arts. 113 [3], 114, and 228 EEC). Consultation with the European Parliament is optional, but Parliament is often consulted on major policy proposals by the commission and also, in a more informal way, on major trade negotiations.

All conditions necessary for the implementation of the CCP were to have been created during the transitional period, which ended on 1 January 1970. Member states were to have coordinated their commercial relations with third countries, and the Community institutions were to have established the necessary procedures and to have taken all other preparatory measures (Arts. 111 and 112 EEC). These tasks, however, were not fulfilled in 1970 and have still not yet been completely achieved. Consequently, in some sectors of the CCP and especially in the relations with the Eastern state-trading countries, there still exist national policy measures that are being progressively coordinated in order that they may finally be replaced by Community measures. This coexistence of measures of CCP and of progressively coordinated measures of national commercial policies is therefore a temporary, transitional situation.

THE INSTRUMENTS OF THE AUTONOMOUS CCP

Customs Duties

The common customs tariff (CCT) was integrally applied in 1968 for industrial products and by 1970 for the remaining agricultural products (compare Art. 23 EEC). The replacement of the national tariffs by the CCT required adjustments of tariff agreements of member states (compare Art. 111 [4] EEC), especially of their lists or tariff concessions under Art. II GATT. As a result, the lists of tariff concessions of the member states were replaced by a sole list for the Community.

The CCT was published for the first time by Regulation (EEC) No. 950/68 of the council.[3] Periodically—as a rule at the beginning of each year—a revised edition is published.[4] This incorporates all amendments to the tariff and the tariff nomenclature that the Community has put into effect since the previous publication, either by unilateral measures or by virtue of agreements concluded with third countries. Temporary tariff amendments, including tariff quotas, and the various preferential tariffs that the Community applies under its preferential trade agreements with a number of countries and under its autonomous General Tariff Preference Scheme[5] for developing countries are not included in this periodical publication. Although separately published, all of them form nevertheless an integral part of the CCT.

The CCT has two columns: the autonomous tariff and the conventional tariff. The latter is applicable to imported goods originating in countries that are GATT members (under the MFN clausula of Art. I GATT) or with which the Community has concluded agreements containing MFN tariff clauses. However, in order to take into account MFN clauses in existing trade agreements of member states with non-GATT members, the community decided to extend its GATT tariff, as an autonomous measure, to all other countries until it has defined its policy on MFN treatment of non-GATT members, either in trade agreements with these countries or by autonomous action (compare preliminary provisions to the CCT Sec. I.B.I).

The administration of Community tariff quotas is, at present, decentralized: They are allocated among member states, which must administer their shares so as to guarantee free and equal access to their share to all persons concerned who are established on their territory. In order to ensure equal and continuous access to the quota throughout the whole community, the allocation among the member states is provisional and flexible: Part of the quota is normally set aside as a Community reserve on which member states must draw whenever their first share has been exhausted and to which are returned the unused portions of their shares.

The duties of the CCT only apply to imports of goods. Exports are not subject to customs duties (either by the Community or by member states).

Autonomous modification and suspension of the duties of the CCT, including tariff quotas, require unanimous council decision; if limited in time (six months, once renewable) and size (20 percent of the duty), they can be made by qualified majority decision (Art. 28 EEC). Conventional modification and suspension, however, can be made in commercial agreements, concluded by qualified majority decision of the council (Arts. 113 and 114 EEC). All modifications are carried out by regulations that are directly applicable and do not allow for implementing legislation by member states. The duties of the CCT are at present collected by the customs authorities of member states, but the revenues largely go (and by 1975 will go entirely) to the budget of the Community.

Since the application of the CCT, member states can no longer apply national customs duties or tariff quotas (except for certain derogations provided in the Act of Accession, discussed in section below entitled "Effects of the Enlargement on the Community"); nor can they autonomously dispose of their share in community tariff quotas, for example, by favoring certain imports under government-sponsored industrial cooperation projects with third countries.

Customs Legislation

The still incomplete customs legislation of the Community already covers the most important sectors of customs law. The customs territory of the Community is defined by Regulation No. 1496/68[6] and corresponds in general to the territories of the member states. The nomenclature of the CCT is based on the "Brussels Nomenclative," and its uniform application is ensured by the Community procedure laid down by Regulation No. 97/69.[7] Rules for the customs valuation of goods have been established by Regulation No. 803/68.[8] The general regime for the definition of the origin of goods is established by Regulation No. 802/68[9] and applies not only to customs duties but also to all Community or national measures of trade policy vis-à-vis third countries. Various association agreements concluded by the Community provide for special rules of origin, and so does the General Scheme of Tariff Preferences of the Community.[10] Customs clearance formalities have been partly harmonized by Council Directives of 30 July 1968[11] dealing with customs treatment and temporary warehousing, No. 69/73 EEC of 4 March 1969[12] on bonded warehouses regime, and No. 69/75 EEC of 4 March 1969[13] on deferred payment of customs duties. Council Directive No. 69/75 ECC of 4 March 1969[14] has harmonized the regime for the free zones (areas where goods are regarded as not being within the Community's customs territory for the purpose of customs duties, levies, quantitative restrictions, or any charge or measure of equivalent effect). The inward processing regime—allowing temporary imports from third countries free of all duties and charges with a view to reexporting the products obtained—has been partly harmonized by the Council Directive of 4 March 1969.[15] The formalities for the free movement of goods within the Community, whether their point of departure or destination is within the Community (internal Community transit) or in a third country (external Community transit), are unified by the Community transit regime, established by Council Regulation (EEC) No. 542/69.[16] Various subjects have not yet been settled by the Community customs legislation, such as the outward processing regime.[17]

Quotas and Liberalization Measures

The common import system has been established by Regulation (CEE) No. 109/70[18] for imports from state-trading countries and by Regulation (CEE) No. 1025/70[19] for imports from the other countries (including almost all GATT members). Both regulations establish a common liberalization list. Importation into the Community of products on these lists is free in relation to the countries concerned— that is, it is not subject to any quantitative restriction. Products thus liberalized may, however, still be subject to other restrictive measures applied by member states, as the common system has not yet abolished such measures or replaced them by Community measures. Moreover, the common system still leaves to member states the choice whether to reserve the liberalization for products originating in and directly imported from the countries concerned or to apply less restrictive criteria.

In fact, the liberalization lists, for the state-trading countries vary from one country to another. The Commission publishes from time to time consolidated versions of the lists. Products not included in these lists may still be under national quantitative restrictions or liberalization measures or may be subject to quantitative quotas established by the Community. The common import system does not preclude the application by member states of prohibitions or quantitative restrictions on imports on grounds of public morality, public policy, or public security; the protection of health and life of humans, animals, or plants; the protection of national treasures possessing artistic, historic, or archaeologic value; or the protection of industrial and commercial property.

A common export system toward all countries without distinction has been created by Regulation (EEC) No. 2603/69.[20] It establishes the principle of liberalization—that is, freedom from quantitative restrictions—by fixing a negative list containing the (rather few) products that are not liberalized in the entire Community and may be either under quantitative export quotas established by the Community or still under national restrictive or liberalization measures. Furthermore, it also provides for measures by member states for the protection of public morality, policy, and security; of health; of national treasures; and of industrial and commercial property.

The administration of quantitative import or export quotas established by the Community, either autonomously or by way of agreement, is governed by Regulation (EEC) No. 1023/70 of the council.[21] The quotas, their value or quantity, and the criteria for their allocation to the different member states are established by the council on a proposal from the commission. Normally, the allocation is fixed and, if necessary, revised, and the increase of the quota is decided by the commission acting upon the advice of the Quota Administration Committee, consisting of representatives of the member states. The quota shares allocated to the member states are generally published in the Community's Official Journal. Licenses must be issued within certain specified time periods by the member states, which have the choice between two procedures: issuing them either as and when applications are received or after examination of all applications together. The council may decide that goods imported under inward processing arrangements shall also be counted against the quota share of the importing member state. With respect to the issuing of the licenses and their limited territorial validity, similar transitional rules apply as in the case of the licenses used in the common import and export systems. Transitional provisions expiring at the end of 1974[22] limit the validity of these authorizations to the territory of the issuing member state and allow any member state to refuse to issue import or export authorizations to persons not established in its territory, without prejudice to the treaty obligations concerning the right of establishment and the free movement of services. This procedure for the administration of quantitative quotas also applies to the administration of voluntary restraint agreements between the Community and exporting countries and to the autonomous increase by the Community of the import ceilings fixed by these agreements (Council Regulation [EEC] No. 1471/70).[23]

The coordination of the national import systems—that is, of the quantitative restrictions or liberalization measures of the member states that have not yet been replaced by Community measures—is organized by the Council Decision of 19 December 1972.[24] Under this decision, all autonomous amendments by member states of their import systems are subject to prior notification and, if need be, consultation in order for the Community to examine the possibility of establishing a common import system for the country and the product concerned or otherwise to coordinate the import systems of all member states in the interest of the Common Market and the further development of the CCP. If the national measure provokes objections, the commission submits appropriate proposals to the council and the member state cannot act before the council has decided. However, in respect to countries that still refuse to negotiate with the Community, member states may, by way of exception and until the end of 1974, put their measures into effect, if the council has not acted within five weeks from the commission's proposal. In urgent and otherwise exceptional cases, liberalization may be withdrawn and quotas abolished or reduced or exceeded by 20 percent, without prior consultation. Once the opening of Community negotiations has been authorized, member states can no longer amend their import system toward the country concerned without authorization by the council.

Until now amendments of the national export systems have been subject only to the procedure established by the Council Decision of 9 October 1961,[25] which provides merely for prior notification of these amendments (and, if need be, prior consultation) and not for preventive intervention by the commission or council.

Safeguard Measures

If imports threaten to cause injury to Community producers, safeguard measures can be taken under the common import system.[26]

Surveillance of imports by automatic licenses, to be issued by member states, can be imposed by the commission, if imports threaten to cause injury to Community producers of like or directly competing products. If such injury is caused or threatens to be caused by imports in greatly increased quantities or on certain terms or conditions (for example, on prices), protective measures can be taken by the council acting by a qualified majority on a proposal from the commission. Such measures can be limited to imports intended for certain regions of the Community. In emergency cases, the commission can take provisional measures for a maximum period of six weeks, which can be abolished, modified, or extended by the council. Moreover, in certain cases member states can take on their own initiative interim protective measures, which normally within five days must be either replaced by a commission measure or abolished. But if the member state refers the commission's refusal to the council, the national measure may be extended for at most one month (or two months, in some cases). A transitional provision expiring at the end of 1974[27] allows member states to refuse to issue or to endorse licenses used for surveillance or protective measures to persons not established in the territory of the issuing state.

In order to prevent or remedy a critical situation caused by a shortage of essential products, similar surveillance and protective measures can be taken with regard to exports under the common export system.[28] Safeguard measures in case of dumping and subsidies are provided for by Regulation (EEC) No. 459/68.[29] This regulation implements, as far as dumping is concerned, the Anti-dumping Code, which was adopted during the Kennedy Round with the view to regulating the application of Art. VI GATT in cases of dumping. Its application, however, is not limited to countries that are GATT members and covers also the granting of bounties or subsidies. It does not set aside special rules on dumping and subsidies laid down in agreements concluded between the Community and third countries nor does it preclude the adoption of other special measures compatible with GATT or the application of the rules of the CCP. Complaints about dumping, bounties, or subsidies by third countries may be submitted by injured or threatened Community industries to member states or the commission. They are examined by the commission in cooperation and consulation with member states. If there is a prima facie case for the adoption of protective measures, the commission advises the exporting country and the exporters and importers and publishes a notice in the Official Journal of the Community allowing interested parties to communicate information and to ask for a hearing by the commission. The commission can ask private persons and member states to supply information and can request the latter to carry out investigations. If exporters voluntarily agree to revise their prices or if protective measures appear unnecessary for other reasons, the commission normally terminates the proceeding and publishes a notice to that effect in the Official Journal. Otherwise it fixes provisional antidumping or countervailing duties pending a definitive decision of the council.

Most association and preferential trade agreements and some other trade agreements of the Community provide for special safeguard measures by the Community. Special safeguard measures may also be taken by the Community with respect to agricultural products.[30] Moreover, the treaties provide for other safeguard clauses that allow individual member states to restrict imports or exports, either after authorization by the commission or the council or sometimes even without such authorization. This is in particular the case in respect of serious monetary problems (Act. 107 [2] EEC), of balance of payments difficulties (Arts. 108 and 109 EEC; compare Art. XII GATT), and of internal or external security problems (Art. 224 EEC, see also Arts. 223 and 225; compare Art. XXI GATT). Finally, member states can in certain cases take national safeguard measures under protective clauses in bilateral agreements concluded with third countries.[31]

Other Charges and Restrictions on Imports
or Exports

On the main agricultural products and on certain processed agricultural products the Community applies variable levies (either in addition to or instead of the duties of the CCT) and various other import or export restrictions such as compensatory taxes and minimum price systems. On other products, the Community usually does not apply charges in addition to the Community customs duties and to the value-added tax, excise duties, and other indirect internal taxes applied by member states (compare Art. III GATT).

The CCP has until now not generally dealt with the application to imports or exports of general internal regulations affecting the exchange of goods—such as turnover taxes (compare Art. 112 [2] EEC)— or monetary regulations such as restrictions on payments for goods and services or on the transfer of such payments (compare Art. 106 [2] EEC). However, such matters have been treated in some commercial agreements concluded by the Community. Monetary questions, such as whether or not to waive a claim for payment in convertible currency, have also occasionally been raised in discussions on the commercial relations of member states with Eastern state-trading countries, as these conditions may have a significant impact on the development of trade and the competition between the enterprises of different member states (compare Art. 112 EEC).

Export Promotion

In the field of export promotion, as distinct from the other instruments of export policy such as tariffs and quantitative restrictions, the Community is still concentrating its efforts on progressively coordinating national export promotion policies and has hardly reached the stage of a real common policy based on common principles and disposing of common instruments. Aids for exports to third countries were to have been harmonized during the transitional period to the extent necessary to avoid distortion of competition between enterprises of the Community (Art. 112 EEC). But even now these aids have on the whole not yet been submitted to coordination procedures.[32] The most significant exception is agriculture, where all national aids for the export of agricultural and processed agricultural products have been replaced by the Community instruments of the CCP.

A coordination of national instruments has started in the more specific field of export credit and credit insurance. A Policy Coordinating group for credit insurance, credit guarantees,and financial credits was set up by Council Decision of 27 September 1960.[33] A consultation procedure in matters of credit insurance, credit guarantees, and financial credits was adopted, which was amended by Council Decision of 15 May 1962 and further amended by Council Decision of 3 December 1973.[34]

Export credits and export credit guarantees granted by member states or by credit insurance institutions acting for the account or with the support of the state are subject to prior notification to other member states and the commission, if they are linked to the export of products or services of the member states concerned and have a duration of more than five years calculated from certain starting points corresponding to those defined by the Bern Union or if they depart from any other common norm adopted by the Community. This last reference covers inter alia the sectoral and other agreements negotiated in the OECD concerning shipbuilding, aviation, and so on. The procedure applies to supplier as well as to financial credits, irrespective of whether the source of the funds is public or private; it applies to individual transactions and also to general credit grants, even if the nature of the individual transactions covered is defined only in general terms. When notifying the other member states, the member state must justify why a derogation from the norms is envisaged (for example, to aid a developing country or to match competition from third countries, whether supported by this country or not). The operation may, and on a request from a majority of member states must, be submitted to prior consultation, but in exceptional cases member states need not delay their decision till the end of the consultation. The consulting member state is not obliged to follow the

61

suggestions of the member states and the commission but must inform them of its final decision. At the end of 1973 the council was considering a commission proposal for a more binding consultation procedure.

Common credit insurance policies for medium- and long-term transactions with public or private buyers have been adopted by two Council Directives of 27 October 1970,[35] whereas in respect of guarantees for the political risk in short-term transactions with public or private buyers the Council Directive of 1 February 1971 has confined itself to harmonizing the basic provisions without drawing up a common policy. However, these common policies and harmonized principles are not yet in force, as the council has not yet been able to decide on commission proposals concerning the common premium system (rates, calculation methods, and classification of importing third countries).[36] Other commission proposals not yet adopted by the council at the end of 1973 deal with the duration and the interest rate of export credits, with guarantees for the risks of monetary and production cost fluctuations, and with a Community guarantee system for investments in third countries.[37]

General export promotion is still mainly a matter of national policies and instruments, which have until now hardly been coordinated by the Community. For trade fairs in third countries, however, some coordination exists, and occasionally Community participation is decided as a complement or a substitute to participation by member states. In the important field of economic and industrial cooperation, the action of member states is increasingly carried out within the framework of so-called cooperation agreements, which are discussed below.

THE INSTRUMENTS OF THE CONVENTIONAL CCP

Agreements with Third Countries

The negotiation and conclusion of bilateral or multilateral agreements on commercial relations with third countries has been, since 1 January 1970 (the end of the transitional period), within the exclusive power of the Community (Arts. 113 [3] and 114 EEC). Consequently, such agreements must now be negotiated and concluded by the institutions of the Community and not by common action of member states. This exclusive power of the Community is not limited to the negotiation of agreements but also covers consultations and other discussions on trade matters, even if they are not intended to result in formal agreements or in other more or less binding acts such as resolutions or recommendations of international organizations. The exercise of this exclusive power requires an adequate participation of the Community in the activity of international organizations dealing with matters within the scope of the CCP, and in many cases full membership is required.[38] Member states should by common action, under Art. 116 EEC, assist the Community in obtaining an adequate position within these organizations but cannot by such common action negotiate on behalf of the Community, as Art. 116 EEC applies to matters of particular interest to the common market that fall outside the scope of the CCP and of other external Community powers.

Procedure for Negotiating and Concluding Agreements Within the Scope of the CCP

This procedure is set out in the Treaty (Arts. 113 [3], Art. 114 and 228 EEC). Negotiations are conducted by the commission in consultation with a special committee appointed by the council and composed of representatives of all member states. The council authorizes the commission to open the negotiations and may issue negotiation directives to it (Art. 113 [3] EEC). The agreements are concluded by the council by qualified majority (Art. 114 EEC). They are binding on the Community and its institutions as well as on its member states (Art. 228 [2] EEC). The treaty does not associate the Parliament with the negotiation and conclusion of trade agreements under Art. 113 EEC. However, repeated requests by the Parliament have resulted in procedures agreed to with the council and the commission that provide for informal consultations before the opening and the conclusion of important trade negotiations. The commission is also the only official spokesman of the Community in all international discussions on trade matters that are not negotiations in the sense of Art. 113 (3) EEC. In negotiating commercial agreements with third countries, the Community intends to unify the existing trade relations, whether contractual or autonomous, of its member states and, if appropriate, also to agree on new reciprocal concessions.

Existing National Bilateral Agreements

Pending their replacement by Community agreements, these bilateral agreements may, by authorization of the council, be extended from year to year, but without negotiation and only insofar as extension does not constitute an obstacle to the implementation of the CCP (title I of the Council Decision of 16 December 1969).[39] Under another, more exceptional, transitional provision, which expired, however, at the end of 1972, the council could authorize member states to negotiate, under directives issued by the council, commercial agreements with third countries as yet unwilling to negotiate with the Community itself—essentially the Comecon countries (title III of the same council

decision). By virtue of this latter provision, member states have
negotiated and concluded commercial agreements with Albania,
Bulgaria, Czechoslovakia, Hungary, Poland, Romania, and the USSR
and in certain cases also with the People's Republic of China.* Most
of these agreements were concluded for a period expiring at the end
of 1974, but in certain cases only one-year agreements were negotiated.
Many agreements contain the reciprocal MFN clause in respect to
tariff matters, a general declaration of intent on progressive liberalization without specification of products, and a safegurad clause for
protection against abnormal prices. They provide, moreover, for
annual protocols to be negotiated in the joint commissions, and for the
establishment of quantitative import and export regimes that both
parties agree to apply in their mutual exchanges. If Community
trade negotiations with these countries remain impossible, the 1973
protocols can be extended for one year in accordance with title I of the
Council Decision of 19 December 1969. Since 1 January 1973, commercial negotiations cannot take place between member states and
these countries.

Cooperation Agreements

A relatively new instrument to influence the commercial and
other economic relations with third countries, and especially with
state-trading countries is the so-called "cooperation agreement."
These intergovernmental agreements usually set out certain general
objectives for the development of economic, industrial, and technological cooperation between the authorities and economic operators of
both parties and define the types of measures to be used and the procedures to be followed in order to attain these objectives. The implementation of these agreements by concrete measures to be discussed
and agreed upon between both parties is usually entrusted to an intergovernmental or joint commission. Such agreements normally do not
create any concrete obligation of commercial policy and often also
cover noncommercial matters such as the right of establishment. Their
negotiation and implementation nevertheless substantially, and intentionally, affect commercial relations with the contracting third countries, especially if the latter have a centrally planned economy and
a foreign trade monopoly, as in the case of Eastern state-trading
countries. Cooperation agreements are therefore an important

---

*Before the conclusion of the basic treaty between the two Ger-
man states, the other member states applied a nonbinding consultation
procedure established in 1961 to their semiofficial relations with the
German Democratic Republic.

instrument of commercial policy that the Community may choose to avail itself of in the future.

Given the still prevailing unwillingness of the countries concerned to negotiate with the Community, the latter is at present mainly limited to ensuring that in negotiating and implementing cooperation agreements, member states conform to the various specific rules and procedures of the CCP, such as the abovementioned coordinating consultations provided for autonomous amendments of import and export systems and for export credit and export credit insurance. In order to facilitate a comprehensive review of the various effects of cooperation agreements on the external economic relations and the evolving common policies of the Community and a progressive coordination among member states, the commission has recently proposed to the council the addition to the existing rules and procedures of an overall consultation procedure for the negotiation and implementation of cooperation agreements between the member states and third countries.[40]

THE CCP AND FREE CIRCULATION OF GOODS WITHIN THE COMMUNITY

Since the end of the transitional period, goods circulate freely within the Community, that is, all customs duties and quantitative restrictions and all charges and measures having equivalent effect are prohibited between member states (Arts. 9, 13, 16, 30, 32, 34 EEC). Even so-called automatic import or export licensing is prohibited.[41] The only exceptions are the prohibitions or restrictions on imports, exports, or transit justified on grounds of public morality, public policy, or public security; protection of health and life of humans, animals, or plants; protection of national treasures of artistic, historic, or archaeological value; and protection of industrial and commercial property (Art. 36 EEC). This free movement applies to products originating in member states and to those coming from third countries that are in free circulation in any member states—that is, for which the import formalities have been complied with and any applicable customs duties or charges having equivalent effect have been levied and which have not benefited from a total or partial drawback of such duties or charges (Arts. 9 [2] and 10 [1] EEC).[42]

However, as long as the CCP has not entirely replaced all national measures of commercial policy, disparities between such national measures may lead to a "deflection of trade"—thereby obstructing the execution of national measures or creating economic difficulties in member states that the CCP is yet unable to solve. In that case, and provided the national measures are in accordance with the treaty, the commission recommends that member states cooperate and, failing this, authorizes them to take certain protective measures (Art. 115 EEC). This safeguard clause should be construed and applied restrictively.[43] Accordingly, it should not be used to solve problems that originate not in disparities between national commercial policies but in the application of the CCP. Thus a member state cannot invoke Art. 115 to prevent imports from a third country via another member state in excess of the share it has received in the Community quota toward that country. Moreover, with the progressive coordination of national import systems, especially since the abovementioned Council Decision of 19 December 1972, the commission tends to limit the application of protective measures to cases of economic difficulties.

The Commission Decision of 12 May 1971, as amended by the Commission Decision of 9 March 1973,[44] has permitted each member state to put into force a licensing system for products originating in third countries and imported through deflection of trade by other member states, if the direct importation into that member state of such products is, in accordance with the treaty, subject to national quantitative restrictions or to voluntary restraints agreed to between the member states and the third country concerned. These licenses must be granted automatically on the supply of all relevant information including country of origin and free circulation of the product in another member state. However, within eight working days following the application, the member state may place a request for the application of Art. 115 before the commission and provisionally withhold the license until the commission's decision (but not longer than 12 working days following the application for the license). Unless agreed with the third country, quotas may not be reserved for imports coming directly from that country—that is, the member state cannot request application of Art. 115 before the quota is fully utilized, for which purpose direct and indirect imports may be totaled. If the commission authorizes protective measures, it may also include the products for which licenses have thus been provisionally withheld. These protective measures usually consist in excluding from free circulation within the common market certain goods from the third country involved that have been imported into the other member states. The commission publishes periodically a list of products for which protective measures have been authorized;[45] the publication of lists of products put under automatic licensing is left to member states.

Art. 115 EEC also applies in case of disparities between national measures concerning the export of goods toward third countries, but the provisional automatic licensing system authorized by the abovementioned Commission Decision does not apply to export restrictions, nor has the commission authorized until now protective measures in such cases.

Other safeguard clauses allowing for exceptions to the free movement of goods within the Community are contained in Arts. 108 and 109 EEC in case of balance-of-payment difficulties. Art. 103 EEC has been applied occasionally to solve difficulties of supply in certain member states during the transitional period and to prevent certain difficulties in the functioning of the common agricultural policy as a result of the recent monetary events. Art. 224 EEC, dealing with threats to internal or external security, has not yet been applied.

EFFECTS OF THE ENLARGEMENT OF THE COMMUNITY

The enlargement of the Community on 1 January 1973 was accompanied by a series of transitional measures for a five-year period. In the present context only the most important such measures are briefly noted, as they may bear on East-West trade.

Free movement of goods between the "old" Community and each of the three new member states, and between the latter three themselves and the application by the latter of the CCT, are being progressively realized over a five-year period (Arts. 31 to 49 and, for agriculture, Arts. 50 to 107 of the "Act of Accession"). Ireland is authorized by Protocols 6 and 7 to the Act of Accession to maintain temporarily certain import and export restrictions toward other member states. Temporary exceptions to the rules concerning the progressive application of the CCT by the new Member States are provided for in Protocols 8 to 15, whereas Protocol 23 regulates the application of the Community General Tariff Preferences Scheme by new member states.

Apart from the CCT and the instruments of the common agricultural policy (CAP), the CCP was generally applicable in the new member states as from 1 February 1973 (Art. 151 [3] Act of Accession), with delays authorized in some areas in respect to particular states. Temporary exceptions to certain acts in the field of customs legislation were laid down in section I of Annex VII, and section VI of the same annex allows Ireland and the United Kingdom during a certain period to apply national antidumping measures and to maintain quantitative export or import restrictions for certain products liberalized in the Community. Finally, some other transitional measures, including temporary safeguard clauses, are provided for in Arts. 133 to 138 and in Arts. 149 to 152 of the Act of Accession.

TERRITORIAL APPLICATION OF THE CCP

The CCP is applicable with certain exceptions and limitations to all territories of the Member States (See Art. 227 EEC; compare Art. 79 ECSC and Art. 198 EAEC).

The CCP applies to West Berlin, which is also within the customs territory of the Community.[46] According to a Protocol on German Internal Trade, annexed to the EEC Treaty, trade between the Federal Republic of Germany and the German Democratic Republic need not be regulated in accordance with the CCP but may be treated under the existing regime. The other member states were allowed to conclude agreements on trade with East Germany in conformity with the principles of the common market and without harming the economies of other member states. In the view of the commission, this latter possibility has expired with the entry into force of the treaty between the two states of Germany, and the CCP is now integrally applicable to trade relations between the other eight member states and the German Democratic Republic.[47] Products imported from the German Democratic Republic into the Federal Republic of Germany are in free circulation within the Community, but the other member states may take protective measures to prevent difficulties.

COMMERCIAL POLICY RELATING TO SPECIFIC PRODUCTS

Agricultural Products

With respect to agricultural products,[48] the CCP is largely defined and implemented within the framework of the common organization of agricultural markets established in accordance with Arts. 39 to 43 of the EEC Treaty. As a result, the CCP is more advanced and more diversified in this sector.

Variable Community levies are applied on the main agricultural products subject to common market organization, either in addition to or instead of the duties of the CCT. The common market organizations usually provide for special import and export systems, including surveillance and safeguard measures, which, if necessary, prevail over the general import and export system.[49] Furthermore, the common market organizations usually prohibit not only national customs duties and quantitative restrictions but also all charges and other measures having equivalent effect (which includes also automatic licenses).[50] Certain market organizations allow the commission to apply specific import measures if it is satisfied that exporting countries observe certain rules, for example, concerning the price of exported products; the commission has from time to time applied such measures to third countries, including certain East European countries. Minimum price systems are also among the safeguard measures provided for by the agricultural market organizations. Certain non-agricultural products that result from the processing of agricultural products are subject to similar import and export measures as agricultural products proper.[51]

Coal and Steel

The ECSC Treaty has created a common market for coal and steel,[52] but confers only limited powers on the Community in matters of commercial policy and leaves most of these matters within the powers of member states (Art. 71 ECSC).

The ECSC Treaty does not create a CCT but provides for harmonizing national customs duties through unanimous council decisions on proposals from the commission (Art. 72 ECSC). The administration of import and export licenses for trade with third countries is left to member states, and the commission can only supervise this administration in order to ensure that it is not unduly restrictive (Art. 73 ECSC). More important is the power of the commission with respect to antidumping and other protective measures (Art. 74 ECSC). The commission can make recommendations to member states (which are binding under Art. 14 ECSC, unlike those issued under Art. 189 EEC) in three cases: (1) dumping or other practices contrary to GATT by third countries or their enterprises (compare Art. VI GATT); (2) price quotations by enterprises in third countries resulting from competitive practices contrary to the competition policy of the ECSC (of special interest with regard to non-GATT state-trading countries); and (3) imports from third countries in relatively increased quantities and under such conditions (for example, prices) that they threaten to cause serious injury to Community industries (compare Art. XIX GATT). However, recommendations for the introduction of quantitative restrictions require in the second case the assent of the council and in the third the conditions set forth in Art. 58 for proclaiming and dealing with a situation of crisis due to a decline in demand. The commission may also under certain condition fix minimum or maximum prices for export to third countries (Art. 61 ECSC). Finally, member states must inform the commission of proposed commercial agreements or arrangements having similar effect where these relate to coal and steel or to the importation of other raw materials and specialized equipment needed for the production of coal and steel. The commission may make binding recommendations to member states in case these agreements contain clauses that would hinder the implementation of the treaty (Art. 75 ECSC).

The ECSC has no general powers with regard to the negotiation and conclusion of commercial agreements on its own behalf but has developed the practice—introduced by paragraph 14 of the convention on transitional provisions, annexed to the treaty—of negotiating certain commercial agreements through the commission.

Goods originating in third countries and brought into free circulation within one member state benefit as a rule from the free movement of coal and steel products between member states provided for by Art. 4 (a) of the ECSC Treaty. Problems may, however, arise as long as the national commercial policies are not sufficiently harmonized.[53] In the absence of a safeguard clause (compare Art. 115 EEC), such problems must be solved by the more general and less stringent provision of Art. 75 (3),ECSC, under which member states must afford each other the necessary mutual assistance in matters of commercial policy, the methods of which may be proposed by the commission.

Important aspects of national commercial policies have on the initiative of the commission been progressively harmonized and co-ordinated by common action of member states (implementation of these common decisions, which legally are beyond the powers of the ECSC, has been left to each member state).

Several coordination decisions have not even been published, such as those dealing with liberalization of steel import from state trading countries and with export restrictions on steel scrap. The Community now has a unified customs tariff for coal and steel products,[54] which is consolidated in GATT, whereas individual member states may under certain conditions be authorized by the commission to establish a national tariff quota. As for liberalization and quantitative restrictions, a substantial coordination exists with respect to imports of steel products from state-trading countries, involving criteria on quantities and prices as well as consultation between all member states and the commission. Export regulations for steel scrap and similar products have been coordinated by several decisions.[55]

Nuclear Energy

The CCP applies in the field of nuclear energy, except for the special rules provided for in the Euratom Treaty, especially with regard to supply policy and external relations (Art. 232 [2] EEC and inter alia Arts. 52 ss., 73 ss., 92 to 95, 101 to 106 EAEC). Consequently, the goods and products specified in the lists of Annex IV to the Euratom Treaty, which fall under the "nuclear common market" established by that treaty (Arts. 92 to 100), were finally included in the CCT of the EEC. Art. 52 of the Euratom Treaty gives the Agency of the Euratom Community a right of option on ores, source materials, and special fissionable materials produced in the territories of member states and the exclusive right to conclude contracts relating to the supply of the same products coming from inside the Community or from outside. Where appropriate, these supply agreements or contracts may be concluded within the framework of agreements concluded between the Community and a third country or an international organization (Art. 64). If the commission finds that the agency is not in a position to deliver within a reasonable period of time or only at excessively high prices, users may conclude directly contracts on supplies from outside the Community (Art. 66). Conclusion or renewal of agreements or contracts between a member state, a person, or an enterprise on the one hand and a third country, an international organization, or a national of a third country on the other, providing inter alia for delivery of the aforementioned products, requires prior consent of the commission (Art. 73). Transfer of small quantities for research may be exempted from these various provisions by the commission (Art. 74). Processing of materials to be returned afterwards to the original person is in general also exempted (Art. 75). These provisions on the agency (Arts. 52 to 76) were due for review in 1965 but are still in force in the absence of new provisions adopted by the council (Art. 76). The Euratom Community may within the limits of its powers and jurisdiction conclude agreements or contracts with a third state, an international organization, or a national of a third state (Art. 101)— that is, its treaty-making power covers all matters within its internal powers. Such agreements or contracts are negotiated by the commission under directives from the council. If their implementation does not require action by the council and stays within the limits of the budget, they are concluded solely by the commission; in other cases they are concluded by the commission with approval of the council (Art. 101). Agreements or contracts concerning matters within the scope of the treaty can only be concluded by member states with a third state, an international organization, or a national of a third state if the commission has no objection (Art. 103). Where an agreement or contract for the exchange of scientific or industrial information in the nuclear field with a third state, an international organization, or a national of a third state requires, on either part, the signature of a state acting in its sovereign capacity, it must be concluded by the commission, unless in accordance with Arts. 103 and 104 the commission authorizes conclusion by the member states, the person, or the enterprise (Art. 29). No person or undertaking concluding or renewing agreements or contracts with a third state, an international organization, or a national of a third state after the entry into force of the Treaty may invoke these agreements or contracts in order to evade treaty obligations (Art. 104). Agreements for cooperation on nuclear energy that member states have concluded with third countries before the entry into force of the treaty must be negotiated jointly with the commission in order to be taken over by the Community, as far as possible (Art. 106). Nonexclusive licenses may be granted on the initiative of the commission, either by arbitration or under compulsory powers, to the Community, to joint enterprises (Art. 48 EAEC), or to other persons or enterprises in respect of patents or utility models relating to inventions directly connected with and essential to the development of nuclear energy in the community (Art. 17 EAEC).

Oil Products and Natural Gas

In this field, the CCP is still rather incomplete. Although the CCT also applies to these products, there is no common definition of origin for oil products. Moreover, member states still apply national measures with respect to liberalization or quantitative restrictions on imports and exports. Member states have been required to maintain minimum stocks of crude oil and oil products,[56] to supply the commission with information on the import of crude oil and natural gas,[57] and to prepare for interventions to be made after consultations with the other member states and the commission in case of shortage of crude oil and oil products.[58] Investment projects concerning the production, transport, stocking, and distribution of coal, oil products, natural gas, and electricity have to be communicated to the commission[59] and certain projects may be financially supported by the Community.[60] Since 1972 the council has been considering various other proposals from the commission;[61] their adoption may be accelerated as a result of the oil crisis of 1973-74.

Sensitive Industrial Products

The Community has already applied the procedures and instruments of its general CCP in order to solve particular problems in certain sectors of industry.

With regard to shipbuilding, Council Directive of 20 July 1972[62] has fixed criteria according to which certain aids and interventions to assist shipbuilding may be considered compatible with the common market with regard to their effect on interstate commerce (which is governed by the rules of Arts. 92 to 94 EEC) as well as on exports to third countries. Extension and amendment of this directive are now under consideration.[63]

With respect to the aviation industry and certain other sectors of advanced technology, the Community participates in negotiations within OECD for sector arrangements on export credit terms. Other proposals from the commission are before the council.

The Community is a party to the multilateral arrangement regarding international trade in cotton textiles[64] and is presently participating in the negotiation, within GATT, of a new multilateral agreement that is scheduled to cover all textile fibers and to enter into force in 1974. Czechoslovakia, Poland, Hungary, and Romania, which were not parties to the present agreement, are participating in these negotiations. Under the present agreement, the Community has concluded a number of bilateral voluntary export restraint agreements with various exporting countries, including Yugoslavia,[65] providing for import ceilings for the Community, which are allocated to member states on a voluntary and provisional basis. These ceilings have occasionally been autonomously increased, especially after the accession of the new member states, by Commission decisions adopted under Council Regulation (EEC) No. 1471/70 (mentioned above in section entitled "Quotas and Liberalization Measures").

In relation to the East European state-trading countries many sensitive textile products are still subject to various conventional or autonomous national quantitative restrictions, which are gradually coordinated and unified under the procedures laid down by Council Decisions of 16 December 1969 and 19 December 1972 (mentioned above respectively in sections entitled "Existing National Bilateral Agreements" and "Quotas and Liberalization Measures"). Disparities between these national measures have repeatedly caused the commission to authorize the exclusion of East European textile products from free circulation between member states in accordance with Art. 115 of the EEC Treaty.

Arms, munitions, and war material are not as such exempt from the CCP and CCT. Any member state may, however (under Art. 223 [1] [b] EEC), take such measures in connection with the production or trade in these goods as it considers necessary for the protection of the essential interests of its security; such measures may not adversely affect the conditions of competition in the common market regarding products that are not intended for specifically military purposes. The list of arms, munitions, and war materials was drawn up by the council in 1959 but has not been published. Furthermore, the EEC Treaty (Art. 224) provides for consultation and common action by member states to prevent the functioning of the common market being affected by measures that a member state may have to take in case of serious internal disturbances affecting the maintenance of law and order, in case of war or serious international tension constituting a threat of war, or in order to carry out obligations it has accepted for the purpose of maintaining peace and international security. Improper use of the powers under Arts. 223 and 224 can be submitted to an in camera ruling of the Court (Art. 225 EEC). (With respect to nuclear energy, see the security and safeguard provisions of Arts. 24 to 27 and 77 to 85 of the Euratom Treaty.)

Legal Remedies

The present survey obviously cannot adequately treat this subject but can only note a few aspects of the relationship between Community law and the municipal law of a member state.

Conflicts between national law and Community law should be solved in favor of the latter. In such cases, the commission can bring an action against the member state before the Court (Art. 169 EEC). Other member states may also introduce such action (Art. 170 EEC), but they rarely do so. If the member state is found in default, it must take the necessary measures to comply with the judgment of the Court (Art. 171 EEC). Private individuals cannot initiate such proceedings; nor can they sue the commission for failure in this respect (compare Art. 175 EEC). They can, however, raise the conflict in proceedings before national courts or tribunals. According to the jurisprudence of the Court, national courts or tribunals must solve the conflict by applying Community law instead of the contrary provision of national law, if the provision of Community law is considered to have "direct effect" within the national legal order. The "direct effect" criterion is wider than that of "self-executing," which is often used with respect to international law. It covers not only regulations, which are "directly applicable in all Member States" (Art. 189), but also other provisions of Community law (for example, in the treaties or in decisions or sometimes even in directives), which leave no discretion to the competent national authorities as to the measures prescribed or prohibited (such as abolition of customs duties). The question whether a Community provision has such direct effect and any other problem of interpretation of the treaties and of secondary Community legislation can be submitted to a ruling of the Court; courts or tribunals against whose decisions there is no remedy under national law are bound to bring such questions before the Court (Art. 177 EEC). It is important to recall in this respect that member states cannot by national legislation "transform" Community provisions with direct effect into national law, with a view to rule out the jurisdiction of the Court under Art. 177 EEC. The possibility of raising questions of interpretation and validity of Community law in proceedings before national courts and having them decided in the last instance by the Court has proved to be an important and frequently used legal remedy for private individuals and enterprises and an efficient procedure for evolving a uniform interpretation and application of the treaties and the secondary legislation.

The Community has to respect international law, and the jurisdiction of the Court to give preliminary rulings under Art. 177 EEC extends to the question whether the validity of secondary Community legislation is affected by a conflict with a rule of international law.

74

A provision of international law that is binding on the Community, such as a treaty concluded by the Community in accordance with Art. 228 EEC, may have this effect if private individuals can claim the right to have that provision applied in litigation. According to the Court, the existence of such a right is to be deduced inter alia from the terms and the nature of the treaty involved. The court therefore denied that right with respect to the provisions of GATT or of tariff agreements negotiated under GATT, although the Court recognized that the Community is bound by GATT because it has within the scope of the CCP gradually taken over the rights and duties that member states held previously.[66] Agreements concluded by member states with third countries before 1 January 1968[67] are not affected but must be amended, to the extent they are incompatible with the treaty or with the secondary legislation created under the treaty (Art. 234 EEC). Agreements concluded after that date need not necessarily be taken into account by the Community in the exercise of its powers. The obligation for member states to respect Community law and avoid obstacles to the further implementation of the CCP has been stressed in council decisions authorizing the extension of national commercial agreements with third countries under title I of Council Decision of 16 December 1969 (see section above entitled "Existing National Bilateral Agreements").

It may finally be observed that the judicial remedies are basically the same under the EEC and Euratom Treaties, but substantially different in the ECSC (the latter has no equivalent to Art. 177 EEC, and has a different system for dealing with treaty infringements by member states).

NOTES

1. Judgment of the Court in case 22/70, Commission v. Council (Recueil 1971, p. 263).
2. Compare the Notice of the Commission on the import of Japanese products into the Community in OJ (Official Journal) No. C 111, 21 Oct. 1972, p. 13.
3. OJ No. L 172, 22 July 1968, p. 1.
4. Last edition: Regulation (EEC) No. 1/74, 17 Dec. 1973, OJ No. L 1, 1 Jan. 1974, p. 1.
5. The scheme for 1973, which was still limited to the six original member states, was published in OJ No. L 296, 10 Dec. 1972. The 1974 scheme, which includes the new member states, is in OJ No. L 358 and 359, 28 and 29 Dec. 1973. For tariff quotas, see, for example, OJ No. L. 356, 27 Dec. 1973.
6. OJ No. L 238, 28 Sept. 1968, p. 1, amended by section I (4) of Annex I to the Act of Accession, and by Regulations (EEC) No.

2744/72 and 3456/73, OJ No. L 291, 28 Dec. 1972, p. 145 and L 356, 27 Dec. 1973, p. 1.

7. OJ No. L 14, 21 Jan. 1969.

8. OJ No. L 148, 28 June 1968, amended by section I (2) of Annex I to the Act of Accession.

9. OJ No. L 148, 28 June 1968.

10. See Regulation (EEC) No. 2818/72 of 22 Dec. 1972, OJ No. L 297, 30 Dec. 1971, p. 13.

11. OJ No. L 194, 6 Aug. 1968, p. 13.

12. OJ No. L 58, 8 March 1969, p. 7.

13. Id., p. 14.

14. Id., p. 11.

15. Id., p. 1.

16. OJ No. L 77, 29 March 1969, p. 1, amended by section I (7) of Annex I to the Act of Accession.

17. For a detailed description, see J. Amphoux, "Customs Legislation in the EEC," (1972) Journal of World Trade Law, pp. 133-184.

18. OJ No. L 19, 26 Jan. 1970; it is applicable vis-à-vis Bulgaria, Hungary, Poland, Romania, Czechoslovakia, and the USSR.

19. OJ No. L 124, 8 June 1970, p. 6; the list of countries in Annex II was amended by section VIII (2) of Annex I to the Act of Accession.

20. OJ No. L 324, 27 Dec. 1969, p. 25.

21. OJ No. L 124, 8 June 1970, p. 1.

22. Art. 14 of the regulation, as amended by Council Regulation (EEC) No. 2747/72, OJ No. L 291, 28 Dec. 1972, p. 150.

23. OJ No. L 164, 27 July 1970, p. 41.

24. OJ No. L 299, 31 Dec. 1972, p. 46.

25. OJ No. 71, 4 Nov. 1961, p. 1274/61.

26. See the Regulations mentioned in section II (3) (EEC) No. 109/70, Art. 6 et seq. and 1025/70, Art. 7 et seq. and compare Art. XIX GATT.

27. Date fixed by Regulation (EEC) No. 2747/72, cited in note 22.

28. See Art. 6 et seq. of Regulation (EEC) 2603/69, mentioned in section of this chapter entitled "Quotas and Liberalization Measures"; compare Art. XI (2a) GATT.

29. OJ No. L 93, 17 April 1968, p. 1.

30. See below, section entitled "Agricultural Products."

31. See Art. 12 (1b) of Regulation (EEC) No. 1025/70 and Art. 9 (1b) of Regulation 109/70, both mentioned in section of this chapter entitled "Quotas and Liberalization Measures."

32. Insofar as these aids also affect trade between member states. they are subject to the rules of Art. 92 to 94 EEC on state aids (see chapter section entitled "Sensitive Industrial Products").

33. OJ No. 66, 27 Oct. 1960, pp. 1339-60.

34. OJ No. 19, 346, 17 Dec. 1973, p. 1.

35. OJ No. L 254, 23 Nov. 1970, p. 1 and 26.

36. Proposals provided for in Annex D of both of the 1970 directives (supra note 35 and accompanying text) were submitted in 1971.

37. Compare Bulletin of the "Agence Europe" (hereafter referred to as "Europe"), 13 Dec. 1972, p. 10 and 27 Dec. 1972, p. 4.

38. The Legal Service of the UN Secretariat recognized the necessity for the Community to participate in negotiations in UN commodity conferences and believed such participation possible without infringing upon UN regulations, in its opinion prepared for the 1968 UN Sugar Conference (1968 UN Juridical Yearbook, p. 201).

39. OJ No. L 326, 29 Dec. 1969, p. 39.

40. OJ No. C 106, 6 Dec. 1963, p. 22; see also "Europe," 23 Oct. 1973 document 766, and "European Report," 13 Oct. 1973, No. 82.

41. Judgment of the Court of Justice of 15 Dec. 1971, cases 51 to 54/71, Recueil 1971, p. 1108.

42. See section of this chapter entitled "Customs Legislation."

43. Judgment of the Court of Justice of 23 Nov. 1971, Bock v. Commission, case 62/70, Recueil 1971, p. 897.

44. OJ No. L 121, 3 June 1971, p. 26 and No. L 80, 28 March 1973, p. 22.

45. See for example OJ No. C 63, 4 Aug. 1973, p. 2.

46. According to the declaration made by the Federal Republic of Germany in accordance with its Berlin Declaration annexed to the Final Act on the EEC and Euratom Treaties.

47. See "Europe," 25 July 1973, p. 10 and 27 Sept. 1973, p. 3.

48. Listed in Art. 38 (3) EEC as completed by Council Regulation No. 7 (a) of 18 Dec. 1959, OJ No. 7, 30 Jan. 1961, p. 71.

49. Compare Regulations (EEC) No. 1025/70, Art. 17, No. 109/70, Art. 13 and No. 2603/69, Art. 12, cited supra notes 19, 18, and 20, respectively.

50. Judgment of the Court of Justice cited in 41, supra note.

51. Compare Regulations No. 170/67/EEC (OJ No. 130, 28 June 1967, p. 2596), (EEC) No. 1059/69 (OJ No. L 141, 12 June 1969, p. 1), (EEC) No. 2682/72 (OJ No. L 289, 27 Dec. 1972, p. 13).

52. Defined in Art. 81 ECSC, as completed by Council Decision published in OJ No. 129, 6 Dec. 1962, p. 2810.

53. See Judgment of the Court of Justice, 14 July 1961 (Vloeberghs v. High Authority, joined cases 9 and 12/60, Rec. VII, p. 39.

54. See Arts. 31 and 39 of the Act of Accession.

55. Mentioned, but not published, in section II of Annex X to the Act of Accession.

56. Council Directive No. 68/414 EEC and Council Decision No. 68/416 EEC, both of 20 Dec. 1968, OJ No. L 308, 23 Dec. 1968, pp. 14 and 19.

57. Council Regulation (EEC) No. 1055/72, 18 May 1972, OJ No. L 120, 25 May 1972, p. 3.

58. Council Directive No. 73/238 EEC, 24 July 1973, OJ No. L 228, 16 Aug. 1973, p. 1.

59. Council Regulation (EEC) No. 1056/72, 18 May 1972, OJ No. L 120, 25 May 1972, p. 7 and Art. 54 ECSC. Compare for nuclear energy Art. 41 EAEC.

60. Council Regulation (EEC) No. 3056/73, 9 Nov. 1973, OJ No. L 312, 13 Nov. 1973, p. 1. Compare Art. 54 ECSC and Art. 48 EAEC.

61. See O J No. C 92, 31 Oct. 1973, p. 10.

62. OJ No. L 169, 27 July 1972, p. 28.

63. See OJ No. C 114, 27 Dec. 1973, p. 23.

64. See OJ No. L 225, 12 Oct. 1970, p. 28.

65. See for Yugoslavia: OJ No. L 182, 5 Aug. 1973, p. 1; for the other countries: OJ No. L 134, 12 June 1972, p. 31; L 220, 30 Sept. 1971, p. 23; L 55, 8 Mar. 1971, p. 12; L 43, 22 Feb. 1971, p. 1.

66. Compare Judgment of the Court of 12 Dec. 1972, International Fruit Company, cases 21 to 24/72, Recueil 1972, p. 1219.

67. For Denmark, Ireland, and the United Kingdom, this date is 1 Jan. 1973 (Art. 5 of the Act of Accession).

4

THE FEDERAL REPUBLIC
OF GERMANY

Axel Lebahn

THE SPECIAL POSITION OF EASTERN TRADE
IN THE FEDERAL REPUBLIC

The Term "Eastern Trade"

The predominantly political significance of "Eastern trade" in
the Federal Republic of Germany (FRG) has had a profound effect on
the FRG's regulatory scheme with respect to this trade, particularly
with the changes in political relations with the Eastern bloc states that
have occurred since the founding of the FRG. The Eastern trade of the
FRG is incomparably more strongly linked with internal policy than
any other frontier-crossing trade. The taboo that public opinion and
official government policy placed on Eastern trade, on the one hand,
together with the politicizing of sometimes purely technical questions,
explain why the term "Eastern trade" has still not found a place today
in any legal provisions of the FRG and only recently is being mentioned
with any freedom in official and unofficial texts. In the drawing up of
common policy guidelines for Western economies by such organizations
as the Committee for Economic Development and the Keizai Doyukai,
the "East" was defined in 1965 with reference to the GATT definition
for the bloc countries as "the Soviet Union and the other European
bloc states, namely Poland, Czechoslovakia, Bulgaria, Romania, Hungary and Albania." Opinion was unanimous that Yugoslovia did not
belong to the bloc; in German eyes, the German Democratic Republic
(GDR) also did not belong, and in American eyes, Cuba, the People's
Republic of China, North Korea, and North Vietnam required separate
treatment.[1] According to internal economic-legal provisions of the
Federal Republic, however, North Korea, the Mongolian People's Republic, North Vietnam, and the People's Republic of China belonged to
the Eastern bloc at the time.[2] The same list of countries is also found

in recent official and unofficial definitions, but the latter refer no longer to the "Eastern bloc" but instead to trade with the "Eastern European and Asiatic state-trading countries."[3] These definitions exclude Yugoslavia from "Eastern trade" on the grounds that the latter has an "economic system of a peculiar kind" and stands "outside the blocs"[4]; the arguments are therefore partly political. A glance at the latest organization chart of the Federal Economics Ministry shows, on the other hand, that the organizational practice of the FRG includes trade with Yugoslavia in "Eastern trade," for in Department V (Foreign Economic Policy and Development Aid), Section VB 2 is responsible for "East-West Economic Relations," in which is included Yugoslavia.[5] Moreover, the abovementioned definitions tacitly overlook the fact that the "List of Countries C,"[6] which as part of Appendix L to the Decree on Foreign Trade enumerates the states to be included under "Eastern trade," has also contained Cuba since 1968. A geographical limitation of the term "Eastern trade" consequently seems questionable, and a definition of the Eastern trading partners of the FRG according to the criterion "socialist planned-trading countries" is more appropriate.

Classification of Trade with the GDR

Such a delimitation made purely according to the economic, social, and governmental structure of the trading partner is in conflict, however, with the official thesis defended since the foundation of the Federal Republic that trade between the FRG and the GDR is not, like trade between other Western countries and the GDR, international and Eastern trade, but internal German trade sui generis.[7] This thesis has been described as fictitious particularly by non-German authors and has been attacked repeatedly by one representative in the European Parliament in questions to the Commission of the European Community.[8] It is also called in to question, however, by individual German authors.[9] A conspicuous feature of this definition question is that not only must systematic scientific principles be derived from it but reliable politico-economic conclusions. The regulating of trade with the GDR is one of the central points in which the self-awareness of the West German state in its classification in a system of peaceful international economic cooperation is concentrated. One would not be doing justice to the historical development of the FRG—to its ideology and practice—if the special nature of its economic links with the GDR were not properly emphasized and if "internal German trade" were equated with the general Eastern trading links of other Western countries to the GDR. If, therefore, "Eastern trade" is defined in the broadest sense as economic relations of Western states with socialist planned-trading countries, it must be clearly emphasized that the corresponding economic relations of the FRG fall into at least two clearly defined categories:

(1) internal German trade and (2) trade with other socialist planned-trading countries (in which the classification of Yugoslavia into a third group can be discussed).

"INNER GERMAN TRADE"

Historical Development, Legal Sources, and Organization

Interzonal or inner German trade can be regarded as the remainder of the "economic unit" of Germany.[10] The safeguarding of the "economic unit" of the German national economy was demanded in the resolutions of the Potsdam Conference.[11] It is not surprising, therefore, that a central problem of the regulation of inner German trade has been not only the economic relations between the FRG and the GDR but, up to the present day, also the economic and political incorporation of Berlin, which has been made an issue expressly or indirectly by both sides.[12] After the Western allies had regulated unilaterally by law the economic trade between the occupation zones, a contractual arrangement between East and West occurred for the first time following the Berlin blockade in the "Frankfurt Agreement" of 1949,[13] the negotiation of which on the Western side was passed in large measure to the FRG authorities.[14] The contracting parties were the "currency areas of the Western DM [deutschemark] and Eastern DM, "thus avoiding making direct reference to the vexing question of recognition of the GDR by the FRG and the unclarified status of Berlin. This neutral compromise formula was retained in later agreements; since the middle of the 1960s, however, the GDR has refused to make any mention of it.[15]

According to Article 7 of the 1st Interzone Regulation of 1951, the authority for the granting of buying permits and bills was granted to the Land (or state) authorities mentioned in Appendix 2 of that Regulation and cooperation licenses to the Federal Office for Food and Industry.[16] As regards the relations with the GDR Ministry for Foreign Trade, according to the official nonrecognition theory of the FRG toward the GDR, no government agency should be responsible; on the instructions of the West German Economics Ministry, therefore, the Trust Office for Interzone Trade was founded in 1949 in Frankfurt under the Deutsche Industrie und Handelstag. Since 1950, the Trust Office has had its headquarters in Berlin. Its employees are appointed by federal authorities.[17] Its head has the title of Commissioner for Inner German Economic Relations in Department IV of the Federal Economics Ministry, Trade and Industry, so that a clear distinction is drawn on the organizational level from the different development of the other Eastern trading links of the federal government.[18]

In addition to numerous agreements of only temporary importance, the Trust Office for Interzone Trade concluded the 1951 Berlin Agreement, which is still valid today (the current text is dated August 16, 1960) and forms the basis of interzone trade as "trade sui generis."[19] This agreement contains the conditions of traffic in goods (Art. II), service transactions (Art.III), and payment transactions (Art. IV ff.). These provisions are given concrete form through annual negotiations on lists of goods and other agreements (partly of a legal nature,[20] partly of a political character—"gentlemen's agreements"[21]) and are embodied in implementing orders, ministerial decrees, and announcements and memoranda of the German Federal Bank,[22] which for its part also concludes agreements with the Central Bank of the GDR (Deutsche Notenbank).[23] The mass of regulations on interzone trade therefore represents a quite special feature of the FRG, namely that an area of foreign relations of eminent importance to the state is not governed by ratifiable treaties but by quasiadministrative agreements[24] the implementation of which under supervision of the rights and duties of the citizens of the FRG does not take place on a legal basis but through administrative regulations. A further peculiarity is that the allied foreign exchange control laws for inner German trade still apply,[25] although they have been superseded for international trade by Art. 47 of the Foreign Trade Law[26] of 1961. This means that inner German trade is still governed by far-reaching prohibitions and orders that were framed at a time when the West German economy appeared weak and in need of protection, whereas the regulating of international trade is governed by the basic concept of freedom in foreign trade as per Art. 1 of the Foreign Trade Law.[27]

The Regulation of Import-Export Relations

All firms engaged in inner German trade have to be licensed. Nearly all goods can be supplied from the FRG and, with the exception of the agricultural sector, nearly all goods can be purchased from it. There are general limits and far-reaching prohibitions on the import and export of goods not manufactured in the FRG or the GDR, in order to limit inner German trade to goods of German origin.[28]

Although two different customs tariffs, differences in customs laws, and different administrations exist in the GDR and the FRG both territories are regarded as a single customs area on the FRG side, so that the frontier between the two states is not a customs frontier.[29] Fiscal control of inner German trade is nevertheless achieved by a turnover tax regulation, which lays down a tax on sales to the GDR of 6 percent (sales taxed at reduced rate 3 percent and for purchases a reduction claim of 11 percent (5.5 percent).[30]

Supplying goods to the GDR. Under General License No. 2-L of January 21, 1969,[31] the supplying for money of goods listed in Appendixes 1 and 2 is licensed as a whole. An individual license is therefore not required for them; the export contract must simply be reported on a form as per Appendix 3 to the General License No. 2-L to the Federal Office for Trade and Industry; a way bill must be attached to the goods in accordance with Appendix 5. About 50 percent of the goods supplied are subject to this procedure.

As regards other goods permitted to be supplied for money, individual licenses are granted on "Application for the granting of a goods certificate," which must be submitted to the highest state (or Land) authority[32] responsible for the residence of the applicant. All deliveries that are announced in the "Bundesanzeiger" are permitted. Certificates for goods will be granted for goods with advertised value limits until the annually specified quota has been exhausted; for the other goods, there are no time limits. Unless it is prohibited by an announcement on the supply of goods, goods purchased from the GDR can also be supplied for outward processing. In this case a purchasing license is required for the import and a goods certificate for the reexport. For the supply of goods from a foreign country into the GDR, a transit trade license is required. The acquiring of the transit goods from the foreign country is then governed by the import regulations (Chapter III, Art. 22ff.) of the Foreign Trade Regulation of August 22, 1961.[33]

Purchase of goods from the GDR. The purchase of goods for money is not subject to license but only to notification in accordance with the General License No. 3-B of December 19, 1969.[34] The purchaser has to submit the notification on a form as per Appendix 3 to the Federal Office for Trade and Industry.

As regards goods not listed in the General License No. 3-B—that is, those subject to individual licensing—application for the granting of a purchasing license must be made to the highest Land authority responsible.[35] An individual license will only be granted if the goods item applied for is announced in the "Bundesanzeiger." Purchases with advertised value limits are limited in time to the accounting year. Purchases with agreed values are not subject to a time limit; they can however be licensed only up to the amount of the agreed values fixed annually. This regulation is aimed at the promotion of long-term contracts, by making possible the granting of premature purchasing licenses for goods scheduled for supply in later years. Lists of goods not subject to a time limit, whose limit values change of their own accord every calendar year, are particularly suited to the long-term planning needs of the GDR.[36]

Purchases without value limits or agreed values are possible on the basis of unlimited announcements not limited in time. Provided the announcements do not specify the contrary, the purchase of GDR goods for inward processing is permitted. A goods certificate for the export and a purchasing license for the reimport are absolutely essential in this case. For the sale of goods from the GDR by a domestic person to foreigners, a special transit trade license is required. The transaction is governed by the export regulations (Chapter II, Art. 5 ff.) of the Foreign Trade Regulation of August 22, 1961.[37]

Trade in units of account with the GDR. As trade with the GDR is strictly bilateral, a bilateral balancing of accounts between the values of the import and export flows must also take place as a matter of principle. The authorities responsible for the conduct of the trade in units of account are the German Federal Bank on the one hand and the Central Bank of the GDR on the other.[38] Payments received in Western DM by the Federal Bank and in Eastern DM by the Central Bank are converted into units of account and credited by each bank to the other.[39] The limitation of the total debit balance of one side to 200 million units of account (as specified in Arts. VIII and IX of the 1951 Berlin Agreement) and the annual balancing obligation were abolished in 1968 by the FRG in accordance with an agreement with the GDR expiring in 1975,[40] so that no balancing has taken place since then. At the end of 1973, the resulting swing of about 620 million units of account came to about 25 percent of the amount that the GDR supplied to the FRG in 1972.[41] Rough estimates for the years 1975-85 put the swing resulting then at DM 1.8 billion and the savings resulting from the freedom from interest at least DM 860 million.[42] A "commercialization" of the swing suggested by West German trade representatives, through an interim solution that would accustom the GDR slowly to the payment of interest,[43] has so far not reached the stage of realization. The discovery that the development of interzone trade in the past has escaped to a considerable extent the influence of economic factors,[44] is causing experts to issue warnings against using economic analyses to gain political ends, through economic enticements or pressure.[45]

The interzone accounts at the German Federal Bank and the State Bank of the GDR are subdivided into three subaccounts, in order to give a better breakdown of the commodity structure between imports and exports, by balancing the values of equivalent goods against each other.[46] Under Subaccount 1 are entered all payments for predominantly "hardware goods,"[47] and under Subaccount 2 are those for predominantly "software goods."[48] The debit balances of the GDR regularly occurring on Subaccount 3 (services) can be balanced by amounts carried forward from Subaccount 2.[49] An S account (cash payment account) makes possible above all the purchase [50] of particularly needed goods for foreign exchange outside the statement on the subaccounts and thus has the function of making possible extraordinary sales, either short-term in particular emergencies or long-term in the purchase of technologically beneficial, expensive goods. The accounting system used in interzone trade therefore represents a fairly widely differentiated legal instrument for the regulation of the flow of trade, but one that is not generally used, mainly for regulation of the flow of trade, political reasons, since many arrangements are arrived at through political statements of good will between the GDR and the FRG.

The payments in Western DM for deliveries from the GDR must be paid through a clearing bank to the German Federal Bank, which sends a credit note to the Staatsbank, whereupon the latter undertakes the corresponding payment to the payee.[51] The clearing banks on the Western side are the central banks and all commercial banks; on the Eastern side they are the Staatsbank, the Berliner Stadtkontor, the Berliner Volksbank eGmbH, and the Deutsche Handelsbank AG. The latter can open letters of credit directly with the West German credit banks.[52] Since 1967, a West German bank consortium in Frankfurt, which ever since 1952 has cooperated as the "Ausfuhr-Aktiengesell-schaft—AKA" in the financing of medium and long-term export deals, has contained the Gesellschaft zur Finanzierung von Industrieanlagen mbH—Gefi, Frankfurt, which is connected in personal union with AKA under uniform management and whose aim is to finance deliveries and sales to the GDR. Its credit guidelines lay down a Ceiling I and a Ceiling II, which correspond to the Ceilings A and B of AKA.[53] A credit insurance for deals with the GDR can be obtained through federal guarantees, which are carried out by the Deutschen Revisions—und Treuhand, Düsseldorf.[54] HERMES Kredit-Versicherung AG, Hamburg, guarantees cannot be applied for, because deliveries to the GDR are not "exports to foreign countries."

The Role of International Treaties

At bottom, the term "inner German trade" can be understood only in terms of the political objective of the Federal Republic to preserve the concept of German unity.[55] The reunification of Germany, which finds its legal basis and control in the Basic Law of the FRG[56] as well as the verdict of the Federal Constitutional Court,[57] has been increasingly attacked by the GDR in recent years and even regarded as questionable by Western states. On the other hand, the FRG can appeal to a more or less explicit partly legal embodiment of its legal standpoint in international treaties. For instance, in 1951 the FRG received within the mining union a special status in trade with the GDR.[58] It was made clear in 1951 that the entry of the FRG requires no changes in GATT rules or the present position regarding

inner German trade in goods of German origin.[59] A Protocol on
Inner German Trade was attached to the Rome Treaty on the founding of the EEC. The first clause of the protocol provides that, as
trade between the FRG and the German territories outside the scope
of the basic law of the FRG is an integral part of inner German trade,
the application of the treaty does not require any changes in the existing
system of this trade.[60] The EEC countries have therefore accepted
and officially respected the legal position of the FRG that the erection
of a customs frontier in Germany is irreconcilable with the thesis of
the political and economic unity of Germany.[61]

As a result of the easier access to the market of the European
Community offered to the GDR on the basis of the protocol on inner
German trade, and particularly as a result of the exemption from duty
in trade with the FRG, some experts have calculated that powerful
economic advantages will accrue to the GDR from its special status.[62]
To the calculation by Professor Merkel (Berlin), which estimates the
special advantages accruing to the GDR from the interzone trade with
the FRG as DM 500 million for the year 1969, Werner Gumpel (Munich)
adds a further DM 500 million of West German direct or indirect
economic aid to the GDR.[63] In the face of such calculations, the official departments of the Federal Republic have always behaved very
reticently. For instance, in Feburary 1970 the then state secretary
in the Federal Economic Ministry, Klaus-Dieter Arndt, denied such
estimates,[64] and the head of the Trust Office for Interzone Trade,
Willi Kleindienst, has grave doubts about the possibility of evaluating
politicoeconomic advantages and disadvantages in money terms.[65]

Although the GDR in principle rejects the West German thesis
of the unity of the German nation and the economic links sui generis
between the GDR and FRG, it nevertheless concedes without further
specification a few special features of the trading relations between
the two German states.[66] In the historic treaty between the FRG and
the GDR of December 21, 1972,[67] the GDR agreed to the future development of economic relations while preserving the mass of provisions of the contactual norms of inner German trade: Trade between
the FRG and the GDR is to be developed on the basis of existing agreements.[68] The parties to the treaty have thus acknowledged inner
German trade in the face of the international problems arising therefrom.[69] Even after the recognition of the GDR as a state by the FRG,
the latter is empowered vis-à-vis the partners of the European Community to maintain its special trading relations with the GDR, thus
evading the provisions of the Community's common commercial
policy.[70] GDR trade with the FRG thus remains an Eastern trade
sui generis.

EASTERN TRADE WITH
OTHER SOCIALIST STATE-TRADING COUNTRIES

Compared with the complicated, detailed, and peculiar regulations of the "Eastern trade sui generis" that govern the trading relations of the FRG with the GDR, the FRG's trading links with other planned-economy countries are determined by the general provisions of its foreign trade legislation and foreign trade treaties, without essential, regional, political, or ideological differences. Despite numerous complaints of discrimination from the socialist countries,[71] the foreign trade law of the FRG contains no regulations designed specifically to ensure different treatment of socialist countries. Unequal treatment only occurs on a small scale and generally reflects differing circumstances. Those regulations that still apply specifically to trading relations with the state-planned countries are today limited in number and importance.

Historical Development, Legal Sources, and Organization

From December 1945 to October 1949 trade between the zones was controlled by the Joint Export-Import Agency (JEIA). Even after the substantial relinquishment of the functions of JEIA to the FRG authorities in 1949, the former retained control over the export of strategic goods.[72] From the beginning of its existence, the Federal Republic considered implementation of the embargo in the FRG as a limitation of its Eastern trade whereby a whole network of regulations originating in international law, law relation to occupation, and of German provenance arose.[73] In an almost unanimously adopted resolution on Eastern trade of May 6, 1952, the German Bundestag demanded full observance of Cocom rules FRG by the FRG (but with equal treatment by other Western countries) and supported the adoption of normal trading regulations with the states of the Soviet block.[74]

Despite the officially demonstrated eagerness of the Federal government to adhere to the embargo rules, there was open criticism of the GDR by the United States for violation of the rules.[75]

The secrecy demanded concerning the restricted list meant that the Eastern trade of the FRG remained in semiobscurity.[76] This practice, observed in some cases for purely political motives in defiance of economic common sense, favored illegal trade.[77] As the Federal government kept in large measure to the Cocom control program, West German traders joined forces and formed the Deutscher Industrie und Handelstag, the Eastern Committee for German Trade, the East Asia Association, the Working Combine for Inter-zone Trade, the Association of German Machine Construction Companies VdMA, and the Rationalisierungskuratorium der Deutschen Wirtschaft RKW. These bodies operated at a time when the regulation and promotion

of Eastern trade was a delicate matter for the state authorities.[78]
In particular, delegates from the Eastern Committee could act in a
quasipublic capacity at a time when the activities of the federal government were limited through the Hallstein doctrine.[79]

Although West German practitioners of Eastern trade, frequently
proud of having been able to achieve considerable success without substantial state support, were often convinced that the status of the FRG's
eastern trade gave them special liberties and opportunities, recognized
experts believed that the German firms could not have been able to
utilize fully the available possibilities because they lacked important
facilities that large competing countries had.[80]

In recent years, a network of international trade treaties with
state-trading countries has been created, affecting the internal Eastern
trade regulations of the FRG.

Although the Eastern trade expert Otto Wolff von Amerongen
had expressed skepticism regarding the chances of a substantial expansion in trade after the August 12, 1970 agreement between the USSR
and the FRG,[81] the curve for the development of trade has actually
shown a sharp increase since 1971.[82] Although a number of other
factors have had a bearing on this trend, there can be no doubt that the
the evolving legal situation, reflected in international treaties and
the removal of internal obstacles to Eastern trade, has had and still
has a considerable influence in promoting trade.

The Regulating of Import-Export Relations

The foreign exchange regulations stemming from Allied legal
sources, which rested on the principle of prohibition subject to permission, were superseded on September 1, 1961 by the Foreign Trade Law
(AWG),[83] together with the Foreign Trade Regulation (AWV)[84] and the
Responsibility Regulation.[85] Article 1 of the AWG states: "Foreign
trade is in principle free." This principle of permission subject to
prohibition has direct legal significance, as it must operate as a yard-
stick and in all doubtful cases favor a liberal view.[86] Eastern trade,
also (provided it is not subject to express limitations), is in principle
free. In addition to the limitations expressed in the AWG and the AWV,
the provisions of a number of other laws in particular must be observed
for trade across borders: a 1909 cattle epidemic law,[87] a 1936 food
law,[88] a 1940 meat inspection law,[89] a 1955 law on protection of German
culture,[90] the plant protection law of 1968,[91] a corn law of 1950,[92] a
sugar law of 1951,[93] a cattle and meat law of 1951,[94] an atom law of
1959,[95] a 1960 law on the import of weapons,[96] a milk and fat law of
1951,[97] and a law regarding residence.[98]

Whereas the FRG has signed specific international administrative
agreements in some of these legal fields (for example, on veterinary
matters) with various states, corresponding agreements with the

socialist countries can only be expected as gradually increasing economic cooperation occurs. For Eastern trade, therefore, the general
trade limitations of the abovementioned laws apply. The following
limitations of the AWG are fundamental here: Art. 5, on the fulfillment of international obligations; Art. 6, on the prevention of harmful effects from foreign trading areas; Art. 7, on protecting the security
of foreign interests; Art. 10, Cl. 3, on satisfying a justified need for
the protection of domestic producers.

Export Regulations. Every export consignment has to be accompanied
by an export certificate under Art. 8 AWV. This declaration procedure,
applying to all items of the commodities list, serves both for foreign
trade statistics and for monitoring exports and turnover tax purposes.
In addition to the declaration procedure, there is a licensing procedure
in enumerated cases (Art. 5-7 AWV). The main case applying to
Eastern trade is the export of strategic goods (Part I, Sections A, B,
and C of the export list, Appendix AL). A license is refused in principle
for the socialist countries in the List of Countries "C."[99] If the FRG
wishes to grant a special license for the delivery of a strategic good,
it would have to secure Cocom's agreement, which is normally only
granted on proof of the civilian use of the goods to be exported.[100]
    The embargo has had its share of difficulties. In early 1963,
for example, a previously granted export license for delivery of a
large-diameter pipeline contracted for between the West German firm
of Mannesmann and the Soviet Union was revoked. West German trade
with the East as a whole suffered a setback as a result of the Eastern
reaction; firms from other Western countries took over part of the
deliveries to the USSR; and the USSR accelerated the creation of its
own pipeline-production facilities. The main damage was suffered
by the FRG.[101]
    Controls over payment terms, which previously were exercised
simultaneously with the export procedure, were abolished in 1967;[102]
This allowed West German exporters to remain competitive vis-à-vis
other Western companies seeking business in Eastern countries. It
remains to be seen whether a similar relaxation of the licensing procedure in the case of strategic goods will result from the long-term
economic tendencies in this direction.

Import Regulations. The import regulations are designed above all
to protect the domestic market from Eastern dumping. According to
Art. 24 AWV, an import declaration must be issued for every imported
commodity for statistical and monitoring purposes. In the case of
most imports with a high value, a certificate of origin must also be
produced as per Art. 29. In the case of imports requiring a license,
an import license takes the place of the import declaration, an

additional certificate of origin being required only if expressly specified in the import license (Art. 31 AWV). Art. 22 AWV stipulates a special license on exchange control grounds if delivery lists are involved that exceed the scale usual in the trade. In view of the promotion of long-term and permanent economic cooperation and a foreign exchange surplus, this license has almost become a mere formality.

Since 1966 a distinction has been drawn in the granting of import licenses between sector subject to quotas (quotas specified in trade treaties) and one not subject to quotas. For the latter, a liberalization has been undertaken by waiving the individual licensing procedure under Art. 10, Cl. 1, AWG and introducing instead licensing based on the "Announcement with Current Application—AmlA." The liberalized procedure has become possible with respect to those countries that bind themselves in trade treaties with the Federal Republic to a common procedure for the prevention of market disturbances in the FRG. A corresponding procedure is at present agreed to with almost all Eastern trading countries, so that every effort to liberalize trade with them is being made. As the liberalization list is being extended in several stages and the list of goods subject to quota has been reduced, the importance of the individual licensing procedure has receded sharply. This autonomous de facto liberalization (which can be withdrawn at any time) has been extended since 1970. Until August 21, 1970, all Eastern imports into the FRG were subject to license; a listed number of commodity items have now been exempted from the licensing.[103] At the beginning of 1974, 91.4 percent of all industrial commodity items were freed of quantitative restrictions.[104]

Export Credit Programs[105]

The general freedom of movement of capital transactions has enabled financial credits to be given to Eastern trading partners of German firms or banks.[106] The federal government has argued continually in the international bodies responsible for these matters (such as the Bern Union, the EEC, the OECD) that the granting of Western credit to the East should be coordinated and restricted. In view of the decline in the volume of FRG-Eastern trade in 1962/63, however, it permitted from 1965 a maximum period of five years for Eastern credits in accordance with Bern Union rules and also provided governmental guarantees. A revival of exports to the East followed.[107] Today, credit terms up to five years are usually agreed on for credits that exceed DM 10 million.[108]

The Federal government promotes Eastern trade through export credit insurance and credit to suppliers. The export credit insurance of the FRG is undertaken on a trust basis by two private companies, HERMES Kredit-Versicherung AG, Hamburg, and the Deutsche

Revisions—und Treuhand AG, Frankfurt. HERMES is responsible for the insurance of all Eastern trade deals. Decisions on applications for cover are made by the Interministerial Committee—IMA, which is composed of representatives of the government, the Federal Bank, and private industry. If credit periods of longer than five years are involved, an information procedure within the Bern Union and a consultation procedure within the European Community are carried out, in order to obtain a picture of the international competitive situation in "matching cases."[109]

Until now, public credits could be granted only through the Kredit Anstalt für Wiederaufbau-KW (the Credit Institute for Reconstruction). The conditions for access to KW funds by foreign recipients specify that the recipient must belong to a developing country. So far, only Yugoslavia (but no Comecon members) is recognized as such. The granting of credit is publicly supported by the Ausfuhrkreditanstalt—AKA, which is part of a private banking consortium that grants credits to suppliers at market rates of interest in accordance with two ceilings.

The future granting of public credit to Eastern trading partners is clouded with uncertainty at the present time. At the January 1974 meeting of the Soviet-German Economic Commission, the FRG rejected such an undertaking on the grounds that a precedent would therefore be created for unforeseeable future credit requirements of the Eastern trading partners, which the FRG could not satisfy.[110]

NOTES

1. Ost-West-Handel. Eine gemeinsame Politik für den Westen 9 et seq. Europaische Vereinigung für wirtschaftliche und soziale Entwicklung, ed. Frankfurt, a.M. 1965.

2. "Osthandel. Die Regelung des Verfahrens im Handel mit Oststaaten," Wirtschaftsverkehr mit dem Ausland 3. Frankfurt a.M. 1963.

3. Osthandel 5, (9 VWV-Reihe zur Aussenwirtschaft, Frankfurt a.M., current loose-leaf); Jahnke and Lucas, "Osthandel-Ostpolitik in der Praxis," Handel zur wirtschaftlichen Zusammenarbeit 5 (Bundesminister für Wirtschaft und Finanzen, Dokumentation Nr. 175, Bonn, 1972); Friderichs, "Chancen im Ost-West-Handel nutzen," Jan. 2, 1974 Nachrichten für Aussenhandel.

4. Osthandel, supra note 3, at 5; Friderichs, supra note 3, at 1.

5. Organization plan of the Bundesministerium für Wirtschaft, Doc. No. ZA 4-000700 (June 1973).

6. Bekanntmachung der Neufassung der Verordnung zur Durch-führung des Aussenwirtschaftsgesetzes (Aussenwirtschaftsverordnung) of Dec. 20, 1966, BGB1. 1967 I, at 1.

7. K. Holbik and H. Myers, Postwar Trade in Divided Germany: The Internal and International Issues 10 et seq. (Baltimore, 1964).

8. Written Questions No. 119, Abl. 1966; No. 54/67, AB1. 1967; Nos. 169/8 and 256/68, AB1. 1969; No. C14/11; No. 261/68, AB1. 1969; No. C29/14 and 79/20; No. 474/69, Abl. 1970; No. C41/4. See Zuleeg, infra note 70, n. 2.

9. Meier, "Grundvertrag, EWG-Vertrag und 'inner-deutscher Handel'," 1972 Betriebsberater 1521.

10. Pentzlin, "Interzonenhandel-Osthandel-EWG," Wirtschafts-beziehungen mit dem Osten 15, 19 (Stuttgart, 1971).

11. Potsdam Conference of August 2, 1945, Art. III (B) (14). See Dokumente zur Berlin-Frage 1944-1962, at 24 (2d ed., Munich, 1962).

12. H. Mendershausen, "Interzonal Trade in Germany," at 1, The Trade and Contractual Relations (United States Air Force Project, RAND Memorandum No. RM-3686-PR, July 1963).

13. Law No. 53 of the U.S. and British Military Government, "Devisenbewirtschaftung und Kontrolle des Güterverkers," Bundesan-zeiger No. 2 (Sept. 27, 1949); Order No. 235, French High Commis-sioner, 1949, Journal Officiel 2155 (Sept. 18, 1949).

14. Bundesanzeiger No. 8 (Oct. 11, 1949).

15. Kleindienst, "Aktuelle Rechtsfragen des Innerdeutschen Handels," 3:2 Beitrage zum Internationalen Wirtschaftsrecht und Atomenergierecht (Göttingen, 1974).

16. First Implementing Order, at the time valid in the version of Dec. 16, 1970. See Beilage zum Bundesanzeiger No. 239 (Dec. 23, 1970).

17. S. Kupper, Der innerdeutsche Handel. Rechtliche Grundlagen, politische und wirtschaftliche Bedeutung 12 (Cologne, 1972).

18. Organization plan of the Bundesministerium für Wirtschaft, Doc. No. ZA 4-000700 (June 1973).

19. 1961 Berlin Treaty Concerning Trade Between the Currency Area of the German Mark (DM-West) and the Currency Area of the German Notenbank (DM-East) (hereafter, "Currency Area Trade Agreement"). See Bundesanzeiger No. 32 (Feb. 15, 1961).

20. Compare "Anhebung der Wertgrenzen von Metallen," Bundesanzeiger No. 220 (Nov. 24, 1973).

21. Compare "Gentlemen's Agreement über beiderseitigen Bezug von Stahlfabrikaten," Frankfurter Allgemeine Zeitung, Oct. 12, 1973, p. 28, col. 5; "Absichtserklarung über Anhebung von Metal-lieferungsmengen," Bundesanzeiger No. 7 (Jan. 1, 1974).

22. IV (7) "Innerdeutscher Handel" 1 (Frankfurt a.M., current loose-leaf).

23. Id. at 11.

24. Kleindienst, "Abwicklung und Praxis der Handelsbeziehungen zur DDR", Wirtschaftsbeziehungen mit dem Osten 61, 62 (Stuttgart, 1971).

25. 18 Entscheidungen des Bundesverfassungsgerichts 353 (1965).

26. Aussenwirtschaftsgesetz of April 28, BGB1, 1961 I, at 481.

27. E. Hocke, Aussenwirtschaftsgesetz. Kommentar und systematische Darstellung mit Rechtsverordnungen und einschlagigen Vorschriften des OWiG, at 19 (Hamburg, 1961).

28. "Innerdeutscher Handel," supra note 22, at 1.

29. G. Heider, Der Interzonenwarenverkehr: Ein Handbuch für die Praxis der Zolldienststellen (Nuremberg, 1964).

30. Allgemeine Verwaltungsvorschrift über die umsatzsteuerliche Behandlung des innerdeutschen Waren und Dienstleistungsverkehrs zwischen den Wahrungsgebieten der Deutschen Mark und der Mark der Deutschen Demokratischen Republik (VwV zu secs. 26 Abs. 4 USTG 1967) of May 16, 1971. See Bundesanzeiger No. 97 (May 24, 1973).

31. Allgemeine Genehmigung No. 7(L) of Jan. 21, 1969, Bundesanzeiger No. 26 (Feb. 7, 1969); revisions of Sept. 28, 1972, Bundesanzeiger No. 168 (Oct. 3, 1972).

32. Appendix 2 to Ersten Interzonenhandels-Durchführungsverordnung of Dec. 16, 1970, Bundesanzeiger No. 239 (Dec. 23, 1970).

33. Aussenwirtschaftsverordnung supra note 6 at 1.

34. Allgemeine Genehmigung No. 3 (B) of Dec. 19, 1969; Bundesanzeiger No. 76 (Dec. 30, 1969); revisions of Sept. 21, 1972, Bundesanzeiger, No. 180 (Sept. 23, 1972).

35. See supra note 32.

36. R. Sieben, Abkommen und Vorschriften zum Interzonenhandel at 11 (Frankfurt a.M., 1961).

37. Aussenwirtschaftsverordnung supra note 6 at 1.

38. See supra note 19, Art. IV.

39. Id., Art. 5.

40. 89. Ergänzung des Interzonenhandelserlasses 94, No. 3, of Dec. 12, 1968, Bundesanzeiger No. 234 (Dec. 14, 1968).

41. See W. Kleindienst, supra note 15.

42. See Frankfurter Allgemeine Zeitung, Nov. 14, 1973, p. 6, col. 2.

43. Press Conference of Otto Wolff von Amerongens at the Leipzig Frühjahrsmesse of 1973, Frankfurter Allgemeine Zeitung, Mar. 13, 1973, p. 13, col. 6.

44. Lambrecht, "Die Entwicklung des Interzonenhandels von seinen Anfängen bis zur Gegenwart," 72 Sonderhefte des Deutschen Instituts für Wirtschaftsforschung 52 (Berlin, 1965).

45. W. Kleindienst, supra note 15.

46. R. Sieben, supra note 36.

47. Appendixes 1 and 2 to No. 1 of the Agreement, Currency Areas Trade Agreement, supra note 19.

48. Appendixes 3 and 4 to No. 1 of the Agreement, id.

49. Appendix 10, id.

50. Appendix 5 to Art. 5, id.

51. Vereinbarung zwischen der Bank deutscher Länder und der Deutschen Notenbank, Appendix 7 to Art. X of the Berlin Treaty of Sept. 20, 1951, Supplement Bundesanzeiger No. 32 (Feb. 12, 1961).

52. Mitteilung Nr. 6003/61 der Deutschen Bundesbank betreffend Bekanntmachung über den Zahlungsverkehr im rahmen des Berliner Abkommens ab 1. Jan. 1961, Bundesanzeiger No. 66 (Apr. 6, 1961).

53. H. Voight, Handbuch der langfristigen Exportfinanzierung in der Bundesrepublik Deutschland, at 73 (Frankfurt a.M., 1971).

54. Id. at 40.

55. Gumpel, "Der innerdeutsche Handel in seinen politischen und ökonomischen Auswirkungen," Wirtschaftsbezihungen mit dem Osten, supra note 24, at 83.

56. Grundgesetz für die Bundesrepublik Deutschland of May 23, 1949: Preamble, Arts. 16, 23, 116, and 146, BGB1 I 1949, at 1.

57. Judgment of the Bundesverfassungsgericht concerning the agreement in regard to Grundlagen der Beziehungen zwischen der BRD und der DDR of June 6, 1973, 73:1 BVerFGE 2 (BvF) (Aug. 31, 1973).

58. Compare section 22 of the Ubergangsabkommen zum Montan-Vertrag.

59. Protokoll von Torquay of April 21, 1951, BGB1 1951 II, at 1980.

60. Protokoll über den innerdeutschen Handel, BGB1. 1957 II, at 984.

61. Wohlfarth et al., Die Europaische Wirtschaftsgemeinschaft, Ein Kommentar zum Vertrag, 662 (Frankfurt a.M. 1960).

62. Nawrocki, "Innerdeutscher Handel und Falsche Optik, 6 Europa-Archiv 590 (1968).

63. Gumpel, supra note 55, at 93.

64. Press conference reported in TAGESPIEGEL, Feb. 26, 1970, at 15.

65. Kleindienst, supra note 15.

66. Interview of SED leader Honecker with the editor of the New York Times, as reported in Neues Deutschland, Nov. 25, 1972, at 4.

67. Vertrag über die Grundlage der Beziehungen zwischen der Bundesrepublik Deutschland und der Deutschen Demokratischen Republik of Dec. 21, 1972 ("Grundvertrag"), 155 Bulletin des Bundespresseamtes 1841 et seq. (Nov. 8, 1972).

68. See sec. I(1) of Supplemental Protocol to Art. 7 of the Grundvertrag.

69. Morawitz, "Der innerdeutsche Handel und die EWG nach dem Grundvertrag," 10 Europa-Archiv 353 (1973).

70. Zuleeg, "Grundvertrag und EWG-Protokoll über den innerdeutschen Handel," 3 Europarecht 209, 225 (1973).

71. Krasnow, "Aussenwirtschaftliche Beziehungen der Sowjetunion zur Bundesrepublik Deutschland," 3:1 Beitrage zum internationalen Wirtschaftsrecht und Atomenergierecht, supra note 15, at 19.

72. G. Adler-Karlsson, Der Fehlschlag. 20 Jahre Wirtschaftskrieg zwischen Ost und West 77 (Vienna, 1971).

73. See Das Ost-Embargo, Dokumentensammlung von Hans Jurgen Lambers 28 et seq. (Göttingen, 1956).

74. Legislative Report of the 207th Session of the German Bundestag, 1. Wahlperiode Report No. 8967 C.

75. G. Adler-Karlsson, supra note 72, at 75.

76. W. Trautmann, Osthandel ja oder nein? 103 (Stuttgart, 1954).

77. E. Hofmann, West-Ost Handel im Zwielicht? 67 (Nurnberg, 1955).

78. M. L. Hoffmann, Problems of East-West Trade 281 (New York, 1957).

79. W. Trautmann, supra note 76, at 124.

80. M. Schmitt, Osthandel auf neuen Wegen 82 (Hamburg, 1968); J. P. de Gara, Trade relations Between the Common Market and the Eastern Bloc 33 (1964).

81. Wolff von Amerongen, "Wirtschaftsbeziehungen mit dem Osten," Wirtschaftsbeziehungen mit dem Osten, supra note 15, at 9.

82. See Table No. 1 in Der Handel mit den Ostblocklander, at 8 (Special Supplement No. 7 to Series 6, Aussenhandel, of the Statistisches Bundesamt, Stuttgart, Dec. 1973).

83. Aussenwirtschaftsgesetz (AWG) of Apr. 28, 1961, BGB1. I 1961, at 481.

84. Aussenwirtschaftsverordnung, supra note 6 at 1 et seq.

85. Verordnung zur Regelung von Zuständigkeiten im Aussenwirtschaftsverkehr of Aug. 7, 1961, BGB1 I 1961, at 1554.

86. For official reasoning regarding sec. 1, see Aussenwirtschaftsgesetz und AuBenwirtschaftsverordnung sowie Abschopfungserhebungsgesets. Textausgabe nebst Auszug aus der amtlichen Begrundung und Sachregister sowie eine Einführung von Joachim Wapenhensch 11 (Berlin, 1961).

87. RGB1. 1909, at 519, in the version made public Feb. 27, 1969, Bekannt, BGB1. 1969 1, at 15 et seq.

88. RGB1. 1936 I, at 18.

89. RGB1. 1940 I, at 1463.

90. RGB1. 1955 I, at 501.
91. BGB1. 1968 I, at 352.
92. BGB1. 1950 I, at 721.
93. BGB1. 1951 I, at 47.
94. BGB1. 1951 I, at 272.
95. BGB1. 1959 I, at 814.
96. BGB1. 1961 I, at 444.
97. BGB1. 1951 I, at 135.
98. BGB1. 1961 I, at 607.
99. C-D. Rohleder, Die Osthandelspolitik der EWG-Mitglieds-
staaten, Grossbritanniens und der USA gegenüber den Staatshandels-
ländern Südosteuropas 53 (Südosteuropa-Studien, Munich 1969).
100. Schmitt-Ott, "Verfahrensfragen im Ost-Gesechäft," Leitfaden
für den Osthandel 12, 22 (Frankfurt o.J., 1969).
101. H. Ernst, Der Osthandel—eine politische Waffe? 60 et seq.
(Stuttgart, 1964).
102. 11. Verordnung zur Änderung der AWV of June 29, 1967,
BGB1 1967 I, at 614.
103. 40. Verordnung zur Änderung der Einführliste (Annex to
the Aussenwirtschaftsgesetz) of Aug 19, 1970, Bundesanzeiger No.
153 (Aug. 21, 1970).
104. Friderichs, "Chancen im Ost-West Handel nutzen," Nachrichten für Aussenhandel 1 (Jan, 2, 1974).
105. See Lederer, "Kreditprobleme im Verkehr mit dem Sudosten,"
4 Sudosteuropa-Jahrbuch 71 et seq. (Munich, 1960).
106. Von Wallenberg-Pachali, "Policy and Practice of the Federal
Republic of Germany," East-West Trade: An Analysis of Trade Between Western Nations and the Soviet Bloc 33 (New York, 1964).
107. A. Schüller, Osthandelspolitik als Problem der Wettbewerbs-
politik 101 et seq. (Frankfurt a.M., 1973).
108. B. Riedrich, Handbuch für den Handel mit der UdSSR 39
(Opladen, 1973).
109. H. Voigt, Handbuch der langfristigen Exportfinanzierung 39
(Frankfurt a.M., 1971).
110. See Frankfurter Allgemeine Zeitung, Jan. 19, 1974, p. 5,
col. 6.

THE UNITED KINGDOM
Julian D. M. Lew

The legal principles applicable generally to the United Kingdom's international trade are equally applicable when such trade is with "Eastern" or "socialist" countries. As a general rule, contracting parties are free to incorporate into their contract any terms, provided such terms are legal, are not for the purpose of avoiding some mandatory provision of English law, and are not violative of English public policy. Socialist foreign trade organizations (or any other foreign trader or trading corporation) may establish themselves and trade in the United Kingdom, subject only to the same laws as any U.K. company. However, as discussed more fully in the following sections of this chapter, exports of certain goods to socialist countries may be restricted, and imports from those countries may be prevented or limited. The availability of foreign currency may also affect trade possibilities with these countries.

As concerns actual contractual capacity, no special license is needed to trade with a socialist trading organization. Subject to the applicant's obtaining an export license or, where necessary, permission to import a particular type of product, the legal right to participate in "East-West" trade is equal for the giant national or public company and the small trading firms or private individuals.

Although there is little direct government interference in East-West trade, certain government departments are responsible for the commercial relations of the United Kingdom with other states. There are also private organizations that provide information and facilities for the promotion of trade between the United Kingdom and the different socialist states.

The Department of Trade and Industry (DTI). The DTI is the government department responsible for all national and international trade. It is through the DTI that government policies are developed, matters of import restrictions and export controls are determined, and short- and long-term trade and cooperation agreements are negotiated.

The DTI will assist and advise British merchants trading or wanting to trade with socialist countries. Information concerning import restrictions and export controls can be obtained from the Overseas Tariffs and Regulations Section of Export Services Division of the DTI. Other general and specific information concerning exports, likely markets, introduction to potential buyers and agents, status reports of foreign firms, details of overseas contracts out for tender, help and advice on participating in overseas trade fairs, assistance in finding licensees to manufacture British products overseas, market research, advertising and publicty, and so on can also be obtained through the Export Services, Division. Information concerning trade fairs and exhibitions can be obtained from the Promotions Branch of the DTI. The British Overseas Trade Board, which is a department within the DTI, is responsible for the annual publication of booklets entitled "Hints to Businessmen," which provide both general and commercial information relating to particular countries.[1]

The Export Credit Guarantees Department (ECGD). The ECGD is a government department responsible for providing credit to U.K. firms wishing to buy goods abroad or to foreign firms wishing to buy goods from U.K. firms. These credit facilities are described in more detail below.

The Ministry of Agriculture, Fisheries, and Food. This ministry is responsible for the supervision and implementation of national policy pertaining to agriculture, the fishing industry, and food and drugs. The import and export of foodstuffs and international cereal agreements[2] are matters dealt with by the Ministry of Agriculture, Fisheries, and Food in consultation with the DTI.

The Ministry of Foreign Affairs. In practice this ministry interferes very little in international trade relations, although it is responsible for the making of any international treaties. In consequence, all international agreements relating to trade and cooperation—although negotiated and signed by the secretary of State for the DTI or some nominee on his behalf—are introduced into Parliament by the secretary of State for Foreign and Commonwealth Affairs.

The Treasury and Bank of England. The Treasury has no direct authority in the area of international trade but does indirectly influence trade by the exercise of its other functions. Such indirect influence could result from controls imposed on public expenditure, measures taken to affect the public debt, and exchange control restrictions. Exchange control restrictions, which regulate the amount of sterling that can be spent abroad, are operated by the Bank of England, to whom application must be made when a merchant wishes to make purchases in excess of the allowed capital exports.

Commercial Department, British Embassy. In every British Embassy or Consulate, there is a commercial department that is responsible for encouraging British trade and facilitating contact between British businessmen and their counterparts from the country in which the embassy is situated. The commercial department attached to a British Embassy is equipped to give advice concerning not only the market possibilities in the particular country but also the most advisable approach to be taken to gain entry to that market.

U.K. firms doing business or wanting to do business with socialist countries are advised when making their initial approaches to keep the commercial department of the British Embassy in that particular country informed of all developments, as embassy commercial staff can be of particular help in advising as to where and how to advertise, how to arrange insurance, with whom to negotiate and contract, and what the relevant legal provisions in the particular socialist state are. (Trade fairs are a major occurrence in socialist states, and it is an important responsibility of the British commercial representatives to inform, help, and arrange for British merchants to participate and show at trade fairs.)

Chambers of Commerce and Other Organizations. The London and Birmingham Chambers of Commerce are particularly active in promoting East-West trade. The Russo-British Chamber of Commerce is concerned with U.K.-USSR trade, and the Sino-British Trade Council promotes trade between Britain and China. These organizations arrange meetings and symposiums on East-West trade, publish information relevant thereto and arrange reciprocal trade missions to visit the different Eastern countries. The East European Trade Council, an autonomous body of the British Trade Board, publishes information on problems of East-West trade and offers help and advice to those participating in East-West trade.

EXPORT CONTROLS AND PROGRAMS

Controls on Exports

The laws and regulations that govern exports from (and imports into) the United Kingdom are regulated by Statutory Instruments made pursuant to the Import, Export and Customs Powers (Defence) Act, 1939. By Section 1(1) of that act, the secretary of State for Trade and Industry ". . . may by order make such provisions as [he] think[s] expedient for prohibiting or regulating . . . the importation into or exportation from the United Kingdom . . . of all goods or goods of any specified description." Pursuant to the powers granted under this enactment, the Export of Goods (Control) Order, 1970[3] was made.

Exports from the United Kingdom are also subject to the Strategic Goods (Control) Order, 1967.[4] Although the former has more significance as regards general exports, the latter is more directly concerned with the exports of goods to socialist countries.

Article 4 of the Export of Goods (Control) Order, 1970,* provides that all those categories of goods listed in Schedule 1 of the order and designated by the letter "A" are prohibited from being exported except "under the authority of a licence granted by the [DTI] . . . provided that all conditions attaching to the said licence . . . are complied with."[5] The categories of goods contained in Schedule 1 are classified under the following subheadings: aircraft, arms and military stores, atomic energy materials, electrical and scientific appliances, chemicals, minerals and metals, engineering products, heavy transport equipment, certain articles of high value, and certain miscellaneous articles. The order itself contains in Article 5(b)(i) certain goods that may be exported under the license of the order and include samples and bona fide gifts not exceeding 25 pounds in value.

Whereas goods not included in Schedule 1 of the order may be freely exported, those included can only be exported under an individual license obtainable from the DTI's Export Licensing Branch. Any person who exports or who facilitates the exportation or attempted exportation of goods that under this order need a special license, may be subject to a fine of up to 100 pounds or two years imprisonment or both, and the goods may be forfeited.[6]

The decision of whether or not to grant an export license is a matter of discretion for the Export Licensing Division of the DTI. The exercise of that discretion is an internal matter. It is known, however, that a decision on a particular matter might take account of the Cocom list.[7]

An indication as to how the discretion is exercised can be obtained from the DTI's Consolidated List of Goods subject to Security Export Control.[8] This list, which is expressly stated to apply principally to exports to Albania, Bulgaria, China, Czechoslovakia, East Germany, Hungary, Mongolia, North Korea, North Vietnam, Poland, Romania, and the USSR (but not Yugoslavia or Cuba) gives an indication of the types of goods that are subject to particularly careful scrutiny before an export license is granted. Those goods included in this list are not totally banned from export, and applications for export licenses

---

*There is in preparation a new order intended to replace this one and giving effect to the changes resulting from Britain's membership of the European Economic Community. This order, which will be in force in the near future, will include changes in the main concerning the exportation of ferrous and nonferrous metals.

will be considered in the light of supporting information and in particular, the nature of the goods, the use to which they are to be put, and the ultimate user.

The Strategic Goods (Control) Order, 1967, was made in pursuance of powers conferred under the Emergency Laws (Re-Enactment and Repeals) Act, 1946. Under Article 1 of this order, it is an offense for a U.K. citizen to dispose of goods of a type described in Schedule 1 of that order situate outside the United Kingdom to the government or any government authority or agency in any country or territory specified in Schedule 2. The goods designated as strategic in Schedule 1 are classified under the same headings as in Schedule 1 to the Export of Goods (Control) Order, 1970, but the 1967 order contains a larger number and wider description of goods, having been made with particular reference to the security and strategic policies of the United Kingdom. The areas listed in Schedule 2 are Albania, Bulgaria, China, Czechoslovakia, East Germany, Hungary, North Korea, North Vietnam, Poland, Romania, Tibet, and the USSR (Yugoslavia and Cuba are thus excluded). As with the 1970 order, those goods contained in the 1967 order may be exported under the authority of a specific license (Article 2[a]). Although the 1967 order appears to overlap with that of 1970, it should be noted that the 1967 order has extraterritorial effect and applies to strategic goods situated outside the United Kingdom. If the goods are within the United Kingdom, they will be dealt with under the 1970 order.

Export Insurance and Guarantees

Under the Export Guarantees Act, 1968, as amended,[9] the Export Credit and Guarantee Department (ECGD) is empowered to provide certain assistance to facilitate exports, both visible and invisible. The ECGD is a separate and independent government department under the secretary of State for Trade and Industry. The ECGD is a member of the Bern Union, to which most of the major export credit insurance organizations belong and through which they coordinate their policies. It is noteworthy that ECGD services are, in principle, equally applicable to countries with market and state-planned economies.

The 1968 Export Guarantees Act divides the services provided by ECGD into two kinds. Section 1 (1) and (2) provides that the "Export Guarantees Advisory Council may with the consent of the Treasury make arrangements for the giving of guarantees to or for the benefit of any person carrying on business in the United Kingdom, the Isle of Man or the Channel Islands in connection with the export, manufacture, treatment or distribution of goods, the rendering of services or any other matter which appears . . . conducive to the purpose of encouraging trade with other countries." (In connection with ECGD, all references hereinafter to the United Kingdom equally apply to the Isle of Man and the Channel Islands.) The words "trade with other countries" are defined to mean any "transaction involving a consideration in money or money's worth" accruing from a person carrying on business or other activities outside the United Kingdom to a person carrying on business in the United Kingdom.[10] The aggregate liabilitie that may be incurred under arrangements made under this section are 6200 million pounds.[11]

The second kind of service provided by ECGD is under Section 2 of the 1968 act. Section 2(i) provides that arrangements may be made with the consent of the Treasury for "giving guarantees to, or for the benefit of, persons carrying on business in the UK where such guarante appears to be expedient in the national interest[12] or for facilitating, where it appears expedient in the national interest so to do, the paymen of sums payable under contracts with persons so carrying on business. These facilities are to be provided for purposes mentioned in Section 1(1) of this act[13] and for "the purpose of rendering economic assistanc to countries outside the UK. . . ."[14] The aggregate liability that may be incurred under arrangements made for the provision of this service is 6000 million pounds.[15]

The ECGD gives effect to the obligations imposed under these statutory provisions in the various ways described below.

British exporters usually obtain normal commercial insurance to cover their contractual obligations,* as commercial risks arising out of such contracts are expressly excluded from ECGD insurance policies. The ECGD insures contracts for extracommercial or politica risks, which most insurance companies do not accept. Thus, where an exporter is selling or proposing to sell consumer or durable goods abroad, particularly to Eastern or developing countries, on terms of payment not exceeding 180 days, he can insure his contract with the ECGD to cover, among other things, losses caused by the insolvency of the buyer; nonpayment by the buyer for goods accepted by him; failure or refusal of the buyer to accept the goods; nonpayment of the goods due to a law or order preventing such payment; the imposition of a law or order preventing the import of the goods into the buyer's country; the cancellation or nonrenewal by relevant authorities of valid import or export licenses; outbreak of war between the United Kingdom and the buyer's country; occurrence of war, hostilities, civil disturbanc revolution, insurrection, and so on in the buyer's country; and failure of the buyer to perform his obligation under the contract. For engineering goods the exporter can, by an endorsement on his policy, obtain cover on contracts with terms of payment of up to five years.

---

*Most East-West contracts for the export of goods from the United Kingdom are made on f.o.b. terms.

102

The major purpose of this type of insurance is that it enables the British exporter to give attractive credit facilities to his foreign buyer. This is known as "supplier credit." Payment is normally made by bills of exchange being handed over by the buyer or his bank in exchange for the bills of lading at the same time as the goods are delivered, such bills of exchange to mature on various specified dates in the future. Having given credit by accepting bills of exchange drawn over a period of time, the British exporter will be able to discount the bills to British banks and so not have to wait for the expiration of the credit period to receive payment. When a contract is covered by ECGD insurance, banks are likely to be favorably disposed to discounting bills drawn as payment for such a contract. If necessary, an exporter can assign to his bank the payment due under his ECGD policy. If subsequently the bills are not honored, the bank will be able to call on the insurance taken out by the exporter from ECGD. (If the buyer refuses to honor the bills of exchange due to the exporter's breach of contract, the bank's remedy will be against the exporter.)

ECGD also provides direct bank guarantees that enable exporters to obtain large money loans at very favorable rates of interest. This is mainly done on the basis of an ECGD comprehensive bank guarantee. On receiving this government-backed security, the financing bank will, on presentation of the bills of exchange, give to the exporter the necessary finance at 0.5 percent above bank rate in the case of business on terms up to two years' credit. If accepted bills are not honored within three months after the due date, ECGD will pay unconditionally the full amount of the bills (ECGD will pay unaccepted bills not honored within one month after the due date).

ECGD also guarantees open bank accounts or export sales on cash against deilvery terms. In this case, the bank will advance money to an exporter and, should the exporter fail to repay the loan, ECGD will repay the bank and then look to the exporter for its own remedy.

Since January 1, 1974, finance for export contracts for two-five years can be obtained by an exporter who has an ECGD guarantee at the fixed rate of 7 percent. For business on credit exceeding five years, a specific rate from 6 to 8.5 percent is fixed for each individual contract, depending on what is needed to "match" the terms of a foreign competitor. Previously, both types of credit were financed at 6 percent.

Where the goods to be exported are "capital goods," ECGD provides specific policies written for the particular transaction. This type of policy covers an individual contract and is appropriate when the goods are of a specialized nature with a long manufacturing period and payment is to be made on the completion of certain specified parts of the contract or where the export project involves overseas installation as well as the supply of the plant.

As an alternative to "supplier credit" for capital projects, the "buyer credit" principle is being used more and more. In buyer credit contracts, the foreign buyer or his bank obtains a loan from a British bank at a special low export finance rate and ECGD will act as guarantc for 100 percent of the loan. (The loan normally amounts to 80 percent of the complete contract price.) Thus, if there is default in repaying the loan, the ECGD is liable to the lending bank under the guarantee. The advantage to the exporter is that he can receive payment from the loan immediately after the goods are shipped, so in effect he is paid on cash terms. This technique now includes general-purpose lines of credit to other countries for broad categories of goods and up to prescribed financial limits for each country.

Before the ECGD will undertake to insure or give a guarantee under an export contract, it may require the contract to contain certain provisions. Unless these provisions are incorporated, ECGD will decline to insure the contract. The provisions required by ECGD as a prerequisite to their cover are to safeguard their positions as guarantors for the repayment of the loan. Thus, the ECGD frequently requires, among other things, the incorporation of provisions concerning the times, places, and money of repayment, the times, places, and circumstances under which delivery is to be made, and provision for the resolution of disputes arising out of such contracts to be resolved by arbitration at an accepted permanent arbitration center or in a neutral country. It is especially important to bear in mind these ECGD requirements when contracting with Eastern countries, as the ECGD will give such contracts close scrutiny in deciding on application for insurance or guarantees.

From April 1, 1974, ECGD is offering a new program—the inclusion of cover against buyer defaults in policies for trade between two foreign countries that is U.K. financed.

Since July 1972, ECGD has offered insurance protection to U.K. residents investing abroad. Under this scheme, a U.K. investor can obtain cover for up to 90 percent of the principal amount invested in respect of such political risks as expropriation, war damage, and restrictions on remittances. As of the end of 1973, ECGD had received no applications for investment insurance to cover investment or participation in a joint venture in a socialist state.

IMPORT CONTROLS

As with those for exports, the laws and regulations governing imports into the United Kingdom are regulated by Statutory Instruments made under the Import, Export and Customs Powers (Defence) Act, 1939. Made pursuant to the powers granted under this enactment, the

Import of Goods (Control) Order, 1954,[16] contains the basic regulations that govern importation.

Article 2 of the Import of Goods (Control) Order, 1954, empowers the DTI to grant a license for the importation of goods, without which no goods may be imported into the United Kingdom.[17] Under this order the secretary of State for Trade and Industry made an Open General Import Licence, dated 5 July 1973, which came into effect in the United Kingdom pursuant to the United Kingdom's joining the EEC, on 1 April 1973.

The Open General Import Licence (hereinafter called the Licence) provides that any goods[18] may be imported into the United Kingdom unless, among other things,* they originate in or are consigned to the United Kingdom from the "Eastern area" and are goods listed in Schedule 1 to the Licence and designated with the letter "E." ("Eastern area" is defined by Article 1 of the Licence as including "Albania, Bulgaria, Czechoslovakia, the German Democratic Republic and East Berlin, Hungary, North Korea, North Vietnam, the People's Republic of China, the People's Republic of Mongolia, Poland, Romania and the Union of Soviet Socialist Republics." Note: Yugoslavia is not considered part of the "Eastern area.") The goods prohibited, which are listed according to a specific classification, include fresh, dried, and frozen fruit and vegetables, different fiber materials including silk yarn, woven fabrics, flax or ramie yarn, cottons, certain types of embroidery, twine, cordage, and elastic fabrics, stockings and certain under and outer garments, certain types of ties, scarves, and handkerchiefs, certain types of footwear or hatwear, certain chromium products, transistor radios and similar electrical equipment, aircrafts, watch movements, and firearms and ammunition. This is a very general description of the contents of Schedule 1 of the Licence.

All goods that are not prohibited from importation by the designation "E" in the Licence may be automatically imported into the United Kingdom without any prior authority. As regards those categories of goods that are so prohibited, they may be imported under an "individual import licence," which is granted as a matter of discretion by the Import Licensing Branch of the DTI. The prohibitions in the Licence are subject to bilateral arrangements made between

---

*Bilateral agreements have been made with Bulgaria, the People's Republic of China, Cuba, Czechoslovakia, the German Democratic Republic, Hungary, Romania, and the USSR. There are no quota agreements with Albania, Mongolia, North Korea, and North Vietnam due to the insignificant levels of trade between the United Kingdom and these countries.

the United Kingdom and certain of the "Eastern area" countries.* The terms of these bilateral arrangements made for the import of goods are published in the DTI publication "Trade and Industry." These arrangements are couched according to the same classification as used in Schedule 1 to the Licence and are subject to certain quota restrictions expressed either in quantity or in value.

Thus, the procedure to be followed to obtain permission to bring the goods into the country varies according to whether or not the particular goods are restricted on the Licence. If the goods are so restricted, the importer must apply for an individual import license for the specific goods. However, where the goods are included in a quota agreement and that quota has been fulfilled, it will not be possible to obtain an individual import license to exceed the quota.

Yugoslavia, which is not considered to be part of the "Eastern area," is treated according to her membership of the General Agreement of Trade and Tariffs (GATT) and is subject to very few import restrictions, those restrictions being designated with a "G" in Schedule 1 of the Licence. Other categories of Yugoslav goods are freely importable into the United Kingdom.

Romania, although considered part of the "Eastern area," is also considered separately in the Licence. Certain categories of goods are designated with the letter "RO," meaning that such goods may not be imported from Romania, even though the same goods may be imported from other "Eastern area" countries. Apart from this, the general rules apply as regards quota agreements with Romania and the import of goods not listed in Schedule 1 of the Licence.

OTHER FACTORS AFFECTING EAST-WEST TRADE

Bilateral Governmental Agreements

An important method by which the British Government can and does influence the volume of trade between the United Kingdom and socialist states is by means of bilateral agreements. These bilateral agreements are, in the main, either long-term trade agreements or cooperation agreements. However, there are also specific agreements regulating the import or export of particular commodities, for example, cereals, or agreements to facilitate the carriage of goods by air, sea, or land.[19]

---

*Although the Open General Import Licence deals with all imports into the United Kingdom regardless of origin, we shall only consider here those provisions strictly relevant to East-West trade.

As long-term trade agreements and cooperation agreements are of special importance to, and a vehicle for, the development of U.K. trade with socialist states, we will consider both types of agreement separately.

Long Term Trade Agreements. These agreements have been made with every European member of Comecon (except the German Democratic Republic—GDR). These agreements do not in themselves provide for a specific level in trade; they neither stipulate for the purchase or sale of certain types or quantities of goods nor provide for particular import/export quotas, tariffs, or charges. Rather, their purpose is generally to create the right atmosphere and the necessary channels to smooth the way for business organizations from the contracting states to improve their trading relations. This is expressed in the preambles to these agreements in which the parties confirm their desire "to promote and facilitate the development of economic co-operation and trade relations between their two countries, to their mutual advantage"—from agreements with Bulgaria and Hungary; similar but different wording in other agreements.

These agreements generally express as the objective of the parties a continuing increase in trade between their two countries. The parties undertake to facilitate (within the scope of the laws and regulations in force in each country) the exchange of goods on mutually advantageous bases. The agreements also have similar provisions for payments for goods and services to be made in freely convertible currency (the agreement with the USSR is an exception); undertakings to facilitate an increase in the exchange of consumer goods, to grant respective credit facilities, to help the other party participate at trade fairs arranged in their country; to follow the principle of free and fair competition in international shipping; to foster and facilitate the development of cooperation between enterprises and organizations in both countries, in various agreed fields (for example, industrial, technical, and scientific projects); and for periodic meetings of the parties, usually through the establishment of "joint commissions."[20]

The agreements handle the problem of imports into the United Kingdom in different ways. The 1969 U.K.-USSR agreement expresses the "expectation" of the U.K. Government that the open import licensing arrangements in force will facilitate imports on normal commercial terms from the USSR, and the U.K. Government "looks forward" to the possibility of progressively reducing during the period of the agreements restrictions on other imports from the Soviet Union. It is also agreed that "an appropriate basis for the import into the UK of goods not covered by open licensing arrangements" is to be established "by mutual agreement and in a spirit of friendly undertaking." Other agreements may go further and involve undertakings to accord MFN treatment in respect of customs duties, tariffs, and other charges,

107

and "to remove progressively any remaining quantitive restrictions on imports" from the territory of a party by a specified date.[21] However, such undertakings are generally subject to the domestic law and the international obligations of the parties (for example, U.K. obligations under the GATT and EEC).

Cooperation Agreements. These agreements have been made between the United Kingdom and most Eastern countries. They have been made for many different purposes, although the largest numbers are to operate in the fields of applied science and technology. As with the long-term trade agreements, these agreements express the desire and interest of the states in the promotion and development of cooperation in particular areas to their mutual advantage. The agreements then attempt to provide the channels and create the atmosphere to facilitate cooperation between their respective enterprises.

Eastern countries view such agreements as a convenient framework for trade in goods and services between states with planned and market economies. The agreements commonly provide for mutual exchange of experts and technicians to study the methods, practices, and procedures in particular areas and exchange of visits for the purposes of studies, training, consultation, and so on. Special emphasis is often laid on arrangements for joint research and development and on an exchange of scientific and technical information.

Perhaps the most important aspect of these agreements is the objective of facilitating the conclusion of agreements for cooperation between the enterprises and organizations of the respective countries. The proposed areas of cooperation are listed in the annexes to the agreements and are those in which the states feel cooperation will be to their greatest mutual benefit.

Most of these agreements also contain provision for review (similar to the review provision in long-term trade agreements). In several of these agreements, there is a joint commission that is given the task of meeting periodically to review implementation of the agreement, to make recommendations as to action required to ensure that its objectives are carried out, to supervise and promote the development of cooperation, and to discuss other related questions.

U.K. Law and Settlement of East-West Trade Disputes

Due to the importance of arbitration in East-West trade, the strict jurisdictional and introverted character of the English arbitration laws, and the nonadherence of the United Kingdom to recent multinational conventions in this field, it is useful to consider the English legal provisions relating to arbitration agreements, arbitration proceedings, and the recognition and enforcement of arbitration awards.

Most contracts between U.K. companies and socialist state-trading organizations contain provisions for the submission of disputes to arbitration. If there is no agreement to submit to arbitration, either in the contract or at the time the dispute arises, the putative plaintiff will have to seek his remedy in the competent court of the state where the putative defendant resides. (If the forum is England, this would be the Commercial Court of the English High Court. The court is presided over by a specialist commercial judge, who, until he became a judge, practiced as a commercial lawyer for at least 15 years.)

By English law an arbitration agreement may be oral or in writing, but to fall within the English Arbitration Act, 1950, the agreement must be in writing, although not necessarily in a formal document. The English courts will also recognize as valid an arbitration agreement that is valid according to the proper law of the contract in which it is contained.[22] It should further be noted that the English court will enforce an arbitration agreement providing for arbitration to take place in a foreign country, where that other country is party to the Geneva Protocol of 24 September 1923 on Arbitration Clauses.[23] So where despite the existence of an arbitration agreement, one party commences an action in England, the English court will stay the action[24] and, except in very rare circumstances,[25] leave the parties to resort to arbitration as they agreed.

Where it is provided that arbitration is to take place in England, the arbitration will be conducted under the Arbitration Act, 1950. This act makes provision, among other things, for the appointment and removal of arbitrators, their powers, the procedure to be followed at the arbitration, the method and time of making the award, and the control exercised by the English court over the arbitration proceedings.

English law follows legal regulations to govern arbitration similar to most countries, with the exception of the "case stated" procedure, which is unique to English law.[26] By this procedure the arbitrators may, if requested by the parties, and must, if ordered by the High Court, state a question of law to be determined by the High Court. This is done by the arbitrator making an award setting out the facts as he found them and stating the questions of law to be determined by the High Court.

This provision is considered by many foreign litigants as a disadvantage of the English law, as it does enable the parties to have recourse to the courts—a second bite at the cherry—causing increased legal costs and the absence of privacy, all of which arbitration is meant to avoid.

It should be noted that the United Kingdom is not a party to the 1961 European (Geneva) Convention on International Commercial Arbitration. After an award has been made in England in accordance with the Arbitration Act, 1950, the award will be enforced by leave of the English High Court in the same manner as any other judgment or order.[27] However, where the award is based on a parole arbitration agreement or is purely declaratory or is unclear, the successful party will have to bring an action on the award. In this case, the plaintiff would have to prove the existence of an agreement to submit disputes of the kind in question to arbitration, that the arbitration tribunal was appointed or constituted as provided for in the agreement, that the award was made, and that it has not been performed.

The United Kingdom has not joined the 1958 United National (New York) Convention on the Recognition and Enforcement of Foreign Arbitral Awards. An award that has been made outside the United Kingdom can be enforced in two ways:[28] under the Geneva Convention of 1927 and under common law.

The 1927 Convention on the Execution of Foreign Arbitral Awards, which has been ratified by the United Kingdom,[29] provides the conditions and circumstances under which an arbitration award made in one country will be enforced in another country. So, where an award is made in pursuance of an arbitration agreement that is valid according to the provisions of the 1923 Protocol[30]—that is, it relates to a dispute between persons one of whom is subject to the jurisdiction of a state party to the 1927 convention[31]—and it is made in a country with whom the United Kingdom has reciprocal arrangements for the recognition and enforcement of arbitration awards under the 1927 Convention,[32] the award will be enforceable as an English award.[33]

Before enforcing an award, the English court will require proof that the award is valid according to the law by which it is governed,[34] was made by the tribunal provided for in the arbitration agreement,[35] was made in conformity with the law governing the arbitration procedure,[36] is a final award,[37] and was made in respect of a matter that by English law may lawfully be referred to arbitration.[38] It should be noted that the English courts will not enforce an award that has been annulled in the country in which it was made[39] or that was made despite the defendant's having had insufficient time to prepare his case.[40] As with the recognition and enforcement of any judgment or award, the English courts will not enforce a foreign award that was obtained by fraud, that was made in an arbitration conducted in a manner contrary to the principles of natural justice, or where to enforce the award would violate English principles of public policy.

The United Kingdom has not made any bilateral agreements with other states for the reciprocal recognition and enforcement of arbitral awards.

A foreign award may also be enforced under common law provided it is an award not requiring any order from the court of the place where it was made (exequatur) to be enforceable there.

Such an award will be enforced if it is provided that there was an arbitration agreement, that the arbitration was conducted in accordance with that agreement and the award made pursuant to that agreement is valid by the law of the place where the arbitration took place. The provisions discussed above concerning the finality of the award, its existing validity, the effect of fraud, and the principles of natural justice and public policy are equally applicable under common law. Such an award is enforced by the plaintiff's suing on the agreement to carry out the provisions in the award.

NOTES

1. "Hints to Businessmen" have been published relating to the following socialist countries: Bulgaria, People's Republic of China, Cuba, Czechoslovakia, Hungary, Poland, Romania, USSR, and Yugoslavia.

2. For example, the U.K.-Romania Exchange of Notes regarding Production and Trade Policies Relating to Cereals, 22 March 1966, Cmnd. 3013, Treaty Series No. 38 (1966).

3. S.I., 1970, no. 1288.

4. S.I., 1967, no. 983.

5. Article 5(1)(a).

6. Customs and Excise Act, 1952, Section 56(1) and (2).

7. See Chapter 1, section entitled "Export Licensing."

8. The current list was published in "Trade and Industry" on 12 October 1972 and 16 November 1972. This consolidated list is only a compilation of the more strategic and security-related goods listed in Schedule 1 of the Export of Goods (Control) Order, 1970.

9. Export Guarantees and Payments Act, 1970; Overseas Investment and Export Guarantees Act, 1972.

10. Export Guarantees Act, 1968, Section 1(3).

11. Ibid., Section 4(1)(a) as amended, Overseas Investment and Export Guarantees Act, 1972, Section 4(1)(a).

12. As provided, amending the 1968 Act, Export Guarantee and Payments Act, 1970, Section 2(1)(a).

13. Ibid., Section 2(2)(a).

14. Ibid., Section 2(2)(b).

15. Ibid., Section 4(1)(b)., as amended, Overseas Investment and Export Guarantees Act, 1972, Section 4(1)(b).

16. S.I., 1954, no. 23.

17. Ibid., Article 1.

18. This is subject to the general overriding prohibition on importation of certain plumage, fur skins, and whale products: Article 6(1)(iii),(iv)(v).

19. The current long-term and cooperation agreements between the United Kingdom and socialist countries are as follows: Albania, Agreement on Commercial Relations, 10 June 1925, Cmnd. 2522 Treaty Series No. 47 (1925); Bulgaria, Long Term Trade Agreement, 27 April 1970, Cmnd. 4337 Treaty Series No. 51 (1970); Cuba, Commercial Agreement with notes regarding navigation 31 July 1939, Cmnd. 5867 Treaty Series No. 67 (1938); Czechoslovakia, Long Term Trade Agreement, 27 June 1972, Cmnd. 5074 Treaty Series No. 101 (1972), Co-operation Agreement, 8 September 1972, Cmnd. 5335 Treaty Series No. 70 (1973); G.D.R., Cooperation Agreement, 18 December 1973, Cmnd. Treaty Series No. 15 (1974); Hungary, Long Term Economic and Trade Agreement with Declaration and Co-operation Agreement, 21 March 1972, Cmnd. 5016 Treaty Series No. 70 (1972); Mongolia, Trade Agreement, 21 March 1973, Cmnd. 5306 Treaty Series No. 53 (1973); Poland, Agreement on Trade and Commerce, 14 August 1935, Cmd. 4984 Treaty Series No. 33 (1935), Long Term Economic and Trade Agreements, 21 April 1971, Cmnd. 4705, Treaty Series No. 47 (1971), Long Term Agreement on Development of Economic, Industrial, Scientific and Technical Co-operation, 20 March 1973, Cmnd. 5286 Treaty Series No. 50 (1973); Romania, Long Term Trade and Co-operation Agreement, 24 August 1972, Cmnd. 5106 Treaty Series No. 107 (1972); USSR, Long Term Trade Agreement, 1 July 1969, Cmnd. 4132 Treaty Series No. 92 (1969); a ten-year agreement for the development of economic, scientific, technical, and industrial cooperation between the United Kingdom and the USSR had been initialed, but not signed, by the end of 1973.

Other agreements have been made between the United Kingdom and socialist countries which affect the commercial relations of the two countries. Cooperation agreements in the field of Applied Science and Technology exist with Bulgaria, Cmnd. 4053, Treaty Series No. 69 (1969); Hungary, Cmnd. 3457, Treaty Series No. 94 (1967); Poland, Cmnd. 3867, Treaty Series No. 8 (1969); Romania, Cmnd. 3295, Treaty Series No. 49 (1967); USSR, Cmnd. 3710, Treaty Series No. 59 (1968); Yugoslavia, Cmnd. 3979, Treaty Series No. 49 (1969). Transport agreements have been made with Czechoslovakia (Road), Cmnd. 4747, Treaty Series No. 59 (1971); Hungary (Road), Cmnd. 4919, Treaty Series No. 29 (1972); USSR (Merchant Navigation), Cmnd. 5008, Treaty Series No. 67 (1972). Cereal agreements have been made with Hungary, Cmnd. 4177, Treaty Series No. 111 (1969); Romania, Cmnd. 3013, Treaty Series No. 38 (1966).

20. See, for example, Article 4, Agreement with Hungary, Cmnd. 5016, Treaty Series No. 70 (1972); Article 7, Agreement with Poland, Cmnd. 4705, Treaty Series No. 47 (1971); Article 11, Agreement with Bulgaria, Cmnd. 4377, Treaty Series No. 51 (1970).

21. See, for example, letters to Hungarian Minister of Foreign Trade, 21 March 1972, Cmnd. 5016, Treaty Series No. 70 (1972), p. 9; Czechoslovak Minister of Foreign Trade, 27 June 1972, Cmnd. 5074, Treaty Series No. 101 (1972), p. 7.

22. Hamlyn & Co. v. Talisker Distillery Co. (1894) A.C. 202; Spurrier v. La Cloche (1902) A.C. 446.

23. The Geneva protocol is given effect to by Sections 4(2) 35(1), and Schedule 1 of the Arbitration Act, 1950.

24. For example, where to stay the action would cause hardship or injustice to one of the parties (Ellinger v. Guinness Mahon & Co [1934] All E.R. 15), where the dispute involves a question of English law, or where England is the more appropriate forum (The Fehmarn [1958] 1 W.L.R. 159).

25. Section 4, Arbitration Act, 1950.

26. Ibid., Section 21.

27. Section 26, Arbitration Act, 1950.

28. Awards made in commonwealth countries may be enforceable under Part II of the Administration of Justice Act, 1920. This is unlikely to affect an award made pursuant to a dispute involving "East-West" trade.

29. Section 35 and Schedule 2, Arbitration Act, 1950.

30. Ibid., Section 35(1)(a).

31. Ibid., Section 35(1)(b).

32. Ibid., Section 35(1)(c). The following socialist states have ratified the convention: Czechoslovakia, Romania, and Yugoslavia. The neutral states that have ratified the convention include Austria, Sweden, and Switzerland.

33. Ibid., Section (36)(1).

34. Ibid., Section 37(1)(a).

35. Ibid., Section 37(1)(b).

36. Ibid., Section 37(1)(c).

37. Ibid., Section 37(1)(d).

38. Ibid., Section 37(1)(a).

39. Ibid., Section 37(2)(a).

40. Ibid., Section 37(2)(b).

ORGANIZATION AND CONDUCT
OF FOREIGN TRADE IN COUNTRIES
WITH STATE-PLANNED ECONOMIES

COMECON
Kazimierz Grzybowski

THE BEGININGS OF COMECON

The first intimation of the economic attitudes that Eastern
European socialist states were to develop in the period that followed
World War II were the statements made by V. M. Molotov, Soviet
Minister of Foreign Affairs at the Paris Peace Conference (1946)
when the plans for European economic integration were being considered. He came out strongly against the policy of equal opportunity
for foreign entrepreneurs in Eastern Europe.[1] At the roots of the
Soviet attitude to the plans for the reconstruction of Europe as a single
economic unit was the awareness that the Soviet Union could not contribute significantly to European reconstruction[2] or act as a source
of capital and technical expertise. Unable to hold its own in terms
of economic assistance, the Soviet Union was forced to erect a barrier
to economic cooperation between East and West.

On July 11, 1947, the Soviet Government announced its own plan
of economic integration, the so-called Molotov plan. Based upon an
extensive network of trade agreements, it was designed to stimulate
the growth and development of Eastern European economies by organizing markets for the disposal of goods and by coordinating supplies
of raw materials and capital goods needed for economic expansion.[3]

The Molotov plan was little more than a propaganda device,
however, and when it became clear that international cooperation under
the aegis of the Marshall Plan was gaining momentum, a conference
of six countries of Eastern Europe—Bulgaria, Czechoslovakia, Hungary,
Poland, Romania, and the USSR—gathered in January in Moscow and
established the Council for Mutual Economic Assistance (Comecon,
or CMEA) announced in a communiqué of January 25, 1949.[4]

Comecon's growth has been slow and uneven. After it was set up in January 1949, the Council held only three meetings in the course of that first year and convened again only after the death of Stalin. The first session of the Council, held in Moscow in April 1949, established a Moscow-based Permanent Secretariat for Economic Cooperation, having technical but not policy-shaping functions. This arrangement, while quite satisfactory in terms of control techniques, was inadequate to carry out over-all planning for the development of the available resources of the various countries.[5]

It was only at the twelfth session held in Sofia (1959) that the Council adopted new statutes for Comecon and approved a draft of the convention on the legal capacity, privileges, and immunities of the Council and its representatives and officials on the territory of the member countries.[6] The charter of the Council was amended during the 16th session (July 1962) by adding to the organization of the Council an Executive Committee.

According to its charter, Comecon is an organization open to all countries of Europe that share the ideas and principles of the Council and that have agreed to assume the obligations contained in its charter. Admission is decided by the session of the Council. Any member country may withdraw from the Council by means of a simple notification addressed to the Soviet Government, which is the depositary of the charter. According to the preamble of the Charter, the founding members have expressed their determination to continue developing comprehensive economic cooperation "on the basis of the consistent implementation of the international socialist division of labor in the interest of building socialism and communism in their countries."

Comecon's position as regards the nonsocialist countries is defined by the statement that its members are ready to "develop economic ties with all countries, regardless of their social and state systems, on the basis of equality, mutual benefit, and noninterference in the other's internal affairs." This is the usual formula for the principle of peaceful coexistence determining relations between socialist and nonsocialist countries.

According to the charter, the function of the Council is to organize economic, technical, and scientific cooperation of the member countries

with a view to the most rational utilization of their natural resources, and to acceleration of the development of the production forces; to work out recommendations dealing with economic ties resulting from the economic plans of individual countries, and to study various economic problems in order to foster the economic interests of member nations. Furthermore, its purpose is to assist the member countries in working out and implementing joint measures assuring the best utilization of resources in industry and agriculture, on the basis of the division of labor, specialization and cooperation in production, transport, and shipping of goods, joint investment projects, and exchange of experience and technical and scientific information.

The Council and its organizations have the right to decide procedural and technical questions concerning its work and duties. In all matters of substance the organizations of Comecon issue recommendations. Only formal acceptance commits the member nations to a policy recommended by Comecon.

The various organizations and bodies of Comecon fall generally into two categories. In the first are those that are created according to the charter; these (the Session of the Council, the Permanent Commissions, the Executive Committee, and the Secretariat) study and recommend various programs in order to accomplish the charter's aims and goals. The second category includes those organizations that are the result of the recommendations, such as cooperative projects, joint enterprises, and organizations for planning various areas of economic activity established by special agreements between the interested parties. The second class of organizations is distinguished from the first by being strictly confined to a concrete field of activity.[7]

TECHNIQUES OF INTEGRATION

Policies of integration have gone through three basic stages. The third, which was spelled out by the Comprehensive Program adopted by the Bucharest session in 1971, envisaged a high degree of coordination in planning, research, and increased flow of investment combined with specialized administrations and joint enterprises, which administer key areas of industrial activity. The process of integration in this third period was to emphasize an increased cooperation with the West, in order to assure the flow of know-how and capital investment, including direct participation of foreign entrepreneurs in the industrial activity (at least in some of the member countries).

Bilateral Trade

According to the official history of the early period of Comecon's existence, when intrabloc bilateral foreign trade was declared to be the main instrument of progress, such trade represented an imperfect but the only available instrument of cooperation.[8] The result was a lopsided and overambitious construction plan which, executed with great energy, dotted the economic landscape of Eastern Europe with grandiose enterprises, industrial cities called upon to be the ideological and industrial citadels of socialism. It became the fashion for each country, whether large or small, to have an iron and steel combine regardless of whether the country had adequate supplies of ores and fuel.[9]

Soviet economists, when examining the situation that confronted the national governments at the end of Stalin's era, credit the phenomenon of "parallel" plans for development of national economies to the absence of controls for the distribution of capital investment adequate to insure its allocation for the most important projects.[10]

Common Industrial Base
(Fuel, Raw Materials, Transport)

The faith that bilateral intrabloc trade would provide all the answers to the problems of integration lasted during the entire Stalin era. When, in 1954, Comecon assembled after more than four years of inactivity, it was confronted with the necessity of devising a method by which the investment program could be considered in terms of the entire area, including all available raw materials, and fuel supplies, all existing capabilities and internal markets. The basic difficulty was that the East European industrial development plans had failed to develop an adequate raw material base.

When the matter came to a head in 1956, the Council recommended "a considerable expansion in the coming five-year period of geological prospecting, reconstruction of existing pits with a view to increasing their capacity, and the opening of new pits and open cast mines, particularly in Poland and Czechoslovakia." In order to overcome the shortage of investment capital in the countries where such reserves of raw materials were available, the Council recommended sharing the capital investment required for building up new capacity in the coal industry. Furthermore, the Council recommended that the Soviet Union undertake to work out a program for the progressive expansion of iron ore deliveries to other socialist countries with steel-producing capabilities.[11]

Not all of the recommendations of the 1956 session were executed. Some agreements were concluded among the three major industrialized countries (Poland, East Germany, and Czechoslovakia), and a new pattern of agreements was initiated providing for the movement of capital from more developed to less developed areas. East Germany and Czechoslovakia granted Poland a credit to expand coal mining; in return, Poland accepted an obligation to supply the two countries with coal and lignite. In a similar agreement Czechoslovakia agreed to finance the construction of a plant in the Soviet Union to process iron ore to be exported to Czechoslovakia's steel factories.[12] It seems that currently supply of coal presents no major problems.

Of even greater importance for the development of future cooperation and the general pattern of Comecon's work was the principle formulated at the sixth session of Comecon (Budapest) that future collaboration must be based on long-term plans aimed at specialization and distribution of tasks among the member nations.

During two subsequent meetings (10th in December 1958 in Prague and 11th, May 1959 in Tirana) Comecon concerned itself with designing technical means for the distribution and development of new sources of fuel and power and with detailed analysis of the various scientific issues of the process of integration. The 10th session recommended the construction of an oil pipeline from the trans-Volga provinces of the USSR, where rich oil fields are located, to the refineries in Poland, East Germany, Hungary, and Czechoslovakia. The Tirana meeting announced a plan for creating a uniform power grid uniting all national power grids with that of the Soviet Union. Simultaneously with these two major cooperative efforts, a series of minor projects involving various countries in Eastern Europe, to be realized by pooling the resources of two or more states, were agreed upon.[13]

As time went by, the general tendency was to include within the Comecon program new areas of economic activity and to expand coordination and integration.

Joint Undertakings and Governmental Economic Organizations

Joint actions taken to cope with the shortage of raw materials and power have been made in three directions: expansion of transport, development of the raw material base, and investment in oil industry. In all these areas the Soviet Union has figured as the main recipient of investment capital. Two joint-action projects are the "Friendship" pipeline, which links the Transvolga oil fields with Central European refineries, and the Joint Power Grid, which links power plants in the Comecon countries in Europe with power plants in the Western USSR.[14] In addition to these joint projects there have been a limited number of joint enterprises, set up by Poland and Czechoslovakia, and Hungary and Bulgaria and owned and operated by the participating countries.

Still another form of direct cooperation between the members of the Comecon are specialized banking and other organizations of multilateral cooperation, the latter including Rolling Stock Park; Inter-metal, an organization coordinating the activities of the smelting industries; Organization of Ballbearing Industry; and Interchem Organization of Chemical Industry. The characteristic feature of these organizations is that although not owners of the industrial establishments involved, they work out a single economic plan assigning tasks, setting up production targets, determining costs and prices, to meet the needs of the member countries and of international trade.[15]

Even before adopting the Comprehensive program of integration in 1965, Bulgaria and Hungary had set up a joint enterprise, Agromash, for the production of specialized agricultural machinery for the cultivation of vegetables, fruit, and grapes, on the basis of the cooperation of the enterprises of both countries. Its activity was limited to planning and technology, and it operates on the basis of a budget funded by both partners. In 1971, the Soviet Union joined Agromash.[16]

One of the major international joint enterprises is the Ust-Illimsk cellulose project in the Soviet Union sponsored by Bulgaria, the GDR, Hungary, Poland, and Romania. There is little cooperation in this enterprise. It probably follows the pattern of Intranmash, a joint Hungarian-Bulgarian enterprise specializing in the production of lifts and transport for internal factory use. Intranmash is a corporation separate from the participating states; it is a foreign trade organization, operates on the principle of commercial accounting, and owns property. Its activity is profitable, and dividends are shared by the participating states.[17]

The Comprehensive Program of 1971 (Chapter VIII) provided for a more intensive approach toward creating new international organizations, both in the area of research, planning, standardization, concentration, and allocation of credits and investments, realization of single projects, as well as actual management of production, sales, and distribution.

The program makes a distinction between international economic organizations and international entrepreneurial organizations. International economic organizations deal with all activities aiming at coordination of planning research and all related questions. International entrepreneurial organizations coordinate production processes, including production, services, trade, and distribution. In the first category, governmental institutions of the administrative type participate. In the second belong enterprises, their association, combines, central bureaus operating on the commercial accounting principle, and other similar organizations organized as separate legal entities. However, even in this category, participants in these organizations preserve full economic and legal independence in terms of organization, ownership of property, and legal status.

Following the adoption of the Comprehensive Program, international economic organizations expanded their ranks. First the International Center for Scientific and Technical Information was added, with the participation of all regular members of the Comecon (excluding Cuba). It is supported from the contributions from the member countries and is in the same class as the Power Grid Peace, Intermetal, Interchem, and the organization for the ballbearings industry.[18]

More recently (December 11-13, 1973) the Executive Committee recommended the creation of the additional international economic organizations: Intertextilmash, Interatomenergo, and Interelectro. Their membership includes all European Comecon countries,with Yugoslavia participating in the Interelectro only.[19]

On September 9, 1966, the USSR and five other Eastern European countries (excluding Czechoslovakia) signed a convention dealing with the status and privileges of so-called "branch organizations," designed for organizations for economic cooperation of an interstate character, if the parties describe such an organization as such.

Each such organization is to be a juridical person according to the laws of the state in which it is located, and to have the power to make agreements, own and acquire property, and sue in courts. However, powers of the state of its location are to be limited by the fact that it cannot be administratively liquidated and is to have a tax immunity, exemption from custom duties, and immunity of archives. In addition, representatives of the participating governments and officials of the organizations are to enjoy personal immunities, according to the regime applicable to the representatives and officials of the Comecon itself.

It seems that joint organizations in the class of international economic organizations (usually supervising and controlling national industries in a certain industrial area, but not directly entrepreneurial in nature) would belong in the category but only when parties designate them as such.[20]

BILATERALISM

While joint enterprises, cooperative projects, investment agreements, joint planning organizations, and international economic organizations play an important role in the process of economic integration in Comecon, they represent a fairly narrow fragment in the general scheme of cooperation. The bulk of the flow of industrial and coordinating activity relies on the institution of the economic plans and of the bilateral trade agreements between the interested countries. None of the Comecon bodies, not even the executive committee established after its reorganization in 1962, has the power to make decisions committing member countries to concrete projects, or plans of economic integration. The progress of the member countries and of the Comecon area as a whole is achieved through action on the national level.

The principle of bilateralism survived into the present period. The communiqué on the 25th session of the Comecon (July 1971) restated the basic principles of the Comecon in their pristine sense. "The Council" the communiqué states

> is an organization of economic cooperation of a new type, uniting the efforts of equal and sovereign socialist states. At the basis of all the CMEA's work are the principles of socialist internationalism, respect for state sovereignty, independence and national interests, noninterference in the internal affairs of countries, full equality and voluntariness, mutual advantage and comradely mutual aid. Socialist integration is not accompanied by the creation of supranational agencies. These principles will guide the Comecon member countries in the process of the further deepening and improvement of cooperation and the development of socialist economic integration, in realizing the comprehensive program adopted at the session.[21]

So, for instance, the Comprehensive Program adopted in 1971 provided for a mechanism for joint planning in certain specific areas of industrial and economic activity (Chapter IV 24, 25). A special committee was established, consisting of the chairmen of the planning agencies of the Comecon countries. Although its ultimate goal is to bring about the unity of planning for the entire bloc of Comecon countries, the ultimate decision must be made within the framework of the national economic plans. Point 25 of Chapter IV or the Comprehensive Program states clearly, "Joint planning does not affect the independent character of the national plan. Joint planning is effected on the basis of the national ownership of the production plants and of the resources."[22] The principle of bilateralism and voluntariness is also applied to the work of the Specialized Commissions.[23]

The USSR ministries have concluded a number of agreements on production specialization and cooperation with corresponding ministries of the other Comecon countries. A considerable number of these provide for an extensive investment of the resources from the socialist countries in the Soviet economy, primarily in the extractive industries to provide their growing industries with raw materials, fuel, and power.[24]

The political implications of these techniques of cooperation as developed in Comecon relations are quite obvious. Statistics of intrabloc trade according to classes of commodities exchanged indicate that Soviet exports during the period 1950-70 emphasized primarily raw materials, semifinished products, and fuels, while its main imports were machinery, factory equipment, and finished goods. Even Bulgaria, which is still at a comparatively low level of industrialization, exported (in proportion to the total volume of exports) more machinery and factory equipment than the Soviet Union. This fact, of course, assigns to the Soviet Union a key role in the economy of the smaller socialist countries in Eastern Europe. At present, the Comecon countries cover their basic raw materials and fuel needs within the group, and Soviet supplies are decisive. The Soviet Union covers nearly all of their oil, gas, pig iron, and electricity imports; two-thirds of their oil products, rolled steel, and phosphorus fertilizers; more than three-fifths of cotton, coal, and manganese ore; and up to 90 percent of iron ore and 80 percent of wood. "Two out of every three tons of the pig iron produced were made out of Soviet iron ore, and half their steel was made out of Soviet raw materials."[25] The political leverage that this situation gives the Soviet Government is beyond dispute. Indeed, prosperity, economic development, and the standard of living of all of Eastern Europe are in Soviet hands. Due to the technique of bilateralism, the Soviet Union is in full control of the flow of its resources, regulating the growth and development of socialist Eastern Europe.

THE TURNING POINT

The 1971 Comprehensive program nonetheless marked a new attitude. The communiqué issued in connection with its adoption contained a statement that integration was seen now in a somewhat different perspective:

> The session declared that any country that is not a Comecon member can fully or partially participate in the implementation of the measures envisaged by the comprehensive program. The CMEA member countries will continue to develop economic, scientific and technical ties with the developing countries and the developed capitalist states on the principles of peaceful coexistence, equality, mutual advantage and respect for sovereignty.[26]

While similar sentiments were expressed before, at this moment this modest statement seems to have acquired a new meaning. It seems to be a result of a conviction that further progress, sophistication, and expansion of industrial expansion call for closer economic cooperation with the outside world.

By the time the comprehensive program was being considered, the need for at least a partial reintegration of the Comecon into the world economic system became quite clear. The main pattern for this new approach was generally accepted. The West was to supply the machinery, factory equipment, technology, and know-how and the general cooperation in the expansion and modernization of the industrial establishment in the East. The East in exchange was to supply cheap labor and raw materials and to export at least some of the goods and commodities produced in the East.[27]

A Soviet economist writing in early 1973 argued for an extensive program of reintegration:

> Obviously, the guaranteeing of security in Europe would make it possible to free substantial material and labor resources and would create conditions for carrying out a number of major all-European projects. At present, the creation of a common power system for Europe by linking the existing power systems of the C.M.E.A. member-countries and the countries of Western Europe, as well as a single system of internal waterways, is technically possible, and the construction of major transcontinental petroleum and gas pipelines and cooperation in the field of environmental protection are feasible. The joint conduct of nuclear and space research, the joint use of nuclear energy for peaceful purposes, the pooling of states' efforts in combating such diseases as cancer, cardiovascular diseases, etc., are also possible. . . .
>
> The C.M.E.A. countries' trade with the industrially developed capitalist countries, which because of the Western powers' policy of prohibitions had been on a low level, at present is one of the most dynamic areas of world trade. In 1960-1970 the average annual growth rates of the socialist countries' exports and imports to the developed capitalist countries were 10.9% and 9.9% respectively, while the growth rate of world trade as a whole was 9.4%. Moreover, in the second half of the 1960s these rates were higher than in the first half. In 1971 the European C.M.E.A. countries' trade turnover with the capitalist states came to $17,500,000,000.

The overwhelming bulk of the C.M.E.A. countries'
trade with the capitalist countries is with Western Europe,
but their trade turnover with Japan is growing rapidly. In
1970 exports to Japan had increased by 650% in comparison with 1960 and were almost three times larger than
exports to the U.S.A. Japan holds first place (734,000,
000 rubles in 1971) in the U.S.S.R.'s trade with the developed capitalist countries.[28]

The argument in favor of extended economic cooperation between
the Soviet Union and the West was given full treatment in a subsequent
article in Pravda that listed three main reasons for closer cooperation
between the socialist and capitalist systems. In the first place specialization is the motor of progress, as no country in the world, even the
largest, is able to develop all aspects of production. The Soviet Union
has large reserves of oil and raw materials, which must not remain
idle, and needs investment, equipment, and know-how, which is available in the industrial West, provided of course that credits to the
USSR can be paid with a part of the goods or materials produced in new
enterprises. Finally, cooperation with the capitalist world will assure
the flow of foreign currency that will permit the raising of the standard
of living of the Soviet people.[29] In effect, this article argued in favor
of the worldwide division of labor, of a world market, and of identity
of economic interest in all countries irrespective of their social system. At the same time, the new direction for the program of development and integration of the Comecon area was not adopted without
serious soul-searching, particularly since it would require an end
to a policy of economic autarchy within Comecon.

The new approach to East-West trade is a threat to the cohesion
and integration programs of the Comecon. It has opened a possibility
that due to its impact on the economic life and industrialization of the
smaller East European nations, these nations may easily return to
the world economic system, in the same sense as Yugoslavia has become a part of it, in spite of that country's connections with the Comecon. Already some of the Comecon countries have imitated Yugoslavia
in providing an opportunity for the foreign investor from the free
economy country to invest in their industries and commercial institutions—as discussed more fully elsewhere in this study. They have
relaxed government controls in certain important areas of foreign
trade, particularly by granting some domestic enterprises the right
to conduct their own foreign trade operations. The obvious purpose
of the new attitude to foreign trade is to permit a greater flexibility
in adapting the product to the needs of the market and to permit an
independent market research in the countries where the product is
sold. Enterprises are encouraged to experiment with technical qualities
and attractiveness of the product for the foreign buyer.

The issue of cooperation with the European Community was one of those that divided Comecon members, with the Soviet Union at first leading the opposition to direct dealings; others—particularly those that depend heavily on foreign trade (Romania, Poland, Hungary, Czechoslovakia)—leaned toward direct links with the Community.

At the time of this writing, there is no clear evidence that there is a common policy binding socialist countries in their dealings with the Community as such or its member countries.

SUPRANATIONAL APPROACHES IN COMECON

Doing business in Eastern Europe and the Soviet Union will seldom require dealing with the Comecon organizations. As a rule, a foreign entrepreneur will deal with a single government and a partner, which will be a cooperative company or governmental corporation. Nevertheless, the tendency to organize the economic activities of the Comecon countries—at least in selected areas—on an international basis is increasingly in evidence. Even at this moment, when the full bloom of East-West economic cooperation is still in the future, an international approach to management of commerce and industry in Eastern Europe is practiced.

For the nonsocialist entrepreneur, three areas are of particular interest: (1) international organizations in charge of certain areas of industrial and commercial activity, (2) international banks of the Comecon, and (3) the law of the Comecon.

Joint Industrial Management

A foreign entrepreneur may have to deal with organizations exercising administrative controls in several countries or joint enterprises that may be the property of more than one country. In the first category belong international entrepreneurial and international economic organizations. Major decisions concerning investment, expansion, production for foreign markets, acquisition of licenses, and foreign patents shall be the concern of all partners.

In the second category belong industrial organizations established with the cooperation of two or more governments. They are comparatively few and as yet not very important. At the same time it must be noted that the December 1973 meeting of the Comecon's Executive Committee recommended creation of such joint enterprises (companies) with the participation of several countries as a desirable form of intrabloc cooperation.[30]

The theoretical implications of this new approach to industrial organizations are quite significant and may indicate a tendency to

128

treat the ownership of means of production as a supranational property. The need is apparently felt for some form that would permit the operation of international economic organizations, representing the interests of a number of socialist countries organized as juristic persons with property rights in factories, installations, and industrial facilities.

Banks

The financing of economic cooperation within Comecon has been the weakest aspect of the general plan for the industrial development of the member countries. Various techniques of financing have been tried, each with little success. In December 1962, it was decided to establish a bank to serve the joint needs of the member countries, particularly in the international aspect of cooperation, including foreign trade, joint projects, and cooperative ventures.[31] In October 1963 a convention was signed to establish the International Bank for Economic Cooperation (IBEC) with its headquarters in Moscow. The statutes of the bank were an integral part of the convention. Simultaneously, member countries signed an agreement on Multilateral Payments and Clearing in Convertible Rubles, which provided a legal framework for the financial operations of the bank. The bank began to function as of January 1, 1964.[32]

The bank handles clearing the accounts resulting from the economic relations between the member countries kept in convertible rubles. The outstanding balances on individual accounts are settled by credit or payment in gold or hard currencies. In addition to this basic function, which is linked primarily to foreign trade among the socialist countries, the bank undertakes to finance joint construction projects.

The capital of the bank was fixed in the amount of 300 million convertible rubles and was to consist of shares bought by the members of the bank. Shares were calculated according to the rise of exports of each country in foreign trade with other member states and were to be paid in convertible rubles, gold, or any other freely convertible currency.

The bank clears the accounts of the member countries as foreign trade operations require it. Ideally, accounts should be cleared every month. When these accounts are imbalanced, the bank credits the accounts with required funds. This is important in the case of countries offering and delivering their products seasonally.

The funds regularly available in the bank are designed primarily to serve foreign trade transactions, and the bank in its activities maintains a policy designed to develop and promote exchange of goods over and above the quotas agreed to in the yearly delivery plans and agreements between the countries. All other operations requiring additional funds are made available to and by the bank according to the specific agreements between the interested parties. Examples of such projects are the construction of the pipeline "Friendship" and the power grid "Peace," the cooperative exploitation of ores, and the construction of power plans.

The bank is an open organization and is not restricted to the members of Comecon, although in practice no other countries have become members. The bank is headed by a council consisting of the representatives of the member countries. Actual management is the responsibility of the board of directors headed by the chairman. Members of the board and its chairman are appointed by the council of the bank. Decisions of the council of the bank are made unanimously. They are binding upon the member countries only when expressly accepted by the governments concerned. Members of the board of directors and the chairman are appointed for five years.

Disputes between the bank and its clients are to be settled by arbitration. A tribunal is either chosen from the already existing arbitration tribunals available in the member countries or especially established for the particular case. If there is no agreement on this point, the Foreign Arbitration Commission in the Soviet Union is the competent arbitrator. The bank has legal personality, may acquire property, and may own assets, according to the law of the country where such assets are located.

While the creation of the bank was certainly a positive factor in the economic life of the Comecon, the measures adopted by Comecon did not go far enough to permit a free movement of capital and an unimpeded flow of commercial transactions among the socialist countries. There is, as yet, no uniform price system, and the bulk of trade still proceeds through the systems of bilateral trade agreements. As a result, the ruble is not yet a truly international, freely transferable currency. Furthermore, the multilateral clearing system is used in transactions involving consumer goods only, while capital goods, tools, machines, and factory equipment, which are in shorter supply, are traded exclusively in bilateral trade agreements.

The aim of new reforms, which will include multilateral clearing and new international credit arrangements, is to produce a truly international, freely transferable currency. However, the reform of the clearing and credit system hinges on the reform of pricing techniques and a uniform price system for the entire socialist market. In other words, before the Soviet ruble can become a transferable currency the socialist international market must be established.

Problems that plagued the bank at its beginnings have thus not been removed. The transferable ruble is still a ledger currency, and not a reserve currency, and a system of national prices is totally unrelated to world prices. Furthermore, accounts in transferable rubles are still handled according to variable exchange rates, depending upon the nature of the accounts. As a result, bilateral clearing of accounts is still the prevailing method.

All these shortcomings are to be corrected when non-Comecon countries shall expand their trade with the Comecon area and avail themselves of the services of the bank. It has been suggested that rubles as the accounting currency used for the settlement of East-West accounts would then be available for the purpose of multilateral accounting, which at the moment represents a minute proportion of bank business.

> To promote this form of settlement, in October 1972 the
> IBEC Council improved the terms for participation in the
> transferable ruble settlement system for countries out-
> side the IBEC. Payments between these countries and the
> IBEC member countries now may be effected in trans-
> ferable rubles for individual commercial transactions or
> for the whole trade turnover on a bilateral or multilat-
> eral basis. The use of the transferable rubles in such
> settlements gives the IBEC member countries certain
> economic advantages. The IBEC can, if and when neces-
> sary, grant credit on easy terms for this kind of settle-
> ment; the current interest rate is 1.5 percent per an-
> num.[33]

Another opportunity was offered by the financial crisis and the floating of the hard currencies in the free economy countries. Following the meeting of the Executive Committee in September 1973, the bank issued a press release on October 24, 1973, which invited foreign business to use its services, in view of the assured stability of the transferable rubles:

> In accordance with recommendations resulting from the
> Comprehensive Programme of socialist economic inte-
> gration of the CMEA countries, the Council of IBEC has
> revised and perfected the terms of participation of non-
> member countries of the IBEC in the system of settle-
> ments in transferable rubles. The banks of non-member
> countries, participating in such settlements, may receive
> transferable rubles in payment for goods delivered and
> services extended to the IBEC member countries, as well
> as in payment for expenses involved in non-commercial
> transactions including expenses of diplomatic and other
> representations, of tourists, etc. These banks may use
> transferable rubles in payment for import from the IBEC

member countries, for repayment of credits received and for payments involved in non-commercial transactions.

Activities of IBEC are limited to settling of accounts and short-term credits to finance foreign trade transactions, particularly of a seasonal nature. Long-term credit until recently was granted and arranged mostly on the basis of credit agreements between the Comecon countries and is now the business of the International Investment Bank (IIB). Its creation was recommended by the 23d (Special) Session of the Council (1970), and the agreement establishing the bank was signed on July 10, 1970 by the seven members of the Comecon (with the exception of Romania, which joined later).

The organization of the IIB is quite identical with that of IBEC. The nominal capital of the bank was set at 1 billion convertible rubles, which in 1972 (after Romania joined the organization) grew up to 1.052 billion rubles, 70 percent in rubles and 30 percent in hard currencies. The contributions of the member countries were calculated according to the size of their exports to other Comecon countries. IIB is governed by a Board of Representatives of all member countries; the board decides by majority vote, except in certain matters that must be decided unanimously, such as admission of new members, increasing the authorized capital, approving annual reports, issuing bond loans, and also overturning the decisions of the administration of the bank.

IIB is theoretically an open organization and may admit as a member any other country that has similar aims and principles and that will accept the obligations arising from the agreement on the Establishment of the International Investment Bank and its charter.[34] At the same time, the bank has no monopoly for channeling credit deals with other banking institutions both within and outside the Comecon.

In addition to the subscribed capital by the member countries, IIB may obtain financial and bank credit and loans, accepting medium and long-term deposits and also by issuing interest-bearing bonds on international markets.

While the purpose of investment operations (granting medium- and long-term loans) is to finance the construction of enterprises within the general plan for the socialist division of labor, IIB may also grant credits to

banks and economic organizations of other states. In keeping with the policies of the bank-member-countries aimed at expanding trade and currency and financial relations with all countries, regardless of their social systems, the bank has been empowered to establish on the basis of equality, business relations with international

132

finance and credit institutions and with banks in capitalist
and developing countries.[35]

The bank mobilizes capital to invest in its projects by various banking
operations:

> The bank will enlist funds in collective currency (trans-
> ferable rubles), the national currencies of the interested
> countries, and freely convertible currency by obtaining
> credits and loans, obtaining contributions, and in other
> ways. It will allocate idle funds, and will also sell and
> buy currency, gold and securities—in other words engage
> in ordinary banking work.[36]

The bank will operate extensively on foreign money markets,
as it cannot buy gold, currency, securities, and so on in the Soviet
Union. The April 1973 session of the IIB Board decided to establish
a credit fund for economic and technical assistance to the developing
countries to be used to grant credits for periods up to 15 years to
build and modernize industrial, agricultural, and other enterprises
in the developing countries, priority being given to projects of high
economic effectiveness.[37]

The Law of the Comecon

The law of the Comecon consists of three classes of rules: (1)
international agreements; (2) charters establishing international economic organizations such as the two banks and other economic organizations and joint enterprises, endowed with a separate corporate
status and capable of making transactions, owning property, and suing
and being sued; and (3) rules controlling foreign trade between the
Comecon countries.

A foreign (non-Comecon) trader is normally little concerned
with the first class of rules, as they deal exclusively with interstate
relations of the Comecon countries. The domestic laws of members
of Comecon provide an adequate framework for commercial transactions with the organizations from free-enterprise economies.

Somewhat more complicated is the situation of a foreign businessman when he enters into transactions with the international economic
or entrepreneurial organizations of Comecon. Their transactional
capacity is strictly defined in their charters and by-laws, and except
in exceptional circumstances, the ultra vires doctrine has full currency in the Comecon area.

This in particular applies to the IBEC and IIB. These banks are authorized to maintain business relations with Western financial and business organizations, and the terms of their charters will control their dealings with the business world of the West.

Join enterprises are legal entities under the law of their location and have a transactional capacity according to that law. However, their charters stand above such law and will determine, as a rule, the law of the contracts.

Finally, of some importance for foreign traders from the West are the following three sets of rules: (1) General Conditions of Delivery (Sales) of Goods; (2) General Conditions of Installation Contracts; and (3) General Conditions of Servicing Contracts.

While these regimes of foreign trade transactions are binding in mutual relations of the Comecon countries, they are not applicable to contracts with Western businessmen or bankers. Nevertheless, they represent a distillation of the usual foreign-trade introduction in the Comecon countries. As such they provide a good introduction to the conditions of trade relations with the Comecon area. There is considerable literature on the subject, and the General Conditions of Delivery are available in English translation.38

Seen in the perspective of East-West economic relations, Comecon is far from an integrated economic organism. The foreign trader will see the entire area differently from the American businessman contemplating a venture in the Common Market. Eastern Europe is a system of markets linked by certain common policies rather than by uniform business opportunities. As it stands at present, it is not an equivalent of the EEC.

Another distinction that makes it a different economic entity is that business deals between foreign investors and their partners in Eastern Europe will only partly depend upon their success in economic terms. It will more importantly depend upon the ability of the foreign partner to meet the demands of the governmental policy that will look at the participation of the foreign entrepreneur primarily as a source of hard currency, which is still in extremely short supply in the Comecon area.

Soviet and Comecon economists are quite hopeful that East-West trade will invigorate and strengthen their economies and raise the standard of living in the Comecon area. And yet the success of this program must depend upon the relaxation of controls and a considerable widening of opportunity for foreign investment.

NOTES

1. U.S. Dept. of State, Paris Peace Conference (Publication No. 2868) 818-19; compare Vishinskii, Voprosy mezhdunarodnogo prava i mezhdunarodnoi politiki 175 (1947).

2. French Yellow Book: Documents of the Conference of Foreign Ministers of France, the United Kingdom and the USSR, Paris, June 27-July 3, 1947, 78-79.

3. Europa Archiv 838, 918 (1947).

4. Za prochnyi mir za narodnoiu demokratiu, February 1, 1949.

5. Grzybowski, The Socialist Commonwealth of Nations 79 (1969).

6. Ibid., 80.

7. Ibid., 75 ff. Compare A. Uschakov. Die wirtschafliche Integration Osteuropas—der Rat für gegenseitige Wirtschaftshilfe (Comecon) 1961 bis 1965, 135-147 (1966); Jean Caillot, Le C.A.E.M. Aspects juridiques et formes de coopération économique entre les pays socialistes, 45-79 (1971).

8. Semin, "Mezhdunarodnoe sotsialisticheskoe razdelenie trude i vneshnaia torgovla," Vneshnaia Torgovla No. 2, 10 (1961);

9. Cf. Grzybowski, supra note 5 at 93.

10. Bogomolov, "0 koordinatsii narodnokhoziaistvennikh planov sotsialisticheskikh stran," Pl. Kh. No. 1, 41 (1960); "Mezhdunarodnoe sotsialisticheskoe razdelenie truda," Vopr. Ek. No. 1, 17 (1960); Semin, supra note 8 at 12.

11. Compare Grzybowski, supra note 5 at 95-96.

12. Bogomolov, "0 koordinatsii narodnokhoziaistvennykh planov sotsialisticheskikh stran," Pl. Kh. No. 8, 45-46 (1960).

13. Grzybowski, supra note 5 at 100-103.

14. Id. at 124-128.

15. P. Bozyk et al., Integracja a wspolpraca gospodarcza w Europie, 42-53.

16. Pravda, August 11, 1972.

17. Bozyk, supra note 15 at 52-53.

18. Pravda, December 12, 1972.

19. Pravda, December 12, 1973.

20. International economic organizations have administrative powers that reflect a most important element in the economic administration of Comecon. See Sobranie postanovlenii soveta ministrov SSSR No. 6, item 34.

21. Pravda, July 30, 1971; Izvestia, July 31, 1971.

22. Soviet ekonomicheskoi vzaimopomoshchi, Kompleksnaia programma dalneishego uglublenia i sovershen stvovania sotsialisticheskoi integratsii stran chlenov SEV, Moskva, Politizdat (1971).

23. O. Chukanov, "Programma sotsialisticheskoi ekonomicheskoi integratsii pretvorajetsia v zhizn," Kommunist No. 13, 1972, 27-38.

24. Pravda, June 30, 1970 and March 27, 1971.

25. V. Moiseienko, "Na princypakh sotsialisticheskogo internatsionalizma," Vneshnaia Torgovla No. 11, 1973, 2-7.

26. Pravda, July 30, 1971. Cf. Chukanov, supra note 23.

27. Compare, for example, Ye. S. Shershnev, Ekonomika, Politika Ideologia No. 4, 3-14, 1972; V. Alkimov, G. Arbatov, N. Inozemtsev, Izvestia, May 8, 1973, 20-21; V. Spandaryan, Pravda, October 20, 1971; Ye. Shershnev, Pravda, June 13, 1973.

28. A. Voinov, "Ekonomicheskie otnoshenia sotsialisticheskikh stran z razvitimi kapitalisticheskimi gosudarstvami," Planovoe Khoziaistvo No. 3, March 1973, 110-120.

29. N. N. Inozemtsev, "Sotsialism i mezhdunarodnoe ekonomicheskoe sotrudnichestvo," Pravda, May 16, 1973. Compare Kaser, "Comecon in Search of a New Direction," Times (London), June 6, 1973.

30. Economist, Aug. 4, 1973 at 84; and Oct. 20, 1973 at 83-84.

31. Kemper, Maskow, "Probleme des Herausbildung zwischenstaatlichen Eigentum gemeinsamer Betriebe der RGW Staaten" 12 Staat und Recht, 1193-1214, 1963.

32. Tsarevski, "Nov etap vev valutno-fiansovite otnoshenia mezhdu stranite chlenki na SEV," Vanshna Turgoviia No. 2, 1-5 (1963).

33. K. Nazarkin, "Mezhdunarodnomu banku ekonomicheskogo sotrudnichestva—10 let," Vneshnaia Torgovla No. 10, 1973, 11-15.

34. V. Vorobjev, "Mezhdunarodnyj investitsionnyi bank: tretti god dejatelnosti," Vneshnaia Torgovla No. 8, 1973, 10, 16.

35. V. Garbuzov, USSR Minister of Finance in Pravda, July 11, 1971.

36. Id.

37. Vorobjev, supra note 34.

38. See, generally, K. Grzybowski, Soviet Private International Law 46 (1965) and his The Socialist Commonwealth of Nations: Organizations and Institutions 29, 57 (1964); S. Pisar, Coexistence and Commerce: Guidelines for Transactions Between East and West 243-316 (1970); Hoya, "The Comecon General Conditions—A Socialist Unification of International Trade Law," 70 Colum. L. Rev. 253 (1970), and sources cited therein.

7

THE PEOPLE'S REPUBLIC
OF BULGARIA
Ivan Apostolov
Yordan Laskov

In the years after September 9, 1944, the economy of the People's Republic of Bulgaria underwent radical changes on the basis of socialist production relations. Bulgarian foreign trade was also consolidated as a socialist foreign trade and assigned tasks in immediate service of the accelerated development of the nation's economy.

The implementation of Bulgaria's foreign trade is effected in accordance with the following democratic principles of the country's foreign trade policy: complete equality in relations between states; respect for the sovereignty and noninterference in the domestic affairs of states; respect for mutual interests and benefit; and good faith in the fulfillment of contracts. Bulgaria's foreign trade is based on the principles of socialist foreign trade; it is alien to inequality, exploitation, and economic dependence; and it is guided by the principles of socialist internationalism and equality and mutual benefits.

At present, about 75 percent of its total foreign trade is with other members of the Council for Mutual Economic Assistance (CMEA), and 55 percent of its trade is with the USSR alone. In Bulgaria's exports, foodstuffs, followed by machinery and equipment, are predominant. Bulgaria is one of the world's major exporters of wines, tomatoes, and cigarettes. Its principal imports are machinery and equipment, followed by fuels, mineral raw materials, chemical products, and industrial consumer goods.

Abiding by the principle of equality and mutual benefit, Bulgaria has maintained and expanded its trade relations with the developed capitalist countries, insofar as they manifest the same desire and respect the country's interests.

The first 1947 Socialist Constitution of the People's Republic of Bulgaria reflected the new character of Bulgaria's foreign trade and its exceptional significance for the development of the country's economy.[1]

All private factories, mines, and banks were nationalized. Conditions were created for the introduction of a state monopoly in foreign trade, to help the socialist reconstruction of the country.

With the adoption of the new Constitution on May 16, 1971, the trends and development of foreign trade were constitutionally consolidated. According to Article 13 of the Constitution, socialist foreign trade is defined as an integral part of the socialist economic system, based upon the public ownership of the means of production.[2]

Article 29 of the Constitution proclaims the principle that "foreign trade is an exclusive right of the state." This constitutional principle establishes the state's exclusive right to carry on foreign trade. The constitutional principle of state monopoly in foreign trade is the basis for the entire system of norms regulating the character, aims and purposes, and organizational structure of Bulgaria's foreign trade. Being an exclusive right to carry on foreign trade, the state monopoly under socialism has a single master, the people,[3] who delegate this right to their political organization, the socialist state, for implementation through those agencies especially authorized for this purpose. The foreign trade state monopoly represents a specific system of organization, methods, and means for carrying on the foreign trade of the socialist state and reflects the requirements of the socialist economy in its relations with the economies of other countries.[4] The constitutional principle is further reflected in a number of other legal provisions.[5]

The state monopoly of foreign trade, according to Article 3 of the Law on Foreign Trade, consists in the exclusive right of the state:

a. to determine the country's foreign trade policy;

b. to set up state economic organizations for carrying on foreign trade;

c. to plan, organize, manage and control foreign trade activities;

d. to delegate to state, co-operative and other organizations the right to carry on foreign trade activities and to determine the object and conditions of their activities;

e. to authorize and determine the participation of Bulgarian organizations in economic activities abroad;

f. to determine the possibility and conditions for the performance of trade or other economic activities in the country by foreign enterprises and firms;

g. to determine the regime for the performance of foreign trade;

h. to direct the country's participation in the international division of labor for the purpose of carrying on effective foreign trade for the nation's economy.

This listing does not exhaust the full extent of the state's foreign trade monopoly, which applies to all transactions that arise in connection with the following:

- the import and export of goods, complete factories, machinery, and equipment;
- rendering and receiving scientific and technological assistance abroad and from abroad;
- operations that have foreign currency as their object;
- the performance of reexport, transit, combined, and other operations;
- purchase and sales and other operations with patents, licenses, copyrights, trademarks, industrial models, and so on;
- publicity, advertising, insurance, and other activities connected with foreign trade;
- international transport, agencies, freighting, and shipment of foreign trade;
- operations connected with international tourism;
- all activities connected with representation, brokerage, commission, servicing, and rendering assistance to foreign physical persons or bodies corporate in the country or to socialist organizations and persons abroad;
- all foreign trade operations in which one of the parties is a foreign physical person or body corporate.[6]

ORGANIZATION AND MANAGEMENT OF BULGARIA'S FOREIGN TRADE

As a result of the socialist reconstruction of the national economy of the People's Republic of Bulgaria after the April 1956 Plenary Session of the Central Committee of the Bulgarian Communist Party, the growth of the country's foreign trade was rapidly increased and its organization was improved. During the 1960s, an experiment was started with a new organization of foreign trade on the principle of a more immediate connection of production with the foreign market.

With a view to improving the effectiveness of foreign trade, the economic impact of the foreign market on production was stepped up. In the process of experimentation, the entire system of organization, management, and control of foreign trade was improved. A new organizational structure of foreign trade was set up and the functions and competencies of the different bodies were determined by laws, in accordance with the requirements of the economic mechanism in operation in the country. The structure, functions, and competencies of the different foreign trade bodies and organizations may be classified as managing, operative, auxiliary, and subsidiary.

<u>Managing Bodies</u>

The managing bodies in foreign trade are the National Assembly, the State Council, the Council of Ministers, the State Planning Committee, the Ministry of Finance, and the Ministry of Foreign Trade.

The National Assembly is the supreme body for management and control of foreign trade. It adopts the laws by which foreign trade is directly or indirectly regulated by the State Plan for the country's social and economic development, and ratifies certain international agreements. The plan is the basic normative act for foreign trade activities.

The State Council, which is a supreme body of the National Assembly, carries out executive and administrative activities in certain basic fields of the government and the state, exercises general guidance and control of the work of the Council of Ministers and the other state bodies, controls the fulfillment of the tasks stemming from the laws and decisions of the National Assembly, represents the country in its international relations, ratifies and denounces international agreements, and exercises control over the activity of the Ministry of Foreign Trade.

The Council of Ministers has the constitutional responsibility to guide, coordinate, and control the activities of all ministries and departments,[7] including the Ministry of Foreign Trade.[8] It draws up and submits to the National Assembly for adoption the draft of the Integrated Plan for the country's socioeconomic development, approves and denounces international agreements that are not subject to approval by the National Assembly or the State Council, and organizes the implementation of foreign policy—and, in this connection, foreign trade policy. A Commission for Economic, Scientific, and Technological Cooperation has been established as an organ of the Council of Ministers. The commission's responsibilities include the fields of economic, scientific, and technological cooperation and the country's participation in the international division of labor and socialist economic integration. The State Planning Committee, in conjunction with the Ministry of Foreign Trade, draws up the section of foreign trade in the Integrated Plan for the country's socioeconomic development. The Ministry of Finance takes part in the elaboration of the country's foreign currency plan and the financial and economic plans of its foreign trade organizations. In conjunction with the Ministry of Foreign Trade, it implements the customs tariff and carries out customs protection. Other ministries and departments have limited managing functions with respect to the foreign trade organizations subordinated to them and only supervise and control their immediate operational activities.[9]

The Ministry of Foreign Trade is the state body in which over-all management and control of foreign trade is concentrated. It is responsible to the Council of Ministers for securing proper implementation of the country's foreign trade activities in accordance with over-all state economic and foreign policy.

According to Article 5, paragraph I of the Law on Foreign Trade, "the Ministry of Foreign Trade pursues the state foreign trade policy and, in accordance with the principle of state foreign trade monopoly, manages, plans, co-ordinates and controls the country's entire foreign trade activity." "It is an organ of the Council of Ministers for the organization and management of foreign trade."[10] The Ministry of Foreign Trade is thus defined as a functional ministry for the implementation of an integrated, centralized state management of foreign trade.

The competencies and functions of the ministry are defined in Article 5 of the 1970 Regulation for the application of the Law on Foreign Trade. Moreover, the ministry takes an active part in planning the country's foreign trade, as provided in Article 6 of the 1970 Regulations.

The functional character of the Ministry of Foreign Trade is underscored by Article 24 of the Law on Foreign Trade, according to which the Minister of Foreign Trade is authorized "to issue instructions on foreign trade activities, obligatory for all institutions, enterprises and organizations."

This managing and controlling role of the Ministry of Foreign Trade is reflected in Article 28 of the Regulations for the Application of the Law on Foreign Trade, according to which

the Minister of Foreign Trade may suspend the carrying out of any orders of the departments and of the socialist economic organizations in their foreign trade activity, which are illegal or harmful to the interests of the state, and in the case of systematic and crass violations of foreign trade discipline, he may come forward with proposals to the Council of Ministers for depriving them of the right to engage in foreign trade activity.

For the fulfillment of the functions of the Ministry of Foreign Trade abroad, the ministry is represented by organs known as "trade representations." At present, Bulgaria has more than 80 such representations. The trade representations, as organs of the Ministry of Foreign Trade, are institutions governed by public law and have nothing in common with the institutions of representation of commercial firms.[11]

Operative Organs

Only foreign trade organizations12 authorized by the Council of Ministers may perform foreign trade activities in Bulgaria. Physical persons do not have the right to engage in such activities. The Council of Ministers decides which organizations are to be entrusted with the right to carry on foreign trade activities.

A foreign trade organization is a Bulgarian socialist body corporate governed by civil law. It represents an independent entity of personal, property, and organizational elements and is the bearer of rights and obligations connected with civil law relations. Foreign trade organizations perform economic activities based on the principle of cost accounting and financial independence, in accordance with the Integrated Plan for the country's socioeconomic development "and in accordance with the laws of the country, the international trade agreements, conventions, protocols and other economic agreements."13 The specific tasks of the foreign trade organizations are determined in the Regulations for the Application of the Law on Foreign Trade.14

Foreign trade activities in the People's Republic of Bulgaria are performed by three kinds of foreign trade organizations: state enterprises, cooperative enterprises, and companies.

The state enterprises are the oldest and most widespread organizational form of foreign trade organizations. The ownership of their basic funds belongs to the state, and the enterprises only have the right of operative management over these funds.

A cooperative enterprise, unlike those of the state, may own its basic funds. Or, ownership may belong to another cooperative organization with only the right of operative management, as in the state enterprises, granted to the enterprise.

The companies are foreign trade organizations with limited liability, in which "ministries, state economic trusts, state enterprises and other organizations, whose activity is connected with that of the company"15 may participate.

The setting up, reorganization, and dissolution of foreign trade organizations is effected by decision of the Council of Ministers, based on the proposal of the Minister of Foreign Trade, the minister of a branch ministry, or the manager of a department.16

In the constituent act of the Council of Ministers for the foundation of a foreign trade organization, the following should be indicated: the firm name, seat, object of activity, and indication of the ministry having administrative authority over it. The constituent act also determines the areas of activity of the foreign trade organization, the funds placed at its disposal, the manner of their obtention, and so on. The formation of state foreign trade enterprises takes place only on the basis of the act by the Council of Ministers from the date of its issuance or the date that is indicated in it. From this moment, it acquires the status of a body corporate. The cooperative foreign trade enterprises are established, reorganized, and dissolved by decision of the corresponding managing body of the cooperative, on the basis of a permit from the Council of Ministers, in which the object and conditions of carrying out foreign trade activity are determined. The cooperative foreign trade enterprise is established, reorganized, and dissolved in accordance with the laws of the People's Republic of Bulgaria, after registration in the people's court. This registration has a constitutive effect.

A company is formed, reorganized, and dissolved[17] on the basis of a decision of its founders, a permit from the Council of Ministers, a decision of the founders for the adoption of its constitution, an approved constitution by the Minister of Foreign Trade and the manager of the respective department under whose administrative authority the company is placed, and registration of the constitution at the people's court. This registration at the court has a constitutive character. The company becomes a body corporate from the moment of its registration at the court.

All Bulgarian foreign trade organizations, after being formed, are obligatorily registered in a special book at the Bulgarian Chamber of Commerce and Industry.[18] The purpose of this registration is to keep an exact record of the foreign trade organizations, so as to be able to determine their status at any moment. This makes it possible for all interested third parties in Bulgaria and abroad to learn all facts regarding a company's areas of activity, representation, organs, rights, and so on. Entered into the register are the following: the firm name, seat, and address of the foreign trade organization and its subdivisions in the country; the constituent act for the establishment of the foreign trade organization; the areas of its activities and the nomenclature of the goods; the amount of its constitutional fund (and for the companies also the amount of their share capital); and the names of the persons representing the foreign trade organization and the scope of their representation rights.

The register is public, and upon demand certified copies or certificates attesting to the facts entered in it may be issued. All entries in the register of the Bulgarian Chamber of Commerce and Industry are published in the State Gazette.

The foreign trade organizations also have an act regulating their inner structure and activity. In the state and cooperative enterprises this act is called a Regulation, and in the others it is called a Constitution. The act contains the name, seat, areas of activities, representative organs, authorized persons, property and financial responsibility, structure and management, and so on of the organization. The regulation is an internal act, which cannot be put up against third parties and from which no rights against third parties may ensue.

In every foreign trade organization, there are operative and functional units. The operative work is performed by "offices," which are not financially independent or juridically separate units. "Departments" are set up as functional units in the foreign trade organizations to serve their over-all activities and to render assistance to the offices. Thus, the Planning and Statistical Department (on the basis of the tasks assigned to it under the plan by the Ministry of Foreign Trade) draws up the plan of the enterprise and supervises its fulfillment by the offices.

Every foreign trade organization, as an independent body corporate, has property of its own enabling it to carry out its activities. This property represents the sum total of the rights and obligations the organization possesses at any given moment.

A characteristic feature of every socialist foreign trade organization is that its basic funds belong to the state. The foreign trade organization has no right of ownership over these funds but only the right of operative management. This enables it to take part in its own name in property owned by another person in the civil turnover and to be responsible with this property for obligations assumed to the amount determined by the law. The foreign trade organization is responsible for the obligations assumed by it only with its turnover funds and with its special funds held in separate accounts at the banks. It cannot be held responsible for its obligations with its basic funds, because they are not its property; they are the property of the state.* Every foreign trade organization, as a separate body corporate, is answerable only for its own obligations. It is not liable for the obligations of the state or of other hierarchically higher bodies or

---

*The term "basic funds" includes all capital investments that have a value over 40 leva and that have a useful life of more than one year—for example, buildings, machinery, equipment, and so on, placed at the disposal of the enterprise by the state for management and use.

The term "turnover funds" means the circulating capital that the enterprise has at its disposal to perform its activity. This circulating capital comprises financial resources and securities, goods, materials, packings, raw materials, fuel, and so on.

The term "special funds" denotes those funds of the enterprise envisaged for expansion and technical improvement, for raising the efficiency of foreign trade, for social, everyday life, and cultural undertakings, and for additional material incentives for its personnel. These funds represent a determined percentage of amortization deductions for a certain period during which the basic funds are used, deductions from the profits of the enterprise, deductions from the total income of the enterprise, and so on.

organizations, just as they are not liable for its obligations,[19] as a result of their complete legal, material, and economic independence.

All foreign trade organizations combine the principle of one-man management with the principle of collective management.

The state and cooperative foreign trade enterprises are managed by a general director, an Economic Committee, and a General Meeting of the industrial and office workers. The general director manages and represents the enterprise in accordance with the principle of one-man management, which principle enjoys priority. In case the general director disagrees with a decision of the Economic Committee or the General Meeting, the dispute is settled by the manager of the respective department or trust under whose authority the foreign trade organization has been placed.

The companies are managed and guided by the General Meeting, a general director, and an Auditing Council. The General Meeting is the main managing body. It decides questions connected with the management and control of the company. It consists of the managers of the organization—members and their proxies. The General Meeting adopts the Constitution of the company, appoints and dismisses the general director and his deputies, adopts the plans, the annual report, and the annual account of the company for the distribution of its incomes, admits and dismisses members, and so on. The general director manages the operative activities of the company and represents the latter before all organs, institutions, and third parties in the country and abroad. The tasks and functions of the Auditing Council are determined by the General Meeting.

The dissolution and winding-up (liquidation) of foreign trade enterprises is governed by the Regulation for the State Economic Organizations.[20] The dissolution and winding-up of companies upon expiration of the time for which they were set up is by a unanimous decision taken by their members or by decision of the Council of Ministers.[21]

In accordance with the Law on Foreign Trade and other provisions such as the Regulation for the State Economic Organizations, the Model Constitution of Foreign Trade Companies, and other acts of the Council of Ministers, the following system of foreign trade organizations has been set up:[22] foreign trade organizations under the Ministry of Foreign Trade; foreign trade organizations for carrying on foreign trade activities of the state economic trusts under the branch ministries and other departments; and foreign trade organizations under the Chamber of Commerce and Industry.

Auxiliary Bodies

Auxiliary bodies of foreign trade in the People's Republic of Bulgaria are those foreign trade organizations that carry on foreign trade activities subordinate to import and export. For the implementation of these activities, a number of foreign trade organizations and institutions have been set up, such as the Despred State Economic Enterprise, the Interpred Association, the Bulstrad Joint-Stock Company, the Bulgarian Foreign Trade Bank, and the Bulgarcontrol State Enterprise.

All shipping activities are entrusted to the Despred State Economic Enterprise, which, on the order of its clients (the foreign trade organizations), concludes in its own name and for their account transport contracts with Bulgarian and foreign transport organizations and performs all services and operations connected with the organizing, reception, delivery, and reloading of cargoes at different ports.

The Bulfracht State Economic Enterprise is entrusted with organizing the freighting of Bulgarian and foreign tonnage for the transport of Bulgarian and foreign cargoes by water. It acts as commissioner in activities connected with the transport of cargoes by water, in the reception and expedition of all kinds of vessels and equipment, and in other areas in the field of maritime trade and navigation.

Operations connected with the insurance of imports, exports, and reexport goods, with their reinsurance, with the insurance of ships, aircraft, motor transport vehicles, and personal and property insurance of foreign and Bulgarian citizens abroad are entrusted to the Bulstrad Joint-Stock Company.

Surveillance of imports and exports, expert examinations and average findings, seed control, and various types of analyses of goods are among the responsibilities of the Bulgarcontrol State Enterprise.

Payment operations with foreign countries, the implementation of foreign currency and credit operations with foreign countries, and the granting of credits to Bulgarian foreign trade organizations and enterprises in foreign currency and leva are entrusted to the Bulgarian Foreign Trade Bank.

The activities connected with the representation of foreign firms and tradesmen in the People's Republic of Bulgaria is entrusted to the specialized Interpred Association, and the activities of commissioners for foreign publishing houses, theaters, agencies, and so on, for the acquisition of publishing and other rights from Bulgarian authors, as well as for the acquisition of rights to use foreign works by Bulgarian publishing houses, theaters, and the like, are entrusted to the director of Copyright Protection.

Subsidiary Bodies

Subsidiary bodies of foreign trade are the Scientific Center of Foreign Trade under the Ministry of Foreign Trade and the Bulgarian Chamber of Commerce and Industry. The Scientific Center of Foreign

Trade conducts research work and studies in various fields—including the planning, forecasting, and efficiency of foreign trade activities.

The Bulgarian Chamber of Commerce and Industry, a public economic organization, organizes the representation of the country at international fairs and exhibitions, issues foreign trade publications in Bulgarian and in foreign languages, and helps Bulgarian foreign trade organizations establish contacts with foreign countries. It issues and attests certificates of origin and other documents necessary for foreign trade transactions. It helps the deepening participation of the People's Republic of Bulgaria in socialist economic integration with the CMEA member countries, and especially with the USSR, and assists in expanding economic relations and cooperation of the People's Republic of Bulgaria with the developing and advanced capitalist countries.

An Arbitration Court has been set up at the Bulgarian Chamber of Commerce and Industry. In accordance with Article 16 of the Law on Foreign Trade, the Arbitration Court is charged with "the hearing and decision by way of arbitration of disputes connected with international trade."

Foreign Trade Planning

Foreign trade in the People's Republic of Bulgaria is regulated by state planning. The foreign trade plan is a constituent part of the Integrated Plan for the country's social and economic development. The tasks of foreign trade are also reflected in the long-term, five-year, and annual plans for the country's socioeconomic development.

The foreign trade plan is drawn up with the active participation of the Ministry of Foreign Trade. It is approved by the National Assembly and is entrusted to the Council of Ministers for its implementation. The State Planning Committee charges the ministries and departments with the fulfillment of the plan.

The foreign trade organizations, on the basis of a plan assigned to them by the Ministry of Foreign Trade, draw up their own plans in which, besides imports and exports, they also reflect the other independent operations necessary for the effective fulfillment of the plan. The foreign trade organizations carry out all their activities on the basis of this plan.

FOREIGN TRADE REGIME

The operative regulation and control of foreign trade activities[23] in Bulgaria is implemented by the Ministry of Foreign Trade. The ministry is the only state body that directs foreign trade activities in the country, directing the foreign trade operations by lines and countries in accordance with the Integrated Plan for the country's socioeconomic development, and international trade agreements, conventions, protocols, and so on.

All import and export transactions and other foreign trade operations are subject to authorization by the Ministry of Foreign Trade. According to Article 17 of the Law on Foreign Trade, "Foreign trade transactions may be concluded with the permission of the Ministry of Foreign Trade. Transactions concluded without such permission are null and void." Transactions concluded abroad by representatives of the foreign trade organizations are subject to the same rules. A special instruction for the order and manner of issuing permissions for foreign trade transactions was issued and approved by the Minister of Foreign Trade on May 20, 1972 and came into force on October 1, 1972.

According to this instruction, for every foreign trade transaction, prior to concluding the corresponding contracts, the competent foreign trade organization files a written request with enclosures in the established form for the issuance of a permission.

Although not envisaged in the legal provisions discussed above, and not recommended, it is possible to conclude a contract on condition that a permission will be obtained. Such a reservation, however, obliges the foreign trade organization actually to take the necessary steps for the obtaining of permission and to inform the contracting party in good time of the result. The conclusion of transactions without permission or the failure to act where a contract has been made subject to obtaining permission and the permission is granted, may lead to the foreign trade enterprise, with respect to its partner, being charged with bad faith and "precontract guilt."

Permissions are required for all kinds of transactions that are the object of foreign trade activities. They are issued for a specific time limit. After the expiration of the time limit, or when the conditions of the transaction have been changed, a new permission must be obtained in the established order, to carry out the transaction.

According to Article 2 of the Law on Foreign Trade, transactions for the assumption of a representation and performance of foreign trade advertising and publicity are foreign trade transactions. Transactions of this kind are subject to the general regime established for foreign trade transactions. Foreign firms may appoint as representatives only the specialized Bulgarian foreign trade organization, the Interpred Association. The latter assumes the representation of foreign firms only after due permission is issued by the Ministry of Foreign Trade. The requests for permits for representation in Bulgaria must indicate the firm that is to be represented, the goods or services that will constitute the object of the representation contract, the remuneration that will be paid, as well as all other essential conditions of the contract.

Foreign trade organizations act in an analogous manner in cases of requests for permission to entrust foreign firms with the right to represent Bulgarian enterprises abroad.

Advertising contracts with foreign firms are also subject to a permission procedure. In granting permission, account is taken of all circumstances connected with the advertising action, including the character of the advertising media, reciprocity in implementing trade advertising, the trends in the country's foreign trade policy, and so on.

The participation of foreign trade organizations in international fairs and exhibitions, as well as of foreign firms in Bulgarian fairs and exhibitions, is also effected on the basis of a permit, which is issued as follows: for the participation of Bulgarian foreign trade organizations, on the basis of a special order and plan approved by the Council of Ministers; and for the participation of foreign firms, in accordance with the rules and regulations of the International Trade Fair in Plovdiv and corresponding lease contracts (for a specific or extended period of time) of exhibition area, which contracts are subject to the abovementioned regime of foreign trade transactions.

Every foreign trade transaction is subject to operative control, which is implemented by the competent bodies of the Ministry of Foreign Trade, the customs houses, and the Bulgarian Foreign Trade Bank.

After a permission for the foreign trade transaction is issued by the Ministry of Foreign Trade, one copy of the request of the foreign trade organization remains on file in the records of the Ministry of Foreign Trade, and the remaining three copies are delivered to the foreign trade organization. The latter sends copies to the Bulgarian Foreign Trade Bank* and to the customs house at the frontier checkpoint through which the goods will pass.

The Bulgarian Foreign Trade Bank gives credits in cash, renders services, and performs all foreign currency and financial operations connected with the foreign trade transactions of the foreign trade organizations as well as payments between them and other enterprises in the country, keeps the funds of foreign trade organizations, and exercises banking control over the financial phase of their activities.

----

*The Bulgarian Foreign Trade Bank is a joint-stock company with a capital of 40,000,000 leva, distributed into 4,000 shares of 10,000 leva each. The activities of the Bulgarian Foreign Trade Bank are prescribed in its Constitution, published in State Gazette No. 19, March 6, 1964.

It exercises its rights and acts in accordance with its Constitution, the Decree on Payments, the Decree on Contributions by the Economic Enterprises to the Budget, the decree on its relations and acts regulating its activities, including the powers given to it by the Bulgarian National Bank, intergovernment agreements, and instructions and orders issued by the bank itself in light of Article 54 of its Constitution.

These acts regulate the granting of credits to foreign trade enterprises, the formation of their income and its distribution, the keeping and use of the funds of the foreign trade organizations, the manner of payment to be made by the foreign trade organizations in connection with transactions with parties belonging to nonsocialist countries, the manner and order of preparing documents for the different kinds of foreign trade operations, and the payments to be made in connection with them—letters of credit, bank guarantees and payments orders, currency control, and sanctions in case of violations. Payment for transactions between enterprises of the CMEA member countries is regulated by Article 49 of the 1968 CMEA General Delivery Conditions.

The foreign trade of Bulgaria is also regulated through customs duties and customs policy.[24] A customs tariff has been in force in Bulgaria since January 1, 1971. It was elaborated on the basis of the Brussels Nomenclature and consists of three columns.

Under Column One are the tariff rates for all goods imported from countries to which Bulgaria has accorded a preferential customs regime. Column Two is applied to imports of goods from countries with which Bulgaria has concluded agreements providing for MFN treatment. Column Three is applied to the import of goods from countries that impose higher duties on goods from Bulgaria than they impose on goods from countries enjoying MFN treatment. The customs duties are collected ad valorem and are paid by the importing organization. The customs duties are calculated on a C.I.F. (cost, insurance, and freight) basis against the following documents: an invoice with attached specification of the goods, transport documents, insurance policy, and certificate of origin. The method of calculating customs duties is prescribed in the Customs Law.[25] On the basis of the export and import permissions submitted to them, the customs authorities supervise the movement of goods and, without such permission, do not allow goods to pass the Bulgarian frontiers.

An order regarding the customs formalities for goods imported and exported by bodies corporate, issued by the Minister of Foreign Trade and the Minister of Finances on April 21, 1971, regulates the following:

1. The calculation of customs duty and customs formalities in connection with goods and objects imported or exported by bodies corporate, as well as the import and export of technical documentation, licenses, samples of goods, and advertising materials.

150

2. The duty-free import of objects and printed matter of a refer-
ential, scientific, and technical character, received free of charge,
the export of similar materials, foodstuffs, and alcoholic beverages
for the needs of Bulgarian representations and the like.

3. The control of the customs houses and the collection of customs duties on imports, exports, or reexports. This control includes
the observance of the state monopoly on foreign trade, the regularity
of the required documents, as well as the factual control over the
goods.

4. The temporary import and export by bodies corporate, the
import and export of samples of goods, the import of samples of goods
by foreign diplomatic and trade representations, and so on.

The customs houses thus assure respect for the established
regime for foreign trade activities prohibitions or limitations on exports and imports, measures of a sanitary and veterinary character,
and collection of customs duties.

All transactions with Bulgarian foreign trade organizations are
concluded and implemented under strict observance of the above-
described legal regime for foreign trade activities. In order to secure
the observance of the regime for foreign trade, a normative system
has been established that provides sanctions for violations expressly
envisaged by the law.[26]

FOREIGN TRADE CONTRACTS

Under Bulgarian law, a foreign trade transaction, in the broad
sense of the word, is every juridical act giving rise to property relations in the field of international trade. The determining criterion
is whether one of the parties is a foreign physical person or a body
corporate.[27] Among the great variety of foreign trade transactions,
purchases and sales occupy a central place.

In the most general outline, the following basic points are of
significance in connection with concluding and carrying out foreign
trade transactions:

1. In Bulgaria, a foreign trade transaction is subordinated to
the regime established by the state monopoly of foreign trade. With
a view to implementing effective control over the observance of this
requirement, the Law on Foreign Trade envisages as a compulsory
prerequisite that every such transaction should be approved by the
Ministry of Foreign Trade. This approval may be given in advance
or subsequently. In every case, however, its presence is an essential
element of the transaction and a necessary prerequisite for its validity.[28]

2. Apart from this requirement, however, the legal subjects participating in foreign trade, which in Bulgaria are state or cooperative foreign trade enterprises within the framework of their approved nomenclature, enjoy absolute autonomy to negotiate and conclude transactions. The parties to a transaction may freely determine the content of the contract under the sole condition that it not be contrary to law, to the State National Economic Plan, and to the rules of the socialist community.[29]

3. The Bulgarian Law on Obligations and Contracts[30] in its basic principles does not deviate from the classic rules to which obligations are subject in most continental legal systems. Thus, this law provides that

a. In conducting negotiations and concluding contracts, the parties must act in good faith. Otherwise, they owe indemnity (Article 12).

b. The offerer is bound by the offer until the expiration of the time set in it, or the time which is usually necessary for the acceptance to arrive (Article 13).

c. A contract is considered as concluded when the acceptance reaches the offerer, and at the place where the offer was made (Article 14).

d. The contract produces an effect between the parties and is effective with respect to third parties only in those cases provided in the law (Article 21).

e. In interpreting contracts, the actual common will of the parties should be sought. Separate agreements should be interpreted in light of their purposes, customary practice, and good faith.

4. Regarding the form of foreign trade transactions, it should be pointed out that Bulgarian law obligatorily requires written form.[31] The character of this requirement is imperative, and its nonobservance leads to the voiding of the transaction.[32] In its constant practice, the Arbitration Court at the Bulgarian Chamber of Commerce and Industry considers this condition as observed if the transaction has been concluded with telegrams or Telex communications exchanged between the parties.[33]

5. The People's Republic of Bulgaria is a party to economic agreements, bilateral or multilateral, with many countries in the world: trade and navigation contracts, trade and payments agreements, and so on. Such international acts have binding force for the state as a subject of international law and serve as a basis for regulating international trade but do not in any way diminish the legal autonomy and independence of foreign trade transactions, under which certain rights arise and obligations are implemented, modified, or extinguished between Bulgarian foreign trade enterprises and foreign commercial organizations, enterprises, or persons. These rights may be exercised, guaranteed, and defended with the methods and means provided

for the transactions and under the domestic laws of the countries concerned. While the nonfulfillment of obligations assumed in connection with foreign trade transactions engages the responsibility of the enterprise participating in the transactions, the nonfulfillment of a foreign trade agreement concluded by the People's Republic of Bulgaria involves the public legal responsibility of the state itself. These two kinds of responsibility are qualitatively different and underline the differences between the two cases. That is why a Bulgarian foreign trade enterprise cannot in any case be identified with the state itself. A Bulgarian foreign trade enterprise is an independent legal subject that has its own legal capacity and competence, separate and different from those of the state.

6. One category of foreign trade transactions is subject to a special regime: the purchase and sale of goods between foreign trade enterprises of the member countries of the CMEA, regulated by the 1968 CMEA General Delivery Conditions.[34]

INDUSTRIAL PROPERTY RIGHTS AND TRANSACTIONS INVOLVING TECHNOLOGY

Industrial Property Rights

In Bulgaria, legal protection is accorded to inventions, industrial models, trademarks, and names of origin.[35]

An author of an invention[36] may, at his option, seek an authorship certificate or a patent. The authorship certificate attests to recognition of the proposal as an invention, its priority, authorship right, as well as the exclusive right of the state to use the invention and to dispose of it as it may see fit.[37] A patent attests to recognition of the proposal as an invention, its right of ownership, the priority of the request for recognition of the invention, and the exclusive right of the owner of the patent over the invention.[38]

According to the law, no patent can be issued and only an authorship certificate may be issued for the following inventions: new methods of prophylaxis, diagnosis, and treatment of diseases in men, animals, and plants; new kinds of varieties of agricultural crops or new animal breeds; technical solutions of problems connected with the use of nuclear energy; inventions made in connection with the author's work in a socialist organization or made on the latter's order; inventions in the creation of which the inventor has received assistance in cash or materials from a socialist organization, and inventions connected with the defense and security of the country.

It is possible for a patent to be transformed into an authorship certificate. When a basic invention is improved or supplemented, upon the request of its author, he may be issued an additional authorship certificate or an additional patent. An additional patent is in force only for the period of time during which the basic patent is in force. Patents are issued for a period of 15 years from the date of the request for their issuance. The owner of a patent may give permission for the utilization of the patent or cede the latter as a whole. For the issuance of a patent, an initial payment of 100 leva is collected. For the maintenance of the patent, an annual fee is paid, which for the second year amounts to 30 leva, and which for every year thereafter up to 15 years amounts to 15 leva more than the fee for the preceding year.

Legal protection of an industrial model[39] may be obtained by a registration at the Institute of Inventions and Rationalizations. A request for the registration of an industrial model may be made by any physical person or body corporate interested in its introduction into production. The registration is of a constitutive character. With the registration of an industrial model, the exceptional right is accorded to use the model in the name of the applicant for a period of five years. This time limit cannot be prolonged. The exclusive right to use an industrial model may be transferred free of charge or as remuneration to another person. For the registration of an industrial model, a fee of 40 leva is collected.

Industrial enterprises, organizations, or persons who produce or sell goods or perform services may register a trademark of their own or a trademark of services.[40] The registration of trademarks and marks of services takes place at the Institute of Inventions and Rationalizations. The trademarks or marks of services may consist of words, figures, graphic representations, spatial or sound elements, or a mixture of these.

No signs can be registered or used as marks that are already universally used; do not have any distinguishing features or are of a descriptive character; do not differ essentially from marks registered in the country; are well-known as world-famous marks; consist of special signs for qualitative control and guarantee; contain false information; resemble international signs for magnitudes; represent coats of arms, flags, signs, or emblems of states or international or intergovernmental organizations; or are at variance with the public interest or socialist morals.

Protection is granted for a period of 10 years from the date of the request for the registration of a trademark. This period may be extended by another 10 years. The right of priority may be used within a period of six months from the date of filing the initial request for registration.

The People's Republic of Bulgaria applies the international classification of trademarks. For a request to have a trademark or a mark of services registered, and for publishing the registration, a fee is collected according to the established tariff. Interested persons and organizations may also request legal protection of the name of origin of the goods.[41]

The registration of every name of origin takes place on the basis of a separate request at the Institute of Inventions and Rationalizations, to which a document is attached attesting the prepaid fee for registration and publication.

The name of origin may be registered by any body corporate or physical person who engages in an economic activity at a given place if the qualitative properties of the goods produced or sold by them correspond to the specific properties typical of the name of origin.

Arranging for the patenting abroad of Bulgarian inventions is entrusted to the Institute of Inventions and Rationalizations.[42] All arrangements regarding the issuing of patents for foreign inventions in Bulgaria and the registration of Bulgarian trademarks abroad and foreign trademarks in Bulgaria are handled through the Bulgarian Chamber of Commerce and Industry.[43]

Licensing

According to Bulgarian law, the following items may be the object of a license contract: inventions enjoying legal protection; inventions, technical achievements, technical know-how, industrial experience, and production secrets not enjoying legal protection; industrial models, trademarks, and legally protected methods for the production of new kinds or varieties of agricultural crops or animal breeds, as well as the results of such production; industrial technologies; and so on.[44]

License contracts may be concluded with foreign organizations, persons, and firms only by the specialized foreign trade organizations entrusted with such activity. For the implementation of the import and export of licenses and models and for foreign trade activities connected with scientific and technical cooperation, a specialized foreign trade organization, the Technika State Foreign Trade Enterprise,[45] has been established.

By way of exception, other foreign trade organizations may also conclude license contracts in specified cases, namely, when a license is acquired for the needs of a state economic trust serviced by the respective foreign trade organization; when a license is connected with production cooperation; or when a license is granted under more favorable conditions in a regular commercial transaction.[46]

The typical object, character, and legal nature of license contracts place the foreign trade organizations that have been charged with their conclusion and fulfillment in a peculiar position. The Technika State Foreign Trade Enterprise is not the "owner" and has no established de jure or de facto monopoly over inventions, industrial models, trademarks, know-how, or other scientific achievements.

The question thus arises as to how the license grantor will be considered as a party in a license contract. The solution involves certain difficulties, as there is no special normative stipulation in Bulgaria governing the order and manner of granting licenses abroad for Bulgarian inventions or other scientific and technical achievements and for the mutual relations arising from such activity.* In order for the Technika State Foreign Trade Enterprise successfully to fulfill the functions assigned to it in this respect and enter into such a contract as licenser, it makes use of a form of representation. It is only in its capacity as a representative of a Bulgarian juridical or physical person having an established de jure or de facto monopoly that the Technika State Foreign Trade Enterprise may conclude such a license contract.

In the case of contracts for the acquisition of licenses by the Technika State Foreign Trade Enterprise or another specialized Bulgarian foreign trade organization, a peculiar situation also arises in that the license is not intended for its needs, but rather for the needs of other economic enterprises—a trust or other domestic enterprise—and, for this reason, all rights ensuing from the license contract have to be transferred to them. The solution to this issue is found by including in the license agreement a special clause that envisages the possibility of transferring the rights acquired under the license to other Bulgarian organizations. In practice, the foreign trade organizations transfer the rights acquired under license contracts to the respective economic organizations through an internal contract, in which all the terms of the agreement concluded with the licensor are obligatorily included.

The purchase and sale of licenses in the People's Republic of Bulgaria is effected mainly with firms and persons of the nonsocialist countries,[47] since the principle of the free-of-charge delivery of scientific and technical achievements has been adopted among the CMEA member countries.

INDUSTRIAL COOPERATION AND
MIXED ENTERPRISES

Industrial cooperation, as a contemporary form of international economic relations, finds increasing application in Bulgaria's foreign

---

*For this reason, it is necessary to rely upon the general regime of Bulgarian civil law and the regime of import and export activities, established by the Law on Foreign Trade.

trade with the nonsocialist countries. This development has led to the setting up of a special legal regulation for such activity.

The basic legal sources regulating industrial cooperation are the Constitution of the People's Republic of Bulgaria and the Law on Foreign Trade.

Industrial cooperation between Bulgarian economic organizations and firms from the nonsocialist countries, whether effected in the People's Republic of Bulgaria, in the partner's country, or in a third country, is a form of international economic relations according to the Law on Foreign Trade and is embraced by the state monopoly over foreign trade. For this reason, contracts for industrial cooperation may be concluded only by organizations to which the Council of Ministers has granted this right.[48]

The conducting of negotiations and the signing of the contract and its fulfillment are effected jointly by the specialized foreign trade organization and the respective state economic trust to which the production of the articles that are the object of cooperation is entrusted.

In the case of contracts for industrial cooperation, the special competence of the socialist organizations must also be observed both with respect to the production activity of the state economic trust and the trade activity of the foreign trade enterprises. The nonobservance of this requirement leads to the nullity of the transaction and more specifically to its nonexistence, as a result of which it cannot be subsequently confirmed or approved by the state bodies. If the fulfillment of the contract is also connected with production activity and the nomenclature of another economic organization in the country, then the Ministry of Foreign Trade decides which organization is to sign the contract. In such cases the organization that has signed the contract is obliged to secure its fulfillment in advance through respective internal contracts.

The normative acts envisage a special procedure for conducting negotiations and concluding contracts for industrial cooperation, which may only take place with the permission of the Commission for Economic, Scientific, and Technical Cooperation, an organ of the Council of Ministers.[49] If there is no such permission, the contracts concluded are null and void.

Contracts for industrial cooperation between Bulgarian foreign trade and economic organizations and firms from Western countries are of various forms, depending on the subject of the contract. Bulgarian organizations, provided they have obtained permission in advance, may conclude contracts for industrial cooperation in the following fields: (1) exploitation of licenses, documentation, know-how, exchange of technical information, and so on, paid for through deliveries of articles produced as the result of such exploitation; (2) delivery of factories and separate complete lines of production, paid for with the articles produced by the delivered factories or production lines; (3) specialization in the production of separate machine types and capacities, and cooperation in sales in third markets; (4) joint production of machinery, equipment, and spare parts, as well as of other kinds of industrial production in the chemical, food, or light industries; (5) subcontracting; (6) joint execution of complete deliveries and assembly work; and (7) joint construction and operation of production capacities outside the People's Republic of Bulgaria.

The wide range of economic purposes defines also the great variety of juridical forms. With the exception of the contract for specialization, all other juridical forms that are used in industrial cooperation are derived from other, simpler international and economic relations. Typically, there is an organic tying up of the separate rights and obligations, under different contracts, of the actual community of interest and the respective juridical interdependence of the obligations of the parties. Production that is the result of industrial cooperation with Western firms is under the same regime as domestic industrial production.

A special department of the Bulgarian Chamber of Commerce and Industry is responsible for facilitating the establishment of contacts between Western firms and Bulgarian organizations interested in industrial cooperation. Through this department, information can be obtained, contacts established, and concrete themes of cooperation elucidated.

A foreign firm interested in industrial cooperation with Bulgarian organizations must submit satisfactory data regarding the level of technology involved; the market possibilities for the sale of the production that will be the object of their cooperation, the relevant juridical and fiscal regime in its own country, and the possibilities for inclusion in the contracts of the necessary guarantees for fulfillment of the contractual obligations and achievement of the necessary technical and economic objectives.

The Bulgarian foreign trade organizations provide any necessary guarantees and financing in accordance with the conditions of the contract through the Bulgarian Foreign Trade Bank.

Foreign firms may also propose industrial cooperation directly to the Bulgarian foreign trade organizations. They may obtain information regarding the areas of interest to Bulgarian foreign trade organizations through (1) direct contact with Bulgarian foreign trade organizations; (2) the Bulgarian Chamber of Commerce and Industry in Sofia; or (3) the Bulgarian sections and mixed commissions, wherever these have been established at chambers of commerce and industry or economic chambers in other countries.

Most Bulgarian foreign trade organizations represent entire branches of Bulgarian industry, a situation that facilitates the examination of proposals for industrial cooperation.

In order to ease industrial cooperation, firms and enterprises of nonsocialist countries may set up their own representations in Bulgaria through the offices of "Interpred," whose activities include those connected with industrial cooperation.

Taking into consideration the fact that in Bulgaria there is no detailed regulation of mixed companies and that there exist certain restrictions of a constitutional character (for instance, the ownership of the basic funds belongs only to the state), the setting up of mixed companies operating in Bulgaria is not desirable. The desired economic results could be achieved by combining different contract forms.

On the other hand, companies established in foreign countries with Bulgarian participation could be successfully used in industrial cooperation, and more particularly for industrial activities in the country of the partner or in a third country. In addition, such companies are of special interest in organizing cooperation in the sales of products that are the result of cooperation agreements.

When concluding a contract for industrial cooperation, specification of the applicable law is of essential significance, to remove all doubts, which is most desirable in the case of long-term economic relations.

Although existing legal regulation and the state and party line favor the development of industrial cooperation with nonsocialist countries, in practice such cooperation is still rather poor. The company form is used very rarely with the seat and activity of the company outside the People's Republic of Bulgaria. Nevertheless, through the contracts for industrial cooperation that have already been concluded, a certain economic effect is being realized—introduction of the achievements of technical progress, mastering the production of new goods, use of the resources of foreign partners together with a more effective use of the production capacities of Bulgaria, expansion of industrial exports, and increased effectiveness and profitability of Bulgarian foreign trade.

SETTLEMENT OF FOREIGN TRADE DISPUTES

The Foreign Trade Arbitration Commission at the Chamber of Commerce in Sofia, a permanent arbitration body, was set up in 1952. The structure, organization, and proceedings of this commission were governed by the Rules for the Proceedings before the Foreign Trade Arbitration Commission at the Bulgarian Chamber of Commerce, approved on February 19, 1952 by the Presidium of the Chamber of

Commerce. This state of affairs was preserved until May 1, 1969, when the new Regulation of the Arbitration Court at the Bulgarian Chamber of Commerce, approved on April 28, 1969, came into force, according to which, in place of the Foreign Trade Arbitration Commission, an Arbitration Court was set up at the Bulgarian Chamber of Commerce. The Arbitration Court is still functioning and is now known as the Arbitration Court at the Bulgarian Chamber of Commerce and Industry, because in 1973 the Bulgarian Chamber of Commerce was renamed the Bulgarian Chamber of Commerce and Industry.50

The Arbitration Court is a special national jurisdiction for the settlement of foreign trade disputes and is not a part of the system of the state courts. Its legislative basis as a body administering justice is contained in Article 19, paragraph II, of the Civil Procedure Code (in force since February 11, 1952), which allows, as an exception, the establishment of a court of conciliation only for cases between socialist organizations based in the People's Republic of Bulgaria and foreign enterprises, firms, and persons. The Regulations of the Arbitration Court widen this competence to include disputes to which only foreign enterprises, firms, and persons are parties. The attachment of the Arbitration Court to the Bulgarian Chamber of Commerce and Industry is justified by the functional link of these two institutions with foreign trade. The link between the Arbitration Court and the Bulgarian Chamber of Commerce and Industry manifests itself both with respect to the nomination of the court staff, the arbitrators, and the administration of its arbitration activity. This structural, organizational, and financial link, and the dependence of the Arbitration Court upon the Bulgarian Chamber of Commerce and Industry, does not mean that in its arbitration activity the Arbitration Court is subordinated to the organs of the Bulgarian Chamber of Commerce and Industry. As a court, it is absolutely independent, because the arbitrators and the Arbitration Courts in general in their administration of justice are subject only to the law and their inner conviction.

The court is made up of arbitrators entered in the List of Arbitrators by decision of the Executive Committee of the Bulgarian Chamber of Commerce and Industry. Their number is not limited; nor is their mandate limited. An arbitrator may lose his status as an arbitrator only by being struck off the list, which is a public document available to any interested party in the People's Republic of Bulgaria or abroad.

The proceedings before the Arbitration Court are governed by the Regulation for the Arbitration Court at the Bulgarian Chamber of Commerce and Industry, which sets forth the basic rules of procedure, which are as follows:

1. The competence of the court, as set forth in paragraphs 8 and 9 of the regulation, extends to

(a) disputes between Bulgarian and foreign enterprises, firms, and persons;

(b) disputes between foreign enterprises, firms, and persons if the parties have concluded an arbitration clause referring the dispute to the court. The regulation also recognizes a so-called tacitly reached arbitration agreement, such as when the defending party, without having challenged the competence of the court, performs actions before it connected with the hearing of the case;

(c) disputes with respect to which the competence of the court has been envisaged in an international treaty or other act that has binding force for the parties.

2. Applicable rules of procedure:

Paragraph 12 of the regulation states that the Arbitration Court hears cases within its competence in accordance with the rules of procedure contained in the regulation. Consequently, the basic law of procedure that governs the arbitration proceedings is the regulation. In all matters not settled by the regulation, the general rules of the Bulgarian Civil Procedure Code are applicable, to the extent they can be applied in view of the character of the arbitration proceedings.

3. A deviation from this basic rule is contained in paragraph 12 (II) of the regulation: When the competence of the Arbitration Court stems from an arbitration agreement between the parties, the rules of procedure agreed upon in that agreement are applicable, provided they do not contradict the principles of the regulation.

4. The official court language is Bulgarian. It is permissible, however, for documents and evidence to be presented in a foreign language. In this case the secretary of the court orders their translation.

The rules of procedure of the Bulgarian Arbitration Court conform to the basic principles that are applied in arbitration proceedings in general. An arbitration procedure begins with the filing of a claim in triplicate, a copy of which is served on the adverse party. A necessary condition to proceeding further is the payment of the arbitration fees in advance, according to a special tariff. Within a month of service of the claim, the defendant may file a reply indicating his position with respect to the claim, setting forth exceptions, and indicating supporting evidence. All service is effected by registered mail, telegram, or Telex notification.

The court in charge of the case, as a rule, consists of three arbitrators. As an exception, when the parties have expressly stated their consent, the case may be heard by only one arbitrator nominated by them. When the court consists of three members, each of the parties nominates its arbitrator, and the two arbitrators within a period of 15 days choose the presiding member of the court.

The hearing of the case takes place at the seat of the court. The hearing may be attended, apart from the parties, witnesses, and experts, only by persons expressly approved by the parties. If needed, a translator is appointed. In the arbitration proceedings, unlike the proceedings before the ordinary courts, foreign lawyers are allowed to appear and plead.

The normal conclusion of an arbitration case is the award of the court. In connection with the issuance of the award, the regulation contains certain basic rules:

The award is decreed after a consultation of the arbitrators, which is secret.

The award is decided by majority vote, the presiding arbitrator being the last to vote.

The award is decreed in accordance with the laws or custom; if these do not exist, then by analogy; and when even analogy cannot be applied, then in accordance with the requirements of justice. The award thus decreed is final and not subject to appeal. Any award for payment entitles the interested party to a writ of execution. If in the award no time has been set for its execution, it must be executed at once. If the award has not been voluntarily fulfilled, it may be compulsorily enforced in the order established by the Bulgarian Civil Procedure Code on the basis of a writ of execution, which at the request of the interested party is issued by the Sofia City Court.

The People's Republic of Bulgaria has ratified the 1958 European (Geneva) Convention on International Commercial Arbitration (the decree for its ratification was published in the State Gazette No. 23 of 1964) and the 1958 United Nations (New York) Convention on the Recognition and Enforcement of Foreign Arbitral Awards (the Decree for its ratification was published in State Gazette No. 57 of 1961). The latter convention was signed by the People's Republic of Bulgaria under the following reservation: "Bulgaria will apply the Convention for Recognition and Enforcement of the Awards decreed on the territory of another contracting country. With respect to awards decreed on the territory of noncontracting parties, it will apply the Convention only to the extent that state recognizes reciprocity."

In accordance with Chapter 3 of the 1958 Convention, the recognition of the effect of an arbitration award and the allowance of its enforcement takes place in compliance with the rules of procedure that are applied in the territory of the country where recognition and enforcement is requested. With respect to Bulgaria, this principle requires application of the Bulgarian procedural norms contained in Articles 303 and 307 of the Bulgarian Civil Procedure Code. That is to say, in the territory of Bulgaria a foreign award will be recognized if it does not contradict Bulgarian laws. A foreign award is not recognized and is not enforced when

(a) a claim for ownership or other property right over real estate situated in the People's Republic of Bulgaria is decided with it;

(b) according to Bulgarian law, the dispute was not within the jurisdiction of the tribunal in the state in which the award was issued;

(c) the defendant was a Bulgarian citizen and did not take part in the case, and proof is not submitted that at least one summons was served for his appearance at the proceedings;

(d) between the same parties, for the same claim, and on the same legal grounds, a Bulgarian court decision has already gone into effect, or if between the same parties, for the same claim, and on the same legal grounds, there is a pending case before a Bulgarian court that was brought prior to the effective date of the award by the foreign tribunal; and

(e) the award is null and void according to the laws of the country in which it was decreed.

NOTES

1. Art. 13 of the Constitution of the People's Republic of Bulgaria, State Gazette No. 248, December 6, 1947, reads: "Foreign and domestic trade are directed and controlled by the state. An exclusive right may be introduced for the state to produce and trade in articles which are of essential significance for the national economy and for the needs of the people."

2. Art. 13/1 of the Constitution of the People's Republic of Bulgaria, State Gazette No. 39/1971.

3. See Art. 2 of the Constitution of the People's Republic of Bulgaria.

4. G. S. Georgiev, Rise and Essence of Socialist Monopoly of Foreign Trade at 59 (Sofia: Research Institute of Foreign Trade, 1967).

5. Such are, for example, the Unified Plan for Social and Economic Development, the Law on Foreign Trade (State Gazette No. 94, December 5, 1969) and the Regulation for the Application of the Law on Foreign Trade (State Gazette No. 101, December 22, 1970).

6. G. S. Georgiev, "Socialist Monopoly of Foreign Trade," Lectures for Postgraduate Specialization of Jurists Vol. 4 at 39-40 (Sofia, 1971).

7. See Art. 103, Paragraph 11 of the Constitution.

8. See Art. 4 of the Law on Foreign Trade.

9. See Art. 5, para. II, of the Law on Foreign Trade.

10. See Art. 4 of the Regulation for the Application of the Law on Foreign Trade.

11. See Arts. 6-9 of the Law on Foreign Trade.

12. According to Art. 12 of the Law on Foreign Trade, "The foreign trade organizations in the sense of this Law are state trusts and enterprises, companies, cooperative and other organizations, which have been granted the right to perform foreign trade activities."

13. See Art. 13 of the Law on Foreign Trade.

14. Art. 13 of the Regulation for the Application of the Law on Foreign Trade.

15. See Art. 1, para. II of the Model Constitution of Foreign Trade Companies, State Gazette No. 11, February 7, 1967.

16. See Art. 3(c) of the Law on Foreign Trade and Art. 10 of the Regulation for the Application of the Law on Foreign Trade.

17. See Art. 2 of the Model Constitution of Foreign Trade Companies.

18. The order for registration and the Regulation for Keeping the Records are determined in a Regulation for Registering Foreign Trade Enterprises in the Register of the Chamber of Commerce, Sofia, State Gazette No. 44, June 6, 1966.

19. According to Art. 14 of the Law on Foreign Trade, "Foreign trade organizations are not held responsible for debts of the state and other organizations, just as the state is not held responsible for debts of the foreign trade organizations."

20. See Chapter VI of the Regulation for the State Economic Organizations, State Gazette No. 4, January 12, 1973.

21. See Section VI of the Model Constitution of Foreign Trade Companies.

22. A detailed list of the foreign trade organizations in the People's Republic of Bulgaria with indication of their activity appears in the manual Bulgarian Foreign Trade Organizations, published by the Bulgarian Chamber of Commerce, Sofia, 1972.

23. According to Art. 2 of the Law on Foreign Trade, "Foreign trade activities in the sense of this Law include all transactions for the export and import of goods, for re-export and transport, representation, foreign trade advertisement and publicity connected with them, for the protection of copyrights and rights over inventions, trademarks and industrial models, transactions in the field of technological experience and other activities connected with international economic relations, when one of the contracting parties is a foreign body corporate or physical person."

24. See Art. 5(o) of the Regulation for the Application of the Law on Foreign Trade.

25. Published in State Gazette No. 21, March 11, 1965, as amended, State Gazette No. 66, August 28, 1966, State Gazette No. 26, May 21, 1968, and State Gazette No. 29, May 11, 1969.

26. See for further details Articles 103, 104, 227, 228, 240, 241, and 242 of the Penal Code (published in State Gazette No. 26, April 2, 1968); the Law on Currency Valuables Transactions and Currency Control (Chapter X, published in State Gazette No. 51, July 1, 1966); Decree for the Conclusion of Foreign Trade Transactions and for Prohibited for Import and Export Currency Valuables, Articles, Printed Matter and Other Materials (published in State Gazette No. 4, January 14, 1955), and so on.

27. V. Koutikov, "Application of Foreign Laws to Bulgarian Foreign Trade Purchases and Sales," in Legal Foundations of Foreign Trade of the People's Republic of Bulgaria, to be published by Naouka i Izkoustvo State Publishing House, Sofia.

28. Art. 17, para. I of the Law on Foreign Trade.

29. Art. 9 of the Law on Obligations and Contracts, State Gazette No. 275, November 22, 1950, as amended State Gazette No. 69/1951, No. 92/1952 and No. 85/1963.

30. Id.

31. Art. 7 of the Law on the Contracts of Socialist Organizations, State Gazette No. 85, November 1, 1963.

32. Compare Arts. 46, 103, 134, 201, and so on of the Maritime Navigation Code, State Gazette No. 55, July 14, 1970 and No. 56, July 17, 1970.

33. Compare Art. 2 of the General Delivery Conditions of Goods between Organizations of the CMEA Member Countries (General Delivery Conditions, CMEA, 1968).

34. Approved by Decree No. 55 of the Council of Ministers of November 26, 1968, published in State Gazette No. 100 of December 24, 1968 and No. 101 of December 27, 1968.

35. The People's Republic of Bulgaria is a member of: (1) the Paris Convention for Protection of Industrial Property of March 20, 1883 in its Lisbon version of October 31, 1958 (pursuant to Ukase No. 633 for Joining, of September 2, 1965 of the Presidium of the National Assembly, published in State Gazette No. 75 of September 24, 1965), and its Stockholm version of July 14, 1967 (pursuant to Ukase for Ratification No. 3 of the Presidium of the National Assembly of January 8, 1970, published in State Gazette No. 5 of January 16, 1970); and (2) the Convention for the Establishment of a World Organization for the Intellectual Ownership of July 14, 1967 (pursuant to Ukase for Ratification No. 3 of the Presidium of the National Assembly, published in State Gazette No. 5 of 1970). The functions of a State Organ according to Art. 12 of the Paris Convention are performed in the People's Republic of Bulgaria by the Institute of Inventions and Rationalizations, Sofia. The legal protection of inventions, industrial models, trademarks, and names of origin is provided for in the People's Republic of Bulgaria in the Law on Inventions and Rationalizations (published

in State Gazette No. 81, October 18, 1968), the Regulation for the Application of the Law on Inventions and Rationalizations (published in State Gazette No. 48, June 20, 1969), the Law on Trade Marks and Industrial Models (published in State Gazette No. 95, December 5, 1967), and the Instruction for the Application of the Law on Trade Marks and Industrial Models (published in State Gazette No. 26 of April 1, 1969).

36. According to Art. 12 of the 1968 Law on Inventions and Rationalizations, "An invention is a new creative technical solution of a problem, more expressive and more useful as compared to the existing level of technology, which refers to any field of the national economy, science, culture, care of public health, and national defense." Bulgarian law recognizes the concept of "discoveries," according to Art. 7 of the 1961 Law on Discoveries, Inventions, and Rationalization Proposals (published in State Gazette No. 10, Feb. 3, 1961): "A discovery is the establishment of hitherto law-governed regularities, phenomena and peculiarities in the material world." The discoverer may request the Institute of Inventions and Rationalizations to issue an author's diploma. No author's diplomas may be issued for discoveries in the fields of social science, geography, archaeology, geology, and paleontology. Discoveries cannot be the object of any industrial ownership under Art. 1 of the 1883 Paris Convention. The 1961 Law on Discoveries, Inventions, and Rationalization Proposals was partially revoked by the 1968 Law on Inventions and Rationalizations noted above, but the provisions regarding discoveries were left in force.

37. Art. 23, para. II of the Law on Inventions and Rationalizations
38. Art. 31 of the Law on Inventions and Rationalizations.
39. According to Art. 24 of the Law on Trade Marks and Industrial Models, "An industrial model is every new outer shaping of an article, consisting in the peculiarities of form, drawings, ornaments, combination of colours and the like, which can be achieved through industrial production."

40. According to Art. 2 of the Law on Trade Marks and Industrial Models, "Trade marks and marks for services are the signs with which an enterprise, the organizations and persons designate the goods which they produce or deliver, or the services which they perform, to distinguish them from the goods or services of the same kind of other enterprises and persons.

"With trade marks can be designated articles intended to be included as component parts, elements or details in other finished articles, regardless of the fact that separate marks exist for them."

41. According to Art. 38 of the Law on Trade Marks and Marks for Services, "The name of the origin of goods is the geographical designation of the country, region, or locality, which serves for

designating the goods originating from that country, region, or locality, the properties or peculiarities of which goods are exclusively or predominantly dependent on the geographical environment, including the natural conditions or production traditions."

42. See Art. 45 of the Law on Inventions and Rationalizations.

43. See Arts. 48 and 49 of the Law on Trade Marks and Industrial Models and Art. 15 of II and III and Art. 16 of the Law on Inventions and Rationalizations.

44. See Art. 2 of the Law on Foreign Trade and Art. 2 of the Regulation for Purchasing Licences (published in State Gazette No. 55 of 1971).

45. The Technika Foreign Trade Enterprise was established by virtue of Decree No. 91 of the Committee for Economic Coordination at the Council of Ministers on March 1, 1971 on the basis of part of the offices of the Technoimpex State Commercial Enterprise, which until then handled the import and export of licenses in the country.

46. Art. 13, para. I of the Regulations for Purchases of Licences reads, "Licenses are bought by the specialized Technika Foreign Trade Enterprise. When the purchasing of licenses is connected with production cooperation, or the license is supplied at more advantageous conditions through a regular commercial transaction, the licenses are purchased by the respective foreign trade organizations servicing the state economic trust."

47. After this manuscript was prepared, Decree No. 39 of the Central Committee of the Bulgarian Communist Party and the Council of Ministers of the People's Republic of Bulgaria for the accelerated introduction of scientific and technical achievements in production was published in State Gazette No. 73, Sept. 14, 1973. This decree settles basic questions connected with the introduction of highly efficient technologies and articles in production; improvement of planning of technical progress in the national economy; creation of the necessary material, financial, and labor conditions for the rapid introduction of scientific and technological elaborations and world experience in production; material and moral incentives in the introduction of scientific and technical achievements in production; improvement of management aimed at introduction of scientific and technological achievements in production; and enhancing the role of the party and other public bodies and organizations along this line. This decree does not change the regime of legal protection of inventions, industrial models, and trademarks established by the Law on Inventions and Rationalizations and the Law on Trade Marks and Industrial Models.

48. Art. 11 of the Law on Foreign Trade.

49. According to Art. 12, para. II of the Regulation for the Application of the Law on Foreign Trade Ministries, "departments and economic organizations may not conduct negotiations to assume

obligations and to conclude foreign trade transactions, except by permission from the Council of Ministers. The Council of Ministers has authorized the Commission for Industrial, Scientific and Technological Cooperation to issue these permissions for conducting negotiations and concluding contracts for industrial cooperation."

50. All normative materials have been published in Foreign Trade of the People's Republic of Bulgaria (Sofia: Naouka i Izkoustvo Publishing House, 1969).

8

THE CZECHOSLOVAK SOCIALIST REPUBLIC

Karl Heřman

Since October 1968 the Czechoslovak Socialist Republic (ČSSR) has been a federation of the Czech Socialist Republic (ČSR) and the Slovak Socialist Republic (SSR).[1] In conformity with the principles of the socialist system, practically all industry and building, all foreign trade, banking, and insurance, a major part of internal trade, and about 45 percent of agriculture are nationalized property. Cooperatives operate mainly in agriculture and in small industries. The private sector is mainly in agriculture and does not have practical importance in economic activity.

The basic principles of Czechoslovak foreign trade, its institutional framework and management, are contained in the 1960 Constitution,[2] the State Organization of Foreign Trade and International Forwarding Agencies Act,[3] and the Czechoslovak Federation Constitutional Act[4] in light of the 1970 Constitutional Act.[5]

INSTITUTIONAL FRAMEWORK, FOREIGN TRADE MANAGEMENT, AND PLANNING[6]

Institutions

The Federal Ministry of Foreign Trade is the central agency of the state administration and has the general power of foreign trade management. It enacts general rules of a juridical, economic, organizational, and administration character and establishes basic foreign trade targets for organizations acting in foreign trade in light of the State Plan of Development of National Economy. Among the various other responsibilities of the ministry are managing the Central Customs Administration;[7] inspecting the quality of exported goods through a body known as the Technical Control of Foreign Trade; and supervising commercial departments abroad (mostly attached to the Czechoslovak diplomatic missions).

The state, as such, does not engage in foreign trade. This is done through a number of entities expressly authorized for the purpose. The most usual organizational form for entities authorized to engage in foreign trade is the so-called foreign trade corporation, established by the Ministry of Foreign Trade. In addition, certain joint-stock companies[8] established by other socialist organizations may engage in foreign trade upon authorization by the ministry.[9] Likewise, certain associations or cooperatives may be given such authorization. The authorizations are framed in such a way as to avoid overlapping responsibilities by the various organizations authorized to conduct foreign trade.* From the point of view of the foreign businessman, this means that (with very few exceptions) there is but one Czechoslovak partner for a given type of foreign trade operation.

When establishing a foreign trade corporation, the Federal Ministry of Foreign Trade provides it with basic capital. In the case of joint-stock companies, associations, or cooperatives, the individual socialist organizations responsible for their creation become shareholders or members in the newly created organization and contribute the capital.

Foreign trade organizations are thus actual owners (not only trustees) of their assets. They are also registered in the land register as owners of immovable property. Therefore, foreign creditors or claimants can, if their claims are not settled voluntarily, attach such property and enforce their claim against the property. Due to this arrangement, any fear that insolvency might occur is quite unwarranted.

All foreign trade organizations are independent juridical persons, distinct from the state. This means that the state is not responsible for the liabilities of these organizations. Nor are particular organizations responsible for the liabilities of other organizations or of the state.

Every foreign trade organization must be registered in the companies register kept with the court of first instance within whose jurisdiction the organization has its seat. Information regarding the legal standing of the organization is entered in the register. Thus, the register would indicate the areas in which the organization is competent to conduct foreign trade activities, its basic capital, the

---

*In addition, the ministry may make exceptions to authorizations previously granted, either for an individual transaction or for all future transactions of a specific type.

names of persons authorized to act on its behalf, and so on. Anyone may consult the register and take abstracts therefrom.

Certain other organizations render services in connection with foreign trade transactions, such as transport;[10] banking;[11] insurance;[12] quantative, qualitative, and technical surveillance of goods as well as other control services;[13] and advertising, publicity, and organization of exhibitions.[14] In addition, a number of specialized entities provide intermediary services[15] in Czechoslovak foreign trade, such as commercial representatives of foreign firms. We might also note two institutions with a promotional role in foreign trade, the Chamber of Commerce of Czechoslovakia and the Research Institute of Foreign Trade.

The Chamber of Commerce is composed of Czechoslovak foreign trade organizations, trusts of industrial branches, most important manufacturing enterprises, and business and other concerns engaged in economic activities, as well as scientific and social institutions, on the basis of voluntary membership. The Chamber fulfills more or less the same tasks as chambers of commerce abroad. Cooperation with other chambers of commerce is institutionalized through joint chambers of commerce or mixed committees. Among the Chamber's many responsibilities are maintaining an independent international trade arbitration court, discussed more fully below.

Foreign Trade Management and Planning

The state monopoly of foreign trade means, in principle, a system of foreign trade management by the state using plans, economic tools, administrative measures, and so on.[16] This concerns foreign businessmen only to the extent that in Czechoslovakia they have to deal with partners known in advance.

The state as such is not directly engaged in trading. Through the Federal Ministry of Foreign Trade, it determines only the subjects (that is, entities) who are solely authorized to carry out foreign trade transactions. To a certain extent this simplifies considerably the task of making contact with Czechoslovak importers and exporters. Deals can be negotiated only with partners authorized under Czechoslovak legislation to engage in foreign trade operations. Any foreign trade deal concluded with a party lacking such an authorization would be null and void.

Like all economic activities in a socialist system of government, foreign trade is, naturally, planned. Economic planning is based on the provisions of the 1960 Constitution[17] and on a 1970 Act on Economic Planning.[18] The approved plan of foreign trade forms an integral part of the entire plan of national economy. The targets of the State Plan of Development of the National Economy bind both the Federal Ministry

171

of Foreign Trade and individual foreign trade organizations. The latter must abide by this plan when negotiating their respective trade deals.

However, the position of foreign partners of Czechoslovak foreign trade organizations is not directly affected by the plan. It is up to the individual organizations to see to it that their contracts are in conformity with the targets of the plan. Once concluded, a contract is valid, and the Czechoslovak organization authorized to deal in foreign trade is not entitled to rely on alleged lack of conformity of the contract with the plan as against its foreign partners.

The targets of the plan are expressed only in values and quantities of commodities, and not by territorial designations or by determination of individual trade partners. The significance of this arrangement may be seen in the fact that no business partner of a Czechoslovak foreign trade organization suffers from any kind of discrimination. Whether a deal will be completed or not depends solely on the terms offered.

FOREIGN TRADE PROCEDURES AND PRACTICES

Individual foreign trade organizations are absolutely free, to the extent allowed by the relevant legislation, to select their partners and to negotiate with them the terms and conditions of individual deals and so on, so that the conclusion of contracts and their execution are, in principle, the same as elsewhere in the world.

Importing and Exporting

In Czechoslovakia, no export or import licenses are needed for individual exports or imports. In most instances, it would be superfluous for a foreign businessman to try to find out whether or not a contract with a particular foreign trade organization involving export or import of goods is subject to any further licensing procedures.

There are exceptions to this rule—for example, contracts relating to industrial property rights (notably the sale and purchase of licenses), cooperation agreements, and agency contracts providing for representation of foreign companies in Czechoslovakia, as well as contracts related to joint ventures in foreign countries. All these contracts need specific prior approval by the Federal Ministry of Foreign Trade.

Customs Regulations and Tariffs

As noted above, the system of customs regulations and tariffs is regulated by the Customs Act.[19] The supreme authority in customs and tariffs is the Central Customs Administration, operating under the Federal Ministry of Foreign Trade. In conformity with the Customs Act, the duty of the Central Customs Administration is to control the goods passing the Czechoslovak border and to carry out the provisions concerning imports, exports, and transit of goods, including all movables such as vehicles, coins, exchange, and payment documents.

The Czechoslovak Customs Tariff consists of two parts: part I, Import, and part II, Export; in part II, no rates are assessed. Part I is set up as a two-column-rate tariff; in the first column are autonomous rates and in the second conventional rates. It is divided into 51 classes and contains altogether 657 items. For the purposes of customs statistics, the customs tariff has been adapted to the Brussels Nomenclature, and a full revision of it in accordance with this nomenclature is anticipated.

The Czechoslovak Customs Tariff provides mostly for specific rates; ad valorem rates apply only to a few items (mostly chemicals). According to the Customs Tariff, materials and minerals, pigments and tanning materials, precious metals, and scrap materials, as well as works of literature and objects of art are duty free.

Most-favored-nation treatment is granted to imports from more than 100 countries, based on Czechoslovakia's membership in the GATT.[20] For imports from these countries, the rates will also be successively reduced in accordance with the obligations Czechoslovakia accepted in the Kennedy Round. Under certain conditions, imports from developing countries are getting preferential rates. There is no customs-free area in the country.

Advertising and publicity material are cleared without duty in conformity with the provisions of the Geneva Convention of November 7, 1952. Samples with commercial value are cleared for temporary import, but security may be required for the appropriate amount of duty plus 10 percent to cover charges and taxes. For imports of samples, ESC (Economic and Social Council) of ATA carnets may be used as well. Special regulations apply to imports of plants, animals, as well as vegetable and animal products.

In the case of exports, the exporting organization has to submit an application to the customs office together with all required documents (including forwarding documents). The customs office compares the application and attached documents with the goods to be exported, checks these against the contract, and supervises packing and marking, and the quantity, quality, and the value of the goods.

Foreign Exchange Regulations

The foreign exchange regulations in Czechoslovakia are based on the Foreign Exchange Act[21] and on the provisions regarding its execution.[22] Some aspects are regulated by further rules, such as the Monetary Reform Act[23] and the State Bank of Czechoslovakia Act.[24]

Any operation involving transfer of foreign exchange across the Czechoslovak border needs approval by the Federal Ministry of Finance. Foreign trade organizations are exempted from this duty. Provided their acts are not ultra vires, these organizations are statutorily authorized to transfer payments to foreign countries for goods purchased or services received, in currencies agreed upon.

Import of foreign coins, notes, and payment documents is unrestricted. Their export by foreign citizens is possible only if their import is duly evidenced. Such proof may be given by presenting the Foreign Exchange Import Declaration. Any Czechoslovak customs authority will hand over the respective form to any foreign citizen crossing the border and certify the data stated therein.

Czechoslovak coins and notes serve only for internal purposes, and, consequently, their export and import are not allowed. Dealing with Czechoslovak money abroad is considered unlawful. Therefore, coins and notes the export or import of which has not been specifically permitted will be forfeited upon seizure at the border, and their holder will be summarily convicted and fined.

As a rule, the Commercial Bank of Czechoslovakia is entrusted with payments connected with export and imports of goods and services that are carried out in accordance with the terms of financial and payments agreements concluded by the Czechoslovak Government and in accordance with the terms governing the individual deals. In the absence of a relevant intergovernmental agreement, the bank abides by the terms of the individual contracts.

Czechoslovak foreign trade organizations have the right to grant as well as accept short-term commercial credits, provided such credits are related to the exercise of their activities (that is, are not ultra vires). Long-term credits are granted by the Commercial Bank of Czechoslovakia, or, if such credit is state credit, their grant has to be approved by the respective governmental agency. The Commercial Bank of Czechoslovakia may also guarantee long-term credits accepted by Czechoslovak foreign trade organizations in connection with imports of goods (especially machinery and equipment).

Representation of Foreign Companies in
Czechoslovakia

A foreign businessman who wishes to be represented on the
Czechoslovak market may conclude an agency contract. Such an agreement can, however, be concluded only with an authorized organization.
This means an organization that has been granted authorization to
engage in foreign trade transactions; also representation of foreign
companies must be within the scope of its activities, or it must receive specific authorization from the Federal Ministry of Foreign
Trade to act as an agent of a foreign company.[25]
It may be worth recalling that direct imports of consignment
stocks of products of a foreign principal can never be affected through
agents. In order to be valid, any contract involving representation of
foreign companies has to be approved in advance under the relevant
provisions of Czechoslovak law by the Federal Ministry of Foreign
Trade. Without such approval, the contract is null and void. Organizations authorized to represent foreign businessmen in Czechoslovakia
may undertake these activities only after receipt of the appropriate
authorization by the Federal Ministry of Foreign Trade.

FOREIGN TRADE CONTRACTS

Rules governing creation and performance of contracts are
enacted in three mutually independent Codes: the Civil Code, the
Economic Code, and the International Trade Code. All economic relations, although naturally in conformity with the socialist economic
system, are by no means uniform, and it is vital to understand this
three-way division by Code in order to determine which law concerns
a particular transaction.
The Civil Code[26] regulates relations between socialist organizations and individuals, and mutual relations between individuals arising
inter alia in the course of satisfying their personal needs. By "individual" is meant a physical person, irrespective of citizenship. It
is interesting to note that the Civil Code imposes a much higher duty
upon socialist organizations (particularly in respect of sales for consumption) than upon individuals in their relations inter se.[27]
The Economic Code[28] governs the relations between socialist
organizations participating in the planned economic activity of the
state, while fulfilling the planned economic targets. Such relations
may not be contrary to the goals of the plan, and the Economic Code
authorizes the establishment, change, or abolition of binding obligations between these organizations without their consent, normally by
order of an Economic Arbitration Court.[29]

The International Trade Code (ITC)[30] regulates relations in international business if according to Czechoslovak conflict of law rules, Czechoslovak law is to be applied.[31] In relations governed by the ITC, the principle of equality under the law for all participants is observed,[32] so that the law does not accord preference to the interests of any one state. The intention is to increase legal security in international economic relations and thereby to contribute to their development on the basis of mutual advantage.

Whether a transaction falls under the ITC depends upon objective criteria based on its business/commercial character[33] and whether it is an international transaction within the meaning of the Code. It should be noted that certain international transactions are governed by special rules—for example, those between member states of the Council for Mutual Economic Assistance (CMEA), which are governed by the 1968 CMEA General Conditions for the delivery of goods (published under no. 12/1969).

The individual provisions of the ITC are relatively detailed, particularly for contracts of sale and legal claims connected therewith. This means that in cases where Czechoslovak law is applicable, the rights and duties of the parties (unless fixed by contract) will be governed by the ITC. Broad contractual autonomy is available to the parties, and they are free to depart from most of the statutory provisions.[34] Only the rules that, owing to their nature, must be mandatory, constitute an exception to this principle. The mandatory rules are all expressly enumerated in the Code.[35] Also, the ITC does not affect certain other legal provisions.[36]

It is significant that under the 1963 Private International Law Act a foreign law chosen by the parties need not have a particular relationship to the transaction.[37] If the parties do not choose a governing law, their mutual relations are governed by the law the application of which "is in keeping with a reasonable settlement of the respective obligation"[38]—surely a nondiscriminatory principle.

During the preparatory work on the ITC,[39] both Czechoslovak experience in international trade as well as foreign legal rules were taken into account. Particular attention was focused on the first attempt to unify the rules of international sale, the so-called Hague Draft of the Uniform Law of International Sale Convention of 1956. The ITC entered into force before the final Hague draft of 1964. Owing to the function that the ITC is intended to fulfill, there was no mechanical reception of existing provisions. Quite the contrary, the rules of this Code form a system acceptable to all participants in international trade. The Code remains, however, a Czechoslovak national legal norm, applicable only in cases where the proper law of the legal relation is—in accordance with the rules of conflicts of law—Czechoslovak law.

It would be impossible to summarize here the more than 700 provisions of the ITC covering such diverse matters as agency, bailment, and insurance. It may be of particular interest, in connection with the international sale of goods, that the ITC does not give the same preference to "commercial usage" as does the 1964 Hague Uniform Sales Law,[40] thus reflecting the view that legal insecurity should be avoided in international trade.

The ITC, like the 1968 CMEA General Conditions of Delivery and the Hague Uniform Sales Law, makes a distinction between substantial breaches (which allow a party to terminate) and minor breaches.[41] The ITC also provides for compensation of damages that are a foreseeable, direct, and normal consequence of the breach.[42] The concept of "directness" can, of course, give rise to difficulties in applying the principle to particular cases.

The ITC reflects support of the principle of objective liability—that is, that a party is liable for damages caused by his failure to fulfill an obligation regardless of culpability. This will entail liability if the other party relies on the validity of the contract and the contract is void because of initial impossibility of performance.[43] Similarly, subsequent impossibility of performance may not preclude liability for damages. The ITC provides that only certain circumstances of an extraordinary nature (such as war and natural disasters), which actually prevent performance (and not merely make performance more burdensome), will extinguish liability for damages.[44] Thus, the failure to obtain necessary licenses would not relieve a party of liability for damages in the event this precludes performance.[45] Likewise, there are situations that may relieve a party from damages, but not of his duty to perform.

PROTECTION OF INDUSTRIAL PROPERTY RIGHTS AND LICENSING AGREEMENTS

The protection of industrial property rights (to patents, industrial designs, registered trademarks, and so on) in Czechoslovakia is regulated by international agreements to which Czechoslovakia is a party as well as by internal legal provisions. Copyright is regulated by a separate set of legal provisions.[46] It might also be mentioned that in Czechoslovak law, there are provisions protecting enterprises as well as consumers from unfair competition and/or deceptive allegations regarding the origin of goods.[47]

Protection of Inventions

The protection of inventions is based on Czechoslovakia's participation in the 1883 Paris Union Convention on the Protection of Industrial Property in its July 14, 1967 Stockholm version.[48] Domestic
Czechoslovak legal provisions of interest to foreigners in this regard
include a statute on discoveries, inventions, improvement suggestions,
and industrial designs that entered into force January 1, 1973.[49] In
principle, foreign citizens enjoy the same rights and are bound by the
same duties, on a basis of reciprocity, as citizens of the ČSSR. The
provisions of international conventions to which the ČSSR is a party
are not affected by the January 1, 1973 act.

An invention, in the meaning of this act, includes any solution of
a technical problem that is now and constitutes, in comparison with
prior art, a progress manifested by a new or higher effect. The invention must be capable of industrial production or applicable in the
course of production or operation. Applications for protection of inventions are to be lodged with the Office for Inventions and Discoveries, whereupon the applicant is vested with the right of priority.
The right of priority, in accordance with the International Convention,
must be claimed by the applicant in the application within three months
thereof.

The rights of authors of inventions are confirmed by a certificate
of authorship or by a patent. In cases where a certificate of authorship
is granted, the invention becomes Czechoslovak national property.

An invention application in which the grant of a patent has been
applied for (this is practically always the case with foreign applicants),
must be filed by the author of the invention, his heir, or assignee.
Foreigners can file their applications only through the authorized
organizations.[50]

Patents are granted to the applicants of the respective invention,
or to their legal successors (patent owners); however, the name of the
author is always quoted in the Patent Letter. The patent owner is
entitled to give consent to Czechoslovak or foreign exploitation of the
invention (by license) or to assign the patent thereto. Both the license
to exploit a patent and a patent assignment must be in writing and
registered in accordance with the law. Patent rights are for 15 years
from the filing date of the invention application.

Protection of Industrial Designs

In the sense of the abovementioned act, an industrial design is
any solution of the external condition of a product both planar and
three-dimensional, new and usable in industrial production. External
condition in this respect consists especially in a particular external

178

appearance, shape, contour, design, color, or in particular arrangement of colors, or in combination of these features. The industrial design is deemed usable in industrial production if, according thereto, products can be repeatedly produced in an industrial way.

The subject matter of an application for industrial design is deemed new unless it has been known in Czechoslovakia or anywhere abroad, prior to the date from which the right of priority has been vested in the applicant, from publicly accessible sources.

The legal provisions for the protection of inventions are generally applicable mutatis mutandis to protection of industrial designs. The industrial design for which a patent has been granted is protected for five years from the filing date of the application; the term may be extended upon request for an additional five-year period.

Protection of Trademarks

The protection of trademarks is based on international agreements to which Czechoslovakia is a party,[51] and on the 1952 Trademarks and Protected Designs Act.[52]

Marks are on application registered in the Register of Trademarks kept by the Office for Inventions and Discoveries. The organization for which the trademark is registered has the exclusive right to its use from the date of application. This right is not effective against former users of the same or a similar unregistered mark for the same products.

Protection lasts 10 years from the date of application. An extension for a further 10-year period is possible on application. Rights to trade marks may only be transferred together with transfer of ownership to the organization on whose behalf they have been registered; in case of a corporate reorganization, consent of the Office for Inventions and Discoveries may be requested.

Licensing Agreements

Contrary to other foreign trade contracts, these agreements may be concluded by Czechoslovak organizations other than foreign trade organizations—that is, by organizations that are the owners of the rights in question. In order to be valid, license agreements have to be arranged through the organization authorized for this purpose by the Federal Ministry of Foreign Trade.[53] All licensing agreements require foreign exchange approval. Only upon receipt of this approval is the Czechoslovak partner in the contract authorized to transfer money abroad through the Commercial Bank of Czechoslovakia.

Royalties or lump-sum payments that the foreign party receives from its Czechoslovak counterpart are subject to taxation in the ČSSR under the relevant provisions of the Income Tax Act. The tax is collected by way of deductions before making transfers to a foreign country.

INDUSTRIAL COOPERATION

If an agreement relates to this kind of cooperation—for example, cooperation in industrial production, scientific research, and technical development including production sharing—it may be entered into by an industrial enterprise as well as a foreign trade organization. However, should such an agreement relate solely to commercial cooperation (without any element of industrial collaboration), it could be concluded only through and by the responsible foreign trade organization.

In accordance with a 1972 act,[54] agreements on industrial cooperation can be concluded by Czechoslovak organizations only with the prior approval of the Czechoslovak authorities. Without such an approval, the agreement would be null and void. The federal or national authority controlling the organization intending to enter into the agreement in question is charged with making this decision, after consulting the Federal Ministry of Foreign Trade, the Federal Ministry for Technical Development and Investments, the Federal Ministry of Finance, and the State Bank of Czechoslovakia. The authority competent to approve the agreement decides on the form of cooperation as well. It is of interest that Czechoslovak organizations are free to associate and to establish consortia for concluding cooperation agreements.

Approval of the cooperation agreement does not automatically supply the authorization needed for participation in foreign trade activities or replace the permission needed in accordance with the Foreign Exchange Act.[55] If the cooperation agreement provides for deliveries of goods to or from Czechoslovakia, the Federal Ministry of Foreign Trade may, upon request of the Czechoslovak partner, grant an exception authorizing him to execute directly imports and exports provided under the terms of the cooperation agreement in question. The same procedures apply mutatis mutandis to discontinuation of cooperation agreements.

Czechoslovak organizations also have the power to enter into joint venture contracts or to acquire shares in foreign companies. Such arrangements need approval by the appropriate Czechoslovak authorities. Capital participation by foreign companies in Czechoslovak organizations is not allowed.

SETTLEMENT OF FOREIGN TRADE DISPUTES

Settlement of foreign trade disputes by arbitration must be considered as the most usual proceeding adopted by the Czechoslovak organizations participating in foreign trade operations.

Foreign Trade Arbitration Machinery

Foreign trade arbitration machinery is based at present on a 1963 Act relating to arbitration in international trade and to enforcement of awards.[56] It deals with such matters as the arbitrability of issues, choice of law governing the validity of arbitration agreements, and enforcement of awards. As noted previously, an international trade arbitration court is attached to the Chamber of Commerce of Czechoslovakia. Its rules[57] are binding for the organization and the procedure of the arbitration. This Arbitration Court has jurisdiction to decide cases if an arbitration agreement has been entered into by the parties, provided the matter involves a property claim arising out of international trade and would otherwise be within the jurisdiction of the courts.[58]

We need not go into detail on the organization of foreign trade arbitration in the ČSSR. However, several aspects may be noted. One is that Czechoslovak citizenship is not a condition for inclusion in the list of arbitrators maintained by the Arbitration Court, from which the arbitrators must be selected. Another is that after the statement of claim has been filed, but before the appointment of an arbitrator, the president of the court may in urgent cases and upon application secure evidence and/or appoint experts for this purpose. A party may apply to the district court or other competent authority for an interlocutory order.

The parties may agree that their claim is to be decided either by one single arbitrator or by three arbitrators. Where reference is to three arbitrators, all decisions are taken by a majority vote, the chairman voting last.

Each party may challenge an arbitrator; in such a case, the Arbitration Board constituted under the rules decides about the justification of the challenge. Awards must be in writing and, unless otherwise agreed between the parties, must state the grounds for the decision. Upon service, an award acquires the force of res judicata and is enforceable in courts of law. The same applies to a settlement concluded before the arbitrators and signed by them.

Recognition and Enforcement of Arbitration
Clauses and Awards

The arbitrability of matters referred to arbitration as well
as other requisites to the substantial validity of an arbitration agreement are governed by the 1963 Arbitration Act, noted above, if the
award is to be made in Czechoslovakia. However, where the legal
relation is not exclusively a Czechoslovak one, the parties may select
a foreign law to govern the arbitration agreement. The act provides,
however, that the choice must not be contrary to a "reasonable arrangement."

Awards rendered in a foreign country are granted recognition
in the ČSSR and enforced as Czechoslovak awards, if reciprocity of
treatment is secured. Recognition or enforcement is withheld in cases
where the award is subject to appeal or to other remedy, suffers from
certain defects (including lack of jurisdiction, lack of procedural due
process),[59] or is contrary to public order.

The 1963 Arbitration Act is applicable only to cases where no
international treaty binding the ČSSR prescribes a different result.
Such treaties are of three types: bilateral treaties on legal assistance
and enforcement of judicial decisions; multilateral conventions on the
recognition and enforcement of foreign arbitral awards; and bilateral
treaties of commerce regulating, inter alia, commercial arbitration.
The individual provisions of the bilateral treaties differ considerably
from each other, and their applicability is to be examined case by
case. It is, however, worth mentioning that the ČSSR has adhered to
the four principal multilateral conventions on the recognition and
enforcement of arbitral awards.[60]

NOTES

1. Czechoslovak Federation Constitutional Act No. 147/1968
(reference is to the annual Collection of Laws of the Czechoslovak
Socialist Republic).
2. Act No. 100/1960.
3. Act No. 119/1948.
4. Act No. 147/1968, Arts. 8 and 16.
5. Act No. 125/1970.
6. See generally, S. Hanak, "Foreign Trade in the Czechoslovak
Socialist Republic" (unpublished paper, 1973) (the author is particularly
indebted to Dr. Hanak for allowing him to draw upon that paper in the
preparation of this chapter); Information on the External Economic
Relations of the Socialist Countries: The Czechoslovak Socialist
Republic, in Czech, ed. J. Hajek (Prague: Chamber of Commerce,

1971); J. Kalvoda et al., Payments and Credits in Relations with Foreign Countries, in Czech (Prague: SNTL, 1971); J. Nykryn et al., Foreign Trade in the Economy of Enterprises, I, English trans. by M. Bachrach (Prague: SPN, 1971).

7. Activities of the Customs Administration are governed by the Customs Act No. 36/1953.

8. Founded under the provisions of Act No. 243/1949.

9. See the Ordinance of the Ministry of Foreign Trade No. 121/1968, amended by Ordinance No. 164/1969.

10. The transport organizations include the Czechoslovak State Railways, Czechoslovak Elbe-Oder Navigation Company, Czechoslovak Danube Navigation Company, Czechoslovak Ocean Shipping Company Ltd., Czechoslovak Airlines, and Czechoslovak Automobile Transport. Forwarding services for foreign trade are concentrated in the Foreign Trade Corporation Čechofracht with its branch offices and operating departments outside Prague, which also act as representatives of a number of shipowners for the ČSSR.

Classification of ships and technical supervision over their construction are carried out by the Czechoslovak Ships Register as an independent specialized classification organization.

11. Foreign trade banking services are rendered by the Commercial Bank of Czechoslovakia Ltd. Apart from services connected with foreign trade payments, it finances foreign trade organizations, grants credits in foreign exchange, purchases and sells foreign exchange to organizations, carries out foreign exchange conversions, and represents the financial interests of Czechoslovak organizations wherever they participate in joint ventures.

12. Especially in connection with transporting goods abroad, insurance of foreign credits, special risks/insurance of trade fairs, factories and/or equipment under construction abroad, reinsurance operations, and so on—provided by a special department of the Czech Insurance Corporation.

13. Carried out by the Foreign Trade Corporation Inspekta, sometimes operating also under contract with foreign surveillance companies.

14. There are two organizations at the disposal of foreign businessmen in this respect. The Czechoslovak Advertising Agency RAPID is mainly concerned with publicizing Czechoslovak goods abroad, whereas the advertising agency of the Czechoslovak Press Office, Made in Publicity, is more involved in giving publicity to foreign goods and services in Czechoslovakia. The enterprise Brno Fairs and Exhibitions not only organizes the international Brno Fairs and administers the exhibition grounds there but also engages in projects, production, and installation of equipment for fairs and exhibitions abroad.

15. In this context, we might also note the foreign trade corporation Transakta, which helps arrange special operations such as barter for foreign as well as domestic organizations, and the foreign trade corporation Polytechna, which specializes in arranging for patents licenses, know-how agreements, scientific and technical cooperation arrangements, and so on.

16. See Act No. 119/1948.

17. Arts. 7-15.

18. No. 145/1970.

19. Supra note 7.

20. Ratification published under No. 59/1948.

21. No. 142/1970.

22. No. 143/1970.

23. No. 41/1953.

24. No. 144/1970.

25. See the Ordinance of the Ministry of Foreign Trade on the representation of foreign firms in foreign trade, No. 136/1968, as amended by the Ordinance of the Federal Ministry of Foreign Trade, No. 165/1969.

26. No. 40/1964.

27. See, for example, Civil Code, secs. 225, 246-255; compare sec. 400 and, more generally, part V of the Civil Code.

28. No. 109/1964.

29. Id., sec. 118. See also Secs. 161-164, 270.

30. Legal Relations Arising in International Business Transactions Act (International Trade Code, hereinafter referred to as the "ITC"), No. 101, 1963. In 1967 the Chamber of Commerce in Prague published an introduction and commentary to the ITC by L. Kopac. See infra note 39.

31. Act concerning Private International Law and the Rules Relating Thereto, No. 97, 1963. See ITC, sec. 3. The 1963 Private International Law Act also governs such matters as recognition and enforcement of foreign judgments in the ČSSR.

32. ITC sec. 1.

33. See ITC sec. 2(2).

34. See also section, entitled "Institutions," of this chapter.

35. ITC sec. 722. It might also be noted that, although Czechoslovak law contains a so-called public-order exception to the application of foreign law (Private International Law Act, supra note 31, sec. 36), this is very strictly defined, and there have been no reported cases where the exception has been invoked to defeat application of a foreign law in foreign trade transactions.

36. The ITC does not affect State Organization of Foreign Trade and International Forwarding Agencies Act No. 119.1948; Corporations Act No. 243/1949; Bills of Exchange and Cheques Act No. 191/1950; or Maritime Navigation Act No. 61/1952.

37. See, for example, sec. 9 of the 1963 act, supra note 31.

38. Id., sec. 10(1); see also sec. 10(2).

39. See Introduction to the English Translation of the International Trade Code, by L. Kopac (Prague: Chamber of Commerce of Czechoslovakia, 1967).

40. ITC sec. 118; compare Hague Uniform Sales Law sec. 9 (2).

41. ITC secs. 235-238.

42. ITC sec. 254(2).

43. ITC sec. 28

44. ITC sec. 252.

45. Id.

46. Notably Act No. 35/1965.

47. See E. Borsky, "Unfair Competition in Foreign Trade" (in Czech), Zahranicni obchod (Foreign Trade Journal) No. 3/1972 at 25-26. Czechoslovakia is a party to the 1891 Madrid Convention on suppression of delusive allegations on the origin of goods (Ordinance of Ministry of Foreign Affairs No. 419/1921) and 1958 Lisbon Convention on protection of indications about the origin of goods and their international registration (No. 81/1970). In this connection, a December 1973 act on protection of indications about the origin of goods may also be mentioned.

48. Not yet published in Czechoslovakia as this chapter was written. For the Lisbon version of 1958, see No. 90/1962.

49. Nov. 1, 1972, No. 84/1972. See also, Ordinances of the President of the Office for Inventions and Discoveries concerning administrative proceedings (No. 104/72) and external relations (No. 107/1972) in respect of these matters.

50. These organizations are UTRIN (Institute for Technical Development and Informations), U Sovovych mlynu 9, Prague 1 (also exclusively authorized Czechoslovak industrial rights registrations abroad); Solicitor's Office (Advokatni poradna), No. 1, Narodni trida 32, Prague 1; and Solicitor's Office (Advokatni poradna), No. 10, Zitna 25, Prague 1.

51. 1891 Madrid Convention on the international registration of factory and trademarks in the 1957 Nice version (published by No. 67/1967) and the 1957 Nice Convention on the international classification of goods and services in relation to factory and trademarks (published by No. 65/1963).

52. No. 8/1952. The section of the 1952 act concerning protected designs has been replaced by the Discoveries, Inventions, Improvement Suggestions, and Industrial Designs Act, No. 84/1972, supra note 49.

53. This organization is Polytechna Foreign Trade Corporation, which may conclude such contracts in its own name but on behalf of the respective Czechoslovak organizations.

54. No. 85/1972, which took effect Jan. 1, 1973.

55. No. 142/1970.

56. No. 98/1963. In 1967 the Chamber of Commerce of Czechoslovakia published an English translation of this act, by S. Hanak, and an English translation (by F. Preisler) of the Commentary to the Act (by M. Stastny and S. Hanak).

57. Rules of the Arbitration Court of the Chamber of Commerce of Czechoslovakia in Prague, approved by the Ordinance of the Minister of Foreign Trade of Dec. 10, 1965, No. 140/1965. An English translation of the rules is available at the Secretariat of the Arbitration Court of the Chamber of Commerce of Czechoslovakia in Prague and is reproduced in Kos-Rabcewicz-Zubkowski, East European Rules on the Validity of International Commercial Arbitration Agreements, at 135 (1970).

58. Act No. 98/1963, sec. 2.

59. Id., sec. 20.

60. Protocol on Arbitration Clauses and Submission concluded in Geneva on September 24, 1923 (No. 181/1931); Convention on the Execution of Foreign Arbitral Awards concluded in Geneva on September 26, 1927 (No. 192/1931); Convention on the Recognition and Enforcement of Foreign Arbitral Awards concluded in New York on June 10, 1958 (No. 74/1959); and European Convention on International Commercial Arbitration concluded in Geneva on April 21, 1961 (No. 176/1964).

9

THE GERMAN
DEMOCRATIC REPUBLIC

Lothar J. Schultz
Clifford A. Rathkopf, Jr.

The German Democratic Republic (GDR) is at present undergoing significant changes in terms of its international political and economic status, as a result of the "normalization treaty" with West Germany, its entry into the United Nations, and its increasing diplomatic recognition by the Western countries. It is already one of the 10 most industrialized countries in the world and has the highest living standard among Comecon members and the second highest foreign trade turnover among these countries.[1] However, the vast majority of this trade has been with other Comecon countries[2] and with developing countries for the raw materials that it generally lacks at home.* Recently there have been signs that the GDR is willing to deal with the West on a somewhat more expanded scale than formerly,[3] and it can be expected, in view of the technology and industrial goods that the GDR is capable of exporting, that such willingness should be reciprocated.[4]

However, in viewing the trade with the West that exists at present, and which is expected to expand, one must always note the special position of West Germany (including West Berlin). Despite the normalization treaty and mutterings from its partners in the European Community,[5] West Germany still maintains that trade with the GDR is "internal trade," a relationship recognized in the 1957 West German Protocol to the Treaty of Rome. This means that the common external tariff walls of the European Community do not apply to "interzonal" trade, and consequently, there are no tariff barriers whatsoever to such trade, a position dear to both Germanys. It is not surprising to

---

*The only raw materials that the GDR has in quantity are bituminous coal and potash, while it must import anthracite coal, oil, iron ore, and wood.

find that in 1972, for example, while import and export trade of the GDR with Western developed countries was 30.8 percent and 21 percent, respectively, of total foreign trade, West Germany's proportions of those figures were roughly 40 percent and 55 percent. In fact, in terms of total trade, West Germany remains the second largest trading partner of the GDR, behind the Soviet Union.[6] One can thus expect that the major portion of increased trade with the West will be with the sister state of the GDR. Still, there is an increasing pattern of trade with other industrialized Western nations, which can be seen as having recently entered its third major phase.

In the first phase, corresponding to the GDR's first five-year-plan (1951-55), during which the newly founded republic (1949) began to expand its productive capacities, the first foreign trade agreements with Western countries were concluded. These agreements were on a nongovernmental basis, concluded on behalf of the GDR by the Chamber of Foreign Trade (Kammer fur Aussenhandel).[7] The Western trading partners were also chambers of commerce or special industrial organizations, because the GDR had not been accorded de jure recognition by the countries in question. These agreements generally ran for one year.

The agreement reached with Austria in 1953 is typical of the early agreements. It was concluded for one year with the Austrian Chamber of Commerce (Österreichische Bundeshandelskammer). Payments were to be in U.S. dollars and to amount to $18 million on both sides. For financial arrangements, a special account in that amount was opened by the state banks of the trading partners. A list of the types and quotas of goods to be delivered was attached to the agreement.[8]

During this first phase, the Chamber of Foreign Trade of the GDR concluded trade agreement with the Scandinavian countries (Sweden, Denmark, and Norway), France, Italy, the United Kingdom, and some other Western European states.

In 1963 the so-called New Economic Policy (Neues Ökonomishes System) was introduced in the GDR. Its aim was to establish a more decentralized system of management and to improve production efficiency, especially in the metal-working and chemical industries, by, for example, seeking more intensive contacts with Western countries. Nongovernmental representative offices of the GDR's Chamber for Foreign Trade were established in various Western European countries, including France, the United Kingdom, and Italy.

During the second phase of GDR foreign trade with the West, which began at the end of the 1960s, long-term nongovernmental agreements were introduced. One of the first long-term agreements was concluded with France, on January 28, 1970. It was to run for a period of five years and provided for a doubling of trade by 1975. In 1970, five-year trade agreements of a rather general nature were also concluded with Italy, the Netherlands, and Austria, and a three-year agreement was reached with the United Kingdom. All these contracts provided for payments to be settled through the State Bank of the GDR and Western banks in hard currency. Within the framework of these agreements, GDR foreign trade enterprises subsequently concluded detailed contracts with Western firms.

The third phase of GDR foreign trade policy began in 1971, with the implementation of the 1971-75 five-year plan, at which time its international political status was improving considerably. During this phase, the GDR has achieved diplomatic recognition by almost all Western states and established diplomatic relations with them. The GDR has now become even more active in its Western trade, and in concluding intergovernmental trade and cooperation agreements with Western nations.

The first such agreement, concluded for 10 years in 1973 between the Foreign Trade Ministries of the GDR and Italy for economic, industrial, and technical cooperation, called for equality of trading rights and reciprocity and stressed cooperation in the industrial field, especially in the metal-working, electrical, and chemical branches. The agreement provides for the establishment of an intergovernmental joint commission meeting alternately in East Berlin and Rome, which is to establish subcommissions to deal with various branches of the economy. At the same time the GDR reached agreement with the Italian Foreign Trade Institute on the mutual exchange of experts, technical documentation, and jointly held fairs and exhibitions. Within the framework of this intergovernmental cooperation agreement, the Italian company Montedison concluded a five-year cooperation agreement with the GDR foreign trade enterprise Chemie-Export-Import calling for an exchange of licenses, know-how, technical documentation, and specialized personnel.[9] Similar intergovernmental agreements on economic, industrial, and technical cooperation were concluded for 10 years in July of 1973 between the GDR and France,[10] and in December of that year with the United Kingdom.[11]

In August 1973, the GDR concluded a five-year trade agreement with Austria, providing for the establishment of a similar intergovernmental joint commission. The partners agreed to abolish the previous financial clearing system and to arrange their payments directly through banks in convertible currency.[12] The GDR is to supply primarily machinery and industrial equipment; and Austria, consumer goods and miscellaneous manufactured metal products.

Despite these new long-term agreements, the GDR has been reluctant to enter into joint industrial cooperative production with Western firms or other forms of direct foreign investment in the GDR, although this is not so in regard to other Comecon countries.[13]

Partially this may be explained by doctrinaire politics and unsatisfactory prior experience. On the other hand, most of such arrangements entered into subcontract out relatively labor-intensive work. This latter element is one that cannot be well utilized in the case of the GDR, however, since the GDR is so labor-poor that is must import workers from other Comecon lands, notably Poland and Hungary. The present situation of not accepting cooperation agreements in regard to foreign plant investment may, however, change.

Aside from such long-term contracts for trade and intergovernmental cooperation mentioned above, the chief area of growth for the GDR with the West appears to be in the area of technological license exchanges. Not only does the GDR have advanced technology that it appears to be willing to license to Western firms, but it also is in need of intensifying labor productivity during the present Five-Year Plan and will most likely be desirous of importing technology, both for consumer and industrial goods. Licensing procedures with the GDR are discussed below.

INSTITUTIONAL FRAMEWORK AND FOREIGN
TRADE PLANNING

As a country with a state monopoly[14] over foreign trade, the GDR has a very centralized system in this field. The Ministry of Foreign Trade acts as a central and controlling authority of all institutions and agencies of foreign trade. It coordinates its activities with the State Planning Commission, which elaborates annual and five-year plans on foreign trade, setting up targets for particular goods. In this way, foreign trade is an integral part of the uniform state plan.

A 1973 Decree of the Council of Ministers on the Work, Rights, and Duties of Publicly Owned Enterprises, Combines, and Associations of Enterprises[15] regulates the legal regime of all forms of the state-owned enterprises. The decree reflects a trend toward more centralized control of the economy. The decision-making power of enterprises is apparently to be more limited, with a greater degree of control to be exercised by the central authorities, namely the ministries, the State Planning Commission, and the Council of Ministers.

The GDR's production enterprises are of three types. The first, of which there are some 13,800, is the individual enterprise (Volkseigene Betriebe, or VEB), headed by a director and directly subordinated to the competent ministry. The second type, a larger group, is composed of large industrial plants, or groupings of individual enterprises belonging to the same branch, the so-called combines (Kombinate). Their member firms are juristic persons with some degree of autonomy and authority to conclude contracts with other enterprises. The third type, the largest group, is composed of so-called associations of publicly owned enterprises (Vereinigung der Volkseigenen Betriebe or VVB). The status of individual members of a VVB is more restricted than in a combine, and their activities are closely integrated under general management. Only the Council of Ministers can establish or dissolve a VVB.

Until nationalization in 1972, the GDR permitted a number of privately (6,479) and semiprivately (3,166) owned enterprises to function. This sector of the economy contributed about 15 percent of the total gross national product, mostly engaged in the textile and light industry fields. About 100,000 artisans have been permitted to continue to work privately.

The foreign trade relationships for almost all of these productive enterprises are supervised by a special ministry, as in most socialist countries. This, the Ministry of Foreign Trade (Ministerium für Aussenhandel), is responsible to the Council of Ministers. Most of the foreign trade operations are conducted by some 53 foreign trade enterprises (Volkseigene Aussenhandelsbetriebe), established either as national enterprises (a VEAHB) or, more likely, as a limited liability company (Aussenhandelsgesellschaft m.b.H.) whose shares are owned by the producing VEB's.

The minister of Foreign Trade names the directors of these foreign trade enterprises and has the right to establish new enterprises and dissolve old ones. Directives and ordinances (Verfügungen und Mitteilungen) of the ministry, not generally available in the West, are directly binding on these enterprises.

The ministry is represented outside the GDR either by special Trade Representatives, who work directly with the foreign trade enterprises and carry out any necessary transactions where they are located, or by the special commercial sections in the GDR embassies.

The foreign trade enterprises are organized according to specific product lines, with authority to conduct import and/or export operations for all productive enterprises in that economic branch. Thus, for example, Industrieanlagen-Import is charged with responsibility for the import of complete plants in the chemical, electrochemical, metallurgical, and other industries. Foreign trade enterprises are juristic persons and not entities of the state, with the result that they are generally to be divorced from any claim against the state, and may sue and be sued on their own. As such they are empowered to negotiate with foreign firms and to conclude contracts in their own name for the account of the productive enterprises, retaining the status of a vendor or vendee. Nevertheless, they work closely with the productive enterprises for whom such foreign trade is industrially significant. Although in regard to imports, such enterprises always act as buyers, they act as commission agents for these productive enterprises in export operations.[16]

The foreign trade enterprises now have contractual relationships with the domestic firms, the so-called "foreign trade internal connections" (Aussenhandelsbinnenbeziehungen), regulated by the 1965 Code of Contracts (Vertragsgesetz)[17] and ordinances thereunder. Under the prior system of autonomy under the relevant foreign trade plan, there was little or no financial incentive or possibility for domestic producers to have the prices of goods delivered to foreign trade enterprises correspond with world prices, since they could not negotiate or conclude export contracts in their own name. This very often resulted in losses for the foreign trade enterprise upon export, which would have to be compensated for by the state. Since the foreign trade enterprises now act as export commission agents, the gain or loss on export is directly reflected in the balance sheets of the producer,[18] forcing them to bring their export prices into a realistic world position and, at the same time, allowing them some discretion in the submission of their own economic plans, rather than having the price in the plans imposed on the basis of extraneous considerations.

In addition, certain large VVB's with manufacturing facilities and certain major manufacturing concerns, such as Carl Zeiss, Chemieanlagen, and Uhrenfabrik, are permitted to have their own combines for centralized foreign sales efforts. Furthermore, for certain products, export contracts regarding deliveries of goods, repairs, construction, and technical performance may be concluded without the intermediary of a foreign trade enterprise.[19] Such export contracts nevertheless remain under state control, since they require the consent of the relevant foreign trade enterprise[20] in order to be effective.[21] Import contracts with non-Comecon country firms, on the other hand, do not have this problem, since prices are not those established by plan; therefore, all import contracts are concluded by the foreign trade enterprises.

Legally independent of the Ministry of Foreign Trade but nevertheless under its supervision is the Chamber of Foreign Trade (Kammer für Aussenhandel, or KfA). Created in 1952 by enterprises and institutions participating or interested in the foreign trade of the GDR, the KfA plays an important role in helping Western firms make trade contacts and resolve disputes in the GDR as well as promoting and supporting the trade activities of GDR producing and foreign trade enterprises.

In addition to maintaining an Arbitration Court, the KfA operates an Average Adjuster Office for overseas and inland shipping averaging problems. The KfA itself is active in establishing and nurturing contacts with foreign chambers of commerce and other nongovernmental organizations, as well as with foreign industries, and of particular significance, has commercial representatives in the Western states that do not diplomatically recognize the GDR. With the GDR's entry into the United Nations and more widespread diplomatic recognition, this latter function is gradually being replaced by GDR Embassy commercial sections. Finally, the KfA issues and certifies certificates of origin and other necessary international documentation.

In addition to the export-import enterprises, there are various enterprises for such related service functions as international freight fowarders (VEB Deutrans), international freight carriage (VEB Deutfracht), sea transport (VSB Deutsche Seerederei Rostock), air transport (Interflug GmbH), and insurance (Deutsche Auslands- und Rückversicherungs AG Berlin, or DARAG). Several others will be mentioned in the next section.

The financial and banking system of the GDR is headed by the State Bank (Staatsbank der DDR). It issues currency, fixes foreign exchange rates, and controls note circulation and all foreign exchange transactions. The commercial bank for GDR foreign trade is the GDR Foreign Trade Bank (Deutsche Aussenhandelsbank AG), a joint stock company. The Foreign Trade Bank carries out those financial operations usually connected with foreign trade, such as credit and payment transactions, and provides hard currency credits to GDR foreign trade enterprises for their transactions with Western trade partners. Also the Deutsche Handelsbank AG, established in 1956, is entitled to provide financial arrangements with foreign trade partners. Other GDR banks have responsibilities only for domestic financial operations including lending money to state-owned enterprises. Perhaps the most important of these is the Industrie und Handelsbank. The Bank für Landwirtschaft und Nahrungsgüterwirtschaft is involved in the agricultural field, and the Genossenschaftsbanken für Handwerk und Gewerbe deal with smaller enterprises and artisans.[22]

FOREIGN TRADE PROCEDURES AND PRACTICES

Within the framework of foreign trade, the GDR places great reliance on the use of intergovernmental agreements as a prior condition to any substantial trade in goods or licenses, examples of which are the agreements mentioned above, concluded with Italy, France, Austria, and Great Britain. While long-term agreements are also in effect as to Comecon, these tend to be of a different nature, regulating the intergroup industrial specialization with delivery and acceptance guarantees to ensure that the various central plans properly mesh. The agreements with the Western countries do not contain such delivery and acceptance guarantees, but rather mutual agreements to grant all necessary import and export licenses for the areas of goods in question. Attempts are generally made in these bilateral agreements to equalize the inflow and outflow of goods and licenses with Western countries, to ease the hard currency burden imposed by the nonconvertability of the GDR mark. Once the agreements have been concluded, the foreign trade enterprises and individual Western firms have a frame of reference within which they can structure their contracts.

Importing and Exporting

Because the economy is structured in advance to accept the level of imports and exports that occur, there is no need for customs duties to be imposed. (Special tariffs are imposed should the country of the foreign exporter specifically discriminate against the GDR in foreign trade, and a basic tariff and a tariff on contracts are imposed should such country have a preference tariff system to which the GDR is not admitted.[23]) The function of customs, therefore, is to ensure that such trade flows are in fact in accordance with the established arrangements, including subsidiary matters such as delivery for repair or of spare parts and the like.

Exports to the West, once agreed upon and permitted by the Ministry of Foreign Trade (through the medium of the foreign trade enterprises), are effected by such permits being transmitted to the exporter, who then makes out an application for export clearance (often merely a waybill showing type and route of transport) and an export report. The application is sent to the inland customs office, and the goods then follow. At inland customs, the goods are checked for quantity, assortment, visible quality, value, packing, markings, and loading, to make certain they correspond with both the contractual terms and the permit (both of which are submitted with the application). The goods are then cleared for consignment to the border customs office, where final export permission is given.

The import of goods does not require any special permit, so long as all waybills and other necessary documents clearly state the contract number of the contract concluded with the relevant foreign trade enterprise. However, a customs clearance application must be made out, used in conjunction with the customs inspection of the goods. The submission of an import notice by VEB Deutrans or the Post Office will suffice in lieu of such an application. The application and the bill of lading must be accompanied by currency invoices and goods specifications, showing also the reason for import.

The import and export of free replacement and spare parts necessitated by warranty obligations are not covered per se by a contract and therefore require a special permit of the relevant foreign trade enterprise if their value exceeds 30 marks, or notification to such enterprise if less. The import of samples and specimens is freely permitted without import licensing; export of such items requires a license if the value is greater than 30 marks. The import and export of hazardous goods and of animals and plants or products thereof require special procedures.

In addition to import and export of goods, there is often the necessity for a commercial inspection of goods at some point prior to or at delivery. The East Berlin firm Deutsche Warenkontrollgesellschaft m.b.H., or Intercontrol, performs this function on a contractual basis for domestic or foreign enterprises. Its personnel examine the goods in question to insure they meet all quality and quantity conditions. This can extend to matters such as production supervision, expert opinions, damage evaluations, quality controls, sample laboratory examination, transport loading supervision, and acting as claims agents. The certificates issued by Intercontrol are often employed as evidence of contract performance and as such recognized by banks to initiate payment procedures.[24]

Credit and Banking

As mentioned in the introduction to this section, long-term intergovernmental agreements for trade have a place of great importance in the foreign trade relationships of the GDR. Such agreements are usually accompanied by another accord on payment and clearing, whereby the goods or licenses to be exchanged are valued in hard currency and overdraft types of credit provisions are established. Either the two central banks involved, or often private bank consortia on the Western side and the Deutsche Aussenhandelsbank AG on the other,[25] create reciprocal accounts for crediting of currency flows to arise from the envisioned trade exchange. Once this is done, both sides work out separate export lists with the estimated values of the exports and negotiate to balance the total trade figures. As stated above, these generally are not guaranteed export volume but represent desired trade goals.[26] Normally under such bilateral clearing procedures, the trading partner with an annual surplus of exports increases its imports with the other partner rather than paying the balance in cash. East Germany, with increased diplomatic recognition, is in the process of beginning to replace these agreements with convertible currency agreements with Western countries, such as the recent one with Austria, but maintains a number of them with developing countries.[27]

Once a currency arrangement is worked out, it is possible to use sight letters of credit or even direct cash against shipping documents for payment terms. When credit is involved, letters of credit against drafts are usually preferred, or, if available, export credit via government-sponsored programs. In lieu of such export credits, forfeiture, or discounting of East German bills of exchange, is possible at rates varying from 6.5 to 8.25 percent with specialized Zurich or

London East-West banks. This procedure involves the sale of an acceptance, promissory note, or other financial claim to the bank without a right of recourse by the Western exporter.[28]

Local Agents

Since it is often difficult for Western firms to establish local offices,[29] they may find it necessary to be represented by local agents within the GDR.* There are nine such agencies located in East Berlin, mostly specializing in certain industrial product areas. The oldest and largest of these is Transinter; others include Metama, Textilvertretungen, Interver, and Kontakta. Agreements with these agencies are based on one- or two-year contracts, automatically renewed absent notice.

Such agencies in the GDR are flexible in their approach to accepting clients, usually on the basis of whether the product has a good possibility of being sold within the GDR—that is, is not manufactured locally or in other Comecon countries. It is possible that competing importers would be using the same agency, but only if the competitors are not from the same country. Exclusive agents may be obtained, which normally means the agency employee working exclusively for the importer will be paid a salary in addition to the commission for the agency.[30]

Reaching the Market

There are two general methods of reaching the market in the GDR other than via a local agent or direct representation: advertising and representation at the Leipzig trade fair.

Advertising by Western firms in the GDR is strictly regulated, and the only statutorily permitted advertising[31] must be done through Interwerbung in East Berlin, which distributes mainly through the media of professional journals. Prior to accepting an order, it will test demand and marketing conditions and various import regulations to ensure satisfactory reception.

For Western trading partners, an occasion to arrange contacts with East German enterprises is provided by the fair at Leipzig.

---

*Increasingly, Western countries are establishing commercial offices per se or within embassies that may take over some of the agency functions. For example, the French introduced a commercial office to represent French industries in East Berlin in 1970, and in the same year the Austrian Chamber of Commerce set up a representation body.

This fair, held twice yearly, is the largest in the Eastern countries. At the September 1973 fair some 6,275 firms from 52 countries were represented, including 1,600 firms from Western countries. The Fair Office (Leipziger Messeamt) at Leipzig is a source of useful information on trade possibilities in the GDR.[32]

FOREIGN TRADE CONTRACTS AND
RELATED MATTERS

Foreign trade contracts—that is, contracts concluded between foreign trading partners and either the foreign trade enterprises or individual firms in the GDR, are to be distinguished from economic contracts. The latter are those made between enterprises within the GDR in order to formalize relationships developed for central economic planning[33] and are the contracts regulated by the 1965 Code of Contracts. The former are still governed by provisions of the 1896 Civil Code (Bürgerliches Gesetzbuch, or BGB) and the Commercial Code (Handelsgesetzbuch, or HGB), both of which are still in force in both Germanies.[34]

However, the GDR is in the late stages of revision of both the BGB and the HGB, to make them conform with socialist legal thought. The BGB, last edition published in 1967 by the Ministry of Justice, will be replaced by the Zivilgesetzbuch to regulate relationships between citizens inter se and citizens and institutions of the state, and those few provisions of its Introductory Law dealing with conflicts of law will be replaced with a Code on the Application of Law (Rechtsanwendungsgesetz). The Commercial Code will be abolished and replaced by several other codes of a somewhat more specialized nature, including one regulation of the substance and procedure of foreign trade contracts (its name at present is proposed to be the Aussenwirtschaftsvertragsgesetz).[35] This latter foreign trade law should govern both contracts and forms used in foreign trade, provide a foundation for the creation and/or acceptance of international norms (such as, at present, the General Conditions of Goods Delivery in Comecon and the Hague Convention on International Sales), and take into consideration both national and foreign trade law.[36] These various new codes may be enacted by the end of 1974.

The present HGB provisions dealing with commercial matters are lex specialis and as such exclude provisions of the Civil Code that might be applicable. It is a law divided into four major sections, or "books." The first book deals with the status of merchants and the manner of their doing business; the second, with various forms of partnerships and commercial juridical persons; the third, with the law of commercial acts; and the fourth, with maritime law.[37] The most important section for foreign trade reference is in the third book, Sections 343-460, dealing with such areas as sales, commission sales, freight forwarding, warehousing, and freight hauling. Most of the original provisions of this book are still in force.[38]

The rules of conflicts of law that apply to contractual relationships are based on the 31 articles of the Introductory Law to the BGB (the so-called EGBGB) and the writings of leading commentators and include the following general principles. The legal capacity of a juristic person is determined by the law of the country where it was established.[39] The form of the contract and its formal validity is determined under the law of the place where the contract is made. Application of a foreign law is denied if it runs counter to the fundamental principles of public order in the GDR[40] or would be inconsistent with the principles of good faith or would run counter to the purposes of GDR laws.[41]

The GDR recognizes the concept of autonomy of will in foreign trade contracts. That is, the parties are free to determine the proper law of the contract. If the parties have not chosen a governing law, the law of the seller's country is to be applied.

For property law conflicts with respect to immovables, the law of the country where the property is situated (lex rei sitae) is to be applied. For movables, the law of the country where the object is situated at the time the claim is raised is considered decisive. The regime of movable goods that are in transport (res in transitu) is determined by the law of the sender's country.[42]

The new Code on the Application of Law is being prepared and will soon replace the somewhat limited EGBGB. According to the latest drafts,[43] it has been decided to extract conflicts rules from most of the various laws and codify them as both general and special norms and in doing so incorporate much of the present commentary and customary law in the area, in so far as not contained in specific international bilateral agreements on mutual legal help.

Certain principles of the new law[44] as presently proposed may clarify the general field of conflicts. In the area of contract law, with the exception of labor contracts, the contracting parties should be able to choose the applicable law, which would govern the form of the contract, with the exceptions of contracts dealing with real property (where lex situs would be applicable) and of labor law. A choice of third-country law would not be expected to occur often but should not be disallowed. Should the parties not express any choice, their choice of law might be inferred from any relevant and conclusive behavior of the parties.

Should the choice of law not be expressed nor be capable of inference from the behavior of the parties, certain statutory norms would become applicable. For example, in contracts of sales or production, one would apply the law of the legal residence or seat of the vendor or producer; if a branch office has been the signatory, the law of its legal residence or seat would be applied. In the case of a license contract, normally the law of the licensor would apply, but if technical or scientific services are required of one of the parties under the license, the law of the person who is so performing would take precedence. However, in the case of postsale customer services, the law of the customer's legal residence applies.

Finally, should a case arise where no statutory norms are applicable, reference would be made to a general principle of conflicts law: The law of the legal residence of the party who must perform under the contract (the payment of money not being considered within the scope of such performance) would govern the contract and the relationship of the parties thereto. When this option is not available, the alternative would be the law of the place of signing of the contract (the determination of such a place being ruled by GDR substantive contract law).

Those special contract rules would also be accompanied by several general rules. In the case of a renvoi, GDR conflicts law looks to the whole of the law of a foreign country and if its conflicts law refers back to GDR law, it would accept the renvoi. The law will probably contain no rules as to reference to third-country law in such an examination. If a reference to substantive foreign law is made necessary by a conflicts rule, this rule may be overridden should the foreign law violate good faith or the public order of the GDR. Since the use of public order to avoid foreign law is not looked on with favor, it would be permitted only in individual cases.

The GDR has accepted certain international standards and is a party to a number of multilateral agreements related to foreign trade that have the effect of "internationalizing" GDR law and practice in certain respects. For example, GDR enterprises readily agree to incorporate the International Chamber of Commerce's Incoterms of 1953 in their contracts with foreign partners. Furthermore, the GDR subscribes to the principles of the 1957 General Conditions for the Supply and Erection of Plant and Machinery for Import and Export, prepared under the auspices of the UN Economic Commission for Europe.

The GDR has accepted[45] several international conventions related to the international transport of goods, such as the International Convention Concerning the Carriage of Goods by Rail of 1954; in 1963 the GDR declared her accession to the international Convention of the Unification of Certain Rules Relating to International Carriage by Air, signed at Warsaw in 1929.

With respect to payments and financial transactions, the GDR has acceded to two important international conventions: the Convention

Providing a Uniform Law for Bills of Exchange and Promissory Notes, signed at Geneva in 1930, and the Convention Providing a Uniform Law of Cheques, signed at Geneva in 1931. The GDR has continued to apply the 1933 German Law of Bills of Exchange and Law on Cheques, both of which are also in force in West Germany. These laws are based on the above-mentioned conventions and follow them rather closely.

INTELLECTUAL AND INDUSTRIAL PROPERTY AND TRANSFER OF TECHNOLOGY

Licensing

GDR trade in licenses has assumed increased importance in recent years. By purchasing foreign licenses, the GDR may expect to improve its technology, stimulate industrial development, economize in domestic scientific research work, and expand opportunities for GDR exports. Frequently, licensing agreements are combined with the import of industrial equipment and complete plants. In recent years, there has also been a substantial reverse flow of technology being exported from the GDR.

A 1964 decree established rules for the purchase and sale of licenses between the GDR and Western countries. In 1968 that decree was replaced by a new licensing decree.[46] According to Article 1 of the 1968 decree, the subject of licensing contracts may be rights of usage under (1) legally protected inventions for products, processes, and technologies, (2) legally unprotected know-how for products, processes, and technologies, (3) commercial samples and models, (4) trademarks, and (5) legally protected and unprotected agricultural cultivating and breeding methods as well as the results of breeding. Such licenses must be in writing.

The nationalized industrial enterprises (both VEB and VVB) and research institutions are authorized to negotiate and conclude license contracts on their own behalf with Western firms and to engage in marketing activities connected therewith.* However, they are legally obliged to consult with and obtain the permission of the Central Office of the International Licensing Trade of the GDR (Zentrales Büro für Internationalen Lizenzhandel der DDR) for instruction and advice on trade, political, commercial, and legal aspects. The office is an organ of the Ministry of Foreign Trade responsible for promoting

---

*The one major exception is the import of complete industrial plants, which falls to the exclusive jurisdiction of the foreign trade enterprise Industrieanlagen-Import.

trade in licenses, and it cooperates closely with the Ministry of Science and Technology and other technical ministries and central government departments. The foreign trade enterprises are also required to assist the industrial enterprises in an advisory capacity with respect to licensing. Licensing agreements are legally binding only after approval by the Ministry of Foreign Trade, and they must be registered with the ministry.

Cooperative societies (cooperatives of artisans, agricultural cooperatives, and so forth), private enterprises, and private citizens are not authorized to conclude license contracts with parties outside the GDR, although they may grant and purchase licenses. Only the Central Office of the International Licensing Trade of the GDR is entitled to conclude such contracts on their behalf for such grants and purchases. This office also may be the direct contracting party to imported licenses in certain branches of the chemical industry.

Licenses for technology flowing into the GDR have often relied more on the transfer of industrial know-how for a lump-sum payment than on attempting to deal with obtaining a GDR patent and the problems of long-term royalty payments in light of nonconvertibility of the currency and uncertainty as to the licensee's future allotments of hard currency. This is now undergoing a change, but it appears that know-how contracts, often with technical assistance and an operating installation included, are still favored. There are no set rules for the manner of royalty payment.

GDR practice varies as to payment procedures on the export of licenses. Both lump-sum and periodic payments are agreed to, depending upon the nature of the license, type of production and volume of production, and other factors. In practice, GDR enterprises may prefer an immediate down payment and fixed annual installments.[47] In any case, incoming and outgoing license payments are almost always handled by the relevant foreign trade enterprise on behalf of the GDR firm involved.

License fees paid to foreign licensors are subject to GDR taxation. According to a 1965 decree,[48] the rate is 25 percent of gross receipts, unless otherwise governed by a bilateral intergovernmental treaty.

The Patent System[49]

The law concerning the property rights of inventors is based generally on the thesis that the means of production are owned collectively and that the inventor's interests must therefore give way to the general interests of the people's economy in the use of inventions. While not giving protection to the interests of private capitalism, however, the state will grant the inventor a material acknowledgement of his labor. Besides compensation for use, for example, other attributes of private property that will attach to the patent include assignability and capability of passing the patent on by inheritance. Thus the patent law has sought to strike a balance between the interests of the state and those of independent innovators and producers. On the whole, the patent system of the GDR is a relatively simple one and is very much aimed at permitting all members of society to obtain and to some degree exploit patents. The system is so designed that (1) patent grants do not lead to monopolies of technology and production in areas deemed economically important and (2) such grants remain beneficial for the entire economy.

Article 22 of the Constitution of the GDR and the Patent Law of September 6, 1950[50] with its subsequent amendment in 1963[51] provide the inventor with certain protections in the forms of economic patents and exclusion patents, the form being at the election of the patentee, unless the patent was developed within a socialist enterprise or research facility or was developed with state aid, in which case only an economic patent will be issued.

This form of patent (a Wirtschaftspatent) is a patent protection that secures for the patentee the use of his patent plus a compensation, payable in a lump sum generally as determined by the Patent Office on the basis of inventive labor involved, the utility of the patent, the degree of the state assistance in its development, and the expense required for industrial exploitation. This sum is normally in practice computed on profits or sales in the first year of the patent's use obtained by all users thereof. Should the benefits subsequently increase beyond expectations, the patentee may receive an additional compensation. Once the first compensation is paid, the rights in the patent rest in the competent ministry for the particular branch of industry where the invention finds use. The Patent Office may also grant exploitation rights under an economic patent to any other person who desires to use such a patent, upon submission of plans for usage and compensation. Both the ministry and any grantees of exploitation rights contribute to the compensation of the inventor.

An exclusion patent (an Ausschliessungspatent), on the other hand, permits only the patentee and his assignees to use the technology, although this patent may be transformed into an economic patent if the inventor desires to retain the patent and receive compensation or permit further third-party use. Often an inventor finds he has no bargaining power as a private individual and cannot use his invention for profitable purposes without making such a transformation. The courts of the GDR make an effort, however, to protect the inventor in his relationship with the state.[52]

For certain production areas, the patent will not be issued for the protection of the products involved but rather only for the specific manufacturing process: foodstuffs, luxury items, medicines, and products of chemical processes.

A patent certificate is granted to a prospective patentee generally without an investigation of the bona fides of the novelty of the application or of the state of the art,[53] investigations being limited to insuring that all necessary supporting papers, designs, and explanations (in German) are attached, along with a sworn statement as to the identity of the inventor, and of the applicant, should another have succeeded to the rights of the inventor, that the subject matter is patentable and not contra bona mores and that the proper fees have been paid. The certificate provides a provisional protection once the subject matter of the patent is recorded in the Patent Register. It should be noted, however, that the patent, despite validity, will not be effective against anyone who was using the invention (or preparing to do so) within the GDR at the time of the application.

Subsequent to the granting of the certificate, the patent will be examined either ex officio by the Patent Office, on challenge by another party, at the request of the patentee in order to exploit the patent himself (for example, examination is necessary for licensing and for the commencement of an infringement suit), or at the request of state enterprises or authorities. Four criteria of patentability are subject to such examination: novelty (not published during the last 100 years in a domestic or foreign document accessible to the public nor publicly used within the GDR in a way that subsequent use by others would be possible, unless such publication or use were based on the invention and within six months of the application or the term of protection under international priority rights), the necessary inventive creativity, capability of industrial application, and technical progressiveness in the area of such industrial application.

Should the Patent Office reject the application, the applicant may appeal to the assessment section within two months for a rehearing. Further appeal lies on the complaints section of the Patent Office and thereafter in the District Court in Leipzig, which acts as a general patent court.

The Patent Office, under the Ministry of Planning and located in Berlin, is composed of a Presidium, a Patent Department, and an Economic Department. The Patent Department itself is composed of five sections: an assessment section (examination of applications and granting of certificates), an administration section (general matters such as fees), and three boards that sit in a body of two technical experts and one legal expert: correction (allowing a patentee to amend or correct his claim), invalidation and revocation (actions for nullity or revocation for exclusive foreign usage), and complaints (to handle contested decisions from other sections). The Economic Department basically looks after the interests of the state in terms of encouraging inventions, giving advice and assistance to inventors and business enterprises (including if necessary financing and testing of inventions and evaluation of possible areas of exploitation), making the patent known to various industrial ministries, and arbitrating disputes on remuneration, exploitation, and revocation. For the latter arbitration functions, there is a special arbitration board of three members, two technical experts, and one member nominated from the Free German Trade Union Federation; other experts may be heard.

Assuming validity, the patent extends for 18 years from the day following receipt of the application by the Patent Office. An issuance fee must be paid prior to the granting of the certificate, and an annual fee is demanded beginning with the second year following issuance. The fees for an exclusion patent are higher than those for an economic patent; fees for the latter may in fact be waived.

A "patent of addition" (Zusatzpatent) may also be granted to a patentee when he wishes to protect an improvement or development of an original patent. The patent of addition expires with the original, unless the latter ceases to be valid, in which case the patent of addition still maintains the same expiration date, but as an independent patent.

Priority of patents within the GDR depends on priority of filing of applications. Since the GDR acceded to the Paris Convention of 1883 (Stockholm version of 1967), effective as of April 26, 1970, an international priority system is provided for a foreign applicant. In addition to the usual application procedure mentioned above, the foreign applicant who wishes to rely on the convention for priority must declare the date and country of prior application within two months of application in the GDR. To enforce his rights subsequently granted, or to dispute any decision concerning the application, if he is not domiciled in the GDR or does not have a trade establishment there, he must further appoint a GDR agent admitted by the Patent Office to represent him before such office. There are two recognized agencies for such purposes: the Internationales Patentbüro and the Patentanwaltsbüro, both located in East Berlin. On the other hand, inventions that were made within the GDR or whose inventor is domiciled in the GDR require GDR registration prior to any application for a foreign patent, unless the respective foreign country has treaty reciprocity with the GDR in such matters.

An inventor who has been granted a certificate must also have notice thereof published in the Patent Office Gazette to insure effectiveness as against third parties. This notice may be withheld, and in fact the patent itself may also, if it is determined that secrecy is in the interest of national security.

In addition to the expiration of the 18-year term of the patent, it may lapse or be extinguished in several other ways. The patentee may surrender it to the Patent Office; should he not pay the annual fee, it will automatically lapse following warning. Invalidity will extinguish protection, and this may be determined on the basis of its not being patentable subject matter, of being the subject matter of a prior patent (although if only partially so, the remainder may be the subject of a valid patent), or of being created from descriptions, drawings, models, or the like, of another person. Should the subject matter of an exclusion patent be requires to fulfill a national economic, social, or cultural need, and the inventor is unwilling to transform his patent to an economic patent, the patent grant may be limited or abolished upon payment of compensation therefor. Finally, if a patent is one that is exclusively or primarily used outside the GDR, unless protected by international treaties, it may be revoked on application of the Economic Department of the Patent Office.

Should infringement occur, the holder of rights in a patent may proceed against the infringer in the Patent Tribunal in the Leipzig District Court for discontinuance of such usage. Should the infringement have been intentional or negligent, damages may be awarded. If the negligence has been minimal, the Patent Tribunal may assess a fine rather than award damages. If the infringement was intentional, the injured party may also petition to have the infringer punished by fine and/or imprisonment and in addition have a monetary penalty assessed and payable to him in lieu of a civil claim for damages. In cases of process patent infringements, all products of the same nature are deemed to have been derived from the process in question, unless otherwise proven.

All infringement claims are barred absolutely 30 years after the infringement, but if the patentee (or holder of patent rights in his place) learns of the infringement and of the identity of the infringer, he has three years from the date of such knowledge within which to assert his claim. Despite such periods of limitations, however, an infringer who has gained at the expense of the patentee may still be liable to a patentee thereafter on a restitutional theory of unjust enrichment.

Trademarks[54]

The trademark law of the GDR is found in the Warenzeichengesetz of February 17, 1954[55] as amended on November 15, 1968[56] and grants rather limited protection to the owner of a trademark.

All industrial products must contain a mark (if not possible, on packaging thereof) that clearly identifies the manufacturer, either by firm name or by a registered trademark or factory mark. Voluntary trademark protection may be registered by any producer of nonindustrial goods who desires to differentiate his goods from those of another, and this may be done by one or a combination of words, pictures, combinations of words and pictures, and the like.

The registration of a trademark is required for it to have any proprietary effect. The registration is done by giving notification to the Patent Office, along with payment of fees for the notification and for the classes of industrial property to which the mark will be applied (limited to 20 at each notification of the Patent Office). The contents of the notification must be sufficient to allow the Patent Office to enter in the Trademark Register the following: day of the notification; the particulars concerning the manner of business carried on for which and the goods on which the mark will be used; a drawing and description of the mark; the name and residence or seat of the owner of the mark as well as legal representatives, and changes thereof; an extension of the 10-year term of the protection (additional 10-year terms are granted freely, so long as fees are paid in the ninth year of each term and no grounds for nullification exist); and, if applicable, the date of cancellation of the mark. This register is open for public inspection.

Certain items, however, are not registrable. Marks that consist entirely of numerals or letters or words referring to manner, date, or place of production, character, price, quantity, or weight of the product unless otherwise having public recognition as being distinctive, or otherwise having no distinctive character, comprise the first category. Any "free mark," one that has lost its distinction by common use of one or more other producers, marks that offend public dignity or make untrue assertions, and marks that are contrary of principles of socialism may not be used. Marks that are official signs of testing, quality, or guarantee and published in the Central Gazette as adopted for certain products inside or outside the GDR may not be registered without authorization or unless the products for which the mark is intended to be used are not similar. Finally in the class of nonregistrable marks are those that are generally known in the commerce of the GDR as marks of another used for the same or similar products, unless authorized by the prior user for registration. Marks that are identical with or similar to or are likely to cause confusion in the public with marks that have already registered or for which registration has been notified for the same or similar goods will not have the notification accepted.

If a foreign applicant wishes to claim priority under an international agreement, he must give notice to the Patent Office of the date and country of prior application within two months of filing the GDR application. The Patent Office may demand certified copies of the relevant foreign application or a certified translation of the prior registration document, or, if an assignment of rights has occurred, a notarized assignment of such rights within the priority period.

Upon receipt of the notification, examinations are made in regard to formal correctness, completion of submitted documents, payment of the proper fees, and registrability. However, there is no publicity given to the notification and no opposition procedure is provided for, other than that of the Patent Office. If foreign applicants who have no business establishment in the GDR wish to make such a notification, it may only be done if there is reciprocity and then only via a power of attorney to one of the two agencies recognized by the Patent Office, the Internationales Patentbüro or the Patentanwaltsbüro. Appeals of nonregistration are handled in much the same way as for patents. The registration per se is in the trademark gazette (Warenzeichenblatt).

Once registration has been completed, the mark may or may not be used, as the owner sees fit. However, the mark may not be the subject of a license, and while inheritable, it is not assignable unless with the sale of the business or part of the business for which the mark was used. Assignments, even when accompanied by a change in ownership of business, are of no effect as against third parties until the assignment has been registered. If the mark is owned by an association as a collective mark, it may not in any case be assigned. Cancellation may be undertaken ex officio by the Patent Office if it appears that the registration was fraudulent or deceptive or the business of the owner of the mark has legally ceased. A third party may request cancellation by the Patent Office on those grounds or because his own mark used on similar goods had priority, but only after a request is made to the owner to cancel voluntarily.

Industrial Designs and Models

Since the repeal of the Utility Model Act in 1963, industrial designs and models have design protection under the 1876 Geschmackmustergesetz, as modified in 1952. Thus, any new and original design, not necessarily of a specific artistic quality but entailing more than simple technical functionality, may be registered for a period of 15 years,* so long as the design incorporates certain aesthetic qualities. This is also handled by the Patent Office. Application for registration may be made for either three-dimensional models or two-dimensional designs, but not both. The parcel containing the design or model may be registered open or sealed,† and there is no examination. The application must be made prior to use of a design

---

*The first application obtains a grant of one to three years, extendable upon application later to 10 and thereafter to 15 years.

†This option may be exercised only in the first three years; thereafter, the parcel will be and remain opened.

or model in a manner so that it becomes known to the public (inside or outside the GDR).

Once the design is registered, rights may be assigned, and neither use of the design or model or marking is obligatory; marking of the article may be undertaken, usually by the words "geschütztes Muster."

Copyright Law[57]

The GDR requires no registration or deposit of creative works in order for an author to receive copyright protection for works of literature, art and science. The right is personal to the author[58] and is exhausted 50 years after his death.[59] The works covered by the Copyright Law include all works in the three fields mentioned, when they are in an objectively perceptible form and are the result of an individual creative act (this can also refer to the Gestalt of a group creativity). Such works mentioned in the statute include, without limitation, writings, speeches, lectures, musical compositions, stage plays, painting, sculpture, graphic art, applied art, films television works, broadcasting works (including script books for the last three), photographic works, and architectural works. If collections, authologies, editions, or other compilations contain a creative effort, they may independently receive protection.

Since the right is a personal one, copyright is not transferable, although rights of use may be (generally for a consideration). Any gratuitous transfer must be expressly agreed upon. Royalty rates are regulated by the Minister of Culture.

Despite this protection, there are important exceptions. For example, free use of a work is permitted without royalties or consent when a new creative work is produced in such use; reproduction is generally permitted if a personal or professional interest is served and the reproduction is not made public; summaries, excerpts, quotations, and collections of such may be reproduced and published if for information or documentation purposes; and broadcasts or reprints by the news media are permitted for topical news coverage.

The copyright statute[60] contains provisions governing contractual relationships between author and "cultural institutions," be they publishers, film studios, theaters, or the like. An important aspect of this is the general provision that these institutions have the dual duty of protecting the rights of the author, on the one hand, and providing for the broadest possible distribution of the works, on the other. Should either of these duties not be fulfilled, the author may rescind the contract, receive pro rata compensation for what has been done, and, if the nonfulfillment was negligent or intentional, claim damages.

Performers also receive a certain protection, should their performance be recorded or broadcast. They must give their consent before such recording is used or before such a performance is broadcast, and remuneration is due in accordance with performance royalty regulations. However, this protection lasts only 10 years from the date of performance and is also subject to the above exceptions regarding free use in the public interest.

A fundamental area of interest to foreign authors is the extent to which they are entitled to protection under the copyright law. The law applies for the protection of citizens of the GDR, whether or not the work has been published. It also applies to works and performances made public for the first time in the GDR, whether or not the author or performer is a citizen or a stateless person. However, in regard to works that have been published outside the GDR, protection is available within the GDR only in accordance with international agreements.[61] In the absence of an international agreement between the GDR and the country of which the author is a citizen (assuming he is not stateless) protection is given only on the basis of reciprocity.

International Agreements

In addition to the various treaties and conventions mentioned above, there are a number of these in the area of industrial and intellectual property. The GDR has declared its adherence to the 1883 Paris Union Convention on the Protection of Industrial Property, originally in the Lisbon Convention version and subsequently in the modified 1967 Stockholm version, and the 1957 Nice Convention (Stockholm version of 1967) concerning the international classification of goods and services in respect to trademarks, as well as the Madrid Convention on the supression of false or misleading indications of origin.[62] It has also accepted the 1891 Madrid Convention (Stockholm version of 1967) concerning international registration and priority of trademarks. On 20 June 1968, the GDR also declared its acceptance of the Bern Convention of 1886 (International Union for the Protection of Literary and Artistic Works) in the 1928 Rome version as was ratified by the German Reich in 1933, and acceded to the 1970 Stockholm Act (World Intellectual Property Organization Convention). It is not however a member of the Universal Copyright Convention in any of its three versions (original, Stockholm version, or Paris revision).

The chief problem in this area is that a number of Western countries (most of whom now recognize the GDR or are preparing to do so) originally disputed and declared reservations as to the validity of the purported acceptance by the GDR of these treaties. There is, for example, a question whether the GDR is a member of the

Bern treaty. Until now the GDR has received no protection in these countries, and it has reciprocated by giving citizens of these countries no protection under its domestic laws. Moreover, bilateral treaties covering some of these matters that were signed with certain of the Western countries, notably the United States, are considered by the GDR to have been de facto canceled by the consequences of World War II, but the treaty partners in some cases consider the treaties still to be in force, but only with West Germany. It may be expected that these problems will be clarified and resolved following recognition of the GDR as a state by these countries.

SETTLEMENT OF FOREIGN TRADE DISPUTES

Foreign Trade Arbitration Court

As with most of Eastern Europe, the GDR utilizes the machinery of arbitration for the settlement of disputes arising in foreign trade. The permanent arbitral body for most* matters is the Court of Arbitration, established as a part of the Chamber of Foreign Trade (KfA) in East Berlin in 1954. Originally set up to deal with matters between parties of the GDR and nonsocialist countries, the Court of Arbitration now also plays a major role in settling disputes arising in the economic cooperation structure of Comecon. Although attached to the KfA, it is legally independent of the state and the Ministry for Foreign Trade and is legally subject to no governmental or administrative instructions, including any of the KfA. Even so, Western business parties are generally hesitant to adopt the standard-form contract clauses calling for arbitration in the GDR, despite GDR claims of impartiality,[63] and prefer, usually with success, to refer disputes to third-country arbitration.[64]

The legal basis of the Court of Arbitration is at present founded on the 1877 Code of Civil Procedure (Sections 1025 to 1047), although this will change when the new Zivilprozessordnung (ZPO) is officially in force. This will not change matters a great deal, since procedures before the Court are laid down in the Arbitration Code (Schiedsgerichtsordnung) of 1957,[65] which is not expected to go through major changes.

The Court of Arbitration[66] has jurisdiction over trade matters, including delivery of goods, license matters, job processing, banking,

---

*There is also the Gdynia Arbitration Court for Ocean and Inland Shipping, based on the tripartite agreement between the chambers of commerce of the GDR, Poland, and Czechoslovakia.

transport, and insurance, if the parties involved have agreed upon submitting disputes to it and at least one of the parties has his legal residence outside the GDR, or if the respondent does not object to arbitration, or if jurisdiction has been agreed upon in an intergovernmental agreement. (This last, at present, refers to the Comecon countries in their Common Conditions of Delivery and of Sale, whereby the arbitration court in the respondent's country has jurisdiction.)

The court is composed of the president, vice president, and secretary, and the Panel of Arbitrators, who sit on Arbitration Boards. These latter are usually experts both in foreign trade matters and legal rules applicable thereto.

A claim is instituted by filing a statement thereof with the secretary, detailing names and addresses of the parties, the requested adjudication and award, the specific dispute and details of the transaction involved, the value of the dispute (important for the imposition of fees based on a sliding scale of amount in dispute), a statement of evidence involved including copies of all contracts, and a declaration accepting the competence of the court. Before this is acted upon, however, there is a mandatory conciliation procedure. Should this fail (that is, an agreement is not reached or a party does not appear), the parties have 60 days to submit the dispute to arbitration in East Berlin* and choose their arbitrators, who will then choose a third member to act as chairman. Should a party refuse to choose an arbitrator, the president of the court will do so rather than allow a discontinuance.

The proceedings are conducted in German; translators are available. Lawyers are not necessary but are permitted, and each party must bear the costs of his own counsel; a lawyer or any other representative requires a valid power-of-attorney. The verbal proceedings supplement the submitted written evidence, but the arbitrators are free to accept or reject any such evidence, including testimony of experts (whom they may interrogate), and may in fact gather their own evidence. Costs are borne generally by the losing party.

Termination is reached by award, compromise of the parties, or dismissal. An award is given verbally shortly (within five days) after the last hearing, and a written copy is served on the parties within a month after such hearing. The award, which is final and nonappealable, sets forth all matters decided and who decide them, the reasons therefor, and costs.

Compromises reached before the Arbitration Board as well as in conciliation procedures have the legal effect of an award. In either

---

*Upon joint request and approval thereof, venue may be elsewhere within the GDR or without.

case, the GDR might have a problem of enforcement against a losing foreign party. GDR efforts to seek execution against a foreign party in foreign courts could pose problems in countries that continue to deny the validity of the GDR's acceptance of the 1958 United Nations (New York) Convention on the Recognition and Enforcement of Foreign Arbitral Awards.[67] This does not affect the validity of an award to a foreign party, however, which may be enforced within the GDR.

Conflicts of Law

A valid arbitration agreement is of vital importance, and the Court of Arbitration has a model written clause that it accepts.[68] As to the capacity of the parties to conclude such an agreement, under present conflicts rules lex patriae is applied.[69] The Introductory Law to the Civil Code (EGBGB) has nothing to say about corporate persons, but leading authorities declare it to be the law of the legal residence or seat of such person.[70] The form of the agreement must also conform to the legal system applicable to formal validity, which under GDR civil law may be chosen by the parties. Since the rules of the Court of Arbitration do not require any given form, the parties may then choose either the law of the GDR of the other country involved. Assuming that GDR rules are chosen, the old BGB, ZPO, and HGB code provisions would at present be applicable.

The results of such a choice would mean that between tradesmen, the arbitration can have any form when in respect to a commercial transaction; if between two nontradesmen, it must be in a separate written agreement. If just one of the parties is a tradesman, the former provision also applies. In any case, a formal defect can be overcome by disregard or noncontest of the parties.[71]

If the parties have not chosen a law, the law that is to be applied is that which corresponds to their presumed will; failing this solution, a "center of gravity" based on whichever law the contract has the most connections to, or finally, the law of the place of execution of the contract (if several, the obligations of the vendor and vendee, by their respective laws) will be used.[72]

NOTES

1. The following statistics for total foreign trade (in billions of rubles) for 1971 are illustrative:

Country	Amount
USSR	23.7
GDR	9.0
Poland	7.1

Country	Amount
Czechoslovakia	6.8
Hungary	4.9
Bulgaria	3.9
Romania	3.4

Source: Dubrovsky, "Der Auusenhandel der RGW-Länder im Jahre 1971," 4 Sozialistische Aussenwirtschafte 30 (1973).

2. In 1972, about 71 percent of the total foreign trade of the GDR was with other Comecon countries, whereas only 26 percent was with the various free-market Western countries (with GDR imports from the West exceeding its exports by about 2.6 billion Valuta-Marks, a foreign trade unit of account officially valued at one West German mark since the GDR mark is nonconvertible). Statistisches Jahrbuch der DDR 1973 at 33 (East Berlin: Staatsverlag der DDR, 1973); see also "Der Aussenhandel der DDR im Jahre 1972," 14 Die Berliner Wirtschaft 557 (1973).

3. GDR statistics (Statistisches Jahrbuch der DDR 1973, supra note 2) show a steady growth in its two-way trade with the industrialized Western countries from 1968 to 1972 (in billion of VM):

Year	Amount
1968	6.0
1969	8.0
1970	9.7
1971	10.3
1972	12.0

The leading Western trade partners of the GDR in 1972, with the exception of the Federal Republic of Germany, were (in billions of VM): France (0.916), the United Kingdom (247), the Netherlands (0.644), and Switzerland (0.621). See also text at note 6. Since 1971, the structure of GDR imports from the West has shifted somewhat. In addition to special machinery and industrial equipment, more consumer goods have been imported. In 1971 the VIII Congress of the governing Socialistische Einheitspartei Deutchlands adopted a decision to improve living standards considerably; this was an aim that could only be achieved by means of increased imports of Western consumer goods.

4. The ability of the GDR to increase its foreign trade with the West depends to a great extent on the availability of hard currency, obtained either by means of increased exports or increased credits extended by Western trading partners. The rather large supply of the latter from West Germany has been one of the critical factors in its large share of the foreign trade of the GDR. Such credits may in fact become progressively more available as political tensions ease further. See, for example, "U.S. Moves to Boost Links with East Germany," Financial Times, Apr. 10, 1973, at 4, reporting certain grants of credit to the GDR by U.S. banks.

5. See Decision of Council of Europe, No. C/57, Official Journal (July 17, 1973); 1332n. s. Europe 10 (July 25, 1973).

6. Statistisches Jahrbuch der DDR 1973, supra note 2 at 10-11.

7. See generally M. Paschke, Die Internationalen Wirtschafts-vereinbaurngen der DDR 78-81, 101-104 (Göttingen, 1970); K. Pritzel, Die Wirtschaftsintegration Mitteldeutschlands 75-79 (Cologne, 1969); H. Tiedke, Der Aussenhandel der DDR 85-86 (East Berlin, 1961).

8. Archiv der Gegenwart at 4299, H. von Siegler, ed. (Bad Godesberg, 1953).

9. Legislazione Economica Italiana at 1219-1220 (Rome, 1973).

10. 92 East-West 1 (Sept. 28, 1973).

11. 652 Trade and Industry (U.K.) (Dec. 20, 1973).

12. Neues Deutschland (Aug. 20, 1973).

13. But see Colitt, "East Germans Negotiating with U.S. Car Makers," Financial Times, Sept. 28, 1973, mentioning that East German officials gave an "enthusiastic and immediate" response to initiatives of U.S. car makers that have West German subsidiaries for possible production in the GDR. It was reported that if such a deal were to go through, the East Germans would insist on controlling financial interests and keeping management control.

14. This state monopoly over foreign trade is dictated by Art. 9V of the Constitution, version of Apr. 6, 1968, Gesetzblatt (the official Gazette of the GDR, hereinafter "GBl") 1968 I, at 199, and reiterated in sec. 1 of the Foreign Trade Law, Gesetz über den Aussenhandel der DDR of Jan. 9, 1958, GBl 1958 I, at 69.

15. GBl 1973 I, at 186.

16. See J. Lieser and K. Pleyer, Das Zivil-u. Wirtschaftsrecht der DDR im Ausklang eines Reformjahrzehnts 99-102 (Stuttgart, 1973).

17. GBl 1965 I, at 104; 4th Durchführungsverordnung (or DVO) zum Vertragsgesetz: Ausführ- und Einführverträge, GBl 1965 II, at 255; see Koch and Osterland, "Rechtsfragen bei der Organisation der Zusammenarbeit zwischen Industrie und Aussenhandel," 2 Vertrags-system 94 (1966).

18. 9th DVO zum Vertragsgesetz—Kommissionverträge beim Export, 5 Feb. 1969, GBl 1969 II, at 133.

19. Sec. 2 et seq., Verordnung über die Durchführung des Aussenhandels, 9 Jan. 1958, GBl 1958 I, at 89, as amended by the 2d Verordnung, id., 16 April 1964, GBl 1964 II, at 288.

20. Id., sec. 6.

21. It might be mentioned here that there are also incentive plans to increase export whereby overplan exporters receive extra allocations of foreign exchange for obtaining foreign goods and licenses not otherwise available. S. Pisar, Coexistence and Commerce 159 (New York, 1970).

22. See K. H. Nattland, Der Aussenhandel in der Wirtschafts-reform der DDR 71 (West Berlin, 1972); I Lexikon der Wirtschaft 126-128 (East. Berlin, 1970).

23. See Gesetz über das Zollwesen der DDR (Zollgesetz) of Mar. 28, 1962, GB1 1962 I, at 42, and especially sec. 11 thereof.

24. DDR Kammer für Aussenhandel, Handbook of the External Economy of the German Democratic Republic 64-65 (East Berlin, 1970).

25. See supra note 5.

26. See S. Pisar supra note 21 at 162, 165.

27. "Shift in East European Bilateral Clearing Agreements" (1973) Business International Eastern European Report 263. This reporter service will be cited hereinafter "BI/EER."

28. "Forfeiting Rates on East European Trade Paper," id., at 229, 265.

29. This is increasingly opening up, and a number of Western firms have opened offices in the GDR. See id. at 87. A 1972 decree states merely that an application should be filed with the Ministry of Foreign Trade, stating name, address, and, in detail, what the nature and activities of the proposed branch office would be; further steps are taken by the ministry. Decree on the activities of branch offices of foreign companies and institutions in the GDR, Dec. 22; 1971; English translation made available by the ministry. For information on recent GDR practices regarding the establishment of offices in that country, see East-West Trade Information Bulletin, March 1974 at 16 (published by U.S. East-West Trade Center, Vienna, Austria)

30. See "Local Agents in Eastern Europe," (1973) BI/EER 73.

31. See GB1 1968 II at 83.

32. See I Ökonomisches Lexikon (2d ed.) 47 (East Berlin, 1971).

33. See Heuer and Klinger, "Foundations of Socialist Economics Law" (1972); 1 Law and Legislation in the German Democratic Republic 5; "Law on the Contract System in Socialist Economy (Contracts Law)" (1965); 2 id, at 61.

34. The BGB has had several major revisions even as it presently exists in the GDR, For example, after nearly complete nationaliza-tion of private enterprise in the GDR during the 1960s, the property law provisions were declared inoperative, and some changes were made in the law of obligations.

35. See, for comment, Maskow, "Konzeptionelle Probleme eines Aussenwirtschaftsvertragsgesetz," 24 Neue Justiz 674 (1970); Maskow, "Überlegungen zum Aufbau des geplanten Aussenwirtschaftsvertrags-gesetz (AWVG) der DDR," 7-8 Recht in der Aussenwirtschaft 1 (1970); Maskow and Mehnert, "Wichtige Gesetzgebungsaufgaben auf dem Gebiet Aussenwirtschaft," 11-12 id. 1 (1968); Standke, "Konstituierende Sitzung der Gesetzgebungsgrundkomission Aussenwirtschaftsvertragsgesetz," id. 12; Maskow, "Gegenstand u. Anwendungsbereich des Aussenwirts-chaftsgesetzbuches," 11 id. 1 (1967); Enderlein and Zimmerman, "Für ein spezielles Aussenhandelsgesetz der DDR," 7-8 id. 10 (1966).

36. Waehler, "Der Aussenhandel der DDR—Institutionen u. Recht," 15 Aussenwirtschaftsdienst der Betriebs-Berater 316, 320 (1969). The author maintains that this will be similar to that of Czechoslovakia, an English translation of which appears in (1964) Bulletin of Czechoslovakian Law 189 et seq.

37. A good introduction to at least the structure and function of the HGB, albeit as found in force in West Germany, is in chapter 7 of E. J. Cohn, II Manual of German Law, 2d ed. (Dobbs Ferry, N.Y., 1971.

38. The latest edition of the HGB was published in a collection of GDR laws relating to foreign trade and entitled Handelsgesetze und Haftpflichtbestimmungen at 25-109 (East Berlin, 1968).

39. Einführungsgesetz des bürgerlichen Gesetzbuchs (or EGBGB), sec. 7.

40. Id., sec. 24.

41. Id., sec. 30.

42. See I Handbuch der Aussenhandelsverträge 65-81 (East Berlin, 1971): Enderlin, "Die weiteren Aufgaben der rechtswissenschaftlichen Forschung zur Regelung der Wirtschaftsbeziehungen der DDR mit nichtsozialistischen Staaten," 22 Staat und Recht 457-63 (1973).

43. See Expig and Lübchen, "Zur gesetzlichen Neuregelung des Kollisionsrecht der DDR," 22 Staat und Recht 69 (1973).

44. Id.,at 75-77, 80-82.

45. But see discussion in section entitled "International Agreements," infra.

46. Lizenzverordnung, Dec. 11, 1968, GB1 1968 II, at 125; see also Anordnung über die Vergutung der Erfinder bei Lizenzvergabe, Dec. 11, 1968, id. at 126; G. Feige and W. Sieffert, Internationale Lizensen (East Berlin, 1965); Eckner, "Gründung der Vereinigung für gewerblichen Rechtsschutz in der DDR," 2 Recht in der Aussenwirtschaft (1972); Ronneberger, "Rechtsprobleme des Abschlusses von Lizenzvertragen," 11 id. 14 (1966).

47. See sources in note 46 supra for a more comprehensive discussion. See also "Selling Licenses to Eastern Europe" (1973) BI/EER at 385; (1974) BI/EER at 27.

48. Compare Anordnung über die Besteuerung der Lizenzeinnahmen von Unternehmen und Bürgern anderer Staaten aus der Überlassung von Urheberrechten an Betriebe der DDR, June 25, 1965, GB1 1965 II at 554; see generally, Pilz, "Zur Besteurung der Lizenzeinkommen ausländischer Partner bei Lizenzvergabe in der DDR" (1965) Der Neuerer 571.

49. See generally Erfinder-und Neuererrecht der DDR (East Berlin, 1968); J. Hemmerling, Komplexe Socialistische Rationalisierung und Neuererbewegung (East Berlin, 1966); Hemmerling, "Das neue Patentprüfungsvenfahren in der DDR," 12 Der Neuerer

1 (1966); von Füner, "Über die Erfordernisse für die Anfassung und Einreichung einer Patentanmeldung in der DDR," Feb. 1965, Gewerbliches Rechtsschutz und Urheberrecht (ausl. u. intl Teil) 76.

50. Patentgesetz, Sept. 6, 1950, GB1 1950 I at 989.

51. Gesetz zur Änderung des Patentgesetzes und zur Aufhebung des Gebrauchsmustergesetzes, July 31, 1963, GB1 1963 I, at 121.

52. Id., sec. 5, at 122.

53. See Rechtsprechung 15 Neue Justiz 109 (1961), reporting a court decision upholding the right of an inventor to claim compensation for a suppressed patent from an enterprise that had contracted to pay on the development and application of the invention. The decision was based on the enterprise's responsibility to put such an invention to use subsequent to acquisition, for the good of both the inventor and the state.

54. See generally, H. Erasmus, Erfinder und Warenzeichenschutz im In- und Ausland (East Berlin, current loose-leaf); Die Neuererbewegung und das Patent-, Muster- und Zeichenwesen (East Berlin, 1964).

55. Warenzeichengesetz, Feb. 17, 1954, GB1 1954 I, at 216.

56. Änderungsgesetz, Nov. 15, 1968, GB1 1968 I, at 357. The entire law was printed in its new version, id. at 360.

57. Gesetz über das Urheberrecht, Sept. 13, 1965, GB1 I 1965 at 209. See generally 19 Neue Justiz 21 (1965) for a collection of explanatory articles. An English translation is found in (1966: 1) Law and Legislation in the DDR 73. See also Püschel, "A New Copyright Code in the DDR," id. at 31.

58. Compare Püschel, "Wesenzüge des socialistischen Urheberrechts der DDR," 19 Neue Justiz 662 (1965) with Samson, "Das Neue Urheberrechtsgesetz der 'DDR'," Oct. 1966, Juristische Rundschau 361,

59. However the state may declare a work to be in the national interest and take over rights to it, in which case the copyright protection will continue. Urheberrechtgesetz, supra note 57, secs. 34-35.

60. Id., secs. 36-72.

61. See section entitled "International Agreements," in text, infra.

62. The effective date of these declarations was Jan. 15, 1965, and the publication thereof Mar. 27, 1965. See GB1 1965 I, at 131. See also Weppe, "Die Pariser Verbandsübereinkommen und der Beitritt der DDR zu ihrer neuesten Fassung," 2 Recht in der Aussenwirtschaft 8 (1965).

63. For the story of a successful U.S. arbitration claim reaching a binding compromise, see "U.S. Company Wins East German Court Award" (1973) BI/EER 42.

64. Id.

65. The text of this may be found in the 1957 Supplement to 1968 Aussenhandel (now entitled Sozialistische Aussenwirtschaft) 580-588, and an English version of the Rules of the Court of Arbitration, in L. Kos-Rabcewicz-Zubkowski, Eastern European Rules on the Validity of International Commercial Arbitration Agreements (hereinafter Eastern European Rules) at 147 (Dobbs Ferry, N.Y., 1970).

66. See generally Strohbach, "Die Kammer für Aussenhandel der DDR und ihr Schiedsgericht," 11 Recht in der Aussenwirtschaft 1 (1972); Strobach, "Zur Problematik von Schiedsgerichtsvereinbarungen in rechtsvergleichender Sicht," 73 Aktuelle Beitrage der Staats- und Rechtswissenschaft 11-40 (1971).

67. 300 U.N.T.S. 3 (1959). Similarly, the GDR declared on Apr. 4, 1958, that it would apply the provisions of the 1923 (Geneva) Protocol on Arbitration Clauses (27 L.N.T.S. 157, 1924) and the 1927 (Geneva) Convention on the Execution of Foreign Arbitral Awards (42 L.N.T.S. 301, 1929), with the same problems of reciprocity.

68. The clause is almost always in standard-form contracts, along with a clause making GDR law applicable. These may be struck out. See Kammer für Aussenhandel der DDR, Taking Recourse to the Court of Arbitration Attached to the Chamber of Foreign Trade of the German Democratic Republic 5 (East Berlin, 1971).

69. EGBGB, sec. 1 (7).

70. Eastern European Rules at 16.

71. Id. at 41.

72. Id. at 42.

218

CHAPTER

10

THE HUNGARIAN
PEOPLE'S REPUBLIC
Joseph Varró

Any attempt to summarize a country's legal system for the use
of businessmen wishing to participate in East-West trade requires
a good deal of self-restraint. A review of the economic political, and
legal background is necessary; and although there are certain general
features common to all socialist countries, there are many particulars
that differ in individual countries according to the practical solution
chosen by them. Also, any such summary requires strict economy of
space, and we agree with the eminent British author who stressed
the difficulties of "miniaturisation."[1]

An understanding of Hungarian legal institutions requires appreciation of the most important principles of the Hungarian Constitution, which is the fundamental law[2] of the Hungarian People's Republic
and helps in construing the legis ratio of more specific legal rules.[3]

Hungary is a people's republic, a socialist state[4] where the
socialist relations of production have become dominant. Social ownership of the means of production is the basis of economic order.[5] The
state promotes and protects all forms of social property[6] but recognizes and protects personal property as well.[7]

Economic life in Hungary is determined by the state's national
economic plans. Relying on enterprises, cooperatives, and institutions
of social ownership, the state directs and controls the national economy.[8]

Implementation of the central economic plan is ensured mainly
by economic "regulators" orienting the economic units toward activities favorable to implementation of the plan, essentially by making

This chapter reflects the legal situation existing at the end of
November 1973. The Hungarian text was translated by Dr. Jenö Rácz.

219

their profits dependent on their economic activities. One of the principal legislative acts regarding planning is a 1972 law on National Economic Planning,[9] subsequently implemented by a Resolution of the Council of Ministers[10] creating a State Planning Commission.

The increased (and in some cases newly created) autonomy of the enterprises and other units of direct economic activity, their wider scope of initiative and economic interests, and their increased freedom of utilizing—within the limits set by their statutes—the socially owned fixed and working capitals entrusted to them are also reflected by the following provisions of the Constitution:

> State property is the property of the people as a whole. Property of the State includes, first, the reserves of subsoil wealth, the state lands, the natural resources, the major producing plants and mines, the railways, the public highways, the waterways and air routes, the banks, the postal, telegraph, telephone, broadcasting and television services. The sphere of State property and of the exclusive economic activity of the State are defended by law. . . .[11] The State enterprises and economic organizations, serving the general interests of society, manage independently the assets and property entrusted to them, in the manner and with the responsibility provided for by the law. . . .[12] The cooperatives are also part of the socialist system of society.[13]

INSTITUTIONAL FRAMEWORK AND FOREIGN TRADE PLANNING

The new system of economic control and management is not codified comprehensively in a single Code or "consolidated Act." As one writer has put it, "no solid codification is possible without practical experience."[14]

Authority to Engage in Foreign Trade

According to a Resolution of the Council of Ministers, foreign trade activities could be pursued after the 23 of July, 1949 only with permits (trade licenses) issued by the Minister of Foreign Trade.[15] The legal rules of the Constitution described above came into force about a month later. Law Decree No. 30 of 1950 on the Planned Management of Foreign Exchange (known as the "Foreign Exchange Code") regulated all foreign exchange transactions, including, in principle, the entire field of foreign trade. It made the minister of Finance the highest authority for all foreign exchange transactions. The former foreign exchange authority, the National Bank of Hungary, "remained the universal organ exercising the state monopoly of foreign exchange transactions," and the minister of Foreign Trade was "authorized to issue export and import licenses."[16] Under this Law Decree, permission was (and, for the time being still is) required for export and import transactions, and related contracts, and for undertaking negotiations.

The Law Decree prohibiting unauthorized foreign trade activity is a lex plusquam perfecta—that is, such activity is null and void and punishable by law. Such a rule is of an absolute nature, and not merely a mandatory rule (ius cogens). Certain authors (Reczei) call it an imperative rule; others identify it with "public order." This, however, is merely a question of nomenclature of private international law. Whatever it is called, the rule excludes application by a Hungarian court of law of any legal rule to the contrary (either in the case of explicit "choice of law" by the parties or according to a "connecting factor" test) that would otherwise be applied as the "proper law of the contract."

On the other hand, if a socialist organization otherwise entitled to conduct foreign trade activity exceeds the scope of its authority, this does not void the transaction, provided the general conditions are satisfied. In such a case, the organization exceeding the scope of its authority is amenable to disciplinary action, but the ultra vires concept in the sense of the common law is unknown in the Hungarian legal system.

On the basis of the introductory rules of the Hungarian Civil Code and the "Foreign Exchange Code," an important decree was issued in 1960 by the minister of Foreign Trade on the Definition of Foreign Trade Agreements and Regulation of Foreign Trade Relations.[17] The new system of economic control and management has left the provisions of this decree in force, but modified in some respects, notably regarding the right to conduct foreign trade activity and the central control of such activity.[18]

As a general rule, foreign trade is conducted or performed by (1) specialized foreign trade companies supervised by the Ministry of Foreign Trade that deal exclusively with foreign trade transactions, and (2) so-called units of production or of domestic trade that are authorized to participate in foreign trade. Since the introduction of the 1968 economic reform, the number of enterprises entitled to engage in foreign trade has greatly expanded, due mainly to enterprises of the second type (which includes both producing as well as trading enterprises). The Hungarian Chamber of Commerce annually publishes a serviceable guide, Directory of Hungarian Foreign-Trade Companies, containing comprehensive details on all Hungarian firms authorized to participate in foreign trade, or from some other point of view important in this respect.[19]

The socialist organizations (mostly state-owned enterprises, but also cooperatives) taking part in foreign trade are independent legal entities free to manage the assets (owned by the state or cooperative) entrusted to them. This relative independence of the economic units, as well as their responsibility toward third parties contracting with them, follows from the constitution.[20]

Control of Foreign Trade

The independence of the socialist economic organizations was markedly increased in the framework of the post-1968 economic mechanism. As a consequence, the methods and tools of central control, as well as the tasks of the cabinet ministers supervising the various economic branches, underwent important changes.

The economic branch of foreign trade is supervised by the minister of Foreign Trade.[21] The monopoly of foreign trade, however, is a state monopoly that is not limited to certain enterprises or to a certain branch. The central control of foreign trade is part of the control of the national economy as a whole and, as such, is exercised by the government. The organ of this control is the Ministry of Foreign Trade, whose authority extends (from this special point of view) over the national economy as a whole. In other words, the minister of Foreign Trade controls and audits all foreign trade activities, whether performed by state enterprises or cooperatives, or by economic units under his own supervision or supervised (in respect to their domestic activities) by any other ministry.[22]

The tools of controlling foreign trade[23] are the following:

● Those tools generally used for influencing economic activity, such as pricing, refunds from the state budget, regulation of investments, credit policy, and so on, that affect the net income (profit) of economic units according to how far they comply with the objective served by the regulator in question.
● Special tools used mainly for short-term regulation of trade flows and commodity patterns by country, and so on (for example, customs duties).
● Administrative controls such as licensing, or central allocation of some products, now used only in exceptional cases.

Entities Involved in Foreign Trade

As mentioned above, the socialist organizations performing foreign trade activities are mostly state-owned enterprises[24]—that is, legal entities entitled to manage independently the assets entrusted to them by the state in order to implement the national economic plan. The state-owned enterprise is responsible for its own obligations to the extent of the assets entrusted to it. The enterprise is led by a director, whose signature suffices to bind the enterprise (otherwise, the signatures of two employees authorized by the director are requested). When a newly founded enterprise intends to perform foreign trade activities, permission by the minister of Foreign Trade is needed.[25] The assets managed by a state-owned enterprise cannot be withdrawn from it.

State enterprises may form joint ventures in the form of trading companies with the consent of the minister of Finance. Such consent is given only after approval by the competent branch minister. In the case of foreign trade activity, approval by the minister of Foreign Trade is required.

"Companies" are of various types under Hungarian law. One is the joint stock company similar to the German Aktiengesellschaft and the French société anonyme. This legal form is common for large enterprises. Another is the limited liability company. The introductory law of the present Hungarian Civil Code[26] (which corresponds approximately to a British "Order in Council") has left in force some rules of the former Commercial Code (Act XXXVII of 1875, as amended), including those regarding the limited liability company. This legal form is related to the German Gesellschaft mit beschraenkter Haftung rather than to the private limited liability company known in the Common Law. Some state-owned Hungarian enterprises are organized in this form, but they are rather exceptional.

Third, the rules of the former Commercial Code relating to corporations resembling the British partnership have remained in force,[27] but this legal form is more closely related to the German concept of the Offene Handelsgesellschaft.

Recent Hungarian legislation has allowed for the creation of so-called joint enterprises.[28] This enactment is important, among other reasons, because it establishes the principle that foreign companies (that is, legal persons) may participate in Hungarian associations, subject to the permission of the minister of Finance and according to the conditions set by him.[29] We will return to this topic below.

Finally, the so-called agency companies should be mentioned. They are state-owned enterprises of various types working as commission agents for and on behalf of foreign firms. Some of them deal mainly with cooperation agreements with foreign firms. At present, 11 such enterprises exist in Hungary, and the volume of their turnover is considerable.

Financial Institutions, Insurance, and Shipping
Services

The most important institutions of this kind are

● the National Bank of Hungary, a joint-stock company, which exercises the state monopoly over foreign exchange transactions and is the largest banking institution of the country.
● the Hungarian Foreign Trade Bank Ltd., whose functions include performing banking transactions connected with foreign trade, for example, issuing letters of credit, accepting and guaranteeing bills of exchange and so on, and dealing with the promotion (and is some respects the coordination) of cooperation transactions.
● the National Savings Bank (OTP), which is primarily engaged in domestic banking services but has a certain role in the field of foreign trade because it handles foreign exchange transactions by foreign tourists and businessmen
● the State Insurance Company, the state-owned enterprise exclusively authorized to deal with all branches of insurance and reinsurance. Insurance is voluntary in Hungary, with the exception of real estate and vehicles for which third-party insurance is compulsory. The civil law rules regarding insurance are contained in the Civil Code.[30]
● The Hungarian General Forwarding Enterprise MASPED,[31] exclusively authorized to handle international shipping, similar to other international forwarding agencies, and available to foreigners as well as Hungarian parties.
● The Hungarian Quality Control Co. Ltd. MERT, exclusively authorized to give and take commissions for quality control[32] and entitled inter alia to check the quality of any goods imported into or exported from Hungary.

We should also mention the Hungarian Chamber of Commerce, which is not an organ of the state administration but a rather business federation of state-owned and social organizations insofar as their foreign trade interests are concerned. The Chamber is primarily a trade-promoting organization.[33] Its members are all Hungarian enterprises dealing with foreign trade, and optional membership is open to any other enterprise with some interest in foreign trade.

Foreign Trade Planning

The recent law on national economic planning and the creation of the State Planning Commission have already been mentioned.[34] According to the law on planning,[35] the national economic plans are short-term plans, medium-term (as a rule five-year) plans, and annual (or operative) plans.

"The basic tool of the planned control of the national economy is the medium-term plan." Among other things, the plan establishes "the main directions of development and structural relations."[36] It follows that the most important part of the "branch plans" of foreign trade is the medium-term plan.[37] In this, among other things, planners must take account of the equilibrium requirements in balance of payments over the plan period, directives regarding foreign trade regulators, the eventual necessity of changing foreign trade price multipliers, principles of applying state subsidies, trade and customs policy, measures to maintain trade equilibrium, and so on. Every medium-term plan, including that for foreign trade, contains a number of prognostic elements that in turn, are closely related to operative decisions taken. Implementation of the medium-term plan is affected by many factors that cannot be foreseen at the time of planning—short-term changes of equilibrium measures taken by other countries, and so on—and that may require intermittent measures such as modification of some "general" or "special" regulators, and eventually in administrative measures such as licensing.

The annual foreign trade plan reflects, firstly and most directly, market relations. Through this plan, the principles of foreign trade policy are put into effect. Plans of enterprises do not depend on central directives. Enterprises make independent decisions as regards their future programs, but under the influence of the economic regulators they necessarily reflect also the centrally established conditions that determine the limits and economic environment within which decisions are made by independent enterprises. Enterprise plans may contain marketing variables, but they give a general picture of anticipated effects of the economic regulators established by the medium-term plan.

Relevant International Agreements

At present, nearly 100 bilateral trade agreements are in force between Hungary and other countries, in addition to a vast number of financial, scientific, technological, and other interstate agreements. In addition to these bilateral agreements, Hungary is a signatory of many multilateral agreements and has ratified a considerable number of these, including the well-known international agreements relating to industrial and intellectual property. Some of the international agreements particularly relevant to our subject matter will be dealt with in subsequent sections of this chapter.

Hungary has signed (but not yet ratified) the Convention Relating to a Uniform Law on the International Sale of Goods, and the Convention Relating to a Uniform Law on the Formation of Contracts for the International Sale of Goods.

The creation of the United Nations Commission on International Trade Law (UNCITRAL), now performing such useful activities, was due to a Hungarian initiative. The representative of Hungary also actively participates in the work of the UN Economic Commission for Europe.

FOREIGN TRADE PROCEDURES AND PRACTICES

Customs Duties

The Hungarian customs system is characterized by ad valorem duties. Its present tariffs have been in effect since January 1, 1968.[38] These are based on the 1950 Brussels nomenclature. Hungarian customs duties[39] have three columns. Column I contains the rates to be applied on goods coming from countries that enjoy preferential treatment in Hungary (mostly in Latin America, Africa, and Asia). Column II relates to goods of countries according Hungary most-favored-nation treatment (about 100 countries belong to this category). The rates of Column III relate to goods of countries that discriminate against Hungarian goods. The rates of this column are, as a rule, double the corresponding rates in Column II.

The arithmetical average of all tariff rates of Column II is about 30 percent ad valorem (raw materials 0-5 percent, semifinished 5-20 percent, finished goods around 50 percent). The average Hungarian rate corresponds to the average of other countries.[40]

The main document for customs purposes is the "declaration of goods," to which various other documents (such as the commercial invoice) are attached as certification. The declaration is drawn up by the Hungarian enterprise authorized for foreign trade activity and serves as a basis for levying customs duty. According to law, it is possible temporarily to exempt certain foreign goods from customs duties. The relevant directives are issued annually by the competent central authorities.[41]

A Decree of the Council of Ministers (No. 23, September 9, 1973) provided for Hungary's Protocol of Accession to the GATT to be effective as of that date. Another Decree (No. 24, September 9, 1973) contains the modified text of the customs tariff and certain new items of Column II, which, from January 1, 1974, will become "concessional duties" in the sense of the GATT. It seems rather premature to say more about these events.

Licensing Requirements

Hungary's foreign trade licensing system is similar to that of other countries applying this administrative method of regulation.

Its dual function is to check transactions and correct foreign trade flows. "In the first instance, the task consists in a regional control of the trade flows, with the purpose of mutual implementation of the trade agreements."[42] The present licensing system is based on the Decree of the Minister of Foreign Trade No. 3 of November 26, 1967 on the Order of Licensing Foreign Trade in Goods and Services.[43]

The minister of Foreign Trade grants licenses exclusively to Hungarian enterprises or other Hungarian organizations authorized to perform foreign trade activity, and only regarding such transactions as fall within the sphere of activity allotted to them.

Occasional licenses are issued for individual foreign trade contracts as defined by the license; general licenses are issued for contracts regarding a defined type of goods or services. The scope of the latter licences may be limited to a particular country and may be made subject to specific conditions. The grant of a license by the minister of Foreign Trade, ipso iure, also constitutes permission by the foreign exchange authority to purchase foreign exchange to the extent and for the purpose defined by the license.[44]

In the absence of the necessary license, a purported contract is null and void. However, permission subsequently granted by the minister of Foreign Trade may validate the contract, with ex tunc effect. From this legal rule, it follows also that a Hungarian enterprise generally entitled to perform foreign trade activity in a defined field may conclude a contract even before the license is granted, with the reservation that the validity of the contract is "subject to the approval of the competent authorities."

> The purpose of the licensing system is to review import and export activities, to keep stable the balance of payments and to secure the execution of trade and payments agreements. The licensing authority does not verify whether sound economic reasons underlie the transaction in question.[45]

Credit, Banking, and Foreign-Exchange System

The role of the National Bank of Hungary has already been noted.[46] The fundamental legal rule relating to it is the Law Decree No. 36 December 17, 1967.[47] Hungary has ratified the Geneva Convention of June 7, 1930 providing for a uniform law for bills of exchange and promissory notes and the Geneva Convention of March 19, 1931 providing for a uniform law for cheques (by Law-Decrees Nos. 1 and 2 of 1965, respectively). In 1963 the National Bank of Hungary and the Hungarian Foreign Trade Bank accepted the International Chamber of Commerce's Uniform Customs and Practice for Documentary Credit and Uniform Rules for the Collection of Commercial Papers.

The basic principles of foreign credits to be granted or contracted by Hungarian enterprises are established by the competent cabinet ministers; the actual permission enabling a Hungarian enterprise to grant or accept a foreign credit relating to the trade of commodities is issued by the minister of Foreign Trade.

Access to the Hungarian Market

According to the legal rule defining foreign trade transactions,[48] advertising in the Hungarian press by a foreign firm can only take place through the intermediary of an authorized Hungarian enterprise, and agency agreements with or representation of foreign firms can be undertaken only by a Hungarian enterprise that has the right to participate in foreign trade. Thus, these basic forms of marketing are open to any foreign firms through the intermediary of an authorized Hungarian organization.

All foreign firms have the right to advertise their commodities or services in any Hungarian publication that accepts advertising through the intermediary of one of the competent Hungarian advertising agencies.[49]

Next to advertising, the most efficient method of canvassing a market is having a local agent. In Hungary, "agency enterprises" are specially organized for this purpose. They know the market thoroughly and are fully able to bring a foreign exporter into contact with potential Hungarian partners. The 11 existing enterprises of this type represent a considerable number of Western firms in Hungary. Under the new order of economic management, they are directly interested in their income from commissions, and they are very reliable representatives of the interests entrusted to them.

Any foreigner may visit Hungary by obtaining an entry visa by way of a quick and simple process. Also, a residence permit is available and is granted by the minister of Internal Affairs.[50] Thus, foreign businessmen may negotiate either personally or through their agents, provided they observe the legal regulations of the country (for example they may negotiate only with Hungarian enterprises authorized to perform foreign trade activities).

For establishing a local office, permission by the competent authority is needed. Such an office does not have the right to conclude foreign trade contracts. Foreigners are free to organize expositions, demonstrations, and so on through the intermediary of an authorized Hungarian organization, which must give prior notice to the Hungarian Chamber of Commerce.[51]

Lectures and performances, especially when they relate to a well-defined branch of the economy or to a limited subject, may prove very useful in canvassing the Hungarian market. This general type of marketing activity is efficiently promoted by the Hungarian Chamber of Commerce, especially by its regional sections. As a rule, lectures, performances, and exhibitions are organized on the basis of mutuality; they may very effectively complement other marketing activities.

FOREIGN TRADE CONTRACTS—LEGAL BACKGROUND

In the foregoing sections, we were mainly concerned with the constitutional, administrative, and organizational aspects of Hungarian foreign trade. In the following discussion, we shall deal with the civil law aspects.

Private International Law

Private international law in its original, narrower sense (that is, the determination of the proper law to be applied), although as important to the businessman as it is to the jurist, may become a source of some insecurity and unexpected difficulties. Trade is based on calculation, foresight, and taking into account such risks as can be covered by insurance or self-insurance. One of these risks is the "legal risk," meaning that the contract may be affected by some legal rule the effect of which was not foreseen by the interested party (or by either of the parties) but that takes place independently of their will. Contracts in international trade require legal security based on clear draftsmanship.

Regarding conflicts of law, two questions are of fundamental importance for the jurist dealing with international trade (including East-West trade):

Is unlimited free choice of law recognized in the country of the other party?

What is the attitude of the legal system of the partner's country regarding renvoi?

Until now, Hungary has had no separate Code of Private International Law. Thus, although its laws sporadically contain some regulations falling under this heading, there is yet no enacted private international law in Hungary. A universal "Code on Conflicts of Law" is in preparation, but its draft has not yet been published. However, Hungarian legal theory provides unambiguous answers to the two questions noted above.

Hungarian legal literature generally accepts the principle of the free choice of law in the field of contracts, whereas it refuses renvoi in this field. In other words, "proper law of the contract" does not mean also the norms of private international law of the legal system referred to.[52] At the same time, the Hungarian legal system generally considers the proper law of obligations to be the law of the place of business or habitual residence (company premises) of the debtor or, in the case of sale of goods, of the seller.[53] As regards contractual formalities, however, the law of the place of contracting is generally recognized as the proper law.

Hungarian Civil Law

The Hungarian Civil Code[54] regulates the entire field of civil law, including trade relations, in a comprehensive manner. Although, as mentioned above, certain rules of the old Hungarian Commercial Code are still in force for the time being, it may generally be said that in Hungary all civil law relations—except family and labor law—are governed by a single code. There is no distinction between civil and commercial law, and there are no separate codes of civil law for domestic and international business transactions, respectively.

The part of Hungarian civil law dealing with obligations includes contract law rules.[55] Here one has to emphasize two principles of fundamental practical importance: (1) the rules of the law of contract are mainly permissive rather than mandatory—that is, contracting parties are free to decide on the content of their contract as they see fit; and (2) the parties are also free to choose the type of contract—that is, they are not bound to any forms or types of contract mentioned in the law.[56]

These principles make it possible for those participating in international trade freely to choose the content of their contracts even if Hungarian law is to be applied.

A formal requirement of Hungarian foreign trade contracts is that they be in writing. This can be telegraphic or by Telex. Apart from a few sporadic cases in some branches of trade, written agreements are common in international trade practice, even in the absence of legal provision to this effect.[57]

Hungarian law makes it possible for the parties to limit, or even to exclude, claims for breach of contract.[58] However, the general legal rule[59] (applicable even to exemption clauses) is that liability for breach of contract caused wilfully or by gross negligence, by committing a criminal offense, or by damaging social property, cannot validly be excluded by the parties.[60] Thus the limitation or exclusion of liability in foreign trade transactions is permitted by Hungarian contract law in the same way as in most European countries.

Formation of Contracts

As between the alternative principles of "will" and "declaration," the latter is accepted by Hungarian law: "A Contract shall come into existence by the mutual and concurrent expression of the intention of the parties."[61] Hungarian law of contracts is similar to that of most other legal systems and distinguishes two stages in the process of formation of a contract—offer and acceptance.[62]

The offerer is bound by his offer (unless expressly excluded in the offer). When the parties are in each other's presence or when communicating by telephone, the offer must be immediately accepted, otherwise it ceases to be effective. When the parties are not in each other's presence, the contract comes into being when the declaration of acceptance reaches the offerer. If the declaration of acceptance includes a modification of the conditions originally offered, this constitutes a refusal of the original offer and a new offer. This, in turn, must be either accepted or refused by the offerer. In the case of contracts concluded between distant partners, the place of contracting is the domicile or place of residence (registered offices) of the offerer.[63]

Performance of Contracts

Contracts have to be performed according to their terms, at the place and in the time specified and according to the quantity, quality, and assortment fixed in the contract. The parties are obliged to cooperate in performing the contract.[64] Under Hungarian law, specific performance is an important remedy.[65] For cases of breach of contract (delay of delivery, faulty performance, anticipatory breach), Hungarian law knows the concept of "implied conditions and/or warranties" and provides appropriate remedies.[66] These range from specific performance, to repair, to substitution, to payment of damages. Survey of the relevant rules would exceed the limits of the present chapter. We might note, however, that the rules of tort apply to questions concerning responsibility for breach of contract and to the measure of damages.[67]

COOPERATION AGREEMENTS AND JOINT VENTURES

Cooperation Agreements

"The term cooperation, applied to a wide range of technico-economic phenomena, has been recurring with increasing frequency in international trade, as a very loosely defined and fairly complex notion." Like the transfer of know-how, cooperation "is not a legal but an economic concept of general character brought about by technic economic requirements."[68]

Although some franchise and exclusive sales agreements (known as "vertical cooperation") have been concluded between Hungarian and foreign partners, mainly for Hungarian export such as motor vehicles, the so-called horizontal type involving interfirm production cooperation is far more common. Production cooperation may cover research and development, shared production, so-called specialization and, in connection with all of these, marketing cooperation. As a rule, production cooperation often involves the establishment of a common network of repair and services, or the common use of an agency network.

The general rules of civil law, briefly reviewed in the previous section, provide broad flexibility for structuring cooperation agreements as the parties see fit.

Of course, a cooperation agreement may be concluded only with a Hungarian company authorized to conduct foreign trade activities. The permission necessary for negotiating and concluding such an agreement must be obtained by the would-be Hungarian partner.[69] Certain special rules[70] are applicable to cooperation transaction; these are part of the general regulation of foreign trade licensing.

Two Hungarian agency enterprises deal mainly with cooperation, but all other companies and other organizations authorized for foreign trade activity also have the right to enter into cooperation agreements. Also an enterprise that does not have such authority may nonetheless be involved in the conclusion of the agreement when it is interested in the cooperation in question (for example, when it produces the goods affected).

In spite of the rapid growth of cooperation agreements, in a legal sense they are not typical international trade transactions. They have no clear-cut system of legal regulation, and one can hardly speak about a uniform practice. In any case, the value of a legal regulation would seem rather doubtful in the case of the protean concept of cooperation, as its distinguishing features are mainly technical and economic, rather than legal.

Joint Ventures

We have already noted that at present there is a possibility not only for Hungarian enterprises to start joint ventures abroad, in community with foreigners, but also for foreign enterprises or other legal persons to enter into Hungarian business association—subject, of course, to obtaining permission and to conditions set by the competent Hungarian authority.[72] Since no uniform practice has yet developed with respect to the latter, let us turn to the exposition contained in a highly informative article:

. . . Economic associations may be created under Law-Decree No. 19 of 1970, implemented by Minister of Finance Decree No. 28 of 1972 (3.10) listing the modes of establishing such associations and the relevant financial rules.

The Decree permits the setting up of associations in which the Hungarian and foreign participants—prompted by their mutual interests—join their efforts for technological development, efficient trade, or servicing activities. The mixed company may even directly participate in production whenever this is warranted economically, provided such a contingency is foreseen in an interstate agreement and the consent of the Council of Ministers is available.

The association may take any of the forms known in Hungarian statutory law, such as joint-stock company, private limited company, unlimited partnership or joint enterprise. The association is managed by a board composed of the delegates of the Hungarian party and the foreign one.

In any association, the material interest of the Hungarian party should generally be not less than 51 percent. The interest of the foreign party may consist of a direct compensation for his economic activity, as well as a share in the profits—both to be regulated in the Articles of Association.

The creation of a mixed association with Hungarian and foreign members and the commencement of its operation is dependent on the permit of the Minister of Finance which is issued by approving the Articles of Association. Apart from this permit the corporation will have to apply for all the permits which a Hungarian company would have to obtain before commencing its operation. For instance, if the company proposes to operate in foreign trade, it must obtain the permit of the Ministry of Foreign Trade to conduct such activities. Similarly, if it wants to erect buildings, it must obtain the permits of the building authority, etc. Thus, the Hungarian statutory rules will apply to the mixed company the same as to any Hungarian company. These rules govern their transactions in foreign currency and loans or credits. The company must pay taxes. Out of its incomes it must set aside a reserve (risk) fund as long as this amounts to 10 percent of the

company assets. After the deduction of the amount of
reserve fund the remaining profit may be used for creating a sharing fund. The sharing fund—whence the employees get their bonuses—cannot exceed 15 percent of
the annual wages total. The net profit remaining after
the deduction of the risk fund and the sharing fund will
be the basis of the company profit tax. The profit tax is
40 percent on profit up to 20 percent of the company
assets, and 60 percent on profits exceeding this limit.
Incidentally, when the company adds the taxable profits
to its assets, it may apply to the Ministry of Finance
for a partial refund of the tax. The company is obliged
to defray the other taxes and similar payments prescribed by Hungarian statutes, such as social security
and superannuation contributions. However, it is not
held to pay other contributions prescribed for Hungarian
state-owned enterprises, such as the charge on fixed
assets engaged, depreciation allowance and wage-increase
levies. The wages of the employees are governed by the
Articles of Association and by the labour contracts within
the limits of the statutory rules and the approved Articles
of Association. Employees who are foreign nationals may
transfer 50 percent of their incomes abroad in the currency determined in the Articles of Association.

The Hungarian National Bank may issue a guarantee
for the reimbursement of the damages arising from any
government measure affecting the foreign party's financial
contribution; such reimbursement may not exceed the
amount of the contribution. The Bank will transfer abroad
the profits due to the foreign member, as well as his share
of the assets in proportion to his quota in the property—in
case he quits the association.

The losses of the association are to be charged
against the risk fund. If this does not cover the losses
and the members do not settle them in some other way,
the Minister of Finance will decide upon the further
operation or on the winding up of the association. In the
case of bankruptcy, when the accumulated debts run above
the assets, the Minister of Finance will decree the liquidation of the association. After settling the debts, the
remaining foreign share of capital may be transferred
abroad free of taxes.[73]

Such joint ventures go beyond cooperation in the sense discussed
in the preceding subsection. Cooperation however, offers a good start

toward the joint venture in that it enables the partners to get acquainted with one another, and with the economic, technical, and human factors of cooperation. If experience in all these respects is favorable, cooperation may be gradually tightened and eventually serve as a firm basis for a future joint venture.

INDUSTRIAL PROPERTY RIGHTS, TRANSACTIONS INVOLVING TECHNOLOGY, AND COPYRIGHT PROTECTION

The Protections Accorded

Hungary joined the 1883 Paris Union in 1909, and the Bern Convention in 1931.[74] Industrial designs have been protected in Hungary since 1907.[75] As regards unfair competition, Act of Parliament V of 1923 (maintained in force by the introductory law of the Civil Code) follows the German regulatory approach. After defining generally the concept of unfair competition, the 1923 statute enumerates examples of the most frequent types thereof, such as unfair advertising, imitation, and slander. In 1969 three modern legal statutes came into effect, namely the laws on patents, trademarks, and copyright.[76]

In 1971 the London Chamber of Commerce, in conjunction with the Hungarian Chamber of Commerce, organized an "Open Forum" on Hungarian legal provisions on patents, trademarks, licensing, and know-how agreements. The report published on the basis of that Open Forum contains much useful information on protection industrial property in Hungary and on related business transactions.[77]

Generally speaking, the Hungarian laws on patents, trademarks, and copyright ensure up-to-date and appropriate remedies and the courts sanction infringements severely, even if only state-owned enterprises are concerned, as in one recent case.

Although in principle, there is a legal difference between the absolute-type legal protection of patents and the merely contractual protection accorded to know-how agreements,[78] practical experience shows that, at the present stage of industrial development, even the best-protected patents can be circumvented. Therefore, many enterprises do not apply for patents for some of their most important inventions, since the invention would then become "public"—although legally protected. On the other hand, a know-how agreement generally offers sufficient protection under the legal rules relating to protection of business secrets and against unfair competition, as well as under the general requirements of civil law.

In our opinion fair business behavior is not only in the interest of all, but is also the general attitude of the majority of businessmen taking part in international trade. Although lawyers tend toward pessimism, we think it important to bear in mind the commercial adage of "trust, not distrust."[79]

As regards new legislation in the field of industrial property, the fact deserving most emphasis is perhaps that, similarly to the Federal Republic of Germany, France, and other countries,[80] Hungary has introduced the so-called system of delayed examination. The complete, thorough examination of the novelty of an invention is "delayed" by four years from the date of the application for the patent.[81] The protection of a patent lasts 20 years from the date when the application for the patent was registered.[82] The Chapter of the 1969 patent law entitled "Contracts for Utilization"[83] establishes the basic rules for licensing. These are not mandatory rules, and the contracting parties are free to depart from them. As regards questions not regulated by specific legal rules, and in the absence of a contractual agreement, the appropriate general rules of the Hungarian Civil Code are to be applied (when according to the rules of private international law, Hungarian substantive law would have to be applied).

In Hungary the registration of patent licenses is not obligatory. However, a licensing contract may be held against a bona fide acquirer of rights who has paid consideration only if it has been recorded in the Register of Patents. The licensor is deemed to warrant that, for the duration of the license contract, the license does not violate third-party rights. In other respects the rules relating to warranties for goods sold apply. When rights of a third party impede or restrict the use of the license, the licensee has the right to rescind the contract with immediate effect. Sublicensing is permitted only with the explicit consent of the patentee. The patentee has to provide for the maintenance of the patent.

According to the new Hungarian Trademark Law,[84] the duration of a trademark is 10 years from the date of application; this may be prolonged by up to 10 additional years. Whereas earlier a trademark could be transferred only when the enterprise itself was sold, at present it may be transferred separately, by means of a contract. The successor of an enterprise automatically acquires the right to use its trademarks. The law makes it possible to grant a trademark license by contract. The relevant rules are also of a permissive character.

In patent and trademark matters, any Hungarian patent attorney can represent a foreign party before the competent Hungarian authority (the National Patent Office). In most cases, foreigners are represented in this respect by a Hungarian patent bureau organized in the form of a state-owned enterprise,[85] but several lawyers' cooperatives also maintain separate patent agency departments dealing with the same tasks.

Transfer of Technology—Patent Licenses and Know-How Agreements

Only Hungarian enterprises or other organizations entitled to engage in foreign trade activity have the right to conclude patent licenses and know-how agreements. This applies both to the granting and the acquiring of licenses. As a rule, the import and export of patent licenses and know-how may be performed only by the enterprise or organization competent to deal in the commodity or technology in question. In addition, a state-owned foreign trade enterprise was specially founded for this purpose;[86] it deals in particular with the granting of licenses to foreign parties. The enterprise or organization entitled to conduct foreign trade activity must obtain a special permission to conclude a license contract, as in the case of the sale of goods.[87]

All international patent license and know-how agreements are subject to very careful preparation. Transactions with Hungarian parties are no different in this respect. Moreover, it bears emphasis, to clear up misunderstandings that seem to persist even today, that the relative ease or difficulty of concluding such agreements with Hungarian companies, and the relative complexity of the agreement, depends exclusively on the technical, economic, and financial factors involved; the view that contracting in this field is not easy with an "Eastern partner" is a mistake. The time required for these transactions is due to their complexity, to their nature and value—as persons with practical experience in East-West trade relations have come to realize.

Patent licenses are acquired when an enterprise wants to manufacture an item that it did not manufacture before, or not in the particular form, quantity, and so on, or when it wants to produce the item by means of some new procedure, technology, and equipment, and so on. For this reason, simple patent licenses, authorizing the licensee to use a patent, but not accompanied by transfer of the appropriate know-how, are becoming a rarity—occurring only in special fields or when the licensor has no particular know-how to transfer and the new product or technology will have to be developed by the licensee or by both parties. The typical license, however, involves transfer of the necessary know-how. As a rule, this also entails a set of accessory contractual elements such as engineering services or design work. Few new products based on licenses do not require new or modified "tools."

From what has been said above regarding the conclusion of license and know-how agreements, and on the possibility of free choice of law, as well as from the fact that, as we shall see, the parties can agree to the jurisdiction of ordinary courts of law or a court of arbitration, it follows that the conclusion and performance of license and know-how agreements involve legal issues similar to those involved in other types of international trade transactions. Licenses and know-how agreements between Hungarian and foreign parties generally refer disputes to arbitration, and arbitration awards are never published, so there is no "case law" to serve as a guide as to legal practice.[88] Nor do the large corporations engaged in important international licensing contracts make these documents publicly available. In our experience, such information is denied even when the other party to the contract would be ready to give his consent. Thus, all important international license and know-how contracts are, as a practical matter unavailable even for the purpose of legal scholarship. The "model contracts" recommended by various authors are, in general, unsuitable for practical application in foreign trade transactions.

Some Typical Provisions of License Contracts Concluded by Hungarian Partners

The following discussion contains the personal observations of the writer and is not intended to suggest any legal regulations or directives in this area. The information may, however, reflect to a modest degree the custom in certain branches of industry where licenses are acquired by Hungarian parties.

Drafting Contracts. Careful, patient preparatory work is indispensable. The parties should have a mutual understanding of the nature and amount of services required, the capacity available, and the steps needed to enable the licensee to start production faultlessly. This will make it possible to determine the need for additional purchases of raw materials, semifinished goods, equipment, or even additional, related licenses, the extent to which the licensor can arrange for these, or whether a consortium of several firms is needed. It is at this stage that the partners exchange information on their respective technical capabilities on any special regulations that may affect the transaction, such as rules on labor safety and fire protection, in the licensee's country. This intensive preparatory stage can help prevent difficulties that might arise subsequently.

The Recital Clauses of the Contract. These clauses normally indicate the identity of the parties and state the common business objective to be served by the contract. As regards the former, the competent foreign trade company must figure as the Hungarian party. Also, the Hungarian enterprise that is going to utilize the license to start up production must be mentioned, since this enterprise—even if it is not entitled to conduct foreign trade activity—is necessarily in direct contact with the foreign party to the transaction in the course of drafting and fulfilling the contract. As a rule, those legal declarations that can independently be made by the user of the license are included in the contract. Although the contract is concluded by a Hungarian foreign trade company on its own account, it serves the purposes of the user of the license. The latter cannot be considered as a stranger to the contract in the sense of the well-known "privity rule" of the Common Law, and the "duty of care" imposed on the licensor must also be observed vis-à-vis the user.

Material and Territorial Scope of the Contract. The material scope of the contract must be unambiguously defined in a technical sense, to indicate the subject matter of the license. It is here that patents covered by the contract have to be enumerated, eventually in a separate appendix. The territorial scope of the contract means, essentially, the geographical areas where items produced by use of the license may be exported. It follows from the fact that the Hungarian national economy is highly export-oriented that, with rare exceptions, a Hungarian firm would not wish to obtain a patent license without obtaining adequate rights to export items produced on the basis of the license. The export markets sought by a Hungarian party usually—and understandably—comprise all or the majority of the CMEA countries. But in most cases, especially when license fees (either lump sum or royalties) are to be paid in convertible currency, the Hungarian partner will also wish to have the right to export to Western markets. In our opinion, appropriate export rights—which is to say, such rights as are compatible with the interests of both parties—are of fundamental importance.

The Licensor's Obligations. The licensor is obliged, first, to deliver sufficient and correct documentation regarding the manufacturing process. Details regarding the quality and extent of such documentation may be conveniently included as an appendix to the contract.

The licensor's obligation to provide technical assistance includes such elements as the transfer of oral or written know-how, training of workers, quality control, and so on, depending on the nature of the agreement and the industry involved. Obligations regarding subsequent improvements are also very important. Here, it is advisable to define precisely the extent of the obligation or, conversely, what is not to be treated as an improvement to be transferred by the licensor.

Payments. In Hungarian contractual practice, all forms of license-fee payment are known and applied—lump sum, annual royalties, and so on. The latter may be based on various factors—for example, value of production—with or without stipulation of minimum rates.

Royalties may be based upon total production in Hungary, or only upon exports. When license fees are calculated upon production or some other quantitative standard, it is possible and customary to stipulate some method of checking and auditing. A common practice is to rely on certificates issued by such authorities as the Hungarian Chamber of Commerce or the Hungarian Foreign Trade Bank Ltd. The conditions and guarantees regarding payments do not differ from those applied in Hungarian foreign trade in goods.

Liability. A fundamental aspect of patent licenses and know-how contractual liability, remedies for breach, and related matters, It seems indispensable to regulate these questions, including third party liability, adequacy of documentation, the consequences of delay, and so on. Hungarian licenses must, in particular, be adequately protected with respect to the manufacturing and marketing provisions of license agreements.

Duration. Generally, the duration of a license contract is 5 to 10 years. Provisions regarding expiry, cancellation, or rescission with or without immediate effect are more or less similar to the corresponding provisions in foreign trade contracts relating to the delivery of goods.

It is most important clearly to provide for the consequences of expiry—for example, whether or not the licensee will be entitled to continue producing and marketing. Certain licenses require great amounts of investment and recurring inputs, and in some large contracts continuation of the right to produce and market after expiry is expressly provided.

Miscellaneous Provisions. It is advisable to provide for the eventualities caused by force majeure and, when the partners are willing to so agree, also for any other ground for relief. In this respect, the general tendency is rather restrictive. In an ever growing number of countries, and for the time being mostly in domestic cases, there is an increasing trend toward recognition of the strict (but not absolute) liability of producers and sellers.

The interests of both parties are best served when they know that they may be exempted from their obligations only in exceptional cases, strictly delimited by objective factors.

Other provisions of license agreements that are of particular significance include those concerning settlement of disputes and applicable law, matters discussed at greater length elsewhere in this chapter.

SETTLEMENT OF FOREIGN TRADE DISPUTES

Every Hungarian enterprise or other organization authorized
to engage in foreign trade activity is free to agree that disputes arising
in connection therewith will be settled by a competent Hungarian or
foreign court. When the parties have agreed upon the exclusive jurisdiction of a particular foreign court, this precludes subsequent litigation before Hungarian courts. Similarly, the parties are free to
stipulate that any legal disputes will be settled by arbitration, either
in Hungary or in some other country.

Foreign Trade Arbitration Machinery in Hungary

Ad Hoc Boards of Arbitration. Any Hungarian socialist organization
and its foreign partner, or two foreign parties, may agree by contract
to stipulate the competence of a Hungarian Board of Arbitration; in
this case no other action before courts of law can take place.[89] A
contract providing for submission to arbitration may be concluded
by an exchange of letters, telegram, or Telex. According to the Hungarian arbitration procedure, the Board of Arbitration is obliged to
hear both parties, to draw up a record of the hearings, and to give
the reasons for its award. The award is equivalent to a final judgment
of a court of law, and execution may take place on the basis of the
award. The interested party may, within 90 days, bring an action
before the Budapest Metropolitan Court for annulment of the award
on the ground that the contract providing for submission to arbitration
did not relate to the legal dispute in question, or that the provisions
of the contract regarding the establishment of the Board of Arbitration
or its award were violated, or that the award was taken without hearing
the losing party, or that the award was not sufficiently reasoned.
However, such an action may relate only to the question of the validity
of the award (or a conciliation settlement reached before the Board
of Arbitration). The party bringing such an action may ask that execution be suspended pending the court's decision.

The Arbitration Tribunal Attached to the Hungarian Chamber of Commerce. The competence of this institutionally organized Arbitration
Tribunal may be stipulated by written contract or by international
agreement. Its awards, and the conciliation settlements reached before
it are subject to execution in the same way as those of the ordinary
courts of law.[90] The Arbitration Tribunal deals mainly with legal
disputes between Hungarian and foreign parties, or between two foreign
parties.[91] Arbitration takes place by a sole arbitrator only on the
explicit wish of the parties; in all other cases the Arbitration Tribunal
consists of three members.

241

It should be emphasized that a foreign party may select his arbitrator from among the persons whose names appear on the Chamber's panel of arbitrators, or he may designate a foreign national whose name is not on the panel.[92] The Arbitration Tribunal of the Hungarian Chamber of Commerce applies the law selected by the parties, or if the parties have not so provided, the proper law of the contract according to the rules of private international law.

Recognition and Enforcement of Arbitration
Clauses and Awards

Hungary has ratified the 1961 European (Geneva) Convention on International Commercial Arbitration (by Law Decree No. 8 of 1964) as well as the 1958 United Nations (New York) Convention on the Recognition and Enforcement of Foreign Arbitral Awards (by Law Decree No. 25 of 1962). Under the applicable procedural rules, final judgments of foreign courts and final decisions of foreign arbitration tribunals on property claims are enforceable if this is allowed under a treaty with the foreign state in question, or when reciprocity of enforcement is ascertained by the Hungarian minister of Justice.[93] Hungary has also concluded bilateral judicial assistance treaties with many countries, some of which include provisions on mutual recognition of court judgments or arbitration awards.

Quite apart from the existence of any multilateral or bilateral treaty relations in this respect between Hungary and a foreign country, it is worth noting that no Hungarian enterprise or organization engaged in foreign trade has ever failed to respect a foreign court judgment or arbitral award rendered in accordance with the provisions of a contract providing for such court jurisdiction or arbitration. Although Hungary is a foreign-trade-oriented country, its international legal disputes are rather rare as compared with the volume of its trade. It seems that Hungarian enterprises find it more useful and effective to resolve legal disputes by means of conciliation rather than litigation.

Of course, the best solution is preventive, by precise drafting of contracts and voluntary fulfillment of the letter and spirit of agreements by both parties. Overriding interests of international trade require mutual good faith and the keeping of promises, and elimination of controversies according to the principle of do ut des, facio ut facias. By adhering to this principle, concrete problems can be solved, and valuable economic relations and invaluable good-will may be kept intact.

NOTES

1. Ph. S. James, <u>Introduction to English Law</u> 9 (Butterworth 6th ed., 1966).

2. Constitution of the Hungarian People's Republic (hereinafter "Const."), sec. 77, para 1. By Act I of 1972, April 19, 1972, Parliament accepted the Amendment of Act XX of 1949, the consolidated text of the Constitution.

3. For a comprehensive treatment of the subject dealt with in this chapter and English texts of many of the legal provisions discussed hereinafter, see I. Szász, <u>Hungarian Statutes Concerning Foreign Trade</u> (Budapest, 1971; published by Corvina Press and commissioned by the Hungarian Chamber of Commerce).

4. Const. sec. 1 and sec. 2, para. 1.

5. Const. sec. 6 para. 1.

6. Const. sec. 6 para. 2.

7. Const. sec. 11.

8. Const. sec. 7.

9. Act of Parliament VII, Dec. 22, 1972, enacted by Council of Ministers Decree No. 1046 of the same date, <u>Magyar Kozlony</u> (Hungarian Gazette), No. 104, 1972.

10. Decree No. 1023, June 30, 1973.

11. Const. sec. 8.

12. Const. sec. 9.

13. Const. sec. 10, para. 1.

14. G. Eörsi, <u>A gazdasagiranyitas uj rendszere atteres jogarol</u> 11 (On the Law of the Transition to the New System of Economic Control and Management) (Közgazdasági és Jogi Könyvkiadó, Budapest, 1968).

15. Government Decree No. 4161 of 1949, sec. 1.

16. I. Mezneries, <u>Penzügyi jog a szocialista gazdalkodasban</u> 537 (Financial Law in the Socialist Economy) (Közgazdasági és Jogi Könyvkiadó, Budapest, 1972).

17. Decree of the Minister of Foreign Trade No. 1 of May 10, 1960, which has general validity in accordance with sec. 39 of the Foreign Exchange Code and sec. 37 of Law Decree No. 11 of 1960 on the Enactment and Execution of the Civil Code.

18. Government Decree No. 2052 of September 17, 1967, on the Tasks, Scope of Authority, and Organization of the Ministry of Foreign Trade.

19. It may be obtained free of charge from the Hungarian Chamber of Commerce or from the Commercial Section of any Hungarian embassy or legation, in Hungarian, English and other languages.

20. See Const. sec. 9 and sec. 10, para. 1.

21. Government Decree No. 2027 of May 28, 1967, on the Tasks and Responsibility of Cabinet Ministers Supervising Economic Branches.

22. Government Decree cited supra note 18, Chapter I, secs. 1, 2, and final provision.

23. For more comprehensive discussion, see J. Biró, A magyar Külkereskelmi Politika (The Trade Policy of Hungary) (Közgazdasági és Jogi Könyvkiadó, Budapest, 1970).

24. Act No. IV of 1959; Hungarian Civil Code secs. 31-38.

25. Government Decree No. 11 of May 13, 1967 on state-owned enterprises, sec. 3, para. 3.

26. Law-Decree No. 11 of April 12, 1960, on Enactment and Execution of the Civil Code, Appendix: on the Former Regulations Remaining in Force. In its time, the old Hungarian Commercial Code was formulated, intentionally, as a near reproduction of the German Allgemeines Handelsgesetzbuch of 1861. This German law preceded the Handelsgesetzbuch of 1895, which is now in force; the 1965 revision of the German law on joint-stock companies (Aktiengesellschaften) is thus the third variant of the original German law that had served as a model for the old regulation of Hungarian company law. The Hungarian Act V of 1930, on the creation of companies similar to the private limited company (Gesellschaft mit beschraenkter Haftung), similarly relied on German inspiration.

27. Also, the rules regarding unlimited partnerships (Offene Handelsgesellschaft) of the old Hungarian Commercial Code have remained in force.

28. Law Decree 19 of 1970, Chapter III and notably sec. 31.

29. Decree of the Minister of Finance No. 28 of October 3, 1972 on Economic Associations Operating with Foreign Participation.

30. Act IV of 1959, Chapter XLV, secs. 536-570.

31. Directive of the Minister of Foreign Trade No. 35 of 1967, Külkereskedelmi Ertesito (Foreign Trade Bulletin) No. 1, 1968.

32. Decree of the Minister of Foreign Trade No. 2, May 30, 1968.

33. Government Decree No. 61 of December 23, 1967, modified by Decree of the Council of Minister No. 21 of May 21, 1972.

34. See notes 9, 10, and 14 supra.

35. Sect. 9 of Act of Parliament VII, Dec. 23, 1972, supra note 9.

36. Id. sec. 7, para. 1 and pt. 9.

37. Op. cit supra note 23 at 86-90.

38. Law Decree No. 2 of 1966 of the Presidium of the Hungarian People's Republic on the Regulation of Customs Law with the enactment regarding its execution; Government Decree No. 9 of Feb. 2, 1966; and Government Decree No. 48 of Nov. 19, 1967, on Commercial Customs Tariffs.

39. The rates effective from January 1, 1972, were fixed by Government Decree No. 26 of Sept. 2, 1971.

40. S. Nagy, A magyar vámjog 25-28 (The Hungarian Customs Law) (ed. by Hungarian Chamber of Commerce and College of Foreign Trade, Budapest, 1973). Compare Szász, supra note 3 at 35-38.

41. By authorization granted in sec. 3 of Government Decree No. 48, supra note 38, the Ministers of Foreign Trade and of Transport and Communications have issued in common Decree No. 10 of Dec. 29, 1972. The Appendix of Decree No. 10 enumerates the commodities temporarily exempt from customs duties. A condition of the exemption is that the commodity in question must originate from a country enjoying the most-favored-nation treatment accorded under Column II of the customs tariff.

42. Biró, supra note 23 at 102.

43. See Szász, supra note 3 at 31-32 and 137-143. The decree mentioned in the text has been amended by the Decree of the Minister of Foreign Trade No. 8 of Nov. 16, 1969.

44. See section of the text entitled "Authority to Engage in Foreign Trade."

45. Szász, supra note 3 at 31.

46. See sections of the text entitled "Authority to Engage in Foreign Trade" and "Financial Institutions, Insurance, and Shipping Services."

47. The statutes of the Bank were published in Magyar Közlöny (Hungarian Gazette) No. 24, March 17, 1968.

48. See note 17 supra.

49. The two agency enterprises operating at present are the Hungexpo Advertising Agency, Budapest 70, P.O.B. 44, and the Magyar Hirdető Full-Service Agency, Budapest V. P.O.B. 367. In addition to advertisements published in daily newspapers, periodicals, and so on, Hungarian importers may effectively be reached by advertising in Magyar Import (Hungarian Imports), a periodical edited by the Hungarian Chamber of Commerce and sent to every Hungarian enterprise that is a member of the Chamber—that is, to the units representing the overwhelming part of economic life, and the majority of potential users of foreign commodities.

50. Trips of foreigners to Hungary and their stay in the country are subject to regulations contained in Government Decree No. 24 of Sept. 25, 1966, and in the Decree of the Minister of Interior No. 4 of Sept. 25, 1966. Depending on the purpose of his stay, a foreigner may obtain a visa, a residence permit, or a permit to stay in the country that includes a labor permit.

51. Decree of the Minister of Foreign Trade No. 1 of Jan. 13, 1970.

52. See I. Szászy, Private International Law in the European Peoples' Democracies 284 (Akadémiai Kiadó Budapest, 1964), cited inter alia by Wittenstein in "Ungarn," No. 1500-AW Gr. W. IV, Auslaendisches Wirtschaftsrecht (E. Schmidt Verlag, Berlin, 1971).

53. Makarov, Quellen des internationalen Privatrechts, I, Gesetztexts (Berlin-Tübingen, 1953). The chapter on Hungary contains the draft of a code of private international law prepared by Professor Szászy in 1947. Sect. 11 of this draft excludes renvoi, and sect. 20, para 1, declares the principle of free choice of law; the same principle is explicitly referred to in sect. 57, para. 1, in respect of the law of obligations and in sect. 58, para. 2, in respect of the sale of goods. Although Hungary is not a participant of the 1955 Hague Convention, Hungarian "conflicts of Law" principles are generally the same as those set forth in Art. 2 of this convention as regards choice of law, and Art. 3 on application of the law of the seller's country. Art. 110, para. 1, of the 1968 General Conditions of Delivery Between Organizations of the Countries Participating in the Council for Mutual Economic Assistance (accepted by Hungary pursuant to Law Decree No. 35 of 1968), although applicable only to the legal relations between organizations of the CMEA countries, reflects a rule that is clearly the same as the principle generally accepted by Hungarian private international law, mentioned in the text.

54. Act IV of 1959, enacted by Law Decree No. 11 of 1959. The Code was amended by Law Decree No. 39 of 1967. The amended Hungarian Civil Code is hereafter referred to as C. C. Hung. Substantial portions of the Code are reproduced in Szász supra note 3 at 165-204.

55. See C. C. Hung., Part Four, Law of Obligations, I. The Contract, Chapters XVII-XXVIII, secs. 198-338; III. Individual Contracts, Chapters XXXIII-L, secs. 365-597.

56. C. C. Hung., sec. 200, para. 1: "The parties shall be free to determine the contents of the contract. They may, by common agreement, depart from the provisions relating to the contract unless such departure is forbidden by statute." And Law Decree No. 11 of 1960 sec. 31, para. 1, provides: "Where the parties may depart by mutual consent from the provisions of the Civil Code relating to contracts, any contractual terms fixed by international agreement or regulation shall be deemed to be agreed upon by the parties."

57. Compare sect. 4 of the United Kingdom's 1893 Sale of Goods Act, repealed by Sect. 1 of the Law Reform (Enforcement of Contracts) Act of 1954.

58. Law Decree No. 11 of 1960, sec. 54.

59. See C. C. Hung., sec. 314.

60. Such a restriction is known in most legal systems of Continental Europe—for example, Art. 100 of the Swiss Code of Obligations.

The "Suisse-Atlantique" case (1966) 2 All E.R. 61 (H.L.), aroused much dispute due to abandonment of the basic concept of "fundamental breach" that had been the rule for almost 40 years, but we cannot dwell on it here. Hungarian law in this respect is unambiguously permissive.

61. See C. C. Hung., sec. 207, para. 1.

62. Compare T. Guhl, Das Schweizerische Obligationenrecht, 110-111 (6th ed., Schhultheiss, Zurich, 1972). The notions of offer and acceptance stem from the older of private contracts between individuals, while the depersonalized mass contract is more characteristic of the present era.

63. See C. C. Hung., secs. 212-213.

64. See C. C. Hung., sec. 277. The principle of performance in kind is only apparently opposed to the Common Law approach, under which "specific performance" is only exceptionally allowed in equity. Under Hungarian law, if additional performance, replacement, or repair, or any kind of restitution in kind (that is, specific performance) becomes possible, the claim for restitution in kind changes into a pecuniary claim that, even in this secondary form, retains the character of restitution, that is, of damages.

65. See C. C. Hung., sec. 300, para. 1 (delay) and sec. 313 (anticipatory breach).

66. See C. C. Hung., secs. 303-04 (delay); secs. 305-308 implied conditions and warranties (faulty performance); sec. 313 (anticipatory breach).

67. C. C. Hung., sec. 318. See also sec. 54, Law Decree No. 11 of 1960, quoted in Szász, supra note 3 at 188.

68. J. Varró, "Different Types of Cooperation as Up-to-Date Forms of Foreign Trade," in Marketing in Hungary (Hungarian Chamber of Commerce) No. 1, 1973 at 13.

69. See section of this chapter entitled "Licensing Requirements."

70. Directive of the Minister of Foreign Trade No. 13 of 1969, Külkereskedelmi Ertesito (Foreign Trade Bulletin) No. 22, 1969, on licensing procedures with respect to industrial cooperation. In this directive reference is made to the general order of foreign trade licensing relating to goods and services and to the legal rules relating to it. See note 43 supra and accompanying text.

71. Intercooperation Co. Ltd. for Trade Promotion (Budapest 13, P.O.B. 53), and the "Hunicoop" Foreign Trade Office for Cooperation in the Engineering Industry (Budapest 5, P.O.B. 111). The activity of the latter extends mainly to branches of the metallurgy and machinery industries.

72. See notes 28 and 29 supra and accompanying text.

73. I. Szász, "The Legal Framework of Cooperation Contracts," in Marketing in Hungary (Hungarian Chamber of Commerce, Nov. 1, 1973) at 19.

74. The Rome Convention of June 22, 1928, on the amendment of the Bern Convention on the Protection of Literary and Art Works, was enacted by Hungary in Act XXIV of 1931.

The Hungarian Law Decree No. 17 of 1962 promulgated the texts of the following Union conventions, as revised in London on June 2, 1934: the Paris Union Convention for the protection of industrial property; the Madrid Agreement on Preventing False Declaration of the Origin of Commodities; and the Madrid Agreement on the International Registering of Industrial or Commercial Trademarks. The Decree of the President of the National Planning Office No. 2 of June 20, 1962 enacted the abovementioned Law Decree. Law Decree No. 7 of 1967 promulgated the texts of the following Union Conventions on the Protection of Industrial Property as revised in Lisbon (October 31, 1958) and Nice (June 15, 1967), respectively: the Paris Union Convention for the Protection of Industrial Property; the Madrid Agreement on International Registering of Industrial or Commercial Trade Marks; the Nice agreement on the international classification of products and services provided with industrial or commercial trademarks; the Lisbon convention on the protection and international registering of declarations of origin; and the Madrid agreement on the prevention of false or misleading declarations of origin. The Decree of the President of the National Planning Office No. 3 of April 1, 1967 enacted Decree No. 7 of 1967.

Law Decree No. 18 of 1970 promulgated the texts of the following union conventions as revised in Stockholm on June 14, 1967: the Paris Union convention on the protection of industrial property; the Stockholm amendment of the Madrid agreement on the prevention of false or misleading declarations of origin; the Nice agreement on the international classification of Products of Services Provided with Industrial or Commercial Trademarks; and the convention signed in Stockholm on the creation of a World Organization of Intellectual Property. The Decree No. 3 of Nov. 5, 1970 of the President of the National Commission for Technical Development enacted the Nice text of the Madrid agreement on the international registering of industrial and commercial trademarks.

75. Decree of the Minister of Trade No. 107, 709, of 1907, is still in force.

76. Act II of 1969 on patents and inventions, Magyar Közlöny (Hungarian Gazette), No. 30, April 26, 1969; Act IX of 1969 on trademarks, id., No. 96, December 23, 1969; and Act III of 1969 on copyright, id., No. 30, April 4, 1969. For analyses of these three statutes in German, see Grur-Abhandlungen No. 5, Verlag Chemie, Vol. 5, 1971 ("Die Neuregelung des gewerblichen Rechtsschutzes und Urheberrechts in Ungarn," by A. Vida, I. Földes, G. Pálos, M. Bognár, and R. Palágyi).

77. Licensing and Cooperation with Hungarian Enterprises and Related Industrial Property Problems, Jan. 26, 1971 (edited by London Chamber of Commerce, 1972). The lectures reported therein include "Economic Cooperation with Hungary and the Legal Background," by I. Szász; "Patent Law and Practice in Hungary," by G. Horvath; "Trade Mark Law and Practice in Hungary," by G. Pálos; and "Patent Licences and Know-How Agreements with Hungary," by J. Varró.

78. To our knowledge, legal protection of know-how exists now only in Peru (Law Decree No. 18.350 of January 25, 1971). This is a general legal regulation "relating to industry"; chap. XV deals with legal protection of industrial procedures, that is, know-how.

79. ". . . Lawyers see only the pathology of commerce, and not its healthy physiological action, and their views are therefore apt to be warped and one-sided." P. Sieghardt, Chalmers' Sale of Goods Act, 195 (13th ed., Butterworths, London, 1957).

80. Act II of 1969, which entered into force on Jan 1, 1970.

81. See secs. 46-47 of the new patent law cited in note 76, supra.

82. Id., sec. 12, para. 1.

83. Id., Chapter III, secs. 17-20.

84. See note 76 supra; sec. 6 regarding the duration of the trademark protection; sec. 12 on transferring a trademark; secs. 8-11 on trademark licenses.

85. Patent Bureau Danubia, Budapest 5, P.O.B. 207.

86. Licencia Hungarian Company for the Commercial Exploitation of Inventions, Budapest 5, P.O.B. 207.

87. See sec. 6, para. 2b, Decree of the Minister of Foreign Trade No. 3 of Nov. 26, 1967, reproduced in Szász, supra note 3 at 139-140.

88. Compare, in this regard, the Common Law doctrine of "ouster," whereby courts of law may intervene (either ex officio or by petition) in arbitration proceedings. In a so-called "special case" under the United Kingdom Arbitration Act 1950 (sec. 21), this may be done repeatedly in the course of the same case.

89. Secs. 360-363, Code of Civil Procedure. The text of Act III of 1952 on the Civil Procedure, as amended by Acts IV or 1954 and VIII of 1957, as well as by the Law Decrees No. 12 of 1960, No. 14 of 1961, and No. 26 of 1972, was revised as a consolidated Act; in this amended form, it was enacted on November 26, 1972.

90. Id., sec. 363.

91. For the text of the procedural rules of the Arbitration Tribunal, see Szász, supra note 3 at 222-232.

92. Sec. 4, para. 1, of the procedural rules referred to in note 91 supra.

93. Secs. 209-10 of Law Decree No. 21 of 1955, as modified, reproduced in Szász, supra note 2 at 235.

11

THE POLISH
PEOPLE'S REPUBLIC
Kazimierz Grzybowski

In the 1960s Polish planners jointly with their counterparts in other socialist countries of Eastern Europe became aware that further modernization of their economies depended upon building up closer ties with the advanced economies in the West. Without such ties, modernization and raising of the technological level of the industries would not be possible, and improvement of the quality of the product could not be achieved. It was essential to assure the flow of foreign investment, establish cooperation with foreign enterprises, and gain access to the inventions, technology, and know-how of the West.

In addition, the socialist market needed cooperation with the West for economic and managerial reasons. Isolated from the West and hamstrung by bureaucratic, centralized managerial techniques, socialist planners in Poland and other countries were unable to raise the level of foreign trade or to resolve problems of dual prices (for the internal and external markets); and they lacked criteria for determination of the efficiency of their industries. These in turn depressed seriously the standard of living. While the socialist nations produced 33 percent of goods and commodities, their share in the world trade was only 10 percent. For Poland, specifically these figures were 2.3 percent and 1.1 percent, respectively.[1]

In order to overcome these shortcomings, following the Bucharest session of the Comecon in April 1971,[2] the Polish Government took a number of steps to reform its economic mechanisms and facilitate closer ties with the West. Powers of the minister of Foreign Trade to further trade and economic cooperation with the West were enlarged; a high-level government committee attached to the State Planning Board was established. A new law on patents and protection of industrial property combining socialist and free economy features of the protection of rights became effective on January 1, 1973.[3]

The new policy has had an impact not only on attitudes and the climate of trade; it has also produced important effects in the foreign trade mechanism and the legal system.

The process is far from finished. New suggestions for a firmer legal foundation for the economic cooperation with private enterprise from abroad are being considered, and some steps in this direction are suggested herein.

The regime of Poland's trade with the West is governed in the first instance by trade treaties and agreements, some of which date back to the pre-World War II period, when Poland's foreign trade was mainly oriented toward the West. In addition to joining a number of multilateral conventions dealing with protection of industrial property (patents and trademarks), authors' rights (copyrights), numerous conventions dealing with private international law, maritime law, and transport and communications, Poland concluded a number of trade and navigation agreements. Western parties to interwar agreements with Poland included Austria, Belgium, Canada, Denmark, France, Netherlands, Sweden, Switzerland, the United Kingdom, and the United States.

Following World War II, Poland's trade agreements changed fundamentally. The only treaty concluded in the old pattern was made with Japan (1958). As Poland was gradually developing into a planned economic country, trade agreements began to emphasize the planned commodity exchange aspect, which was adopted as a basic technique in its relations with other socialist countries. Recent agreements of this type were concluded with France (1969), the Benelux countries (1971), West Germany (1970), Italy (1970), and the United Kingdom (1971). These agreements were concluded for varying periods and usually implemented by means of yearly protocols setting up classes of goods to be mutually delivered. Actual commodity exchanges are arranged by the Mixed Commissions, which explore new trade avenues and exchange information on export and import opportunities in the respective countries.

Poland also began to conclude agreements providing for economic, industrial, scientific, and technical cooperation, planned and supervised by Mixed Commissions. Poland has concluded cooperation agreements of various types with the Benelux (1965), Italy (1965), the Netherlands and Denmark (1967), Sweden (1969), France (1972), Belgium, and the United Kingdom (1973),[4] and more such agreements are likely.

Agreements on exchange of goods and cooperation provide for the MFN clause according to the General Agreement on Tariffs and Trade (GATT), to which Poland has been a party since 1967.[5] However, it is recognized that while GATT is effective as regards the level of tariffs and custom duties, it is unable to affect nontariff barriers.

Of major significance was the series of agreements on basic commercial and economic issues including reciprocal availability of trade credits, expanded arrangements for business facilities, and third-country arbitration, reached between the United States and Poland in late 1972.[6] These two countries have since June 1972 operated a joint intergovernmental trade commission, similar to those established between Poland and a number of other Western nations.[7] In late 1973 the United States and Poland signed an Agreement Relating to Port Access Procedures,[8] and a U.S.-Polish treaty on avoidance of double taxation was under active negotiation in early 1974. It is also significant that Warsaw was chosen as the site for the U.S. Government's first Trade and Information Office opened in an Eastern country.

FOREIGN TRADE REGIME

Higher Administrative Authorities— The Ministry of Foreign Trade

The Polish constitutional principle[9] of the state monopoly of foreign trade is the basis for Polish foreign trade. Next in importance are the five-year plans, followed by a number of legal provisions dealing with (1) the organization and functioning of the foreign trade apparatus and (2) the substantive law and rules of procedure applicable to foreign trade transactions.[10]

Foreign trade policy is shaped and regulated by the Council of Ministers. The council is assisted in this task by the Committee of Economic Ministers and the State Planning Commission. Actual control over the implementing of these policies and regulations is the responsibility of the minister of Foreign Trade. While a decision to establish a foreign trade enterprise belongs to the Council of Ministers, the minister of Foreign Trade—in agreement with the minister of Finance—makes actual arrangements for its actual setting up, issuing it with a charter, determining its legal capacity, and allocating assets (credits in foreign trade banks) to finance its activity.

Following the 25th session of the Comecon in Bucharest, in 1971, and in order to encourage expanded economic cooperation with the West, the Council of Ministers adopted the Ordinance on Functions of the Minister of Foreign Trade and His Powers in Coordinating Economic Relations with Foreign Countries (July 9, 1971). This ordinance transformed the Ministry of Foreign Trade into an important center of decision with powers going in five main directions:

(1) Formulation of the foreign trade policy in the broadest sense, in order to stimulate industrial investment; promoting international

division of labor and the integration with the Comecon system, as well as cooperation with the market economy countries in the West.

(2) Supervision, control, and regulation of foreign trade mechanism, including granting concessions to conduct foreign trade operations, chartering the new foreign trade organizations, and granting export and import licenses.

(3) Management of financial resources and hard currency funds to finance foreign trade operations. In this respect, the Ministry of Foreign Trade employs the services of the banks of foreign trade.

(4) The Foreign Trade minister negotiates and signs foreign trade agreements, appoints trade counselors and attachés to Polish diplomatic missions abroad, appoints representatives to the Mixed Commissions set up to promote economic cooperation with the Western countries, and represents Polish economic interests in international organizations.

(5) The minister authorizes foreign entrepreneurs (natural and juridical persons) to conduct economic activities in Poland and determines the objectives, scope, and conditions of these activities.[11]

Two classes of enterprises come under the jurisdiction of the minister of Foreign Trade. To the first category belong those that are set up by the Ministry and are organizationally, financially, and administratively under his jurisdiction. To the second category belong enterprises within the jurisdiction of other ministries, controlled by the Ministry of Foreign Trade only as regards their trade activities abroad. Their scope and area of foreign trade activity is determined by the license issued by the minister of Foreign Trade.[12]

Foreign Trade Organizations

These fall into three categories: government enterprises; cooperatives and their unions; and corporations (limited liability or stock companies). In addition to these three classes of legal entities authorized to make foreign trade transactions, a new category is emerging, the so-called production-commercial enterprises, major industrial enterprises that have been given authorizations to conduct their own foreign trade transactions.[13]

Foreign trade enterprises are owned by the state and are chartered, set up, merged, and liquidated by the minister of Foreign Trade (acting in agreement with the minister of Finance) in accordance with the provisions of the Decree of October 26, 1950[14] and appropriate sections of the Civil Code that came into force in 1965.[15] The charter of each determines its name, seat, and scope of activity; the supervisory authority; and whether the enterprise may establish branches or offices in other locations. The ministry of Foreign Trade provides the enterprise with funding, equal to the nominal capital of the enterprise specified in its charter (Art. 8/1 of a 1950 decree on governmental enterprises).

The enterprise management is headed by the director, who represents the enterprise. He is assisted by the deputy director and the chief bookkeeper.

In order to make binding declarations involving proprietary rights and enter into obligations, the cooperation of at least two persons forming the management of the enterprise is needed, including at least one of the two mentioned above (special rules apply where an enterprise has no deputy director). In case of need additional persons (plenipotentiaries, representatives) may be appointed. The supervisory authority may authorize the director of the enterprise to make binding declarations in specified areas of activity (Art. 16 of the decree of 1950).

However, to represent the enterprise in court or before the Commercial Court of Arbitration, the presence of one authorized person is required (Art. 1 of a decree of June 2, 1961 concerning the representation in courts of the government authorities, bureaus, and government enterprises).[16]

A special exception from these rules was made as regards the representation of interests and proprietary rights of the foreign trade organizations. Instructions of the minister for Foreign Trade of March 11, 1961 allow the director to authorize a single representative to make binding declarations for the enterprise as regards specific transactions. This is used frequently on occasions such as signing the contract abroad or appointing a representative with powers of attorney to handle a litigation.

The names of the representatives (with the exception of those who are appointed to perform a single act, or to represent the enterprise in court) must be entered into the register of enterprises (in case of foreign trade organizations, this register is maintained by the Chamber of Foreign Trade). Powers of the representative should clearly specify the purpose and the scope of his authority. Full powers must be issued in writing.

The organization of cooperatives is provided for in a law of February 17, 1961.[17] A cooperative has an organization that differs basically from that of a governmental enterprise—as reflecting the social character of its functions. The cooperative's role in the socialist economy of Poland is far greater than the usual economic role of the cooperative suggests, as cooperatives may be organized with the participation of governmental enterprises and other juridical persons. Of great importance are statewide unions of cooperatives, cooperative centrals, or other unions of cooperatives for specific purposes. Foreign trade organizations representing economic interests of groups of cooperatives, sometimes in association with other juridical persons such as governmental enterprises, are particularly important in the area of foreign trade involving agricultural products.

The cooperative foreign trade organizations follow closely the foreign trade techniques used by governmental enterprises, except that functions of the director are performed by the board of the cooperative. Two members of the board of the cooperative must act together in order to make declarations binding the cooperative as regards their proprietary rights and obligations.

In the area of their foreign trade activity, cooperative organizations are controlled by the minister of Foreign Trade equally with all other foreign trade organizations.

The third form of the foreign trade organizations is that of limited liability companies and joint stock companies organized according to the provisions of the Commercial Code of 1934, amended and adapted for the conditions in a socialist country where industrial and commercial activity and foreign trade are the monopoly of the state.[18] A number of foreign trade organizations are organized as limited liability companies (Polimex, Elektrim) or as joint stock companies (International Shipping and Transfer Co., Hartwig Co., Poliglob, and so on). The internal setup of these companies is quite orthodox. Their affairs are managed by the board of directors and the management, and their representation in foreign trade transactions and the function of the minister of Foreign Trade follows the general pattern described above.

With the enactment of a resolution of the Council of Ministers on the organization of the industrial unions on December 7, 1966,[19] some of the major industrial establishments also now have the right to handle their foreign trade operations directly. In such a case, the enterprise sets up its separate foreign trade department and itself becomes a foreign trade enterprise, or cooperates with an already existing foreign trade organization and sets up a foreign trade office which formally is a branch institution of that organization.

The motivation behind this decision was to bring the enterprise producing for a foreign market closer to his foreign business partner. It was a measure to encourage exports and direct relations with Western business circles. In addition to granting foreign trade status to producing enterprises, the Council of Ministers also encouraged broad associations of producers to establish their own foreign trade agencies.[20]

Sometimes smaller firms are encouraged to organize a joint stock company (of which they become stockholders) to handle their foreign trade transactions, and to represent their interests exclusively.[21]

A related economic reform would allow foreign trade organizations more flexibility in arranging deals; and opportunities not merely to act as intermediaries between domestic producers and foreign companies but to approach the Western model of the trading firm. In late 1973, the Polish foreign trade organization Polimex-Cekop was the first to be authorized to experiment with the new structure. It is now permitted to purchase goods directly from domestic manufacturers and sell them abroad on its own account. It need no longer transfer the "profit" earned on the transaction to the state budget and has freedom to establish its own monetary reward scheme for personnel.[22]

The scope of the foreign trade activity of foreign trade organizations is determined by the branch specialization of each such enterprise. In the area of that specialization, they have legal capacity. Outside of that assigned field of responsibility, any contracts would be null and void.

Under article 12 of the 1950 decree on government enterprises and article 40 of the Civil Code, the state is not responsible for the obligations of the governmental enterprises established on commercial accounting. At the same time governmental enterprises are not responsible for the obligations of the state. The civil law status of these governmental enterprises had additional consequences. In the first place governmental enterprises organized on the principle of commercial accounting are not covered by the sovereign immunity of the state. They may be sued not only in the country of their incorporation but also before foreign courts under the general rules of jurisdiction. In the second place, a foreign trade organization is not imputed with responsibility on account of refusal by the competent organ of the state to grant an export or import license required for an import or export transaction.[23]

The question of the liability of Polish trade organizations in the event of refusal to grant an export license was the subject of litigation between an East German enterprise and a Polish export organization that failed to deliver a certain quantity of coal and coke due to the order of the chairman of the Polish Council of Ministers who stopped the delivery. The defendant claimed impossibility, and therefore dissolution of the contract; while the claimant refused to recognize the order as absolving the respondent. The Polish Arbitration Tribunal ruled for the Polish defendant. It pointed out that certainly the defendant could do nothing against the highest authority of the state. At the same time, it pointed out that while this result is binding on the civil law level, it does not exhaust the possibility of recovery on the political level on the claim that an international agreement between two governments was breached.[24]

Polish foreign trade experts argue in favor of a strict delimitation of actum imperii from actum gestionis. Not every administrative act shall have the character of the act of the sovereign. Certainly normal administration has no such character. However, decisions such as granting a permit, license, or concession to establish an enterprise or to introduce a commodity on the market; export and import licenses; or a permit to transfer an amount of foreign currency abroad— all have a sovereign character and must be treated as exculpating the contracting party from performing on the contract.

Whether a given enterprise has a juridical personality under civil law is decided by the personal law of the legal person, in the case of Polish juridical persons, the law of Poland. This has important implications as regards the status of the Polish foreign trade organizations also before foreign courts.

Other Important Agencies and Organizations

The Chamber of Foreign Trade, established in 1949, has an important role in developing and strengthening economic relations between Poland and other countries, not unlike its counterparts in the other countries examined in this study.

Of special interest to the Western trader is the Chamber's duty to collect and publish Polish practices and usages in the areas of foreign trade and sea transport, as well as its authority to issue certificates of origin, verify invoices and other documentation, appoint experts, and so on. The Chamber is an organization of social and economic interests, consisting of regular, corresponding, and honorary members. Its regular members include all foreign trade organizations, the National Bank of Poland, the Bank of Commerce, Ltd., and state insurance, shipping lines and other agencies. Other similar institutions may be admitted on request by the Chamber with the approval of the minister of Foreign Trade. The Chamber also serves as a center for organizing a Court of Arbitration for Foreign Trade.[25]

Poland's central bank is the Narodowy Bank Polski, or National Bank of Poland, which handles financial relations with foreign national banks. The Bank Handlowy a Warszawie, S.A., or Bank of Commerce, Ltd., in Warsaw, carries out all types of foreign trade banking transactions. It has a network of representatives throughout the world and is in the process of establishing offices in major Western trading centers.

Bank Polska Kasa Opieki S.A., or the Polish Welfare Bank, is an affiliate of the Post Office Savings Bank in Warsaw, providing usual banking services and facilities. Established in the interwar years, it had numerous branches in countries with large Polish emigration (such as the United States and France). After the war the bank developed a scheme under which a recipient in Poland may purchase goods— either imported or made in Poland or foreign markets—if the goods are paid for in foreign currency.

Insurance is a state monopoly in Poland, handled by Panstwowy Zaklad Ubezpieczen (PZU), or State Insurance Company. Foreign traders carrying out transactions with Poland who insure their goods with the PZU can obtain the required cover for risks involved in sea and overland transport as well as in air and inland freight carriage. PZU effects marine insurance on world market terms and is a member of the International Association of Marine Insurance.

WARTA, Towarzystwo Reasekuracyjne, Sp. Akc., is the state monopoly for reinsurance. It is in close touch with foreign insurance companies and brokers and effects reinsurance.

Advertising is a state monopoly handled by the State Advertising Agency AGPOL.

Agencies and Commercial Representation

Foreign interests in Poland are represented by Polish commercial agencies or branch representations of foreign enterprises.

Commercial agencies are chartered and organized as stock companies (on the basis of concession granted by the Ministry of Foreign Trade). These commercial agencies act on the basis of long-term contract with firms abroad, or on a commission basis. The services include all commercial aspects in connection with a foreign trade transaction, such as gathering information, presentation of offers, assistance in trade negotiations, advertising, and furnishing samples.[26]

Until recently, only a limited number of offices of foreign firms had been allowed to establish in Poland, on a very restricted basis, to provide technical information and to supply spare parts, excluding buying, selling, and other commercial activities. Permits are issued for one year only. These restrictions did not apply to the travel industry, in particular foreign airlines, which may open offices on a basis of reciprocity.

During the November 1972 session of the Joint U.S.-Polish Trade Commission[27] accreditation procedures for commercial representation offices were agreed to be needed, and a new more liberal policy was adopted by Poland in 1973. A number of U.S. and other Western companies have since been given permission to open representation offices, although the latter must continue to work through the established foreign trade apparatus, and are now subject to a new tax regime.

Polish interests abroad are often represented by mixed stock companies organized jointly by Polish foreign trade organizations and local commercial interests specializing in trade relations with Poland. Usually these mixed stock companies represent specific lines of goods, either in the export or import business. Such firms have been established in such countries as England (Anglodal and Daltrade), France (Metalex-France), and Italy (Ital-Mex).[28]

FOREIGN TRADE CONTRACTS; TRANSACTIONS INVOLVING TECHNOLOGY

There is no provision in Polish law, whether specially concerning foreign trade transactions or generally civil law relations, that deals with the transactional capacity of aliens in Poland. The only rule in this area is Art. 8 of the Polish Private International Law of 1965, which states generally that aliens may acquire rights and obligations equally with Polish nationals, except when the law provides otherwise. This provision certainly does not cover foreign trade transactions with Polish foreign trade organizations, which are the exclusive monopoly of the government.

Art. 124 of the Soviet Principles of Civil Legislation of 1961 states that

> Foreign firms and organizations may, without any special permission, effect transactions in the field of foreign trade in the USSR, as well as connected insurance and accounting operations, with foreign trade associations and other Soviet organizations empowered by the law to enter into such transactions.[29]

While a similar provision in the Polish law is lacking, there is ample evidence that the Polish Government adopts an identical position. Polish trade agreements with other countries usually contain clauses assuring foreign traders a free hand in transactions with domestic corporations in accordance with the laws and regulations in force.[30]

A basic question arising in all foreign trade contracts with Polish parties concerns the law applicable to the transaction. The 1965 Polish Private International Law Act lays down detailed rules in this regard[31] although certain specific rules are contained in specialized statutes such as the Law of Checks and Bills of Exchange of 1936.

With respect to contractual obligations, the 1965 Act reflected a liberalization of the earlier (1926) law under which parties to a contract were not completely free to choose governing law: There had to be some "connection," either through citizenship of the parties or subject matter. The 1965 statute, while retaining the "connection" test,[32] eliminates characterizations based on citizenship or subject matter (other than in respect of immovables with respect to which contracts are still controlled by lex situa).[33]

The 1965 act does not clearly state whether the choice of law must be expressed or whether it can be inferred from the parties' conduct.[34] Where the parties who have failed to make a choice have domicile or residence in different countries, they are presumed to have made the following choice:

(1) for contracts of sale of movables or of delivery—law of domicile or residence of seller or consignor at time contract was made;

(2) for contracts of manufacture, agency, brokerage, carriage of goods, or bailment—law of domicile or residence of the manufacturer, agent, broker, carrier, or bailee at time contract was made;

(3) for insurance contracts—law of country in which insurance company had its principal place of business at time contract was made;

(4) for copyright transfers—law of domicile or residence of purchaser of copyright at time of purchase.

If domicile or residence cannot be determined, or in the case of other types of obligations, lex loci contractus governs.[35] Tort liability is subject to different rules.

It might also be noted here that the 1965 act contains a so-called "public policy" proviso, forbidding the application of a foreign law if this would produce effects contrary to the fundamental principles of the country's legal order.[36]

Should Polish law be found applicable, the 1965 Civil Code is applied. The next question that is to be resolved is which of the provisions dealing with contractual relations apply, as the Civil Code deals both with commercial transactions between units of the public sector as well as between private citizens (the latter are more liberal compared to the legal rules applicable to commerce between entities in the public sector).[37]

The Civil Code (particularly its provisions on private-sector contracts) does not differ substantially from the civil legislation of such typically civil-law countries as Switzerland, France, or Austria.[38]

Civil law applies to contractual relations between the foreign trade organizations and foreign traders. It assures the equality of the parties, and under the Private International Law Statute of 1965 will guarantee recognition of the legal capacity and the right to sue in Polish courts and before the Court of Arbitration to foreign partners. The civil law provisions will not, however, question governmental determinations as to the limited legal capacity of Polish foreign trade enterprises, or formalities to be complied with in making an agreement, or the required form of the agreement (which will be null and void unless strictly adhered to).

Under Article 384 of the Civil Code, the Council of Ministers or another supreme organ of state administration acting under the authority of the Council of Ministers may adopt general conditions of sale and forms of contract different from the Civil Code. These regulations have a force equal to that of the Civil Code. They exist in the form of general conditions of contracts of sale for export, and general conditions of sale of commodities imported, attached to the instruction of the chairman of the State Planning Committee with the Council of Ministers, of February 13, 1967.[39]

It is perhaps worth noting here that terms of trade worked out by the International Chamber of Commerce (Incoterms of 1953 and 1957; International Customs and Practices for Documentary Credits 1962; and International Rules for Collection of Documents 1967) are frequently referred to in foreign trade transactions between Polish and foreign business organizations.

Licensing transactions have assumed increasing importance in Poland's foreign trade over the last few years. In fact, it is reported that in the three years 1970-72 Poland purchased more licenses from the West than in the preceding 10 years.[40] A specialized foreign trade organization, Polservice, handles all "pure" license transactions and is presumably consulted when other Polish organizations conclude licensing arrangements directly, in connection with the import of plant and equipment.[41]

Licensing transactions with Poland are facilitated by Poland's participation in the various international conventions on protection of industrial and intellectual property, its bilateral treaty commitments, and its own statutory scheme of protections.

A new patent law enacted on October 19, 1972 (effective January 1, 1973) modernized a number of the aspects of the preexisting situations, governed by a 1962 act, as discussed more fully in Chapter 16. Trademarks are governed by a March 28, 1963 statute, which is not unlike similar recent statutes introduced by its neighboring East European countries. Poland's copyright law is based on a July 10, 1952 statute, which prescribes a 20-year period of protection from the death of the author for most works, and 10 years from date of first publication for certain classes of works.

Poland's membership in international conventions includes the Paris Union Convention, and it has indicated its intention to apply the transitional provisions of the 1967 Stockholm revision as well as the 1967 Stockholm Convention establishing the World Intellectual Property Organization. Poland is also a member of the 1891 Madrid Agreement for the International Registration of Marks. With respect to copyrights, Poland is a party to the Bern Union, including its 1928 Rome revision, and has longstanding bilateral copyright relations with a number of countries including the United States.

COOPERATION AGREEMENTS AND JOINT VENTURES

Developments in this area are of singular interest for Poland's partners abroad. Although generalizations are hazardous, the expansion of cooperation with Poland may be said to reflect a complex situation due in large part to the traditional structure of exports and imports between the East and West. Raw materials, fuels and agricultural products have tended to flow westward, while industrial products and goods have been sent eastward. That situation hardly could promote the expansion of trade, particularly in view of the Common Agricultural Policy (CAP) of the European Community (discussed more fully in Chapter 3) and the growing crisis in the fuel and raw materials market.* It was essential to seek new ways of broadening the exchanges, and at least some socialist countries were able to offer cheap labor and low-cost production.

Poland has encouraged the conclusion of contracts that provide for "cooperation" between a Polish enterprise and a capitalist enterprise in certain lines of goods. The Polish side is especially interested in projects that move beyond mere subcontracting to partnership, involve a division of labor and export markets, and allow for long-term planning of imports over a 10-15-year period, rather than resulting in single ad hoc purchases.

A typical arrangement is a contract between the Polish foreign trade organization Metalexport and a Swedish state concern, MST Machine Company AB, signed in February 1971, to run for a period of 10 years. It provides for the delivery of elements for the production of lathes and tools. It is a complex agreement covering such matters as innovations in the process of production and the exchange of experience. Mixed technological teams are to be set up, and experts are to be exchanged. Another complex cooperation deal involves the production FIAT automobiles in Poland.

Cooperation agreements with American firms are of relatively recent date. In 1972 three such agreements were made, with Koehring for the production of hydraulic excavators, with Clark Company for the production of driving axles for earth-moving equipment and construction cranes, and with International Harvester of heavy crawler tractors for construction and earth moving.[42]

In 1973, examples of cooperation with U.S. firms included the conclusion of Honeywell's first cooperation agreement in Eastern Europe—with a Polish partner. The arrangement contemplates that

---

*A serious obstruction in the expansion of the Polish foreign trade, particularly with Britain, is the CAP, which includes import quotas for Polish agricultural products. As an article by a Polish economist explained, "The present structure continues to be dominated by the export of raw materials, semifinished products, and farm and food products with the percentage of industrial production being still very low and disproportionate to Poland's current economic potential" (Foreign Trade, 1972, at 237).

Honeywell-designed automation equipment will be made in a plant near Warsaw. It runs for five years and can be renewed. Honeywell is to be repaid for its equipment, materials, know-how, and other items partly in cash, but mainly in the form of automation equipment produced under the cooperation. It is understood that price adjustments are to be negotiated with respect to equipment to be delivered to Honeywell as costs change. The Polish side apparently has sales rights anywhere in Comecon, with Honeywell to act as exclusive distributor in the West and with the products specially labeled for each area. Detailed quality control standards are to be imposed, and there will be extensive training and exchange of personnel.[43]

Socialist regimes of property relations in which ownership of land and of means of production is vested exclusively in the state represent a serious obstacle in promoting investments in direct participation in the business activities in socialist countries. Unless the government of a socialist country provides a special legal framework for the setting up of an enterprise with the participation of foreign capital and guarantees property and management rights of investors, their legal position is uncertain and in constant jeopardy.

A socialist state of the Soviet type (such as Poland) has the power to dispose of the property rights of individual enterprises and by a simple administrative act to merge, divide, regroup, and rearrange industrial branches in accordance with the economic plan or current line of economic policy. It seems essential, therefore, in order to create a climate promoting direct investment in a socialist country, that these powers of the state, which are the essence of the socialist management of industry and commerce, be restricted in the area of the economic sector in which private investment is to play an important role.

To illustrate points made above, two approaches towards stabilizing and guaranteeing property rights of foreign investors may be described. The first and most important is the example of Yugoslavia, which, as discussed elsewhere in this study, now has detailed legislation providing for extensive for protection of the property rights of foreign investors.

The other approach is reflected in two joint enterprises established in Poland with the cooperation of Czechoslovakia and Hungary, respectively. A joint transfer and shipping company (Spedrapid) to handle Czechoslovak imports and exports through Polish ports was organized by a contract between Hartwig (a Polish Government enterprise) and Metrans (a Czechoslovak Government company). It was set up as a Polish joint stock company in which both governments shared on a 50/50 basis. However, the contract alone was unable to settle matters vital to the orderly cooperation of the two partners. Under the contract and Polish law, as the enterprise operated in

Poland, the assets of the Spedrapid were the property of Polish Government and legally under its unlimited control. In order to provide for the special situation of this organization, an international agreement was made in 1956, which declared that the enterprise was the property of the two governments, that it could be liquidated exclusively by agreement of the two governments concerned, and that, were it dissolved, Czechoslovakia would receive her share of the assets.[44]

Another joint stock company (Haldex) was set up by the governments of Poland and Hungary to exploit tailing at Polish coal mines in Silesia. The company was created by a straight agreement between the two countries, which contributed the capital and the assets of the company. Both governments are company shareholders, and although Haldex is a Polish company it is the property of both.[45]

Examination of Polish legislation that is adduced in order to argue that it is possible to provide for the participation of foreign capital in a business enterprise in Poland suggests that it hardly meets the needs of the situation under discussion here.

According to the Commercial Code of 1934, foreign stock and limited liability companies may be granted a permit to establish themselves in Poland.[46] The right to grant the permit is within the competence of the minister of Foreign Trade, according to the 1971 Ordinance noted above.

Polish foreign trade experts argue that enactment of special legislation to permit involvement of foreign capital is not necessary.[47] And yet the present legal framework that can be successfully used to encourage foreign investment in joint enterprises in Poland is hardly specific. The Commercial Code regime was devised for a social and economic order in which private enterprise and ownership of the means of production was a rule and not an exception. Under the present regime, a law drafted along the general lines of the Yugoslav Act of 1971 is needed.

It is understood that legislation is in fact under active consideration by the Polish authorities.*

Another solution, presenting an even more effective guarantee, would be an international agreement between a Western country and Poland, providing for special protections in the case of joint enterprises

---

*At a press conference in Vienna in September 1973 the Polish Foreign Trade Minister, Mr. Olechowski, declared that his ministry was formulating the terms on which foreign capital would be able to participate in joint ventures with Polish enterprises. There was nothing in Poland's constitution to prevent joint ventures with Western firms, he said, though joint ventures were only one form of cooperation among several others. (Neue Zurcher Zeitung, Sept. 22, 1973.)

involving investments by their nationals, possibly including dispute settlement procedures. This solution would recommend itself as providing an even stronger guarantee of the property rights of aliens in Poland. Some aspects of the international protection of foreign investment in Poland could be met should Poland become a member of the World Bank and at the same time accede to the 1965 Convention on the Settlement of Investment Disputes Between States and Nationals of Other States, which was elaborated under the auspices of the World Bank.[48] The convention, which has been ratified by many Western countries, but no Comecon members (Yugoslavia is, however, a party), created an International Center for the Settlement of Investment Disputes and provides for a conciliation and arbitration procedure in case of litigation involving foreign investors.

FOREIGN TRADE ARBITRATION

Poland is a party to the 1923 Geneva Protocol on Arbitration Clauses; the 1958 United Nations (New York) Convention on the Recognition and Enforcement of Foreign Arbitral Awards; and the 1961 European (Geneva) Convention on International Commercial Arbitration.[49] Four permanent arbitration institutions function in Poland: the Court of Arbitration of the Chamber of Foreign Trade, the Gdynia Court of Arbitration for Maritime Trade, the Gdynia Wool Association, and the Gdynia Cotton Association. We discuss below the first two, which are of more general interest.

Court of Arbitration of the Chamber of Foreign Trade

Unless an international agreement that covers the case provides otherwise, the procedure before the Polish Foreign Trade Court of Arbitration is regulated by the Rules of Procedure adopted by the Polish Chamber of Foreign Trade on December 28, 1968.[50] These rules came into force on January 1, 1970. The Code of Civil Procedure of 1964[51] applies subsidiarily to questions not covered by the rules.[52] Also important are those provisions of the Code of Civil Procedure that deal with the procedure to establish foreign law and reciprocity, foreign judgments, and their execution. Finally, the provisions of the 1965 Statute on Private International Law will apply.

The rules provide for a College of Arbiters, consisting of a Presidium, which includes the chairman and his four deputies, a minimum of 30 arbiters, and the secretary and his four deputies. They are appointed and dismissed by the Chamber of Foreign Trade. Actual cases are handled by arbitration tribunals, which are composed

265

of as many members as the agreement to arbitrate provides for. Should the agreement to arbitrate be silent on the matter, a tribunal of three, one of them the presiding arbiter, shall be selected. The 1970 Rules provide (in Sec. 4.3) that nationals of other countries as well as Polish nationals may be enrolled in the College of Arbiters (not, however, to serve on the Presidium or Secretariat). However, in practice the College until now has apparently consisted exclusively of Polish nationals.[53]

According to Section 1 of the rules, the Court of Arbitration has jurisdiction to consider cases involving commercial transactions including sales, transport, shipping, insurance, and other commercial transactions, and also service contracts, between parties of whom at the time of filing the case at least one has a seat or residence abroad. Jurisdiction must be provided for in the international agreement between the countries concerned, or in an arbitral clause included either in the original contract or separately in writing, or by its acceptance by the respondent after filing the complaint. In such a case, the plaintiff may ask the secretary of the College of Arbiters to request the other party to agree within a determined time limit to accept the jurisdiction of the court. Agreements to submit a dispute or disputes to arbitration must be made in writing.

The initial phase of the proceedings is handled by the Presidium, which resolves issues of jurisdiction. The secretary, who receives the complaint, sees to it that documents supporting the jurisdiction of the Court of Arbitration Tribunal are supplied; that proper translations (in case the foreign party submits its claim or rejoinder in a foreign language) are supplied; that parties appoint arbiters and their substitutes from the list of the arbiters maintained by the College of Arbiters. Polish, French, English, German, or Russian may be employed. Should there be more than two parties involved, each of them has the right to appoint an arbiter and his substitutes. Should one of the parties fail to appoint such an arbiter, he will be selected by the chairman of the College. Arbiters appointed by the parties select the chairman of the particular arbitration tribunal to hear the case.

The Presidium of the College decides the case when an arbiter is challenged by one of the parties as not competent to hear the case. In such a case, provisions of the Code of Civil Procedure apply.[54]

After the initial phase of the proceedings is completed, and the tribunal validly selected, the chairman of the Court sees to it that the case should be decided in one public and oral hearing. To that end he may order additional documents and an exchange of briefs so that the issues are clear and the required evidence is available. Parties may request that the hearing take place in camera. However, members of the Presidium and the secretary of the College have the duty to

266

attend such hearing. Parties may also ask that additional persons in their trust be also present.

Admission of evidence is controlled by the chairman of the tribunal, who admits evidence relevant in the case. While the case is handled by the tribunal, the Presidium may be requested to provide clarification of legal questions, in particular as regards those that concern issues of foreign law, and the previous practice in Polish foreign trade arbitration.

Polish is the official language of the oral hearings. However, the court may decide—should that serve the purpose—to hold the hearing in one of four foreign languages—German, French, English, and Russian.

At all times, the chairman of the Court may approach the parties with a proposal to settle the matter amicably.

Parties may agree that a single arbiter may decide the case and that no oral hearing shall be held and the decision made on the basis of written evidence.

In general, the proceedings before the Polish Court of Arbitration are marked by a heavy reliance on documentary evidence. Jurisdiction, the content of agreements between parties, and their mutual obligations, as well as all other incidents of the transaction must be proved by written evidence, either relating to relations between the parties or by statements of proper authorities and experts regarding such matters as insurance, damage to the goods, or shortages.

The autonomy of the will of the parties as to choice of law is stressed by the 1970 rules (Sec. 29), and the arbiters are enjoined to decide the case with regard to equity and commercial practices, inasmuch as this is allowed by the law that governs the transaction.

There seems to exist an important omission in the provisions of the 1970 rules, namely, with respect to the question of jurisdiction in cases involving disputes between partners in the enterprise set up with the participation of the foreign investor, when the enterprise is a juridical person under Polish law (limited liability or joint stock company) or makes claims against the Polish state in connection with the violation of guarantees as to disposal of profits and ownership of assets claimed by the foreign investor. Such questions might usefully be clarified when the Polish authorities promulgate new provisions on investment joint ventures, as discussed above.

Court of Arbitration for Maritime
Trade in Gdynia55

The Chambers of Foreign Trade of Poland, Czechoslovakia, and East Germany signed on June 17, 1959 an agreement to establish an International Court of Arbitration for Maritime and Inland Navigation.

All three countries depend on Baltic ports for access to the International sea lanes, and Czechoslovakia depends both on Polish as well as on East German ports for shipment of her exports and imports from and to overseas destinations. The court was established to deal with disputes concerning the activities of the shipping organizations of the three countries, with the exception arising from labor relations (which come under the jurisdiction of the domestic courts of the contracting parties).

The Gdynia Court is the result of close cooperation of the three countries in the field of international shipping and maritime commerce. All three countries handle a sizable amount of goods in transit to other socialist countries. Furthermore, Polish and East German shipyards serve international shipping in the Baltic.

Gdynia Court is an elaborate structure. Its operation is regulated in detail in a number of documents that constitute the Treaty of 1959 including: (1) an agreement on the creation and maintenance of the Court of Gdynia; (2) rules of procedure; (3) an agreement on costs of procedure; (4) an ordinance on the honorarium and fees of the members of the court; and (5) an additional protocol regulating various incidental problems.

Procedure and organization of the court follows the pattern of the Warsaw Court of Arbitration. Each contracting party appoints a member of the Presidium and his deputy, and the office of the president goes in rotation to a member of the Presidium from each of the three countries each year. The secretary is appointed by the Presidium. Each of the three countries appoints at least 10 members to the panel of arbiters. The Rules of Procedure follow closely the Rules of the Court of Arbitration in Warsaw.

NOTES

1. Ciamaga Rola Handlu Zagranicznego w Gospodarce Narodowej Polski 18 Handel Zagraniczny (1973), 323-327; Dlugosz, "Przeslanki udzialu kraju socjalistycznego w miedzynarodowym podziale pracy," 18 Handel Zagraniczny (1973), 79-80; Bozyk Grabska and Lytko, Integracja a wspolpraca gospodarcza w Europie (1972), 244-256.

2. See Chapter 6 of this study, on Comecon.

3. Dzuennik Ustaw (afterwards D.U.) 43/272. See also "1973, The Year of Poland," Commerce International (London Chamber of Commerce, November 1973), 26-45.

4. Sadowski, "The Law of Foreign Trade in the Polish People's Republic," 37 Law and Contemp. Probs. 506-507 (1972); Zaremba, "Umowy i komisje mieszane—instytucjonalne formy wspolpracy gospodarczej Polski z Europe Zacholnia," Handel Zagraniczny, No. 9, 324 (1972).

5. For discussions of Poland's adherence to the GATT, see Note, "East-West Trade: The Accession of Poland to the GATT," 24 Stan. L. Rev. 748 (1972); Laczkowski, "Poland's Accession to GATT," 5 Jour. World Tr. L. 110 (1971).

6. U.S. Commerce Dept., "Fact Sheet-Joint American-Polish Trade Commission, 2d Sess., Nov. 4-8, 1972."

7. See Sadowski supra note 4 at 508.

8. Dept. State. Bull., Nov. 5, 1973 at 580.

9. Art. 7, para. 2 of Constitution of July 26, 1952.

10. Sadowski supra note 4 at 508-509 contains a succinct summary list of the principal texts.

11. D.U. 19/183. Compare Sadowski supra note 4 at 510-11.

12. Licensing of enterprises to engage in foreign trade operations is controlled by the internal regulations of the Ministry of Foreign Trade, Instructions of January 21, 1963.

13. See Grzybowski, "The Foreign Trade Regime in the Comecon Countries Today," 4 N.Y.U. J. Int'l L.Pol. 183, 188 (1971).

14. Consolidated text in 1960 D.U. No. 118, text 111.

15. Notably Secs. 33-43 and Sec. 128, para. 2.

16. D.U. No. 25/93.

17. D.U. 12/61.

18. D.U. 57/61, 1964.

19. Monitor Polski, No. 69/327 (hereafter M.P.).

20. Vaganov, Gosudarstvennaia monopolia vnieshnej torgovli v sotsialisticheskikh stranakh in Vnieshnaia torgovla sotsialisticheskikh stran (Moscow, 1966).

21. Compare Kalensky, "Pravny Otazky rizeni zahranicniho obhodu clenskich statu RVHP," in Studie z Mexinarodniho Prava (1966); Knapp, "The Function, Organization and Activities of Foreign Trade Corporation in the European Socialist Countries," in Sources of the Law of International Trade (ed. C. M. Schmitthoff, London, 1964) at 52.

22. East-West, Jan. 11, 1974 at 2.

23. Ordinance of the Council of Ministers of March 27, 1962, D.U. 21/94.

24. Polska Izba Handlu Zagranicznego, Orzecznictwa Kolegjum Arbitrow 1/XI 1957, 31/X, 1959, 17-22.

25. Sadowski supra note 4 at 514-515. Grzybowski, The Socialist Commonwealth of Nations, 218 ff.; Kos-Rabcewicz-Zubkowski, East European Rules on the Validity of International Commercial Arbitration (1970) 163 and passim; Pfaff, Die Aussenhandelsschiedsgerichtbarkeit der sozialistichem Länder im Handel mit der Bundesrepublik Deutschland (1973), 338 ff.

26. Polska Izba Handlu Zagr (Polish Chamber of Foreign Trade), Information for Businessmen Trading with Poland, Information Publication Series 42 (1972); Sadowski supra note 4 at 514.

27. U.S. Dept. of Commerce, Fact Sheet, Joint American-Polish Trade Commission, 2d Sess., Nov. 4-8, 1972, 4. One of the reasons why the Polish Government is reluctant to admit a larger number of commercial offices of foreign firms in Poland is lack of office space. A Swedish firm has been commissioned to build a 38-story office building in Warsaw, which is now nearing completion. However, even under the liberalized conditions, the activities of the foreign commercial agencies may not conclude deals with commercial or productions enterprises in Poland. They can deal exclusively through foreign trade organizations.

28. See Jakubowski, Przedsiebiorstwa w Handlu Miedzynarodowym 1970, 191-192.

29. Grzybowski, Soviet Private International Law (1970) at 70.

30. Kobryner, "Struktura polskich umow handlowych i platniczych z krajami kapitalistycznymi," Prawo w Handlu Zagranicznym, 1964, No. 5/6, 44; Jakubowski, Umowa sprzedazy w handlu zagranicznym (Warsaw, 1966).

31. See, for example, Lasok, "The Polish System of Private International Law," 15 Am. J. Comp. L. 330 (1967); Rajski, "The New Polish Private International Law," 15 Int'l and Comp. L. Q. 457 (1966).

32. Art. 30.

33. Art. 25(2).

34. See Art. 25(1); compare Art. 26.

35. Arts. 27 and 29.

36. Art. 6.

37. See Jakubowski, Prawne ramy obrotu handlowego Miedzy krajami socjalistycznymi Panstow i Prawo, 536 (1961); compare Grzybowski supra note 13 at 281-282.

38. Trammer, "The Law of Foreign Trade in the Legal Systems of the Countries of Planned Economy," in Sources of the Law of International Trade, op. cit. at 42.

39. M.P. No. 12/64.

40. Business International (B.I.), Eastern Europe Report, Dec. 14, 1973 at 365. See also Janiszewski, "Polservice Experience in Licensing to and from Poland," 8 Les Nouvelles 146 (1972).

41. See, for example, B.I. Eastern Europe Report, Jan. 12 and 26, 1973 at 2 and 20, respectively, for discussion of some practical aspects of licensing trade with Poland.

42. Handel Zagr. No. 10, 1973.

43. See, for example, B.I., Eastern Europe Report, Dec. 14, 1973 at 361.

44. Jakubowski supra note 28 at 191-192.

45. Id., 195.

46. Arts. 161 and 310, para. 3.

47. Rybak, "Joint venture-wspolne przedsiewziecia i wspolne ryzyko," Handel Zagraniczny 331 (1973).

48. 14 Am. J. Comp. L. 892 ff (1966). Compare Sassoon, "Convention on the Settlement of Investment Disputes," Journal of Business Law 335 (1965).

49. See, for example, L. Kos-Rabcewicz-Zubkowski, East European Rules on the Validity of International Commercial Arbitration Agreements (1970), 90-91, 238.

50. Art. 1096, 1964 Code of Civil Procedure, D.U. 43/296.

51. Id.

52. In particular those included in Book Three, on arbitration between private persons, in Arts. 695-715 of the Code of Civil Procedure.

53. Grzybowski supra note 29 at 40.

54. Code of Civil Procedure, Arts. 40-50, 703.

55. Domke, "Schiedgerichts und Kostenanordnung, des 1959 errichteten international Schiedsgericht für See und Binnenschiffahrt in Gdynia," 6 Ost Europa Recht 74-82 (1960); Spitzner, Osmar, und Fellhauer, "Die internationale Schiedsgericht für See und Binnenschiffahrt in Gdynia," 9 Aussenhandel 31-33, No. 13 (1959); compare Grzybowski supra note 13 at 219 and passim; see also Kos-Rabcewicz-Zubkowski, op. cit. at 163-209.

12

THE SOCIALIST REPUBLIC
OF ROMANIA

Jay A. Burgess

POLITICAL AND CONSTITUTIONAL SETTING

Under its constitution, Romania is declared to be a socialist republic and a sovereign, independent, unitary state.[1] Power is vested in the working people under the leadership of the Romanian Communist Party (Partidul Communist Roman—PCR). The sole legislative body and focal point of state power is the Grand National Assembly (Marea Adunare Nationala), which supervises and controls the functions of all other state organs. The Assembly is vested with broad powers, which include authority to amend the Constitution. The major part of Romania's legislative work is performed by the Council of State, which passes decrees that must be submitted to the Grand National Assembly at its next session but come into full force as law immediately upon passage by the Council.

The chief administrative organ under Romania's Constitution is the Council of Ministers. The Council of Ministers is given broad powers including the general implementation of Romania's domestic and foreign policies; the application of laws; the establishment and implementation of the state plan and state budget; and the coordination and control of all ministries and other state organs. In fulfilling its functions, the Council of Ministers is authorized to issue orders or rules called decisions. Such decisions are meant to implement and elaborate laws in force, and they stand as legal norms. None of the courts, including the Supreme Court, has authority to review the

---

The views expressed herein are the author's and are not intended to reflect the views of the U.S. Government.

constitutionality of Romania's laws, but the Supreme Court does supervise and assure the uniformity of judicial procedures.

Real power rests with the leadership of the Romanian Communist Party. Under the Constitution, the party is granted the leading role in both government and society. It makes all major decisions and appointments, notwithstanding that they are publicly adopted and promulgated by the government.

INSTITUTIONAL FRAMEWORK FOR FOREIGN TRADE

Primacy of Law No. 1

Since the spring of 1971 the cornerstone of Romanian foreign trade has been law No. 1,[2] which represents the culmination of years of economic reform aimed at increasing Romania's commercial trade with the West, in order to achieve a balance with her already heavy trading pattern with the USSR and other Eastern countries.[3]

Under Law No. 1 Romanian foreign trade activity is established as a state monopoly and is conducted strictly in accordance with the national economic plan.[4] General control over foreign trade is vested in the Council of Ministers while implementation is left to the Ministry of Foreign Trade and its subordinate units—the economic and industrial ministries, foreign trade companies, industrial centrals, and other central bodies and producing units. These implementation units are directly responsible and answerable to the Council of Ministers for implementing state policy and the directives of the PRC, fulfilling the foreign trade plan, and organizing foreign trade activity.

At the top of this implementation structure is the Ministry of Foreign Trade, which formulates the annual foreign trade plan, issues instructions and compulsory regulations to its subordinate foreign trade units, and approves and issues export and import licenses for each product and group of products.[5] The next level of foreign trade activity is represented by the economic and industrial ministries. They are responsible for over-all planning in their respective industrial or economic sectors, which they in turn coordinate with the Ministry of Foreign Trade in its formulation of the over-all foreign trade plan. In so doing, these ministries draw heavily on the support of the planning, research, and design institutes. The ministries also coordinate and check the activities of lower foreign trade units and appoint many of their chief personnel. Below these ministries are the foreign trade companies, which represent the various industrial and economic sectors. These state companies are independent, autonomous units that support themselves from a percentage of the

273

transactions they complete. Next in line are the industrial centrals and other central units, which combine in horizontal or vertical fashion several enterprises and/or suppliers having similar products, functions, or structures. As will be shown later, these are relatively new economic units designed to decentralize Romania's foreign trade system and make it more responsive to trade with the West. Finally, there are the producing enterprises and end-users, which are the basic units of production in the Romanian economy. They can be a part of an industrial central, become involved in international transactions through the foreign trade company operating in their respective sectors, or even, in some cases, deal directly with foreign clients. Thus, at the operational level it is the state trading companies, the industrial centrals, and other units having the status of centrals, and, in some cases, producing units and end-users that carry out foreign trade transactions, negotiate, and actually sign contracts and other trade documents as principals.

Economic Reforms and Foreign Trade

The Ministry of Foreign Trade has always been the real focal point of Romania's foreign trade system. Until recently, all authority for the implementation of foreign trade activity was placed in the ministry, with subordinate foreign trade units responsible directly to it for all their activities.

Rigid centralization of the foreign trade system continued up until the dramatic economic reforms of the late 1960s, which not only facilitated trade with the West but also opened a whole new era of Romanian economic development. Several key legislative acts made this reform possible. First, the Romanian Bank of Foreign Trade was created in 1968.[6] As an independent organization and a separate legal entity, the bank was given wide authority to organize and carry out financial matters concerning all operations of the foreign trade system and all transactions involving foreigners. Additionally, the bank was granted the power to buy and sell hard foreign currency; to give credits to state trading companies; to authorize imports and exports; to enter into financial arrangements with foreign banks; to guarantee payment by Romanian foreign trade entities; and to present to the Council of Ministers plans and programs for the foreign trade banking system.[7]

Second, in 1969 the Ministry of Foreign Trade was reorganized to make it compatible with the new foreign trade system being created by reform.[8] This new act set as its objective the development of Romania's international commercial relations, including the expansion of Romania's foreign-exchange-producing reserves. Specifically, Decree No. 622 attempted to decentralize the ministry's control over

the foreign trade process and to facilitate the industrial centrals concept (see below) by encouraging direct foreign contact with Romanian
enterprises and end-users, opening up planning authority to subordinate
economic entities, and promoting the idea of collective responsibility
in foreign trade decision-making. By doing so, much of the day-to-
day contact and negotiating was taken out of the Ministry of Foreign
Trade and placed in subordinate economic units, more familiar with
the practical operational matters that lead to productive foreign trade
activity. This is not to say, however, that the ministry lost its authority or ability to control foreign trade implementation. On the
contrary, under the reorganization law, it retained these powers but
assumed more of a supervisory posture in the foreign trade system.

Third and most important was the passage in 1969 of a law
establishing the "industrial centrals" within Romania's economy.[9]
In order to make economic reform and foreign trade reorganization
successful, it was necessary to create a new type of economic unit
in the industrial sector. This need was answered by the industrial
centrals, which along with the restructured economic ministries and
enterprises, molded a new three-level economic structure.

Industrial centrals are defined as autonomous economic units
made up of a union of enterprises making similar products or having
similar functions or structures. In setting up the centrals, Romanian
authorities hoped to bring together under a unified management related
plants and manufacturing processes, raw materials, sources, and
distributive facilities.[10] The industrial centrals are grouped according to the principle of homogeneous, horizontal, vertical, or geographic
concentration depending on the specific nature of production. The
concentrations are not mutually exclusive and are often grouped into
combinations reflecting several different concentrations.

Under HCM No. 586[11] the industrial centrals combine organizational, managerial, and developmental functions and attributes of
industrial sectors formerly found in the industrial ministries, the
state trading companies, and other central units and enterprises.
The industrial centrals, thus, function as independent, profit-making
units with their own economic administration, and they exist in Romania
as corporate legal entities having financial autonomy. Basically,
industrial centrals are geared first toward improving and increasing
production, research, and marketing in the Romanian economy and
specifically in the foreign trade sector and second toward freeing the
industrial and manufacturing processes from the centralized control
of the national ministries. Their scope of economic activity is quite
broad, in keeping with these objectives. Industrial centrals have the
authority to make proposals for both the national economic plan and
the foreign trade plan through their respective economic ministries;
to manage and direct their subordinate economic units by issuing them

275

instructions and directives; to organize and control manufacturing operations; to direct and coordinate the production process to engage directly in foreign trade activities by selling their products abroad or purchasing the raw materials and equipment necessary to manufacture their product; and to manage their own financial affairs and support their activities through profits earned or through bank financing.

The philosophy behind Law No. 1 is a relatively simple one— "to integrate foreign trade activities with production activities" by means of establishing direct contacts between Romanian producing units and foreign markets and by removing the excessive centralism of Romania's previous foreign trade structure.[12] Its practical application has resulted in the transfer of many foreign trade activities from the Ministry of Foreign Trade to the economic ministries, foreign trade companies, industrial centrals, and producing units. In most cases, this means that the industrial centrals producing units and end-users have the right to effect foreign trade transactions themselves. Unlike Romania's previous foreign trade structure, the basic economic units under Law No. 1 were given the authority to carry out market research, choose foreign partners, and negotiate and conclude contracts.[13]

All this is not to say, however, that Law No. 1 has not retained in the Ministry of Foreign Trade considerable control over the foreign trade process. Basic decision-making remains with the ministry, and all foreign trade must fall within the guidelines issued by the minister of Foreign Trade and under the scope of the foreign trade plan. These retained controls include the authority to license export/ import transactions and the right to set rules and regulations concerning foreign exchange and prices. The main advantage of Law No. 1 rests in the opportunity it provides the basic producing economic units to seek out and develop direct customer relationships.

Recent Legislative Changes

In 1973 additional legislative modifications were made that cause no real conceptual changes in the foreign trade system but that attempt to streamline it and make it more efficient. Both in 1971[14] and more recently in 1973,[15] Law No. 16 of 1968, establishing the Romanian Bank of Foreign Trade, was modified. Further legislative modification occurred in March 1973, when two decrees were passed that affected structural changes in the Ministry of Foreign Trade.[16] Decree No. 103 spelled out a general structural reorganization, which applied to all ministries and other central state organs. In particular, it provided for a system of departmentalization complete with personnel designations and administrative headings, which were to be adhered to by the ministries. Even more important, however, was Decree No. 127, which reorganized the structure of the Ministry of Foreign Trade so as to place more emphasis on export and import planning and to make the ministry more responsive to trade with the West. This was accomplished inter alia by establishing separate new departments of economic relations with capitalist Europe, on one hand, and with Asia, America, and Africa on the other. Even more recent modification occurred in November 1973, with the passage of another act restructuring the Ministry of Foreign Trade.[17] Decree No. 600 established a further new department within the ministry (the Office of International Economic Cooperation) and also set out a long list of ministerial functions regarding bilateral economic and technical-scientific cooperation, not the least of which firmly establishes the ministry's participation in developing the joint venture concept, both in Romania and abroad.

Finally, industrial centrals and enterprises themselves have been restructured recently in an attempt to facilitate the foreign trade process. In March 1973, the State Council passed legislation aimed at consolidating the structures of industrial centrals, state enterprises, and other economic units.[18] While Decree No. 162 contains some questionable provisions, such as those establishing fixed numbers of personnel for various departments in all economic units of a common type, it does contain some significant changes with respect to industrial centrals. In reducing the total number of industrial centrals from almost 200 down to 71 and changing ministerial responsibilities over the centrals, Romania hopes to "add appreciably to their overall effectiveness."[19] This reorganization and consolidation seem to represent a return to a more centralized type of economic structure. It is probably more accurate, however, to say that the Romanians had decentralized too far and that for purposes of efficient management and production it was necessary to combine many of the centrals.

Planning and Foreign Trade

Another key aspect of Law No. 1 is its heavy emphasis on planning. Comprehensive economic planning is a critical element in the development of any socialist economy, and this is no less true in Romania, where the Constitution gives the state plan equal status with the state budget. Traditionally, economic planning in Romania has been rigidly centralized. Under the direction of the Council of Ministries, a series of long-term, five-year and annual plans were developed by high government organs such as the Ministry of Foreign Trade, the National Bank of Romania, the Romanian Bank of Foreign Trade, the Ministry of Finance, and the State Planning Committee after receiving inputs from lower state organizations and economic units. The key to this process was the five-year plan, which was approved by the

Grand National Assembly and which then served as the basis for developing the annual national plans. It was from this national plan, in turn, that departmental plans, such as the foreign trade plan, were derived.[20]

The deficiencies of this traditional system of central planning were reorganized during the late 1960s and administrative and organizational reforms were enacted that attempted to improve the quality of planning by granting more planning autonomy to individual economic units yet still maintaining and strengthening the directing role of the central planning organs. The most recent of these reforms, and by and far the most comprehensive, is Law No. 8 of November 1972. This law sets out the basic principles and objectives of Romania's planned economic and social development. It reaffirms the central importance of a comprehensive national plan and sets out regulations for the organization of planning and the functions and responsibilities of the Romanian Communist Party, state organs, and other basic economic units. Law No. 8 and these other reforms, it can be seen, closely parallel the reforms taking place in the foreign trade system and again show Romania's desire to improve and develop her over-all economy and make it more responsive to international commerce.

In terms of foreign trade, rigid central planning has meant that all imports and exports are usually planned in advance and that there is no impulse buying by foreign trade entities. Law No. 1 does not change that basic philosophy, but it does provide that, in harmony with the other planning reforms seen above, producing units and end users, with the support of their industrial centrals and economic industrial ministries, work out their own detailed foreign trade plans. These are brought together and formalized into a final foreign trade plan by the Ministry of Foreign Trade and the State Planning Committee. The individual plans of the producing units and end-users are not intended as simple recommendations to the Ministry of Foreign Trade but rather are to be based on extensive market research and past experience of these foreign trade units. They are to serve as the fundamental components of the larger foreign trade plan.

Membership in GATT, IBRD, and IMF

In addition to the changes and reforms introduced by Law No. 1 and subsequent legislative acts, Romania has also shown an interest in joining various international economic organizations in order to improve her economic relations with the West. In November 1971, for instance, Romania achieved full membership status in GATT (General Agreement on Tariffs and Trade), after having been an observer since 1957. In joining the GATT, Romania pledged to increase her imports from GATT members at a specified rate and gave verbal assurance that she would "not discriminate against fellow GATT members in favor of Comecon trading partners."[21] In return, GATT is working to remove existing quota restrictions on Romanian exports, and thus far, Romania has received generalized trade preferences from most developed countries (Common Market countries, Canada, Japan, and Australia) except the United States. More recently (in December 1972), Romania was accepted for membership in both the International Bank for Reconstruction and Development (IBRD, or World Bank) and the International Monetary Fund (IMF).[22] Romania sought status, and has been recognized by the IBRD, as a developing country for purposes of obtaining low-interest World Bank development loans. The IMF does not recognize members as developed or developing, but simply by attaining membership in the IMF, Romania qualified for assistance in the form of access to the IMF's Special Drawing Rights Account.

FOREIGN TRADE PROCEDURES AND PRACTICES

Agencies Involved in Foreign Trade

While the Ministry of Foreign Trade, the economic and industrial ministries, the industrial centrals, producing units, end-users, and the Foreign Trade Bank all play vital roles in Romania's foreign trade structure, there are several important state organs among others that also facilitate the foreign trade process. First, the Chamber of Commerce has as its main objective the development of Romania's international economic relations.[23] It serves as a valuable source of market information for prospective buyers and sellers and is an excellent way to make trade contacts in Romania, since its membership consists of all the foreign trade companies, most of the large enterprises and associations, many smaller enterprises, and trade-related industrial organizations. All of the country's general service and trade promotion functions in the international area are under the jurisdiction of the Chamber, and it offers through itself and other agencies a wide variety of services to help foreign business partners buy and sell in the Romanian market. In addition to the normal dissemination of trade information and the use of promotional techniques, the Chamber also provides arbitration machinery for disputes between domestic enterprises arising out of foreign trade transactions and has a bureau for foreign patents and inventions.

Second, international shipping, transport, and forwarding for foreign trade transactions is handled by the state company, Romtrans. With a network of in-country agencies and subagencies and with contacts and correspondents in most countries of the world, Romtrans carries out three basic activities—international forwarding, chartering, and ship-agent services.

Finally, in connection with the transport of export, import, and transit goods, ADAS serves as the state company with sole authority to insure such shipments. ADAS provides insurance of all types for goods traveling by every means of transport.

Importing and Exporting—Customs Controls

In addition to all foreign trade being conducted in accordance with the national economic plan and foreign trade plan issued by the Minister of Foreign Trade, each foreign trade transaction requires an import or export license issued by the ministry. The rules and regulations under which such licenses are approved or denied are matters of an internal nature and are not published. It is believed, however, that these regulations are quite flexible and that a broad range of considerations go into determining whether a license will be approved or not. These include balance of payments and other financial considerations, shipping terms, availability in other markets, the foreign trade plan, and even political factors. In particular, the plan sets quotas and obligations that must be met, and where possible exceeded. Whether import and export requirements in a certain area are being met can be the key factor in determining the approval of a license.

The emphasis under Law No. 1 is clearly upon production for export, with an eye toward competitiveness in the international market-place. It is not enough merely to meet production targets, since failure by economic units to discharge their export obligations adversely affects their profits even if such targets are met. This is so because "the production plan is considered underfulfilled by the value of the undelivered exports."[24] In order to increase production for export, economic units have established export bonuses and production incentive systems. These bonuses and incentives for exceeding the plan are especially important to economic units manufacturing for export, which—unlike their suppliers—are allowed to keep a portion of their foreign exchange earnings for such incentive funds. Generally, it can be said that exporting economic units are given considerable latitude to market their products abroad at the best possible price. Ministry of Foreign Trade controls, rules, and regulations can all be adjusted or modified if a good hard-currency-earning export transaction is agreed upon.

Importing is a different situation. With hard currency reserves usually in short supply, it is vital for Romania to control carefully its importing activities. Importing economic units are given

considerably less authority than their exporting counterparts, and the
Ministry of Foreign Trade approves import licenses only after careful scrutiny. Romanian trading enterprises have shown interest in a
very broad range of imports, but the reality of Romania's economy
dictates that most imports must be weighted in favor of capital goods.
Goods and products designed to develop and expand Romania's industrial base are stressed, such as machinery, equipment, plant installations, fuels, and raw and processed materials.

The extreme importance of controlling imports was expressed
clearly on June 20, 1973, when the Grand National Assembly passed
a new law on import duties, which came into effect on January 1, 1974.[25]
This new law does several things, not the least of which is to classify
various imports according to their importance for the Romanian
economy, to encourage increased production and eliminating certain
superfluous commodities. In addition, the law hopes to give Romania
some leverage against countries that do not grant Romania most
favored nation (MFN) trade status (such as the United States) by providing increased tariffs on goods imported from such countries. Those
nations that grant Romanian exports MFN status, however, will receive MFN tariffs on their exports. The law seems to be a direct
challenge to the United States for its reluctance to pass MFN legislation for Romania, but Bucharest has softened the blow somewhat by
making this act of an experimental nature and in force for only one
year as of January 1, 1974.

In 1961 a comprehensive customs law was enacted and was
modified in 1969.[26] These laws established categories of goods that
could be exported and imported; customs organs and border control
points; authorities to inspect and verify customs approval; duties,
exemptions, and penalties; and customs procedures and rules. Most
recently, Law No. 1 establishes that the determination of customs
policies will be in the hands of the Ministry of Foreign Trade. It
emphasizes that goods and their means of transport may enter and
leave Romania at designated customs control points and that such
goods are subject to customs control as established by law, such as
Law No. 6 (including its modifications) and its complementing legislation.[27] Actual customs clearance for imported goods is the responsibility of the foreign trade companies, and it consists basically of
checking the goods to ascertain that they comply with the shipping
documents under which they have arrived in Romania.

One further form of customs control is exercised by OCM
(Oficiul de Control al Marfurilor), the Goods Control Office. This
organization carries out a number of services designed to determine
the quality and quantity of exported and imported goods, as well as
control over their packing, storage, marking, and means of transport.
OCM's services to a foreign client can include: inspection of products

to be imported from Romania throughout the manufacturing process; assistance in counting and weighing the goods; and supervision of packing, marking, and storage arrangements on board the means of transport. Such services and controls must be requested by the foreign client in the case of Romanian exports; but they are apparently carried our routinely in the case of Romanian imports. OCM's inspection certificates act as guarantees for the quality, quantity, and condition of the goods that are delivered.

Banking, Credit, and Financial

In the financial sector, as noted above, implementation of foreign trade activity occurs through the Romanian Bank of Foreign Trade. A major aspect of its broad authority and functions is the bank's ability to facilitate both exports and imports through strict controls over allocations of foreign exchange and domestic currency. The bank receives credits from foreign countries and grants credits to various underdeveloped countries, as well as to Romanian foreign trade companies and entities. Short-term credits usually go to the producing enterprises but in some cases may be granted to the foreign trade companies. As in matters of production, the emphasis is clearly on exporting.

Besides controlling credit policy, the Bank of Foreign Trade, in conjunction with the Ministry of Finance and the National Bank of Romania, carefully restricts the use of hard currency. All foreign trade entities, for instance, must apply to the bank for convertible currency necessary to pay for imports. Also, all foreign exchange realized by foreign trade exporting entities (or any other foreign operations) must be surrendered to the bank. Once application for hard currency has been made, the bank and the foreign trade entity look to the terms of payment established in the import sales contract.

A further indication of the Foreign Trade Bank's efforts to expand its economic ties with the West and increase its financial cooperation there is seen in the formation in 1973 of a joint British-Romanian bank. This bank was set up between the Romanian Foreign Trade Bank, Barclay's Bank of London, and Manufacturers' Hanover Trust of New York. This new bank will give the Foreign Trade Bank considerably more financial latitude than it had before by giving it a higher profile in international banking circles and bringing to it advice and expertise it would not otherwise receive.

Romania's national currency, the leu (plural: lei), is nonconvertible and is usable only within the country. Based on the realignment of the dollar in February 1973, the official rate of exchange is 4.97 lei to the dollar. However, Romania also has a tourist rate that is normally used in international business transactions and also is applicable to nonresident accounts created by transfers of foreign currencies in Romania. This tourist rate is currently at 14.38 lei to the dollar. The flow of both Romanian and foreign currencies is carefully controlled by the National Bank of Romania, either directly or through other state organs that it authorizes, such as the Bank of Foreign Trade and the Ministry of Tourism.[28]

As with all products in centrally-planned economies, the prices of goods in the foreign trade area are set by the government and tend to be somewhat rigid. For instance, the selling price of goods imported into Romania, irrespective of origin, is usually set at the price level of similar or substitute Romanian goods, with some adjustment allowed for differences in quality. There have been several legislative acts passed dealing with prices since 1968, the most important of which were a 1970 law that reorganized the State Committee for Prices and gave it authority to control all prices and a 1972 comprehensive new law on prices.[29] Among other things, this latter act contains provisions that establish prices for imports and exports. It also shifts the authority to set prices and control price implementation policy from the Council of Ministers to the Grand National Assembly and the Council of State. It is hoped that this new law will define responsibilities more clearly in the intricate area of price control and create a more responsive price system.

Western Access to the Local Market

Western companies may open up commercial offices in Romania or be represented by specialized Romanian economic organizations and offices.[30] Such representation requires approval by both the Ministry of Foreign Trade and the Council of Ministers, and approval is generally based on reciprocity (that is, foreign agencies are permitted in the country only if Romanian economic organs can be established in the country of the company making the request) after initial recommendation by the Chamber of Commerce.[31] The approval process can take many months, and firms engaged in licensing-type projects or activities promoting Romanian exports are most likely to receive permission. At present there are more than 70 foreign companies operating commercial offices in Bucharest.

Foreign company representation offices may engage in commercial operations, including the negotiation and conclusion of contracts; the issuance of commercial information and advertising; technical assistance and the servicing of machinery and equipment; the servicing of international transportation services; and other economic and commercial activities related to foreign trade. The office may be staffed by either Romanian nationals or resident foreigners. Foreign personnel can be paid directly and are subject to Romanian legislation in force concerning the status of foreigners in Romania, but Romanian nationals working for foreign agencies are strictly controlled.[32] Such Romanian personnel cannot be hired directly by foreign firms but are employed through the Chamber of Commerce. Similarly, they are paid by the Chamber of Commerce, with the foreign office making special foreign exchange deposits with the Bank of Foreign Trade to cover their salary and social insurance payments.[33] Furthermore, salaries paid to Romanian personnel are not set by the foreign company, but rather are dictated by the Ministry of Finance and are based on the employees' qualifications, not on the work actually performed for the foreign agency.[34]

In addition to the above factors, the very high cost of opening and maintaining a commercial office makes such a venture difficult in practice. Suitable office space and housing for foreign personnel are limited and expensive, and many office supplies must be imported due to nonavailability in Romania. Salaries for local personnel have been very high, although in March 1972 the government lowered them considerably in an attempt to keep Western companies from limiting their hiring of Romanian nationals.[35] Finally, a rather heavy tax burden is placed upon the offices of foreign companies. This includes a corporate income tax, a personal income tax for resident foreign personnel, and customs duties on imported items that must be paid in foreign exchange through specially opened accounts with the Bank of Foreign Trade.[36] Generally, there are two corporate tax rates, depending on whether or not the office operates on a commission basis. Where commissions are received for representing other firms, the tax is based on a percentage of the office's income after deductions for expenses, with minimum taxes assessed on the number of employees in an office, even though no taxable income is reported by the company office. In this case, the maximum tax on corporate income cannot exceed 60 percent of the total taxable income. Where commissions are not received, the office is taxed at a fixed rate on the basis of contracts signed in Romania, again, with minimum taxes assessed on the number of personnel employed, regardless of office income.[37]

An alternative to the problems and expense of opening and maintaining a local office is Argus, a state agency specifically created by the Chamber of Commerce. Argus represents foreign firms in Romania "on a commission basis and can negotiate but not sign on its clients' behalf," or it can provide local agents who will represent a company exclusively.[38] The procedures for obtaining the services of Argus are similar to those required for opening an office, including the annual stamp fee and concessional tax. However, income taxes, office rental, and maintenance are avoided. There are currently some 30 Western companies being represented by Argus; it is especially useful for the small- and medium-sized firms unable to afford the high cost of establishing a local office.

Advertising and all promotion of foreign companies are under the jurisdiction of Publicom, the Romanian international advertising agency. One other unique form of advertising and promotion is the Bucharest International Fair, first held in October 1970 and subsequently rescheduled for the autumn of each even-numbered year. The Bucharest Fair, unlike many other East European fairs, is aimed at promoting trade with the West and attracts many Western exhibitors. It usually emphasizes a broad range of industrial, electrical, chemical, and matallurgical products, and it can be a particularly effective way for Western traders to make useful contacts in Romania.

FOREIGN TRADE CONTRACTS

Origins of Romanian Law

Romanian contract law traces its origins to the French civil code, which Romania adopted in 1865 along with the Belgian constitution and Italian criminal code.[39] The post-World War II period, of course, saw the establishment of a socialist legal system, as the civil law system gave way to socialist legal principles and procedures. Nevertheless, the civil law concept did not entirely disappear, as is evidenced by the existence of the Romanian Civil Code, the Code of Civil Procedure, and the Commercial Code. These codes were not abrogated as such after the founding of socialist Romania. Rather, their provisions were modified, amended, or abrogated to reflect socialist legal norms, particularly in the areas of planning and economic law. Complementing these changes in the codes were an extensive series of legislative acts—laws, decrees, and decisions—that reflected the social, economic, and legal transformation of Romania.

Current Legal Rules

While the basic rules of contract law are established in the Civil Code,[40] it is really Law No. 71 of December 29, 1969[41] and its amendments[42] that establish the fundamental contract norms and rules for effecting all forms of economic relations, including those pertaining to foreign trade. This law ties the economic contract very closely to the basic factor and central concept of socialist economics-planning. In fact, the law confers on the economic contract its character as an instrument of planning.[43] Therefore, this law sets down specific, procedures whereby economic contracts must be negotiated and signed within the over-all time frames of both the annual and five-year plans.

Among other things, Law No. 71 also confers contracting authority on various types of economic units (including foreign trade entities); provides specific instructions regarding terms and conditions of delivery of both goods and services; establishes rules regarding the duration of economic contracts; sets down the various rights and obligations of the contracting parties, including risk-bearing; proscribes strict rules regarding renunciation and modification of signed contracts; provides for the determination of prices for goods and services; provides a definition of force majeure; and prescribes penalty provisions for failure to execute or for breach of contract.[44] Of particular significance is a provision that vests in the foreign trade companies, economic ministries, and other central units, such as the industrial centrals, the obligation to negotiate and execute foreign trade contracts within the guidelines of this law. Finally, in one of its later provisions, the law states that its provisions are intended to complement and interact with the applicable provisions of the Civil Code, thereby creating continuity and a unified body of contract law.

Specifically, in the area of foreign trade law, Law No. 1 addresses itself to contracting, although not in great detail. The main thrust of Law No. 1 with respect to foreign trade contracts is its emphasis on autonomy. It includes both the authority to negotiate and execute foreign trade contracts and to observe obligations and enforce rights under those contracts.[45] Thus, contracting authority extends to industrial centrals, some basic producing units, and certain end-users, as well as foreign trade companies, economic ministries, and the Ministry to Foreign Trade.

Beyond these general provisions regarding the authority of Romanian economic units to enter into foreign trade contracts, there is very little addressing the nature and form of these contracts themselves. Law No. 1 does require that foreign trade contracts and any modifications thereof be in writing and that such contracts be in conformity with Romania's international agreements and conventions and further that these contracts protect and promote the interests of Romania's national economy. In its only other direct reference to contract form, Law No. 1 permits the managers, or their delegates, of all economic units authorized to conduct foreign trade activities, to sign foreign trade contracts. There are several indirect references to the contracting function, such as the provision that notes the availability and applicability to such contracts of the Arbitration Commission for the settlement of foreign trade disputes operating under the Chamber of Commerce. Another indirect reference is the provision that labels nonperformance (and presumably other forms of breach) of export obligations (that is, contracts) as a failure to fulfill the national plan, which, we have seen, is at the very center of the Romanian economy.

Contract Practices

As far as actual contract form is concerned, the foreign trade companies use a relatively standard Western sales contract format.[46] All contract documents and modifications must be in writing and it is cautioned that verbal assurances and understandings cannot be relied upon. Due to the extensive amount of time needed to negotiate and approve a contract, during which time compromises are usually reached, it is generally difficult to modify written contracts.

While Romanian authorities are generally reluctant to be flexible in their approach to performance under a contract, they have frequently been willing to accept Western preferences as regards force majeure, third-country arbitration, choice of law, and means of transportation. Force majeure, for instance, is often defined broadly by the Romanians as "all events beyond the control of the parties which are unforeseen, or if foreseen, unavoidable, and resultant delays and nonfulfillment of obligations are not subject to claims, penalties, interest, or compensation."[47] One area of particular difficulty in negotiations is the penalty and guarantee clauses. These often include penalties for the late submission of documents, for late delivery (usually 5 percent), and for delay in commissioning (also 5 percent). The Romanians also insist in most cases on a 5 percent performance guarantee. Western practice has been to compensate for these inflexible penalties and guarantees by upward adjustment of the final sales price.[48]

In larger import transactions, Romanian authorities often seek to add to the contract a counterpurchasing commitment for the seller for specified Romanian products. This is done, of course, to offset the loss of hard currency and is in keeping with the export-oriented objectives of Law No. 1. A common way of dealing with this problem has been to commission an outside trading company (usually in Western Europe) to handle this aspect of the contract, thereby avoiding the Western seller's having to dispose of these counterpurchases.[49]

INDUSTRIAL AND INTELLECTUAL PROPERTY AND TRANSACTIONS INVOLVING TECHNOLOGY

Industrial and Intellectual Property Rights Protection

In the area of industrial property, authority to approve and grant such protection is vested in the Bureau for Foreign Patents and Inventions (Rominvent) attached to the Chamber of Commerce.[50] While the General Directorate for Metrology Standards and Inventions,

State Office for Inventions, acts as the Romanian patent office by administering patent laws, inventors' certificates, and trademarks, it is Rominvent to which one must turn, both for protection of foreign industrial property in Romania and for Romanian industrial property abroad. All such applications for protection are made through this organization. Rominvent carries out the patenting of inventions and protection of trademarks and trade names; provides for the modification of same by transmission or extinction of the patent or trademark right; and investigates and offers advice on the technical and legal validity of all patents, trademarks, and trade names, and any other industrial property rights. The charges and fees levied by Rominvent are said to be consistent with those charged abroad for similar services.[51]

Romania is a party to the 1833 Paris Union International Convention for the Protection of Industrial Property and has adhered to all its revisions, including its most recent two, in Lisbon in 1958 and in Stockholm in 1967. Romania also subscribes to the 1891 Madrid Agreement for the International Registration of Trademarks, as revised in London in 1934 and again in Nice in 1957. This means that foreign nationals will be entitled to receive the same patent and trademark protection and rights as Romania extends to her own citizens. Certain countries, such as the United States, enjoy a "right of priority" for patent applications. This means that after first filing a patent application in the United States, for instance, a U.S. national has one year in which to file a corresponding application in Romania, yet still receive his U.S. application date on his Romanian application, thereby preserving his earlier filing date. A similar right is also available for trademark applications, except that the right of priority extends only six months, not a full year.[52] Other benefits enjoyed by certain countries, such as the United States, include protection against arbitrary cancellation of a foreigner's Romanian patent.[53]

The applicable Romanian law concerning patents is Decree No. 844 of September 8, 1967.[54] This act permits foreign nationals to apply for and receive patent registration for their inventions. Upon receipt of the patent, the owner gains the exclusive right to use the invention in Romania. However, the patent owner cannot personally exploit and capitalize on his patent registration, which can only be licensed to the state. Therefore, Romanian inventors prefer to rely upon the inventors' certificate system (also provided for in Decree No. 844).[55] Certification entitles the inventor to payments based on the invention's use and the right of promotion or a better job, but the state assumes complete ownership of the invention. Unlike Romanian inventors, foreigners usually prefer to secure patents.

Under Decree 844, application for a patent may be made by the inventor, his heir, or his assignee, whether he be an individual, a firm, or a corporation. In most cases it should be filed before the invention has been used or exploited in Romania and prior to its publication or patenting in any country. The decree permits patents to be used for a period of 15 years running from the date of filing of the application, subject to the payment of annual renewal fees. Furthermore, any patent must be worked in Romania within three years from the date of patent issue or four years from the date of filing, whichever is later. Also, work on the patent must not be discontinued for more than two years in succession, and if a patent is not worked during this three-or four-year period, it automatically becomes subject to compulsory state license. Finally, if a Romanian-origin patent is considered to be of national interest and agreement cannot be reached with the inventor for its transfer to the state, the invention may be expropriated for the national good upon payment of compensation.

In the area of trademarks, Law No. 28 governs.[56] Under it, there is no requirement of prior use (that is, the applicant can register a trademark without prior registration in his native country), and the first user is entitled to registration and exclusive use of a trademark. As noted above, there is a six-month "right of priority" for trademarks, and a registered trademark vests exclusive rights in the owner and is enforceable by him against its unauthorized use. To be acceptable for registration, a trademark must be sufficiently distinguishable from other trademarks; it must not be a copy or imitation of a foreign trademark; it must not be of a generic character; and it must not be a name and/or insignia that is false, deceptive, or contrary to the rules of socialist society. Acceptable applications are published for challenge, and those opposing have three months from the date of publication to block a registration. Trademarks may then be challenged within five years of registration for failure to meet registration criteria or because of prior ownership. Registration lasts for 10 years from the application filing date and may be renewed for similar periods. Application for renewal must be made prior to the expiration of the current registration.

With respect to copyrights, Romania is a member of the Bern Convention for the Protection of Literary and Artistic Works. Even if a foreigner's country is not a member of this convention, he can obtain automatic protection for his work in Romania and other member countries by simultaneous publication in any other member country at the time of first publication in his native country. The applicable Romanian law here is Decree No. 321,[57] which provides that an author's copyright protection is good for the duration of his life. After an author's death, the copyright can continue by succession, according to certain rules.

Licensing

Licensing occupies an important place in the Romanian foreign trade system. The buying, selling, and promotion of license is handled chiefly by Uzinexportimport. In addition to this organization, contact should also be made with the end-user involved in the licensing transaction, as well as the industrial ministry involved. Much of what has been said above with respect to contracts applies to licensing agreements.

A particularly attractive aspect of concluding licensing agreements with Romania is that she has the ability to penetrate third markets, via her bilateral agreements, to which access would normally be difficult at best.[58]

JOINT VENTURES AND COOPERATION
AGREEMENTS

Opportunities for Direct Foreign Investment
in Romania

Nowhere has Romania's move toward increased commercial cooperation with the West been more pronounced than in its recent effort to attract foreign capital by permitting direct foreign private investment in the form of joint ventures. The concept was first codified in Law No. 1, which generally authorized the establishment of joint business ventures between Romanian enterprises and foreign companies in areas critical to the development of the Romanian economy— industrial and agricultural production, transportation, trade services, construction, and technical-scientific research and services. In several brief but significant articles of the Law, the general principles under which joint ventures are to operate are set out as follows: direct contact between Romanian enterprises and foreign markets is allowed; the formation of joint companies, either in Romania or in other countries, between Romanian enterprises and foreign companies is permitted; the foreign company is allowed to own up to 49 percent of the equity in such joint companies in Romania, and the Romanian financial contribution to the joint venture, as well as the repatriation of profits in hard currency, is guaranteed.

Legislative Basis. Despite these innovations (Romania had become the first Comecon country to allow direct foreign private investment), the few provisions of Law No. 1 were vague as to operational terms and conditions for joint ventures. Conditions regulating the operation of joint ventures were to be set down in the contracts negotiated by the parties. Clearly, specific details in the form of implementing rules and regulations were needed if foreign investors were to be attracted. The Romanians had a legal skeleton that needed to be fleshed out in the form of implementation legislation. This was accomplished in November 1972, with the passage of Decree No. 424 on constitution, organization, and operation of joint companies in the Socialist Republic of Romania and Decree No. 425 regarding tax on profits of joint companies constituted in the Socialist Republic of Romania.[59]

Decree 424 restates and elaborates the basic provisions of Law No. 1. In Chapter 1 of the decree, entitled "General Stipulations," there are eight articles that set the tone of the decree and reveal the intentions of the Romanian authorities in promoting the joint venture concept.

Under Law No. 1, Romanian economic organizations are permitted to directly contact foreign companies and to enter into joint ventures (also called joint companies) with them. Articles 1 and 5 of the decree restate those principles in somewhat more detail. Article 1 discusses the formation of joint ventures with foreign participation on Romanian soil. In particular, it outlines a broad range of economic sectors in which such joint ventures may be formed—"industry, agriculture, construction, tourism, transportation, and scientific and technical research." It also establishes the commercial scope of joint venture activity in these areas—"with the object of producing and marketing material goods, performing services or carrying out their work." Article 5, on the other hand, details the types of commercial organizations permitted to enter into joint ventures. On the Romanian side, this encompasses economic units having legal status that are charged with the responsibility of carrying out foreign trade activity, and it includes both individual enterprises and groups of enterprises, such as industrial centrals. On the foreign side, it includes individual companies or groups of foreign companies involved in trade, banking, or finance. Article 4 restates the basic rule that with any joint venture in Romania, the Romanian share must be at least 51 percent, thus preserving the Marxist principle of state ownership.

Especially important to foreign investors is the provision of Law No. 1, which guarantees both the Romanian financial contribution to the joint venture and the repatriation of profits in hard currency to the foreign partner. Article 7 of the decree repeats and expands the latter of these guarantees. It establishes the Romanian Bank of Foreign Trade as the primary guarantor of profit repatriation or other sums due the foreign investor, either from the sale of shares to the Romanian partner or from the distribution of assets subsequent to dissolution and winding up of the joint venture. It should be noted, however, that both Law No. 1 and Decree 424 make it very clear that such repatriated sums are, prior to transfer abroad, subject to deductions for taxes, contributions to social insurance, and any other financial obligations imposed under Romanian law or in the contract.

In addition to restating the main features of Law No. 1, Chapter I ("General Stipulations") sets out other important objectives and principles. Article 3, for instance, establishes that all joint ventures will enjoy the status of Romanian corporate bodies and will operate subject to the laws of Romania. Article 1 declares that joint ventures are organized and governed by a contract of association and statutes. These are roughly equivalent to the articles of incorporation and by-laws of a U.S. corporation, respectively.

Although not formally spelled out in the Law or the Decree, joint ventures may take either of two forms. They may be joint stock companies with actual stock certificates issued to the partners, a joint board of directors, and a general meeting of the shareholders. On the other hand, they can also be limited liability companies with no stock certificates issued, but with capital subscription covered in the original contractual agreement. Such limited liability joint ventures have a management committee rather than a board of directors but do hold a general meeting for shareholders. This distinction is familiar and meaningful to Western business interests but may not be of much practical significance in Romania, since the terms do not have the same connotations in a Romanian context and since there are special restrictions and constraints in Law No. 1 and Decree No. 424 not found in most foreign investment laws.

The most significant objective of Article 2 is its call for the joint ventures to promote exports, expand markets, diversify products for export, and develop collaboration activities in third markets.[60] As Romania is in need of hard currency to expand her industrial base and develop her economy, she makes no secret of the fact that the joint ventures will export a substantial percentage of their production. While there is no set percentage earmarked for export in the decree, we must assume that during contract negotiations for joint ventures the Romanians would be very interested in setting high export percentages.

Formation and Organization of Joint Ventures. In order to form a joint venture, the partners must first carry out a "study of technical-economic efficiency." This feasibility study is essential before proceeding further. Following the completion of this study, the partners draft a memorandum of association expressing their intent to enter into a joint venture, and the economic justification for so doing, and setting forth the objectives and purposes of the joint venture.

Once these two steps have been taken, the partners then draw up the contract of association and statutes of the joint company. Among other things, these two documents stipulate the contracting partners;

the name, object, and registered office of the joint company; its duration; the capital of the joint company, and procedures for subscription and transfer of the same; the quantity and value of capital shares; the rights and obligations of the partners; and the form and operation of management. In addition, the company statutes shall include organizational and operational provisions, such as the attributes of the company's general meeting, including voting rights, types of decision-making, selection of a board of directors, and the responsibilities of company managers and directors; the accounting methods and principles to be used; and the means of settling disputes between the partners.

It is particularly important to note the elaborate approval procedures the Romanian partner must go through before it can enter into a joint venture. First, the decree states that before the necessary abovementioned documents are executed, they shall be reviewed and approved by the State Planning Committee, the Ministry of Finance, the Ministry of Foreign Trade, the Ministry of Labor, the Bank of Foreign Trade, and other financing banks.

Control Data Corporation, the first U.S. company to sign a joint venture agreement (on April 4, 1973) in Romania, has indicated that preliminary discussions and studies for some form of economic cooperation were made as early as 1968.[61]

With the advice and consent of these ministries and state agencies obtained, the partners must take the four basic documents, accompanied by a request, to the Ministry of Foreign Trade. It is here that the documents are reviewed and studied to ensure compliance with Romanian law.

With the approval of the Ministry of Foreign Trade, the joint venture proposal is submitted to the Council of Ministers, which—if it also approves the application—drafts special legislation incorporating the joint venture into local law. Before passage into law, this proposed legislation—which embodies the constitution, contract of association, and statutes of the joint venture—must be sent to the Council of State for approval. Thus, each approved joint venture will be a legal entity created by law. The number of approvals required and the high levels of government at which such scrutiny takes place suggest that approved joint ventures may not be too numerous at first.[62] Once the Romanian authorities have had some experience with joint ventures and established streamlined review procedures, the number of viable joint ventures may increase.

Once approved and enacted into law, the joint venture must be registered with both the Ministry of Foreign Trade and the Ministry of Finance, the two state organs that will be most concerned with its economics and financial operation. The joint venture is legally constituted and formally comes into existence upon registration with the Ministry of Foreign Trade, at which time publication of the same is also made in the Official Bulletin of the Socialist Republic of Romania. Any subsequent alteration of either the contract of association or the company statutes must also be submitted for approval to the Council of State, in which case all of the formation procedures referred to above must again be carried out.

In addition to stipulating formation procedures, Chapter II also sets out financial provisions for the joint ventures. The decree states, for example, that the contract of association and statutes shall list the assets initially contributed to the joint venture, as well as those subsequently acquired. These contributions to capital by the parties may consist of "a financial contribution, a contribution in goods required for carrying out the investment activities in which the company is currently engaged, and a contribution of the industrial property rights or other rights." All contributions shall be assessed in the currency agreed upon in the contract of association and statutes, as will the value of the contributed goods. Since the joint venture must operate in world markets and in order to facilitate its operation, foreign convertible currency (hard currency) will be used.63 Furthermore, the Romanian partner may include the right to use Romanian land in the joint venture as part of his contribution. If land is not included in the Romanian partner's contribution, then the joint venture must pay rent to the state for the use of the land.

Several questions arise here, including both the definition of industrial property rights and the extent to which these contributions shall be divided up. While Article 14 states that the contributions shall be established in the joint venture's contract of association and statutes, it is uncertain how much of a cash contribution the Romanian partner will generally be willing or able to make, particularly in view of the fact that such joint ventures will operate on a hard currency basis. An even larger question is posed by the uncertainty surrounding the value of Romanian soil or, in lieu of a Romanian contribution of land, its rental value. Critical questions remaining unanswered include how the value of the land, or alternatively its rental value, is to be assessed and by whom.

The Control Data and Resita-Renk agreements are somewhat enlightening, though they leave most questions still unanswered. It would seem that initially, at least, the Romanian authorities appeared willing to make substantial capital investments, although it is still unclear what percentage of this capital investment is land, buildings, equipment, and so on, and what percentage is actually hard currency.64

Other pertinent financial provisions in Decree 424 provide that the partners' financial contributions shall be placed—in the name of the joint venture—in Romanian banking institutions (that is, the Bank of Foreign Trade). Also, as seen earlier, the Romanian Government guarantees the transfer abroad of both company profits and contributed capital. The decree further provides that all such transfers will occur through the Bank of Foreign Trade or other authorized financial institutions, thus emphasizing the bank's central role in handling joint venture accounts.

Profit repatriation is really more the subject of Decree 425, regarding taxation of profits, which is analyzed separately in this chapter. Generally, however, several points can be mentioned here. The terms and conditions of profit repatriation are to be spelled out in the contract of association and statutes. There is no limitation on profits which may be repatriated, but such repatriation must occur on an annual basis. Reinvestment of profits is, of course, allowed and the specifics of this aspect are detailed in the discussion of Decree 425. Both the Resita-Renk and Control Data joint ventures are guaranteed through the Bank of Foreign Trade. Furthermore, the Control Data agreement provides for repatriation and transfer of profits without limitation by Control Data at any time, along with a provision for reinvestment of profits in the company, but without stipulating any minimum percentage. (See Postscript, page 310.)

Chapter III of Decree 424 describes the operation and activities of joint ventures. To begin with, joint companies are required to work out both annual and five-year plans of economic and financial activity. Such plans must have the proper approvals as outlined in the statutes of the joint venture. It is not clear from the decree to what extent, if any, these plans must coincide with or complement the annual and five-year national economic plans of Romania, but it would seem that the requirement of approvals indicates some degree of coordination. The Control Data agreement, for instance, provides for both annual and five-year plans, taking into account such matters as the substitution of later, more advanced equipment at the appropriate time, working conditions and wages, overhead and prices, as well as sales projections.

Decree 424 emphasizes that joint companies shall gear their production for export. It also states that sales in Romania (that is, not for export) shall be in the agreed-upon hard currency of the company. Production for export may be traded either directly by the joint venture or through Romanian foreign trade organizations. This latter approach raises several other questions not the least of which is the financial relationship between the joint company and its Romanian exporter.

The Resita-Renk joint venture, which will manufacture gears for ships, does not really bear out this heavy emphasis on exports. Approximately 50 percent of production will go to the Romanian market and 25 percent will go to other Comecon countries. Only 25 percent will be exported to the West. The Control Data joint venture, which will produce computer printers, card-readers, and card punch systems, plans to sell approximately 55 percent of its production in Romania, with the other 45 percent to be marketed initially in Western Europe. At some later date, part of this 45 percent will be marketed in Comecon countries, where sales will be for dollars only.

One of the key elements in Decree 424 is that all operations and expenses of a joint company shall be in a convertible foreign currency, as agreed to in the contract of association and company statutes. Hence, virtually all of the company's transactions will take place in a stipulated hard currency—including the purchase of raw materials and supplies, both abroad and in Romania, the sale of joint venture products in both the home market and abroad (as noted above), and the salaries of foreign and Romanian employees. Some petty expenses and minor transactions, such as supplies where no prices can be established, will be met out of a special lei account, which the joint venture company will keep with the Bank of Foreign Trade.

All financial transactions of the joint company (either in hard currency or in lei) must be conducted through the Bank of Foreign Trade or other authorized Romanian bank. The joint company shall have the right freely to dispose of these balances, which shall also draw interest, but payments in hard currency by the company can only be drawn from these accounts and loans that are secured (that is, the joint venture cannot draw upon other hard currency accounts of the Foreign Trade Bank, the Romanian Government, or other Romanian foreign trade companies to meet its costs of operation).

A point of uncertainty is Article 26, which requires the establishment of reserve funds out of joint venture profits. The size of these funds and the conditions under which they are drawn off company profits are to be made clear in the statutes of the joint company. Thus, distribution of profits to the partners, proportionate to their contributions to the subscribed capital, can occur only after deductions for taxes, reserve funds, and future development requirements, which constitute a further uncertainty in the decree. As there are several unknowns here that could radically affect the amount of profit distributed to a foreign partner, it is imperative to determine during contract negotiations the amounts to be deducted, whether by percentage or fixed fee, and the scope of their application.

The decree provides that the salaries of Romanian personnel will be computed in the stipulated hard currency but paid directly to the bank holding the account of the joint company. The bank will then pay the Romanian personnel in lei out of the joint venture's Romanian currency account. Such a system avoids the complicated accounting task of keeping separate expense ledgers for Romanian and foreign personnel. It does, however, raise an interesting question concerning the conversion rate of Romanian workers' salaries to lei, which could leave room for considerable discrepancy in figuring the earnings of the joint venture.

Finally, Chapter III of Decree 424 provides general guidelines for accounting procedures to be used, although precise accounting methods are not specified and may be quite flexible according to the statutes of the joint venture. The decree does provide for the full depreciation of the company's assets as an expense, since under Romanian law such "assets are considered fixed funds until their value is fully written off." The write-off periods are to be established under the statutes or by a general meeting of the partners, but in no case shall these be longer than the "standard operating lifetimes" as stipulated in Romanian law.

The area of accounting methods and procedures was one that required a great deal of negotiation between Control Data and the Romanians, particularly with respect to depreciation of assets. The result was a 38-page appendix that establishes accounting priorities for the joint venture. U.S. general accounting methods will be followed.

Chapters IV and V of Decree 424 discuss what collectively may be referred to as management and control of the joint ventures. These chapters are somewhat lacking in defining the scope of joint venture management, and if there can be said to be a major weakness of the decree, it is precisely these management chapters.

Indirect reference to management is made where the decree refers to "the joint company's body controlling its accounting activity." It should be noted that this body must list as members one or two delegates from the Ministry of Finance. What is uncertain is the relationship of the officials of this accounting body to the joint venture itself (that is, how much control does the joint company have over these officials and, more importantly, over the company books, of which this body is custodian). Other critical questions remaining unanswered with respect to these accounting bodies are the weight to be given their recommendations and suggestions; their function as policy-makers or bookkeepers; and their status within the joint company, particularly whether they are counted as representatives of the Romanian partners or merely as neutral parties.

The Control Data agreement has shed some light on the meaning of these accounting bodies. It provides for the joint venture to be audited by a three-man Treasurer's Commission and spells out the duties of the commission. Elsewhere in the decree, mention is made of a "managing committee," although such a committee is never defined. The decree states only that the board of directors or managing committee shall establish the rights and obligations of the foreign personnel. On the other hand, the decree also provides for representatives of the working people to serve on the board of directors or the managing committee. The issue is further confused by a later reference to the joint company's collective managing bodies. This provision, which states that the working method of the collective managing bodies shall be agreed upon by the parties and provided for in the company's statutes, suggests, however, that the ambiguity may be intentional (that is, each individual joint venture may actually have considerable latitude in setting up whatever type of managing committee or group it wishes). One point that is very clear is that foreign personnel are allowed, and in fact may be expected, to fill managerial roles in the joint venture. As seen earlier, this sharing of managerial expertise is one of the major objectives of Romania's joint venture legislation.

The Control Data agreement again clarifies some of these uncertainties. It establishes a General Assembly of shareholders (consisting of Control Data and the Romanian Government) to be called each year and within three months following the close of the company's fiscal year, and sets out the duties of the General Assembly. In addition to the General Assembly, Control Data's agreement provides for a board of directors whose chairman alternates annually between a Control Data representative and a Romanian. It also establishes a Management Committee that will have a Romanian managing director (to be appointed for three years and renewable by agreement of both parties) and an assistant managing director (to be provided by Control Data for two years and also subject to renewal by agreement of both parties). Furthermore, company employees will designate representatives to the Managing Committee, which will also include representatives of the partners to the agreement.[65]

While Chapter V of the decree is relevant to the management question, its main thrust is to define the rights and obligations of joint venture personnel. Generally, the decree provides that Romanian personnel are entitled to the same rights and obligations provided for personnel of the state enterprises by Romanian legislation in force.

As noted earlier, the decree provides that representatives from the general meetings of the working people shall serve on the board of directors or the managing committee. In addition, it states that the Romanian law applicable to these general meetings shall also apply to the joint ventures. This would seem to indicate that Romanian labor laws, union rules and regulations, and local and municipal ordinances applying to the labor force all will be strictly applied through the company's statutes. Obviously, this is an area of considerable uncertainty for Western joint venture partners and one that will require clarification in the negotiation process.

One particular aspect of Romanian law regarding a joint company's obligation to the Romanian labor force is spelled out in the decree. It provides that the joint venture must make a contribution to the social insurance fund (a type of social security) for all Romanian employees. This fee is established by law and in this case must be paid in foreign currency. Again, the Control Data agreement is enlightening. The

Romanian authorities handle the hiring of all Romanian personnel, under five-year employment contracts. In addition, there is a five-year labor plan setting forth precise rules governing labor, wages, overhead, and prices.

The decree provides that the rights and obligations of all foreign personnel of the joint venture are established by the board of directors or the managing committee. This provision also authorizes foreign personnel to hold managerial positions and permits the transfer of their wages abroad, as provided by the management of the company. At their choosing, foreign personnel may or may not be covered by Romanian social insurance programs, but it should be noted that the company must pay the contribution unless social insurance benefits are specifically renounced.

Lengthy and detailed negotiations took place between Control Data and the Romanians over the rights and obligations of foreign personnel. As with Romanian personnel, the hiring of all foreign employees will be formally conducted by the Romanians, although Control Data will have the right to propose various foreign personnel. In addition, the Romanian Government has worked out various benefits for these foreign employees, such as duty-free import. Medical coverage, however, is not included in these benefits. Furthermore, it is the company's Managing Committee that handles all personnel matters not specifically covered in the agreement, such as how much of the salary of foreign employees may be transferred out of Romania in hard currency and how much vacation time will be granted to foreign personnel. Finally, foreign personnel may leave the employ of the joint venture merely by giving notice.

The life of any joint venture must be agreed upon by the partners and specified in the company's contract of association. Beyond that, Chapter VI of the decree provides for the dissolution and winding up of the joint venture. In essence, it provides that dissolution and liquidation procedures, company obligations and responsibilities, and asset distribution are all to be spelled out in the company statutes. All documents of dissolution and winding up must be registered with both the Ministry of Foreign Trade and the Ministry of Finance and published in the Official Bulletin.

The duration of any joint venture depends on both its objectives and operation. The Resita-Renk joint venture is set for a duration of 15 years but with an added provision that prevents termination of activities without Renk's (the foreign partner) agreement. Control Data's agreement calls for a 20-year term of operation, with an option for renewal.

Finally, in a very brief Chapter VII, "Final Stipulations," the decree provides for the settlement of disputes, either in the local law courts or by arbitration, as agreed to by the partners. Details as to arbitration procedures are to be spelled out in the contract of association and statutes.

This provision (Article 38), allowing the use of foreign arbitration tribunals, and another provision (Article 23), permitting the direct sale of joint venture production, rather than through Romanian foreign trade companies, both point up one of the most interesting aspects of the joint venture concept as applied in Romania. In both instances, the traditional principle of a state monopoly in foreign trade, which we have seen is established by the Constitution, is compromised and adjusted in the interests of developing the country's commercial relations with the West and expanding her economy.

In an apparent effort to be precise and answer the types of questions Western investors were most commonly asking about Law No. 1, the Romanian authorities passed, as a companion act to Decree No. 424, Decree No. 425, which pertains to taxes on joint venture profits.

Decree 425 provides for an annual tax rate of 30 percent, computed on annual profits. These profits appear to be based on the company books, with no special mention made of allowable deductions and determination of depreciation, except for the reserve fund. This fund is to be created at the rate of 5 percent of the annual profits until the total reserve fund reaches 25 percent of invested capital. Furthermore, a reinvestment incentive is offered in the form of a reduction of 20 percent from the normal tax rate for profits reinvested for a period of at least five years. This means that a 20 percent reduction is applied against the nominal tax rate of 30 percent so that profits would be taxed at 24 percent, rather than a 20 percent point reduction from 30 percent down to 10 percent. The Resita-Renk and Control Data agreements are both believed to contain such tax provisions.

Decree 425 also permits the Council of Ministers to grant a full tax exemption through the year in which taxable profits began to be made and, in addition, a one-half tax exemption for the following two years.

There are several uncertainties here that are readily apparent. The relationship between the tax exemption, the reserve fund deduction, and the special deduction for reinvested profits is vague. Are these various provisions mutually exclusive or do they overlap, and more importantly, can incentives, such as the reserve fund deduction, be deferred in such a way as to maximize the benefits of their creation? In addition, there is nothing in this decree to indicate whether operating losses could be carried back or forward to offset profits and whether these losses might be used to defer the full-year tax exemption.

A further significant tax rate provision of the decree provides that profits remaining for distribution after payment of all the above-mentioned taxes shall be taxed further at a rate of 10 percent where such profits are transferred abroad. Furthermore, this provision emphasizes that taxation of the income of joint venture employees and consultants shall be in accordance with Romanian law in force regarding income taxation. Such taxable income includes both wages and other forms of remuneration. Thus, any particular tax exemptions for employees or consultants must be negotiated. This is particularly significant in the case of highly skilled, highly paid foreign personnel who remain in Romania for any length of time.

The decree makes no mention of exemptions from customs duties or import taxes on equipment of the joint venture or the personal effects of its foreign personnel. Law No. 1 contains several provisions applying to customs regulations, none of which, however, speak of any exemptions. In fact, one provision of Law No. 1 provides that "imported goods are liable to customs, fiscal or other duties, and taxes established by law." As they are not provided for in the decree, necessary provision for such tax exemptions must be made during contract negotiations.

Cooperation Agreements

While the joint venture is currently the focal point of interest for Western business interests, cooperation agreements have traditionally been (and continue to be) a more significant element of Romania's economic relations with the West. Cooperation may take many diverse forms depending on the interests and needs of the cooperating parties.[66] Cooperation with developed Western countries occurs in almost all fields of economic activity, particularly in the areas of mechanical engineering, electrical engineering, electronics, chemical and petroleum industries, aviation, transportation, telecommunications, textiles, and agriculture.[67]

Cooperation agreements are a unique form of contract that bring together commercial, technical, and financial elements for purposes of achieving complex economic objectives. In many cooperation activities several contracts may be involved. The conclusion of such contracts, however, follows normal commercial and juridical practice.

SETTLEMENT OF FOREIGN TRADE DISPUTES

Arbitration in Romania[68]

The Romanian arbitration system has three different forms, one of which governs domestic disputes, while the other two are for foreign trade disputes. Of these two latter forms, the first is an ad hoc arbitration that can be used in foreign trade situations. It is the second form of foreign trade arbitration, however, that is the most important. This is the arbitration that is handled through the Arbitration Commission of the Chamber of Commerce. The commission is established by law but works under the authority of the Chamber of Commerce.

The commission, like the Chamber of Commerce, is not a state organization per se, and its activities are not subject to the control of the state's judicial and administrative organs. Because it is not subject to other judicial and administrative organs but rather has executory power, the awards issued by the commission are binding and are not subject to judicial review.[69]

Under Article 2 of the commission's rules, its jurisdiction is defined as competence "to settle patrimonial disputes arising from foreign trade transactions between Romanian foreign trade companies and foreign private persons or corporate bodies, provided the parties have chosen to resort to arbitration or if such a procedure is stipulated by international agreements." In addition, the commission may settle foreign trade patrimonial disputes arising between foreign parties, but only if the parties have so agreed to in writing. Actual disputes are judged by a panel of two arbitrators and an umpire.[70] Commission rules of procedure are those set out in the formal Rules of the Arbitration Commission, supplemented by the Code of Civil Procedure.

With regard to choice of law under the contract, the commission will rely on the autonomy of the contracting parties and look to choice of law as expressed in the contract. Generally, the law so chosen by the parties is accepted by the commission so long as it is a valid law in force in a definite state and so long as it has a direct connection with the contract itself.[71] It must not, however, be contrary to Romanian public policy, and the commission is entitled to review the choice of law and to change it in the contract should they deem it necessary.[72] Furthermore, if the parties remain silent regarding choice of law for the contract, the commission may decide what law should govern the contract based upon conflict-of-laws principles. In such a case either the law of the place where the contract was concluded (lex loci contractus) or the law of the country where the contract is executed (lex loci executionis) shall apply.[73]

As noted above, commission awards are final and executory.[74] Their enforcement is carried out in Romania according to the Code of Civil Procedure and abroad according to the provisions of international treaties and agreements or, should such treaties and agreements not be applicable, then according to the legal provisions of the country where the award is to be executed. It should be noted at this point that Romania is a party to the 1958 New York Convention for the Acceptance and Enforcement of Foreign Arbitration Awards and to the 1961 Geneva European Convention on International Commercial Arbitration. Furthermore, in Romania's relations with countries that are parties to the 1923 Geneva Protocol on Arbitration Clauses and the 1927 Geneva Convention on the Enforcement of Foreign Arbitration Awards, both to which Romania is a party, she applies the provisions of these two conventions so long as the countries are not yet parties to the 1958 New York Convention.

Third-Country Arbitration

While the institutionalization of arbitration is provided for by the Arbitration Commission of the Chamber of Commerce, in practice many foreign trade contracts provide for third-party arbitration at some neutral country, typically under the Rules of Conciliation and Arbitration of the International Chamber of Commerce in Paris.

SOME RECENT DEVELOPMENTS

Romania's drive for economic development and increased commercial cooperation with the West was seen especially clearly in the December 4-7, 1973, visit to the United States of President Nicolae Ceausescu, who has emphasized his country's recent focus on international economic cooperation in the form of joint ventures and, in particular, its hope of establishing such joint companies with U.S. corporations.[75]

The Romanians have been seeking most-favored-nation tariff treatment since 1969. Bucharest has enjoyed Nixon Administration support for MFN status for several years but has not as yet been able to hurdle Congressional obstacles. Currently, Romanian MFN status is stalled because it is linked with an administration request to give MFN status to the Soviet Union, a move that has attracted considerable opposition because of the Soviet position on Jewish emigration.

During the Ceausescu visit, a bilateral agreement between the U.S. Chamber of Commerce and the Romanian Chamber of Commerce was concluded that established a joint U.S.-Romanian Economic Council. Probably most significant, the visit produced a number of agreements that further strengthened U.S.-Romanian relations. A joint statement was issued on December 5, 1973, which contains the principles on which U.S.-Romanian relations are based.[76] In addition to this statement, bilateral agreements were signed regarding fisheries in the Western region of the middle Atlantic Ocean and relating to civil air transport.[77] Also, a joint statement on economic, industrial, and technological cooperation was signed on December 5, 1973, and an income tax treaty was signed on December 4, 1973. The joint statement seeks to give a new impetus to economic cooperation by promoting trade, joint ventures, joint marketing, and other commercial arrangements.[78]

The income tax agreement[79] is especially important because it will remove tax barriers to the flow of both investments and individuals. The agreement itself incorporates the same basic principles with respect to taxation of business, personal service, and investment income; and it assures nondiscriminatory tax treatment in that citizens and business establishments of one country receive the same tax treatment as the nationals and commercial enterprises of the other country. Of importance to U.S. business firms with resident personnel in Romania will be the provision stipulating a reduction of withholding taxes on interest derived by foreign residents to not more than 10 percent (with the exception that interest paid to the other government on loans granted or guaranteed by a government agency will be exempt from tax at the source). The maximum rate of tax on industrial is set at 15 percent. Also, a reciprocal withholding rate of not more than 10 percent on dividends is established. It should be noted that this maintains the present Romanian statutory rate, which, when combined with their corporate tax rate on joint ventures (now at 30 percent, as seen above), is within the limits of the U.S. foreign tax credit. Also significant to investors is the fact that equipment rentals will no longer be subject to the 20 percent Romanian withholding tax, provided that such equipment is not connected with a Romanian office (that is, a permanent establishment). Finally, the agreement comes into effect on January 1, 1974, after approval by the U.S. Senate and the proper authorities in Bucharest. It will remain in force for a period of five years, after which it would continue in force indefinitely unless terminated by either nation.

NOTES

1. Constitutia Republicii Socialiste Romania (1969), hereinafter "Constitutia," Article 1; see generally Keefe et al., Area Handbook for Romania, hereinafter Area Handbook, 116 (1972); and U.S. Department of State, Background Notes—Socialist Republic of Romania, hereinafter Background Notes (August 1970), 3.

2. Law No. 1 (Legea Nr. 1), March 17, 1971 (on foreign trade and economic and technicoscientific cooperation activities in the Socialist Republic of Romania), published in the Official Bulletin of the Socialist Republic of Romania, hereinafter B.Of., No. 33, on March 17, 1971; see also 11 International Legal Materials No. 1 (January 1972), 161. Note that Legea Nr. 1 of 1971 replaces Decret Nr. 317 of 1949.

3. J. A. Burgess, "Romania Looks West: An Analysis of Legislative Change in the Foreign Trade Sector During the Sixties," 2 Calif. West. Int'l. L. J. 22 (1971).

4. Legea Nr. 1 at Articles 2 and 16, and T. R. Popescu, "Probleme Juridice" in Relatiile Comerciale Internationale Ale R. P. R. (Bucharest: Editura de Stat, 1955), 15-20.

5. "Trading and Investing in Romania," Overseas Business Reports, U.S. Department of Commerce, August 1973, 6.

6. Legea Nr. 16; June 21, 1968 (privind infiintarea, organizarea, si functionarea Bancii Romane de Comert Exterior) B.Of. Nr. 80 din June 22, 1968. Prior to 1968 all financial matters involving foreign trade were handled by the National Bank of Romania.

7. Id., at Article 2; and G. Florescu, "The Law on Finances," 4 Romanian Foreign Trade, 1973, 90.

8. Decret Nr. 622, September 12, 1969 (privind organizarea si functionarea Ministerului Comertului Exterior), B.Of., Nr. 107 din September 12, 1969.

9. HCM Nr. 586, March 24, 1969, Hotarire pentru aprobarea Statutului Centralei Industriale (cadru), B.Of., Nr. 47 din April 2, 1969.

10. "Doing Business with Romania," Business International, 1973, 13.

11. HCM stands for Hotariri ale Consiliului de Ministri (decisions).

12. G. Florescu, "General Principles in Foreign Trade Activities in the Light of Law No. 1/1971," 3 Romanian Foreign Trade No. 84, 1972, 34.

13. Id. at 34 and Legea Nr. 1, at Article 25.

14. Decret Nr. 127, January 25, 1971 (pentru modificarea articolului 10 din Legea Nr. 16/1968 privind infiintarea, organizarea si functionarea Bancii Romane de Comert Exterior), B.Of., Nr. 10 din January 27, 1971.

15. Decret Nr. 134, March 15, 1973 (pentru modificarea Legea Nr. 16/1968 privind infiintarea, organizarea, si functionarea Bancii Romane de Comert Exterior, cu modificarile ulterioare), B.Of., Nr. 40 din March 28, 1973.

16. Decret Nr. 103, March 12, 1973 (privind stabilirea normelor unitare de organizarea a ministerelor si a celorlatte organe centrale de stat), B.Of., Nr. 29 din March 14, 1973, and Decret Nr. 127, March 15, 1973 (pentru modificarea Decretului Nr. 622/1969 privind organizarea si functionarea Ministerului Comertului Exterior, devint Legea Nr. 41/1969 cu modificarile ulterioare), B.Of., Nr. 40 din March 28, 1973.

17. Decret Nr. 600, November 3, 1973 (pentru modificarea Decretului Nr. 622/1969 privind organizarea si functionarea Ministerului Comertului Exterior, devenit Legea Nr. 41/1969, cu modificarile ulterioare), B.Of., Nr. 173 din November 3, 1973.

18. Decret Nr. 162, March 22, 1973 (privind stabilirea normelor unitare de structura pentru unitatile economice), B.Of., Nr. 65 din May 11, 1973, and HCM Nr. 367, April 9, 1973 (privind unele masuri de reorganizare a centralelor industriale, unitatilor asimilate acestora, precum si a unor intreprinderi de stat), B.Of., Nr. 128 din August 17, 1973.

19. "Eastern Europe Report," Business International August 24, 1973, 245.

20. Economic and Commercial Guide to Romania 1969-1970 (Romanian Chamber of Commerce, Bucharest), 27-28.

21. "Gatt Membership Welcomed," Journal of Commerce, January 27, 1972, 5.

22. Romanian membership was made possible by the passage of two acts—Decret Nr. 493, December 7, 1972 (privind aderarea Romaniei la FMI), B.Of., Nr. 146 din December 9, 1972 and Decret Nr. 494, December 7, 1972 (privind aderarea Romaniei la BIRD), B.Of., Nr. 146 din December 9, 1972.

23. Decret Nr. 623 of November 21, 1973 (privind organizarea Camerei de Comert si Industrie a Republicii Socialiste Romania), B.Of., Nr. 184 din November 22, 1973. The name of the Chamber has been officially changed to the Chamber of Commerce and Industry.

24. Area Handbook at 249.

25. Legea Nr. 12, of June 20, 1973 (privind tariful vamal de import al Republicii Socialiste Romania), B.Of., Nr. 92 din June 22, 1973.

26. Legea Nr. 6, of December 28, 1961 (privind reglementarea regimului vamal al Republicii Socialiste Romania), B.Of., Nr. 29 din December 30, 1961. This was modified by Decret Nr. 47, of January 29, 1969 (privind modificarea articolelor 54 si 55 din Legea Nr. 6/1961 privind reglementarea regimului vamal al Republicii Socialiste Romania), B.Of., Nr. 15 din January 30, 1969.

26. See, for instance, HCM Nr. 2415, of October 28, 1968 (privind punctele de control pentru trecerea frontierei de stat), B.Of., Nr. 135 din October 28, 1968.

28. Decret Nr. 210, of June 17, 1960 (privind regimul mijloacelor de plata straine, metalelor pretioase si pietrelor pretioase), B.Of., Nr. 8 din June 17, 1960, and Decret Nr. 211, June 17, 1960 (pentu acordarea unor posibilitati de predare, cedare si declarare a mejloacelor de plata straine si a metalelor pretioase, precum si pentru gratiereu unor pedepse si incetarea procesului penal pentru unele infractiuni), B.Of., Nr. 8 din June 17, 1960.

Decret Nr. 210 was then later modified by Decret Nr. 885, of September 11, 1967 (pentru modificarea Decretului Nr. 210/1960 . . .), B.Of., Nr. 80 din September 11, 1967; Decret Nr. 25, of January 30, 1970 (pentru modificarea Decretului Nr. 210/1960 . . .), B.Of., Nr. 3, of January 31, 1970; and Decret Nr. 132, of April 19, 1972 (pentru modificarea Decretului Nr. 210/1960 . . .), B.Of., Nr. 39, of April 19, 1972.

29. Decret Nr. 12, of March 17, 1970 (privind organizarea si functionarea Comitetului de Stat pentru Preturi), B.Of., Nr. 23, din March 18, 1970 and Decret Nr. 388, of October 11, 1972 (privind stabilirea preturilor si tarifelor fixe sau limita la produsele grupele si subgrupele de produse sau servicii, precum si la obiectele de constructii care constituie momencaltura Consiliului de Stat), B.Of., Nr. 122 din November 6, 1972.

Other important acts concerning prices that were passed during this period include Legea Nr. 19, of December 16, 1971 (cu privire la regimul preturilor si tarifelor), B.Of., Nr. 154 din December 16, 1971, and Decret Nr. 317 of August 22, 1972 (privind organizarea si functionarea Comititului de Stat pentru Preturi), B.Of., Nr. 95 din August 29, 1972. It should also be noted that the December 14, 1973, edition of Romania Libera referred to discussions undertaken by the Executive Committee of the PCR and the Council of Ministers concerning possible new legislation concerning prices. The Council of Ministers is expected to make appropriate legislative proposals to the Council of State.

30. Decret Nr. 15 of January 25, 1971 (on authorization and working regulations of commercial agencies set up by foreign trading firms and economic organizations in the Socialist Republic of Romania), published in B.Of., No. 10, of January 27, 1971. See also 11 International Legal Materials No. 1, January 1972, 157. Note that Decret Nr. 15 has been modified by Decret Nr. 396 of July 10, 1973 (pentru modificarea Decretului Nr. 15/1971 . . .), B.Of., Nr. 105 din July 17, 1973.

31. Foreign companies interested in establishing an office in Romania must apply initially to the Chamber of Commerce. Decret Nr. 15, Arts. 5 and 6, provides that this application should include information and documentation as to the following: country of incorporation, including certification of the company's capital and financial soundness; proposed scope of activities of the agency; the number, responsibilities, and nationality of proposed staff members; and a description of the proposed agency's movable assets.

32. Decret Nr. 15, supra note 30, at Article 12.

33. Id., at Article 21; and "Trading and Investing in Romania," supra note 5 at 13.

34. "Doing Business with Romania," supra note 5 at 44.

35. Id.

36. Decret Nr. 15, supra note 30 at Articles 15, 16, and 17.

37. See Decret Nr. 153 of May 11, 1954 (provitor la impozitul pe veniturile populatiei), B.Of., Nr. 22 din May 11, 1954, as amended by Decret Nr. 650 of 1968. Also, see HCM Nr. 545, of April 30, 1970

(privind reglementarea unor impozite pe veniturile populatiei), B.Of., Nr. 41 din April 30, 1970.

38. "Trading and Investing in Romania," supra note 5 at 13.

39. G. W. Nash, "Rumanian Contracts of Delivery: A Comparative Analysis," 17 Buffalo Law Review 375, 377 (1968).

40. See Civil Code (Ministerul Justitiei, (1958) beginning at Article 242. Title III of the Civil Code beginning at Article 942 discusses the general nature and specific attributes of Romanian contract law.

41. Legea Nr. 71, of December 29, 1969 (contractelor economice), B.Of., Nr. 154 din December 29, 1969.

42. Legea Nr. 71 was amended by HCM, Nr. 306, of March 24, 1970 (privind unele masuri pentru aplicarea legii contractelor economice), B.Of., Nr. 35 din April 15, 1970. Legea Nr. 71 was also modified by Decret Nr. 395, of July 10, 1973 (pentru modificarea legii contractelor economice Nr. 71/1969), B.Of., Nr. 105 din July 17, 1973.

43. Legea Nr. 71, supra note 115 at Article 2, as amended by Decret 395, supra note 42, at Article I, 1.

44. HCM (Decision) No. 306 of March 24, 1970, which both elaborates and makes more definite the penalty provisions of Law No. 71. In particular, fines for various forms of nonperformance have been increased as much as five- and six-fold.

45. Legea Nr. 1, supra note 2 at Article 22(b) and (f), and (g) Florescu, "General Principles . . .," supra note 12 at 34.

46. See "Trading and Investing in Romania," supra note 5 at 11.

47. Id. at 12.

48. Id.

49. Id.

50. This authority is granted in Decret Nr. 623 of November 22, 1973, which establishes the Chamber of Commerce and Industry, and in Law No. 1, Article 47.

51. Economic and Commercial Guide, supra note 20 at 205.

52. "Trading and Investing in Romania," supra note 5, at 14.

53. Id.

54. Decret Nr. 844 of September 30, 1967 (privind inventiile, inovatiile si rationalizarile), B.Of., Nr. 85 din September 30, 1967.

55. Decret Nr. 844, supra note 148 at Article 6+.

56. Legea Nr. 28, of December 29, 1967 (privind marcile de fabrica de comert si de serviciu), B.Of., Nr. 114 din December 29, 1967.

57. Decret Nr. 321, of June 27, 1956 (privind dreptul de autor), B.Of., Nr. 18, din June 27, 1956, as modified by Decret Nr. 358 of August 3, 1957 (pentru modificarea alineatului 3 din articol 41 al Decretului Nr. 321/1956, privind dreptul de autor), B.Of., Nr. 21, din August 3, 1957, and Decret Nr. 1172, of December 28, 1968 (pentru

modificarea Decretului Nr. 321/1956 privind dreptul de autor), B.Of., Nr. 174, din December 30, 1968.

58. R. S. Kretschmar and R. Foor, The Potential for Joint Ventures in Eastern Europe, 41 (1972).

59. Decret Nr. 424, of November 2, 1972 (pentru constituirea, organizarea si functionarea societatilor mixte in Republica Socialista Romania) and Decret Nr. 425, of November 2, 1972 (privind impozitul pe beneficiile societatilor mixte constituite in Republica Socialista Romania), both published in B.Of., Nr. 121 din November 4, 1972. See also 12 International Legal Materials, Nr. 3 (May 1973), at 651 and 656.

60. N. Manescu si Al. Detesan, "Societatile Mixte de Comercializare," Viata Economica, XI, Nr. 9 (496), of March 2, 1973 at 1.

61. "Questions and Answers on Investing in Romania," Overseas Private Investment Corporation (1973), at 9.

62. Since passage of Decrees 424 and 425 in November of 1972, five joint venture contracts have been signed. (Press Bulletin of November 7, 1973, with statistics taken from "Joint East-West Ventures in Production and Marketing," Institute of Soviet and East European Studies, Carleton University, Ottawa, Canada, 1973).

63. For example, the Control Data Corporation agreement with CIETV of Romania calls for a joint venture operating on U.S. dollars. Another joint venture agreement, signed October 6, 1973, between Zahnraderfabrik Renk AG of West Germany and the Industrial Central for Machine Construction at Resita, Romania, will operate with deutschemarks. ("Romania's Two Joint Ventures with the West," Business International/Eastern Europe Report, November 16, 1973, pp. 332-333.)

64. See "Joint Venture Agreements in Eastern Europe: Guidelines for Drafting Joint Venture Agreements," Control Data Corporation (1973) at 2; "Eastern Europe Report," Business International (November 16, 1973) at 332.

65. In the Resita-Renk joint venture, all decisions of the administrative council (that is, the managing committee) and the board of directors must be unanimous. "Eastern Europe Report," Business International (November 16, 1973) at 332.

66. According to G. Cristea, "Cooperation in Production, the Modern Form of Commercial Exchanges," Romanian Foreign Trade No. 3, 1973, 88: "Among the forms of international cooperation practiced at present by Romania, production cooperation holds the greatest share, over 160 cooperation ventures having been concluded with firms in 20 industrially-developed countries."

67. Id. at 88-89.

68. Kleckner, "Foreign Trade Arbitration in Romania," 5 NYU J. Int'l L. and Pol. 233, 237 (1972).

69. Id. at 238.

70. Id. at 204, and Ion Nestor, Arbitrajul in Comertul Exterior al R.P.R. (Bucharest, 1957) at 58-63.

71. O. Capatina, "Conflictele de Legi Referitoare la Contractele de Vinzare Internationala de Marfuri," Revista Romana de Drept No. 9 (1972) at 26.

72. Id.

73. Kleckner supra note 68 at 244.

74. In some special situations some forms of extraordinary recourse are available, such as nullity, judicial review, and reversal. For a more complete discussion of these, see id. at 242.

75. "Inside Romania: A Talk with Ceausescu," Business Week, Dec. 1, 1973 at 44.

76. See text of "Joint Statement of the President of the United States of America, Richard Nixon, and the President of the Council of State of the Socialist Republic of Romania, Nicolae Ceausescu," issued by the Office of the White House Press Secretary on December 5, 1973; and "Ceausescu, Nixon Sign Agreement," Washington Post, Dec. 6, 1973 at A2.

77. See U.S. Department of State Press Bulletins No. 436 ("United States and Romania Sign Air Transport Agreement") and No. 437 ("United States and Romania Sign Fisheries Agreement"), Dec. 4, 1973.

78. See text of "Joint Statement on Economic, Industrial and Technological Cooperation Between the United States of America and the Socialist Republic of Romania," issued by the U.S. Department of State on Dec. 5, 1973 at 1-2.

79. See text of "Convention Between the Government of the United States of America and the Government of the Socialist Republic of Romania with Respect to Taxes on Income," issued by the U.S. Department of the Treasury on December 4, 1973 at Art. 22.

Postscript: After submission of this study to the publisher it was ascertained that the foreign partner's right to repatriation of profits will almost certainly depend upon exports to hard currency areas. The Romanian authorities have apparently decided that joint venture operations will, at least for foreign exchange purposes, give rise to two types of transactions: "contract" hard currency transactions (in the case of most domestic and intra-Comecon operations) and "convertible" hard currency transactions (mainly those with hard currency countries). It appears that only the latter will provide a source of repatriation of profits for the Western investor. See East European Trade Council, Mixed Companies in Romania 11 (London, 1974): 14-19.

13

THE UNION OF SOVIET
SOCIALIST REPUBLICS

Albert Kiralfy

The Soviet law of foreign trade is closely linked with Soviet
law generally and with the socialist system of economy. Foreign
trade is not regulated by the law of the market but by the needs of
the USSR as understood by its rulers. This means that it is a state
monopoly administered at the Union (federal) level and that it is highly
centralized. Products are only imported if they cannot be produced
in sufficient quantity in the USSR and they are urgently needed by it.
Products are exported in order to earn foreign exchange needed for
other purposes.

The partial reversal of socialism under the New Economic
Policy made foreign trade especially vulnerable to pressure for liberalization and away from strict control. Lenin feared that this would
lead to a rebirth of capitalism within the Russian socialist republics
themselves, and therefore he eventually overruled Stalin and other
leaders who considered the centralized foreign trade administration
too bureaucratic and unwieldy to cope with capitalist enterprise.[1]
But a few foreign firms were allowed to operate within Russia, and a
few Russian production enterprises were allowed to deal with their
products abroad.[2] In November 1923 the constituent statute of the
Foreign Trade Department was approved and the state monopoly system tightened.

Under the first Constitution of the USSR in 1924, the conduct of
foreign trade was made a matter for Union (federal) competence.[3]
A Union Foreign Trade Department was established.[4] The USSR then
concluded a number of trade treaties with foreign countries.[5]

The trading unit was a special Soviet foreign trade organization,
of which a number were established in 1925. In February 1930 the
modern system was instituted, under which various import and export
organizations are created by the Ministry of Foreign Trade, each

311

enjoying a monopoly in particular product lines. In 1933 the constituent statute of Soviet Trade Delegations was enacted. From July 1953,
Soviet foreign trade organizations have entered into direct contracts
with foreign firms, but under various types of official control.

The main change in recent years has been the development of
the Comecon trading bloc in Eastern Europe, with which we are not
directly concerned, and the elaboration of sophisticated foreign aid
programs, involving large projects in underdeveloped countries. It is
Soviet policy to trade with its socialist partners wherever possible,
but trade with the West is still growing, on the theory of the peaceful
coexistence of different economic systems on the basis of mutual
benefit.

INSTITUTIONAL FRAMEWORK
AND FOREIGN TRADE PLANNING

Soviet Foreign Trade Agencies and
Organizations

The State. At the international level, the Soviet state, through the
Soviet Government, represents the republics of the USSR, and foreign
trade is assigned exclusively to the competence of the union federation).[6] The Soviet Government negotiates trade treaties and maintains diplomatic representatives abroad, through the Ministry of Foreign Affairs. On the other hand, the Soviet state and its government
have no legal personality at the level of civil law and private transactions. For the purpose of making foreign trade contracts, it acts
through the Soviet foreign trade organizations.

Where the USSR is party to a treaty, it will generally conform
the terms of foreign trade contracts to the requirements of such treaty
to fulfill its obligations to other sovereign governments. But the
treaty is not incorporated in the contract and the contract is not invalid if, for some reason, it has been made in violation of the treaty.[7]

A trading contract is normally based on the state plan, and not
directly on an international treaty. If the plan or contract violates
the treaty, that is a matter for discussion between the states involved.
In particular, a treaty does not affect liability under a contract already entered into, unless both parties to the contract consent to a
change.

The Ministry of Foreign Trade. The ministry was set up as a People's
Commissariat, but otherwise in much its present form, by a law of
November 1923, now supplemented by the General Statute on Soviet
Ministries of July 1967.[8] The ministry has exclusive powers over

import and export trade, customs, and transport, freight, and insurance in foreign trade.[9]

The minister of Foreign Trade is appointed by the Supreme Soviet, the highest legislative body in the USSR. The ministry is divided into sections, one dealing with research and preparations for trading negotiations, another supplying detailed information on different classes of product, and a third conducting the actual trading administration, including financial and transport matters.[10]

The Chamber of Commerce and Industry of the USSR. This is a body to which various domestic and foreign trade organizations of the USSR belong. Besides the more usual promotion of foreign trade, it also has public functions: It handles patenting by foreigners in the USSR and Soviet patents abroad; it provides a translation service for foreign firms trading with the USSR; and it inspects goods exported from or imported into the USSR. Perhaps its most striking feature is that it maintains a Foreign Trade Arbitration Commission (FTAC, in operation since 1932), which is an important forum for deciding foreign trade disputes submitted to it.[11] Since 1930, it has also maintained a Maritime Arbitration Commission, now operating under a decree of 1960.

State Banks. The financing of foreign trade[12] is handled by a special Foreign Trade Bank of the USSR (Vneshtorgbank), which exercises the state monopoly of banking in this field. It is a joint-stock company in which the State Bank of the USSR (Gosbank) has the largest interest. Vneshtorgbank provides credit, issues letters of credit, and makes payments. It will have creditor's rights, as a result, in many cases. It may also undertake to act as guarantor for the performance of a foreign trade contract. The bank also acts an an official controller of all financial dealings in the field, verifying that they are in conformity with the provisions of the state export or import plan and are justified by the contract in pursuance of which they are made. Loans or credits to foreign states, however, are made by the bank itself.

Soviet Foreign Trade Organizations (SFTOs). These are set up by the Ministry of Foreign Trade and are limited in number. The name of each SFTO expresses its field of interest. It has operational funds and legal personality and enters directly into foreign trade contracts.[13] The SFTO acts as a screen between the foreign firm and the actual Soviet internal production enterprise supplying export goods or the enterprise importing goods. There are no legal links between these and the foreign firms.[14] The SFTO acts for all interested Soviet enterprises in its field of interest and may have to coordinate their desires and decide among them.

The head office of each SFTO is generally in Moscow, but the SFTOs may set up branches elsewhere and also combine with foreign firms in mixed companies outside the USSR, as discussed more fully below. Each SFTO is headed by a president and deputy presidents appointed by the Soviet Foreign Trade Ministry. The president has wide powers of executive management. He is also the representative officer for legal purposes as well as administration.[15] The signature of two authorized officers of an SFTO are usually a prerequisite of any binding contract with it.[16] One of these is generally the president of the SFTO, if the contract is signed in Moscow. The president may authorize other persons to sign elsewhere. The journal of the Ministry of Foreign Trade (Vneshnaya Torgovlya) publishes the names of all such authorized persons.

As discussed more fully below, SFTOs are civilly liable on their contracts, and assets allocated to them by the Soviet authorities may be attached by their creditors. However, they seldom have extensive assets since they have little need for them, acting as intermediaries and relying on bank credits. Imports in their hands may not be attached in the USSR, as SFTOs are regarded as mere agents for Soviet firms. The Soviet Foreign Trade Bank may also have preferential liens on goods in order to recover credits. Fortunately SFTOs have a good credit record, and resort to compulsion is unnecessary.

State Insurance. The Soviet Finance Ministry operates State Insurance (Gosstrakh) and Foreign (Trade) Insurance (Ingosstrakh). Insurance is a state monopoly exercised at Union level.[17] Ingosstrakh has legal personality and enters into insurance contracts. The foreign trade contract may stipulate that it should do so. Marine insurance is also handled by Ingosstrakh.[18] The Finance Ministry has approved special rules of transit insurance.[19]

Soviet Transport Organizations. The Soviet Constitution places railways under Union competence.[20] They are operated by the Soviet Ministry of Transport.[21] The various railway systems are legal persons, operating on separate budgets. The present statute is of April 1964, regulating economic relations with the public, including freight contracts.[22] The internal administration of the railways is governed by an ordinance of March 1959.

As between the socialist countries, and between the USSR and its immediate neighbors, special treaties regulate international through traffic by railway. In through shipments to the West, the situation depends on the terms of the contract made with the first carrier, who is liable for any loss or damage throughout the journey, subject to a right of recourse against the system actually at fault.[23] The USSR is not a party to general international conventions on uniform regulation of rail shipments.

Sea transport is a state monopoly[24] and the responsibility of the Maritime Ministry.[25] There is no constituent statute for Soviet shipping as such.[26] There is a Maritime Code, which regulates operations at sea, like most Merchant Shipping Acts, and deals with carrier's liability.[27] The present code is of September 1968. There are also General Freight Conditions of February 1957. There are 11 state shipping lines.[28] Each is a legal person, with funds allotted to it, and enters into contracts of carriage of goods by sea.

Civil aviation is an activity of the Union. The Civil Aviation Ministry operates under a decree of July 1964. In its trading aspect, the ministry appears as the Soviet airline, Aeroflot.[29] There are Rules of Carriage of July 1965 and of Air Freight of November 1967. Each republic has a subdivision of Aeroflot, with legal personality. General rules of air law are laid down in the Air Code of the USSR of December 1961,[30] which also deals with the liability of the carrier of goods by air.

Soviet Trade Delegations. The Soviet Government often establishes, with the consent of the host country, a local trade delegation, usually in the country's capital but sometimes also with regional branches. The present constituent statute of these trade delegations is a law of September 1933. Trade delegations may also be provided for in treaties and are governed in some respects by the general rules of public international law.

The local trade delegation assists in the conduct of Soviet trade with the host country. It helps SFTOs make contracts with local firms and to perform such contracts. It examines the legality of all foreign trade contracts and issues import licenses for goods going to the USSR.[31] It supervises direct dealings between SFTOs and local firms.

The trade delegation is subject to a dual subordination. It forms part of the Soviet diplomatic representation in a country and is the proper channel for Soviet ministries and government departments in commercial matters. But it is also functionally subordinate to the Soviet Foreign Trade Ministry in conducting foreign trade with local firms. The trade delegation claims diplomatic privileges and immunities as an official organ of the Soviet state monopoly of foreign trade. This situation is usually confirmed, but can be occasionally waived, by the terms of a particular treaty.[32] Local courts generally have no jurisdiction over members of the delegations. Their assets are also exempt from claims of creditors, unless a treaty provides to the contrary. The 1972 U.S.-USSR Trade Agreement, discussed more fully in Chapter 1, for example, makes detailed provision for the exchange of commercial representation between the two governments, including the status of the Soviet trade representation in the United States.

Trade delegations do not generally make commercial contracts. They may make international agreements as representatives of the USSR, which will bind the USSR internationally. The 1933 constituent statute on Soviet Trade Delegations provides, however, that these delegations may also sue and be sued in foreign courts in matters arising out of commercial transactions. This provision will only apply where there is a special treaty or official Soviet declaration to that effect, subordinating delegations to the local jurisdiction. It will also only apply where delegations act as direct parties to contracts and not merely as negotiators and where the contract is made in the host country.[33] A separate treaty provision or submission is required before assets of the delegation can be taken to satisfy a judgment against it.[34] The 1972 U.S.-USSR Trade Agreement does not authorize the Soviet Trade Representation in the United States to trade directly. This restriction may be removed by legislation, but such a change would probably involve the loss of immunity from civil proceedings.[35]

The Soviet Planning System

The entire economic life of the USSR is centrally planned to a remarkable degree, not only for efficiency but in order to carry out political policy.[36] The planning apparatus is known as Gosplan and is at present regulated by a constituent statute of September 1968.

Annual plans and prospective five-year plans are in continuous preparation, modification, and execution. The appropriate ministries notify industrial enterprises and transport bodies as to what is expected of them. They in turn report in detail on their productive capacity and potential. The state plan is an administrative document, but it has the force of law once it is approved, and all transactions in the USSR must then conform to it.

Foreign trade is an important element in the state plan, and export and import requirements are incorporated in it. There are separate plans for the supply of goods for export, the allocation of imports, and transport and financial aspects.[37] The detailed operation of the plan is realized by subdividing the various plan assignments among the appropriate subordinate governmental bodies such as the Ministry of Foreign Trade. In the case of foreign trade, the SFTOs are then assigned responsibility for practical, concrete implementation. The planning authorities keep foreign trade under constant review and help guide its direction and policies. Thus, it is of interest that an important newspaper article on the arrangements with foreign firms to supply capital to develop Soviet minerals and timber resources in return for deliveries of the resultant products was written by an official of the plan.[38]

A system of licensing and license numbers is used to ensure that all exports and imports conform to the directives of the plan. Customs officials at ports and frontiers examine the goods for these indications.

FOREIGN TRADE PROCEDURES AND PRACTICES

These are regulated by government-to-government agreements as well as Soviet law, and in certain cases the former may override legislative provisions; for example, the Soviet Basic Customs Code governing documentation, inspection, and so on can be overridden.[39] Similarly, rates of customs duty (which are established by a Customs Tariff confirmed by the Council of Ministers of the USSR) are reduced in favor of countries that give the USSR MFN treatment. The unlawful financing of goods legally imported and the exporting and importing of currency and securities are punished as smuggling.[40]

Financial Aspects

Financing of USSR trade with Western nations takes various forms, and a full discussion would take us far beyond the scope of the present survey. It is perhaps useful, however, to distinguish financial transactions of three main types.[41] First, there are current transactions covering such matters as sales of goods and services to supply entire factories. Financial arrangements for current transactions may be based on underlying intergovernmental and/or bank-to-bank arrangements. A second type of financial transaction—the capital transaction—is not concerned with financing a particular commercial deal but with the provision of credit to the USSR by Western banks. Finally, there are special transactions involving the financing of business conducted cooperatively by the USSR and other countries, commonly by each partner providing part of the products or services, or by the provision of equipment and technical advice by one partner in return (in whole or in part) for products to be made of raw materials acquired by the other with this assistance.

Cooperative projects in the USSR are designed to make use of foreign capital without direct equity investment as such by Western firms and to avoid the balance of payments difficulties that would arise when normal credits had to be repaid. Such agreements go back at least as far as 1968 (with Japan, when credits for $160 million being granted for the purchase of equipment for the timber industry were repaid in part by timber shipments).[42] Negotiations in 1973 included a direct reduction iron manufacturing complex from Germany involving iron shipments to Germany for 10-15 years; and two multi-billion-dollar projects involving the development of the natural gas resources of the USSR.

Role of Government-to-Government
Agreements[43]

In the June 3, 1969 Long-Term Trade Agreement between the United Kingdom and the USSR,[44] both governments agreed to facilitate, within the scope of laws and regulations in force, the exchange of goods and services on a mutually advantageous basis (Art. 1). Representatives of the governments shall meet once a year (or more often if one of the parties so proposes) to examine the working of the agreement (Art. 6). Both governments are to allow each other's ships to participate in trade between the two countries on the principle of free and fair competition (Art. 7) and shall resume negotiations for a Treaty of Commerce between the United Kingdom and the USSR to replace the Temporary Commercial Agreement of February 16, 1934 (Art. 9). The agreement came into force on July 1, 1969 and remains in effect until December 31, 1975, being automatically extended thereafter from year to year. In November 1973 the two governments initialed a long-term agreement on economic, scientific, and technical cooperation apparently along the lines of similar agreements concluded by the USSR in recent years.[45]

The 1972 U.S.-USSR Trade Agreement is discussed in Chapter 1. The U.S.-USSR Agreement on Financing Procedures, October 18, 1972, extends Export-Import Bank (Eximbank) credits and guarantees to the USSR. Relations with Eximbank will be handled exclusively by the Soviet Bank for Foreign Trade (Vneshtorgbank), which it authorized to receive credits and repay them and to deal with Soviet purchasers in respect of credits and guarantees. The Soviet Government guarantees the repayment of any credits extended or guaranteed by Eximbank. The United States agrees to apply the same criteria to Vneshtorgbank applications as to other Eximbank transactions and to grant credits and guarantees to the USSR on terms no less favorable than those usually extended to similar purchasers.

By letter dated October 18, 1972 the Soviet minister of Foreign Trade informed the U.S. secretary of Commerce that the USSR would also make financing available for U.S. purchases of Soviet goods and services on terms no less favorable than for financing available from government and commercial sources in the United States for comparable export transactions.

In related negotiations, the United States and the USSR signed a three-year maritime agreement providing for access to 40 specified ports in each country by commercial vessels and certain other flag-carriers (excluding warships) on four days' advance notice. This does not apply to fishing boats or fishery research or fishery support ships, which are covered by other arrangements. MFN treatment is to apply with respect to tonnage duties, and the parties state an intention that vessels flying their national flags will each carry equal and substantial shares of the trade between the United States and the USSR (not less than one-third of all ocean-borne cargoes).

On June 20, 1973, the United States and the USSR negotiated a double taxation agreement, which covers such matters as treatment of interest payments, royalties, personal service, and sales through brokers or agents. It provides, inter alia, that income derived from commercial activities in one contracting state by a resident of the other contracting state will be taxable in the first contracting state if the income is derived through an office or representative bureau in the USSR or an office or other place of business in the United States; however, it is understood that sales or services through a broker or general commission agents would be exempt from tax and that SFTOs are deemed to be brokers or general commission agents in purchasing for Soviet industry from foreign suppliers. This agreement is subject to Senate advice and consent to ratification by the United States.

Western Access to the Soviet Market

All advertising is passed through the Soviet agency Vneshtorgreklama, which has representatives in a number of Western countries including the United Kingdom. Vneshtorgreklama has now concluded an agreement with a U.S. agency, Marsteller Inc., whereby Marsteller will organize advertising campaigns in the USSR for U.S.-based firms. Most advertisements are placed in scientific and technical publications in the USSR because import approval is most readily obtained for Western capital goods. It is easy to choose the right publication for advertising capital goods, because each specialized periodical covers a particular field and has a clearly defined function.

Establishment of Local Offices

At present, the alternative for a Western firm are to apply for accreditation (some 40 Western firms have been accredited since 1968) or use a hotel room as an office, a practice that is usually tolerated by the authorities. However, the hotel room will be without services such as Telex, and visas for those who staff these hotel room offices are not always freely available. Even an accredited firm would be well-advised to bring in its own office equipment, especially Telexes. A number of Western banks, including the First National City Bank of New York, Chase Manhattan Bank, and the Bank of America, have also been given permission to open Moscow offices.

In September 1973 a joint American-Soviet undertaking for a large international trade center in Moscow was announced. This development suggests a great expansion in numbers of accredited companies and possibly a relaxation of the de facto rule that only firms with an annual turnover of 5 million pounds would be considered for accreditation.[46]

Local Agents

The USSR has no state-owned agencies for representing foreign firms, and private Soviet citizens are prohibited from so doing. If a Western firm does not wish to open an office in Moscow for its trade with the USSR (and until recently, it has been quite difficult to establish and maintain either an accredited or a hotel room office), it can send in representatives when required or appoint a local agent. Local agents may be either duly authorized by the Soviet Government or merely tolerated, working on a hotel-room basis.

Personal contact is vital in dealings in the USSR, and a resident agent is likely to have made such contact. The normal term of an agency contract is reported to be three years' minimum (one year to introduce the new product, and one year or more years to conclude the first deals). The rates of commission are normally 5-10 percent.[47]

FOREIGN TRADE CONTRACTS

Rules Governing the Creation and Performance of Contracts

Parties. SFTOs are traders, not producers. The goods they export are produced by the productive state enterprises in the USSR, and the goods they import are ordered through them by other state enterprises in the USSR. In the case of exports from the USSR, the SFTOs order goods from domestic enterprises; and they can insist on the latter entering into the relevant contracts with them and supplying the goods in accordance with the export plan in general and the contract in particular. The SFTOs have a right of recourse against these suppliers for failure to perform their contracts.[48] In the case of the importation of goods into the USSR, the SFTOs normally act as agents in the USSR for domestic enterprises that have been authorized by their superior authorities to obtain the imports in question.[49]

The foreign customer is never in any legal relationship with the domestic Soviet enterprises producing or ordering goods, even where deliveries are made directly to or by such domestic enterprises, as they are not themselves authorized to participate in foreign trade.[50] The relations between the SFTO and its domestic contractor are regulated by internal Soviet civil law. The internal contract will probably provide for various penalties—for example, for delay in delivery of goods—and the SFTO will try to ensure that it is in a position to pass these penalties on to its Western contractor if the latter is at fault, by incorporating similar penalty provisions in the foreign trade contract.

The Limited Capacity of Soviet Organizations. The Soviet Constitution and Soviet law provide that all major economic assets, such as mineral ores, timber, factories, and machines, belong to "the people."[51] The Soviet state is not a legal person in civil relationships, but it establishes by administrative action a number of autonomous state economic enterprises through ministries. These ministries control the enterprises. Technically, enterprises do not own the assets allocated to them, which remain state property.

A recent Soviet reform (to be put into operation during the 1973-75 period) has provided for the creation of a system of industrial associations, which will administer the productive enterprises. The enterprises will retain their legal personality and can sue and be sued, but the industrial associations will also have legal personality and power to enter into legal relations. The associations will be taking over many powers of administration formerly exercised by government departments and agencies.[52] In the field of foreign trade, the associations will coordinate import requirements (probably administratively rather than legally) for the due production and eventual delivery of goods ordered for export.[53] Research and development is also being encouraged by the establishment of research and production associations, which cover an entire branch of industry and maintain their own plants to develop technical innovations.

Some 60 SFTOs have been set up by the Soviet Ministry of Foreign Trade. Each of these is concerned with a particular area of commerce, such as export and import of machine tools (V/O Stankoimport). The charter creating each organization circumscribes its range of activity accordingly. Under Soviet law, a juridical person or corporation can only act for the purposes for which it was created, a strict ultra vires rule.[54]

Normally, foreign trade transactions by SFTOs are invalid unless made in writing or similar form and signed by two specially authorized officials.[55] This invalidity is complete in all circumstances and cannot be waived.[56] This strict rule is probably designed to ensure the working of the planned economy by preventing transactions that violate the plan from escaping notice. It has led to a great deal of legal controversy. Some writers consider that it is a

requirement of "form."[57] In private international law, such a requirement is usually governed by the law of the place where the contract
is made, and if the contract is made in Moscow, this would raise no
difficulty. But such a contract might be made outside the USSR in a
country without such strict requirements. Soviet law still insists
on the rule's being observed. To justify this position, some Soviet
lawyers regard the requirements of writing and signatures as matters of capacity, and, since SFTOs are created in the USSR by Soviet
law, this would be a good justification. Some Soviet lawyers see the
rule as a matter of sovereignty, the state monopoly of foreign trade
being delegated specifically for certain purposes to a given organization, and otherwise retained or delegated to different organizations.[58]
This argument may be based on the fear that in some situations Soviet
law would not necessarily govern the capacity of an organization—for
instance, where some legal system allowed foreign corporations to
trade only on the same conditions as its own.

An even greater legal difficulty would be created if the requirements of writing and signatures were treated as mere evidence of
the existence and terms of the contract, since in this case the rules
of private international law allow the court or arbitration tribunal to
apply its own local law of evidence. Thus, if the foreign trade contract submitted disputes to arbitration in London, English law would
apply and might accept informal proof of the making of the contract.

The argument that the limited capacity of SFTOs is linked with
Soviet state sovereignty is a dangerous one. The Soviet authorities
have insisted all along that these organizations and enterprises are
independent persons in law and not merely emanations of the state.
Any attempt to identify them with the sovereign power would threaten
this position.[59]

Soviet authorities are prone to repeated reorganizations, and
this applies to the administration of the economy. This may mean
that even if a long-term foreign trade contract is made with a SFTO,
that SFTO may lose its identity through some act of higher authority.
In the case of merger or subdivision, all obligations continue to attach, and there is no problem.[60] In the case of complete liquidation
the position is less clear, however.[61] In practice the Soviet authorities will make provision for performance of outstanding obligations.
When two organizations were merged by the Soviet Ministry of Foreign
Trade in 1966, the foreign contractor was duly notified; he made no
objection but later argued that the contract prohibited assignment.
Soviet arbitration rejected this claim and held that the contract sub-
sisted with the new organization.[62]

Contracts with Western Firms. Soviet law recognizes that a corporation or other legal person lawfully constituted in a foreign country

322

may enter into any otherwise lawful transaction in the field of foreign trade in the USSR.[63] In principle, Soviet law recognizes limitations imposed on the capacity of such corporations in their countries of origin; in practice this is not a problem since their charters or constitutions are open to public inspection by Soviet officials in the host country and since the ultra vires rule has been very much diluted in the West. Foreign law might impose requirements of signature like those of Soviet law already discussed. In one case a Western company pleaded before the Moscow Foreign Trade Arbitration Commission (FTAC) that the contract had not been signed by the officials specified in its constitution. The tribunal was able, however, to find that the proper officials had later ratified the contract, and it thus held that this surmounted the difficulty.[64]

General Law of Contracts. Soviet law recognizes the possibility of a contract's being modified by subsequent agreement and will spell out a contract from correspondence. However, such letters must be signed by the proper officials.[65]

The Soviet law of contracts is not very different from that of France and other European countries. A contract is binding only when the offeror receives the offeree's acceptance, so that both parties are aware that agreement has been reached.[66] The offeree must send off his acceptance promptly. The offeror may fix a deadline for acceptance, which must then be strictly observed.[67] SFTOs generally fix such deadlines in correspondence through the mail. If the offeree changes the terms of the offer, this is regarded as a counter-offer.[68]

Language of the Contract. Contracts with SFTOs may be drawn up in Russian as well as in the language of the Western party, or only in the Western language.[69] The contract may provide that one or the other or both languages are to be authentic, or that both texts are to be equally valid.[70] No linguistic problems appear to arise in practice, possibly owing to the community of understanding of commercial and technical terms and to the very detailed and often exhaustive discussions of all the terms of the contract before it is finally signed.

Some insistence on the use of Russian texts as authoritative has been due in part to considerations of prestige rather than commercial convenience. One theory that has developed regarding international treaties is that a party should be bound only by the obligations as expressed in his own language.[71] In the case of a private contract, it may be that the language of the country whose law is applicable to the obligation (the proper law of contract) will prevail.[72]

If a dispute arising out of a foreign trade contract is submitted to arbitration in Moscow, the text may be in any language but must be accompanied by a translation into the language of the arbitration agreement or of the contract containing the arbitration clause.[73] Foreigners may enter into notarial acts in the USSR, where the law requires notarization.[74] The state notary must translate, on request, any document written in a language that the person consulting him does not understand.[75]

Terms of the Contract. Soviet organizations are restricted in the contracts into which they may enter. In internal trade, there are model terms that are used in most contracts, such as the General Delivery Conditions of 1969, which apply to dealings in goods between Soviet state economic enterprises. Any variation from these terms is subject to scrutiny by higher officials and to possible cancellation by the state arbitration tribunals. In trade within the East European socialist bloc (Comecon), there are similar General Delivery Conditions (1968).

No such over-all model terms are prescribed for foreign trade, and commercial treaties between East and West deal with tariffs and similar government action and do not prescribe the terms of contracts.[76] Hence there appears to be considerable room for negotiation. In fact, however, SFTOs tend to negotiate on the basis of model draft contracts and are slow to depart from them in any major particular.[77] Any attempt to vary this will inevitably lead to delays, since the Soviet negotiators will have to obtain authorization from higher authorities to allow the changes.[78]

A contract becomes binding in Soviet law only when all essential terms are agreed to. This includes not only such matters as price and identity of goods but also any terms that either side stipulates to be essential.[79]

Soviet negotiators will leave little of importance outside the words of the contract, as they must know, for plan purposes, exactly what is required. They recognize the legal effects of universal mercantile rubrics like c.i.f. and f.o.b. clauses.[80] But, generally speaking, they will not leave the contract terms to be filled out by custom or practice or tacit terms. Not only is it difficult to postulate a common custom for different economic systems, but the Soviet authorities cannot deal with a contract if its effects are unpredictable without judicial interpretation and if its operation is difficult to control.

Plan and Contract. The influence of Soviet planning is two-sided. The positive side is that the Soviet contractor can be expected to perform his bargain precisely as agreed. The negative side is that he will not easily tolerate delays or defaults, since a number of other operations in the USSR may depend on performance of the particular contract. There is no competition in the USSR, and there are no alternative sources of goods or services to those provided in the plan. Soviet foreign trade contracts will usually contain percentage penalties based on the price of the goods for late deliveries. In the case of a prescribed period of grave delay, the contract may entitle the Soviet party to cancel the contract, obtain the return of any payments plus interest, and sue for damages. Quality guarantees will also be required, which may involve Western exporters in heavy after-sales service obligations. Performance on the Soviet side will depend on performance on the other side unless the contract otherwise provides.[81]

Basis of Liability for Breach of Contract. In the Anglo-American law of contract, the question of fault does not generally arise. In theory, the position is different in Soviet law, though the practical consequences may be slight. In principle, breach of contract is a wrong, liability for which depends on some kind of fault (unless otherwise provided by contract). However, where a contractor has failed to perform according to his contract, the burden of proof rests on him to show the absence of fault.[82] If, for example, there is only one possible source for the goods, and this source becomes lost without any blame attaching to the contractor, he is not liable for failure to supply the goods.[83] Objective impossibility is here referred to; it is no excuse that he is unable, for example, to get the goods because he cannot pay for them.

Since articles to be exported from the USSR are part of a planned system of production, the SFTO would probably be unable to show impossibility of performance, unless the plan broke down in practice. This may happen and may require internal adjustments, but the desire for foreign exchange would generally mean that foreign trade goods would be spared.

Problems might arise, however, apart from actual inability to produce the goods. The question of impossibility of performance was raised in an interesting case arising out of the Suez crisis of 1956, which deserves detailed study. An SFTO, V/O "Soyuzneft export," contracted to supply 650 tons of fuel, f.o.b. Black Sea ports, to the Jordan Investment, Ltd., for export to Israel. The Soviet firm duly applied to the Soviet Ministry of Foreign Trade for an export license. The ministry, on 5 November 1956, refused to issue the license and ordered the Soviet organization not to perform the contract. The Jordan company sued for $2 million damages. The FTAC in Moscow made its award on 19 June 1958.[84] The SFTO had pleaded that it was freed from liability, since performance had become impossible through circumstances beyond its control.[85] The ministry had been actuated by political opposition to Israel. The Jordan company argued that the ministry and the organization were both instruments of the

Soviet state and that the organization could not rely on its own wrong. This argument failed. Such a situation could also have arisen where a Western government interfered with performance of a contract by a Western nationalized corporation like a railway or airline.

Trade embargoes have been used by the USSR on other occasions. When Yugoslavia broke with the Cominform in 1948, the USSR placed an embargo on all trade with Yugoslavia, which was only lifted in 1955. In 1957 the Soviet Union brought about the downfall of a Finnish Government by stopping trade. Of course, Western governments have also acted to prevent the supply of strategic materials to the USSR.

Public Policy and Contract. Soviet codes contain general provisions invalidating any transaction that violates the fundamentals of the Soviet system.[86] In internal affairs, this contemplates such matters as private speculation, employment of labor by private persons, accumulation of dwellings by one citizen, and the like. In the nature of things, such problems would hardly arise in a foreign trade transaction. The Soviet contract partners have no capacity to do anything of this kind, and their contracts are thoroughly scrutinized by all kinds of official agencies and incorporated into the public state economic plan. In fact, Soviet writers repeatedly state that this public policy requirement has never been raised on the Soviet side to invalidate any foreign trade contract.[87] The converse is not true. Western contractors have at times refused to keep a contract or a term thereof on the pretext that the basic legal principles of their home country are violated by it.[88]

Effects of the State Plan. The Soviet state plan will take into account a foreign trade contract and will create an administrative duty on the part of the Soviet foreign trade enterprise to perform it. Soviet internal law recognizes an act of planning as a source of civil rights and duties[89] and requires a contract based on a task imposed by an act of planning to conform to it.[90] However, Soviet lawyers are in disagreement as to whether this applies to foreign trade transactions. An alteration of the state plan may discharge the obligation of a contract.[91] Since the foreign contractor has no power to influence such an act of Soviet administration, it would seem unreasonable to subject him to such a consequence, but some writers believe he should be bound by it.[92] The Soviet party may be bound by the plan to enter into a specific foreign trade contract, but the foreign firm referred to in the plan appears to have no right to force the Soviet party to make the contract, as the obligation is administrative and not legal until the contract is signed.[93]

Legal Status of SFTOs. SFTOs are not part of the Soviet state, which establishes them. They do not, therefore, claim immunity from suit. They are liable, in principle, to the extent of their assets,[94] but with numerous exemptions, for instance, for buildings.[95] A treaty may specifically provide for their liability and its extent.[96] SFTOs are not responsible for the obligations of another Soviet organization and cannot have assets seized as a reprisal.[97]

Scope of Autonomy of the Parties

Union or Republican Law. The basic rules of Soviet private international law are Union-wide and are included in the Fundamentals of Civil Legislation, which apply in all parts of the Soviet Union and are incorporated in the Civil Codes of each Union Republic.[98] The Civil Codes vary slightly among themselves but not substantially, and certainly not in the foreign trade field, which is a union matter. In practice, the law of the principal Russian Republic is generally applied and presumably on the basis that the contract was made at the Moscow head office of the Soviet organization.[99] The fact that actual production, and even shipment, occurred in a different republic—for example, that goods were made in Kiev and shipped from Odessa, in the Ukraine—would not affect the legal position of the foreign contractor, although it might affect the relations of the Soviet export organization and its internal supplier. In any case, most of the rules affecting the Soviet economy are Union-wide and do not vary from republic to republic.[100]

Freedom of Will. In the case of an internal contract, the Soviet system chooses the contract partner and dictates most of the terms of the contract, so that the autonomy of the parties is rather nominal. Obviously, foreign contractors are not bound to accept such dictation. However, the practical position is not so different. If he wishes to buy Soviet timber, he can only contract with the timber-export monopoly organization, and this monopoly weakens his bargaining position in insisting on its own terms of purchase. His only possible advantages are that he can threaten to buy elsewhere, and at prices reflecting the market situation. The decision of the SFTO to buy or sell, however, may be politically and not economically determined.

The Law Governing the Operation and Effects of a Contract. Unless contrary provision is made in a treaty, a statute, or the contract, Soviet law generally follows the internationally accepted rules of private international law. There are some important Soviet statutory provisions in this regard—for example, in the absence of other provisions a contract is governed by the law of the country in which it was made.[101] In practice, it is unusual for parties to Soviet foreign trade contracts to specify some particular law.[102] A contract is deemed to be made in Soviet law, as we have seen, when the offeror receives the acceptance.[103] Logically this would mean that the place from which the offer was made would be the locus contractus, the place where the first initiative was taken and the final agreement of wills consciously realized. Soviet arbitration practice has applied this result in several decisions.[104] As the offeror tends to be the exporter, therefore, in contracts concluded by correspondence, the exporter's rather than the importer's law would apply. This solution has the added advantage that the main problems of performance of a contract arise on the side of supply and not payment—for example, delays in delivery, excuses for nonperformance, effects of strikes—whereas the payment of a fixed sum of money does not raise complicated questions.

The 1968 Romulus Films case is instructive in this regard. The film The Sleeping Beauty had already been made in the USSR. It was booked by Romulus Films for sole rights of exhibition in England and the contract was signed in London. The FTAC applied English law to a dispute arising out of this contract, because the contract was made in London. The lex loci contractus was also the law of the place of performance, in the sense of exhibition; nothing remained to be done in the USSR in this connection.[105]

Soviet law is adamant on the point that Soviet law is to govern the question of classification or qualification of the preliminary determination of the place of contract.[106] Other matters may have to be qualified—for example, whether a statute that requires legal proceedings to be taken within a limited period of time is a matter of substantive law to be governed by the law of the contract or of procedure to be governed by the law of the court of arbitration. In internal Soviet law, as in most continental systems, limitation is regarded as substantive,[107] but in Anglo-American law it is usually treated as procedural. Soviet law will follow the classification of the law of the contract on such matters.[108]

An interesting point arises on the sale contract itself. Although Soviet law provides for sale contracts in the proper sense, most deals between state enterprises are classified as delivery contracts, since the state remains owner throughout. The delivery contract (Postavka) is in other respects a kind of sale of future goods by description. In the field of foreign trade, where ownership of goods clearly passes, such contracts are classified by Soviet lawyers as proper sales, and thus they are conveniently dealt with by the private international law on that subject.[109] The title of sale is even applied, for want of a better title, to elaborate contracts for the supply of information, patent licensing, installation of equipment, and other matters that might seem better classified as other types of contract.

How is a particular system of law chosen by the parties? Soviet law requires a specific choice, not one by implication only. Reference to submission of disputes to arbitration in a country does not necessarily mean that the law of that country is to apply. The place may have been chosen as a safe neutral point to satisfy both sides, and not because its law is favored or even known.[110]

Can the parties select a foreign legal system arbitrarily and whimsically, without any real relevance to their contract? Many Western legal systems require a selected system to have some real connection with the contract, to be one of several obvious competitors for application quite apart from the conscious choice. In theory Soviet law imposes no such restriction.[111] Once chosen, the legal system will apply to the performance of the contract, discharge of obligation, breach of contract remedies, statute of limitations, and any other matters arising out of a contract once duly entered into.[112]

Renvoi. Where the law of some country is specified in a contract, or indicated by a law or statute, a further problem is whether the internal law of that country is to be applied, as if the contract had been made there between local residents, or whether the whole of that country's law is to be applied, including its version of the rules of private international law applicable to cases with a foreign element. Many legal systems apply the latter solution, which may result in a third system's being applied in the event the applicable law (without special agreement to the contrary) applies the renvoi doctrine. Soviet law considers that the parties wanted a named system to apply and will apply the internal rules of that system, without a renvoi. Had the parties wished some other system to apply, they could have chosen it specifically.[113]

Passing of Risk of Loss, Transfer of Ownership. The usual rules of c.i.f. and f.o.b. contracts apply. The Hague Uniform Law on the international sale of movables has not been ratified by the USSR, but the effect is similar in Soviet Law. Risk[114] generally passes with the ownership of the goods (res perit domino), and ownership passes according to the law of the country where the goods are situated (lex situs).[115] If Soviet law is applied, as the appropriate system, ownership passes by delivery unless the contract otherwise provides.[116] In business, such matters are generally dealt with by insurance, and the important matter is to know who must insure. A well-drawn foreign trade contract will solve this problem by making clear provision for this—for example, by requiring the foreign party to insure the goods with Ingosstrakh.[117] The risk of nonpayment for the goods may also be covered.[118]

Law Applicable to Financing of Foreign Trade Transactions. This general topic has been previously discussed.[119] The applicable law is universal in character, based on old mercantile custom—for example, the use of letters of credit or cheques.[120] An interesting legal feature is the irrevocable credit established by the buyer's bank in favor of a seller, although the seller has not provided any consideration to the bank, an arrangement under which the bank cannot raise any defense the buyer might have against the seller.[121] This is possible in continental law and now in U.S. law,[122] but not in English law. Soviet law governs all guarantees made by the Soviet Foreign Trade Bank, including those concerned with opening credits.[123]

Law Governing Arbitration Clauses. Foreign trade contracts generally provide for arbitration in a named city.[124] In Soviet law most aspects of arbitration clauses are governed by the law of the place of arbitration (lex fori)[125] unless the contract otherwise provides. In practice, the stumbling block is usually that one party wishes to resort to a regular court of law. If a treaty between the USSR and another country provides for the recognition of arbitration, no resort to a court will be allowed.[126] On the other hand, in the absence of such treaty, the result may be different—for example, where the law of a Western country guarantees access to the courts in spite of the existence of an arbitration clause in a contract.[127]

COPYRIGHT, INDUSTRIAL PROPERTY RIGHTS, AND TRANSFER OF TECHNOLOGY

Copyright

Copyrights apply to "works of science, literature or art regardless of the form, purpose and merit of the work or of the method of its reproduction."[128] Copyrights apply to published works, and those expressed in objective form, such as films, tape recordings, drawings, public utterances, and performances. The author and his heirs, regardless of their citizenship, own the copyright in a work published for the first time in the USSR, and in those in objective form existing in the territory of the USSR. Where a citizen of the USSR has work published for the first time, or existing in objective form, in a foreign country, the author and his heirs are recognized as owners of the copyright. Otherwise, copyrights in foreign countries are only recognized according to the terms of relevant international agreements to which the USSR is a party; the USSR recently adhered to the Universal Copyright Convention (UCC), as discussed below.

An author retains his copyright for life and passes it to his heirs according to USSR and Union-republic legislation. Reduced periods of copyright may be established, and here the heirs retain the copyright for the period of time unexpired on the author's death. Limits for the exercise of copyright by heirs and payment of royalties are established in Union-republic legislation.[129]

The rights of the author are threefold.[130] He may publish, reproduce, and circulate his work legally either under his own name or under a pseudonym or anonymously; his work is inviolable; and he may receive royalties for the use of his work by others, where legally allowed (see below), the rates being established by USSR and Union-republic legislation. Coauthorship is also recognized.[131] USSR and Union-republic legislation also recognizes, in certain cases, the copyright of a juristic person.[132] Where a work has been produced as the result of an official assignment in a scientific or other organization, the copyright belongs to the producer, but a special procedure is laid down for the use of such work by the organization concerned and the cases in which royalties are to be paid.[133] Under the amendments made at the time of accession to the UCC, Soviet law now requires the author's permission for translations.[134]

An author's work may be used by other persons only on the basis of a contract with the author or his heirs (there are approved standard contracts), except in cases stipulated by law.[135] The following cases are permitted without the author's consent and without payment of royalties, but with mandatory acknowledgment to author and source.[136] Where a new, creatively independent work is produced; for reproduction in scientific, critical, educational, and political-enlightenment publications of individual published works of science, literature, and art and excerpts from them; for use as information in periodicals and films and on radio and television about published works; for reproduction in newspapers and films and on radio and television of public speeches, reports, and published works; and for reproduction by any method except mechanical contact copying of works of fine art in places open with free entry except exhibitions and museums.

The following cases are permitted without the author's consent but with payment of royalties and acknowledgment to the author:[137] public performance of published works (if performance is free, royalties are only payable in certain cases); recording for the purpose of public reproduction, or dissemination of published works on film, record, tape, or other device, with the exception of the use of works in motion picture theaters or on radio or television; use by a composer of published literary works in order to create a musical composition from the text; and use of works of fine art and also of photographic works in manufactured articles (here acknowledgment is not mandatory).

The state may compulsorily purchase a copyright in the publication, public performance, or other use of a work from the author or his heirs under a procedure established by Union-republic legislation.[138]

On May 27, 1973 the USSR signed the UCC with immediate effect.[139] The USSR will now have to contract and pay royalties on every Western book that appears in the USSR. The main reason for signing (after declining to do so for many years) may be to control writers who are disapproved of, and to limit the dissemination of their literature, and possibly also to increase hard-currency income. Under Article 3 of the Convention, no contracting state shall be precluded "from requiring formalities or other conditions for the acquisition of enjoyment of copyright in respect of works first published in its territory or works of its nationals wherever published."[140]

The Copyright Agency set up by the Soviet Union on September 20, 1973[141] is thus within the terms of the Convention. The Soviet press was at pains to stress certain amendments to the law in favor of the author made at the same time as the setting up of the agency[142] and the fact that the agency is a voluntary, not a state organ. The disguise, however, is a little thin, for though the claim is that the agency will protect Soviet authors, the fact is that the agency is to be the sole channel for negotiations between foreign publishers and Soviet authors, and for the first time it will be an offense for an author to by-pass the agency.[143] Before his deportation, Alexander Solzhenitsyn could have become the first test case under the new arrangement, for he had previously announced permission for publication in the West so long as he was unable to publish in the USSR.[144] On the other hand, he seemed also to have attempted to turn the tables on the Soviet authorities, since he had also announced that two unpublished chapters of a work of his were circulating in samizdat underground form and that this constituted sufficient publication for him to be able to claim copyright and ask for injunction against unauthorized Western publication, a frequent happening for which the authorities had previously blamed him.[145]

A more mundane explanation for Soviet accession is that hard currency is needed by the authorities, and income from authors' earnings would be welcomed; certainly the 30 to 70 percent taxes on royalties earned abroad, announced in Moscow on September 27, 1973, could support such a notion, though equally these rates balanced against 1.5 to 8 percent on Soviet authors who publish at home could indicate merely another facet of the authorities' determination to discourage publication in the West.[146]

Trademarks

Soviet legislation on trademarks embodies a registration system and not the "first-user" system of common law.[147] Trademarks are protected by a 1962 Statute on Trademarks (last amended in 1967) and by the Paris Convention.[148] A trademark or service mark (mark used to identify services) is defined as

an artistic representation, original in its form (original names and words, separate combinations of letters and figures, vignettes, different forms of packing, artistic compositions and drawings whether combined or not with letters, figures, words, etc.), used to distinguish goods or services of one enterprise from similar goods or services of other enterprises, and to advertise them.[149]

Not registrable as trademarks are[150] free marks (those used to denote well-known goods); marks constituting national emblems and insignia; marks of international organizations—for example, the Red Cross and Red Crescent; business-summary information about the product and the producer; marks containing false or misleading information about the manufacturer or place of origin of the product; marks contrary to the public interest or the requirements of socialist morality; or marks that conflict with international conventions to which the USSR adheres. Trademarks cannot be used for liquid gaseous, or unconsolidated substances supplied or sold without packing or for other goods exempted from all kinds of marking according to state standards or technical specifications.[151]

Trademarks of foreigners can only be registered in the USSR if Soviet citizens, organizations, and enterprises enjoy reciprocal rights in the applicant's country.[152] Application must be made to the All-Union Chamber of Commerce and Industry, which follows the necessary procedures and must be appointed as agent. Soviet citizens apply to the State Committee for Inventions and Discoveries.

When granted, a trademark or service has legal effect over the whole territory of the USSR.[153] It may be registered for a term indicated by the applicant up to a maximum of 10 years and may be extended for periods not exceeding 10 years each time, provided that applications for extension are made not later than six months before expiration is due.[154] The appropriate committee examines the application as to form, legality of registration, and the existence of trademarks for the same class of goods in another person's name.[155] In the case of refusal of registration, reasons must be given, and there is a right of appeal to be exercised within two months.[156]

The Paris Convention covers trademarks, and "priority rights" therefore apply in the USSR. A Convention member country applicant may request priority of his trademark as from the date of first filing in his country, provided he applies in the USSR within six months.[157] The use of a trademark is not essential to its validity, and it is registered for a definite class of goods.[158] The trademark classification of the USSR comprises 42 classes of goods and services according to international classification. With regard to infringement, Section 21 of the Statute on Trademarks states,

> During the term of validity of the certificate granting the right to the exclusive use of a trademark, the proprietor of the certificate may demand, in the number prescribed by law, the cessation of unlawful use of an identical or analogous trademark or service mark in connection with goods or services of the same class, and damages for any loss caused to him.

Patents and Certificates of Authorship

Soviet law creates property and personal rights attaching to persons who produce inventions and innovations. Inventive activity is also regulated by the provisions of international agreements to which the USSR is a party, such as the Paris Convention on the Protection of Industrial Property (the USSR joined in 1965). According to the 1973 Statute on Discoveries, Inventions, and Innovation Proposals,[159] "a solution of a technical problem distinguished by its essential novelty in any field of national economy, culture, public health or national defense which produces positive results" is recognized as an invention. Inventions and technical improvements relating to national defense are kept secret.

There are two types of protection of inventions in operation, both of which may be extended to a foreigner on a reciprocal basis; they are the author's certificate and the patent. Both certify the recognition of a suggestion as an invention, the priority of invention, and the authorship of the invention.[160] However, there are important differences. An author's certificate is permanent; a patent expires after 15 years. The certificate gives the state the exclusive right to the invention and guarantees the inventor regulated compensation as well as some other rights and privileges specified by law. The patent gives the inventor the exclusive right to the invention within the boundaries of the USSR, and the invention may be utilized only by agreement with the patent owner. Where an invention is of particular importance to the state and utilization is in the interests of society, the patent may be compulsorily purchased by the state, or a compulsory license for use of the invention by a state enterprise or organization may be established. However, before this can be done, the enterprise or organization must have failed to reach agreement with the patent owner. The Council of Ministers decides whether to purchase compulsorily and the amount of compensation payable.

Applications for both certificates and patents by Soviet citizens are made to the State Committee for Inventions and Discoveries attached to the Council of Ministers of the USSR. Foreigners must apply to the All-Union Chamber of Commerce and Industry, which conducts all the necessary procedures (the Soviets stress that the use of third-party patent firms as intermediaries serves no useful purpose). In view of the specific features of the economy of the USSR, it is natural that author's certificates are most usually applied for by Soviet citizens, whereas foreigners tend to apply for patents.

Author's certificates are issued for new substances of chemical means, atomic fission and medical and food products.[161] A certificate must be applied for in the event of new and improved breeds of farm animals and poultry, species of silkworms of varieties of agricultural crops, any of which have been obtained through selection. Also, where an invention is produced in connection with work in a state or public enterprise or under its direction or with its financial or other aid, only a certificate may be applied for.[162]

The right to file an application for a patent attaches to the inventor, his heirs, and an assignee (such as an enterprise or firm). A patent may be exchanged for an author's certificate by the owner or his heirs provided it has not been previously assigned or licensed. An author's certificate may be applied for by the inventor or his heirs. It cannot be assigned but may be inherited. Foreign applicants receive help and guidance from the USSR All-Union Chamber of Commerce, to which they must apply.

The exclusive right of the patent owner may be limited by the "right of prior use." If a Soviet enterprise has been using the invention before an application is filed, it may continue to use the invention freely after it is patented and the patent owner is not entitled to collect compensation from that enterprise.[163] The Soviet Union, as a party to the Paris Convention, is bound by the principle of "priority rights." This means that the date of the filing of a patent application in another Convention member country is taken as the theoretical date of filing in the USSR, with the proviso that the application for a patent or author's certificate is made within 12 months of the first application. Otherwise, the date of the receipt of the application is considered to be the date of priority.[164]

Each invention is examined by an expert committee to determine its novelty and its industrial utility. A check on previously issued Soviet author's certificates and patents is made, as well as on foreign patents. After examination (which should take six months but may take longer), the application is approved, or rejected with reasons given. There is a right of appeal, to be exercised within two months.[165] Detailed rules are laid down with respect to royalties and lump-sum payments.[166]

Industrial designs may also be protected by the grant of a patent or an author' s certificate. These are designs that are applied to actual products so as to give them a particular appearance. The term of the patent is only five years, subject to extension. Under the Paris Convention, a foreign applicant will be protected if he applies within six months of his original application abroad. Scrutiny of the novelty, utility, and aesthetic quality of the design is similar to that in the case of applications for patents for inventions.[167]

Licensing

Soviet interest in Western technology is keen.[168] At the end of 1970, the Soviet Planning Committee (Gosplan) published a new regulation on the acquisition of patent and know-how licenses from the West. Soviet license trade is thus likely to expand over the coming years. V/O Licensintorg, which is an SFTO under the control of the Ministry of Foreign Trade, has a special responsibility for purchasing licenses from abroad and selling Soviet licenses to foreign countries. Where the license deals primarily with acquisition of technology and no equipment of plant is to be furnished, Licensintorg negotiates the agreement.

The USSR has a number of industrial ministries, each of which supervises certain industries and is responsible for identifying needed foreign technology. The concerned ministry is also involved in the Soviet decision-making process with respect to acquisition of foreign licenses.

A foreign firm interested in exploring exchanges of technology involving more than one industrial ministry is advised to contact the important State Committee for Science and Technology (SCST), one of the principal committees of the USSR Council of Ministers and alone responsible for technical research and development throughout industry including economic research. It establishes priorities as to acquisition of foreign technology and makes final decisions on whether to acquire such technology and/or purchase of machinery and so on.

The research and development institutes, through their planning departments, may be expected to play an increasingly important role in initiating Soviet action leading to the purchase of foreign technology (and sale of Soviet technology), particularly as the Soviet industrial reforms noted above come into full effect. Only when a specific foreign technology transaction has been approved by the SCST and funded in an annual foreign trade plan will V/O Licensintorg (or, as discussed below, another SFTO) have formal responsibility for its acquisition

Mention should also be made of the role of V/O Vneshtechnica, a national association subordinate to the SCST, organized in 1967, which arranges for the performance of all kinds of scientific research and design services in the USSR and abroad, for Soviet and foreign entities, and of the State Committee for Inventions and Discoveries (SCID), which reports directly to the Council of Ministers and is responsible for various bodies concerned with patent questions. The SCID apparently is playing an increasingly important role in Soviet acquisition of foreign technology.

If the agreement involves primarily the sale of plant or equipment (even if accompanied by transfer of technology), the appropriate SFTO, rather than V/O Licensintorg, would have primary responsibility for the negotiations. Even if Licensintorg is not the primary negotiator, it may be consulted by the SFTO directly responsible for the negotiations.

Soviet law provides that trademarks (and service marks) registered in the name of an enterprise (or organization) may be licensed for full or partial use to another enterprise. (Here, the licenses agreement must provide that the quality of the goods of the license shall not be inferior to the quality of the proprietor's goods. The latter is responsible for seeing that this condition is carried out.) The agreement is invalid unless registered with the SCID. A patent may also be licensed, which agreement must be registered with the SCID. However, if no patent application has been filed, the license agreement need not be recorded.

In general, licenses acquired by the USSR run from 5 to 10 years. Payment may be on a lump-sum basis (particularly for licenses sold together with a turnkey plant, where there is no patent protection, or where it is impossible or impractical to control the volume of production), or by periodic payments, or by some combination of the two methods. The USSR readily agrees to payments in hard currency. Periodic payments can be determined with reference to number of units produced, or sold, or on some other mutually agreed basis. The USSR has agreed to neutral, third-country auditing of records (these are maintained apart from the enterprise's regular accounting records). Payments are not subject to Soviet taxes. Normally, licenses are acquired by the USSR in order to make use of them for production anywhere in that country; and often they will seek exclusive production rights from CMEA countries. Reaching agreement on selling rights is frequently difficult, as the USSR will usually insist on nonexclusive sales rights in CMEA countries as well as in a number of developing or even Western industrialized countries.[169]

COOPERATION AGREEMENTS AND JOINT VENTURES

The USSR has encouraged Soviet organizations to participate with Western firms in joint-stock companies organized under the law of a Western country,[170] usually to promote Soviet exports, but thus far the USSR has taken the position that no "investment joint ventures" on Soviet soil (that is, along the lines of recent Romanian and Hungarian law) would be permitted—though there are some indications that the USSR may be increasingly flexible as to legal structures for promoting "cooperation" deals with Western firms.[171] Such cooperation is welcomed, and examples are numerous. A common approach involves the supply by a Western company (or consortium) of equipment, technology, plant, know-how, and so on, on extended credit terms, with repayment generated at least in part in natural resources or resulting products. The USSR frequently seeks to promote these deals in implementing the many agreements on trade and cooperation it has concluded with other governments. Under the intergovernmental agreement, there is normally a joint commission, with subsidiary working parties, charged with examination of various matters of common interest, including specific areas of cooperation. The working parties often include industry representatives.

The United States and the Soviet Union have agreed to work through the Joint U.S.-USSR Commercial Commission, established in May 1972, in overseeing and facilitating implementation of the 1972 Trade Agreement in accordance with the terms of reference and rules of procedure of that commission. Although the Trade Agreement has not yet come into force, the Joint Commission has continued to function, apparently quite actively. It has established joint working groups on such matters as status of reciprocal business facilities in the two countries, project financing, and U.S.-USSR participation in specified types of industrial projects, including cooperation projects to develop natural gas resources in the USSR, in the construction of power-consuming productive facilities in the USSR, and cooperation in a number of other projects.

The SCST has concluded a number of so-called "framework cooperation arrangements with Western firms, usually contemplating exchanges in the scientific or technical field, or joint research and development projects—normally to be implemented by specific contracts. Or the Soviet partner may be an SFTO such as V/O Prommashimport, which concluded a cooperation agreement in 1973 with Finnish firms for the joint development of iron ore fields at Kostamus in Soviet Karelia. Any general statement about the nature of cooperation agreements with the USSR, and the parties thereto, tends to have built-in exceptions.

Even when a special area of likely interest has been identified by a working party of an intergovernmental commission, further exchanges of delegations between the parties directly concerned are virtually indispensable. The binding contracts are not agreed to by the governmental commissions but have to be negotiated by the enterprises concerned.

FIAT began negotiations in 1961, and some 50 delegations in each direction were reportedly required before a contract was signed in 1966 for the construction by FIAT of a large automobile plant in Togliattigrad.

The recent Soviet preference for deals with multinational concerns, with their similarity to the Soviet ability to commit immense amounts of resources over a wide range, is particularly evident in the field of cooperation. The giant concerns also have the ability to match the Soviet hierarchy with a hierarchy that, while it may not interlock precisely, at least bears a resemblance to the Soviet system.

Interestingly, the chairman of the Soviet FTAC, who ultimately could often be involved in adjudicating disputes arising out of cooperation contracts, has noted that the growth of the cooperation agreements between East and West has not been matched by a growth in legal forms to accomodate the realities of the situation;[172] his specific point seems to be that many complex and sophisticated agreements on technological and scientific matters are formulated, and thus have to be adjudicated, in the strait-jacket of an old-fashioned contract for the sale and delivery of goods.

We have already noted that Soviet organizations participate with Western firms in joint ventures organized in Western countries. These have been based on post-World War II experience with former German companies, which in turn were reflected in joint-stock companies set up by the USSR in China under agreements made in 1950.[173] With these experiences in mind, the Soviets have recently established a number of joint-stock companies in the West, mainly to promote the sale of Soviet products. The SFTO responsible for exporting the particular product line usually establishes the company jointly with a Western firm (which usually has been a selling agent for the Soviets prior to creation of the joint venture). The tendency is for the Soviets to retain a majority holding (usually 51 percent) in the equity capital.[174] There have also been some Soviet investments in industrial ventures in Western countries, such as the 1970 agreement between the French Ministry of Economic Affairs and Finance and the Soviet Ministry of Iron and Steel Production, for Soviet participation in a French steel complex.[175]

SETTLEMENT OF DISPUTES

The usual Soviet method of settling foreign trade disputes is arbitration.[176] The preferred forum, perhaps not unnaturally, has been the Soviet FTAC in Moscow, established in 1932[177] and operating under Rules of Procedure laid down in 1949, as amended in 1959 and 1967.[178] In general, the Soviet preference is for a permanent and not an ad hoc body.[179] Within the Comecon bloc, disputes may also be governed by the General Conditions of Delivery of 1968.[180] Arbitration with other countries may be governed by the 1961 European (Geneva) Convention on International Commercial Arbitration and by the 1958 United Nations (New York) Convention on the Recognition and Enforcement of Foreign Arbitral Awards, to both of which the USSR is a party.

The FTAC has a panel of 15 arbitrators appointed annually by the All-Union Chamber of Commerce and Industry from representatives of trading and other appropriate organizations and other people possessing specialized knowledge.[181] The parties to an arbitration each choose one arbitrator, and the two arbitrators thus chosen decide on an umpire, although, by consent a single arbitrator may be appointed.[182] Once the tribunal is constituted, the parties can choose any person to represent them, including foreigners.[183] The parties are expected to file copies of their documents for each other's use, to be served by the FTAC.[184] The arbitrators can hold preliminary meetings without the parties and can make orders for the handing over of documents.[185] Indeed, the chairman of the FTAC has recently pointed out that in some cases the arbitrators' orders for more precise documentation of claims can themselves result in sufficient information being revealed to enable the parties, especially in technical contract cases, to arrive at a settlement.[186] The arbitrators may request the opinion of experts,[187] but each of the parties must prove the facts relied on as grounds for its claims or defense.[188] The validity and the weight to be given to any item of evidence is in the discretion of the arbitrators.[189] The tribunal may give a majority decision.[190] A brief award in writing must be made at the hearing, a full award and the reasons for it being delivered within 15 days.[191]

The Soviet attitude to arbitration is a very positive one, and it is generally acknowledged that the Moscow FTAC has a good record for sensible, impartial decisions.[192] It is perhaps regrettable, if understandable, that many Western firms feel it necessary to oppose Soviet suggestions of Moscow as an arbitration forum.[193] Western firms usually favor third-party "impartial" arbitration, in Stockholm, Paris, Bern, or Zurich, though some Germans firms now avoid Stockholm, since, if the law of the forum is to be applied, they believe Swedish rules favor the buyer.

Soviet anxiety to underline its firmly respectable record in this field is found in Ramzaitsev's point, that rules developed by socialist arbitration courts have been considered, and in some cases adopted, by international conventions, and that the uniformity encouraged by these conventions is to be welcomed.[194] Bratus similarly concludes that more international conventions are desirable for the sake of certainty and the strengthening of international trade links[195] and that, conversely, to be effective, conventions should be firmly rooted in arbitration practice, an observation that is doubly interesting because of its specialized context.

The central theme of the Bratus address is that modern conditions have produced huge numbers of highly technical contracts that go to arbitrators and yet are drawn in a form (that of a contract for the sale and delivery of goods) that is inappropriate and obliges the arbitrator to resort to an unhappy mental posture, not unlike that of the old common lawyer applying a legal fiction.[196] Bratus would like to see a clearer legal approach to these contracts and indeed mentions that in January 1972 a draft convention was approved by the CMEA executive on the settlement by arbitration of civil law disputes arising from economic, scientific, and technical cooperation.[197]

It should perhaps be emphasized that the acceptance of Moscow as the forum for arbitration does not necessarily imply acceptance of Soviet law as the law to be applied. In fact, the Soviets are generally quick to make the point that it has long been their rule that, where the contract is silent, the FTAC applies the law of the place where the contract was made. However, it is fair to add that in most cases involving the sale of Western plant or equipment, the contract is signed in Moscow.[198]

The Soviet rules of procedure provide that the arbitration agreement must be in writing, either as an integral part of the entire agreement or by a separate paper, including a later arrangement made by exchange of letters.[199] Ramzaitsev emphasizes and appears to approve the acceptance of jurisdiction where no arbitration agreement was entered into, but where there was de facto recognition of arbitration in that one party submitted a claim to arbitration and the other party approved such submission.[200]

The Soviet position gives rise to an interesting theoretical difficulty in this area of law, in that an arbitration clause that forms part of a larger contract that is invalid ought itself to be invalid so as to preclude a submission to arbitration. Similarly, once a contract is fully performed, any arbitration clause should cease to be effective. However, arbitration precedents appear to have established a rule that the arbitration clause in any case constitutes a separate agreement that does not stand or fall with the rest of the contract in which it is contained.[201]

A related question is that of clauses in the agreement that are in conflict with the rules of the FTAC itself. Jurisdiction has been declined where an agreement contained a provision for an appeal, in conflict with the FTAC's constitutive decree,[202] though other rules, whether under the decree, the CMEA General Conditions, or the Geneva Convention, are specifically stated to be subject to contrary agreement.

The enforcement of awards, not voluntarily compiled with, is provided for in the Russian Civil Procedure Code (and the corresponding codes of other republics of the USSR).[203] The 1958 New York convention also applies. However, Soviet sources insist that compliance with awards is invariably voluntary.[204]

As noted previously, there are public policy provisions in Soviet law that deny enforcement to any foreign law that contradicts the fundamentals of the Soviet system,[205] but these have never been resorted to in the field of Soviet foreign trade arbitration.[206]

NOTES

1. V. S. Pozdnyakov, Gosudarstvennaya Monopolia Vneshnei Torgovli v SSSR (State Monopoly of Foreign Trade in the USSR) at 28 (Moscow, 1969).

2. Id. at 40.

3. Arts. 1 amd 51.

4. Triska and Slusser, The Theory, Law and Practice of Soviet Treaties, Chs. 18-22 (Stanford, Cal.: Stanford University Press, 1962).

5. Details of the many agreements of this kind can be found in relevant Soviet publications and Bratus, "Arbitration and International Economic Cooperation," 27 Arbit. J. 230 (1972); Triska and Slusser, supra note 4 at 284-287, 290-294, notes 3, 9, 12.

6. USSR Const., Art. 14.

7. Pozdnyakov, supra note 1 at 141.

8. Art. 75 of 1967 Statute. See Pozdnyakov, supra note 1 at 97.

9. Pozdnyakov, supra note 1 at 74-75.

10. Id. at 78-80.

11. D. M. Genkin, Pravoye Regulirovanye Vneshnei Torgovli SSSR (Legal Regulation of Soviet Foreign Trade), secs. 75, 76 (Moscow, 1961). See also, section entitled "Settlement of Disputes," infra.

12. See section entitled "Foreign Trade Procedures and Practices," infra.

13. See section entitled "Foreign Trade Contracts," infra.

14. See Fundamental Principles of Civil Legislation of the USSR, Sec. 124 (hereinafter referred to as "Fundamentals"). An English translation by the author is contained in 7 Law in Eastern Europe 263 (Szirmai, ed., 1963).

15. Pozdnyakov, supra note 1 at 112-113.

16. Fundamentals, sec. 14.

17. USSR Const., Art. 14. See B. Rudden, "Soviet Insurance Law," in 12 Law in Eastern Europe (Szirmai, ed, 1966). In 1973 the Chubb Corp. and the London-based Black Sea and Baltic General Insurance Co. Ltd., agreed to the joint establishment of a property liability insurance facility for the USSR and other Eastern Europe countries.

18. Maritime Commerce Code, Art. 194 (1968).

19. Adopted Oct. 20, 1958, published in Sbornik Normativnykh Materialov po Voprosam Vneshnei Torgovli SSSR I (Moscow, 1970) at 184.

20. USSR Const., Art. 14.

21. Id. Art. 77.

22. Sobranie Postanovlenii Pravitelstva SSSR (Collection of Decrees of Government of the USSR), 1964, No. 5.

23. Genkin, supra note 12, sec. 35.

24. USSR Const., Art. 4.

25. It has been in its present form since August 1954.

26. Pfaff, Das Sowjetische Transport Recht 57 (Hamburg, 1970).

27. See The Merchant Shipping Code of the USSR 1968 Translated and edited by W. E. Butler and J. B. Quigley, Jr. (Baltimore, 1970).

28. Pfaff, supra note 26 at 66.

29. Id. at 124.

30. See D. A. Cooper, The Air Code of the USSR (Charlottesville, Va., 1966); and H. J. Spanjaard, "The Air Code of the USSR," 14 Law in Eastern Europe 66 (Szirmai, ed., 1967).

31. Pozdnyakov, supra note 1 at 88-91.

32. Id. at 125.

33. Triska and Slusser, supra note 5 at 331.

34. Pozdnyakov, supra note 1 at 129. The extent of assets privileged from seizure depends on the terms of the treaty.

35. R. Starr, "A New Legal Framework for Trade Between the United States and the Soviet Union: The 1972 US-USSR Trade Agreement," 67 AJIL at 72-73 (1973).

36. USSR Const., Art. 11.

37. Pozdnyakov, supra note 1 at 92-93, 132-133.

38. Pravda, May 8, 1973, article by V. Spandarian.

39. See Art. 20 of the Code.

40. Art. 100, Basic Customs Code. See, generally, S. M. Kachalov and A. V. Mugilianskii, Pravovoe Regularovanie Importa (Legal Regulation of Import) (Moscow: Izd-vo Iuridicheskaia literatura [Iur. Lit.,] 1972).

41. See Colloquium on Banking, Money and Credit in Eastern Europe 17-23 (NATO Directorate of Economic Affairs, Brussels, 1973).

42. See, for example, A. Nove, "Russia's Credit-Barter Dealing," Times (London), June 12, 1973; and more generally, N. Patolichev, "Soviet Foreign Trade; Its Role and Prospects," Foreign Trade, 1973, No. 4, at 3.

43. In recent years the USSR has concluded trade and/or long-term cooperation agreements with France, Italy, the Federal German Republic, and many other countries. See, for example, Patolichev, supra note 43.

44. Cmnd. 4132, Treaty series No. 92 (1969).

45. In the view of the British Government, prior approval by the European communities for renewal or extension of this agreement is not required. See Trade and Industry (publ. by U.K. Department of Trade and Industry), Vol. 11, No. 10, at 460-61 (June 7, 1973).

46. "£45m Moscow Trade Centre for the West," Times (London), Sept. 21, 1973.

47. BI, Eastern Europe Report, June 1, 1973.

48. Pozdnyakov, supra note 1 at 144.

49. Id. at 145-146.

50. L. A. Lunts, Dogovor Prodazhi vo Vneshnei Torgovli SSSR (Foreign Trade Sales) at 15-16 (Moscow: Iur. Lit., 1972).

51. USSR Const., Art. 6.

52. Decree No. 140 of March 2, 1973 of Soviet Council of Ministers, secs. 6, 7, 36. For analysis of the Soviet research and production association (a Soviet innovation that, unlike the creation of industrial associations, has apparently not yet been applied in other CMEA countries), see East-West Monthly Supp-1, Oct. 1973.

53. Soviet decree cited note 52, secs. 110, 111.

54. Fundamentals, sec. 12; Civil Code of the Russian Republic of the USSR (RSFSR), Art. 26.

55. See, for example, sec. V., para. 11, of the Charter of the All-Union Export-Import Association "Soyuzgazexport," Foreign Trade, No. 10, at 57-58 (1973).

56. Fundamentals, sec. 14; RSFSR Civil Code, Art. 45.

57. Ramsaitsev, Vneshnetorgovy Arbitrazh v SSSR (Foreign Trade Arbitration in the USSR), 142-145 (Moscow, 1957)

58. L. A. Lunts, Mezhdunarodnoye Chastnoe Pravo-Osobennaia Chast' (International Private Law, Special Part), at 157-162 (Moscow, 1963); and Lunts, supra note 51 at 100. See also K. Grzybowski,

"Soviet Private International Law," in Law and Eastern Europe, Vol. 10 (Szirmai. ed., 1965).

59. T. Hoya, "The Legal Framework of Soviet Foreign Trade," 56 Minn. L. Rev 32-3 (1971); see also H. J. Berman, "The Legal Framework of Trade Between Planned and Market Economy Countries: the Soviet-American Example," 24 Law and Contemp. Prob., 482, 487-492 (1959).

60. RSFSR Civil Code, Art. 37.

61. Id., Arts. 37, 38.

62. Lunts, supra note 50 at 95 citing the 1969 "Textile" case.

63. Fundamentals, sec. 124; RSFSR Civil Code, Art. 564.

64. Hoya, supra note 59 at 36; Soviet Chamber of Commerce Legal Report 5 (23d. ed., 1970).

65. In practice, Soviet and East European lawyers recognize that a contract may be concluded by telegram as well as by letter (see, for example, Genkin, supra note 12 at sec. 19. This is obviously convenient, as Soviet telegraphic services are much quicker than Soviet postal services, but it is difficult to reconcile with the requirements of authenticity and proof of authority of an official to sign a contract.

66. RSFSR Civil Code, Arts. 162-164. This differs from the English "mailbox theory," under which a contract is generally completed by mailing the acceptance, if the offer was by mail.

67. RSFSR Civil Code, Art. 162.

68. Id., Art. 165. This rule is fairly universal.

69. See generally Triska and Slusser, supra note 5 at 60.

70. See, for example, Business International, Doing Business with the USSR at 196 (hereinafter referred to as Doing Business with the USSR) (1971) (reference is to Standard Purchase Contract of V/O Stankoimport, final clause).

71. V. D. Degan, L'Interpretation des accords en droit international 84 (Hague 1963).

72. See The Industrie (1894) A.C.581.

73. Handbook of Soviet Foreign Trade Arbitration Commission 11, 23 (1965 ruling) (in Russian and English) (Moscow, 1972).

74. Notarial statute, 1965, Chapter XVI. In 1973 the USSR Supreme Soviet enacted new legislation (effective Jan. 1, 1974) on the Office of the Notary, which, inter alia, permits foreign companies direct access to the office. See N. Belyk, "Duties of Office of Notary," Soviet News, July 24, 1973. See also, Lascelles, "USSR Extends Foreign Concerns' Legal Rights," Financial Times (London), July 25, 1973.

75. Notarial statute cited in note 74, sec. 24.

76. Hoya, supra note 59 at 22.

77. See, for example, Doing Business with the USSR, supra note 70 at 188-196 (standard purchase contract of V/O Stankoimport).

78. Id. at 85 and see Chapter 8 generally.

79. RSFSR Civil Code, Art. 160.

80. Lunts, supra note 50 at 60 et seq.

81. RSFSR Civil Code, Art 177.

82. Id., Art. 222.

83. Id , Art 235.

84. A translation of the record of the proceedings was provided by G. W. Haight in 8 ICLQ 416 (1959). See also Domke, "The Israeli-Soviet Oil Arbitration," 53 AJIL 787 (1959); Berman, "Force Majeure and the Denial of an Export License under Soviet Law: A Comment on Jordan Investments Ltd. v. Soyuzneftexport," 73 Harv. L. Rev. 1128 (1960).

85. Relying on provisions of the older Russian Civil Code now contained in articles 222 and 235 of the present (1964) RSFSR Civil Code.

86. RSFSR Civil Code, Art. 568.

87. Lunts, supra note 58 at 70.

88. See section below entitled "Settlement of Disputes" and sources cited in note 206 infra.

89. RSFSR Civil Code, Art. 4.

90. Id., Art. 159.

91. Id., Art. 234.

92. Pozdnyakov, supra note 1 at 136.

93. Id., at 135.

94. RSFSR Civil Code, Art. 32.

95. Id., Art. 98.

96. For example, Art. 6, para. 2 of the 1972 U.S.-USSR trade agreement. See Starr, supra note 36 at 74.

97. Prelude Corp. v. the Owner of M/V Atlantic, (N.D. Cal. 1971), 65 AJIL 806 (1971), 13 Harv. J. Int. L. 316 (1972). This was an attempt to attach a Soviet cargo ship as security for alleged damage caused by Soviet fishing boats.

98. For example, Part VIII of the 1964 RSFSR Civil Code.

99. D. Genkin, Sovetskoe Gosudarstvo I Pravo (Soviet State and Law Periodical), 1965, No. 2, at 51 and 55, cited by Hoya, supra note 59 at 30.

100. Art. 14 of the Soviet Constitution gives the union over-all powers in this area, even where a republic legislates.

101. Fundamentals, sec. 126; RSFSR Civil Code, Art. 566; see generally Mádl, Foreign Trade Monopoly, Private International Law (in English) (Akademiai Kiado, Budapest, 1967).

102. Lunts, supra note 50 at 38, 55.

103. Id., at 44.

104. Citing Soviet Chamber of Commerce Legal Report 32 (7th. ed. 1956).

105. Lunts, supra note 50 at 53, citing Soviet Chamber of Commerce Legal Report 38 (22d ed., 1969).

106. RSFSR Civil Code, Art. 566 (2).

107. Id., chapter VI.

108. Lunts, supra note 50 at 42.

109. Id., at 18.

110. Id., at 46-47.

111. Id., at 48.

112. Id., at 50, 56.

113. Id. at 55, citing Soviet Chamber of Commerce Legal Report at 38 (22d ed., 1969).

114. Art. 97 of Hague Uniform Law of Sale, 1964.

115. RSFSR Civil Code, Art. 138.

116. Id., Art. 135.

117. See notes 17-19, supra, and accompanying text.

118. Doing Business with the USSR, supra note 70 at 197.

119. See section entitled "Foreign Trade Procedures and Practices," supra.

120. See A. B. Altshuler, Valiutniye Otnoshenia po Vneshnei Torgovli SSSR (Legal Problems of Currency Relations in Soviet Foreign Trade), Chs. 3, 5, 6 (in Russian) (Moscow: Mezhdunarodnye Otnoshenia, 1968).

121. Lunts, supra note 50 at 65; USSR Uniform Rules on Letters of Credit, 1962.

122. Uniform Commercial Code, Section 5-105.

123. Lunts, supra note 50 at 67; Soviet State Bank statute, sec. 59.

124. See section entitled "Settlement of Disputes," infra.

125. Compare 1961 European (Geneva) Convention on International Commercial Arbitration, Art. VI, 484 UNTS 364 (1963-1964).

126. Lunts, supra note 50 at 81, citing the 1971 Soviet FTAC arbitration award in the Prodintorg case.

127. Oscar Meyer case, Soviet Chamber of Commerce Legal Report 24 (19th ed. 1965).

128. Fundamentals, sec. 96. See generally, S. L. Levitsky, "Introduction to Soviet Copyright Law," in Law in Eastern Europe, Vol. 8 (Szirmai, ed., 1964), and Y. Matveev, "Copyright Protection in the USSR," Bull. Copyright Soc., Vol. 20 at 219 (1973).

129. Fundamentals, sec. 105.

130. Id., sec. 98.

131. Id., sec. 99.

132. Id., sec. 100.

133. Id.

134. Soviet News, Sept. 7, 1973.

135. Fundamentals, sec. 101.

136. Id., sec. 103.

137. Id., sec. 104.

138. Id., sec. 106.

139. See, for example, consequent amendments to U.K. legislation by Stat. Inst. No. 963 (1973).

140. N. Bethell, "Authors' Rights, or Authors Wronged?" Times (London), March 2, 1973. See also "Soviet Law Could Restrict Outflow of Banned Works," International Herald-Tribune, March 16, 1973; "Russia's Accession to Copyright Convention May Result in Tighter Curb on Dissident Authors," Times (London), March 16, 1973.

141. Id., Sept. 21, 1973; Soviet News, Sept. 25, 1973.

142. See, for example, Soviet News, Sept. 25, 1973.

143. Times (London), Sept. 21, 1973.

144. Id., Sept. 21 and 22, 1973.

145. Id., Sept. 22, 1973.

146. Id., Sept. 28, 1973.

147. See J. M. Lightman, "Domestic and International Trade Aspects of the USSR Trademark System," IDEA, The Patent, Trademark and Copyright Journal of Research and Education, Vol. 12, at 792, 797 (1968).

148. See Doing Business with the USSR, supra note 70 at 116-117, for additional details.

149. Statute on Trademarks, sec. 1.

150. Id.; see also Lightman, supra note 147 at 803.

151. Statute on Trademarks, sec. 3.

152. Id., sec. 27.

153. Id., sec. 4.

154. Id., secs 19 and 20.

155. Id., secs. 12, 15.

156. Id., sec. 16.

157. See Doing Business with the USSR, supra note 70 at 116.

158. Statute on Trademarks, sec. 8.

159. Law of Aug. 21, 1973, sec. 21, Russian text appears in Sobranie Postanovlenii Pravitelstva SSSR (Collection of Decrees of Government of the USSR), 1973, at 408-458.

160. Id., sec. 7.

161. Id., sec. 25.

162. Id., sec. 24.

163. Id., sec. 29.

164. Id., sec. 52.

165. Id., secs. 48, 50, 59.

166. Id., secs. 108, 118; the courts deal with most disputes about authorship, royalties, and questions of anticipation, sec. 155.

167. See generally, M. Boguslavsky, "Legal Protection of Industrial Designs in the USSR," Nordiskt Immateriett Rattsskydd, 1973, at 240.

168. See M. L. Gorodisskiy, Licenses in USSR Foreign Trade at 13 (English translation of the 1972 Russian-language study, U.S. Dept. of Commerce, NTIS, COM-73-10738, 1973); US/USSR Technology Licensing Prospects (Summary Report of U.S. Delegation Visit to USSR, U.S. Dept. of Commerce, Sept. 1973).

169. See BI, Eastern Europe Report, Sept. 21 and Oct. 5, 1973, as well as references cited supra notes 168.

170. See, for example, V. Andreyev and L. Yezhov, "Development of Business Co-operation between the USSR and France," Foreign Trade, No. 11, 1973 at 25. See also A. Lebedinskas, "Effectiveness of Participation in Construction of Enterprises Abroad," Id. at 47.

171. See, for example, R. Kaiser, "Russia Invites U.S. Companies to Explore Investment Areas," International Herald-Tribune, Aug. 24, 1973.

172. Bratus, supra note 5 at 232-233.

173. Triska and Slusser, supra note 4 at 309-311.

174. Doing Business with the USSR, supra note 70 at 134.

175. Id., at 135.

176. For more detailed information on Soviet foreign trade arbitration practices, see Bratus, supra note 5; Leff, "The Foreign Trade Arbitration Commission of the USSR and the West," in New Strategies for Peaceful Resolution of International Business Disputes (American Arbitration Association 1971): Pisar, Coexistence and Commerce, Chapters 20-24 (1970). See also authorities cited in note 84, supra.

177. By decree of the Presidium of the Supreme Soviet (June 17, 1932), Collection of laws of the USSR, 1932, No. 48, sec. 281.

178. Chamber of Commerce decisions of Jan. 21, 1949, Mar. 25, 1959, and Aug. 12, 1967.

179. D. Ramzaitsev, a member of the Moscow FTAC, in a contribution to the forthcoming Encyclopaedia of Comparative Law, Vol. 3, Ch. 20 (b), section I.

180. Bratus, supra note 5 at 247-248.

181. June 17, 1932 Decree, supra note 177, sec. 2.

182. Id., secs. 4, 5, 6; Rules of Procedure, sec. 10.

183. Rules of Procedure, sec. 20.

184. Id., secs. 5, 6.

185. Id., sec. 12 (a).

186. Bratus, supra note 5 at 249.

187. Rules of Procedure, sec. 23.

188. Id., sec. 21.

189. Id., sec. 22.

190. Id., sec. 25.

191. Id., sec. 26.

192. See Starr, supra note 35 at 76 and authorities cited at note 34.

193. Id., at 76-78. See also Doing Business with the USSR, supra note 70 at 88.

194. Ramzaitsev, supra note 57, II(a).

195. Bratus, supra note 5 at 250-251.

196. Id., at 230-234.

197. Id., at 242, citing Izvestiia, Jan. 21, 1972.

198. Doing Business with the USSR, supra note 70 at 88.

199. Rules of Procedure, sec. 1.

200. Ramzaitsev, supra note 57, II(d)(iii). This was not a Russian case, however.

201. Id., V, citing, inter alia, an unnamed and undated case decided by the Soviet FTAC.

202. Sec. 11 of 1932 Decree; case between Lebanon and a Soviet enterprise in 1965, cited in Ramzaitsev, supra note 57 at II(d)(vii).

203. See Pisar, supra note 176 at 462-463.

204. Ramzaitsev, supra note 57, II(c).

205. Fundamentals, sec. 128. See note 87, supra, and accompanying text.

206. Ramzaitsev, supra note 58, VI. See also Ramzaitsev, "The Law Applied by Arbitration Tribunals—I," in The Sources of the Law of International Trade 138, 151-152 (Schmitthoff, ed., 1964).

For recognition and enforcement by Western courts of East-West arbitration clauses and awards made in socialist countries, see Ramzaitsev, supra note 57; compare Pisar, supra note 176 at 463-469.

14

THE SOCIALIST FEDERAL
REPUBLIC OF YUGOSLAVIA
Drago Marolt
John R. Liebman

No discussion of modern Yugoslavia and its institutions could be successful without some historical preface. Yugoslavia has been referred to as one country with two alphabets, three religions, four languages, five nations, and six federal states called republics.[1] It comprises the hub of the Balkans, which in itself says a great deal about Yugoslavia. In the nations constituting the Yugoslav Socialist Federal Republic have occurred most of the significant confrontations between the Roman Catholic West, the Greek Orthodox East, and the Moslem South. The analogy applies to Yugoslav economic organization: the capitalist West, the centrally planned East, and the underdeveloped South.

It has been observed that the present generation of Yugoslavs has experienced all three known modern economic systems: capitalism before World War II, a centrally planned economy after the war, and self-government socialism in more recent years.[2] The latter is particularly and uniquely Yugoslav in its origins and its present application today.

Much of what is true of Yugoslavia today has its origins in its volatile and colorful history. The region now comprising Yugoslavia was settled in the 6th century A.D. by Slavic peoples, after having been dominated in its eastern reaches by the Turks and its western reaches by the Romans. The cultural and linguistic differences between these peoples was exacerbated in A.D. 1054 by the schism between the Eastern Orthodox and the Roman Catholic Churches.

Most of present-day Yugoslavia was the scene of military confrontation between Turks, Austro-Hungarians, and Russians, each of whom sought to subject Yugoslavia to its hegemony. It is, of course, well known that this rivalry served as a trigger for the outbreak of World War I, marked by the assassination of Archduke Franz Ferdinand at Sarajevo in the summer of 1914. Indigenous independence movements within the regions of Serbia and Montenegro were also destined to play an important role in the history of Yugoslavia and resulted in short-lived independence for these republics at the end of the 19th century.

Modern Yugoslavia emerged from the Treaty of Versailles and essentially embodied a unification of Slovenia and Croatia with the Kingdom of Serbia. The Yugoslav monarchy under the hegemony of Serbia survived until the collapse of the Third Reich in 1945, and Yugoslavia emerged from World War II as a republic.

The Yugoslav Republic today is truly federal in its character and has been shaped by the enactment of three constitutions since the end of World War II. Under the current constitution, which was promulgated on April 9, 1963, Yugoslavia is governed by the president of the Republic, a Federal Assembly comprised of five chambers, a Federal Executive Council having broad executive and administrative powers, and a Constitutional Court. Of the five chambers in the Federal Assembly, each of which is composed of 120 members, the most important is the Federal Chamber, the delegates of which are elected partly by the Chambers of each of the Yugoslav Republics from among their respective members, and in part by the Communal Assembly in each of the constituencies of each Republic, as confirmed by the voters in that constituency. The remaining chambers of the Federal Assembly include the Economic Chamber, the Chamber of Education and Culture, the Chamber of Social Welfare and Health, and the Organizational-Political Chamber.

The Socialist Federal Republic of Yugoslavia now consists of the seven Socialist Republics of Serbia, Croatia, Slovenia, Bosnia-Hercegovina, Macedonia, and Montenegro, together with the two autonomous regions of the Kosmet and the Vojrodina. These constituent republics have been the recipients in recent years of increasing delegations of responsibility and autonomy from the federal government. In sum, political development in Yugoslavia has obliterated most, if not all, Yugoslav political tradition, in the process creating a tradition of change.

THE ECONOMIC SETTING

Yugoslav Economic Ideology

"Social Ownership." Yugoslav economic life has passed through three stages following World War II. During the years 1947 through 1951, Yugoslav economic life was modeled on the Soviet Russian pattern. The state budget absorbed by far the bulk of the national income. The economy was administered directly by ministries and directors on a centralized level, culminating in 1950 with a totally centrally planned economy. It is fair to observe that the favored dogma of that period was that socialism was equated to the concepts of state ownership and central planning.[3]

Beginning in 1952, the Yugoslav economy entered its second phase, a phase of decentralization, marked by enactment of the Law on Management of Government Business Enterprises and Economic Associations by Workers Collectives in July 1950. The essence of this law, which remained in effect as a transitional measure until 1960, was that workers' collectives were to conduct all activities of their respective enterprises through their management organs, workers' councils, and managing boards. The workers' council, in turn, was to be elected by all employees of any given enterprise by secret ballot. More importantly, the introduction of concepts of self-government, as reflected in the workers' collective, emphasized the state as the economic raison d'etre but deemphasized the centrally planned and administered economy. The focus of economic effort became the enterprise, and, on an economic plane, this meant a shift from central planning to a market economy and its concomitant, a shift from state ownership in its purest form to "social ownership." The shift to a market economy brought with it the climate of competition, which, in turn, implied more independent economic entities. Interestingly, the converse of that proposition bears great weight as well: If an enterprise is in fact autonomous in respect to the decision-making process, a free market must be present.

Thus, the second phase of modern Yugoslavia brought about the dismantling of the central planning apparatus together with its numerous ministries, directorates, and artificially and administratively fixed price system.[4]

The third and present phase of the Yugoslav economy, otherwise known as "self-government socialism," is the result of a series of political, economic, and constitutional reforms that were instituted during the period 1958-63. Its bellwether was the new platform of the League of Communists in 1958, which defined the Yugoslav version of socialism as "social ownership," best defined as the absence of nonlabor income and exploitation.

The implementation of social ownership was given impetus by the enactment of numerous new measures, the aggregate effect of which was to institutionalize the trend toward decentralization and greater autonomy for unit enterprises; the development of a more competitive market economy; an accelerated movement toward integration of Yugoslavia into the world economy; and a massive reorganization of the monetary and banking systems. The old state banks, which were depositaries for state-owned capital, were replaced by new commercial banks, and state-owned capital was redistributed.

The old Yugoslav National Bank, as discussed in detail below, is now restricted in its activity to the execution of monetary policy.

It is important to observe here that Marx held that ownership relations are the basic determinants of social relations and, therefore, of the socioeconomic system. The class that owns (that is, that has economic control over) the means of production rules society. This theorem found its first application in Yugoslavia following the end of World War II in an economic policy that required that over-all economic control must be vested in the state and perforce must be hostile to private initiative and private enterprise. In modern Yugoslavia, however, this theory has been drastically revised and is seen now as "social ownership."5

The implementation of social ownership in terms of the economic structure of Yugoslavia and its microeconomic units has resulted in a unique and complex structure. The difference between Yugoslav economic concepts and capitalist economic concepts does not lie in the manner or structure in which the enterprise is managed but in the nature of the ownership over the means of production. While the means of production are the property of the entire nation, which accords with more orthodox Marxist ideology, the Yugoslav Constitution places the means of production at the exclusive and full disposal of the working collective or enterprise. It is fair then to describe a typical Yugoslav enterprise as a community of associated workers and employees that form a legally independent juridical personality. The managing organs of these enterprises are free to make all decisions for the benefit of the enterprise, although their decisions are subject to scrutiny by the workers' councils. The latter, while resembling closely shareholders' committees, are in fact empowered to establish business policy for the enterprise, to confirm the remuneration policy of the enterprise and to approve the purchase of substantial assets as well as the sale of substantial assets, and therefore bear some resemblance to "working" boards of directors.

From an economic standpoint, the Yugoslav enterprise operates within a sophisticated market economy. The individual enterprise carries out its day-to-day activities on an autonomous basis and makes its own decisions respecting long-term development, investment, changes in product mix, pricing, and any and all other business activities, including prospective ventures with partners both inside and outside the country.

Legal Analysis of Social Ownership. The basic principles determining the legal status of a Yugoslav enterprise are found in the Constitution of 1963. Although the trend toward autonomy originated as early as 1953 with the enactment of the law discussed earlier, the Constitution of 1963 provided a mature and complete framework of social

354

organization founded on the concept of self-management by workers. In this system, the legal independence of an enterprise becomes a cornerstone for the drive toward self-management. For example, Articles 6 and 7, Chapter 2, of the Constitution of 1963 provide that self-management shall entitle workers of an enterprise to participate in the acquisition and distribution of the output because the product has been created by the use and application of the social means of production. The interrelations of the workers within a given enterprise, as well as the relations of an enterprise vis-à-vis other enterprises and the state, are governed by legal mechanisms established by commercial, civil, financial, and administrative ordinances.

The fundamental source of law governing the status of Yugoslav enterprises was the Basic Law on Enterprises of 1965. This law has its origin within the Constitution of 1963, which defines a working organization as "an autonomous and self-managing organization," prescribing that it should (1) have the status of a legal person; (2) have specified rights to the socially owned assets managed by it; (3) be bound to maintain without diminution the value of the social assets within its control; and (4) be liable for its obligations incurred in respect to the assets managed by the enterprise. It is interesting to note that in respect to conferring the right to manage socially owned assets, the law expressly forbids the imposition of restrictions on or the confiscation of such assets by the government unless necessitated by "common interest," but, in any event, such action will be subject to payment of compensation therefor to the enterprise.

The foregoing provisions of the 1963 Constitution found more detailed expression in the Basic Law of Enterprises. In Article 1, the law stated that "an enterprise shall be an autonomous basic working organization of the unified social and economic system of Yugoslavia." Article 13, Chapter 2, provides that a working organization shall be formed as an enterprise for economic activity. Article 21 lends specific detail to the matter of proprietary liability of enterprises, emphasizing that the state shall not be liable for obligations incurred by enterprises arising out of their proprietary activities, except in cases provided by law or where such obligation has been assumed pursuant to an agreement between the state and a given enterprise or between a state and a third party.

It is thus seen that Yugoslav economic enterprises are bodies corporate, possessing rights and duties not unlike those found in their Western corporate counterparts. Business enterprises in Yugoslavia are the keystones of economic life in that country, along with more traditional forms of agricultural and other workers' cooperatives common to Yugoslav business life. It is essential, therefore, that the concepts of "enterprises," "working organizations," and "social ownership"—especially the latter—be comprehended.

To understand fully the concept of "social ownership," one must turn to a comparative analysis of other juridical forms. Mentioned freely throughout the Constitution of 1963 are phrases akin to "rights of use," but social ownership is far broader than usus fractus because it extends to the sale of capital goods. On the other hand, social ownership is more restrictive than classical norms of ownership because the right of sale is not absolute. Legal writers differ widely in their descriptions of social ownership, dependent in many instances on whether the interest of the writer is in the public law aspect or the private law aspect of social ownership. The only consensus to be found among these writers is that "social ownership" and "social property," as those terms are applied in Yugoslavia, are unique, that they do not imply an unlimited right over things characteristic of classical concepts of property, and that they include elements of both public and private law. And there the consensus ends.

"Working Organizations." The Basic Law of Enterprises of 1965, as replaced by the new law on enterprises of 1973, has seen the transfer of autonomous management rights to individual economic units in the past years. Direct decision-making by all members of work units at meetings called for those purposes has become more common and has found formal approbation in the 1973 amendments. Thus, in view of the fact that the vast majority of decisions affecting economic life in Yugoslavia are implemented on a unit level, it becomes essential to comprehend the manner in which the Yugoslavian concept of "enterprise" finds its application through the "working organization."

As seen above, a "working organization" is considered a community of associated workers and employees who combine their individual efforts with socially owned means of production that have been acquired by them as a "right of use," to produce goods and services. The working organization is managed by all of its workers and only by all of its workers, thus implementing the concept of "self management." This concept is considered the pivotal ingredient of the Yugoslav socioeconomic system. Through the evolution of Yugoslav constitutional law, the concepts of association of workers and self-management have been blended into "organizations of united work," otherwise known as working organizations. The essential ingredient of a working organization is that it be an economic unit, which, in turn, may comprise a portion of a larger association, referred to in the aggregate as an "enterprise."

Should a working organization desire to sever its relationship with its enterprise and either enter into association with another working organization or become an independent enterprise, Yugoslav law provides a procedural framework for this purpose. Similarly, since 1967, it has become possible for an enterprise to invest in another enterprise and share in its profits. As will be seen elsewhere in this study, the structure exists for similar arrangements, as between Yugoslav enterprises and foreign corporations.

Transactional Analysis of "Working Organizations"

Organization. Yugoslav enterprises are defined by Article 3 of the Law on Formation of Organizations of United Work,* which provides in part that "the workers, combining their own work with the social means of production and who are organized in basic organizations of united work, and between themselves bound through the working process, economic and other common interests, shall constitute the working organization as an independent and self-managed organization for social production." The actual formation of an enterprise must be accomplished in two stages. Initially, the founder or founders prepare the articles of formation that set forth the name of the working organization, its location, scope of activities, value of assets at the disposal of the working organization at the onset of operations, and the name of the persons acting in the name of the working organization. The law further specifies those who may act as a founder, including other organizations of united work, organizations of business association, political entities, local communities, and other juridical persons. The second stage of formation of an enterprise is the actual establishment of the working organization, including the following: (1) the formation of the basic organization of united work, (2) the execution of a self-management contract among basic organizations uniting to form the working organization and the election of its workers' council, and (3) the formulation and adoption of by-laws. By-laws determine the internal organization, jurisdiction, and responsibilities of the various management entities within the working organization, the status of the workers, and the management of the enterprise, and define specifically policy and decision-making processes. Irrespective of the final form assumed by the working organization, these documents must be registered with the District Economic Court (Okrozno Gospodarske Sodisce). It is seen at once that working organizations formed under the LEECR are similar in their juridical characteristics to classical corporate entities in that their characteristics are determined by the contract between the principals who have united to form the working organization.

---

*Law on Establishment and Entry into Court Register of Organizations of Associated Labor, Official Gazette 19 of 1973, referred to herein as LEECR.

Treatment of Assets and Income. Under Article 15 of the 1963 Constitution, a working organization has vested rights with respect to the assets placed at its disposal and the right to manage those assets. Like those assets, income derived by the working organization is social property but nonetheless may not be appropriated by the state except as specified elsewhere in the Constitution and described earlier.

The power of an enterprise or working organization to manage its assets is the most extensive substantive right that may be established in relation to social property ("quasiownership") and includes the following powers: (1) to use the assets as prescribed by management; (2) to alter the nature and location of the assets; (3) to invest or reinvest the assets of the enterprise; (4) to combine the assets with those of other enterprises; (5) to sell, lease, or otherwise transfer the assets of the enterprise on such terms and conditions as management deems to be in its best interests; and (6) to allocate the income of the enterprise to its various activities as management may require.

The right of use as regards assets of Yugoslav enterprises is a substantive right that may be pursued through such legal action as provided for by civil law. This derives from the notion that the right of use carries the concomitant obligation to the community (that is, the state) to protect and utilize the assets prudently. Accordingly, as noted earlier in this discussion, the state may not deprive an enterprise of its right of use over social assets unless required by common interest and adequately compensated.

Similarly, an enterprise is held accountable for all of its obligations. Article 15 of the Constitution of 1963 provides that all enterprises are liable for their obligations arising out of the assets over which control and management is exercised. An enterprise that becomes insolvent, therefore, may have a receivership imposed in respect to its assets.

Finally, Yugoslav enterprises have the rights of disposition of income derived from their assets. Income is distributed for the most part as personal incomes or salaries to the workers (including the managers), with the balance being held as retained earnings. The decisional authority in respect to income distribution is now within the exclusive control of the basic organizations of the united work. Previously, distribution of income rested with the workers' councils of each enterprise and could be distributed as required by the charter and by-laws of the particular enterprise. Inflation and other economic pressures, however, led to the imposition of salary freezes by the state, leading ultimately to enactment of a constitutional amendment, which now provides that income distribution is to be determined by the basic organization.

Functional Autonomy. The Constitution of 1963 is unusually explicit in respect to the delegation of autonomy to working organizations, and specifically protects the rights of aliens in and to Yugoslav working organizations after a contract of investment has been concluded. But the real substance of functional autonomy is found in recent amendments to the Constitution, which confer autonomy upon basic organizations of united work if the results of the activity generated by such basic organizations can be expressed in real value, that is, either in market terms or in productivity terms. Thus, both basic organizations of united work and working organizations have the same legal status and no founder of such organizations has a right to interfere in the activities of an enterprise except to the extent that it has attained a contractual right to receive certain benefits from the enterprise based upon the investment made by such founder.

By virtue of its autonomy, an enterprise may alter the scope of its business activities, either in matter of degree or of function. In the latter case, changes must be registered in their same manner as the organization has been chartered. In addition to the activities the enterprise may be authorized to conduct, an enterprise may exercise all other activities that are in furtherance of its avowed business objectives without the necessity of an amended registration. In terms of the applicability of the ultra vires doctrine of common law, however, all contracts between enterprises and third persons are honored, irrespective of any necessity for registration of a new activity by the enterprise that has gone unheeded.

Workers' Management Bodies. Once a Yugoslav enterprise is organized and commences operations, its management must be delegated to the working collective, which thereupon elects its organizations of workers' management. As seen above, the decision-making process thus delegated pertains to business matters of essential significance, including the use and disposition of assets, organization of operations, distribution of income, employment relations, and so on. The organs of workers' management include both the workers' council and the individual executive organ, the latter usually being called the director, general director, or managing director of the enterprise and are appointed by the workers' councils. The director's status is quite special because of his dual function. As the executive of the workers' council, the director prepares and carries out the decisions of the workers' council. Simultaneously, he also exercises a public function of supervision of the legality of decisions made by the workers' council and other management bodies of the enterprise and, in this role, assumes direct responsibility to the state.

It has been pointed out earlier that not all working organizations in Yugoslavia need have basic organizations as their founders. Such working organizations not having such basic organizations are totally liable for all of their obligations. Other working organizations comprised of one or more basic organizations, while held responsible for their obligations, do not impose such obligations on their underlying basic organizations except to the extent that such obligations have been assumed in the self-management agreement between the component units establishing the enterprise, negotiated and registered at the outset. In the event that no such specific limit on such obligations has been established pursuant to the self-management agreement, the basic organizations comprising an enterprise are jointly and severally liable for the obligations of each other.

Representation of working organizations is usually accomplished by that individual who is so designated by its management organs and registered accordingly with the economic court as specified in the by-laws of his organization. That person may, in addition, delegate his authorization to act to another individual pursuant to procuratory letters (Prokura). Prokura entitle an individual to conclude agreements and other legal acts in connection with the activities of the enterprise and also define the limits of his authority. On the other hand, Prokura do not empower an individual to conclude contracts or agreements that refer to the sale of fixed assets, and, in any event, Prokura are transferable and are subject to cancellation in a manner similar to the revocation of power of attorney.

Relations with Third Parties. Consistent with the autonomy conferred upon working organizations, Yugoslav enterprises are quite similar to classical corporations in respect to their relations with third parties. In these dealings, working organizations must use their own names (firma) and adhere to their by-laws. This assumes special significance where there are a number of enterprises engaged in the same or similar activities, and Yugoslav law prescribes that the name or firma of all enterprises not confuse third parties regarding the scope or nature of the business activities of the working organization. This requirement is enforced through the process of registration, to which each working organization must submit.

The firma of working organizations may also be used as the trademark of the enterprise and are thus regulated by the Law on Trademarks of 1961 as well as the International Convention on the Protection of Industrial Property, to which Yugoslavia is a signatory. Thus, trademarks employed by Yugoslav working organizations are protectable in accordance with conventional civil law.

The approach employed in Yugoslavia to matters of free competition and monopolization are, like the Yugoslav concept of self-management and social property, unique in comparison to both classical civil law and the civil law of other socialist states. Amendment 25

to the Constitution of 1963 provides that enterprises, as juridical
entities, may enter into business relations inter se freely, and prescribes that competition in the marketplace should be free and un-
fettered. But the law also provides that there is no inconsistency
between free competition and agreements between enterprises respecting joint development and production, sales, or other forms of
business combinations. The only apparent restraint on such agreements or combinations is a general proscription against retention of
any advantages deriving from monopolized markets.

Other Legal Considerations. As discussed earlier, it is rare for the
state to assume operational positions in enterprises. However, it
must be noted that the state will intervene to create market conditions
that accord with economic policy and are expressed principally through
"economic-administrative measures." Such measures may be directed
either toward all enterprises or toward specific enterprises, and they
include such measures as product allocation, quota applications, system-
ization of export and import licenses for specific goods, and restrictions pertaining to dealing in particular goods, price controls, and the
like. Amendment 23 to the Constitution of 1963 (adopted in 1971)
introduced two legal instruments previously not employed in Yugoslavia;
the first was the self-management agreement, concluded between basic
organizations of working organizations or between working organizations
inter se, and the second was a "societal agreement," concluded between
working organizations, their associations, trade unions, and other
sociopolitical organizations.
    In sum, the entire thrust of Yugoslav constitutional law as it
pertains to commercial life is based ultimately on the principle of
self-management, where the social plan adopted by the state is indi-
cative, rather than directive, in nature. Any legal act or deed accomplished by an enterprise that threatens the unity of the Yugoslav
market is deemed anticonstitutional, invoking both conventional legal
concepts of unfair competition, monopoly, market division, and speculation and, as well, notions of socialist public policy as expressed
through the Yugoslav Constitution.

Termination of an Enterprise. The LEECR lists six conditions that
will invoke the termination of an enterprise. These conditions reveal
clearly that state interest in the existence of any given enterprise
may be exerted if that enterprise fails to discharge its obligation to
the state. Thus, in addition to classical criteria of insolvency or
bankruptcy, the existence of which may lead to the termination of an
enterprise, Yugoslav law permits the termination of an enterprise in
the event that a given enterprise fails to fulfill all of the conditions
prescribed for doing business in the field of its registered activity

or if the "natural conditions" necessary for the perpetuation of the enterprise no longer exist.

We may thus turn to an examination of the specific rules and practices governing Yugoslav commercial life, both domestically and in respect to joint ventures with foreign business entities, with a basic comprehension of the underlying theory and practices characterizing economic life in Yugoslavia.

YUGOSLAV FOREIGN TRADE REGIME

Parity of Foreign Trade with Internal Trade

The Yugoslav Law on Trade of Goods and Services with Foreign Countries (also known as the Foreign Trade Law) provides that the flow of commodities into and out of the country shall be free. In theory, at least, foreign trade is regulated in the same manner as domestic trade. In practice, however, foreign trade is closely regulated owing to its close interface with international monetary and domestic development considerations.

Article I (a) of the Foreign Trade Law states that foreign trade may be restricted by federal law or judicial or administrative determinations based on federal law. Further Article 37 posits that the Federal Executive Council (that is, the state) is entitled to restrict foreign trade of certain commodities or group services on the basis of quotas, permits, or approvals.

Compared to earlier periods, however, Yugoslav foreign trade today has been largely liberalized. Immediately after World War II, foreign trade was a state monopoly, exercised through state foreign trade enterprises. In 1951 to 1952, at the onset of the new economic system and the market economy, foreign trade became gradually decentralized along with other sectors of the economy. Multiple exchange rates were employed to adjust foreign prices to domestic prices, both in export and import transactions. Besides organization difficulties, at that time a shortage of foreign exchange made any import liberalization impossible.

In 1967, a new foreign trade and exchange system was introduced, based on the principles of the economic reform of July 1965. These principles of mutatis mutandis are still valid today. The foreign exchange reform liberalized an important import sector, introduced a uniform rate of exchange, and brought about the enactment of customs law by substituting customs for earlier regulations. A temporary customs tariff was introduced in 1961 followed in 1965 by a permanent tariff, which is based on the Brussels nomenclature and represents a sharp reduction from previous rates. The present tariff is a one-column schedule of rates, applicable to imports from those countries that extend most-favored-nation status to Yugoslavia. At present, these rates apply to all countries. The tariff provides that the schedule rate is to be increased by 50 percent and applied to goods from nations that do not extend MFN treatment to Yugoslavia.

The Foreign Exchange Act, published as Official Gazette No. 36 in 1972, provides that payments and collections in connection with foreign trade transactions may be effected in foreign exchange or in dinars. Article 8 of the act reestablished the domestic foreign exchange market but extended market privileges only to Yugoslav banks. A juridical person therefore may obtain foreign exchange legally only by doing business with foreign countries on the basis of other relations with foreign countries, or by buying at authorized banks for dinars

The trend toward liberalization of foreign trade and exchange, while visible in Yugoslavia, is limited by extant circumstances. In 1967, for example, about one-fourth of imports were liberalized. Thereafter, imports began to expand faster than exports, so import restrictions were reintroduced, especially in 1972. However, in 1973, imports were liberalized again, due to a significant increase in foreign exchange reserves.

Yugoslavia is a high contracting party of the General Agreement on Tariffs and Trade (GATT), a member of the International Bank for Reconstruction and Development, the International Monetary Fund, an associate member of the Organization for Economic Cooperation and Development (OECD), and a member of many specialized international agencies. It maintains an observer status with Comecon and has a special agreement with the Common Market but is not an active member of any trade organizations. Yugoslavia has established trade agreements with 86 countries, including bilateral clearing arrangements, primarily with Eastern European and developing countries.

Customs System; Import Tariff System

Yugoslav import duties follow traditional principles: They are low or even nonexistent for raw materials and certain semimanufactured products, and high for consumer goods. Most of them are in the range of between 20 percent and 35 percent.

Many agricultural products and foodstuffs are subject to an additional, variable levy. The purpose of this levy is to protect domestic producers and sellers from wide fluctuations in the import prices of these commodities. Because import duties are not flexible enough to safeguard against foreign competition, Yugoslavia follows the pattern used by the European Economic Community. The value of the import for duty purposes is the cost of the goods plus transport costs to the Yugoslav border, plus insurance, packing, and other costs, incurred during shipment to Yugoslavia. As a rule, the invoice value, indicating free or c.i.f. Yugoslav border value, will be taken as the basis for computing import duties.

Special Customs Provisions. Transit. Goods in transit through Yugoslavia require only a transit declaration.

Storage fees. Goods must be cleared within three days after they enter the customs warehouse in order not to be subject to storage fees. After three days, the merchandise is subject to storage fees.

Customs warehouses. Yugoslav regulations allow the establishment of customs warehouses or depots but only in cities with a customs office. The local customs office issues the necessary permit.

Enterprises with foreign subsidiaries in Yugoslavia may establish bonded warehouses for temporary warehousing of imported goods. While held in bond, these goods are not subject to import duty. The appropriate permit may be obtained from the Federal Director of Customs.

Free zones. Free zones may be established upon issuance of permits issued by the Federal Secretariat for Finance, in accordance with the Federal Secretariat for Foreign Trade and the Federal Secretariat for Transport and Communications. The following operations are permitted within free zones: (1) receipt and dispatching of domestic export or import goods, or goods in transit that have not been cleared through customs; (2) receipt and storage of the abovementioned groups of goods; (3) normal operations attendant to preparation of goods for market, such as sorting, weighing, labeling, and packing; (4) processing, mixing, manufacturing, and repairing of goods.

Retail trade in the free zone is prohibited. Joint ventures between foreign and Yugoslav enterprises also can be established in free zones, but activities allowed in these zones for these ventures are specifically delineated. Subject to prior approval of the Federal Secretariat for Foreign Trade, foreign firms may establish offices within the zone in connection with the joint venture arrangement and may employ both foreign and Yugoslav citizens.

Restrictions, Quotas, Licenses, and Foreign Exchange

Considerations. The liberalization trend in Yugoslav foreign trade practices that has become increasingly dominant in recent years has been tempered by the necessity to maintain strict control over domestic inflation and chronic payments deficits. Thus, Yugoslav restrictions of imports have generally emerged in the form of exchange regulation rather than as direct import barriers.

The administration of import restrictions. All import commodities fall into six categories. The first five categories are regulated
through different methods of allocating foreign exchange. The sixth
is subject to a license, the granting of which does not carry with it
an allocation of foreign exchange. The commodities are grouped as
follows:

(1) LB—Free Imports. Foreign exchange is freely available
for imports of these items when a firm deposits the equivalent amount
of dinars. This group encompasses primarily raw materials but also
includes some semimanufactured and consumer goods.

(2) LBO—Conditionally Free Imports. The goods specified in
this category may be imported freely, as described under category
(1), but only after each enterprise has fulfilled its obligation to import
these goods in compliance with the prescribed exchange allocations
for countries with which Yugoslavia has concluded bilateral trade
agreements, including relative commodity lists, and with which it
maintains clearing arrangements.

The allocation of specific kinds and amounts of foreign exchange
for payment of goods under this import regime is effected by internal
agreement among related enterprises through the Economic Chamber
of Yugoslavia, with regard to the amounts and kinds of foreign exchange
previously used by the enterprises. With the approval of the Federal
Chamber of Economy, domestic enterprises may make contracts with
banks approved for the purchase of allocated amounts of foreign currency. The aim of this restriction is to compel enterprises to purchase
listed commodities first from Yugoslavia clearing partners in kinds
and amounts concluded between Yugoslavia and related countries.
After the enterprise fulfills the allocated contract, it is free to import
further quantities from any country under the conditions of category
1 above.

(3) GDK—Global Quota of Foreign Exchange. The total yearly
allocation of foreign exchange for import of goods in this list is set
by the Federal Secretariat for Foreign Trade for each enterprise.
Before allocations are issued, enterprises must divide the total quota
between themselves at meetings in the Federal Chamber of Economy.
In the event agreement cannot be reached, the Federal Secretariat
for Foreign Trade issues the allocations under its discretionary
power.

An enterprise may, during a given year, import the goods specified in this list only as prescribed by the allocation. However, this
allocation represents the right of an enterprise to convert the allocated
amount of dinars in any foreign exchange, and it does not limit the
quantities an enterprise can import, if it possesses its own foreign
exchange.

(4) BK—Quota of Ultimate Foreign Exchange. There are
relatively few items in this list. These commodities may be imported

365

only in the amount of predetermined value for each year. Quotas for each item on this list are specified as per the amount of convertible exchange available.

(5) RK—Quantitative Quota. For items listed here, maximum quantities, not values, are restricted for importation. Allocations for goods under either category (4) or (5) are based on agreement among importers, retailers, wholesalers, and domestic manufacturers, although the Federal Secretariat for Foreign Trade ultimately establishes restrictions in cooperation with the Federal Secretariat for Economy.

(6) Import Licenses. The articles enumerated in this list may be imported by a license issued by the Secretariat for Foreign Trade. This license may be issued conditionally to a Yugoslav importer on the basis of his level of exports of Yugoslav goods. The issuance of the license does not carry with it an allocation of foreign exchange; that is, exchange must come from some other source, such as retention quota or unused portions of GDK.

To summarize, the goods listed in categories (4), (5), and (6) can be imported only in limited quantities. Importation of goods included in categories (1) and (2) is free, while the import of articles listed in (3) depends on allocated amounts of foreign exchange, plus unlimited imports, paid for by an enterprise's own foreign exchange— that is, its retention quota and a 10 percent depreciation allowance. Certain goods are marked in the import list by an asterisk. To import these articles from LBO and RK lists, prior agreements between retailers, wholesalers, importers, and domestic manufacturers of these products is necessary. Such agreements establish timing of imports, quality requirements, and so on.

These are the basic legal norms regulating imports, but there are some additional modifications. For example, the metallurgy, electronics, and shipbuilding industries generally import reproductive materials, the import of which is restricted on the basis of a fixed percentage of realized earnings of foreign exchange. Further, to import wool, cotton, rubber, or tires, agreement among the importers is necessary. Additionally, there are some products, expecially in foodstuffs, timber, pulp, and paper where consent of the Federal Secretariat for Foreign Trade is required. Consent is granted upon consideration of (1) the demand on the domestic market, (2) market prices, and (3) the purposes grounding the desire to import these articles from foreign countries.

Variations from these regulations are allowed only in exceptional cases, and for each variation a permit issued by the National Bank of Yugoslavia is required.

Foreign exchange regulations. Authority for the distribution and administration of foreign exchange remains with the National

Bank. All foreign exchange must be sold to the bank, except that foreign exchange that businesses may keep as their own in foreign exchange accounts. This foreign exchange is called the retention quota. The amount of allowable retention quota has recently been increased and is generally determined after consideration of an enterprise's earnings of foreign exchange. These relate to its economic activity with foreign countries, exports, tourism, shipping, and so on. As a rule the retention quota now represents 20 percent of the earned foreign exchange, but certain groups of enterprises enjoy even greater retention quotas. Thus, enterprises engaged in selling tourist services have 45 percent of their foreign exchange earnings at their disposal. Similarly, enterprises engaged in printing books, offering graphic services, producing records or motion pictures, or dealing in foreign investment are allowed to dispose freely of 100 percent of their foreign exchange earnings.

In addition to the retention quota, businesses may have a portion of their annual depreciation allowances converted into foreign exchange for the purchase of foreign equipment, spare parts, and know-how.

Foreign exchange available through retention quotas and depreciation allowances may be used freely to import all goods, except those in BK, RK, and Import License groups. This foreign exchange may also be used to transfer registered capital to foreign partners and joint ventures to pay royalties and other foreign business expenses, but depreciation allowances may not be applied in repatriation of profits to foreign partners.

Working Organizations Engaged in Foreign Trade

Article 4 of the Law on Foreign Trade defines the subjects of foreign trade and the organizations of united work that may engage in foreign trade operations. The authority to carry on foreign trade operations may be acquired by economic enterprises (working organizations, cooperatives, or business associations) that are formed in conformity with Yugoslav regulations.

Article 4 (a) allows the organization of united work to decide independently the forms and ways in which it will conduct its foreign trade operations. An organization may be authorized to carry on foreign trade operations exclusively, or it may be authorized to carry them on together with domestic trade operations. It may be either a manufacturing or a commercial organization, or a combination of both. Consequently, foreign trade operations may be carried on by manufacturing organizations, by domestic and foreign trade organizations, and by strictly foreign trade organizations. It is legally possible, and widely practiced, for all such organizations to represent foreign firms, maintain stocks on consignment (in bonded warehouses), and export or import for their own account or for another. Each organization must be registered for foreign trade operations, and to be registered it must fulfill basic requirements—for example, it must maintain minimum working capital, employ a minimum number of personnel, and be experienced in foreign trade operations.

The organization has to register its foreign trade activities in the Register of Enterprises and Institutions with the appropriate district court. The organization must specify in its entry in the register the class of foreign trade operations it will entertain. Under Yugoslav law, natural persons cannot acquire authority to exercise foreign trade activities.

It should be noted that an economic organization, duly registered for foreign trade activities, can lose its authority to carry on foreign trade operations if it fails to fulfill any prescribed conditions or if a penalty is imposed on it by judicial decree.

Import Channels

Import trading companies, individual manufacturers, and wholesalers are permitted to import on their own account or for the account of others. Because of the Yugoslav approach to trade, which favors foreign-exchange-earners, it is often a part of a foreign exporter's marketing strategy, where import channels permit, to sell on the Yugoslav market.

Import channels may vary depending upon the kind of merchandise to be imported. For equipment, raw materials, and technical materials to be utilized in manufacturing operations, the end-user is the actual buyer, regardless of whether he imports directly or through another importer. Therefore, it is necessary for a foreign exporter to be in direct contact with the end-user. However, the export-import company remains an equally important channel into Yugoslavia because many smaller manufacturers are not registered for foreign trade operations and because there are financial and other arrangements between export-import organizations and many manufacturers. Moreover, recently, numerous export-import organizations have merged with manufacturers.

Large manufacturers generally prefer to import directly to avoid middle-man costs, though these costs are not high when compared with their counterparts in Western Europe. Import channels for these goods involve direct contact with manufacturers and with export-import trading organizations. For consumer goods, domestic trade is carried on mostly by wholesalers. Many wholesalers engage directly in foreign trade, though many of them compete with export-import trading companies in foreign trade operations. There are also many chains of stores, operated by enterprises (often including related manufacturing units), which function as importers and wholesalers, directly importing goods for their outlets.

Occasionally, manufacturing organizations import technical consumer goods, thereby enlarging the types of goods received. This import channel may be very useful for articles that require servicing beyond the date of purchase by the end-user.

Therefore, it is useful for a foreign exporter to have business associations in Yugoslavia. Several hundred Yugoslav enterprises are authorized to perform this activity. These are usually commission agents who promote the sale of their clients' goods in Yugoslavia. They may maintain warehouses, sell from consignment, or import for their own account.

Individuals are not permitted to represent foreign firms. The importance of personal contact in Yugoslavia, however, has been emphasized many times, and it is generally advisable to ensure a profitable and acceptable trade. Without such contacts, considerable time and persistence is required to establish relations with potential purchasers.

Commercial Practices

Terms of Trade. As usual the contract is the most important document between the parties. All details and procedures should be specified in detail, as well as penalties for breach of a contractual provision. The essential documents on freight shipments to Yugoslavia are the generally used commercial invoice and a direct order "to order" bill of lading. A consular invoice is usually not required. As a rule, certificate of origin is not necessary.

However, Yugoslav regulations do prescribe the presentation of the certificate of origin for certain kinds of imports, and often this certificate has to be confirmed by a Yugoslav consulate, in the country of origin.

The Decision on Obligatory Procurement of Certificates of Origin for Imports of Specified Goods (Official Bulletin 51, 1969), makes the certificate obligatory for import of certain goods, primarily those articles of higher technological degree such as TV sets, radios, refrigerators, washing machines, home appliances, watches, tape recorders, and enamel ware. To be acceptable, the certificate of origin must be completed by a qualified Chamber of Commerce, Board of Trade, or manufacturers' association. If it is completed by the shipper of the goods, his statement as to the origin of the goods must be certified either by a Chamber of Commerce or another of the abovementioned organizations.

The sale of technical consumer goods in Yugoslavia is possible only if the warranty is offered to the end-buyer and servicing is offered (Official Gazette 21, 1969). These conditions must be fulfilled by the Yugoslav importer, who must cooperate in this regard with the foreign exporter.

Yugoslav authorities control the sanitary conditions of imported foods, forest plants, and so on at the Yugoslav border or at their destination cities. This requires that relative quality descriptions be clearly defined in the contract of sale.

The documentary requirements for air shipments are the same as for other shipments to Yugoslavia, except that the air-way bill replaces the bill of lading.

There are no special requirements in Yugoslavia for the labeling of general merchandise or for indicating the country of origin of the goods, but the usual prohibitions as to false indications of origin are in effect.

Quotations by foreign suppliers are usually made "Free Yugoslav border" or "c.i.f. Yugoslav Port." It is also quite common that the quotations "c.i.f. Yugoslav Port" or "Border and f.o.b. Exporters' Port" are required. The principal Yugoslav port is Rijeka.

The method of payment between Yugoslav and foreign partners is not statutorily regulated but is part of the contract among partners. The purchase of consumer and other goods (apart from equipment goods) formerly was financed by commercial credit, extended to the buyer by the foreign exporter, either by open credit or by bank guarantee; more recently, "credit" has lost much of its previous significance owing to internal Yugoslav regulations regarding obligatory deposits. However, the purchase of equipment goods continues to require long-term credits. There are no collection agencies in Yugoslavia, although Yugoslavia enterprises are generally noted for prompt payment. Sophisticated credit information service in Yugoslavia of a "Dun and Bradstreet" variety is also nonexistent. Credit information may be obtained either at Yugoslav commercial banks or Chambers of Economy.

In Yugoslavia there are no governmental purchasing agencies. Government purchases are generally made through a foreign trade enterprise specialist in the product. This is the usual way in which goods for use by specific governmental agencies are acquired.

Credit Facilities. During the series of economic reforms in Yugoslavia, banks, like manufacturing enterprises, were freed largely of central control and operated as independent profit-making enterprises. Control over credit has been effectively transferred from the state budget to commercial banks, with the Yugoslav National Bank supervising the monetary and credit policy.

Commercial credit and consumer credit have become widespread in Yugoslavia. The usual terms are a 20 percent down-payment, the balance to be repaid within one to three years. Wholesalers generally sell to retailers on credit, with payment due within 60 to 90 days.

Yugoslav importers are interested in concluding import deals on credit, especially when extending credit to their buyers. Because it is known that Yugoslav enterprises represent minimal credit risks to foreign suppliers, Yugoslav importers are able to obtain very attractive credit terms. However, present Yugoslav regulations in this field do not stimulate Yugoslav enterprises to negotiate importation of consumer goods on credit. Pertinent regulations stipulate that the enterprise must deposit the countervalue of the import deal, concluded on credit terms in dinars, with the commercial bank interest free—that is, two-thirds of the total value at the date of concluding the contract and one-third on the day of clearing the shipment through customs. These regulations nullify the advantages of foreign credit arrangement and thereby cause them effectively to disappear.

On the other hand, the provisions regulating the import of capital goods on credit terms are liberal. Official Gazette 22 (1972) provides that the enterprise must deposit the dinar countervalue in percentages depending upon the duration of the credit period. If the foreign supplier grants credit for three years, a deposit in dinars of 20 percent of the total value of the import has to be made at the bank interest free before conclusion of the contract. In the event the duration of credit is not less than three years and not more than five years, a 10 percent deposit is required. Where credit has been extended for more than five years, only a 1 percent deposit is necessary. Therefore, it is customary that Yugoslav buyers of foreign equipment insist on credit arrangements extending beyond five years.

Marketing. The Yugoslav market is a dynamic market, not only due to a high rate of economic growth but also because of changing organizational principles. Such factors makes direct contact on a permanent basis very important.

In Yugoslavia, there exist several institutions for market research, especially in the three largest cities, Belgrade, Zagreb, and Ljubljana. However, these institutions are not yet highly developed, engaging primarily in research efforts connected with new investment projects. Considerable effort is spent exploring future export possibilities or researching various economic problems for association or governmental agencies. Nevertheless these institutions do exist and can perform a market research function. Clearly, such research institutions possess greater insight into the Yugoslav market than could a similar organization outside the country.

Further, all Yugoslav enterprises are required to be members of the Economic Chamber of Yugoslavia, which embodies organizational departments embracing specific industries and sectors of the economy as well as the Secretariat for Foreign Economic Relations. This chamber is not government-controlled and could become an important contact in exploring the sale possibilities within Yugoslavia. The same holds true for the abovementioned professional associations.

The Chamber of Economy is organized on a territorial principle, so that there are Chambers of Economy for each Yugoslav Republic located in their respective capitals—Belgrade, Zagreb, Sarajevo, Ljubljana, Skopje, and Titograd. These agencies can offer great assistance in exploring local markets.

Commercial Representation of Foreign Firms in Yugoslavia

Under Yugoslav Law, foreign firms may seek representation of their interests through commission agents. These firms may establish subsidiary offices within the country. Article 86 of the Law on Foreign Trade restricts such branch offices to the following operations: actions on behalf of foreign business associations in matters related to the establishment and performance of contracts for sale of goods and services; and exercising operations of commercial representation, such as warehouses, service agreements in connection with imported equipment, durable consumer goods, and other technical services.

Yugoslav law regulating the representation of foreign commercial interests is similar to such legislation in other countries. However, Yugoslav law bars natural persons from exercising the activities of commercial representation of foreign firms. Thus, foreign firms may seek representation in Yugoslavia only through authorized enterprises, registered as foreign trade organizations. A contract for commercial representation must be executed in writing. Approval of the state authority is not a prerequisite to the contract's validity.

In practice, these contracts are generally for a term of at least one year. However, a trial contract of representation is permissible, though it may not extend for a term of less than six months. Additionally, a Yugoslav foreign trade enterprise may represent a foreign association in markets outside of Yugoslavia. Alternatively, a foreign business association may establish its own representative office in Yugoslavia, its operations being regulated by the Decision on Conditions for Operating Representative Offices of a Foreign Firm in Yugoslavia, published in Official Gazette No. 22 (1969). The decision permits operation of the foreign representative where there exists a joint venture with a Yugoslav corporation; contracts have been concluded with a Yugoslav firm; exports from Yugoslavia are anticipated; long-term business regulations have been developed on the Yugoslav market for exports; and imports will enter Yugoslavia from the foreign business association.

These regulations control the flow of goods into Yugoslav markets. In the case of contracts for technical services, foreign representatives are permitted where qualitative or quantitative control of professional services is required; the services are for shipbuilding or modification of existing vessels; or the services are for operations in the field of river transportation.

Representative offices may be established only after acquisition of permits from the offices of the Federal Secretariat for Foreign Trade, the Federal Secretariat for Economy, and the Federal Chamber of Economy. Prior to establishment of the office in Yugoslavia, the foreign corporation must initially deposit 600,000 dinars in convertible exchange (roughly equivalent to U.S. $40,000 with the National Bank of Yugoslavia. This deposit is waived however, where the foreign corporation has a direct investment in a Yugoslav enterprise; concluded a production cooperation contract with a Yugoslav enterprise; contracted for the supervision of shipbuilding; or contracted for operations in river transportation.

Finally, the representative office of a foreign corporation must first register with the Federal Secretariat for Foreign Trade before initiation of business operations, and at least half of its employees, including the manager, must be Yugoslav nationals.

Advertising and Trade Fairs

A number of advertising agencies, though not very large, operate in Yugoslavia. Most domestic advertisers have established their own advertising departments within their enterprises and deal directly with the media, which in turn carry advertisements as supplied or create additional material.

Product advertising is carried in newspapers and periodicals. Because there are three languages and two alphabets within Yugoslavia, there is no single newspaper that can offer distribution throughout the country. Therefore, any advertisement in newspapers or periodicals must be distributed on a regional basis if the entire Yugoslav market is to be covered. The advertising rates vary greatly but are relatively inexpensive. For example, a full-page advertisement can run from as low as U.S. $200 up to a maximum of $2,000. Commercial radio is a widely used medium in Yugoslavia, though it is not necessarily the most effective because Yugoslav automobiles do not generally carry radios and because TV sets have lessened the use of the radio in the home. Nevertheless, radio is effective in rural areas, where TV sets do not predominate.

More Yugoslav families possess TV sets than ever before, and thus this medium is probably the most important. Television programming includes network shows watched throughout the country with subtitles in other languages. The cost of television advertisement runs under U.S. $1,000 per minute. Advertising may also be accomplished through films and slides shown in theaters. Alternative methods include the display of signs in sport arenas, on buses, and along the highways.

There is a variety of trade fairs in Yugoslavia of both national and local importance. Trade shows represent an excellent medium through which new products may be introduced to the Yugoslav market, as they attract wide attendance from potential buyers, importers, and wholesalers. The largest Yugoslav trade fair, held each fall and spring, is the Zagreb International Trade Fair, a general fair with special trade shows. Additionally there are the specialized trade shows, which offer excellent opportunities for initial contract negotiations and the introduction of new products. These trade shows are seen throughout Yugoslavia; of special importance are specialized fairs held in Belgrade, Ljubljana, Zagreb, and Novi Sad. Typically the fairs are organized by independent trade show enterprises, which offer all necessary services to participants or arrange for such services through forwarding agents.

Samples with no commercial value enter Yugoslavia free of duty and other taxes. However, foodstuffs and beverages cannot be imported as samples. Conversely, samples with commercial value are subject to regular duty consistent with ordinary commercial shipments. However, customs authorities have the discretionary power to exempt temporarily samples from duties and other fees provided the samples are returned within a given period. Finally, samples without commercial value may be sent by mail or hand-carried by travelers, but in either case they enter duty free.

Chambers of Economy

One of the most important elements in government-business relations in Yugoslavia are the Chambers of Economy. Each of the constituent republics and autonomous regions of the country has its independent Chamber of Economy, which in turn is a member of the Federal Economic Chamber. The express mission of the Chambers of Economy is to establish policy and procedures in respect to economic matters and to cooperate with the state in the implementation of these policies. The Chambers of Economy also provide a forum for the resolution of any policy conflicts that may occur between the business community and the government, including such matters as import allocations. Policy conflicts in these areas are resolved through "self-management agreements" (between enterprises) or "society agreements" (regulating interests of various sectors of the economy as a whole).

Among its many functions, the Federal Chamber of Economy, which is composed of some 18 Industrial Councils, coordinates marketing efforts in respect to foreign markets and economic relations with foreign countries, representing all Yugoslav enterprises. The Assembly of the Chamber of Economy, which is the Chamber's highest management body, is charged with the codification of commercial law, the appointment of arbitrators to adjudicate commercial disputes, the coordination of public relations and advertising abroad, and the establishment and operation of representative offices in foreign countries. More importantly, the Chamber of Economy takes a substantive position in respect to foreign trade and foreign exchange policy, development of export and import trading, and assistance in the area of foreign trade documentation. Thus, while the Chamber of Economy resembles superficially the chambers of commerce common to the capitalist world, it can be seen that it exercises quasigovernmental powers as well.

CREDIT, BANKING, AND FOREIGN EXCHANGE

Banks

Role of Banks and Organization. The recent decentralization of the Yugoslav economy, which began in the early 1950s, did not include the banking system, which remained essentially centralized and subject to central planning influences until 1965. Banking enterprises on a local level were limited to day-to-day commercial functions, while all major investment decisions, including matters pertaining to long-term credits, remained within the province of federal budgetary and investment mechanisms. This fact is attributable to the perceived need on the part of the federal government to redistribute income among the different federated republics of the country, rather than to any notions of federal control of investment policy or principles of socialist planning. Nonetheless, the decentralization of the banks opened investment decisions to political influences not dissimilar to those found in many systems where distribution of wealth is determined on a federal level.

The Law on Banks and Credit Operations[6] overhauled the Yugoslav banking system completely. Under the new law, banks have been redefined as associations of producers who pool their resources to promote a more effective utilization of social assets and are authorized to conduct typical banking operations in accordance with the country's social and economic plans. Although banks are deemed to be autonomous in the exercise of their various activities, they are obliged to follow federal guidelines in the conduct of credit operations. One of the more significant facets of the law of 1965 is that of "de-territorialization." As applied in Yugoslavia, this principle now permits all banks to conduct their business throughout Yugoslavia. However, enterprises may work only with banks located within their respective republics. By the same token, enterprises are free to work with whatever bank or banks they desire to work with, and each enterprise is free to maintain its accounts with one or more banks, both as regards local currency and foreign exchange. In other respects, banks are treated in the same manner as other Yugoslav enterprises and are held responsible for their obligations to the extent of assets that are placed under their control.

The Law of 1965 established two types of banks. The first, the National Bank of Yugoslavia,[7] is regulated under the Law on the National Bank of Yugoslavia. The National Bank is primarily a central bank and is responsible for the maintenance of the liquidity of Yugoslavia's balance of payments and the creation of foreign exchange reserves, but the National Bank is also authorized to carry on a limited number of commercial bank operations. The second category of banks is denominated business banks and included (until 1972) commercial banks, investment banks, mixed banks (which have commercial and investment functions) and, finally, savings banks. Commercial banks are concerned primarily with short-term credits to the business community and similar types of commercial operations. Investment banks are chiefly involved in the establishment of credits for the acquisition of fixed assets and long-term working-capital loans, accompanied occasionally by some short-term credits and commercial banking operations. Savings banks have not yet been established under Official Gazette 16 of 1965, and their authorized functions encompass banking operations oriented to personal requirements, including those common to Western thrift institutions. Because no savings banks have been established under this enabling legislation, the authorized functions are generally carried on by the other banks discussed above.

There is no limit to the number of banks that may be established in Yugoslavia. In order to establish a bank, there must be at least 25 founders, the majority of whom are to be Yugoslav enterprises, and a minimum capitalization of 10 million dinars (commercial banks must have an additional 20 million dinars in demand deposits). Investment banks on the other hand must have available 150 million dinars of funds for credit, whereas a mixed bank must have no less than 50 million dinars and a savings bank no less than 1 million dinars available for credit functions. The result of these requirements, in part, has been a consolidation among Yugoslav banking institutions. In 1966, at the outset of the new banking legislation, Yugoslavia had 112 chartered banks with 365 branch offices. By 1971, however, many of the smaller banks had been absorbed into major banks, leaving

55 banks in the country with 682 branch offices. This set the stage for additional legislation, which was designed to rationalize further the Yugoslav banking system.

The amendment of 1972 removed the distinction between commercial, investment, mixed, and savings banks, consolidating their functions, and established a single capital requirement of 50 million dinars for any bank chartered under Yugoslav law. The amendment also introduced negotiability to evidences of equity participation in the banks, authorizing the transfer of a founder's certificate to another legal entity in compliance with the articles of association of the bank in question. It should be noted, however, that such certificates of participation carry with them the principle of assessability, invoked in the event that the bank's resources are inadequate to meet its obligations.

Regulation of Foreign Exchange Banking Operations

Until 1966 all foreign exchange operations were channeled through a handful of banks, whose obligations in this regard were underwritten by the central government. Under the circumstances, foreign creditors were not concerned with the legal status of the banks with whom they dealt. Under the new banking system, however, central government guarantees have been abolished for all banks, except for the National Bank, and all Yugoslav banks may now conduct foreign exchange operations and become involved directly with foreign creditors.[8]

Foreign credit operations are defined under the above law as any undertaking wherein a Yugoslav bank incurs a debt payable in foreign exchange or issues guarantees to enterprises on the basis of an agreement concluded abroad, extending credit to foreign borrowers or granting credit to domestic borrowers for the purpose of financing exports or for the execution of investment projects outside of Yugoslavia. Any bank engaging in these types of operations is required, so long as any of those obligations are outstanding, to set aside a reserve fund in foreign exchange to cover these types of obligations, to the extent (expressed as a percentage of such obligations) as required from time to time by the Federal Executive Council. In other respects, banks dealing in foreign exchange operations must have stated capital of not less than 500 million dinars and deposits of not less than 1 billion dinars.

All agreements relating to foreign exchange credits must be written and must specify the terms upon which credit is granted, the terms and conditions pertaining to its utilization, and the terms respecting the payment and other rights and obligations of the parties. Following the conclusion of foreign exchange agreement, the bank is required to notify the Yugoslav National Bank, which notification shall have been preceded by written notice to that bank of the granting bank's intention to enter into the agreement. These regulations are designed to afford the Yugoslav National Bank an ongoing means of monitoring foreign exchange transactions and provide an exclusive means for clearing all foreign exchange operations accounts.

As the vast majority of foreign exchange operations conducted by Yugoslav banks involve current transactions in goods and services, it is important to note that Yugoslavia has adopted uniform rules and practices pertaining to documentary credits prepared by the International Chamber of Commerce together with the uniform rules for the collection of commercial paper and other negotiable documents.

Foreign Credits

One of the more important areas of concern of the Yugoslav National Bank pertains to loans obtained by Yugoslav enterprises in foreign exchange from abroad. Official Gazette 29 of 1971 prescribes that all working organizations and banks must register a Notice of Intent to negotiate credit arrangements with foreign institutions in advance, as well as the registration of a concluded credit arrangement. The bank is entitled to reject the notification of intent if the proposed credit could be detrimental to Yugoslavia's international payments position. Any credits included with a Yugoslav working organization or a bank without registration vitiates the underlying obligation. In this respect, Yugoslavia has chosen a path well known to many other developing countries.

Similarly, where foreign credits are to be used for payment for imported equipment, retention quotas must be established by the borrower-importer, which will vary in accordance with the tenor of the credit arrangement. If the period of repayment is less than three years, the compensating balance required is 20 percent of the total loans; if the period of repayment is more than three but less than five years, the compensating balance is 10 percent of the total loan; and, for credits of maturities exceeding five years, 1 percent is required as the compensating balance.[9]

For credits not tied to imports, the retention quota is regulated by Official Gazette 62 of 1972. This provision requires Yugoslav enterprises to maintain interest-free deposits with the National Bank of Yugoslavia in dinars in an amount equal to the foreign credit for the term of the obligation and so long as it remains outstanding. This deposit must be made, accordingly, in the case of financial credits prior to the conclusion of the credit arrangement and for foreign deposits at the time such deposits are received by the Yugoslav enterprise. The deposit in question must be made in an amount equal to 75 percent of the total foreign credit irrespective of the duration of the credit arrangement and must be made in local currency. In no event, however, may a foreign credit be repaid in the term of less than two years from the date of the initial disbursement. It must be noted that these regulations apply only to foreign credits extended directly to Yugoslav enterprises and do not obtain in connection with existing joint ventures with foreign business entities.

Basic Regulation of Foreign Exchange Transactions

Convertibility of Yugoslav currency. The hallmark of Yugoslav monetary policy in the past 10 years has been to achieve convertibility of the Yugoslav dinar. This policy has resulted in the progressive liberalization of trade, and particularly of Yugoslav imports from abroad. This trend has gathered further momentum from the increasing degree of autonomy granted to Yugoslav enterprises, which, in turn, has generated increasing demand for imported capital goods.

Subject to a number of restrictions regarding foreign exchange transactions, Yugoslav enterprises may establish their own credit arrangements with foreign lenders, limited only by their own financial strength. The restrictions applicable in this instance fall into the two categories of retention quotas and monetary correction. Otherwise, Yugoslav enterprises may convert local currency freely into foreign exchange for the financing of foreign travel, for advertising in foreign markets, and for fees and other administrative expenses incurred in connection with international operations, including expenses attendant to operating branch or representative offices abroad.

As noted previously, foreign partners' shares of profits earned by joint ventures between Yugoslav enterprises and foreign companies may be freely converted into foreign exchange and expatriated up to one-third of the total inflow of foreign exchange to the joint venture acquired through the export of products or services from the joint venture.

Regulation of Foreign Credit Arrangements. All Yugoslav transactions involving the use of credits granted abroad are governed by the Law on Credit Operations with Foreign Countries,[10] which replaced a similar law enacted in 1966. In essence, this law applies to the following types of transactions: the export and import of goods and services if payment for the same extends beyond 60 days; the extension or receipt of nonbank loans abroad; and the extension or receipt of bank loans abroad. These regulations also apply to the creation of demand deposits, guarantees, and refinancings of preexisting credits outside of Yugoslavia.

Although foreign credit arrangements may be entered into by virtually all forms of Yugoslav enterprise, including the banks and "sociopolitical communities," any liabilities that are incurred by Yugoslav entities to foreign entities and that are payable in foreign exchange are authorized only if the Yugoslav entity can assure the National Bank of Yugoslavia that the necessary foreign exchange and local currency will be available to service the debts to be incurred. As all credit operations must be registered with the National Bank of Yugoslavia, the latter exercises ultimate authority on all questions of this sort.

FOREIGN TRADE CONTRACTS

Parties. Yugoslav law defines foreign transactions as those having a commercial character—that is, those transactions that are effected by working organizations involved in economic activities. In exceptional cases, statutory provision authorizes foreign trade transactions effected by noncommercial parties—this is ad hoc authorization. Nevertheless, only Yugoslav enterprises authorized for operations in foreign trade may be a party to any agreement that contemplates foreign trade.

A foreign trade contract is a bilateral agreement in which one of the contracting parties is a Yugoslav national and the other party is of foreign citizenship. Internationality of the agreement is provided by the contractual relationship of the foreign partner; consequently, the agreement is classified according to its respective foreign nationality. These agreements are formed either (1) on one's behalf for one's account, (2) on one's behalf for the account of another, or (3) by the acts of a commission agent. Organizations authorized for extraterritorial transactions may employ all three modalities. Contracts involving transport services, the postal system, or telephone and telegraph services may be accomplished only on one's behalf and for one's account.

Creation and performance of contracts. Yugoslav business associations, by law, may incur contractual obligations only to the extent of their financial holdings. Although a foreign trade transaction is governed by the general provisions of Yugoslav Civil Law, it may also come under the purview of administrative law. Thus, official interference in the area of exchange regulations should be anticipated. Through administrative-legal prescriptions, the state may influence indirectly the formulation of foreign trade contracts. Yugoslav legislation requires administrative permits for certain transactions of foreign trade. Despite the fact that foreign trade has been greatly liberalized, present legislation imposes a system of quotas, permits, and approvals upon foreign trade agreements.

Nevertheless, contractual arrangements are not rendered invalid simply because a required permit has not been obtained. Rather, such an agreement is not enforceable unless the contracting parties subsequently agree to recognize those regulations in force. If the contract cannot be adapted to the regulations, a suit for damages may be filed by a bona fide party against the party responsible for the breach to the extent of damages incurred.

In general, Yugoslav courts recognize the general presumption of validity of contracts and therefore will avoid if possible construing a law so as to invalidate an agreement. But beyond matters of basic validity, the parties to an agreement cannot avoid the application of Yugoslav law where public policy is involved and which may place a ban on imports or exports, for example.

The Foreign Exchange Law and provisions regulating the monetary aspect of foreign trade transactions are considered an integral part of Yugoslav administrative law and as such influence the nature of foreign trade agreements. Parties are obliged to follow these laws during the process of negotiations. In the event that a debtor defaults in payment by failing to adhere to pertinent regulations, the creditor cannot compel execution of payment.

LICENSING AND INDUSTRIAL COOPERATION AGREEMENTS

License Agreements in General

Yugoslav regulations with regard to licensing in the field of industrial property, inventions, trademarks, designs, and know-how follow in general the same principles characterizing most patent and copyright laws elsewhere in the world. The Law on Patents and Technical Improvements of 1960 defines a license agreement as an assignment by an owner of the patent, in part or in whole, of the right to use an invention to another party. Such a license may extend to either patented or nonpatented technology or know-how, may specify the territorial limits of the license, and may be exclusive, nonexclusive, or a combination thereof.

The salient difference between Yugoslav law and classical law lies in the Yugoslav requirement that a license agreement be concluded in writing, whereas in most other jurisdictions no special form of license is required. Additionally, international licensing agreements are regulated by the Decision on the Method and Conditions of the Contract on Assigning and Receiving Industrial Property Rights Abroad,[11] which prescribes that all licensing agreements, as well as other kinds of agreements respecting business-technical cooperation be made in writing and be registered with the Federal Secretariat for the Economy. Prior to the enactment just referred to, license agreements were required to be recorded but did not need official approval as a condition to their legal effect. Under the new law, official approval following registration is an absolute necessity to the legal efficacy of a license agreement. In the normal course of affairs, the Federal Secretariat issues its decision in respect to a proposed license agreement within 30 days following submission; and, if approval is given, the agreement is registered without further act of the applicant. If approval is denied, or approval is conditional upon the satisfaction of additional conditions imposed by the Federal Secretariat, the applicant is notified to that effect, whereupon the application may be either withdrawn or resubmitted in the form required by the Federal Secretariat.

Criteria typically applied in these matters are that the underlying technology that is the object of the license agreement be based on the highest state of the art, that production thereof has a prospect of profitability, and that the proposed Yugoslav licensee be able to use the technology on a continuous basis. It should be noted, however, that trademark and design patent licenses are exempt from these requirements.

Rights and Duties Under Yugoslav Licensing Agreements

Under Yugoslav law, a licensor is obliged to deliver the subject matter of the license agreement, together with all appropriate technical documentation, engineering designs, and operation instructions to the licensee, but the licensor need not warrant the profitability or the competitiveness of the technology being licensed. The licensor's title is implied under Yugoslav law and, if the license purports to be exclusive, the licensor relinquishes his rights to use the technology himself.

Other legal considerations attendant to licensing agreements, such as the obligation on the part of the licensee to use the license technology, are treated much in the same manner as classical licensing law and are generally left to the parties to determine in the contract. Most license agreements in favor of Yugoslav licensees provide for payment of royalties in a fixed amount per unit produced or as a percentage of the sales price of the articles produced, or a lump sum.

One controversial facet of licensing law in Yugoslavia is set forth in Article XXVII of the Law on Patent and Technical Improvements, which provides in pertinent part that

> If any organization has obtained an exclusive license, and
> the agreement between the owner of the patent and the
> organization [licensee] does not contain specific

limitations, the Council of Arbitration may grant, on the request of an interested organization, the right to use the invention to other organizations within the limits of and subject to the conditions on which the license has been obtained. The organization which is granted the right to use the invention shall be bound to compensate to the proprietor of the patent a proportionate share of the cost of obtaining the license, together with royalties to the licensor, in proportion to such licensee's participation in respect to the use of the invention covered by the license.

Article 97 of the foregoing law further stipulates that "technical documentation, processes, methods of construction, and trade secrets of an organization may be used by other organizations pursuant to the provisions on the use of inventions developed in such organizations." Since these provisions quoted above are inconsistent with other statutory provisions set forth in the Basic Law on Enterprises, as well as the Criminal Code, they have come under heavy attack by legal experts in recent years and remain as law only in the most nominal sense.

Long-Term Industrial Cooperation Arrangements

Yugoslav law provides a manner in which it is possible for a Yugoslav enterprise to enter into a cooperative agreement with a foreign company, in which the Yugoslav organization would manufacture certain components of certain products, importing the necessary materials attendant thereto, together with licenses, know-how, and other technology necessary for the Yugoslav party to carry out its part of the agreement. The provisions governing these kinds of arrangements are found in the Law on Long-Term Technical Cooperation Between Domestic Organizations of Associations and a Foreign Person[12] and require that such agreements be concluded for a term of not less than five years and that the Yugoslav party to the agreement must have an untrammeled right to obtain all necessary technical information together with improvements thereon, pertaining to the articles or products that are the subject of the agreement. Like the more common license agreements discussed above, these agreements must be in writing and are validated only by registration by the Federal Secretariat.

Foreign exchange regulation plays an important role in these agreements as well. The Yugoslav party to the agreement is authorized to use its foreign exchange earnings derived from exports stemming from the agreement to import freely any and all products relating to the cooperative venture, together with other products that may appear on the free import list, the conditionally free import list, or the

383

global foreign exchange import list. Finally, if the Federal Secretariat for the Economy and the Federal Secretariat for Foreign Trade issue their respective consents upon the validation of the agreement, even the imported products appearing on restricted lists may be freely imported up to the total amount of the foreign exchange earned on account of products exported pursuant to the joint venture.

SETTLEMENT OF FOREIGN TRADE DISPUTES

Contractual Default in Yugoslavia

Yugoslav law, as expressed in the General Usages, recognizes two types of default; default on the part of the debtor and default on the part of the creditor. Each contracting party is both debtor and creditor, depending on the particular facet of the agreement involved in the dispute. Thus, where a contract of purchase and sale is involved, the purchaser commits a creditor's default if he refuses to accept goods duly delivered by the seller, and the seller commits a creditor's default if he refuses to accept the purchase price tendered by the buyer.

A delay in performance of an agreement is treated in accordance with whether it is a fixed-term agreement or a transaction not having a fixed term. In the case of an indefinite transaction, where a debtor's default occurs, the creditor may elect to require performance of the agreement or to repudiate the contract and claim damages for nonperformance. In the event that the agreement is repudiated, the debtor nonetheless has a grace period in which to cure the default, which grace period is only prescribed as reasonable in light of the circumstances of the particular case.

In the event of a fixed-term transaction, default brings about a rescission ipso facto, and no grace period is granted. For the purpose of equating a fixed-term transaction to classical commercial agreements, an agreement to be considered a fixed-term transaction in Yugoslavia must contain a "time of the essence" provision.

Damages, like all other contractual problems, are governed by the General Usages, and assume one of two forms: unliquidated damages (expressed as the difference between the contract price and the average prevailing market price) or liquidated damages (expressed as the aggregate of the "cover" purchase and attendant loss of profit).

The General Usages also define the limits of penalty clauses that will be enforced. Generally, penalty clauses will be enforced only if specifically agreed to in the underlying agreement by the parties, and only in cases of nonmonetary obligations. The creditor must elect to claim the penalty or require performance of the obligation in question, which election is mutually exclusive. However, in cases where performance of the obligation in question is deficient (rather than nonexistent), the claimant may require both performance of the agreement and the penalty. Should the penalty be established at a figure deemed excessive by the Economic Court, it may be reduced accordingly.

Problems of Deficient Deliveries

In the event that delivery of goods pursuant to an agreement fails to conform to the contractual conditions regarding either quantity or quality, the buyer is obliged to protest the same to the seller as a condition precedent to the exercise of rights conferred upon the buyer by General Usages.

Specifically, in the event of a delivery deficient in quantity, the buyer is obliged to accept the quantity delivered, but, following inspection of the goods and protest to the seller, the buyer may reject the entire shipment and refuse to pay. In the event of a "long delivery" the buyer may return the excess portion of goods contracted for, assuming that the goods are divisible; if not, the buyer may refuse the entire delivery.

Deficiency of quality in the sale of goods confers upon the buyer, following protest, the right to demand replacement of the goods, repudiation of the contract in toto, or a fair price reduction against the contract. Should the buyer elect to repudiate the agreement and place the goods in question at the disposal of the seller, no judicial action is required. In the event that the grade of goods delivered to the buyer exceeds the grade ordered, the buyer may accept delivery thereof (although he is not obligated to do so), and to pay only the contract price. If such an error causes any damages to the buyer, such as higher sales tax, import duty, and so on, the seller may be liable to the buyer accordingly.

Other problem areas in sales of goods that do not appear in the General Usages are generally covered under various international conventions, such as the Convention for the Unification of Specified Rules of Air Transport (1929), the International Convention on Carriage of Goods by Railway (1952), and the Convention on International Transport of Freight by Road (1956).

Before concluding this section, there are two principles enunciated in the General Usages that deserve mention at this point, and those pertain to the release of the debtor's liability for reasons of force majeure and the principle of changed circumstances. Inasmuch as the basis of legal liability in Yugoslavia is a subjective one, force majeure is an unusual principle because of its reliance on an objective standard. In the second instance, however, Yugoslav subjectivity is very much present. In the case of a claimed change of circumstances, either party to an agreement may seek a revision of an agreement through the Economic Court if the circumstances prevailing at that time are fundamentally different in comparison to those existing at the time the agreement was entered into, and relief may be granted if such changed circumstances could not have been anticipated and would otherwise work an extreme hardship on the petitioning party if left unchanged.

Choice of Law Rules

Yugoslav law contains no special choice of law of rules for commercial agreements and disputes, leaving the resolution of such questions to Yugoslav private international law. It should be noted here that Yugoslavia is not a signatory to the Hague Convention of 1955.

Yugoslav private international law is fairly typical of many of the approaches to choice-of-law questions found in Europe today, because so many classical systems operated in Yugoslavia prior to the Republic. Nonetheless, some basic principles of private international law unique to Yugoslavia have emerged since 1945.

The first is that in the event that parties to an agreement do not specify the governing law, the law of the "closest connection" applies, an approach quite similar to the "contacts" theory found in many Anglo-American jurisdictions. If choice of law is specified in the agreement, Yugoslav law generally will respect such choice of law provided that it does not contravene public policy or constitute an evasion of public policy. In general, however, Yugoslav private law may be avoided by an appropriate choice-of-law clause in the agreement.

Arbitration

Although the Courts of Arbitration are seldom used by domestic Yugoslav enterprises for settling commercial disputes, which generally resort to the Economic (Commercial) Court in these cases, they are exceedingly important in resolving disputes between Yugoslav enterprises and foreign entities. These procedures are found in the Law on Settling Disputes Arising from Mutual Business Relations Among Organizations of United Work at Permanent Arbitration Courts.[13] Thus, with increasing Yugoslav involvement with foreign companies, arbitration procedures are being used more frequently.

Since Yugoslav juridical persons are free to choose any arbitration form, whether in Yugoslavia or abroad, Yugoslav civil law gives full faith and credit to the autonomy of the parties, including the method of choosing arbitrators, the composition of the arbitration tribunal, the procedure to be applied, the law to be applied (with the limitation noted above), as well as the choice of the arbitration tribunal itself. The latter extends to the choice of foreign arbitration courts, as well as Yugoslav tribunals.

All disputes under Yugoslav law must be submitted to the Arbitration Court in writing, and, if the court chosen is the Federal Chamber of Economy, at least one of the parties to the dispute must be a foreigner, and none of the Yugoslav parties may be a natural person. In addition to this limitation, there are certain types of disputes that under Yugoslav law must be resolved by specific agencies created for that purpose and may not be submitted to arbitration. Included in this category are disputes respecting the possession of real estate, chartering of ships, and claims against the state arising out of military affairs.

It is not necessary that an arbitrator be a Yugoslav national, but the number of arbitrators chosen must be an odd number. The only limitation over the identity of arbitrators is that the arbitrators selected by the parties to the dispute must choose the President of the Court from an approved list issued yearly by the Assembly of the Economic Chamber of Yugoslavia.

As the parties may agree as to the procedure to be employed in connection with the arbitration process, such procedure must be followed by the arbitrators chosen by the parties. Notions of due process insofar as summonses are concerned also apply to Yugoslav arbitral procedures. In addition, the parties may be represented by their counsel; and, should one of the parties to the arbitration be a foreign national, he may choose a foreign counsel to represent him at such proceedings.

The award is given the same status as a judicial judgment and may be executed in a manner similar to that accorded a judicial judgment. Foreign arbitration awards as well are executed in Yugoslavia under the same terms and conditions applicable to foreign judgments. The principal condition to be met is that there be reciprocity between the foreign jurisdiction involved and Yugoslavia. Such reciprocity need not be formalized on a diplomatic level but need only exist de facto. Obviously, any foreign judgment that is contrary to Yugoslav public policy will not be enforced. The United Nations (New York) Convention on Recognition and Execution of Foreign Arbitral Awards of 1958 has not been ratified by Yugoslavia, although Yugoslavia participated in the conference that led to the enactment of the convention.

NOTES

1. Horvath, "Yugoslav Economic Policy in the Post-War Period: Problems, Ideas, Institutional Developments," 61 American Economic Review 71 (June 1971).

2. Ibid.

3. Kidrič, "Kvalitet robno-novčanih odnosa u FNRJ," 1 Komunist 33-51 (1949).

4. Horvath, op cit. at 80.

5. Id. at 82. The concept of "social ownership" found its origin in the 1958 Program of the League of Communists, which defined it as "the social system based on socialized means of production in which social production is managed by associated direct producers, in which income is distributed according to the principle to each according to his work and in which, under the rule of the working class, itself being changed as a class, all social relations are gradually liberated from class antagonisms and all elements of exploitation of man by man." See Program Saveza Komunista Jugoslavije (Belgrade, 1958).

6. Official Gazette 12 of 1965.

7. Official Gazette 16 of 1965.

8. Official Gazette 29 of 1966, as amended in 1972.

9. The foregoing regulations are subject to frequent adjustment.

10. Official Gazette 36 of 1972.

11. Official Gazette 6 of 1973.

12. Official Gazette 7 of 1973.

13. Official Gazette 22 of 1973.

BIBLIOGRAPHIC NOTE

The reader may wish to consult the following studies for further information concerning Yugoslavia's foreign trade and related matters:

Bombelles. Economic Development of Communist Yugoslavia (Hoover Institute, 1968).

van Doren. "Ownership of Yugoslav Social Property and United States Industrial Property, a Comparison," 26 Rutgers L. Rev. 73 (1972).

Drăskić. "Régime juridique des investissements étrangers dans les entreprises yougoslaves," 23 Rev. Trim. Dr. Comm'l 662 (1970).

Finžgar. "Unternehmungen u. Anstalten im jugoslawischen Recht," 90 Juristiche Blätter 19 (1968).

——. "Grundlegen Neuerungen des jugoslawischen Zivilrechts," 87 Juristiche Blätter 134 (1965)

Glickman and Sukijasovic. "Yugoslav Worker Management and Its
    Effect on Foreign Investment," 12 Harv. Int'l L. J. 260 (1971).

Goldstajn. "Gemeinsame Investitionen in—u. auslandischer Firmen
    in Jugoslawien u. der Bereich staatlicher Garantien," 9 Jahrbuch
    für Ostrecht 155 (1968).

——. "Law of Sales in Yugoslavia," 14 Law in Eastern Europe 25
    (1967).

Horvath. "Yugoslav Economic Policy in the Post-War Period: Prob-
    lems, Ideas, Institutional Developments," 61 American Economic
    Review 71 (June 1971). This fine discussion also contains an
    extensive bibliography, much of which is primary reference
    material by noted Yugoslav authorities.

Legendre. "Droit Maritime Yugoslave," 24 Dr. Mar. Fr. 696 (1972).

Lew. "Commercial Arbitration in the Socialist Federal Republic of
    Yugoslavia," 13 Rassegna Arb. 97 (1973).

——. "Commercial Arbitration in the Socialist Federal Republic
    of Yugoslavia," 28 Arb. J. 34 (1973).

Meichsner. "Zahlungsort bei Geldschulden nach jugoslawischen
    Recht," 13 Osteuropa Recht 81 (1967).

Mitrovic. "Jugoslawische Rechtsprechung zum internationalen
    Privatrecht," 27 Rabels Zeitschrift 136 (1962).

Montias. "Economic Reform and Retreat in Yugoslavia," 37 Foreign
    Affairs 295 (1959).

Moore. Self-Management in Yugoslavia (Fabian Society, London,
    1970).

Neumann. "Joint Ventures in Yugoslavia: 1971 Amendments to
    Foreign Investment Laws," 6 N.Y.U. J. Int'l L. and Pol. 271
    (1973).

Pavolic. "The protection of Private Rights in a Socialist State: Recent
    Developments in Yugoslav Copyright Law," 14 Harv. Int'l L. J.
    111 (1973).

Peselj. "Yugoslavia's Economy Looks to the West," 2 L. and Pol.
    Int'l Bus. 46 (1970).

———. "Yugoslav Laws on Foreign Investments," 2 Int'l Lawyer 499 (1968).

Pfaff. "Probleme der Anerkennung u. Vollstreckung jugoslawischer Schiedssprüche in der BRD," 16 AWD des BB 55 (1970).

Prica. "Know-How in Yugoslav Law," Rapports Nationaux Yougoslaves au XIIe Congrès International de Droit Comparé, 97 (Belgrade, 1970).

Savezna Privredna Komora. (Conference organized by Yugo. Inst. Comp. L. and AALS) Articles by Kalogera, "Arbitration as a Method of Setting the Disputes Arising from Commercial Agreements According to Yugoslav Law"; Kapor, "Consequences of Default in Performance of Contracts Under Yugoslav Law"; Prica, "Foreign Trade Transactions, and Authority for their Exercise Under Yugoslav Law"; Tasic, "The New Yugoslav Foreign Exchange System"; Janjic, "Licensing Agreements in the Sphere of Industrial Property Under Yugoslav Law."

Spaic, "Neue Entwicklungstendenzen im jugoslawischen Urheberrecht," 50 Archiv für Urheber-, Funk- U. Theaterrecht 92 (1967)

Stojanović. "Privateigentum im jugoslawischen Recht," 16 Osteuropa-Recht 170 (1970).

Stolz. "Jugoslowische Investitionsbank," 17 Osteuropa-Recht 266 (1971).

M. Sukijasovic. Yugoslav Investment Legislation at Work: Experiences So Far (New York, 1970).

———. "Legal Aspects of Foreign Investment in Yugoslavia," 37 Law and Contemp. Prob. 474 (1972).

Verona. "Neuordnung des Geschmacksmusterrechts in Jugoslawien" (Oct. 1963) GRUR (AIT) 477.

Yugoslav Chamber of Economy, Institute of Comparative Law. The Legal System of Foreign Capital Investments in Yugoslav Enterprises (Belgrade, 1972).

15

THE PEOPLE'S REPUBLIC
OF CHINA

Anthony Richard Dicks

POLITICAL AND CONSTITUTIONAL
BACKGROUND

Of the world's major countries, the People's Republic of China (PRC) probably most nearly approaches economic self-sufficiency.[1] Trade, as a result, has remained more obviously subordinate to political stategy in China than in other countries[2] and has to some extent been a shuttlecock in the country's internal politics.

From the foundation of the PRC, China's foreign trade has been the subject of an official policy, laid down in 1949 as follows: "The People's Republic of China may restore and develop commercial relations with foreign governments and peoples on a basis of equality and mutual benefits."[3] For the internal regulations of the country's foreign trade, the prescription was even simpler: "Control shall be exercised over foreign trade and the policy of protecting trade shall be adopted."[4]

The planned nature of the Chinese economy has fundamental implications for the legal objectives that PRC foreign trade officials must set themselves in international transaction.[5] In this chapter the attempt is made to describe, in outline, the legal and administrative structure adopted by the PRC to permit what they see as fundamentally different economic and commercial systems of socialism and capitalism to function in harmony. It is a structure uniquely Chinese in design. The centralized control of foreign trade, and its subordination where necessary to political requirements, has ensured that the PRC has largely retained the initiative in determining the conditions under which Chinese trade with market-economy nations is carried on.'

THE INSTITUTIONAL FRAMEWORK FOR
FOREIGN TRADE[6]

Ministry of Foreign Trade

The Ministry of Foreign Trade (MFT) is directly subordinate to the State Council, of which the minister is a member. Up to the Cultural Revolution period, the MFT was one of a number of ministries that were subject to the coordinating functions of the Office of Finance and Trade within the State Council organization;[7] it is believed that the office was abolished in the State Council reforms following the Cultural Revolution,[8] but it is not known whether any form of coordinating organization replaced it.

The MFT has under its jurisdiction three principal administrative systems that reach down to the local level. The first is the administrative organization of the MFT itself, consisting of foreign trade bureaus in each province, and departments or administrative offices in those of the smaller territorial units. There are also believed to be bureaus in many of the more important ports and border railheads, and it was reported in 1963 that there was in Canton the office of a special commissioner empowered to take major decisions on the spot, an office that may well be of special importance (and perhaps only then is fully staffed) during the Kwangchow Spring and Autumn Commodities Fairs.

These local foreign trade organs are jointly controlled by the MFT at the center and the local government in which they are located. They are in this sense typical of the whole Chinese system of local administration, and as with other branches of that administration, there is considerable uncertainty outside China how far decisions are taken at the center and how far they are local, though it is known that since 1957 a policy of decentralization of many aspects of economic control has been pursued fairly consistently.[9]

Besides the foreign trade organs proper, the MFT is at the head of a family of foreign trade corporations, the agencies that actually carry on foreign trade business with both domestic and foreign partners; they are described in more detail below. The MFT also controls the Maritime Customs, a network of bureaus and subordinate offices that are situated not only in administrative centers where foreign trade is of importance but also in ports and at border points where they can carry out their primary function, physical control of the import and export of goods.

The MFT controls various other institutions, of which the most directly important to the foreign trading partner is the chain of China Commodity Inspection Bureaus (CCIB), which, with their subbureaus, are established at the principal import and export points. The whole chain is subordinate to a General Bureau within the MFT.[10] The list of commodities subject to compulsory inspection by the CCIB and the official rules and standards used for inspection of goods are laid down centrally by the MFT. Other subordinate bodies include the Foreign Trade Institute (believed to be concerned with teaching and research) and, it is said, a market research institute.[11]

Foreign trade research and planning in the realm of technology and technical cooperation is outside the competence of the MFT, for it is an integral part of the functions of the State Scientific and Technological Commission (SSTC). However, while the SSTC has the responsibility to "develop international technological interchange and technical cooperation," the MFT "shall continue to have the responsibility for organizing the work of foreign negotiations regarding international technological exchange and technical cooperation."[12] This quoted provision is a good illustration of the role of the MFT as a mere external representative in respect to some aspects of Chinese foreign trade policy. In other fields, it is the the prime mover. In the major commodity trades, for example, the organs or corporations of the MFT have frequently acted directly within the internal economy in the ordering and purchasing of goods for export and sometimes the organizing of new lines of production.[13]

The China Council for the Promotion of International Trade (CCPIT)

In form the CCPIT is an autonomous corporate body, which legally does not form part of the government hierarchy. In the past, it has been responsible for the opening of trade contacts with countries that have no relations with China, for exchanging commercial delegations, and where appropriate for concluding unofficial trade agreements with similar bodies in such countries. Over the years, however, the CCPIT has come to assume wider and more permanent functions. It acts as the initiator of unofficial Chinese commercial delegations going abroad and as host to similar delegations coming to China. It also makes arrangements for Chinese participation in foreign exhibitions and trade fairs and assists groups of foreign companies in holding fairs in China. The CCPIT has proved an appropriate organization to conclude agreements (for example, as to trade fairs) with nongovernmental representatives of the business community in other countries, such as trade councils and chambers of commerce. In some respects the CCPIT itself fulfills the functions of a chamber of commerce. It has sometimes undertaken certain promotional functions, such as producing the magazine Foreign Trade of the People's Republic of China,[14] and it has occasionally sponsored publication of books on foreign trade subjects.[15]

The CCPIT includes in its organization the two arbitration bodies to which Chinese arbitration clauses make reference, the Foreign Trade Arbitration Commission (FTAC) of the CCPIT and the Maritime Arbitration Commission (MAC) of the CCPIT. The Legal Department of the CCPIT acts as secretariat for both the FTAC and the MAC. The CCPIT is also the body to which reference is made in standard Chinese foreign trade contracts as the competent body to issue force majeure certificates.

Finally, under Article 15 of the Detailed Rules for the Implementation of the Regulations for the Control of Trademarks,[16] the CCPIT acts as an agent for foreign companies wishing to register trademarks in the PRC.

Foreign Trade Enterprises

The great majority of China's foreign trade is conducted exclusively through the state-owned foreign trade corporations established for this purpose under the aegis of the MFT—presently nine in number.

In addition to these trading companies, there are two corporations under the MFT that are concerned with the transport of foreign trade goods, the China National Chartering Corporation and the China National Foreign Trade Transportation Corporation.

Three other Chinese state enterprises are also closely involved in external trade: the Guozi Shudian (China Publication Center), the China Film Distribution and Exhibition Corporation, and the China Stamp Export Corporation. These bodies do not belong to the foreign trade system proper, for the commodities they handle are deemed to be cultural rather than commercial in character. In the conduct of their commercial relations overseas, however, they appear to conform to the practices laid down for organizations subject to the MFT.[17]

The foreign trade corporations have from the outset been organized as state enterprises. Like other state enterprises, they are endowed with juridical personality, enabling them to conclude contracts both with other legal or national persons within China, and also with persons outside China. Their contractual relations with other enterprises and organizations are governed by civil law and by the system of "economic accounting," which enables state enterprises to take part in economic activity as independent legal entities but at the same time ensures that such enterprises act in conformity with their obligations under the state plan.[18]

Most of the foreign trade corporations have establishments in several major cities, or places of particular significance to foreign trade.[19] Foreign businessmen are encouraged in many instances to negotiate and contract with particular branches rather than with the national company,* and in such cases payment is normally made for the credit of the branch.

The precise relationship of the branches to the corporations as a whole is difficult to determine; given the size of the PRC and the complexity of its economic and administrative system, it would not be surprising to discover that it varied from corporation to corporation, and even from place to place. There is little doubt that the national corporations have important coordinating functions—such as in adopting contract terms and conducting research into external markets and world prices—but it is much less certain whether they take final decisions over price and other conditions; nor is it clear how the central company is compensated for such services, if at all. What does seem clear is that it is the policy of the foreign trade authorities in the PRC to present the corporations to the outside world as single entities.

With certain very limited exceptions, the foreign trade corporations have no branches or representative offices overseas. It seems probable that one of the resaons why the PRC has not sought to extend its commercial contacts in this way is that it has attached great importance to avoiding so far as possible submission to the jurisdiction of the courts of foreign countries by any of its organizations.† It is therefore not surprising that the very few exceptions to this self-denying rule have been in Eastern state-trading countries.

Chinese foreign trade corporations have also been very slow to employ agents in foreign countries, though again a number of exceptions should be noted.‡ The most important are the networks of agencies and subagencies for the foreign trade corporations in Hong Kong

---

*The present writer's impression is that this tendency is more marked in the case of exports of agricultural produce and the products of rural and traditional industry than with sales of machinery and the like.

†This restriction has not prevented the Bank of China, which had overseas branches before the PRC's establishment in 1949, from continuing to operate successfully abroad. It has also not affected the strategy of the Hsinhua (New China) News Agency, which, perhaps taking courage from the decision in Krajina vs. TASS Agency (1949) 2 All E.R. 274, has established many offices abroad.

‡Of the foreign trade corporations proper, The China National Chartering Corporation has always employed brokers on the Baltic Exchange to see to its chartering requirements, and it also makes use of ship brokers in Hong Kong for the same purposes. The purchase of ships is also concluded by brokers. The Bank of China and the People's Insurance Company of China have a network of agency relations throughout the world.

and, to a lesser extent, Macao (both of which are considered by the PRC technically to be Chinese territory). In Hong Kong the most important agencies are the China Resources Company, the Teck Soon Hong, Limited, the Hua Yuan Company, and the Ng Fung Hong, all of which undertake representative, and to some extent agency, functions for both Chinese exports and imports. China Resources has been of major importance in China's trade with Western countries, though its special role in arranging large-scale and, in effect, intergovernmental transactions with countries that had no diplomatic relations with the PRC will clearly be of diminishing significance in the future.

Lastly, the foreign trade corporations are represented in fact, though probably not in law, by particular members of the commercial staffs of Chinese diplomatic missions overseas. In the larger missions, there is at least one office to look after the interests of each corporation. While they are in the host country, these persons are, of course, diplomatic officers, but they appear to carry out many of the functions of ordinary commercial representatives. It is believed, however, that they are not normally authorized to conclude contracts, though there have certainly been exceptions of this rule, if indeed it can be described as such.[20]

Within China, the corporations act, in effect, as agents of the various Chinese organizations that have export goods to sell or import requirements to fulfill. Whether they are agents in a precise legal sense must presumably depend on the facts of each particular transaction.

As state enterprises, the foreign trade corporations are expected, to an extent that varies from time to time, to cover their expenses and to make a profit, which must come from the margin between internal prices and the converted Renminbi (RMB) equivalent of the foreign contract price. Little is known of the precise way in which the corporations earn their profits, although there is some evidence to suggest that in situations when the role of the corporations approximates most closely that of the agency—namely in the import of machinery, whole plants, instruments, and industrial raw materials (all of which are ordered by or on account of an enterprise or institution)— they are paid the RMB equivalent of 2 or 3 percent of the cost by way of commission.* In other cases, it is said that internal prices are agreed on a country-wide basis between the corporations and the

---

*It is not clear whether cost in this instance is the c.i.f. price. If so, the import corporation would presumably have to recompense the China National Foreign Trade Transportation Corporation for its services in the procurement of shipping and insurance, as well as for the cost of those items.

Ministry of Commerce, with a factor for their own charges presumably included.[21]

Profits made by the corporations are handed over to the state. To what extent and in what way they are divided between the central and local (for example, provincial) organs of government is a matter for speculation; but it seems likely that provincial foreign trade companies are financially as well as operationally subject to the governments of their provinces.

Financial Institutions

The financial side of China's foreign trade is administered by a series of institutions separate from, though parallel to the MFT and foreign trade corporations, notably the Ministry of Finance (MF) and the People's Bank of China (PBC), the former primarily a fiscal department and the latter concerned with the banking and accounting activities of almost every sector of the economy.

The MF's position in the foreign trade system seems to be confined to authorizing the expenditure of state funds for the purpose of financing foreign trade and receiving by way of revenue the proceeds of the duty levied by the Maritime Customs, and such part of the profits of the foreign trade corporations as is handed over to the central government.

The People's Bank of China

The PBC combines the functions of a central bank with those of a nationwide banking system. Although it does not serve the whole economy in the latter capacity,* it is responsible for the monetary affairs of the whole of the industrial and commercial sectors, and it has extensive powers of financial supervision over the organizations to which it lends money, a fact that has been responsible at times for a certain amount of resentment.[22] Its control and supervision of the financial affairs of enterprises is all-embracing.

In the field of foreign trade the PBC acts in three capacities. As a central bank, it monopolizes the foreign exchange holdings of the PRC, operates the system of exchange control, and lays down exchange rates against various foreign currencies.† Once the annual

---

*The agricultural sector maintains its own banking and credit institutions.

†The exchange rate is fixed by notice of the PBC communicated to correspondent banks of the Bank of China (a subordinate institution of the PBC, described infra). A change in the rate, particularly against

and quarterly foreign exchange plans are settled, foreign exchange is released to the Bank of China for the accomplishment of the planned transactions.

Secondly, as a central bank, the PBC has responsibilities in the settlement of payments on a bilateral basis under trade agreements made between China and various other countries. Normally, in such agreements it is provided that the PBC and the central bank of the other contracting state shall make the necessary arrangements for a bilateral payments system.

Thirdly, the PBC, in its capacity as the banker to the Chinese foreign trade corporations in respect of their dealings inside the country, advances the necessary funds by way of loan to the corporations[23] and supervises their disbursement and eventual repayment. This aspect of its functions are carried out by the State Enterprises Department of the External Affairs Bureau of the PBC, a department that appears to exist chiefly to control the foreign trade corporations.

There are several Chinese banks operating outside the PRC as state-private joint enterprises. Of these the most important is the Bank of China, which among other things has specific responsibilities for foreign trade.

The Bank of China

The Bank of China is a state-private joint corporation, in which part of the capital is held by the PBC, while part is in the hands, supposedly, of private shareholders. At present, two-thirds of its authorized capital of 19.8 million yuan are said to belong to the government.* It is, however, in effect a wholly controlled agent of the PBC that chiefly functions in the field of foreign exchange and trade. The bank has a subsidiary in Macao and branches in Hong Kong, Southeast Asia, and London. As well as its function of carrying out the financial transactions in China's foreign trade and overseeing the monetary affairs of the foreign trade corporations, the bank has always been an important source of commercial, economic, and political information.

---

sterling and against the Hong Kong dollar, usually follows any devaluation or revaluation of a major world currency and more recently has followed major movements in floating rates. As a nonparticipant in the the IMF, the PRC has never considered itself tied to fixed parities by international obligation.

*According to its December 1971 balance sheet, the bank's total assets were 8,386,768,615.15 yuan, a sum in excess of 1 billion pounds at the rate of exchange then current.

Other Banks

Two British banks, the Hongkong and Shanghai Banking Corporation (incorporated in Hong Kong) and the Chartered Bank (incorporated in England), retain branches in Shanghai, which, although reduced to doing very little business in the Cultural Revolution, were more recently said to have substantial dealings in foreign exchange and trade finance.[24] Both banks are on the list authorized by the Bank of China to undertake financial business arising out of U.S.-China trade.

Insurance

The principal institution in this field is the People's Insurance Company of China, (PICC) a state enterprise that has its head office in Peking, with branches in many major cities. There are also two state private joint companies in the insurance field, China Insurance Company and Tai Ping Insurance Company, both of which have branches in Hong Kong and various places in South east Asia.

In the field of marine insurance the PICC insures both hulls and cargo and evidently employs only its own policy and clauses, which are a considerably modified version respectively of Lloyd's policy and the London Institute clauses. It seems likely that the policy is governed by Chinese law.[25] The other two companies, however, also often use policies of a standard English form, which are probably better known and thus more acceptable in the Southeast Asian ports where they chiefly operate. All these companies are believed to reinsure part of their foreign currency risks in Western markets.

Shipping Services

Chinese corporations, in their trade with Western countries, almost invariably insist on buying f.o.b. and selling c.i.f.[26] The only contracts known to the present writer that are exceptions to this rule are those in which the goods sold (for instance, certain chemicals) require carriage in ships of a very specialized kind. In the great majority of cases the whole shipping and insurance operation is arranged by the China National Foreign Trade Transportation Corporation which acts as agent for the foreign trade corporations and which is usually the party to be notified under the terms of the contract of sale.

Although China has for some years followed a policy aimed at self-sufficiency in shipping and has been building and purchasing tonnage at an increasing rate, the majority of her foreign cargo is still probably carried by foreign vessels. In some cases, these are liners operating regular services to Chinese ports; many others are under charter to the PRC, the charters being secured, normally through foreign agents, by the China National Chartering Corporation, a part of the foreign trade system.

The operational side of Chinese shipping activities, whether the vessel concerned is Chinese or foreign, is the responsibility of a number of state enterprises under the aegis of the Ministry of Communications. The most important of these bodies is the China Ocean Shipping Company, which is the largest operator of seagoing tonnage under the Chinese flag. Other services are performed by or through the China Ocean Shipping Agency,* a separate corporation that performs the very varied services normally provided by a ship's agent.

There can be little doubt that those countries that are linked to Chinese ports by regular liner services have definite trading advantages, in particular with regard to delivery dates, a factor that can have important implications in such major contracts as the supply and installation of whole plants.[27]

Foreign Trade Delegations

In the absence of more extensive informal contacts between China and other countries, the visits to China of foreign delegations, and even more important, the visits abroad of Chinese groups, provide almost the only opportunities (other than trade exhibitions) for direct inspection of the selling and purchasing opportunities available in the countries concerned. This is particularly important in technological fields, and it is no coincidence that the great increase in the number of Chinese technical delegations coming to Europe in the early 1970s has been accompanied by a similar increase in the purchase of important technology and equipment.

Official delegations are arranged through intergovernmental channels, while unofficial delegations are usually arranged on the Chinese side by the CCPIT, and on the foreign side by bodies representative of the particular industries and trades concerned or by special chambers of commerce or similar groups established for the purposes of trade with China.

Chinese Export Commodities Fair

A special feature of China's foreign trade is the Chinese Export Commodities Fair, held twice each year at Kwangchow (Canton), from

---

*A further organization of some importance is the Register of Shipping of the PRC, the Chinese ship classification organization, which also (like the CCIB in the field of import and export goods) has a monopoly of surveying work in China.

15 April to 15 May and from 15 October to 18 November. It is attended by large numbers of foreign and overseas Chinese businessmen, and in recent years, with a constant increase in the number and importance of China's commercial contacts, there has been a certain amount of overcrowding, with consequent difficulties for those trying to transact business. The authorities responsible for the management of the fair (it is jointly sponsored by the national foreign trade corporations) have recently expanded the accommodations available.

The fair is concerned with both imports and exports, although as its name implies it is specially designed to exhibit the ever growing range of Chinese products available for sale abroad (some products not for export are also shown). Businessmen anxious to negotiate contracts for sale to China often find the fair a convenient starting point for negotiations, which are frequently continued in Peking after the fair ends. An invitation to Peking in such circumstances is usually interpreted by foreign businessmen as an expression of serious interest on the Chinese side.

Role of Planning

Very little is known of the role of planning in present-day China, particularly as regards foreign trade. While there is no doubt that the PRC remains committed to the idea of planning as such, there are reasons for doubting that the attitude toward the planning process has remained stable in recent years.

In all probability, the center both coordinates the various foreign trade plans submitted annually by the provinces and also adjusts them by a consensus in the overall national interest. The larger a particular planned purchase is (for example, a complete plant), the greater is the probability that the center has the final decision, particularly having regard to the special responsibilities of the SSTC in planning of this kind.[28] As regards the import of machinery of a more general kind (and particularly transport equipment, such as trucks) the likelihood is that some sort of bargaining process between the center and the provinces produces an agreed annual plan.

If it is correct that the PRC has always sought to balance its imports against its exports, the annual foreign trade plan must be a somewhat provisional document, which can only crystallize during the course of the year as the actual foreign exchange balances become clear. The PBC's accounting procedure for foreign trade enterprise accounts calls for balance sheets to be drawn up promptly every month, a requirement probably in part due to the need to know the state of the nation's foreign trade figures.

On the basis of the annual foreign trade plan, quarterly plans are evidently prepared, within which the foreign trade corporations

401

(each of which has its own annual export and import plan) draw up their contracts with both domestic and foreign trading partners. The basic requirement of the foreign trade corporation, particularly with regard to export contracts, is to be sure that contracts made with the (foreign) buyer can be matched by performance of the contract made with the (domestic) producer. It is clear that this basic requirement, on which much of the PRC's excellent reputation for the performance of its trade obligations depends, can only be met by a particularly strict planning and contractual discipline,* which, it must be assumed, continues in force.[29]

An important element in the planning process is clearly the fixing of the price levels to be applied at the Export Commodities Fair, where the great bulk of China's export trade sales are initiated if not concluded. In all probability, the sales plans of the various corporations are approved in draft before the fair starts and only finally approved by the MFT after careful soundings of the market have been taken in the form of negotiations with the foreign traders. It is believed that this is the reason for the length of negotiations, in many cases, and for the well-known fact that a large part of the business of the fair is only finalized in the last few days.

FOREIGN TRADE PROCEDURES
AND PRACTICES

Importing and Exporting

Licensing. The import or export of all goods, unless specifically exempted by regulations of the MFT, requires an import license or export license, issued by the MFT or by a local bureau of foreign

---

*In a series of regulations made in 1960 on foreign trade payments, a number of provisions make it clear that a strict regime was the objective. One instance is the rule that suppliers of export goods could only receive payment where the goods had been delivered to the foreign trade corporation (unlike the usual case in Chinese domestic trade, where cash is paid against shipping or railway documents). On the other hand, a foreign trade corporation reselling imported goods to a domestic buyer is entitled to obtain cash against documents, though whether these are the international shipping documents, or fresh documents issued in respect of internal carriage, is not quite clear. If it is the former, and the goods are sold afloat to the end-user, the corporation would be able to generate a considerable amount of credit.

trade.[30] Prescribed forms must be submitted, in duplicate by the
foreign trade corporations and other state enterprises involved in
foreign trade, such as Guozi Shudian. Private individuals and foreign
merchants have to submit the applications in quadruplicate, however.
A single license can only cover a consignment of goods arriving at
a single port, since the authenticated license has to be presented to
the Maritime Customs at the port as authority for releasing the goods.
Where there is no license, or where the license has expired, does not
tally with the other documents, or is otherwise invalid, the Customs
may detain the goods. The goods exempted from licensing are listed
in two lists, one for imports and one for exports.[31]

The law relating to trade samples and promotional materials,
incorporating the exemptions noted above, is further elaborated in
the more detailed special provisions of the Maritime Customs Regulations for the Inspection and Control of the Import and Export of Samples
of Goods and Advertising Materials.[32]

The Tariff. The Import and Export Tariff of the Maritime Customs
of the PRC was first brought into operation by decree of the (former)
Government Administration Council on 16 May 1951. The most recent
edition available in the West, incorporating amendments up to 1 July
1960, was published in 1961.[33] It is divided into 17 major sections,
89 sections, and comprises 939 items, some of which are subdivided.
The import tariff is divided into two rates of duty, a general rate and
a lowest (that is, MFN) rate. In the majority of cases the general
rate is 25-30 percent higher than the lowest rate, but in the case of
some luxury items the general rate is 100 percent higher.[34]

The number of items attracting an export tariff is very small,
the principal examples being two kinds of groundnuts,[35] which are
rated for export at 15 percent, and peppermint oil and menthol, both
rated at 20 percent.[36] It is not known why these commodities have
been singled out for special treatment.

The exact economic function of tariff controls, since all foreign
trade enterprises were either under state control or state-private
joint management, is not easy to determine. It is arguable that the
principal object of maintaining the tariff structure in the state-directed
economy was to provide a weapon for negotiating for MFN treatment
in other countries, but it seems doubtful whether this can be the only
reason. Its significance may well lie in its contribution to the revenue
of the central, as opposed to local, government.[37]

The responsibility for administering the tariff and collecting
the duty falls upon the Maritime Customs.[38] The Customs has the
power to apply tariff designations to items not included in the existing
classification.[39] Duty is charged ad valorem on the c.i.f. value of
imported cargoes,[40] and the Customs may estimate the value in the

absence of satisfactory proof. Import duty may be reduced or exempted where cargo is damaged or lost,[41] but otherwise exemptions or reductions can be granted only in accordance with specific government decrees.[42] Where export goods are made substantially of imported raw materials on which duty has been paid, a drawback may be allowed.[43] Whether the general rate or preferential rate is applied depends on the existence of a trade agreement with the country of origin.[44] Goods imported as samples or for exhibitions may be exempted from duty on condition that they are reexported within six months, or such other period as is laid down by the Maritime Customs; should they not be exported within this period, duty is payable.[45] Advertising matter, however, and free samples for distribution that have no other use and no commercial value will be exempted from duty altogether.[46]

Where goods are imported under contract by the foreign trade corporations, the Maritime Customs also has the responsibility of assessing the goods for the payment of the "consolidated industrial and commercial tax."[47]

Customs. The Maritime Customs of the PRC is a uniformed service under the control of the MFT. Its principal function is the physical control of goods and currency across the national borders, which it exercises under the authority of the Provisional Maritime Customs Law of the PRC[48] and a substantial body of subsidiary legislation. With regard to foreign trade, its principal functions, the control of goods in accordance with the licensing system, and the assessment and collection of duty in accordance with the tariff, have been described above. There are, however, many other specific regulations with which the Maritime Customs is concerned that may affect foreign trade, such as the legislation that controls the export of antiquities[49] or the import of films.[50]

One particular responsibility of the Maritime Customs that is of general importance to foreign trade is the obligation to examine cargo for loss, damage, or defective packing and to make reports thereon, a function that can be of considerable importance where cargo or insurance claims are concerned.[51]

Credit, Banking, and Foreign Exchange
System

Credit. Since the completion of the repayment of the early Soviet loans in 1965 the Chinese leadership has again and again reiterated the importance, both political and economic, of avoiding foreign indebtedness.[52] This policy of self-reliance has thus far prevented the PRC from contracting further long-term external debts. Foreign trade, as far as possible, has been balanced, so that imports have been paid for, where possible, by exports.[53] In some years (notably 1967), imports have visibly exceeded exports, but China has generally made efforts in succeeding years to correct the imbalance.

Since 1970, however, the dramatic expansion in Chinese imports of major capital equipment, together with the interest shown by Chinese trade officials in purchasing further major items in the near future have made it clear that substantial lines of credit will be required by the PRC.

It is perhaps worth emphasizing that the policy of self-reliance has not been formally abandoned, and Chinese officials are not prepared to admit that loans of a conventional kind have been contracted. Up to mid-1973, the majority of large purchases were probably being financed by "seller credit," the Chinese importers paying on deferred terms with an interest factor either incorporated into the contract price or separately stated.* There is every reason to suppose that this type of arrangement will continue to play the most important part in China's arrangements to finance foreign trade, though its attractiveness for her trading partners must depend on many other financial factors.

Since mid-1973, however, it seems that China may have started to make use of a somewhat different facility, "deposits" in foreign currencies by Western banks with the Bank of China in Hong Kong. It has been suggested in one report that the deposits were for three years initially, with an interest rate of 6 percent, and that "roll-over" facilities would be available if required by the Chinese side when repayment becomes due.[54] The fact that they have been made is an indication that the PRC is gradually starting to participate in normal international banking arrangements.

Banking. The banking arrangements that have been used in the PRC's foreign trade since 1949 have been both varied and highly complicated, as a result, chiefly, of the need to develop different techniques to deal with capitalist and socialist trading partners and with states that recognized the PRC and states that did not. A full consideration of China's payment system is beyond the scope of the present discussion, since in East-West trade it may be expected that, at present, most transactions will be financed on the private level.[55]

---

*It is believed that China attaches great importance to the way in which this type of arrangement is described. Chinese bank officials have reacted sharply to suggestions that deferred payment terms are in reality a form of loan or credit.

In China's trade with most Western countries (in contrast to its trade with other areas), over-all settlement arrangements have not played a major part. Financial terms have been incorporated into the various individual contracts. At the present time, the standard-form contracts used by China's foreign trade corporations usually call for settlement by an irrevocable letter of credit, issued through one of the increasing number of banks that have correspondent relationships with the Bank of China.* Chinese buyers in particular tend to insert very strict terms of payment, the letter of credit being opened after presentation of a minutely specified set of shipping documents and being payable against drafts. The letters of credit used by the Bank of China and other Chinese banks overseas are of the usual international types.

It is not easy to generalize as to the currency used in Chinese payments. Normally payment is effected in one of the major European currencies, of which sterling is the most used, but since the mid-1960s the Chinese foreign trade corporations have become increasingly enthusiastic about the use of the Chinese (RMB) as a currency not of settlement but of account. As a result, foreign importers requiring RMB for settlement purposes have in recent years been able to buy it up to six months ahead of time from the Bank of China branches outside the PRC itself, as well as from the bank's various associated banks in Hong Kong and Southeast Asia. A copy of the contract is usually required by the Chinese bank before purchases of forward RMB are permitted, it being the policy of the PRC to prevent speculation abroad in the national currency as far as possible. In fact where purchases of this kind are made, the RMB is, once again, merely the unit of account. In Hong Kong, for example, a foreign purchaser of forward RMB would pay for it in Hong Kong or other currency; on withdrawal, he would be paid once more in Hong Kong or other currency, but in accordance with the prevailing RMB rate.

Exporters to China who earn RMB in the country may open an internal Chinese account and retain their currency unconverted, for use subsequently.

Except in the now somewhat unusual case just described, the Chinese foreign trade corporations must have access to foreign

---

*A recent significant addition to the list is the Chase Manhattan Bank, the first American bank to open such a direct link since the relaxation of the U.S. trade embargo against China. The arrangement probably signifies Chinese willingness to use U.S. dollars for the purposes of trade settlements, though it was said by Chase Manhattan that at present the correspondentship would only relate to individual transactions. (Financial Times, 4 July 1973.)

exchange to pay for their own purchases. It is the function of the Bank of China, under the supervision of the PBC, to provide the foreign currency required for settlement of each transaction of the foreign trade corporations.

Exchange Control. The banking arrangements discussed above illustrate the working of the Chinese foreign exchange control system. In monetary matters, the separation of the internal from the external economy is almost complete, and rigid controls both within the banking and foreign trade systems (and also of the actual movement of currency) are designed to maintain this barrier. The few remaining foreign banks, for instance, are under rigid supervision, and virtually all foreign trade transactions are passed through and monitored by the Bank of China or one of its subsidiaries. Regulation of the access to foreign exchange reserves by the corporations is secured by the requirement that transactions conform to the foreign trade plan of the MFT and to the foreign exchange plan drawn up by the MFT, the MF, and the PBC to enable the foreign trade plan to be carried out. Transactions outside either plan require special permission.

The main legislation to establish the exchange control was introduced soon after the establishment of the PRC.[56] In 1956 the PBC introduced rules to enable both residents and nonresidents of China to establish accounts in China in foreign currency.[57] Under these regulations, two types of account were established, to serve residents of China and nonresidents, respectively. Of these types the nonresident or "external" account ("A" account) appears to have fallen into disuse inside China,[58] presumably because few people resident abroad wish to maintain convertible RMB accounts within China, particularly when the main advantages of such an arrangement can be obtained from an account with the Bank of China or one of its associated banks in Hong Kong denominated in RMB. However, it would seem that in an appropriate case, a nonresident could be allowed to open a "B" account within China with funds primarily intended to be utilized within the country. Having regard to the organization of the foreign trade system, however, it is unlikely that such an arrangement would be required, or authorized, in the ordinary course of East-West trade.

Western Access to the Chinese Market

Advertising. There is in theory no reason why Western companies should not purchase advertising space in Chinese newspapers and periodicals, and in the period before the Cultural Revolution such advertisements occasionally appeared. Advertisements were placed exclusively through three agencies.[59] Advertising space was generally very limited, because Chinese publications do not depend for their existence on advertising, and such space as was for sale was sought after for official and other local advertisements. Spaces available were usually rather small.

As far as is known, no advertisement space in newspapers or magazines has been made available since the Cultural Revolution. Advertising on radio, television, or in the cinema is unknown.

Engaging Local Agents. Although enterprises in China make agency arrangements with one another for various commercial purposes within the internal economic sphere, they do not accept agency business from foreign companies. The foreign trade corporations themselves act as agents for their various enterprise customers within the internal economy, and are thus obviously unable to undertake such duties for their Western trading partners. Since the closure of the last Western trading company's office in 1962, the only effective Western commercial representatives resident in China are the offices of certain foreign banks.

It is accordingly not possible to establish conventional agency arrangements inside China. It should be borne in mind, however, that some of the larger trading companies of Hong Kong and Japan have personnel traveling in and out of the country with such frequency that they are represented there on a virtually permanent basis.

Any individual citizen of the PRC, whether an official or not, who entered into a private arrangement with a foreign company to act as its agent would expose himself to grave political and legal risks, particularly if in the course of his activities as an agent he procured economic or commercial information for his principals.[60]

Establishing Local Offices. There is probably no definitive reason in law why a foreign corporation could not establish a branch office in the PRC,* or even incorporate a privately owned enterprise, since none of the various forms of corporate organization that are to be found on the Chinese statute book[61] specifically exclude foreign capital participation. In theory, indeed, as the law stands, it would be possible to form a state-private joint enterprise in which a foreign partner provided the private investment element, although the degree

---

*Chinese law recognizes the corporate status of foreign companies within its legal system and accords them legal capacity, for example to own various forms of property in China, tangible and intangible. See, for example, Article 12 of the Regulations for the Administration of Trademarks, 10 April 1963 (13 F.K.H.P. 162) which clearly recognizes such proprietary rights. However, to license such a corporation to trade within China is a different matter altogether.

of control exercised by the state side according to the regulations for such enterprises would make it unlikely that a foreign investor would regard such a company as a serviceable corporate vehicle for a joint venture in the Western sense.[62]

However, at each stage in the formation, registration and licensing for operation of all the various forms of enterprise or organization known to the law of the PRC since 1949, there is a requirement for a government permit, in the granting or withholding of which the authorities clearly have the fullest discretion. At present the policy of the Chinese Government appears to be wholly opposed to the establishment of branches, representative offices, or any other form of corporate presence on Chinese territory. The few offices of foreign enterprises that now operate in China are either survivals from the past or the more recently established offices of representatives essential to the operation of airlines that have traffic rights in the PRC. There is no sign at present of any expansion of this very restricted category.

FOREIGN TRADE CONTRACTS

Introduction: The Extracontractual
Relationship

In theory the legal problems that surround transactions between the Chinese corporations and their foreign trading partners are legion. In practice, however, as Chinese officials concerned with foreign trade like to point out, it is only very rarely that problems of this kind give rise to serious difficulties.[63] The great majority of the multitude of individual transactions that together comprise China's trade with the West are completed without serious problems. If a statistical comparison were possible, there is no reason to doubt that the record of the PRC would compare favorably with that of many other countries as regards the discharge of its contractual obligations.

The foreign trade corporations, it is true, have acquired a reputation for driving hard bargains, and those who regularly deal in those commodities of which the PRC is a major producer have good reason to admire the skill with which Chinese negotiators work to secure the most favorable possible terms for their country. Once a contract is concluded, however, the Chinese corporations have a reputation for performing their obligations promptly and scrupulously. Although the Chinese corporations often have difficulties in delivering their exports on time, the goods they deliver are almost always of the standard and quality specified in the contract and well packed. Most buyers could ask for little more.

It would be wholly wrong to assume, then, that the absence of a more conventional legal regime for trade between China and the West is, in normal circumstances, an obstacle to commerce. A further feature of Chinese practice that requires mention in this connection is the importance attached by the officials of the foreign trade corporations to the establishment and continuation of long-term relationships with particular foreign companies and individuals. Expressions of long-standing cooperation, mutual respect, and friendship, which are from time to time made by Chinese communist officials, are sometimes regarded by Western businessmen as of little more practical importance than mere courtesies; they should in reality be highly prized, for it is precisely with companies that they know well that Chinese officials feel most secure in dealing. An obvious illustration of this policy, which is familiar to countless Western businessmen who regularly go to the Export Commodities Fair is the length of time required to establish a full trading relationship: The first or even the second visit to Canton is often disappointing for the representatives of new companies entering the China trade, even though they may be seeking nothing more than to purchase well-established Chinese export commodities. Gradually, however, as companies and individuals become well known at the fair, their business becomes more and more satisfactory in terms of scale and, even, on occasion, of price. On the other hand, companies that attempt to conclude single, large-scale purchases of Chinese commodities, even on apparently very profitable terms from the Chinese point of view, evidently have little attractiveness for the corporations. (As will become clear, it is precisely this kind of transaction that is most likely to strain the legal framework within which it is carried out.)

To those familiar with trade between China and the West, there will be nothing new in these observations, and, indeed, they would be trite were it not for the great emphasis put on such relationships in Chinese trade practice. It is fair to say that only within these continuing larger extracontractual relationships of mutual confidence that the details of contractual practice can be understood. In particular, the extracontractual relationship provides an extralegal framework within which adjustments may be made to compensate for failures in individual contracts without recourse to the making of a legal claim, far less to any dispute-setting machinery. In such cases, indeed, no "dispute" arises. Thus, for example, where a relatively minor shortage or quality defect occurs in a delivery under a Chinese export contract, if the buyer notifies the export corporation, and requests a settlement, the chances are that it will be made without difficulty in the course of negotiating the next contract, often by way of a price concession, but without any admission of fault on the Chinese side. A much less favorable atmosphere for settlement is created on the other hand if a legalistic point of view is adopted by the Western buyer—if a formal claim is made under the contract, or if the goods are repudiated* or payment is withheld, so that Chinese agreement to settle the claims becomes dependent on an admission, express or implied, of legal fault. Such further steps as resort to arbitration, even in accordance with a clause in the contract providing for arbitration in Peking, can have an even more serious effect on long-term relationships.

As a model or framework for the regulation of trading relationships, this system has a number of obvious advantages, and it has proved acceptable over the years to many companies doing substantial regular business with China. With some reservations, it has also proved acceptable to the banks and other institutions that underwrite this trade. It is, however, essentially a structure designed for what may be called the traditional sector of China's trade, that is, the regular, large-scale export of Chinese products and commodities, and to a more limited extent, the import of "run-of-the-mill" goods and commodities. It is, a priori, inapplicable to transactions that by their nature are unique or at least occasional. As Chinese technological capability and industrial capacity increase, the quantity and variety of regular exports of Western products will, with a few exceptions, tend to fall off. Western companies exporting to China will increasingly, therefore, have to search for other ways of establishing satisfactory relationships than the long-standing extracontractual relationships that are relevant to the commodity trades. The PRC, on the other hand, will increasingly have to establish trading relations with companies with which it has not had many, or any, previous dealings if it wishes to acquire their products or technology.

Terms of Contract

It is in this context that the legal aspects of Chinese foreign trade contracts must be examined. To many experienced importers of Chinese goods the whole legal aspect may appear as an academic exercise that has little or no relevance to their essentially simple transactions.† The exporter or would-be exporter of complicated

---

*In one known case of serious discrepancy between the goods and the contract description, refusal by the foreign buyer to take delivery has not impaired the extracontractual relationship.

†To others, it has proved all too important. Even allowing for instances of misunderstanding that might have been avoided, the number of cases of serious dispute over legal questions should not be minimized or forgotten. In many such cases before the Cultural

machinery or technology, however, has to contemplate a multitude of potential areas of misunderstanding or disagreement that would never occur to an importer, notwithstanding 20 years' experience in the purchase of dried eggs or tung oil.

One important feature of China's trade with Western countries has been the general absence of an over-all legal framework within which individual tarnsactions can take place, such as exists in the case of most of the PRC's trade with Eastern Europe,[65] as well as in the special case of Japan.[66] Although a party to certain public international conventions in the field of transport law,[67] the PRC has not thus far adhered to conventions that directly affect commercial law, and its long absence from the United Nations and UN agencies precluded Chinese participation in the formulation of sets of conditions equivalent to those adopted for East-West trade by the U.N. Economic Commission for Europe. Similarly, political problems long prevented Chinese participation in private bodies interested in the establishment of uniform trade practices, such as the International Chamber of Commerce.[68]

The various foreign trade corporations each have their own standard forms of contract for imports and exports. Those that relate to trade with the West* have been formulated entirely on the initiative of the Chinese side. Although modifications of these terms are not unusual in certain kinds of contract, the changes in the standard forms over the years † have tended to reflect unilateral decisions by the Chinese side, rather than a process of consultations or negotiations with representative bodies from other countries (a principal

---

Revolution, Western companies were obliged to waive fully justified claims in the interests of future business, a consideration that puts a slightly different light on the "extracontractual" relationship referred to above. Other cases led to a more or less permanent breach with the Chinese side, to attempts at arbitration, and even to litigation.[64]

*The corporations must have different forms to meet the requirements of trade with other socialist states, whether or not subject to internationally agreed conditions of delivery (though none have been reached the attention of the writer); and they have also in the past used separate standard forms for imports and exports under "private" trade and "agreement" or "memorandum trade" with various classes of Japanese companies. Separate forms have also been used in some trade with Chinese firms in Hong Kong and Macao, and these have been inspected by the writer.

†The earliest contracts within the author's experience date from 1958.

exception being Sino-Japanese trade, in which various sets of contract terms have been negotiated by commercial delegations of the two sides), and, given the continuing competition among Western countries for the Chinese trade, it is likely that this situation will not change.

Problems Arising from the Standard Forms of Contract

A detailed discussion of the terms that occur in these standard forms would require far more space than is here available. There is, in any event, some doubt how far valid generalizations may be made as to the meanings of these clauses when taken out of the context of particular transactions, or at any rate particular classes of transactions. It seems questionable, for example, whether a comparison of the wording (or even the application in practice) of two different force majeure clauses, one in an import contract for chemicals, the other in an export contract for tea, will yield a clear enough principle to assist the reader in considering a third formula adopted in a contract for the installation of a polymer plant.[69]

One of the facts noted by most observers is the marked difference between contracts in which Chinese corporations are sellers and those in which they are buyers. While the former tend to be simple statements of the terms of purchase, payment, and shipping, the latter usually contain formidable penalties and other conditions for noncompliance.[70] These inequalities could be multiplied, to include, for example, the most invariable rule whereby the Chinese corporations sell c.i.f. but buy f.o.b.; or the Chinese insistence on the inspection by the CCBI as the conclusive contractual determination of quality, a provision that has come to present special difficulties to sellers of intricate machinery or other products requiring special handling, deprived as they are by the f.o.b. terms of any control over ocean carriage and handling at the destination.

Many of the standard forms used in trade with the West are bilingual, in Chinese and English, but certain corporations issue some forms at least in English only. Where the form is bilingual, it sometimes has a clause providing that the two texts shall be equally authoritative but this is by no means always the case. However, it would seem that little turns on the insertion or omission of such a clause, for where there are two texts they would normally be construed together in any event. No instance is known to the writer of a clause providing that in case of doubt one of the languages should be authoritative; in this respect the policy of those corporations that use bilingual texts appears to be consistently in favor of putting both parties in an equal position as regards language.[71]

The language of the English text is very much in the mold of similar documents used elsewhere in the world, though the drafting, especially of export contracts, is less precise than might be desired. Many of the terms employed are expressions with a familiar meaning in English law, and hence with a familiar, if possibly less precise, meaning in the general usage of international trade. In those instances where there is an English text alone, the Chinese corporations are clearly content to rely on terms of this kind, without any attempt to impose on them a meaning drawn from Chinese notions of contract. Where, however, there is also a Chinese text, the question arises how far the notions of Chinese internal law must be imported into the construction of the contract, for many of the Chinese expressions used have a significance in Chinese domestic usage that does not necessarily correspond to the "internationally accepted" meaning of the English text.[72]

By way of example, Clause 13 of the purchase contract of the China National Chemicals Import and Export Corporation makes provision for the late delivery or nondelivery as a result of "generally recognized 'force majeure' causes . . .," an expression that is patently open to as many interpretations as there are such causes that may arguably be said to be included or excluded by the definition. The Chinese text of the clause is equivalent, save that the meaning of the expression for force majeure has slightly different connotations in Chinese domestic law.[73]

A particularly obvious gap in the provisions of these contracts is the lack of a choice of law clause. As a result of the PRC's political emphasis on equality between trading partners and between states, the Chinese foreign trade corporations will never subject their contracts to the law of their partner's country, and it is believed to be very rare indeed for the law of a third state to be expressly chosen as the governing law.* In many instances, however, the inference that would be drawn by a court in a foreign country that examined a Chinese standard form contract would probably be that the parties had by implication chosen Chinese law as the governing law. There are also indications that the arbitral tribunals in Peking, the FTAC and MAC, would start their consideration of such contracts from the assumption that Chinese law applies, though foreign usage might have persuasive force.[74]

---

*Provisions for arbitration in third states might prompt the arbitration to imply a choice of the law of the third state, as discussed in Chapter 20 of this study.

Chinese Internal Law of Contract[75]

Chinese law lays down no special rules, so far as is known, that govern the formation, construction, or discharge of foreign trade contracts as a class. So far as Chinese law may be held to apply to such contracts, therefore, they must be subject to the ordinary domestic law, which, with few exceptions, has no general rules applicable to all types of contract.[76] Instead, the precise terms of most Chinese contracts between enterprises are to be found in specific statutes that regulate a particular branch of the economy. In examining contract practice within the PRC, therefore, it seems prudent to avoid attempts to generalize and rather to consider different kinds of contracts under the separate headings of sale, supply, capital construction (for example, plant installation), personal service, transport, loan, and insurance.[77] Some basic rules are doubtless common to all of these clauses, such as the provision of Article 4 of the Provisional Contract Regulations: "The contents of a contract must be specific and precise, and in the interpretation of the text every effort shall be made to achieve certainty." Other equally basic provisions of the Provisional Contract Regulations, however, have been superseded in respect of particular classes of contract by the more detailed provisions of the relevant legislation.[78]

Reference to Chinese domestic law for guidance in the construction of foreign trade contracts is accordingly not always a simple matter quite apart from the difficulty of procuring the relevant texts. The different types of foreign trade contracts, insofar as they can be said to be equivalent to contracts within the internal economy, are likely to correspond in function to widely different classes of internal contract.

Within these limits, reference to the Chinese law seems reasonable. If, for example, a capital construction contract for which there are statutory terms in Chinese law lays down certain percentages by way of penalty for delay after the due completion date of an installation, there seems to be no reason why this standard should not also be regarded as reasonably suitable for application to a whole plant installation agreement concluded between the China National Technical Import Corporation and a foreign manufacturer. Similar considerations would apply with regard to internal supply contracts as setting standards for the construction of import contracts by, for example, the China National Machinery Import and Export Corporation.

Scope of Autonomy of the Parties

The law of the PRC appears to lay down no restrictions on the extent to which foreign trade corporations can vary the terms of their standard form contracts, and subject to political considerations, there would appear to be no rules of law that restrict the terms that they can negotiate in foreign trade contracts that do not adhere to standard forms. By and large, however, the corporations pursue a policy of requiring adherence to the unmodified standard forms; the principal exceptions are large-scale sales or purchases or other contracts of special importance or novelty, such as sales of complete plants. Even in the negotiation of large-scale or other special contracts, the foreign trade officials are by no means free to adopt any terms that they choose, for there are without doubt certain prescribed commercial and legal strategies to which all the corporations are expected to adhere in their foreign dealings, in the absence of special circumstances that doubtless have to be approved at a very high level. In general, the Chinese side appears concerned to avoid the creation of publicly known precedents for concessions of this kind, and contracts that contain important concessions are often made on the understanding that their contents are kept strictly secret.

Most of the problems that have been discussed above with regard to standard-form contracts are, in the context of run-of-the-mill trade, more theoretical than practical. In the preparation of very large-scale contracts, however, the greatest attention should be paid to every detail, and the foreign party or parties* will wish to guard against even theoretical difficulties as far as this is possible.

In practice, the most serious drafting problems arise not from the legal principles set out above but from the lack of close contact between the contractor and the end-user, the enterprise that ultimately is to use the equipment that is to be supplied. A lack of information as to the likely uses (and stresses) to which equipment may be subjected, to give an obvious example, many make it very difficult to insert the proper and highly necessary protections into the all-embracing guarantee clauses that the Chinese corporations customarily exact. Even more fundamental problems can arise in matters of design and installation as a result of inadequate knowledge of the terrain and of the human and other resources available for installation work. Once these questions are resolved (as far as they can be resolved within the present Chinese framework for dealing with foreign business) the preparation of detailed terms for the contract is far less difficult. When such terms clearly correspond to the technical needs

---

*It must be remembered that in a consortium contract, the terms of, for instance, a China National Technology Import Corporation Contract may ultimately become the subject of dispute between the Western partners.

of the project, moreover, the Chinese negotiators are normally more
than willing to be accommodating.

TRANSFER OF TECHNOLOGY; INDUSTRIAL AND INTELLECTUAL PROPERTY RIGHTS[79]

Since 1970, it has become clear that although dependence on
foreign ideas and techniques is still eschewed, the import (by purchase
or otherwise) of technology, with or without equipment, is playing an
increasingly significant part in the development and modernization of
all aspects of the Chinese economy.

Chinese Law of Property in Inventions

In the internal economic life of China, the notion that a design,
invention, or process that might be economically useful should exist
as a form of private property is subject to strong social disapproval.
From 1950 until 1963,[80] Chinese law protected private property in
inventions and patents, thus showing that as a matter of law such proprietary rights were recognized. After the virtual disappearance of
private enterprise from the industrial life of the country in the late
1950s, such provisions became irrelevant to the internal economy,
and the 1950 Regulations were repealed.[81]

They were replaced by the Regulations on Awards for Inventions,[82]
which appear still to be in force. For the purpose of the Regulations,
an invention[83] is defined as "a new achievement of science or technology which must at the same time satisfy the following three conditions:

(1) It must not have existed previously or if it existed in a foreign
country must not have been published;

(2) Its utility must be proved by practice;

(3) It must be advanced in relation to what exists at present."[84]

An invention that satisfies these requirements may be reported
in accordance with a statutory procedure and if it successfully under-
goes examination may be registered in the name of the person or
group of persons responsible for its introduction. After registration
a certificate of invention is then given to the applicant, together with
a monetary award, in accordance with a fixed scale, which divides
inventions, accordancing to their significance, into five classes. The
largest sum payable is 10,000 yuan, the smallest 500 yuan. However,
by Article 17 of the Regulations, it is also provided that inventions of
exceptional importance may be nominated by the State Scientific and

417

Technological Commission* for special award, subject to approval by the State Council.

The law lays down clearly that all inventions (including, it seems, those not registered in accordance with the Regulations) are the property of the state, specifically excludes the acquisition of a monopoly by individuals or "units," † and provides that all units throughout the country may employ any invention they may require. The state is also empowered to transfer inventions to foreign buyers, whether in the course of foreign trade or "for other reasons," in which case the transaction is effected by the Ministry of Foreign Trade with the approval of the State Scientific and Technological Commission.

It follows from this state monopoly of inventions that foreign companies or individuals are unable to acquire in China rights in respect of inventions analogous to patents in the Western sense. On the contrary, any patented technique or design, once available inside China, becomes the property of the state and (with certain exceptions on security grounds) is available for exploitation throughout the country.

Nevertheless, the foreign inventor may apply to be rewarded in accordance with the Regulations. Foreign "units" (an expression that includes commercial firms and corporations of all kinds) and individuals, as well as overseas Chinese, may apply for and receive rewards in accordance with the Regulations, applications being made in such cases directly to the Bureau of Inventions of the State Scientific and Technological Commission in Peking.

The Western owner of an invention, apparently regardless of whether he had patented the invention elsewhere, would by applying for a reward in China appear to accept the provisions of Article 23, whereby all inventions belong to the state, and of Article 25, which empower the state to sell inventions abroad. It is probable, by Chinese law, that all inventions that reach China, whether with or without the consent of the inventor and whether for a consideration or otherwise, become Chinese state property automatically, and as such they are no doubt subject to Article 25, but in the event that a Chinese corporation sold either the invention, or goods incorporating it, abroad, then the inventor would not be precluded from taking proceedings under any patent that he had obtained outside China. He might, however, by applying for registration and award under the Regulations, be said to

---

*A bureau at the ministerial level directly subordinate to the State Council. It exercises general control over the application of the Regulations.

†That is, corporations, cooperatives, or government organs.

418

approbate any subsequent dealing with the invention by the Ministry of Foreign Trade.

Secondly, although a foreign applicant is clearly entitled to bene- fit from the provisions of Article 17, allowing the commission to in- crease the award in a suitable case, there is no way of knowing, when the application is made, whether the commission will take a favorable view. Indeed there is no way of bargaining, as the Regulations stand, over the award to be given even under the prescribed table. Thirdly, even in the event that a substantial award were paid, it would appar- ently be paid in an unconvertible currency, and there is no certainty that exchange control permission would be given for export of the proceeds.

The only circumstance in which the Regulations might provide a useful device for a Western trading partner would be in the event that an invention was already being utilized in China, without any formal transfer of technology, for example, if a machine containing an original device had been copied in China without the inventor's agreement. In such case, assuming that the originality of the inven- tion could be established to the satisfaction of the State Scientific and Technological Commission, some compensation would presumably be payable. The foreign applicant would, in effect, have nothing to lose, and an application in China might offer a better chance of amicable settlement than, for example, an infringement action in a third country in respect of machines imported from China.

Transfers of Technology Outside the Law of Inventions

In the absence of any closer approximation to a patent system, most transfers of technology from Western countries to China will have a purely contractual character, rather than being transfers of legally recognizable property rights such as dealings in patents in Western countries. It is doubtful whether, as a matter of Chinese law, this is affected by the fact that many such transfers are drafted in the conventional way used for patent licenses, and that they are in the view of the foreign seller, dealings in patents; for a patent right can only exist, as a form of property, in a particular territory. In the great majority of cases, of course, the sale of technology is com- prised, often without any special terms, in a sale of some product, typically machinery, with which it is connected.

More sophisticated contracts for the supply of whole plants and so on call for much more elaborate "know-how" arrangements, some- times involving the exchange of personnel for training or installation purposes. In such cases, a payment has usually been made for the technology as such, either as an ingredient in an over-all price or as a separately calculated item. In some cases, separate collateral contracts have been signed with respect to know-how and design fees. It is asserted by one source[85] that in the majority of contracts for the purchase of whole plants in the 1960s, the know-how factor represented at least 10 percent of the purchase price.[86] In some cases, the agreement as regards technology has been verbal.[87] On the other hand, in a more recent instance, Western Union International, a United States company, sold the Chinese an earth satellite station for $4 million, in which the technology was reportedly supplied free of charge.[88]

An interesting variation of these arrangements occurred in the contract signed in January 1974 between Snam Progetti, an Italian state-owned engineering company of the ENI group, and the China National Technical Import Corporation for the sale to the latter of a process for the manufacture of polypropylene, which will be incorporated in a polymer plant to be designed and constructed by the Italian company in China. The process is the property of the Standard Oil Company of Indiana and was licensed to Snam Progetti for the purpose. Standard, however, will be responsible for the training of Chinese personnel.[89]

Until recently, it was unusual for a Chinese corporation to purchase technology without also buying equipment. In 1967 the French Berliet Company sold licenses to manufacture four different types of trucks to a Chinese corporation for a lump sum, without furnishing either plant or other technical assistance (both of which would have presented special problems in the political situation of that period). A number of other instances have been reported more recently,* and there seems every prospect that such sales will continue and perhaps increase in number and importance.

Contracts for sales of technology between Chinese and foreign trading partners normally contain restrictions on Chinese exports that cover both the products concerned and the technology.

Thus far, no instance has been reported of a transfer of technology in exchange for royalties, although most of the major purchases

---

*A particularly important projected sale is that of the right to produce the Rolls-Royce (1971) Spey jet engine. It is reported that the agreement sought by the Chinese side would expressly permit not only manufacture of the existing Spey but also the development, by China and for Chinese use, of further models and improvements, without any interference from the British sellers, thus acquiring, with the Spey rights, the basis for a gas-turbine aero-engine industry. At some point, independent development of this kind would probably have to be saleable outside China, a matter of some delicacy. Financial Times, 1 October 1973; see also Observer, 27 January 1974.

of technology, or of whole plants together with technology, have been
financed by deferred payments, normally up to five years.

Although royalties have not been agreed in purchases of technology, other forms of continuing arrangement have been reported.
Two Japanese food-processing companies are said to have entered
into technological exchange arrangements with Chinese corporations,[90]
and it is also known that companies that have provided technology are
often favored with subsequent orders for equipment, but no generaliza-
tion of the circumstances surrounding such arrangements seems apt.

An important element in any transfer of technology must always
be the restriction of further unlicensed transfers by the purchaser.
Such terms have been included in some of the larger sales of technology to China,[91] but they have required special negotiation in each
case. In the absence of such arrangements, it is believed that there
can be no question of any protection within China, having regard to
the nature of Chinese law and policy regarding inventions and copyrights (see below).

Copyright in Trade Between China and the West

The Chinese attitude toward industrial and intellectual property,
discussed above, applies, if anything, with greater force to publications.
Although individual authors within China may be rewarded for their
work, there exists no copyright as such, and any publication that
reaches China may, subject to the various laws regarding official
secrets and censorship, be reproduced, published, and distributed
within China without legal hindrance. Moreover, there are provisions
of law that specifically contemplate the photocopying for distribution
of selected books and journals of foreign origin and provide for the
deposit of a certain number of copies in central libraries.

It follows that any book, journal, or other writing, as well as
any map, plan, picture, or drawing that is exported to China must be
sent on the full understanding that within the country, there is no legal
restriction whatever on its duplication or resale.

It should also be noted, however, that in cases where Western
books have been translated and published in China without the consent
or knowledge of the Western publisher, the existence and ownership
of the foreign copyright has been marked on the fly leaf in the conventional way. Copies of such books that find their way out of China are
thus marked correctly, and any remedy that the copyright holder may
wish to pursue outside China is accordingly available to him.*

---

*This practice contrasts favorably with that of the previous
Chinese Nationalist Government, which permitted the publication of
translations without any acknowledgment of copyright.

Trademarks

The right to a trademark exists in the PRC solely by virtue of
its registration in accordance with the provisions of the Regulations
for the Administration of Trademarks[92] and of the rules made under
them.[93] Both the Regulations and the Rules are designed primarily
to apply to the registration of trademarks in China. As might be expected in the context of the Chinese state-managed economy, the object-
tives of the Chinese trademark system are rather different from those
of free enterprise countries. By Article 1 of the Regulations, the
legislation is intended to "strengthen administration of trademarks
and to encourage enterprises to guarantee and improve the quality of
their products." Article 3 defines a trademark as a "mark representing a fixed standard of quality" attaching to the particular product or
commodity to which it applies, and also makes provision for the supervision of this standard. A number of the other provisions of the Regulations and of the Rules are directed to the same end.

Special provision is also made for the registration of trademarks
in favor of "foreign enterprises." A foreign enterprise may only register a mark in respect of which it already had proprietary rights in
the country to which it belongs, and in making application for registration it has to furnish proof of such proprietorship by a copy of the
original registration. The spirit of the Chinese legislation is to recognize the validity and exclusiveness of foreign marks when used in
China, rather than to grant entirely new Chinese marks to foreign
applicants. As a result, not all the conditions relating to quality control that apply to marks registered in favor of Chinese domestic enterprises will affect the foreign proprietor's products, although there
might be circumstances in which a foreign enterprise (which could
probably include an organization designed to protect the quality of a
particular commodity) might regard it as advantageous to try to go
beyond what is required of foreign applicants by law by registering
a mark in conjunction with a product of a specified quality. Foreign
marks in the nature of "certification marks" might benefit from such
a strategy, as would marks related to products already made in Western countries to very precise specifications for special uses, such as
pharmaceuticals. It could only be beneficial to an exporter if the trademark under which its goods were sold came to be associated in the
mind of end-users, or of intermediate authorities involved in purchasing, with a precise standard of quality.

It is a condition of registration by foreign applicants that the
enterprise should "belong" to a state that, in the words of Article 12
of the Regulations, "has already reached agreement" on the reciprocal
recognition of trademarks with the PRC. Two questions arise from
this provision, the first regarding the meaning of "belonging" to a

particular state and the second the meaning of "reached agreement."
As regards the first, the Chinese expression used—literally translated
as the state to which the enterprise "belongs"—gives no indication as
to the precise nature of the connection between the foreign enterprise
and a particular state. However, the Rules provide some guidance,
for Articles 16 and 20 provide that an applicant shall lodge a "certificate of nationality" with the application, suggesting that nationality
would be conclusive on the question of "belonging." This construction
is supported by the text of one of the few explicit agreements concluded
between the PRC and a Western country regarding trademark protection, in which the protection is extended to the "citizens, commercial
firms and cooperative organizations of the other party."[94]

Assuming the provisions of Article 12 of the Regulations to refer
to nationality, the meaning of nationality when applied to a business
organization is always a matter of some doubt. In view of the requirement of a certificate, it seems likely that the test of nationality is,
prima facie, the place of incorporation, for the "certificate of nationality" can scarcely (in the case of common law countries at least)
refer to any document other than the certificate of incorporation.

As regards the second question, the requirement that an applicant's country must have "reached agreement" with the PRC in respect of mutual trademark protection is much less precise than the
wording of the equivalent expression in the earlier legislation, which
provided that an agreement must have been concluded between the
countries concerned. The change in wording suggests an intended
liberalization of the Chinese rules, which accords with the removal
of the requirement in the old law of diplomatic recognition between
the states. It seems quite possible therefore that an enterprise belonging to any state that has trademark legislation that would permit
registration of and afford protection to Chinese trademarks can effect
registration in the PRC, for the reciprocal functioning, in fact, regardless of express undertakings by the states concerned, might be
said to amount to the reaching of agreement by them, even though the
agreement was implied rather than expressed.

Certain words and designs, identical with or similar to the
symbols or flags of the PRC, other states, or the Red Cross or Red
Crescent cannot be used for trademarks. There is also a prohibition
on "words or designs that may have a politically undesirable effect."
A registrable mark must be in the Chinese language, although it is
probably unobjectionable for the foreign language of the original mark
to appear side by side with the Chinese.*

---

*It is not clear, in view of the wording of Article 5, but it is
understood that in practice the objection is not raised. English may
only be used on domestic marks if the goods concerned are for export.

A trademark only attaches to the class of products or commodities in respect of which it is registered. The classes of goods are set out in a table attached to the Rules, and a separate application for registration must be made in respect of each class. A registered mark can be extended to new kinds of goods within the same class by a simple permit, however.

Registration confers an exclusive right to the user within the territory of the PRC for a certain term prescribed in the grant, subject only to cancellation on certain grounds. The duration of a registration granted to a Chinese proprietor is unlimited, but for foreign enterprises a definite period must be designated in each case by the authority that grants registrations, the Central Administrative Bureau for Industry and Commerce (CABIC). This rule confers a discretion on the CABIC, designed to enable it to assimilate the Chinese registration to the terms on which grants are made in the country of the applicant, in order to ensure the greatest possible reciprocity.

Trademarks are within certain limits assignable, but assignment requires the consent of the CABIT in order to take effect. Applications made by foreign enterprises must follow an established procedure, laid down by the Rules. The application must be made to the CABIT by the Trademark Registration Department of the CCPIT, which acts as agent in all respects for the foreign enterprise. For this purpose the CCPIT must be given a power of attorney in the form prescribed, which must be executed before a notary, and, if executed abroad, legalized; similar formalities must be procured for the other documents required. The power of attorney evidently lapses as soon as registration is granted, for the same formal procedures attend applications for renewal, alteration, or assignment of the mark. Each transaction also attracts a modest fee.

COOPERATION AGREEMENTS AND JOINT VENTURES

Background

Up to the present time, those responsible for Chinese economic policy toward the West have shown little interest in any form of continuing partnership with foreign industry or commerce. The PRC has shown itself willing to make long-term or standing arrangements with Western financial institutions for cooperation in the provision of certain commercial services, principally banking and shipping, but, presumably in furtherance of the policy of self-reliance, cooperative arrangements with manufacturers have been avoided.

During the earliest days after the proclamation of the People's Republic, four joint enterprises were established by agreement between the Chinese and Russian governments. Although little is known of either the structure or activities of these four companies, it appears that they were owned by the partner countries in equal shares, so that the USSR was the joint owner of four important enterprises functioning in Chinese territory.* The experiment, which was considered by the Chinese side to operate very much to the advantage of the Soviet Union, was brought to an end in 1954.

An agreement was signed in June 1951 for the establishment of a Sino-Polish Joint Stock Shipping Corporation.[95] Little is known of its corporation organization, but it appears to be a creature of public international law rather than municipal law. It continues to play a significant part in the provision of shipping services between China and Europe. A similar organization was established between China and Albania in December 1961, which is also evidently still functioning, although its operations are on a smaller scale than the Sino-Polish Corporation. Finally, a Sino-Tanzanian Maritime Transport Joint Stock Company was established by a series of agreements in July 1966 and thereafter, to operate a joint shipping service between Chinese and Tanzanian ports. Once again, the company is of an international character, though as with the other two shipping companies, its vessels are registered in one of the two countries concerned and form a part of the national fleet.

Cooperation Agreements

In the commercial and industrial sphere, there are thus far very few known examples of agreements for technical or commercial cooperation between Chinese enterprises and Western companies. One obvious problem of policy for the Chinese side in contemplating the establishment of such arrangements in the future would be the requirement for a permanent relationship between a foreign company and an enterprise functioning purely within the Chinese internal economy.

The only known cooperation agreements operating at present may illustrate the point. According to one report,[96] two Japanese foodstuffs firms signed long-term cooperation agreements with China (presumably with the China National Cereal, Oils, and Foodstuff Import and Export Corporation). In one of these, QP, a major Japanese foodstuff company, undertook to supply Japanese strawberry seedlings in exchange for the Chinese-grown crop from these seedlings. Clearly,

---

*It is believed that the corporations were, however, international and were not formed under the law of the PRC.

the Chinese foreign trade corporation would not itself perform the operations of planting, growing, and harvesting the crop, but it may be remarked that these are all functions that can be easily enough discharged by a subcontract between the corporation and a Chinese agricultural unit, without the need for intensive or constant direct collaboration with Japanese personnel. (Some mutual consultation would most probably be required from time to time.) As regards the special transport equipment, this can doubtless be provided either by the Japanese side or by the corporation. It would seem, then, that few organizational problems are posed by this contract that would take it outside the ordinary course of Chinese import and export operations. It would be otherwise, however, with an arrangement that required the constant presence of foreign technicians in Chinese laboratories or vice versa. The problems that might arise in the latter case can only be gradually resolved, and it is likely that the experience gained in exchanges of personnel on a short-term basis for training under the various current contracts for transfer of technology will be examined carefully by the Chinese authorities with a view to further developments in long-term cooperation.

In July 1972 China expressed interest in acquiring information and assistance relating to advanced Japanese fishing techniques, but no details of subsequent developments have come to hand. It is significant, however, that at the same time at least one Japanese fishing company was given the right to trade its catch directly at Chinese ports. (South China Morning Post 12 July and 22 July 1972.) More recently, there have been reports that Chinese representatives have shown interest in purchasing helicopters from the United Aircraft Corporation, with engines to be supplied by Pratt and Whitney. According to "high sources" within United Aircraft, the Chinese interests, "extend to a co-production agreement," which "implies an assembly plant in China." (Times, 12 December 1973). Since the aircraft are to be used for border patrolling, there is a national security interest, which would probably take the decision of principle out of the hands of the ordinary foreign trade authorities in China, but it seems premature to comment further on a report that may still express more hope than probability.

Joint Ventures

No instance is recorded of Chinese participation in a joint venture of any kind with a Western company, either inside or outside Chinese territory, and since the policy of the People's Republic seems to be firmly opposed to the direct exploitation of the resources or labor of the Chinese people within Chinese territory by foreign capital, the prospects for the establishment of jointly owned enterprises inside the country seem to be slim. Equally, China has shown little interest in entrepreneurial activity abroad, and there is reason to believe that, with the exception of the various branches of the Bank of China established abroad, the government's policy is as opposed to investment and "exploitation" by the PRC in foreign countries as it is to the converse in China.*

An apparent exception to the policy just stated might be the various enterprises operated in Hong Kong. In a significant number of cases, it would seem that both Chinese Government and local private interests are in collaboration in what is, in effect, a joint venture. Such ventures may be found in the fields of import and export, shipping and chartering, storage, and wholesale and retail marketing.

It seems doubtful, however, whether in Chinese terms these enterprises represent a true exception in principal to the general policy, for in accordance with the Chinese view they are incorporated in Chinese territory (albeit in accordance with alien law provisionally in force there), and other than the Chinese Government or its nominees, the shareholders are Hong Kong or overseas Chinese, who for certain purposes, at least, are deemed to have Chinese nationality, enjoy a privileged status under the Chinese Constitution,[97] and have been allowed within certain limits to invest in Chinese domestic enterprises.[98]

SETTLEMENT OF FOREIGN TRADE DISPUTES

Chinese Policy Toward Dispute Settlement[99]

In the field of dispute settlement more than any other, the PRC has adopted legal strategies deliberately designed to exclude from its foreign trade arrangements the institutions familiar in Western countries. In particular, the Chinese state-trading corporations have consistently sought to avoid situations that might involve them in litigation before the courts of other states, particularly as defendants.[100] In some countries they are assisted by the application of the doctrine

---

*A recent proposal to open a department store in Tokyo dealing only in Chinese goods made by a visiting Japanese delegation in Peking met with a very cautious response. The report (by the Kyodo Agency) continued: "It was believed that since the Chinese Government does not authorize joint ventures with foreign business interests Chinese capital participation would be impossible." (Japan Times, 5 September 1973.)

of state immunity to state-trading organizations.[101] Elsewhere they have been less successful, notwithstanding vigorously expressed pleas of immunity.[102] With the exception of the banks and insurance companies, none of the foreign trade corporations has branches or representative offices in countries where the jurisdiction of the courts might be invoked against it by Western trading partners, and as far as possible Chinese agency arrangements abroad are made in such a way as to avoid possible subjection to foreign jurisdiction by joinder of defendants.[103]

The Chinese dislike of litigation in foreign courts[104] is extended also to foreign arbitral tribunals.[105] China might in the long run be prepared to accept bilateral East-West trade agreements providing for arbitration in the defendant's country, an arrangement that clearly provides for formal equality between the two sides. (Such arrangements have been common in the various "conditions of delivery" agreed between the PRC and various East European states. They have also been inserted in Sino-Japanese agreements.) At present, however, in the great majority of cases, China pursues a now well-established policy of insisting, so far as possible, on arbitration in Peking in all events. Most of the standard forms of contract employed by the foreign trade corporations incorporate a Peking arbitration clause, and only in circumstances where the Western partner has strong negotiating advantages is it possible to displace such a provision.* In such cases China usually favors arbitration in Stockholm or Zurich under local rules, though on occasion other venues have been agreed to.† Such provisions are usually to be found in major contracts, such as the installation of whole plants, or in contracts for the sale of advanced equipment that the Chinese side is particularly anxious to acquire.

Economic Disputes in China Generally

The formal system of people's courts is not much used in China for the settlement of commercial disputes, either in internal or external trade. This is not to say that they are lacking in jurisdiction,

---

*In chartering vessels, on the other hand, the China National Chartering Corporation, while always endeavoring to secure Peking arbitration, is often obliged by market conditions to accept Baltic arbitration.

†For example, arbitration by a foreign diplomat in his legation in London, evidently in an attempt to escape the application of English arbitration law, which permits recourse to the ordinary courts.

for the Constitution of 1954,[106] and the Organic Law of the People's Courts,[107] which was enacted in pursuance of the Constitution, both confer on the people's courts a very wide jurisdiction in civil as well as criminal matters. Moreover, a number of statutes that regulate internal commerce have expressly conferred jurisdiction on the people's courts, particularly in the field of transport. It seems, nonetheless, that the Chinese leadership has in general preferred to settle disputes between state enterprises by less formal means.[108]

Thus, the courts—although in principle available to foreign litigants in commercial as in other disputes—are in practice so little used for commercial litigation of any kind as to be in all probability unsuitable for the determination of foreign trade problems. In their place, the PRC has established two arbitral commissions, the Foreign Trade Arbitration Commission of the CCPIT (FTAC)[109] and the Maritime Arbitration Commission of the CCPIT (MAC).[110]

Although acceptance of their jurisdiction normally operates to oust the jurisdiction of the courts both in China and elsewhere, they are evidently not wholly independent of the people's courts. In the first place, as their respective regulations make clear, they depend in the last resort on the courts for the enforcement of their awards. Secondly, it would appear that in certain instances (considered below) the courts have a power to intervene in foreign trade disputes without regard to the arbitration clause.

Before turning to a discussion of the FTAC and MAC, mention should be made of provisions in various statutes connected with foreign trade for the settlement of disputes arising out of "vertical" relationships—that is, between enterprises (whether Chinese or foreign) and the various administraitve organs of the government. Thus, Article 8 of the Trademark Regulations provides that an applicant who is dissatisfied with the rejection of an application for registration of a trademark may appeal against the decision within one month, whereupon the application will be reconsidered. Article 9 of the Provisional Regulations on the Inspection and Testing of Import and Export Commodities lays down a procedure both for retesting or reexamination if objection is taken to the first result, and if the objection is still maintained, for review by a special adjudicatory committee.[111] All of these procedures may in certain circumstances be of importance to foreign trading partners of the PRC.

Foreign Trade Arbitration Machinery

There has been remarkably little discussion in Chinese legal books or periodicals of the two arbitral commissions of the CCPIT,[112] and little is known in the West of their practice or jurisprudence.[113] Moreover, as a result of the marked preference of Chinese corporations for settling disputes informally rather than going to arbitration, it seems clear that the number of disputes in respect of which arbitral proceedings are started is comparatively small, and the number in which an award is finally given is smaller still. It follows that any attempt to analyze the machinery available for arbitration in China must be based very largely on the statutory texts that form the basis of the commissions' activities, amplified, where possible, from various oral sources.[114]

Both the FTAC and the MAC are founded on the statutory basis of a decision of the State Council. They are, however, established within the CCPIT, which as has already been seen, is a quasiprivate body. In pursuance of the powers conferred on it by the respective State Council decisions, the CCPIT has in addition made a set of procedural rules for each commission.[115] The respective statutory texts of the two commissions show great similarity. The jurisdiction of each commission is based in each case on the consent of the parties, which must be expressed in writing, though it is immaterial whether it is expressed in an arbitration clause of a contract or in a special submission agreement made either before or after the dispute occurs.

It would seem that notwithstanding the written consent of the parties, neither body is legally competent to undertake arbitration outside its statutory sphere of operation. In the case of the FTAC, the commission is empowered by the FTAC Decision, Article 1, "to settle such disputes as may arise from contracts and transactions in foreign trade, particularly disputse between foreign firms, companies or other economic organizations on the one hand and Chinese firms, companies or other economic organizations on the other." This definition is repeated in the FTAC Rules, Rule 2, with the addition of the following words:

> It may also exercise jurisdiction for the arbitration of similar cases arising between foreign firms, companies or economic organizations as well as between Chinese firms, companies or other economic organizations. Such disputes include all disputes arising from contracts for purchase or sale of merchandise in foreign countries or contracts for commissioning an agency to purchase or sell merchandise in foreign countries, disputes arising from transportation, insurance, safe keeping or delivery of the merchandise in question and disputes arising from other matters of business in foreign trade.

The first of these two sentences, besides permitting joinder of third or fourth parties to a particular dispute (for example, an end-user enterprise in China in addition to the foreign trade corporation), permits the resale in the West of goods (especially bulk commodities) bought from China on "back-to-back" terms—that is, on exactly the same terms as the previous sale. In such cases the jurisdiction of the FTAC has sometimes been invoked. This Rule also enables parties in two countries other than China to select the FTAC for third-country arbitration. There are no limitations in the MAC Decision or in the MAC Rules as to the nationality of the parties.

The procedure whereby an arbitration is initiated is conventional enough, as are the rules for selecting arbitrators and for the appointment of an umpire. The arbitrators are all chosen from among the members of each commission; all are citizens of the PRC and are experts in various appropriate fields.

Even prior to the commencement of the arbitration proper, the chairman of the commission may at the request of one party prescribe "preliminary measures" for the protection of the rights of the parties,[116] and in the case of the MAC, "measures of security" prescribed under this rule may be enforced by the people's courts, a provision that enables the MAC to order the arrest of vessels and cargo within Chinese waters.[117]

Proceedings may be written as well as oral. Parties may appear in person or must, where a corporation is a party, be represented by an attorney, who may be a Chinese citizen or a foreigner.[118] Hearings must be held in China, though not necessarily at the seat of the commission, and they may be in public or in camera. There are provisions for counterclaims by defendants, to which the procedure for initiating complaints applies mutatis mutandi.

A number of rules also provide for the collection of evidence and empower the commissions to obtain expert evidence from either Chinese or foreign experts, but there are no express provisions governing the admissibility of evidence, nor the difficult and important question of the admissibility and proof of foreign law. The present writer was told by an officer of the commissions that in appropriate cases foreign law would be applied; in cases submitted to the commissions, it was said, there would be "no difficulty in understanding what law was to be applied."[119]

In answer to a question regarding choice of law before the commissions, the writer was told:

> If a case is to be settled in China, it must clearly be settled in accordance with Chinese law. Of course, a particular concrete dispute may be very complex in character, so that other considerations may have to be taken into account in settling it and other rules applied. There is no single legal procedure that will suit every case. But the first matter for consideration is Chinese law, after which we take into account the international practice.

The solution of conflict problems was a matter of practice, for which Chinese law had no written rules. One such rule of practice, evidently, is that foreign law or international commercial practice is only applied insofar as it is regarded as reasonable.[120]

Once the case is decided, an award is given, which must be reduced to writing within 15 days. It is final and cannot be impeached in any court, under the Decisions and Rules of both bodies, quite apart from the parallel provisions of any arbitration clause. A sum of money to cover an arbitration fee (not exceeding 2 percent of the sum claimed) and the costs of the successful party may be made against the unsuccessful party at the discretion of the arbitrators, and both amounts form part of the arbitral award and are thus final.[121] The award as a whole may be executed, if necessary, by application to the people's courts.

The machinery set out above represents the formal arbitration process of the PRC. It is necessary to emphasize once more, however, that it has up to now been so rarely used, in East-West trade at any rate, as to be almost an academic model. In the few cases that are brought before one or other of the commissions at all, almost invariably conciliation methods are employed. It is therefore of importance to note both the power of the commissions to initiate conciliation procedures at any stage of the reference and the great importance attached by the personnel of the commissions to achieving agreed settlements in this way rather than resorting to what in China is regarded as the much more "antagonistic" device of a compulsory award to which one party does not give his agreement.

Rule 19 of the MAC Rules specifically empowers the MAC to make efforts to bring about an agreed settlement in the following terms: "19. The MAC may endeavor to settle by conciliation any dispute of which it has taken cognizance." The FTAC Rules contain no such provision, but as a matter of practice the FTAC is just as free to embark on conciliation.[122]

Where a settlement is achieved through conciliation, it is drawn up in writing and signed by both parties as well as by the members of the arbitral concerned. It is understood that, as a matter of practice, such an agreement, known as a "conciliatory conclusion," where embodied in the accepted form, is considered to have the same enforceable character as an award.

Recognition and Enforcement of
Arbitration Clauses and Awards

So far as is known, the PRC has entered into no treaties with Western countries, either bilateral or multilateral, for the enforcement of arbitral awards. In a number of treaties of commerce and navigation concluded between the PRC and other socialist states,[123] there are such provisions, but it is not known in what way they operate.

The Decisions and Rules of both FTAC and MAC provide that awards of those bodies shall be enforced by the people's courts when necessary.[124] Beyond this, however, the Decisions and Rules of each body provide that neither party may have recourse to a court of law by way of appeal or otherwise against a decision of the commission. The extent to which these two rules are supposed to be read together is not clear; if they are read together it would seem that once an award or, perhaps, a record of conciliation is secured, the people's court has no option but to enforce it forthwith.

Whether this is in fact the proper view must be doubted, for the very slender evidence available suggests that the people's courts have, in some circumstances at least, a power to disregard the arbitral procedure altogether. The exact limits of this doctrine are not clear, but it would seem that an arbitral award that endangered or offended the fundamental ordre public of the state would in all probability be refused enforcement by the people's court.

This conclusion may be drawn from the somewhat anomalous Vickers-Zimmer case,[125] arising out of a contract for the supply and installation of a synthetic fiber plant at Lanchow made between Vickers-Zimmer and the China National Technical Import Company, which contained a clause providing for arbitration in Stockholm. Notwithstanding the arbitration clause, the Intermediate Municipal People's Court of Peking entertained proceedings against Vickers-Zimmer on grounds of fraud, which resulted in the annulment of the contract by the court and an order to pay an indemnity of 650,000 pounds. The defendants were not represented at the court, the jurisdiction of which they did not accept.* The court found, among other things, that the defendants had deliberately sought to undermine China's national economy and security.

Despite the wide implications of this decision in terms of legal principle, it should be emphasized that the decision arose out of somewhat exceptional circumstances, in which the Chinese authorities evidently decided that the dispute had become an "antagonistic contradiction between the enemy and ourselves."† It certainly is not

---

*It should be added that the case, which took place at the height of the Cultural Revolution, was closely connected with criminal proceedings in which two of Vickers Zimmer's technical staff were convicted of espionage.

†The expression quoted is that of Chairman Mao Tse-tung and is used to describe serious disputes, in contrast to "contradictions among the people," that is, disputes in which the element of class hostility is involved. See Mao Tse-tung, "On the Correct Handling of

representative of the normal practice of Chinese foreign trade corporations in complying with arbitration clauses.

Arbitration Clauses and the
Negotiated Settlement of Disputes

The majority of arbitration clauses inserted by the Chinese into
foreign trade contracts with the West contains a provision requiring
the parties to settle all disputes arising in connection with the contract or its execution by amicable negotiation. Obligations of this
kind are taken much more seriously by Chinese parties to a contract
than is often the case with those Westerners who are new to trading
with the PRC. Such provisions embody deep-seated Chinese social
beliefs in the virtue of compromise and adjustment, which stand in
contrast to the belief in an inflexible defense of one's legal rights,
which characterizes the social morality of much of the Western world.

Where disputes occur in the course of trade transactions, it is
usually advisable to maintain the most flexible possible approach. A
hasty insistence on arbitration (even if in fact it leads only to conciliation proceedings) is not appreciated by the Chinese side, whereas
patient and flexible negotiations (often lasting for several years) usually
produce a result that, if not wholly satisfactory, is nonetheless a reasonable compromise.

The foreign negotiator is presented with formidable obstacles,
however, for Chinese corporation officials are often surprisingly ill-
informed about the more complicated ramifications of commercial
disputes that are not their immediate concern. Thus, estimates of
loss, particularly of a financial or consequential kind, are often dis-
believed or not understood on the Chinese side. Negotiations toward
settlement of claims are thus quite frequently complicated by mutual
misunderstanding and are correspondingly discouraging. There is a
danger that as contractual relations become more and more sophisticated, the opportunities for such misunderstanding could increase.

It is thus in some ways a remarkable fact that the great majority
of disputes are in fact solved by negotiations, however long drawn-out
these may be, and very few, in China's trade with the West at any rate,
go before the FTAC or MAC. This is in part due to the ordinary pressures of business in a competitive market, but it also owes something
to the belief among many Western businessmen (however ill-founded)

Contradictions Among the People," 27 February 1957 (5 F.K.H.P.
1-34). It must be noted that during the Cultural Revolution period a
substantial number of serious disputes arose over charter parties
and in other areas of maritime law. Happily, in the great majority
of cases, the difficulties were of a temporary nature.

that if they were to initiate arbitration proceedings in Peking, the outcome would invariably be unfavorable to the foreign side.

It should be stressed, in conclusion, that the Chinese side is generally willing to make some gesture of compromise in the early stages of a problem, for the prospect of a commercial dispute is as unattractive to the foreign trade corporations as it is to the Western company. Gradually, no doubt, as China and her Western trading partners each become more appreciative of the other's requirements, and thus better able to modify their own expectations, the mutual confidence in legal arrangements that is a requisite for successful and stable long-term trade will take deeper and deeper root.

NOTES

The following abbreviations are used in these Notes to refer to Chinese materials:

F.L.H.P.:   Chung-yang Jen-min Cheng-fu Fa-ling Hui-pien (Collection of Laws and Decrees of the Central People's Government) (Peking: Legal Press, Volumes 1-5, 1952-55) covering the years 1949-54. Cited by number of volume.

F.K.H.P.   Chung-hua Jen-min Kung-ho-kuo Fa-kuei Hui-pien (Collection of Laws and Regulations of the People's Republic of China) (Peking: Legal Press, Volumes 1-13, 1956-64) covering the years 1954-63. Cited by number of volume.

C.J.F.K.H.P.   Chin-jung Fa-kuei Hui-pien (Collection of Financial Laws and Regulations), Collected by the Head Office of the People's Bank of China (Peking: Financial and Economic Press, 1956-62, 1954, 1955, 1956, 1957, and 1958-60. Cited by year covered—for example, (1956) C.J.F.K.H.P.

T.Y.C.   Chung-hua Jen-min Kung-ho-kuo T'iao-yüeh-chi (Collection of Treaties of the People's Republic of China) (Peking: World Knowledge Press, Volumes 1-13, 1960-65) covering the years 1949-64. Cited by number of volume.

JPRS   Reports of the Joint Publications Research Service of the United States Government Department of Commerce (Washington D.C.: Government Printing Office, current). Cited by serial number and date of publication.

S.C.M.P.   Survey of the China Mainland Press (Hong Kong:
                  U.S. Consulate General, current). Cited by serial
                  number and date of publication.

1. Among many recent books on China's foreign trade, mention
may be made of Eckstein (ed.), China Trade Prospects and U.S. Policy
(New York, 1971) in which the chapter by Jerome A. Cohen, "Chinese
Law and Sino-American Trade," is of special relevance to the present
subject; also Stahnke (ed.), China's Trade with the West (New York,
1972).

2. See Starr, "Developing trade with China," 13 Virg. J. Int'l L.
13 (1973) for an account of developments in this area.

3. Article 57 of the Common Programme of the Chinese People's
Political Consultative Conference, adopted 29th September 1949, in
Blaustein (ed.), Fundamental Legal Documents of Communist China
53 (South Hackensack, 1962). The Common Programme served as the
constitution of China until the adoption of the Constitution of the PRC
on 20 September, 1954 (Blaustein, 1).

4. Part of Article 37, Common Programme, in Blaustein, op.
cit. at 48.

5. On the law of the PRC in general, see Li, "The Role of Law
in Communist China," 44 China Quarterly 66 (1970); on the legal system, see Leng, Justice in Communist China (Dobbs Ferry, 1967). The
constitutional structure may be found in the various constitutional
documents set out in Blaustein, op. cit. For some observations on
recent developments in the legal system, see Cohen, "Chinese Law:
At the Crossroads," 53 China Quarterly 139 (1973).

6. See generally Hsiao, "Communist China's Foreign Trade
Organization," 20 Vand. L. Rev. 303 (1967).

7. See Donnithorne, China's Economic System at 517 (London,
1967).

8. Nai Kaku Kambo, Na Kaku Chosa Kanshu (Cabinet Research
Directorate), Chuka Jimmin Kyowakoku Soshiki Betsunin Meikyo 71-72
(Directory of Personnel and Organizations of the PRC) (hereafter
cited as Meikyo) (Tokyo, 1972).

9. Donnithorne, op. cit., Chapter 8.

10. Provisional Regulations for the Inspection of Import and
Export Commodities, 3 January 1954 (5 F.L.H.P. 71), Article 2. An
unofficial translation of the Regulations appears in Trade with China:
A Practical Guide 95 (Hong Kong: Ta Kung Pao, 1957).

11. Donnithorne, op. cit., at 322.

12. Proposal Submitted by the Premier of the State Council to
the Standing Committee of the National People's Congress for the
Reorganization of Economic and Financial Departmental Organs Subordinate to the State Council, as adopted by Resolution of the Standing

Committee of the National People's Congress of the PRC Regarding
the Reorganization of Organs Subordinate to the State Council, 12
May 1956 (3 F.K.H.P. 79). Article 2(2) establishes and defines the
functions of the State Technological Commission, which was merged
with the Scientific Planning Commission to form the SSTC in November
1958; see Resolution of the Standing Committee of the National People's
Congress, 23 November 1958 (8 F.K.H.P. 95).

13. A humble but instructive example may be found in the Directive of the Ministry of Agriculture, Ministry of Commerce, MFT and
of the Central Committee of the Communist Youth League of China
Regarding the Development of Domestic Rabbit Production, 28 December 1959 (10 F.K.H.P. 378).

14. Ceased publication in 1966.

15. For example, Tui-wai Moa-yi Chung-ts'ai Shou-ts'e (Foreign Trade Arbitration Handbook) (Peking: Legal Press, 1957).

16. 25 April 1963 (13 F.K.H.P. 164).

17. See, for example, the Regulations for the Issue of Licenses
for the Import and Export of Goods, 23 January 1957 (5 F.K.H.P.
163), Article 3, which specifically applies the rules governing the
foreign trade corporations to these three bodies.

18. Chung-hua Jen-min Kung-ho-kuo Min-fa Chi-pen Wen-t'i
(Basic Problems of the Civil Law of the PRC) (Peking: Legal Press,
1958; hereafter referred to as Basic Problems of the Civil Law) 27-
28. An English translation may be found in the JPRS series, JPRS No.
4879, 15 August 1961. The book has undergone considerable criticism
in the course of successive political movements in China, but it is
believed that the basic assumptions to which this reference relates
still hold good.

19. See, for example, National Organizations of Foreign Trade
and Organizations of Other Foreign Business of the PRC (Peking:
CCPIT, 1972). The Chinese expression commonly used is fen-kung-
ssu, literally "branch company" or "branch corporation." The expression used for the central organization is either kung-ssu ("company"
or corporation") or sometimes tsung-kung-ssu, meaning "general"
or "principal" company or corporation. Fen-Kung-ssu is a term that
usually denotes a branch of a company in the English sense, but it
could also refer to a separate but associated entity. No legislation
is known to have been published that conclusively defines its meaning
in the context of foreign trade corporations. For a full list of the
branches, see T. Watanabe and K. Okagawe, Chunichi Boeki Nyumon
(Tokyo: Japan Economic News Co., 1972).

20. Foreign trade contracts are sometimes signed inside Chinese
diplomatic premises. A legal adviser to the Ministry of Foreign
Affairs of the PRC has doubted whether such a circumstance would
displace any local rule of private international law in favor of the

lex loci contractus. Ni Cheng-ao, Kuo-chi-fa-chung-te Ssu-fa Kuan-hsia Wen-t'i (Problems of Jurisdiction in International Law 74-75 (Peking: World Knowledge Press, 1964).

21. Donnithorne, op. cit., 327; the evidence dates from 1957.

22. For the banking system generally, see Donnithorne, op. cit., Chapter 15. A further useful account of the system is Jones, "People's Banking," Far Eastern Economic Review, 15 July 1965, at 137.

23. For the conditions under which such loans are granted, see the General Regulations for Loans of the PBC, 23 January 1951 (1949-51, C.J.F.K.H.P. 93) as amended by various subsequent regulations. Note in Particular Notification Regarding Certain Problems in Foreign Trade Credit and Settlement Work, issued by the PBC, 8 May, 1956 (1956, C.J.F.K.H.P. 132), which included provisions for relieving certain corporations of liability where they have suffered losses.

24. Financial Times, 7 June 1972.

25. The jurisdictional clause of this policy, which if applied would mean that the PICC could only be sued in China, reads, in part, "All disputes arising between the Insured and the Company shall be settled by friendly negotiation on the principles of seeing truth from facts and of reasonableness and fairness."

26. See also Reghizzi, "Legal Aspects of Trade with China: The Italian Experience," 9 Harv. Int'l L. J. 35, 99-100 (1968).

27. A fuller account of the legal framework of Chinese shipping arrangements will be found in Dicks, "Some Aspects of Chinese Maritime Law and Practice," in Victor H. Li (ed.), "Law and Politics in China's Foreign Trade" (University of Washington Press, forthcoming).

28. On the subject of central and local influence in planning, see Donnithorne, op. cit. Chapter 18, and for more recent evidence, Donnithorne, "China's Cellular Economy: Some Economic Trends in the Cultural Revolution," 52 China Quarterly 605 (1972).

29. It is likely that the system in force in 1960 has undergone some changes if only in the direction of simplification of regulations. See Dicks, "A New Model for Chinese Legislation: The 1972 Shipping Regulations," 57 China Quarterly 63 (1974).

30. Regulations for the Issue of Licenses for the Import and Export of Goods, 23 January 1957, 5 F.K.H.P. 163, Articles 1 and 2. The Regulations replaced earlier legislation on the subject.

31. Id., Tables 1 and 2.

32. As amended, 27 March 1959, 9 F.K.H.P. 192.

33. Chung-hua Jen-min Kung-ho-Kuo Hai-Kuan Chin-ch'u-k'ou Shui-tse (Import and Export Tariff of the Maritime Customs of the PRC) published on the authority of the Maritime Customs Administration Bureau of the MFT (Peking: Legal Press, 1961).

34. In the case of imported whiskey, for example, the lowest rate is 200 percent while the general rate is 400 percent. Id., 11, item 108(b).

35. Id., 17, items 175(a) and (b).

36. Id., 43, items 423 and 424 respectively.

37. Donnithorne, supra note 7 at 380.

38. Provisional Maritime Customs Law of the People's Republic of China (Customs Law) 23 March 1951, Chung-hua Jen-min Kung-ho-kuo Hai-kuan Fa-kuei (Customs Laws and Regulations of the PRC) (Peking: Legal Press, 1961, 5), Article 113. See also Provisional Regulations of the Maritime Customs of the PRC for the Implementation of the Import and Export Tariff, 4 May 1951, supra note 30.

39. Provisional Regulations for the Implementation of the Import and Export Tariff, Article 2.

40. Customs Law, Article 115.

41. Customs Law, Article 120.

42. Customs Law, Article 118.

43. Customs Law, 140.

44. Provisional Regulations for Implementation of the Import and Export Tariff, Article 5.

45. Customs Law, Article 123.

46. Customs Law, Article 121.

47. For the nature of the tax, see Donnithorne, supra note 7 at 372.

48. Supra note 38.

49. Provisional Regulations Prohibiting the Export of Valuable Art Objects, Pictures and Books, 24 May 1950 (1 F.L.H.P. 558.)

50. Provisional Regulations Regarding the Import of Foreign Films, 11 July 1950 (1 F.L.H.P. 573).

51. Maritime Customs Regulations for the Investigation and Exposure of Accidents in the Import and Export of Goods, 5 September 1958, 8 (F.K.H.P. 192).

52. A high point in the articulation of this policy, which coincides with the Cultural Revolution, was an article by "Tsai Cheng" ("Finance") in the Jen-min Jih-pao (People's Daily) 11 May 1969, and printed in translation, with the title (in part) "Hail China, a Socialist Country Without Internal or External Debts," in China's Renminbi: One of the Few Most Stable Currencies in the World (Peking: Foreign Languages Press, 1969), 1. A more moderate statement was made by Li Hsi-Fu, vice chairman of the CCPIT, in March 1973. Admitting that China accepted imports on an installment payment basis, he said "normal" commercial credits were not being considered. "We are not in a position to float loans on the international monetary market because we are a socialist country." Times (London), 26 March 1973.

53. A further source of foreign exchange that has been of particular value in lean years has been the remittances by overseas Chinese. See Donnithorne, supra note 7 at 513. A recent estimate of the value of such remittances was $500 million per annum. Financial Times, 15 January 1974.

54. Financial Times, 7 December 1973. The report concerned a particular loan of $100 million, but it was suggested that over-all indebtedness of the Chinese is already much higher than that.

55. See Münzel, "Ways of Payment in China's Foreign Trade," to be published in Victor H. Li (ed.), "Law and Politics in China's Foreign Trade" (University of Washington Press, forthcoming).

56. Regulations for Prevention of the Movement of National Currency Across the National Frontiers, 6 March, 1951 (2 F.L.H.P. 147). See also Regulations for Control of Foreign Remittances, 27 February 1951, Selections from China Mainland Press No. 78 (6 March 1951) 12.

57. Regulations on Foreign Currency Deposits, 15 October 1956 (1956 C.J.F.K.H.P., 133). Translation in K. C. Chao, Economic Planing and Organization in Mainland China, A Documentary Study (1949-1957) Vol. 1 (Harvard University Press, 1963) 244.

58. Münzel, supra note 55.

59. Hints to Businessmen Visiting the People's Republic of China (London: Board of Trade, 1963).

60. Regulations of the People's Republic of China Regarding Penalties for Corruption, 21 April 1952 (3 F.L.H.P. 25: translated in Blaustein, supra note 3 at 227), Article 9.

61. The Provisional Regulations Regarding Private Enterprises, 30 December 1950 (1 F.L.H.P. 539) has in all probability fallen into desuetude, though its repeal has not been reported. An isolated case of a foreign-owned private enterprise in operation as late as 1967, however, is reported in South China Morning Post, 18 October 1972.

62. Provisional Regulations on State-Private Jointly Operated Enterprises, 2 September 1954 (5 F.L.H.P. 65). It is notable that of the state-private enterprises of which the articles of association are available, most have a specific internal rule requiring all shareholders to be citizens of the PRC.

63. The writer has heard such remarks made by Chinese officials, on a number of occasions. The observations that follow are based on the writer's numerous conversations with businessmen who have dealt with China over the past 12 years. Like the remarks of the Chinese officials, they are generalizations based upon subjective perceptions and as such should be treated with due caution; but as generalizations they seem rarely to be disputed.

64. See Boone, "The Foreign Trade of China," 11 China Quarterly 169, 175 (1962). There were further instances of a similar kind as a result of disruptions of industry and transport, at the time of the Cultural Revolution, and commercial relations became particularly difficult with the persons then in charge of the People's Insurance Company of China, which chose that time to revoke its "strikes, riots, and civil commotions" cover. South China Morning Post, 11 July 1968 and 22 September 1968. There were also widely reported difficulties

in dealing with the various maritime authorities. In view of the extent of economic disruption believed to have occurred in China at that time, however, it is notable that a very large number of export contracts were fulfilled, subject to delays, of which the Western side was sometimes warned at the time of contracting.

65. Although China is not a party to the Comecon General Conditions of Delivery, conditions of delivery of a similar kind have been incorporated into commercial treaties and agreements with several East European states, including the USSR. Hsiao, "Communist China's Trade Treaties and Agreements, 1949-64," 22 Vand. L. Rev. 623 (1968).

66. Discussed more fully in Chapter 2 of this book. The conclusion in early January 1974 of a trade agreement and the "normalization" of Sino-Japanese relations may result in Sino-Japanese trade practices becoming a precedent for more fully spelt-out legal arrangements between China and Western countries. On the Japanese experience up to 1972, see Dan F. Henderson and Tasuku Matsuo, "Japan's Trade Experience with the PRC" in Victor H. Li (ed.), Law and Politics in China's Foreign Trade (University of Washington Press, forthcoming). For example of contracts used in both private and Agreement or Memorandum trade, see Hsiao, "Communist China's Foreign Trade Contracts and Means of Settling Disputes," 21 Vand. L. Rev. 503 (1968).

67. For example, the International Load Line Convention, 1930, to which China adhered on 23 October 1957 (6 T.Y.C. 294).

68. For some comments on the ICC's position as an arbitral body, see the CCPIT publication, Tui-wai Mao-yi Chung-ts'ai Shou-ts'e (Handbook of Foreign Trade Arbitration) (Peking: Legal Press, 1957), postscript, 449-450. The present writer was told by an official of the CCPIT in 1965 that the ICC was unacceptable as an arbitral body because it was a "tool of U.S. imperialism," and the same taint presumably extended to its activities in the field of unification of contract terms.

69. This is not to suggest that an analysis of such clauses is not valuable. Both Smith, in "Standard Form Contracts in the International Commercial Transactions of the People's Republic of China," 21 Int'l and Comp. L. Q. 133 (1972), and Reghizzi (supra note 53) make very useful observations on the clauses to be found in the standard import and export contracts, to which the reader is referred.

70. See, for example, Clauses 15, 17, and 19 of a recent contract form of the China National Machinery Import and Export Corporation. It seems the Corporation rarely enforces the penalty provisions.

71. This contrasts with the practice of the various organs of government with which foreign companies may have to deal, such as the CCIB and the Harbor Administration Bureau under the Ministry

of Communications, which include in their official certificates a clause to the effect that in case of doubt the Chinese version shall prevail.

72. For example, Jen-li pu-k'e k'ang-chü yüan-yin (literally, "causes that human force cannot resist"), the term usually translated as force majeure, has a somewhat different meaning as used in Chinese statutes from the expression force majeure, embracing a larger number of possible causes.

73. See supra note 72.

74. Conversation between the writer and legal officials of the FTAC and MAC, May 1965. These officials also took the view, however, that all the rules required for the settlement of any dispute that might arise under Chinese foreign trade contracts could be found in the provisions of the contract.

75. The literature in English on the modern Chinese law of contracts is sparse; the principal articles are the following: Pfeffer, "The Institution of Contracts in the Chinese People's Republic," Pt. I (1963) 14 China Quarterly 153, Pt. II (1963) 15 China Quarterly 115 (largely based on the text of Basic Problems of the Civil Law supra note 27); Hsiao, "The Role of Economic Contracts in Communist China," 53 Calif. L. Rev. 1029 (1963); Pfeffer, "Contracts in China Revisited" (1966) 28 China Quarterly 106.

76. The principal exceptions are the basic rules contained in the Provisional Regulations Issued by the Financial and Economic Commission of the Government Administration Council of the Central People's Government Relating to the Conclusion of Contracts by Organs, State Enterprises and Cooperatives, 27 September 1950, 1 F.L.H.P. 532 ("Provisional Contract Regulations"). Although some of these provisions relate only to contracts of loan or guarantee (Articles 3 and 6) and others may have fallen into desuetude (such as Article 10: settlement of disputes), others seem to apply to all types of contract in the commercial sphere.

77. This view appears to have the support of the principal academic work on Chinese civil law. Basic Problems of the Civil Law, supra note 18.

78. Most of the statutory forms of contract available have more specific provisions regarding damages and penalties for nonperformance. However, a recent example of such a statute suggests that there may currently be a movement back toward less precise formulations of contractual liability between enterprises. (Dicks, supra note 29, where such provisions, largely in relation to internal shipping, are discussed in more detail.)

79. For more detailed consideration of some aspects of the internal legislation, see Hsia and Haun, "Laws of the People's Republic of China on Industrial and Intellectual Property," 5 Law and Pol. Int'l. Bus. 743 (1973).

80. Provisional Regulations for the Protection of Invention Rights and Patent Rights, 17 August 1950. Text in 1 F.L.H.P. 359.

81. Notice of the State Council Regarding Promulgation of the Regulations for Awards for Inventions" and the "Regulations on Awards for Technical Improvements," 3 November 1963, 13 F.K.H.P. 241.

82. Promulgated by Notice of the State Council, 3 November 1963 (13 F.K.H.P. 241). At the same time there were also introduced the Regulations on Awards for Technological Improvements (id., 246), but these appear to have no relevance to international trade, although foreign residents of China may benefit from them: Article 19. Quaere whether this would include a temporarily resident technician employed in China to help install a plant under a turnkey contract.

83. "Fa-ming."

84. Article 2.

85. "How China Buys Foreign Technology," Business International, 15 December 1972 at 396.

86. The Japanese Company Kuraray were reported to have obtained approximately $21 million for a whole vinylon plant sold in August 1963; about 23 percent was specified as being for know-how, and 10 percent for design fees. Loc. cit.

87. Loc. cit. Apparently these cases all involved Japanese companies, and it may be that this precaution was designed to reduce liability for Japanese taxation. However, the possibility cannot be excluded that Chinese purposes were also served by this service.

88. Loc. cit.

89. Financial Times, 9 January 1974.

90. See supra note 85.

91. For example, the Kuraray contract, supra note 86.

92. 10 April 1963 (13 F.K.H.P. 162); in this section referred to as the Regulations.

93. Detailed Rules for the Application of the Regulations for the Administration of Trademarks, 25 April 1963 (13 F.K.H.P. 164); in this section, referred to as the Rules.

94. Exchange of Notes Between the Governments of Sweden and the PRC Constituting an Agreement Concerning the Mutual Registration of Trademarks, 8 April 1957 (428 U.N.T.S. 268). This agreement was made during the currency of an earlier statute, the Provisional Regulations on Registration of Trademarks, 28 August 1950 (1 F.L.H.P. 528), but on the question of "belonging," the wording of Article 5 of the Provisional Regulations is similar to that of Article 12 of the Regulations. Moreover the survival of the agreement and three other such agreements without amendment following the repeal of the Provisional Regulations of 1950 and the adoption of the Regulations indicates that no change in this respect was thought necessary. The other trademark agreements are the exchanges of notes with the United

Kingdom, 1 June 1956 (5 T.Y.C. 68); Switzerland, 14 April 1957 (6 T.Y.C. 178); Denmark, 12 April 1958 (7 T.Y.C. 37); and Finland, 26 January 1967. The texts available to the writer appear to support the same view.

95. For references, see Johnson and Chiu, op. cit. at 7.

96. See supra note 86.

97. Articles 23 and 98. Blaustein, op. cit. at 11 and 31.

98. Regulations for the Preferential Treatment of Overseas Chinese Investment in State-operated Overseas Chinese Investment Corporations, 1 August 1957 (6 F.K.H.P. 570).

99. The subject has attracted a considerable literature; see, for example, Cohen, supra note 1.

100. On a number of occasions they have sought relief in foreign courts with unfortunate results. The most famous case is Central Air Transport, Inc. v. Civil Air Transport Corporation (1953) A.C. 70, in which a successful suit by the Chinese state corporation in the courts of Hong Kong was revised on appeal by the Judicial Committee of the Privy Council. The decision has been the subject of a considerable amount of unfavorable comment. A more recent case, in which the merits were very much on the Chinese side, though the legal principle was not, was China State Bank Ltd., v. Dairy Farm, Ice and Cold Storage Co. Ltd. (1967) H.K.L.R. 95.

101. See for example Baccus SRL v. Servicio Nacional del Trigo (1957) 1 Q.B. 438 (C.A.)

102. See note in 64 Am. J. Int'l L. 371-5 (1970) for an account of the prosecution of the Bank of China in Singapore. On the other hand in Synn Lee and Co. Ltd. v. Bank of China (1962) M.L.J. 395, the bank defended an action in the Malaysian court without any indication that it was waiving a plea of immunity.

103. This subject is discussed in the context of a critical analysis of the jurisdictional attitudes of English and U.S. courts in a book by a legal adviser of the Chinese Ministry of Foreign Affairs; Ni Cheng-Ao, Kuo-chi-fa-chung-te Ssŭ-fa Kuan-hsia Wen-t'i (Problems of Jurisdiction in International Law) (Peking: World Knowledge Press, 1964), especially at 79-80. The book was reviewed by the present writer in 15 Int'l and Comp. L. Q. 913-5 (1966).

104. Current Chinese attitudes to foreign trade dispute settlement in general are often attributed by Western writers in part, at least, to the traditional Chinese antipathy to litigation, a point discussed by several authorities, such as Cohen, supra note 1.

105. Conversation between the present writer and officials of the FTAC and MAC, May 1965. Criticism was directed particularly at the monopolistic tendencies of the International Chamber of Commerce and of the Arbitration Committee of the Baltic Exchange.

106. Blaustein, op. cit., 26 (Article 73).

107. Id., 131-132 (Articles 1 and 3).

108. This question is considered in Li, "Role of Law in Communist China," supra note 5.

109. Decision of the Government Administration Council of the Central People's Government on the Establishment of the FTAC within the CCPIT, 6 May 1954 (pamphlet issued by the CCPIT, 1956).

110. Decision of the State Council on the Establishment of the MAC Within the CCPIT, 21 November 1958 (8 F.K.H.P. 177).

111. The jurisdiction of harbor administration bureaus with regard to inquiries into marine casualties should also be noted. See Dicks, "Some Aspects of Chinese Maritime Law and Practice," in Victor H. Li (ed.), Law and Politics in China's Foreign Trade (University of Washington Press, forthcoming).

112. Two exceptions, both written in English, are Shao Hsun-yi, "Foreign Trade Arbitration in China" (1960) Foreign Trade of the People's Republic of China, Part 3, 21; and Wang Wen Lin, "People's Republic of China," in P. Sanders (ed.), International Commercial Arbitration: A World Handbook, Volume III (The Hague: Martinus Nijhoff, 1965). The latter work includes the official English translation of the statutory texts relating to the MAC.

113. See, however, "How the Case of M.S. Varild was Settled" (1963) 3 Foreign Trade of the People's Republic of China 4, in which there is a short account of the proceedings in respect of a disputed salvage claim, which was ultimately settled by conciliation.

114. In particular, from a lengthy interview that the present writer was fortunate enough to obtain with legal workers in the joint secretariat of the FTAC and MAC in May 1965. The account that follows also draws on the experiences of a few Western companies that have been before the Commission.

115. The statutory texts are as follows. FTAC: Decision of the Government Administration Council of the Central People's Government on the Establishment with the CCPIT of the FTAC, 6 May, 1954 (the FTAC Decision): Provisional Rules of Procedure of the FTAC of the CCPIT, 31 March 1956 (the FTAC Rules); MAC: Decision of the State Council of the PRC on the Establishment Within the CCPIT of the MAC, 21 November 1958 (the MAC Decision); and Provisional Rules of Procedure of the MAC of the CCPIT, 8 January 1959 (the MAC Rules). The texts of the FTAC Decision and and FTAC Rules were published in Chinese and English by the CCPIT in 1956, and tt those of the MAC Decision and MAC Rules in 1959.

116. FTAC Rules, Rule 15; MAC Rules 15.

117. MAC Rules, Rule 16. In practice arrest is usually carried out by the harbor authorities, which have special powers in this respect. See Dicks, op. cit.

118. FTAC Rules, Rule 18; MAC Rules, Rule 20. It should be

pointed out that from the Chinese text it is clear that the expression "attorney" does not refer, as in American usage, to lawyers, but rather to attorneys in the strict sense of representatives. It would seem that such a representative would have to be armed with a properly legalized power of attorney to enable him to act.

119. Interview, May 1965, supra note 114.

120. Id.

121. FTAC Rules, Rules 33-34; MAC Rules, Rules 35-36. The arbitration fee may be shared between the parties.

122. Wang Wen Lin, op. cit., at 127-129.

123. USSR (Treaty of 23 April 1958); GDR (Treaty of 18 January 1960); Albania (Treaty of 2 February 1961); and Korea (Treaty of 5 November 1962). The discussion in the text does not take account of the 1974 Sino-Japanese trade agreement.

124. Wang Wen Lin (op. cit.) writing in 1965 states that questions of enforcement have not as yet arisen.

125. China Mail, 4 May 1968, 5 July 1968; South China Morning Post, 6 July 1968.

INTRODUCTORY NOTE ON
CONTRACTING WITH ENTERPRISES
IN STATE-PLANNED ECONOMIES
Robert Starr

In their relations inter se, the members of Comecon have developed the world's most advanced unification of international trade law, notably in the 1968 General Conditions for the Delivery of Goods. These General Conditions, discussed more fully in Chapter 6, go far beyond the standardized terms (for example, Incoterms, 1953, International Chamber of Commerce) or form contracts used in the West and regulate with the force of law sales concluded between foreign trade organizations in member countries.[1]

Trade between planned and market economy countries is not governed by any detailed set of rules such as embodied in the 1968 General Conditions. Foreign trade organizations (FTOs) in planned economy countries have "standard form" contracts specially designed for transactions with Western trading partners, which to a degree reflect the influence of Comecon practices. Not surprisingly, however, the "standard form" contracts vary considerably, depending upon whether the state-trading partner is seller, buyer, licensor, or licensee.

Negotiations with Western companies are normally conducted on the basis of these "standard form" contracts. Whether and to what extent a Western firm can obtain provisions that vary form those contained in such contracts depends on a number of factors, including the relative bargaining power of the parties in the context of the particular negotiation. In general, an Eastern contract negotiator will press for agreement on his "standard form" clauses or on certain alternative clauses to which he may have authority to agree. Proposals that exceed his scope of authority must be referred to his superiors for approval and are likely to require more prolonged negotiations. A long-term contractual relationship between an FTO and a Western firm may result in the development of certain mutually acceptable terms and conditions that are readily incorporated into subsequent contracts.

Considerable effort has been made to bridge gaps between trade practices in different countries and areas by the development of general terms and conditions for international trade relations (particularly for relations between Western firms and Eastern FTOs) and by the preparation of guides for drafting different types of international contracts, notably within the United Nations Economic Commission for Europe (ECE).

The ECE has published a number of "General Conditions." Broadly speaking, they may be grouped into two main categories: (1) a series of General Conditions drafted primarily by experts from market economy countries and (2) a series of General Conditions drafted with the participation of Eastern as well as Western representatives and designed mainly for the special needs of East-West contracts.[2] The latter group include General Conditions No. 574 for the Supply of Plant and Machinery for Export (December 1955); No. 574A for the Supply and Erection of Plant and Machinery for Import and Export (March 1957); No. 574D for the Erection of Plant and Machinery Abroad (August 1963); No 730 for Import and Export of Durable Consumer Goods and of Other Engineering Stock Articles (March 1961); and Additional Clauses for Supervision of Erection of Plant and the Machinery Abroad No. 574B (April 1964). The ECE has also issued preparatory texts to serve as guides with respect to contracts for large industrial works and the international transfer of know-how in the engineering industry.[3]

These ECE efforts appear thus far to have had relatively little impact on East-West contract negotiations. Nevertheless, it is important that a Western contract negotiator be familiar with such efforts, as well as the 1968 Comecon General Conditions and related earlier efforts (including the predecessor 1958 General Conditions for the Delivery of Goods; the General Conditions of Assembly and Provision of Other Technical Services in Connection with Reciprocal Delivery of Machinery and Equipment, 1962; and the General Conditions for the Technical Servicing of Machinery, Equipment and Other Items, 1962)[4] as he seeks to overcome difficulties on particularly sensitive aspects of the contract negotiations with his Eastern counterpart.

SOCIALIST FOREIGN TRADE CONTRACT PRACTICES

As discussed more fully in the respective chapters of Part II of this study, Soviet and East European legal regimes generally accept the commercial custom and commercial law inherited from the law merchant,[5] and their laws relating to foreign trade contracts are broadly similar to those of Western nations, with certain important differences stemming mainly from different conceptions about the role of the contract in state-planned economies.

By and large, socialist contract law on such matters as contract formation and responsibility for risk of loss and damage is rather orthodox in terms of Western traditions. In contrast, socialist law regarding breach of contract and remedies for breach tends to exhibit considerably differences from Western concepts.

From the perspective of an Eastern country, a foreign trade contract is essentially one of a series of bureaucratic orders designed to assure fulfillment of a particular planning objective. In a planned system, many terms of performance may be dictated by higher authority, and incentives vary from those in a market economy. Not surprisingly, remedies for nonperformance in a planned system are also different from those in a market economy. In a planned system, performance itself, and not monetary profit, is viewed as a principal economic objective. Accordingly, specific performance is typically the remedy sought for nonperformance in the domestic commercial contract practice of a planned system, with delays to be compensated by a schedule of penalty payments keyed to duration of the delay. Such payments may go well beyond what would be considered liquidated damages by a Western tribunal, yet they would be strictly enforceable under the laws of an Eastern country. Eastern foreign trade contract practices are, not surprisingly, strongly influenced by domestic requirements and practices.

SOME PROBLEM AREAS IN CONTRACT NEGOTIATIONS

We briefly note here some contract issues of particular significance in the East-West context, with special reference to contracts involving export sales to the USSR and Eastern Europe. The reader is cautioned that contracting practices vary greatly among the Eastern countries, and even among trading organizations of a particular country. Contracting with China, while raising many of the same issues discussed here, tends to involve special considerations and is discussed more fully in Chapter 15.

Scope for Free Choice of Law. Given the basic dissimilarities between the market and state-planned economic systems noted above, the Western contract negotiator is inclined to ask whether and to what extent his Eastern counterpart is free to agree to the application of a foreign law to the transaction.

Soviet and East European legal regimes recognize the principle of free choice of law with respect to foreign trade transactions, though with varying nuances from country to country.[6] In general the Eastern legal systems impose two basic obligatory limitations on the principle of free choice of law.

The first limitation is that the formal validity of a foreign trade transaction entered into by an organization of a socialist country, including the signature of the contract on behalf of the organization, is deemed to be governed by the laws of the socialist country, regardless of the place where the transaction is concluded. A Western firm should assume that under the law of its trading partner the contract (and any modification or amendment) must be in writing and in accordance with certain formalities, and the firm should satisfy itself that these requirements have been met.

The second limitation is that under Soviet and East European legal systems, capacity and authority of the parties to a foreign trade transaction are deemed to be governed by their respective national laws. Here again, the Western firm must take steps to assure compliance with the national law of its contract partner. This requirement does not normally create practical difficulties, as it is most unlikely that representatives of an FTO would attempt to conclude a contract beyond the actual scope of authority of the FTO. Were this to happen, however, the purported agreement would normally be considered null and void under the law of the Eastern country in question. The Western firm is unlikely to prevail on a theory of "apparent authority" in most Eastern countries.

Provided the two obligatory limitations discussed are not contravened, an Eastern trading partner normally has considerable freedom with respect to determination of the substantive law that is to govern the contractual rights and duties of the parties. The extent of this freedom varies from country to country, depending generally on whether there is a requirement that the law selected by the parties has some connection with the legal relation in question. The Western negotiator should make it his business to determine the freedom enjoyed in this regard by his Eastern counterpart.

Soviet law recognizes a "public policy" limitation, precluding application of a foreign law in the USSR if this would contravene fundamental principles of Soviet law. Similar clauses are to be found in the laws of other socialist countries. While in theory such legislation allows considerable scope for curbing the free-choice-of-law principle discussed above, it does not appear that the "public policy" exceptions have been applied in such a manner.[7]

It is normally in the best interests of the contracting parties to determine in advance the law that is to apply in the event of dispute. Quite frequently the parties agree to application of a third-country legal system, yet the Western partner may not have fully explored the implications of such a clause

452

If the contract provides for arbitration of disputes in another country but does not specify governing law, the arbitrators might apply one of various legal systems, including the law of the Eastern partner. The choice will turn on the language of the arbitration clause and the applicable legal principles in the country of arbitration.

The matter of deciding on governing law is perhaps most complex in the case of large-scale projects in an Eastern country involving the supply and erection of industrial plant and building and engineering work—sometimes involving a number of Western companies pursuant to separate contracts or a comprehensive contract (including "turnkey" contracts). In such projects, it may be necessary to take account of certain legal provisions in the Eastern country that may have an obligatory character (such as work safety rules), and a Western contractor will wish to ensure that, to the extent possible, the law applicable to his relations with an Eastern contracting party is the same as the law applicable in his relations with subcontractors or other contracting parties with whom he may share liability.

In light of such problems, it is highly advisable that East-West contracts be drafted in as specific and detailed a manner as possible, to minimize the need to have reference to any national law and to anticipate in advance needs arising under a particular law.

Export and Import Licenses. In their buying contracts, Eastern FTOs may seek to ensure that Western sellers bear all risks connected with obtaining export licenses; that if a license is not granted or is revoked, the buyer may cancel the contract and obtain the return of payments already made and reimbursement of losses; and that penalties attach to delays caused by failure to obtain an export license. These clauses vary greatly. The Western seller will normally seek to make the obtaining of an export license a condition precedent to his contractual obligations and to ensure that he will not be subject to a claim for damages, or penalties, in the event subsequent revocation of the license prevents him from performing or completing performance. As Western governments have liberalized their regulation of East-West trade to preclude the need for specific licenses for most items, this contract issue is of less serious concern than in the past. A related question concerns the possible need for an import license by the Eastern FTO and the risk that the Eastern government may delay, refuse, or revoke an FTO's import license.

Force Majeure and Excuses for Nonperformance. This can be a most difficult and contentious aspect of the contract negotiation, mainly because of the well-known opposition of Eastern negotiators to clauses including circumstances such as industrial disputes within a definition of force majeure.

453

The 1968 Comecon General Conditions provide that the parties shall be relieved of liability for partial or total nonperformance, inter alia, "if such nonperformance was the consequence of circumstances of insuperable force"(sec. 68, para. 1). "Insuperable force" is defined as "circumstances that arose after conclusion of the contract as a result of events of an extraordinary character that were unforeseen and unavoidable by the party"(sec. 68, para. 2).

A similar approach is reflected in those ECE General Conditions prepared with special reference to East-West trade relations, such as General Conditions for the Supply of Plant and Machinery for Export No. 574, December 1955, sec. 10.1:

> Any circumstances beyond the control of the parties intervening after the formation of the contract and impeding its reasonable performance shall be considered as cases of relief. For the purpose of this clause circumstances not due to the fault of the party invoking them shall be deemed to be beyond the control of the parties

In contrast, the parallel section (sec. 10.1) of the ECE General Conditions for the Supply of Plant and Machinery for Export No. 188 (March 1953) specifies particular grounds for relief, including industrial disputes.

Typical relief (force majeure) clauses in Eastern FTO standard form contracts are more narrowly drawn, specifically referring only to certain circumstances. Thus, one Soviet FTO's standard contract mentions only "fire, flood, earthquake and war, provided these have directly affected the execution of the present Contract" as "force majeure circumstances"; and the clause allows either party to invoke force majeure and to cancel the contract or any part of it if the circumstances last longer than six months. Allowing both parties, and not merely the seller, to invoke the clause can be a matter of grave concern, particularly if the clause would permit the buyer to cancel the contract in the event an import license is withdrawn—for example, as a result of a change in import plans.

Related problems arising in this regard are categorizing the extent to which performance must be affected for a party to claim relief, and clearly defining the effects of force majeure and how performance is to be resumed when the force majeure circumstances are removed. In this regard it is especially important to consider the applicable rules of the legal system that is to govern the contractual relation.

Whatever the formulation agreed upon in a particular negotiation, it should clearly establish the procedure under which it is to be invoked and applied.

Guarantees. Eastern "standard form" purchasing contracts normally contain comprehensive guarantee clauses. A typical clause provides for the seller to guarantee that the equipment supplied corresponds to the highest technical standard in the seller's country for this kind of equipment at the time of execution of the contract and reflects high quality of materials and first-class workmanship and assembly; that the equipment and documentation delivered conform to the contract; and the "normal operation" of the equipment for a given period of time from the date the equipment is put into operation. Some clauses seek to impose on the seller guarantees regarding delivery dates or dates for completion of plant construction and detailed performance or output commitments. The guarantee clauses in "standard form" purchase contracts often provide for penalties in the event of defects and give the buyer a right to cancel the contract if more than a certain period of time (for example, four months) is required to eliminate the defects. The buyer may also have the right to demand the return of payments made for delivered equipment and compensation for losses suffered.

Obligations to repair or replace defective equipment or parts should be carefully drafted to cover such matters as the presentation of claims, transportation, and servicing costs.

In some contracts, it will be appropriate for the seller to insist upon strict rules for proper maintenance of equipment and require that detailed records be kept.

It is not possible to generalize about these problems, as different negotiations tend to raise special questions. By and large, the Western negotiator should not expect to obtain acceptance for his own standard guarantee clauses. Some concessions are likely to be required. However, he should be especially wary of any formula that provides a guarantee in respect of any matter beyond the control of the seller (for example, skill of Eastern workmen or quality of input materials); allows the buyer a unilateral right of cancellation; or exposes the seller to penalties, liability for indirect or consequential damages, or open-ended cost commitments to remedy defects.

Inspection and Testing. Eastern purchasing contracts often contain comprehensive provisions on this subject. A typical clause gives the buyer the right to send an inspector to the seller's works, upon appropriate notice that the equipment to be shipped is ready for testing, "to observe the manufacturing process of the equipment, to check the quality of its separate units and materials used as well as to take part in the tests of the equipment," with the buyer to be provided "technical facilities and premises" necessary for this purpose and at no cost to the buyer. The seller is to carry out preshipment testing of equipment in the presence of the buyer's inspector, who may insist that the seller eliminate defects or noncompliance of equipment with contract specifications (without, however, the seller's having the right to extend delivery dates). If the buyer does not send an inspector, the seller must nonetheless conduct the tests and issue a test report for the buyer.

Neither the presence of the buyer's inspector at the seller's tests nor the issuance by the buyer of a "release note" authorizing shipment serves to free the seller from any contractual guarantees or commitments regarding the capabilities of the equipment to be supplied. A further testing program after delivery is frequently provided for in the contract.

Penalties. Perhaps the most striking aspect of "standard form" contracts of Eastern enterprises is that they commonly call for penalties (often referred to as "agreed and liquidated damages") in the event of delays in delivery dates both with respect to equipment, necessary parts, and technical documentation. (Defects in the equipment delivered or incompleteness of technical documentation is often treated as delayed delivery and is accordingly subject to the same penalty provisions.) A typical penalty clause may be calculated weekly at a specific percent of the "value" of the delayed equipment (for example, 0.5 percent), with the rate increasing after the first month (for example, to 1 percent weekly), and with the total amount of penalty for delay not to exceed a specific percent (for example, 10 percent) of the value of the equipment not delivered in time. If the delayed delivery of parts prevents the operation of previously delivered equipment, the penalty will apply to both. The penalty rates are often expressly excluded from the scope of the arbitration clause. Should the delay in delivery exceed a certain period (for example, four months), the buyer usually has the right to cancel the contract in whole or in part without compensation to the seller for any expenses or damages caused by such cancellation, and should the buyer do so he is entitled to the maximum penalty as well as the return of any payments plus interest.

Eastern practice is by no means uniform even in this area of the contract negotiation, and generalizations are risky. Some sellers are able to avoid altogether inclusion of penalty clauses, while others find it difficult to move far from the language of the "standard form" contract clauses. Aspects of these clauses that give rise to particular concern include the fact that they do not take account of delays occasioned by events beyond the seller's control (though not excused as force majeure) or by the buyer.

It is also important to ensure that a penalty is not imposed twice if both machinery and related documentation are delayed, and that any agreed maximum amount of penalties does not allow for overlapping of penalties in excess of this amount.

456

The date or dates for purposes of applying penalty clauses (usually the date of the bill of lading) may differ from the date when the buyer may have assumed or was to assume expenses connected with the delivery of the goods, from the date when risk of loss was to have passed, and from the date of payment.

The choice of governing law may be a particularly important factor in determining the scope of the parties' respective rights and obligations under penalty clauses.

Cancellation. We have already seen that under standard cancellation clauses in an Eastern purchasing contract the parties may have the right to cancel the contract in the event of force majeure circumstances that last longer than a stated period, and the buyer may have the right to cancel the contract (in addition to other remedies) in the event delays in delivery exceed a certain period. In addition, the guarantee provisions of such contracts may give the buyer the right to cancel in the event of defects in equipment that cannot be eliminated, as well as the right to compensation for losses suffered (or a corresponding reduction in the price of delivered equipment). The combined effect of these clauses is to give the Eastern buyer an extraordinary measure of protection and unilateral discretion as to the exercise of certain rights, thus exposing the seller to great risk.

Payment. It is not possible to generalize about payment terms in East-West contracts, as they differ greatly depending on the nature of the contract, the country involved, and a host of other factors such as availability of credit facilities and possible barter or counter-purchasing commitments.

East-West contracts tend to rely on the same well-settled financial techniques commonly encountered in other international transactions, such as sight letters of credit, letters of credit against acceptance of draft, bills of exchange, and so forth. Eastern countries have individual preferences with respect to payment practices and techniques that are well known to most Western banking and other financial institutions involved in East-West trade. Thus, a Polish FTO may agree to pay the cost of export credit risk insurance upon presentation of the premium charge, while FTOs in other countries may expect the seller to reflect any insurance in his prices.

The contract may lay down rules regarding such matters as the status of advance payments and whether and under what conditions (if any) they are to be considered as "conditional" and/or subject to repayment, and the rights of the seller in the event the buyer delays in making any payment (including possible entitlement to interest).

Payment clauses normally reflect such considerations as freight, insurance, packing requirements, delivery terms, and monetary or other factors that may significantly affect seller's costs subsequent to the making of the contract.[8]

Eastern countries vary as to the pressures that may be brought to bear on the Western supplier to conclude a barter or counterpurchase arrangement. If this issue arises in the contract negotiation, some Western companies are effectively able to deal with it through a generally worded clause expressing willingness in principle to make counterpurchases of a stated type and value if the products are offered at competitive prices and terms, and subject to the conclusion of specific contracts. Where possible this is normally best handled through legally separate contracts. If a Western seller finds that a barter or counterpurchasing arrangement is unavoidable, he will have to consider how best to protect himself against such risks as substandard quality of Eastern goods and unreliability of Eastern deliveries. If the deal involves Eastern goods that are not of direct use to the Western party, the latter's risk is that much greater.

Other Contract Issues. The foregoing discussion is intended to highlight certain areas of East-West contract negotiations. One especially important issue, that of dispute settlement clauses, is treated more comprehensively in Chapter 18.

If the contract is to involve export credits, insurance, guarantees, or other financial support from a government-backed export financing agency, it is indispensable to ensure that the contract fully conforms to any legal requirements of the agency. And, of course, the structuring of the contract must also be carefully reviewed for its tax implications, a matter beyond the scope of this discussion.

East-West contracts raise many other questions. For example, Eastern FTOs often seek to include detailed provisions regarding drawings and technical documentation, and as we have seen they often wish to impose penalties for delayed or incomplete documentation. Proposed clauses imposing obligations on the Western supplier of drawings and technical documentation must be carefully reviewed, for they may involve the transfer of valuable technical data and manufacturing know-how, sometimes with respect to items that are not of the seller's manufacture.

The Western negotiatior will also have to consider the risks and financial implications of any obligations involving translation of documents or the supply of interpreting services. FTOs may propose a contract in both the seller's and buyer's languages and a clause to the effect that "both texts are equally valid." Understandably, a Western company prefers to contract only in its own working language and does not wish to have a responsibility to determine whether there is conformity of texts. Also, a clause such as described above provides no guidance in the events a language discrepancy should appear.

However, it does not appear that such language problems have been a cause of disputes submitted to East-West arbitration.

Contracts calling for after-sales servicing involve a number of added complexities, mainly regarding the supply of spare parts and defraying expenses incurred by the seller in the buyer's country.

Where erection or installation and start-up of machinery or plant on site, or supervision thereof, is required,[9] particular care must be paid to the special problems of sending Western personnel to work in the buyer's country for example, living quarters; transportation arrangements; translation and interpretation; information and responsibilities concerning local laws and regulations; organization of work and the role of seller's personnel vis-à-vis local employees; working conditions including safety regulations; overtime rules and work outside of the contract; rules concerning leave, medical care, and insurance; responsibilities in case of interruption of work; allocation of responsibility for personal injuries or damage to property; liaison communications between seller and his personnel; and rules for liaison between representatives of the parties. Most importantly, the contract must lay down rules for determining and allocating all charges that may arise, and the rights and obligations of the parties during the erection, installation, and start-up or supervision period should be fully spelled out in the contract. FTOs often propose detailed conditions for such contracts (so detailed, in fact, that they may even cover the expenses connected with the death of the seller's personnel).

In negotiations for erection or installation and start-up of plant, and particularly in the case of large industrial works projects, a number of contract issues such as those noted above take on added complexity. Thus, calculation of penalty clauses relating to completion of work projects or failure of the plant to attain certain parameters is considerably more complex than calculation of penalties for delay in delivery of particular items.

The above discussion is not intended as an exhaustive treatment of the issues covered or to suggest that these issues will necessarily be the most difficult ones in a particular negotiation. Certain other issues commonly encountered in most international trade contracts, such as packing of goods, shipping requirements, insurance, delivery terms, passing of risks, and title, may also give rise to special considerations in the East-West context.

The Western negotiator should be on the alert for subtle but important differences that may be reflected in Eastern usage of similar or even identical terms, or apparent differences that on careful analysis prove to have similar significance. Take, for example, the term "value," used in the English text of many Soviet "standard form" contracts. It is not clear whether this is the same as "price," or "fair market value," or whether it might have still another meaning. Such uncertainty should be resolved in the contract negotiation.

In general, it may be said that contract clauses with the USSR
and Eastern Europe tend to be rather more detailed than the corresponding provisions in contracts between firms in market economy countries.
This detail perhaps reflects a desire on the part of Eastern trade
partners to leave as little doubt as possible concerning the contractual
relationship. They appear disinclined to draw up a contract in general
terms and rely on custom to fill in the gaps.

NOTES

1. See T. W. Hoya and J. B. Quigley, Jr., "Comecon 1968
General Delivery Conditions for the Delivery of Goods," 31 Ohio S.L.J.
1 (1970); and T. W. Hoya, "The Comecon General Conditions—A
Socialist Unification of International Trade Law," 70 Col. L. Rev.
253 (1970).
2. The work of the ECE in this regard has been analyzed by,
among others, P. Benjamin, "ECE General Conditions of Sale and
Standard Forms of Contract," J. Bus. L. 113 (1961); S. Michida, "Possible Avenues to Preparation of Standard Contracts for International
Trade as a Global Level," Unification of the Law Governing International
Sales of Goods 251 (ed. by J. Honnold, Paris, 1965); and C. M. Schmitthoff, "The Unification or Harmonization of Law by Means of Standard
Contracts and General Conditions," 17 Int'l and Comp. L. Q. 551- 559-
562 (1968). For a useful recent comparative analysis of many different general conditions of sale and standard contracts, see the Report
of the Secretary General to the United Nations Commission on International Trade Law, "General Conditions of Sale and Standard Contract," Doc. A/CN. 9/78, 16 March 1973.
3. DOCS TRADE/WP. 5/23 and TRADE/222, IM/WP. 5/83, respectively. The ECE is currently examining the possibility of a guide
on drawing up international contracts on industrial cooperation.
4. For texts, see Register of Texts of Conventions and Other
Instruments Concerning International Trade Law, Vol. 1, published
in 1971 by UNCITRAL.
5. H. J. Berman, "The Legal Framework of Trade Between
Planned and Market Economies: The Soviet-American Example,"
24 Law and Contemp. Probs 490 (1959).
6. See, for example, D. F. Ramzaitsev, "The Law Applied by
Arbitration Tribunals—I," and T. Ionasco and I. Nestor, "The Limits
of Party Autonomy—I," in The Sources of the Law of International
Trade 138, 167 (ed. by C. M. Schmitthoff, London, 1964); S. Pisar,
Coexistence and Commerce 438 et seq, (1970).
7. See, for example, The Sources of the Law of International
Trade, supra note 6 at 150-151 (Ramzaitsev) and 200 (Ionasco and
Nestor).

8. See, for example, the Supplementary Price Revision Clause in ECE General Conditions for the Supply and Erection of Plant and Machinery for Import and Export No. 574A.

9. See ECE General Conditions No. 574 and 574A, and Additional Clauses No. 574B.

17

**PROTECTION OF INDUSTRIAL
PROPERTY RIGHTS**
E. M. Jucker
H. Streitzig

In the past decade the traditional exchange of goods manufactured in the East and exported to the West against imports of highly sophisticated machines, fine mechanical equipment, chemicals, and so on has been increasingly complemented by a new type of trade, namely the exchange of technology. Indeed, technology is an independent productivity factor of the same order as labor or capital and is now recognized as one of the decisive elements for economic growth.

East-West commercial relations today reflect an increasing number of scientific, technological, and economic arrangements. Long-term agreements for delivery of completely equipped plants, exchange of patents and know-how, and joint ventures in manufacturing, research, and marketing are the results of the new trend. East European countries have increased their scientific and technological output to such an extent that partnership on an equal basis has become possible with the highly sophisticated capitalist enterprises of the West. This development is demonstrated by the number of patents sold by the East to the West and by the number of know-how agreements based on innovations achieved in the East.

In the long run, an Eastern socialist country turns into an economically and legally powerful state competitor, especially after expiration of patent and know-how licenses. Despite this theoretically justified concern, the general experience of Western companies in the field of exchange of technology with the East is positive, and apprehensions are as a rule exaggerated. Licensing of the latest

Editor's Note: For complementary discussions of this subject, and more detailed references to the relevant national laws, see the respective chapters of Part II.

technology to the East is a very interesting and promising new kind
of commercial transaction: However, we must keep in mind that this
trade cannot be oneway. Soviet leaders, for example, often claim
that it is insufferable that their first-class equipment and their newest
technology are less than willingly accepted by the West and still
encounter considerable emotional barriers.

PROTECTION OF INVENTIONS IN
EASTERN COUNTRIES

Legal regimes of industrial property protection are more extensive in the socialist countries than in the West and embrace not
only the examination and granting of protective rights but also the
encouragement of inventions. They also deal with the application of
the results of inventive activities to production processes.[1] Owing
to the state monopoly of the production facilities, as a rule the individual inventor in a socialist country is not in a position to put his
invention into practice himself.

After perfecting his invention, the inventor may hand it over
to the state, receiving a "certificate of authorship" as proof of his
original work. By granting a certificate of authorship, the state
assumes the obligation to exploit the invention. The inventor obtains
a right to remuneration depending on the savings achieved or other
beneficial effects accruing from the application of his invention. A
certificate, once granted, is subject to no time limit.

Soviet law governing inventions provides the model for industrial
property rights in Eastern Europe, although only Albania, Bulgaria,
and recently Czechoslovakia operate a system of certificates of
authorship that follow the Soviet model very closely. Mainly on
account of the development of their economies, the other socialist
countries have moved away from the Soviet system and introduced
special forms of protection. Hungary and Yugoslavia, which had
previously introduced the certificate of authorship, have given it up
again.

Industrial property rights in the wider sense include not only
inventions but also scientific discoveries and technical improvements
(rationalization proposals, innovations, and so on),[2] though for the
latter no certificates of authorship are awarded usually, only diplomas
or other documents.

In all the East European countries there exists protection of
inventions by patents apart from protection by certificates of authorship. With the exceptions of Albania and the Soviet Union, these
countries were in fact among the first to join the Paris Convention
of 1883 (the USSR became a full member only in 1965, and Albania
has not yet joined the Paris Convention).[3]

The conditions that have to be satisfied before a patent is granted in the socialist countries are comparable with the corresponding requirements in the West. However, the possibilities of exploiting the invention are far smaller in the socialist countries. Apart from the exclusive privilege, the patentee in a socialist country can only transfer his patent together with the licensing rights to a state organization or enterprise. In contrast to the certificate of authorship, patents have a limited period of validity. Generally (with the exception of Czechoslovakia), patents may be converted into certificates of authorship at any time during their period of validity, but certificates of authorship cannot be changed into patents.

In the survey of industrial property rights in the socialist countries that follows, mention will also be made of forms of protection that do not concern inventions and are unknown in the Western countries, dealing with discoveries and rationalization proposals.

Albania[4]

A degree enacted in 1950 reflected the influence of the Soviet legal system. This influence was again apparent in the law of July 1956 and in the decree of January 12, 1960, currently in force, governing discoveries, inventions, and rationalization proposals. Both laws are supplemented by an implementation decree dating from 1963. Albania is the only socialist country in Eastern Europe that is not a party to the Paris Convention.

Protection Categories

Discoveries. Protection is granted for discoveries in the fields of the natural sciences, medicine, and astronomy.[5] (The relevant legal provisions do not name these discovery categories specifically. As in the Soviet model, it is merely stated that discoveries in the fields of the social sciences, archaeology, geology, and palaeontology do not qualify for protection. Essentially, this means that in Albania and in the other socialist countries discussed below, the previously mentioned discovery categories are protected.) Discoveries submitted are examined by the Patent Office, with the assistance of the Academy of Science. If the application is granted, the discoverer receives a single payment and a diploma.

Inventions. Inventions may be protected by certificates of authorship or by patents, chemical substances as such being excluded from protection. In the case of inventions of substances produced by chemical means, both certificates of authorship and patents may be granted for the new manufacturing process. Only certificates of authorship are granted for medicaments, new methods for treating diseases that have been tried in practice and are in regular use, inventions concerning the cultivation of new seed strains by seedsmen and seed cultivation stations, and the breeding of new and improved livestock strains.

Though absolute novelty is stipulated for inventions, the novelty criterion is based only on Albanian certificates of authorship and patents.

Patents of addition are possible in Albania. The inventor of the supplementary invention (if the main invention was also his) is granted a priority of six months against third persons.

Patents remain valid for 15 years from the date of the application. Applications regarding inventions are examined for novelty (see above), while applications regarding certificates of authorship are examined for utility as well. Organizations that were in possession of the invention before the application was lodged and that have been exploiting or were preparing to exploit the invention independently of the inventor, may continue to exploit it after the patent is granted.

Rationalization Proposals. Rationalization proposals are protected and reimbursed, but absolute novelty is required.

Conflicts

The settling of disputes connected with the granting of patents and certificates of authorship, as well as remuneration for these, is left to the courts. The law does not lay down which kind of court has to deal with disputes regarding patent infringements.

Bulgaria[6]

In 1950, when legal protection for industrial property was brought into line with the country's new socialist system, the Soviet legal system was copied to a large extent. The law now in force dealing with inventions and rationalizations dates from 1968 (effective January 1, 1969). The protection of discoveries is regulated by a 1961 law.

Protection Categories

Discoveries. Protection is granted in respect of discoveries in the natural sciences, medicine, and astronomy. After recognition by the Academy of Science, a diploma is granted to the discoverer by the Institute for Inventions and Rationalizations. He is entitled to remuneration on the strength of this.

465

Inventions. A new, creative, and technical solution for a task is regarded as an invention. To merit protection the invention must be new, progressive, and useful, compared with the existing state of the art. It may relate to any field of the national economy, science, culture, public health, and national defense. Absolute novelty is required against Bulgarian and foreign patents and publications and against notorious use in Bulgaria and other countries.

Both patents and certificates of authorship are issued for inventions. The certificate of authorship is obtainable only by individual inventors. Bulgaria has not adopted the Soviet provision whereby these certificates may also be granted to enterprises and organizations. Socialist organizations with whose aid the inventors have made their inventions are, however, entitled to exploit these inventions and be named in the certificate of authorship. The exclusive right of the state to the inventions remains unaffected by this.

Only certificates of authorship are granted for the following:

● Substances obtained by chemical means.
● Medicaments, foodstuffs, semiluxury articles, and cosmetics produced by chemical and/or other means.
● New methods of prophylaxis, diagnosis, and treatment of diseases in human beings, animals, and plants.
● New strains of agricultural plants or new breeds of animals.
● Technical solutions to problems associated with the utilization of nuclear energy.
● Inventions made in conjunction with the work of the author in a socialist organization or with the authority of such an organization.
● Inventions for the development of which the inventor has received financial or material assistance from a socialist organization.
● Inventions in connection with the defense and security of the country.

Patents also may be issued for new processes for the manufacture of the substances in the first two categories mentioned above. The patent endows the patentee with the exclusive right to the invention, including the right to transfer the patent or grant a license. Express provision is made for the possibility of a compulsory license. Enterprises, institutions, and persons who have already exploited the invention independently of the subsequent patentee retain the right to claim the invention as joint users.

An additional invention is defined as an invention that constitutes an improvement to another invention for which a patent or certificate of authorship has been granted and that cannot be exploited on its own without the use of the main patent. For additional inventions, a dependent certificate of authorship may be granted up to 15 years after the issuing of the main certificate of authorship; otherwise, the additional invention becomes independent. For an additional invention to an original main patent, an application may be lodged optionally for a dependent patent or a dependent certificate of authorship. An additional invention can be exploited only with the agreement of the owner of the main patent. Any application referring to an additional invention lodged by the inventor of the main invention within three months of the publication (that is, date of permission to print in the Official Gazette) of the main invention enjoys priority over applications submitted by others during this period.

A patent remains valid 15 years from the date of application.

Rationalization proposals. These are defined as technical solutions to a problem that constitute a novelty at least within the enterprise or organization and are regarded as a useful and progressive change in existing production processes, designs, projects of technology, scientific organization, or material. The state is greatly interested in inventions and rationalization measures, and there are accordingly state bodies occupied solely with the encouragement of inventions.

Conflicts

The Institute of Inventions and Rationalizations is responsible for the appraisal of a patent, its nullity and its priority. For other disputes, such as infringement lawsuits, the courts are competent. Injunctions and compensation for damages may be claimed, subject to a limitation period of three years. Provision is made for prosecution.

Czechoslovakia[7]

On April 1, 1952, a new patent law came into force. Though in general it followed the principles of invention legislation in other socialist countries, among other things introducing protection for improvement proposals, it did not adopt the certificate of authorship. Inventions could be protected only by patents. This law was not in force very long and was replaced by a new one on July 16, 1957. This new law provides for protection of authorship, though only in exceptional cases. A law that came into force on January 1, 1973 introduced the certificate of authorship as a major form of protection, taking the Soviet certificate as its model to a large extent.

Protection Categories

Discoveries. A discovery is defined as the establishment of previously
unknown but objectively existing phenomena, properties, or laws of
the material world. As with the Soviet model, however, only discoveries in the natural sciences, medicine, and astronomy are recognized.
Descriptions of discoveries are submitted to the Academy of Sciences.
If the academy considers the discovery to be new, it arranges publication in collaboration with the author and the Patent Office. If the
novelty is not effectively contested within a year of publication, the
Patent Office issues the discoverer a diploma at the recommendation
of the academy.

Inventions. Czechoslovakia's patent law defines an invention as a
solution to a technical problem that (related to the worldwide state of
the art) is new and constitutes an advance on the previous state of the
art, reflected in a new and higher effectiveness.
     Certificates of authorship or patents are issued for inventions.
Only certificates of authorship are granted for inventions made by
the author (or coauthors) as part of his activities within a socialist
organization or with the material support of such an organization.
Moreover, only certificates of authorship are granted for substances
resulting from nuclear reactions and for technical solutions associated
with the generation or exploitation of nuclear energy, as well as for
medicaments, chemically produced substances, foodstuffs, and industrial production microorganisms. When a certificate of authorship is
granted for an invention, the invention becomes national property.
The state has not only the right to exploit the invention but in fact the
duty to see that it is exploited.
     Processes for the production of foodstuffs, medicaments, and
substances produced chemically may be protected by patents. Patent
validity is 15 years from the application date. The patentee has the
exclusive right to exploit the invention—that is, to produce the object
individually and put it on the market or apply it in production as the
case may be. He is also entitled to grant licenses. This positive
exploitation right is, however, restricted by constitutional provisions
governing the possibility of owning production facilities. A patent can
be converted in a certificate of authorship within seven years after
grant.
     The rights conferred with the patent are ineffective against
anyone who, independently of the patentee, was exploiting the invention
before the application was submitted or was preparing to exploit it.
     For an invention dependent on another invention for which an
earlier application has been submitted and for which a certificate of
authorship or a patent has been granted, a dependent certificate of

468

authorship or a dependent patent is issued if exploitation is conditional upon exploitation of the basic invention.

Improvement Proposals. An improvement proposal is defined as a concrete solution to a problem of manufacturing technique, technical organization, or organizational economics within an organization. It must be new to this organization, and its application must bring benefits for society. Novelty implies that no analogous solution must exist in regulations or directives (such as technical standards and instructions). If the proposal is accepted, the applicant is entitled to remuneration. In addition he receives a diploma.

Conflicts

The Patent Office decides on the nullification of patents, on the compulsory granting of licenses and petitions by the patentee or a third party with a legal interest, and whether a patent has been infringed or not. Against any ruling by the Patent Office an appeal may be made to its president, whose decision is final and binding on the courts. Patent infringement disputes are settled by the courts.

The German Democratic Republic[8]

A 1950 Patent Law introduced the economic patent in addition to the exclusive patent. An amending law in 1963 introduced the delayed examination and abolished the protection of utility patents. A decree concerning innovators was enacted in 1963, together with a regulation governing license traffic with other countries.

The law concerning inventions in the GDR presupposes collective ownership of the means of production and subordinates the interests of the inventor to those of the socialist economy. Allowance must however be made for the fact that there are still capitalist producers in the GDR, who must retain the possibility of exploiting exclusively the inventions developed by them. The GDR law is influenced by the interests of the state and by the interests of certain independent producers so that it differs not only from Soviet law but also from the laws in other socialist countries.

Forms of Protection

Inventions. Inventions must be new (this refers to printed publications during the last 100 years as well as obvious prior use in the GDR) and industrially applicable. Besides novelty and applicability, in practice two further requirements must be met before protection is granted:

The invention must be technically progressive and embody the necessary level of invention. In the cases of foodstuffs, semiluxuries, and medicaments and substances produced by chemical means, patents can be granted only for particular manufacturing processes. An invention may be protected either by an exclusive or an economic patent. In principle, the applicant has the choice between the two forms. If, however, an invention has been made in a socialist enterprise or research institute in connection with the activities of the inventor or with state assistance or is the result of an invention assignment, only an economic patent may be granted.

The right to exploit an economic patent rests with the patentee and with the person nominated by the Patent Office. In principle, every socialist organization is free to exploit the patent, subject to the payment of a single lump-sum remuneration. The amount of this payment depends on the importance of the invention to society, the achievement of the inventor, and the contribution of society toward the invention. In the case of an economic patent granted for an invention made under assignment, the patentee also requires the permission of the Patent Office before he can exploit the invention patented in his name. In the case of an exclusive patent, only the patentee has the right to exploit it. At his request, however, the exclusive patent may be converted into an economic one.

The Patent Law is based consistently on the inventor principle. Both with the exclusive and the economic patent, the rights reside with the inventor or his legal successor. Exceptions are envisaged only in the case of an economic patent resulting from an assignment invention where the inventor refrains from lodging a patent application. In that case, the enterprise may apply for an economic patent. Furthermore, in the case of an assignment invention, the person who gave the assignment also has the right to apply for a patent.

The validity of a patent, either exclusive or economic, is for 18 years, calculated from the day following the date on which the application was lodged at the Patent Office. If the patent is granted for a process, the protection extends also to the immediate products of the process. The patent is not effective against anyone who, at the time of the application, was already exploiting the invention in the GDR or was making appropriate preparations to do so. An application may be submitted for a patent of addition in respect of a further development or improvement to a patented invention.

Upon receiving an application, the Patent Office first issues a patent without examining the application for fulfillment of the material requirements for patent protection, in particular novelty, technical progress, level of invention, existence of prior patents, and so on.[9] There is only a formal examination as to whether the application is patentable at all, and the state of the art is recorded. If the requirements are satisfied, a provisional patent is granted. With the issuing of the patent, protection is provided for the time being. Actual examination follows only in the event of exploitation—that is, at the request of the patentee if a protected process product is imported into the GDR and also at the request of enterprises or authorities. It is mandatory where licenses negotiations have reached an advanced stage or when an infringement suit is filed. If the subsequent examination reveals that the invention is wholly or partly unpatentable, the patent is annulled wholly or in part. Otherwise the original patent is confirmed.

Innovations. Innovations are defined in an innovators' decree of 1963 and an amending decree of June 1967 as proposals for (1) improving machinery, equipment, and so on, (2) raising work productivity, or (3) improving hygiene, work safety, fire prevention, or working conditions—proposals that secure economic or other advantages for society. In principle, an innovation is any proposal that alters the existing method of working and brings benefits. A level of invention is not necessary. Provided that their innovation is exploited, those submitting proposals for innovations or methods or owners of economic patents or their legal successors are entitled to remuneration.

Conflicts

The examination of inventions and the nullification of patents are performed by the Patent Office. Against the decision of the Patent Office, an appeal to the Supreme Court is possible in certain cases. Patent disputes, especially infringement suits, are handled by the District Court in Leipzig. Against the decision of this court, an appeal may be made to the Supreme Court of the GDR.

Hungary[10]

In 1969, Hungary enacted unified and up-to-date legislation governing industrial property rights. For the patenting of inventions, this law provides for the so-called complete examination and postponed examination. The complete examination includes in particular an examination for novelty and technical progress in the invention for which a patent is requested. For many fields—for example, for chemical inventions—an examination is officially prescribed. In all other cases, a complete examination may be requested by anyone within four years of the publication of the application.

Protection Categories

Inventions. A patentable invention is defined as any new, progressive
technical solution that can be applied in practice. An invention is
regarded as new if there has been no printed description or notorious
use anywhere in the world during the 100 years prior to the date of
the application. Plant strains and animal breeds can be protected
under provisions specially stipulated in the law. Excluded from patent
protection, however, are medicaments, products produced by chemical
means, and foodstuffs. On the other hand, production processes for
these are patentable, as are also alloys. With all inventions, the
employer is entitled to lodge patent applications, the moral rights of
the inventor being secured.[11] Remuneration is linked with the exploitation of the invention and not with its formal protection.

The licensing provisions have been drafted with special care.
Enterprises that are owners of patented inventions may transfer
exploitation rights to other enterprises, a payment being agreed as
a rule. The purpose of this provision is to encourage economic competition between enterprises and thus technological progress as well.

Patents are valid 20 years from the date of the application. The
protection afforded by process patent also extends to the immediate
product of that process. Any person who was using the invention in
good faith before the priority date or preparing to use it is entitled
to continue using it after the patent is granted. No provision is made
for patents of addition in the new law.

Innovations. An innovation is any proposal (in the technical, organizational, or business fields) that, if implemented, will bring useful
economic or other results for the national economy, at the same time
improving quality or at least maintaining it. An innovation may also
be a proposal of this kind taken from technical literature (book,
periodical, description of lapsed patent). In contrast to an invention,
an innovation is required to embody only a relative novelty. This
relative novelty does not exist, however, if the proposed idea is being
used or applied by the enterprise to which it is submitted or if the
enterprise or its controlling bodies certify that the implementation
of the proposal was planned before the date of its submission. With
innovations the exclusivity principle also applies: The author of the
innovation may transfer it to other enterprises only with the approval
of his own enterprise. The entitled enterprise may place the innovation
at the disposal of other enterprises against remuneration, though it
is not compelled to do this.

Conflicts

The nullity procedure, the negative declaratory procedure, and the interpretation of the patent description are performed by the Patent Office in the first instance. Against the decision of the Patent Office, however, an appeal may be lodged with the court in Budapest within 30 days. An appeal against the decision of the court may be lodged with the Supreme Court. In case of infringements, civil claims (such as confirmation of the patent infringement and injunctions) may be advanced against the infringer.

Poland[12]

After the establishment of the Polish Republic in 1918, patent laws were promulgated in 1919, 1924, and 1928. The last of these remained in force essentially until 1962. In order to conform with the socialist legal system, however, in 1950 the provisions of the 1928 law were supplemented by a decree regulating the rights of employees in connection with their inventions. It was laid down that, when a patent is granted to a state enterprise, the inventor is entitled to a certificate of authorship. In this way, patents and certificates of authorship were linked. The 1950 decree also introduced protection for technical improvements and perfections. A 1962 law brought no significant changes, merely coding systematically all the regulations introduced previously. On January 1, 1973, a new law came into force, bringing an alteration of the provisions of the 1962 law as they affected the protection of inventions and useful models.

Protection Categories

In Poland there is protection for a useful model, but scientific discoveries are not recognized as a special protection category. Accordingly, the following may qualify for protection: inventions, useful models, and rationalization proposals.

Inventions. Inventions are protected only by patents that recognize the ownership of the invention and the exclusive right to exploit it. Patents are not granted for foodstuffs, pharmaceuticals, and substances produced by chemical and radioactive processes, though the processes for producing them may be patented. Exploitation of patents is compulsory. The patentee must exploit his invention within three years of the granting of the patent. Exploitation must be within the framework of the national economy and continued for the duration of the validity of the patent; otherwise a license may be issued unilaterally by the Patent Office. Novelty may be prejudiced by the general world-wide state of the art and notorious exploitation or exhibition within Poland.

The 1973 law provides for the granting of two kinds of patents: a temporary patent with a validity of five years, and the patent usual hitherto, with a validity of 15 years from the date of the application.

A limited examination (as to novelty in Poland) is stipulated for granting the temporary patent. The patent with a validity of 15 years is issued after full examination (as to worldwide novelty). After examination, a temporary patent may be converted into one valid for 15 years. The Patent Office announces the submission of the application 18 months after the date of priority. The protection afforded by a process patent also covers the immediate product of the process. Anyone who, on the priority date, is exploiting the invention in good faith or is preparing to do so may continue to exploit it on the same scale after the patent is granted. The owner of a patent for an invention may obtain a subsequent patent (patent of addition) for improvements or supplements to this invention if these improvements or supplements constitute an invention but cannot be applied on their own. The position is different in the case of employees' inventions. Such inventions are made under assignment from or with the help of an enterprise of the socialist economy or by an employee in an enterprise. The unit of the socialist economy applies for a patent on the invention under its own name and obtains the patent to its favor.[13] Other units of the socialist economy may use the invention only in return for compensation.[14] The inventor concerned gets a certificate of authorship, and his data together with the data of the patent are entered in the Patent Register. The legal definition of an employee's invention is thus valid only within the socialist economy. Inventions resulting from employment in a nonsocialist enterprise are not regarded as employees' inventions, and in such cases a contract between the employee and employer may assign the patent with its exclusive rights to the enterprise. The author of an invention proposal accepted for exploitation is entitled to remuneration commensurate with the economic results obtained with it.

Useful Models. A useful model is defined as the technical design, hitherto unused in Poland, of an object, its system, construction, and assembly in durable form, making the object more useful or easier to employ. Protection for a useful model lasts five years and can be extended for a further five years by application of the owner. Protection for useful models is granted after a limited examination.

Rationalization Proposals.[15] Rationalization proposals are defined as new projects not having the characteristics of an invention or useful model that in the field of the national economy bring about an improvement in the application of a technique, in the quality of a product, in methods of technical control, in testing or safety, and in working hygiene or that improve the results of work or contribute toward a better utilization of the working media. Rationalization proposals must be generally applicable and new for the socialist economy (limited novelty stipulation). The author of a rationalization proposal is entitled to remuneration.

Conflicts

The Patent Office decides on the nullification of patents, useful model certificates, certificates of authorship, and rationalization certificates. An application for a negative declaratory procedure may also be lodged with the Patent Office. For infringement disputes arising from patents granted and from registered useful models as well as in disputes regarding the authorship of a patent application or patent or useful model, there are competent courts.

Romania[16]

The first Romanian patent law, dating from 1906 remained in force until 1950, when a decree introduced certificates of invention for inventions belonging to the state. The law was reformulated in 1967.

Protection Categories

Inventions. Romanian patent law defines an invention as the solution of a technical problem in any branch of the economy, science, culture, social services, and national defense that constitutes a novelty and an advance over the known worldwide state of the art. Anyone who was exploiting the invention in good faith before the priority date of the application or was preparing to do this may continue these activities on the same scale after the patent is granted.

Patents for substances produced by nuclear processes or methods, chemical products, disinfectants, foodstuffs, and spices together with new plant strains are granted only to state enterprises and other state organizations.[17] For chemical substances, medicaments, foodstuffs, and semiluxuries, foreigners may obtain only patents for the processes by which these are produced. Patents are issued to enterprises for service inventions and inventions under assignment. In all cases, the inventor receives an invention certificate together with all rights associated with this.

Patents of addition are granted for inventions constituting an improvement or supplement to another invention for which a patent has been granted and that cannot be exploited without making use of the main patent. Patents of addition must satisfy the same conditions as main patents.

Protection is afforded to the inventor and his legal successor. In addition to his claim to the patent, the inventor is entitled to transfer his rights to an enterprise. In this case, the patent is granted to the enterprise, and the inventor receives an invention certificate.

The only form of protection for inventions is the patent.[18] The invention certificate issued to the inventor or inventors when an invention is transferred to an enterprise in the cases just mentioned constitutes the certificate of authorship for the invention and at the same time the entitlement to remuneration of the beneficiary.[19] Patents are valid for 15 years from the application date.

Despite the standardized form of protection afforded by the patent, there is a considerable difference between patents granted to an inventor and those to an enterprise. With the patent, an exclusive exploitation right is conceded to the inventor, but not to a state enterprise, because all socialist enterprises possess a license by law allowing them to exploit any invention for which a patent has been granted to any socialist enterprise. Such exploitation takes place without any prior formalities, though the patentee or Patent Office must be notified of the exploitation.[20] The question of remunerability of exploitation is not mentioned in the law, but in practice exploitation is remunerable—first, because of civil law generally and, second, because the state desires to stimulate enterprises to make and patent inventions.[21]

Innovations and Rationalization Proposals. Romanian law recognizes both innovations and rationalization proposals. The difference is qualitative and quantitative in nature. An innovation is a useful and progressive solution to a technical problem; rationalization means a solution to an organizational problem. If, however, benefits during the first year exceed 20,000 lei, a rationalization measure is regarded as an innovation. If they are below this sum, a solution that is actually a technical one will be regarded as a rationalization. In both cases, the criterion is the relative novelty in the organization in which the innovation or rationalization is to be applied. The author of an innovation or rationalization proposal or his legal successor is entitled to a remuneration if his proposal is exploited.

Conflicts

Disputes concerned with patents are settled by the appeals commission of the Patent Office. Disputes in connection with the rights associated with invention patents, transfers, and licenses may be submitted to the courts.

The USSR[22]

In 1919 a decree was promulgated governing industrial property rights. It supplanted all prerevolutionary legislation, introducing the certificate of authorship as the basic form of protection for inventions and with it the general exploitability of inventions. Since, however, a large part of the production facilities were privately owned at that time, the arrangement did not work well. The decree was replaced by a new one in September 1924, which abandoned the certificate of authorship in favor of the patent once more. The decree also contained provisions for compulsory licensing and nationalizing patented inventions, as well as some modern rules for regulating the legal position with regard to inventions by employees.

During the first five-year plan (1927-32), in 1931, the 1924 decree was repealed and the certificate of authorship was reintroduced. As the new protection form, the certificates of authorship covered minor technical improvements and rationalization proposals. This coverage was intended to encourage workers to submit inventions, innovations, or rationalization proposals. In 1961 a further patent law entered in force comprising the revisions of the 1931 law together with subsequent decrees of 1941 and 1942 improving the material position of inventors. The patent act now in force dates from January 1, 1974. In 1965 the USSR became a full member of the Paris Convention (Lisbon text).

Protection Categories

Discoveries.[23] Soviet patent law defines a discovery as the "establishment of objectively existing but previously unknown laws, properties and phenomena of the material world," though it excludes "geographical, archaeological and palaentological discoveries as well as discoveries of mineral deposits and discoveries in the social sciences etc." In practice this means that, as in Albania, Bulgaria, and Czechoslovakia, only discoveries in the natural sciences, medicine, and astronomy qualify for protection. A diploma is issued to the discoverer (or enterprise in the case of discoveries made by an enterprise).

Inventions. An invention is defined as a fundamental new solution to a technical problem, one that makes a substantial contribution in any field of the national economy, culture, hygiene, or national defense. Certificates of authorship may be granted for medicaments, substances produced by chemical means or resulting from nuclear reactions, semiluxuries, foodstuffs, technical solutions associated with the exploitation of nuclear energy, and strains of microorganisms. Patents may be issued for processes for producing medicaments, semiluxuries, and foodstuffs as well as chemical substances.

Patents and certificates of authorship are granted only for new, inventive, and technically progressive solutions to technical problems. The state of the art includes publications all over the world as well as older applications in the USSR.

The certificate of authorship also grants protection for achievements in the field of bioengineering, establishing new, economical plant strains and animal breeds.[24] These achievements are not inventions in the usual sense of the definition and are placed on the same footing as inventions only in respect of the form of protection. Only certificates of authorship are granted if the invention has been made by an employee or under assignment in a state, cooperative, or social organization, or if it is the result of financial or other material aid. Otherwise, in principle, the inventor has the right to choose between a certificate of authorship or a patent. The certificate of authorship is the form of protection used chiefly by Soviet inventors. If his invention is exploited, the author receives a remuneration of 1.5 percent of the saving resulting from putting the invention into practice (calculated for the first 12 months).

The patent allows foreign applicants to protect their inventions in the USSR. Throughout the time of the patent's validity, however, the patentee is entitled to apply for the conversion of the patent into a certificate of authorship if no license has been granted for it. A certificate of authorship cannot be converted into a patent. A patent is valid 15 years from the date of the application. If a patent has been issued contrary to the legal regulations, it may be contested and nullified throughout its period of validity.

An enterprise that independently of the inventor was using the same invention before the application was lodged or had made preparations to use it enjoys the right of prior use against the invention. Toward other Soviet organizations, however, the exclusive right conferred by the patent is maintained in this case.

Legal transactions involving patents, in particular licensing, are valid only if registered with the State Committee for Discoveries and Inventions. Provision is made for the compulsory granting of licenses, though no use has as yet been made of this. A decision on compulsory licensing must be made by the Council of Ministers of the USSR, which at the same time fixes the amount of compensation to be paid.

Additional inventions are defined as inventions that constitute a further development of another (main) invention for which a certificate of authorship or patent has already been granted and that cannot be exploited without using the main invention. It is not required that the same party apply for the main invention and the additional invention.

Rationalization. Rationalization proposals are defined as proposals that as applied technology (machinery, equipment, tools, devices, apparatus, plants) improve the products manufactured, the production technology, supervision and research methods, safety engineering and work safety, as well as proposals allowing increased work productivity, efficient exploitation of energy, equipment, and material. The authorship of a rationalization proposal is confirmed by a written certificate (diploma). In addition to the authorship and the date of the application in the enterprise, the certificate states that the rationalization proposal has been put into effect. From this, the author of the proposal can claim the moral and material rights prescribed by law.

Conflicts[25]

The Patent Office decides certain categories of disputes, chiefly those concerning the recognition of the invention and priority. The criminal courts deal with the following types of cases: infringement of authorship; disclosure of the nature of an invention before the application and without the approval of the inventor; bureaucratic delay of the procedure after lodging the application; delay in the procedure for exploiting the subject of the protection; and fixing remuneration due to authors. The civil courts are competent for disputes involving authorship of a discovery; priority of a rationalization proposal if this has not been settled within the particular organization; fixing the remuneration for inventors or authors of rationalization proposals; and patent infringements (mainly declaratory or injunction actions). An action for compensation in the case of patent infringement is possible only in accordance with the general principles of civil law.

Yugoslavia[26]

After the introduction of the self-administration system in the state factories, a 1948 patent law was replaced by a new one, in 1960, which was adapted to the new economic system. The 1960 law provide only patent protection. Certificates of authorship and state patents are abolished.

Protection Categories

Inventions. An invention is defined as a new (in relation to Yugoslav and foreign publications and patents as well as notorious prior use in Yugoslavia) solution to a particular technical problem, which can be exploited in industry or in any other economic field. In the cases of chemical substances, medicaments, semiluxuries, and foodstuffs, only production processes can be protected. Alloys as such qualify for protection. In principle, the inventor or his legal successor has a right to patent protection. If the inventor or inventors cannot be established or a corresponding contract exists between the inventor and an enterprise, the application may be lodged in the name of the organization. An invention developed in an organization and patented in its name may be exploited solely by this enterprise. Exploitation by other enterprises or organizations without the permission of the patentee is possible only on the strength of a legal exploitation license. This is granted if the patentee is not exploiting the invention or not exploiting it sufficiently for the national economy. This license is also remunerative and is issued only if no contractual agreement can be reached. In this case, a special arbitration court must decide whether the license is to be granted and what compensation must be paid.27

Every patentee has the exclusive right of exploitation, with due allowance for the restrictions imposed by the socialist economic system. Thus, everyone can exploit his patented inventions within the framework of the economic activities permitted by law. Since, however, the great majority of the production facilities in Yugoslavia are nationalized, licensing between private patentees and socialist organizations is usual.

A patent remains valid 15 years from the publication of the decision to grant it. The exclusive right is, however, in force from the date of the application, provided that the patent is subsequently granted. The protection afforded by a process patent also covers the immediate product of the process. If an applicant or patentee supplements his invention, an additional patent may be applied for in respect of the extension or perfection achieved. Any unauthorized exploitation of an invention covered by a patent application or patent constitutes an infringement. Any person who, independently of the inventor, has already exploited the invention not publicly before the date of the application or has made preparations to do this, retains the right to further exploitation after the patent is granted.

Technical Improvements.28 Technical improvements may refer to all known technical media and technologies. A level of invention is not necessary. On the other hand, an application of an existing technique to a new field does not constitute a technical improvement. Besides his right to moral recognition, the author of a technical improvement is also entitled to commensurate remuneration.

Conflicts

Against all decisions of the Patent Office, an appeal may be made to the Supreme Court. Other disputes—in particular, infringement suits—are left to the higher economic courts.

EXTENT OF INDUSTRIAL PROPERTY RIGHTS PROTECTION—SOME COMPARISONS BETWEEN EAST AND WEST

Considerations Regarding the Strength of Patent Protection

The benefit that the holder of a patent derives from his patent is closely connected with his ability to discover infringement and thereafter to act appropriately, for example by suing for infringement. In the chemical field, discovery of imitation may be effected by analysis of the allegedly infringing product. Per se protection is the strongest form of protection available and is clearly of particular advantage as regards unauthorized importation.

In comparison with compound protection, the process protection afforded in many countries is of course very weak. In assessing the strength of process protection, it is important to consider two concepts, namely "derived compound protection" (or product-by-process protection, as it is sometimes called) and "reversal of the onus of proof." In some countries, as in Hungary and Czechoslovakia, the patentee has to make out a prima facie case of infringement (based on at least some evidence) and the alleged infringer is then required to prove noninfringement. This, however, cannot be considered as reversal of the onus of proof in the classic sense, where there is presumption of the use of the patented process, unless evidence to the contrary is provided.

Both legal concepts are extremely valuable tools, and in countries where neither concept exists, only the actual carrying out of the process in the country concerned constitutes infringement. Importation of a product produced abroad by the patented process will not infringe. In these countries, a patentee must prove that his process has actually been employed in the country concerned. In practice this is often extremely difficult, particularly when there are a number of alternative processes available in addition to that or those actually patented. In countries that provide for derived compound protection, unauthorized importation of the compound prepared abroad by the patented process constitutes infringement. However, where there is no provision for the reversal of the onus of proof, the practical difficulties of proving that the process employed abroad is in fact the patented process, which are often insurmountable, render this type of protection of dubious value. Consequently, from the practical viewpoint, process protection is of very limited value unless the law provides both for the reversal of the onus of proof and for derived compound protection, but even then the strength of the protection is fairly limited in comparison to product protection.

Patent Protection for Chemical Inventions

For purposes of comparison, the following West European countries will be considered: Austria, Belgium, Denmark, the Federal Republic of Germany, Finland, France, the Netherlands, Norway, Sweden, Switzerland, and the United Kingdom.

Countries Providing for Compound Protection Per Se. This form of protection is provided in Belgium, the Federal Republic of Germany, France, the United Kingdom, and, except for pharmaceuticals, Norway, Sweden, Denmark, and Finland. No East European socialist country provides for the patenting of compounds per se.

Countries Providing Only for Process Protection, But with Derived Compound Protection and Reversal of the Onus of Proof. This protection is provided in Austria, the Netherlands (if two processes are disclosed, it is possible to have protection for all analogy—or non-inventive—processes) and Switzerland, and also is applicable, following jurisdiction, in Finland, Norway, and Sweden (pharmaceuticals only). The following socialist countries fall within this category: the GDR, Poland, and Yugoslavia.

Countries Providing Only for Process Protection with Derived Compound Protection, but Not for the Reversal of the Onus of Proof. Of the West European countries, Denmark (pharmaceuticals only) falls into this category (pending jurisdiction) and, of the socialist countries, Hungary.

Countries Providing Only for Process and with Neither Derived Compound Protection nor Reversal of the Onus of Proof. None of the West European countries under present consideration fall into this category, whereas the following socialist countries do: Albania, Bulgaria, Czechoslovakia, Romania, and the USSR.

Maximum Term of Patent Protection

The term of patent protection in the socialist countries is often shorter than that in the West. For instance, the term of protection in Albania, Bulgaria, Czechoslovakia, Poland, Romania, and the USSR is 15 years from the date of application, in the German Democratic Republic 18 years from the day following the date of application, in Hungary 20 years from the date of application, and in Yugoslavia 15 years from the date of publication. Some examples of the terms of patent protection in the West countries are in Belgium and France 20 years and in Denmark, Finland, Norway, and Sweden 17 years from the date of application.

Protection for Nonchemical Inventions

For inventions not dealt with in the two sections on pages 481-83, especially inventions of objects, machines, and so on, protection in the socialist countries is comparable to the West European countries, though differences may arise due to official practice. With respect to protection of computer programs, there is a measure of uncertainty in many countries, both East and West.

Protection of Compositions

In almost all the West European countries, compositions (with the possible exceptions of those relating to pharmaceuticals and foodstuffs) are patentable. Conversely, in socialist countries, compositions are either unpatentable or allowable only in very restricted form—for example, in Albania, Bulgaria, and the USSR, restriction to the specific components of the compositions is required. In the GDR, composition claims, in so far as they relate to the use of the compound produced by an analogy process, were held to be unallowable following a decision of October 1972. However, it is felt that it may be possible to gain allowance of composition claims even when the active componds are produced by analogy processes, providing that the compositions are novel and clearly recite each component, and the quantity thereof, of the compositions. In Yugoslavia, similar difficulties arise in the protection of compositions since claims to compositions are regarded as attempts to protect the compounds per se.

Problems Arising from the Different Practices Adopted by Patent Offices in Process Countries

Apart from the previously described differences between the strength of process and compound protection, additional problems arise from the different approaches adopted by the Patent Offices in process countries. In several Western countries, the application is considered uniform, provided that at least one process is covered by which all of the final products involved can be produced. In the Netherlands, very broad protection is allowable, and normally all analogy processes can be claimed in one application. Of the socialist countries, only the GDR and Hungary take a comparatively broad view of unity. Only a single process may be claimed in one application in Austria and Switzerland, and similar requirements exist in Albania, Bulgaria, Czechoslovakia, Yugoslavia, Poland, Romania, and the USSR. Generally, where disunity occurs, the original application must be restricted according to the requirements of the Patent Office and, if the remaining processes are to be protected, the appropriate number of divisional applications must be filled. This leads to a considerable increase in expense. Expenses in the socialist countries tend to be high compared with those in the West, and the need to file divisionals adds to cost problems.

RECENT DEVELOPMENTS IN INTERNATIONAL PROTECTION OF INDUSTRIAL PROPERTY

In the last few years, there have been important developments in the European Communities. Of particular interest are the European Economic Community (EEC) Patent and the European Patent Convention. In the near future, it will be possible for an inventor from East or West to file a single application that will result in a patent with validity in all EEC countries. Protection of compounds per se and pharmaceuticals is foreseen, and the term of the European Patent will be 20 years from the date of filing. It will be possible to file one patent application that, if approved, will result in a bundle of national patents in all European countries adhering to the European Patent Convention. The rights stemming from an EEC patent or from the bundle of European patents will be very effective. Inventors from East European countries will certainly make the best use of these new possibilities and will achieve a very strong position in the West.

In comparison, as discussed above, the inventor from the West still encounters many difficulties in the socialist countries. He must file a large number of individual applications in each of the socialist countries, and he has to face the fact that the rights conferred on him in the socialist countries are inadequate compared with the rights conferred on the Eastern inventor in the West. This situation creates various problems for East-West trade and cooperation. However, it should be noted that it is especially the Soviet Union today that is aiming at a harmonization of these aspects. During the last few years, the Soviet Union has concluded various bilateral agreements—for example, with France, Italy, West Germany, and Austria—and is now negotiating similar agreements with other countries. These agreements aim at a closer scientific, technological, and economic cooperation and contemplate certain legislative measures in the field of industrial property to facilitate patenting of inventions stemming from such cooperation. It is hoped that this development will continue.

CONCLUSIONS

The patent systems of industrialized countries in the West generally offer more effective protection to foreign inventors, including also inventors from Eastern Europe, than the patent systems of Eastern countries offer to inventors from Western countries.

In both the socialist and capitalist countries, patents represent a right to exclude others from using inventions. This "negative" right, which does not allow an invention to be utilized, materially, is practically the only right to which a foreign inventor is entitled in a socialist country. Thus, he is dependent on the agreement of the civil authorities for any utilization of his invention. The situation for the foreign inventor in a capitalist industrial country is quite different. He can, with complete freedom, choose the optimal utilization of his invention, be it by sale of the invention, granting of exclusive or nonexclusive licenses, or setting up of production alone or with others. In the chemical area, there is discrimination as a consequence of the ban on product protection in socialist countries, which ban has already been lifted or will be lifted in the near future in industrialized capitalist countries. The institution of the Certificate of Authorship is also felt to be de facto discriminatory on the following grounds: Admittedly, a Certificate of Authorship grants the same rights to a foreign inventor as to a native inventor. However, these rights amount only to compensation in the form of a limited sum in the local currency or practical privileges generally relating to improvement in living standards. Such rights are attractive only for the national inventor and not for the foreign inventor.

Abolition of, or at least a reduction in, this threefold discrimination (namely, the restricted possibilities of utilization, the lack of product protection for chemical inventions, and the nature of the compensation for Certificates of Authorship) would very significantly contribute to an improvement in trade relations between socialist and capitalist countries.

Exchange of technology over national barriers cannot proceed without a proper protection of this technology through patents. An important unpatented invention would soon be copied all over the world if it remained unprotected and would lose its market value if it could be obtained freely by competitors. In order to have tradeable technology, one must be able to obtain effective patent protection all over the world. This fact has been fully appreciated by Western enterprises. The number of their patent applications in Western and in Eastern countries has been rising, and the number of patents granted in the East to Western enterprises clearly demonstrates this Western strategy. Eastern enterprises have now also started to recognize the importance of patenting their own inventions in the West. On the basis of protected inventions, East and West can negotiate their trade transactions in peace and security, and both partners have a better bargaining position. In recent years the importance of mutual protection of industrial property has been recognized by the East and by the West. Improvements in the protection of industrial property rights are under way in the West and should also be envisaged in the East. With more effective patent systems, all trade partners will achieve more rapid expansion in various branches of industry and more dynamic growth of the national economy. Peaceful coexistence between the socialist and the capitalist systems based on a better political climate will greatly improve if trade relations receive an adequate stimulus from harmonized systems for the protection of industrial property.

NOTES

1. Hiance-Plasseraud, La protection des inventions en Union Soviétique et dans les républiques populaires, 12 (Paris, 1969).
2. Id., 14.
3. Pasquier, "Les brevets et licenses dans les pays d'économie socialiste," Le courier des pays de l'Est, 1967, No. 83, at 26.
4. See Hiance-Plasseraud, supra note 1 at 127-143; von Füner, "Gewerblicher Rechtsschutz in den VR. Albanien," Recht in Ost und West, Vol. 10, No. 1, at 22 (Jan. 15, 1966).
5. Erfinder-und Neuerrecht der DDR, 107 (collective authorship) (Staatsverlag der DDR, Berlin, 1968).
6. See Hiance-Plasseraud, supra note 1 at 150-177; Dietz, "Die Neueregelung des gewerblichen Rechtsschutzes in Bulargien" (August 1969) Gewerblicher Rechtsschutz und Urheberrecht Ausl. u Intl. Teil) 243 (hereafter, GRUR/AIT); G. Dobrev, Der Schutz des gewerblichen Eigentums in der VR. Bulgarien (Bulgarian Chamber of Commerce, Sofia, 1972).
7. See Hiance-Plasseraud, supra note 1 at 347-380; "Uebersicht über das neue Patentgesetz Nr. 84/1972 in der Tschechoslowakie," Transpatent (Dusseldorf), 1973, No. 56, 895-2010-401.

8. See Hiance-Plasseraud, supra note 1 at 265-302.

9. Hemmerling, "Das neue Patentprufüngsvefahren in der DDR," Der Neuerer, 1966, No. 12.

10. See Hiance-Plasseraud, supra note 1 at 181-219; Vida, "Das neue ungarische Patentgesetz" (May 1970) GRUR/AIT 149.

11. Vida, supra note 10 at 153.

12. See Hiance-Plasseraud, supra note 1 at 223-261; A. Kopff, "Das neue polnische Gesetz über Erfindungsgewesen" (Sept. 1973) GRUR/AIT at 583; Gruszow, "Nouvelle loi polonaise sur les brevets . . . ," Revue Gewers des Brevets, Aug. 1972, secs. 1-001, 1-002.

13. Kopff, supra note 12 at 585.

14. Id. at 587.

15. Id. at 585.

16. See Hiance-Plasseraud, 303-341; Holban, "Grundzüge des neuen Erfinderrechts in Rumänien" (May 1968) GRUR/AIT at 155; Eminescu, "Zur neuen Erfindergesetzgebung in Rumänien" (March 1969) GRUR/AIT at 223; Eminescu, "Das Recht der Erfindung in Rumänien und die Perspektiven seiner Entwecklung" (May 1967) GRUR/AIT at 86.

17. Holban, supra note 16 at 155-156.

18. Id. at 156.

19. Id. at 156-157.

20. Id. at 157.

21. Eminescu (May 1967) GRUR/AIT supra note 16 at 86.

22. See Hiance-Plasseraud, supra note 1 at 47-123.

23. Id. at 62.

24. Hiance-Plasseraud, supra note 1 at 78.

25. Id. at 105-113.

26. See Hiance-Plasseraud, supra note 1 at 381-409; Pretnar, "Die Neuordnung des Erfinder-und Patentrechts in Yugoslawien" (June 1961) GRUR/AIT at 265.

27. Pretnar, supra note 26 at 272.

28. Id. at 269.

CHAPTER

18

EVOLVING PATTERNS OF
EAST-WEST BUSINESS TRANSACTIONS:
INTRODUCTORY NOTE ON
COOPERATION AGREEMENTS
Robert Starr

During the last decade East-West trade has taken on a new and more complex character. This trade is still primarily conducted along traditional lines, by the sale and purchase of goods and services. However, business relations between Western companies and their counterparts in countries with state-planned economies are increasingly being established on a long-term basis; they go beyond straightforward sale and purchase contracts to include complementary or reciprocally matching operations between legally independent enterprises in such areas as production, marketing, research and development, and exchange of technology.

Such cooperative relations are frequently governed by special legal rules in Eastern countries. Also, cooperation agreements may provide a basis for obtaining preferential tax treatment and access to credit and foreign exchange, special treatment of imports or exports with respect to quotas and/or customs duties, preferential exchange rates for export sales, and possibly other benefits under long-term intergovernmental agreements and/or under national laws.

For the purpose of convenience we shall refer to such cooperative relations as "industrial cooperation." There is no internationally-agreed definition of this term.[1] A useful working definition is contained in a 1973 study of the Economic Commission for Europe:

> Industrial co-operation in an east-west context denotes
> the economic relationships and activities arising from
> (a) contracts extending over a number of years between
> partners belonging to different economic systems which
> go beyond the straightforward sale or purchase of goods
> and services to include a set of complementary or
> reciprocally matching operations (in production, in the

development and transfer of technology, in marketing, etc.); and from (b) contracts between such partners which have been identified as industrial co-operation contracts by Governments in bilateral or multilateral agreements.[2]

ROLE OF INTERGOVERNMENTAL AGREEMENTS[3]

The role of intergovernmental agreements has already been mentioned. These take various forms. Some long-term intergovernmental trade and payment agreements—for example, the May 13, 1970 agreement between the Benelux countries and Bulgaria, and the December 17, 1970 agreement between the Federal Republic of Germany and Czechoslovakia—specifically refer to "most-favored nation" treatment in the context of industrial cooperation. Under other intergovernmental agreements, such as the February 23, 1970 agreement between France and Czechoslovakia, and the February 12, 1971 agreement between the Federal Republic of Germany and Bulgaria, items traded under cooperation agreements enjoy a special status vis a vis import restrictions in the importing country. Still other agreements, such as the April 21, 1971 agreement between the United Kingdom and Poland, and the November 15, 1969 agreement between Italy and Hungary, express support for industrial cooperation in more general terms.

Advantageous conditions of credit for industrial cooperation projects is sometimes contemplated, as in the January 23, 1970 agreement between France and Bulgaria. Intergovernmental agreements on industrial cooperation generally contemplate the establishment of intergovernmental joint commissions to promote industrial cooperation links between Western firms and their Eastern counterparts. These intergovernmental commissions may help identify and remove legal and/or administrative problems; serve as a clearing house of information on proposals for industrial cooperation; and serve as a point of contact for interested enterprises and organizations, through working groups established under the aegis of the commissions.

REASONS FOR CONCLUDING INDUSTRIAL COOPERATION AGREEMENTS[4]

Industrial cooperation agreements are of special attraction to countries with state-planned economies for a number of reasons. Such agreements may facilitate the acquisition of advanced technologies, often at great cost savings; allow the Eastern partner to acquire management and production expertise; provide a stable and predictable framework consistent with planned development of national economies; permit balanced financing and result in foreign exchange economies; allow increased competitiveness in export markets; and and may offer opportunities for acquiring valuable marketing know-how and access to new and enlarged market outlets.

However, the benefits are not necessarily one-sided. A Western company may find that industrial cooperation expands market opportunities for its products and/or technology in Eastern countries and sometimes in certain third markets (particularly developing countries); lowers production costs through access to needed natural resources, a less costly and more stable labor supply, or additional productive capacity; or permits it to benefit from economic, financial, tariff, or tax concessions. Still other benefits may include the profitable use of resources that are already outdated (or becoming so) in Western markets, and access to Eastern technology in areas where it is more advanced.

It is impossible to make valid generalizations in discussing the benefits of industrial cooperation, since they tend to vary from country to country, and from industry to industry, in Eastern Europe, and they may depend upon such other circumstances as geographical proximity, tariff regimes, or problems of labor unrest in Western plants. The different types of industrial cooperation are outlined in the following discussion, although it should be noted that the categories are somewhat artificial. A particular cooperation deal may overlap various of these categories.

TYPES OF COOPERATION ARRANGEMENTS

Coproduction and Specialization

Perhaps the most frequent forms of industrial cooperation, and also the most complex, are coproduction and specialization. Each partner may produce certain components of a final product for subsequent assembly by either partner or both; or each partner may produce certain components within a range of inal products, for exchange with the other partner—usually on the basis of technology supplied by one of the parters but sometimes on the basis of the partners' respective technologies or as a result of joint research and development. Such arrangements also tend to involve marketing cooperation as well, with the partners acting as agents for each other in their respective markets. The products usually carry the trademark of the selling partner, but sometimes carry a joint trademark.

Subcontracting

Under this common form of cooperation, the Eastern enterprise typically produces in accordance with designs and specifications supplied by its Western partner (sometimes machinery and equipment and parts are also supplied) and delivers an agreed-upon quantity of finished or semifinished goods or spare parts. Such arrangements may be for a short period of time, merely to supplement the capacity of the Western partner; more frequently, they entail long-term relationships between the parties.

Cooperation Involving Licensing

The bare license of the right to exploit industrial property rights does not in itself constitute a cooperation arrangement. However, licensing agreements can involve cooperation, as when payment is to be made in products or components related to or resulting from a license. Frequently, a cooperation agreement contemplates a licensing arrangement accompanied by the supply of machinery, equipment, and/or technical assistance, and sometimes component parts.

Supply of Complete Plant or Production Lines

This type of cooperation involves the sale of a complete plant or production line with at least partial payment in resulting product; frequently, the Western partner also supplies drawings, equipment and know-how, trains the buyer's personnel, and assists in the start-up and operation of the Eastern plant.

Joint Ventures

The most common form of joint venture involves marketing of products made in Eastern countries through a jointly-owned enterprise established in a Western country, with both partners contributing capital and sharing in management decisions as well as profits and losses. In some cases these enterprises are also concerned with assembly of products supplied by the Eastern partner, and not infrequently they are involved in two-way trade as well.

As discussed more fully in the respective chapters of Part II and in the following chapter, investment joint ventures are now permitted in Yugoslavia and in two Comecon countries, Romania and Hungary, under legal provisions specially enacted for this purpose (Poland has similar legislation under active consideration and there have been reports that Czechoslovakia and possibly the German Democratic Republic may follow suit). In Yugoslavia, Romania, and

Hungary it is now possible to establish joint ventures within their territories that have legal characteristics similar to joint ventures in market-economy countries—with co-management, co-ownership of of capital, and sharing of profits and risks—to undertake production, marketing and other operations. In view of the special significance of these developments, the subject will be treated at greater length in the next chapter.

Joint Tendering and Other Joint Projects

Examples of cooperation in joint tendering for work projects in either country, or more frequently in a third country (often a developing country), are numerous. Usually one of the partners acts as the main contractor—depending upon a variety of political, financial, and other factors. The Eastern partner normally acts as the main contractor on a project in another East European country.

Research and Development

Cooperation in research and development generally involves the exchange of information on research and development activities by the partners, frequently with exchanges of inspection missions, joint conferences and even the establishment of joint committees to examine common problems. More intensive cooperation in this field may re-involve joint research and development projects, often with respect to equipment produced by each of the partners.

Other Forms of Cooperation

This brief listing of categories is intended only to illustrate in broad outline the main forms of East-West cooperation; it is by no means complete. Indeed, one of the most fascinating aspects of East-West trade is the challenge posed by the need to devise new legal patterns to meet perceived needs. Frequently a cooperation arrangement may involve a combination of elements, such as the sale of machinery and equipment, licensing of know-how; and repurchase of product by the Western partner. Within any listing of categories of East-West cooperation, it would also be necessary to include contracts that have been identified as cooperation agreements under intergovernmental agreements and/or pursuant to applicable law in a particular country.

Some projects do not fit neatly into any of the above categories —for example, a recently concluded deal whereby a group of Japanese companies is to undertake a major hotel construction project in Sofia, with the hotel to be operated jointly by the Japanese and the Bulgarian Tourism Commission under a new management cooperation system, and the Japanese investment protected by financial guarantees of the Bulgarian Foreign Trade Bank.

East-West cooperation is also expanding in fields related to industrial activities, notably in financing. The past few years have witnessed a number of new banking institutions jointly established by Western banks and their East European counterparts to promote East-West trade. Thus, the Anglo-Romanian Bank Ltd. was formed in London in 1972, with 50 per cent of its capital contributed by the Romanian Foreign Trade Bank and the other 50 per cent shared by Barclays Bank (30 per cent) and Manufacturers Hanover Trust (20 per cent).

One of the most interesting developments in the financial field was the formation by the Moscow Narodny Bank and Morgan Grenfell of a jointly owned (50-50) leasing company in London to promote capital goods leasing deals between East and West. In recent years equipment financing has become widespread in the West (particularly in the United States) because of its unique advantages in certain situations.

There have been relatively few instances of leasing of Western equipment to Eastern countries; the Eastern countries have been slow to recognize the attractions of equipment financing in promoting their own exports in world markets. However, the Soviet Union has now made it clear that this situation is to change.[5] It would not be surprising if leasing were to play an increasingly important role in East-West trade, and especially in industrial cooperation between Western manufacturers and Eastern organizations. Leasing arrangements might offer particularly interesting possibilities as an alternative to establishing investment joint ventures in certain Eastern countries.

NEGOTIATING COOPERATION AGREEMENTS

Identifying the Appropriate Eastern Partner

The Eastern partner to a cooperation contract may be a producing enterprise, a foreign trade organization (FTO), or even a governmental body such as a Ministry or State Committee, depending upon the country in question, the nature of the agreement, and the field in which cooperation is envisaged. Or there may be more than one Eastern partner.

A number of Western firms have concluded "framework" cooperation agreements with the Soviet State Committee for Science and Technology (SCST)—and occasionally with an industrial ministry such as the Ministry of Electrical Engineering—for scientific and technical cooperation. Such Agreements are of a very general nature, envisaging future cooperation in certain areas and leaving all commercial, financial, and legal matters to be resolved separately. Similar links have been established between Western firms and governmental bodies in other Eastern countries.

Compliance with Local Procedural Requirements

Industrial cooperation agreements are often subject to special legal rules in Eastern countries.* It is common to encounter a requirement of special authorization or prior approval by the competent authorities. (This normally means that coordination with a number of agencies may be necessary—for example, the ministry of foreign trade, the foreign trade bank, the finance ministry, and the industrial ministry having general supervisory authority over the producing enterprise that proposes to enter into the cooperation agreement.) Industrial cooperation agreements may have to be registered with an appropriate local office. Special approval may also be required under the local law to terminate the agreement.

Drafting the Agreement

The form of the agreement will depend on the type of cooperation to be established. In general, two basic contract approaches may be distinguished: (1) a "framework" agreement establishing the guidelines for cooperation, which is implemented by individual contracts prescribing specific rights and obligations of the parties; (2) a comprehensive cooperation agreement establishing the detailed rules for all aspects of the cooperation program. The first approach would include both scientific and technical cooperation agreements, such as those concluded by the Soviet SCST, as well as agreements on more intensive industrial cooperation where cooperation is likely to extend over a period of years and it is difficult to anticipate and provide for future circumstances at the outset. Since amendments to to the second type of agreement would normally require an elaborate and time-consuming approval process in the Eastern country, it is often found useful to adopt a legal formula that precludes the need to amend the basic agreement between the parties in the event that future negotiations are likely to be conducted with respect to a new development. Another advantage of separate agreements is that they may facilitate the task of establishing with greater legal clarity the respective rights and responsibilities of the parties in the various

---

*See the respective chaters in Part II of this book.

areas of their cooperation. This may facilitate the settlement of any disputes that may arise.

Where certain provisions are likely to be common to many similar contracts implementing the cooperation program, these can usually be reduced to standard terms and conditions and incorporated by reference as required.

The absence of well-tried standard form cooperation agreements, internationally agreed upon general terms and conditions, or even comprehensive guidelines for the preparation of such agreements, can be a hindrance to cooperation negotiations—particularly for parties without previous experience in this field.[6] However, a number of the legal forms common in international transactions (licensing agreements; sales and purchase contracts; technical assistance agreements; leasing; agency, or distributorship arrangements; etc.) are readily adaptable to the cooperation context. Some cooperation forms, notably coproduction and specialization, tend to involve very detailed rules for the division of labor, responsibilities, and so forth, and these are less amenable to standardized rules.

The operation of a cooperation program frequently involves training Eastern personnel and assigning Western experts to the Eastern country for considerable periods of time to provide technical assistance. It is indispensable to anticipate all possible items of expense in this regard and to clearly allocate these costs between the parties.

Many a cooperation deal has run into trouble when the Eastern partner encountered difficulties in obtaining raw materials, semifinished goods, or needed components, even though they may in principle have been entitled to priority access to such items. The Western partner should avoid a situation of dependence on promised delivery schedules and should seek maximum contract protection—for example, through penalty clauses.

Cooperation agreements often lay down detailed rules for controlling the quality of goods manufactured in the Eastern country, particularly if they are to be sold under the Western company's trademark or under a joint trademark. The Western partner will frequently insist on the right to take measures to remedy defective performance by the Eastern partner and to recover expenses caused by the replacement of defective parts.

Warranty clauses are commonly found in East-West sales contracts and take on special significance in cooperation agreements, where the relatively close and long-term relationship to be established between the parties requires particularly clear and workable provisions. It is most important to sort out questions of responsibilities to third parties.

The Western partner will above all wish to avoid any minimum purchase commitments—unless he has had sufficient experience with the Eastern partner to satisfy himself as to the latter's ability to meet delivery schedules and quality standards.

The marketing provisions of cooperation agreements are often most complex in the case of joint-production or specialization-type agreements. Marketing may be conducted independently by both partners, or jointly (frequently through a jointly owned sales company), or by a combination of these methods (for example, independently in the partners' home markets and jointly in third markets). Clauses commonly found in marketing provisions cover such issues as handling inquiries from potential customers in the other partner's marketing area, accounting and inspection of records, and provision for reasonable marketing expenses. It may also be necessary to consider the question of pricing products resulting from the cooperation, in trade between themselves as well as with third countries.

Particularly in the case of long-term joint production or specialization agreements, it is often found appropriate to require a periodic balancing of accounts, taking into consideration such factors as currency fluctuations, with provision for settling accumulated credit balances. Frequently one of the parties may accumulate credits during the initial stages.

The financial questions are among the most difficult aspects of negotiating a cooperation agreement, especially if, as is often the case, the Western party will wish to obtain assistance from Western banks or government-backed export financing facilities, and the contract involves repayment in kind.

Cooperation agreements sometimes provide for the establishment of a joint body, composed of representatives of the parties, to meet periodically to discuss problem areas, often with subsidiary bodies in technical, commercial, financial, and other fields. Such joint efforts may be useful in fostering a sense of true community of interests that, in the final analysis, is the distinguishing feature of these agreements.

NOTES

1. See, generally, Economic Commission for Europe (ECE), Analytical Report on Industrial Co-Operation Among ECE Countries (hereafter "ECE Analytical Report"), Doc. E/ECE/844 and Addenda 1 and 2, March 14, 1973, May 4, 1973 and April 9, 1973, respectively.

The International Chamber of Commerce's Liaison Committee with the Chambers of Commerce of Socialist Countries has established an ad hoc Working Party to examine practical ways of facilitating East-West trade. The Working Party has conducted an inquiry on East-West industrial cooperation agreements and has under preparation a report that will examine, inter alia, legislative and regulatory provisions in the socialist countries governing East-West industrial cooperation projects, forms of industrial cooperation permitted in these countries, and administrative, fiscal, and other facilities that Eastern and Western governments grant or may grant to facilitate cooperation agreements. See ICC Docs. No. 555-22/7, October 26, 1973 and No. 555/28, November 14, 1973.

2. ECE Analytical Report, Doc. E/ECE/844, para. 3.

3. The intergovernmental agreements referred to are collected in Register of Intergovernmental Agreements on Industrial Cooperation (Report by the Executive Secretary of the ECE), Docs. TRADE/ 252, November 10, 1971 and TRADE/252 Add. 1-13, October 4, 1971 and April 22, 1972. See also, Activities of the Intergovernmental Joint Commissions in the Field of Industrial Cooperation (Note by the ECE Secretariat), Doc. COOP. IND./2., April 5, 1972.

4. See ECE Analytical Report, Doc. E/ECE/844, paras. 14-40; East European Trade Council, Industrial Cooperation in Eastern Europe (London 1972); Business International (BI), Doing Business With Eastern Europe 146-47 (1972)

5. See, for example, K. Baranov, "Construction Plant Hire on the Capitalist Market," Foreign Trade, No. 12, 1973, at 46 (published by USSR Ministry of Foreign Trade).

6. Efforts are underway in the ECE to develop a guide on drawing up international contracts on industrial cooperation, initially in connection with construction of industrial works in the country of one of the parties to the cooperation agreement. See Doc. TRADE/GE.1/ R.4, August 22, 1973 (Secretariat Note).

19

JOINT VENTURES IN
EASTERN EUROPE
James C. Conner
James R. Offutt

The subject of this chapter is equity-type joint ventures between local and foreign capital in productive enterprises in Eastern Europe. Laws enacted in Yugoslavia in 1967 were the first to permit domestic enterprises to enter into such ventures with foreign investors. Since 1967, these laws have been further refined by the Yugoslavs and have been followed by laws authorizing joint ventures in Hungary (1970) and Romania (1971). In addition, Poland is reported to be preparing joint venture legislation for enactment in 1974,[1] and at least one other East European country, the German Democratic Republic, has indicated it is considering expanding business relationships with the West to include joint ventures.[2] The potential, therefore, for East-West partnerships in productive joint ventures is steadily increasing, and many foreign firms, in varying degrees, are interested in exploring the possibilities of such ventures.

Joint ventures are to be distinguished from the traditional methods of cooperation between foreign and local parties in socialist countries such as industrial property, licensing, trading agencies, and coproduction arrangements.[3] In a joint venture, however, the local enterprise may also be the licensee of one of the partner's industrial

---

The views expressed herein are those of the authors and not necessarily those of the International Finance Corporation or the Overseas Private Investment Corporation, where the authors are, respectively, senior counsel and counsel.

The authors gratefully acknowledge their indebtedness to Dr. Branko Vukmir, general counsel of the Business Association, INGRA, of Zagreb, Yugoslavia, for his invaluable assistance in the preparation of the discussion of joint ventures in Yugoslavia.

property rights; it may, like a typical trading agent, market the product locally or abroad; and it may, as in a coproduction arrangement, produce parts to be supplied to one of the partners for assembly with parts he has manufactured.

There are several reasons why foreign investors and host countries may prefer joint ventures over other forms of industrial cooperation. From the standpoint of the foreign investor, a joint venture offers the best means of participating in the management, control, and profits of the local enterprise and of avoiding the strictures of local legislation, particularly foreign exchange controls, which may make it unprofitable or undesirable for foreign manufacturers to supply the local market except by means of a joint venture. The host country, on the other hand, may view joint ventures as offering greater assurance that the foreign partner will continue to update his technological input, more fully utilize his existing and future market outlets in the West, and have a continuing financial stake in improving the management and technical skills of local employees.

Although East European joint ventures with foreign participation are referred to herein as "equity-type" ventures, it must be recognized that, for obvious reasons, the same property rights that flow naturally from equity investments in the West do not technically exist in Eastern Europe. Instead, the emphasis in Eastern Europe is placed on contractual rights—that is, those derived from agreements between co-venturers. This emphasis on contractual rights is due not only to the different property concepts prevailing in the socialist countries but also to the absence of a comprehensive "companies act" to govern the rights and obligations of the parties. With these points in mind, however, and once they understand the ground rules for investing in Eastern Europe, foreign investors are generally able to negotiate agreements that give them most of the rights of an equity investor in a capitalist country.

The ensuing discussion is designed to provide the potential investor a survey of the relevant laws as well as a close look at some of the practical problems he may encounter in negotiating a joint venture in Eastern Europe. Because actual operating experience has thus far been limited primarily to Yugoslavia, where there are now some 100 joint ventures with foreign participation, Section I of this chapter is devoted to a detailed description of the Yugoslav law and practice, and Section II compares the Yugoslav law and investment setting with those of Romania and Hungary. A more detailed exposition of the Romanian and Hungarian laws can be found in chapters 12 and 10, respectively. Since no discussion of joint ventures in a socialist country can be meaningful without reference to the political and economic system of the country, this chapter should also be read in conjunction with the country analyses in Part II of this book.

SECTION I: JOINT VENTURES IN YUGOSLAVIA

Background of Yugoslav Laws Permitting
Joint Ventures

From an early date, the post-World War II communist regime
in Yugoslavia allowed cooperation with foreign business firms through
licenses of foreign technology and, later, coproduction arrangements.
The legislation enacted in 1967[4] to permit foreign firms to make direct
equity-type investments in Yugoslavia was a logical outgrowth of the
economic reforms beginning in 1965 that were intended to increase
Yugoslavia's productivity and wealth by exposing its industry to the
stimulus of free market competition, both internally and vis-à-vis
the rest of the world, and to speed up development of Yugoslavia's
less developed regions. By allowing investments by foreigners, Yugoslavia hoped that it would increase its industrial productivity and product quality through the introduction of new technology and equipment
and the training of workers and also increase the country's exports.
Like their brethren in other East European countries, the Yugoslavs
viewed the acquisition of additional foreign exchange and investment
capital as only an incidental, secondary benefit of ventures with foreign technical partners.

An important feature of the Yugoslav joint venture legislation
is that it fits foreign investments into the normal Yugoslav framework of self-management industry instead of creating a special class
of foreign-owned companies. As explained in greater detail in Chapter
14, industrial activity in Yugoslavia is carried out primarily by "self-
managed" business entities. These are not state-owned enterprises
but are, instead, organizations of workers who have joined together
to manage and, in a sense, "own" certain productive assets and receive
the fruits of their labor without direct control by governmental authority. These "working organizations," which are generally referred to
by their traditional name of "enterprises" in this chapter, usually
comprise two or more so-called basic organizations of associated
labor (herein referred to as BOALs or units). As indicated in Chapter
14, BOALs may be organized by any group of workers (within or outside an existing enterprise) if they meet certain statutory tests that
require, in essence, that they generate something that can be meas-
ured as a separate or separable income.[5]

Both the enterprise and each of its BOALs usually have their
own statutes (roughly comparable to articles of incorporation), other
regulations (somewhat akin to corporate by-laws), and their own
workers' council, managing director, and other organs of self-management. Each BOAL has juridical personality, agrees on its own

working conditions, manages its own productive assets, and decides upon the distribution of its income and other fundamental matters in accordance with a "self-management agreement" by which it and one or more other BOALs form a "working organization" (enterprise). The self-management agreement prescribes all the fundamental intra-enterprise relationships, for example, the allocation of the units' liabilities vis-à-vis one another and third parties, the constitutional structure of the enterprise (organs of management, their methods of selection, and so on), and general principles regarding the sharing and division of assets and income of the component units.[6]

Basic Rights of Foreign Investors
in Yugoslav Joint Ventures

The present law authorizing foreign equity-type investments in Yugoslav industry is the Law on Investments of Resources of Foreign Persons in Domestic Organizations of Associated Labor (the Foreign Investment Act, or FIA).[7]

In brief, the FIA permits foreign investment in most of the business sectors that might interest foreigners and allows them to participate directly in Yugoslav productive enterprises (including the control and management thereof), to limit their liability to the amount of their invested capital, to withdraw a proportionate share of the profits after deduction of taxes, and to sell or repatriate their capital investment. The federal Constitution guarantees that a foreign investor's rights will not be diminished by any changes in the laws (other than tax laws) enacted after the investment is made.

In granting foreign investors these rights, the Yugoslav law imposes certain conditions and limitations. As a practically universal rule, the foreign investor's capital contribution to a joint venture may not exceed the value of the Yugoslav partner's contribution. The Yugoslav partner must be treated on the basis of equality and fairness. The workers in the joint venture enterprise cannot abdicate their constitutional right of self-management, although they may exercise this right by making binding decisions with respect to certain matters at the outset of the joint venture. The investment must be of a long-term nature, must promise to advance the economy of Yugoslavia (as defined by the statutory criteria), and must, in most cases, generate all foreign exchange that will be needed to repatriate the foreign partner's invested capital and his share of the profits.

The Fundamental Rules of the Game

The Joint Venture Agreement

Every foreign investment in a joint venture is made pursuant
to a written contract between the Yugoslav and foreign coventurers
(sometimes herein referred to as partners).[8] This contract is a crit-
ically important document, since the legislation on joint ventures is
designed to allow the parties to regulate the joint venture's internal
relationships by comprehensive contractual arrangements.

Negotiation of the contract may take many months. When completed, the contract must be approved by the workers' council of the
enterprise or the unit thereof in which the investment is being made
and must, as well, be approved by a majority of the workers of any
other Yugoslav party to the agreement.[9] If the entity that is to carry
out the joint venture is a new one, it will be founded by the Yugoslav
"mother enterprise" as soon as the parties settle the final terms of
the joint venture contract* (which will often include, as an appendix,
the proposed statute of the new entity.)

Registration of the Joint Venture

According to the FIA, the joint venture agreement enters into
force, and is entitled to the law's protection against subsequent changes
in the law, as soon as it is signed; however, it does not become fully
effective unless and until it is registered by the Federal Secretariat
of the Economy.[10]

Conditions of Eligibility for Registration. The Secretariat will register
the agreement if it satisfies the requirements set forth in the FIA.
These requirements are relatively few in number and are fairly objective and easily understood. However, it is obviously advisable to clear
up any doubtful points before completing and filing the agreement for
registration. If the Secretariat rejects the application, the parties
may either revise and resubmit the agreement or appeal to the Federal
Executive Council.[11]

The requirements[12] that a joint venture agreement must satisfy
in order to be registered are as follows:

1. It must not violate any provision of the FIA or any other applicable regulations. Examples of such provisions include the
following:

---

*If the new entity will be a unit within the over-all structure
of the Yugoslav partner, rather than an independent new enterprise,
it cannot be fully, legally constituted until it begins production.

(a) The amount of capital contributed by the foreign partner (other than by loans) must be less than the amount contributed by the Yugoslav partner. This is often referred to as the 49/51 percent rule. The Federal Assembly may declare specific sectors of the economy exempt from this restriction[13] but has not done so up to the present time.

(b) Foreign investment is not allowed in banking, insurance, internal transportation, trade, public utilities, or other public services. An exception may be granted by the Federal Executive Council if the joint venture would contribute to a more rapid development of one of those sectors.[14]

2. It must provide for an increase of the local enterprise's output, exports, and productivity and the introduction of modern techniques, technology, or organization of production and business operations in the local enterprise or must provide for the promotion of scientific research by the local enterprise.

3. It must make adequate provision for the acquisition of sufficient financing to achieve the objectives mentioned in paragraph 2 above.

4. It must not depart substantially from internationally recognized norms of joint business ventures.

5. It must not materially discriminate against the Yugoslav partner. The FIA's literal wording on this point is somewhat misleading. Article 4 says the contract cannot give the foreign partner "rights other, or greater than" the rights of the Yugoslav partner. Article 12 says the contract will not be registered if it "substantially impairs" the equality of the parties. In practice, the Secretariat allows differences in the rights of the parties that flow fairly from differences in their respective roles.

6. It must not attribute an unrealistic value to the foreign partner's contributions of nonfinancial assets (such as patents and know-how) to the equity account of the venture.

7. It must not contain any provisions inimical to the security or defense of Yugoslavia. No appeal may be taken from a rejection of a contract on this ground.

Registration Procedure, Effects. The Yugoslav coventurer must apply to the Federal Secretariat of the Economy for registration of the joint venture agreement within 30 days after it is signed.[15] As a general rule, the Secretariat of the Economy first asks for the rulings of the Federal Secretariats for Defense and Internal Affairs as to whether the project might harm the national security or defense. If these rulings are favorable, the Secretariat of the Economy proceeds to examine the other aspects of the agreement. If it then has questions or doubts, it informally advises the Yugoslav partner and gives it an opportunity to rectify the defect. A problem frequently encountered is the agreement's failure to show clearly enough that the venture will produce the favorable economic effects required by the FIA. For this reason, either the joint venture agreement or some supporting documents should contain clear evidence that the parties (especially the foreign partner) are legally obligated to take action that should produce the desired economic benefits.

The Secretariat must rule upon the request within two months. The Yugoslav party may appeal from a negative decision (except for rulings based upon a determination of adverse effects to the national security or defense) to the Federal Executive Council within 15 days.[16]

The register of joint venture agreements is open to public inspection, but the agreements themselves are not. The public register shows the names and headquarters of the contracting parties; the amounts of their respective capital investments; and the dates of the signing of the agreement, the application for registration, and the Secretariat's ruling thereon.[17] All other information is supposed to be treated as confidential.

Upon registration, the agreement "becomes valid"[18]—that is, it enters into full force and effect retroactively to the date it was signed, with prima facie official sanction as to its contents. However, it would still be possible for the courts or other interested governmental bodies to rule thereafter that some provision of the FIA or another law of more general applicability (such as the formula for determining or allocating profits) is violated. Moreover, the agreement may contain conditions that prevent the parties' mutual obligations from being fully effective until certain actions are completed.

Since 1971, the federal Constitution has provided that "the rights of foreign nationals to resources invested in an organization of associated labor in the country may not be curtailed by statute or some other enactments after the formation of the contract."[19] A 1971 enactment elaborated on this by providing that if the laws regulating investments by foreigners are amended after the registration of an investment contract, the law in effect when the contract becomes effective will continue to apply if that law is more favorable to the foreign investor, unless the contracting parties agree otherwise.[20] Article 20 of the FIA makes this protection effective as of the date of signature of the agreement.[21]

There are, however, several limitations on the scope of this protection. The first is explicit: There is no protection against changes in the laws regarding "obligations to the social community" (such as taxes).[22] The second is implicit in the text of FIA Article 20(1), which purports only to protect against changes in "the law which regulates investment of resources of foreign persons in a domestic organization of associated labor." Although this language would seem to encompass all laws that directly regulate foreign investments (such as the foreign exchange regulations regarding transfer of profits and repatriation of capital), it could be interpreted as referring only to the Foreign Investment Act and its predecessors. It may therefore be prudent to incorporate a provision in every joint venture agreement whereby the foreign partner may terminate the contract prematurely if the tax laws or any other laws are modified in a way that has a substantial adverse effect on his investment and the profits therefrom.[23]

A Background Note on Yugoslav Accounting Concepts, Determination and Allocation of Profits, and Business Taxes

To make various portions of the following discussion of joint ventures more meaningful, the following primer on Yugoslav accounting and taxation is included here.

Yugoslav accounting concepts and practices differ from their "Western" counterparts in various ways. Foreign investors find that sometimes unfamiliar terminology is used, and sometimes familiar terminology has unfathomable meanings. This, in fact, is one of the greatest obstacles to the successful evaluation and exploitation of potential joint venture possibilities. Accordingly, at an early point in the appraisal and planning stage, the prospective investor should assign one of its best accountants or financial managers to the task of learning everything possible about Yugoslav accounting and the prospective Yugoslav partner's particular accounting practices.*

––––––––––––––

*The financial reports of every Yugoslav enterprise, including joint ventures, are examined annually by the Social Accounting Service (SDK), a state accounting agency. However, these examinations and occasional reviews by SDK personnel are made primarily for the purpose of determining whether the enterprise has fulfilled various legal obligations. They are not audits in the "Western" sense. Most of the auditing practices and standards considered to be essential by international accountants are not followed by the SDK. The joint venture agreement should therefore require the accounts of the enterprise to be audited by an independent accounting firm of international standing.

A federal law (the law on the Bookkeeping of Working Organizations, O.G. 46/48, 56/69, 71/72) enforced by the SDK establishes the basic accounting principles to be followed by all Yugoslav enterprises.

The Yugoslav Balance Sheet

Unlike the Yugoslav equivalent of a profit and loss statement, discussed below, the Yugoslav balance sheet does not differ greatly from its "Western" counterpart. However, some terms do not mean quite the same thing in both systems. Also, for analytical purposes, a Western accountant would want to regroup or ignore various accounts to conform the balance sheet to the Western format.

The balance sheet of an enterprise or any component basic organ-ization of associated labor shows three basic "equity" accounts: The business fund, reserve fund, and collective (or general) consumption fund. If the accounting unit is a joint venture, it will also have equity accounts for the respective coventurers, which need not necessarily conform to the composition of the "Nominal Capital Account" used by the parties to determine their respective shares of the joint venture's profits.

The business fund (also called the operating fund) is sometimes loosely called the net worth of the enterprise (or the enterprise's own means, in Yugoslav literature). More accurately, the net worth of the enterprise includes the business fund, foreign and domestic investors' "equity" interests (if it is a joint venture), and various reserve funds that may be used for business operations.

The reserve fund corresponds roughly to the monetary and other assets reserved to cover future operating losses and, if necessary, to pay the workers' "basic" (or "reckoned") wages. The collective con-sumption fund corresponds to the assets being used or destined to be used for the common benefit of the enterprise's workers—for example, for construction of a canteen or health facility.

Yugoslav enterprises use the "indirect" method of depreciation; hence, accumulated depreciation of fixed assets is reflected in a sep-arate account, the depreciation fund.

Two minor balance sheet accounts are the loans for the underde-veloped regions of Yugoslavia and joint reserve funds accounts. The first consists of low-interest-bearing loans the enterprise must make each year to the federal government for relending to the underdeveloped regions of Yugoslavia. The second is built up by compulsory loans made annually to the "joint reserves" of the local commune and re-public to provide funds for loans or grants to enterprises in financial jeopardy or desperately in need of modernization.

Income Statement: Business Taxes

The Income Statement is actually a combination of three state-ments: an Income Formation Statement, an Income Disposition State-ment, and an Absorption of Loss Statement; of which only the first two are discussed herein. The calculations used for these statements must conform to the requirements of the Law on Establishment and Calculation of Gross Income and Profit of the Basic Organizations of Associated Labor.[24]

The Income Formation Statement shows the organization's "realized income" (dohodak) —that is, the economic value generated by the year's business operations. "Realized income" is determined by deducting the cost of goods sold (materials and services, opening inventories minus closing inventories, and depreciation, but not labor costs) and extraordinary expenses from the revenues ("gross income") derived from sales of goods and services, interest earnings, and other revenue.

The Income Disposition Statement shows the remaining items that Western accountants would deduct as costs but that the Yugoslav system treats as appropriations out of "realized income." These items are classified as contractual liabilities (such as interest on debt and insurance premiums), legal liabilities (taxes and mandatory payments) and realized personal incomes (salaries and wages).

Legal liabilities include taxes and obligatory "contributions" of various kinds.* In recent years the only significant taxes on business enterprises have been turnover taxes (for sales to the end-user), customs duties, and, beginning in 1973, a tax on, or compulsory low-interest loans out of, income in some republics.[25]

Mandatory "contributions" have at various times included small contributions for the reconstruction of certain areas damaged by earthquake; a contribution for housing construction (mostly retained and used by the enterprise itself); charges for the use of water and urban land; social insurance surcharges on gross personal incomes; and, in some republics, contributions for education.

The final appropriation out of realized income is for the personal incomes of the workers. These are, in essence, the gross wages paid according to a schedule of wages payable for work performed (for instance, hourly rates). Since 1972, the basic or "reckoned" wages have been determined by the enterprise in accordance with tripartite "social agreements" established in each republic between government, trade unions,† and chambers of commerce[26] on the basis of complex

---

*Under the current constitutional structure, the federation establishes only the over-all system and the basic rate of the indirect (turnover) taxes to be charged by the republics. The republics establish their own direct taxes, with almost complete freedom from federal control.

†Each enterprise has its own trade union group. Yugoslav trade unions not only have the traditional union function of protecting the interests of members of the work force but also play a quasimanagement role in seeking to improve the functioning of workers' self-management. They also provide vocational and academic training.

rules that are intended to influence the savings practices of enterprises and to reduce wage differentials among Yugoslav workers that result from factors other than the efficiency of the respective firms. Each republic has its own set of such rules.

If an enterprise does not have sufficient earnings to pay the workers' basic personal income as well as the enterprise's contractual and legal liabilities, the basic personal income must be paid out of the reserve fund. Profitable organizations may (subject to certain legal and other constraints, including those imposed by joint venture agreements with foreign partners) pay a bonus out of the profit remaining after all other required payments have been made.

Allocation of "Remaining Income"

The income remaining after all of the above appropriations have been made is called the remaining income or profit (dobitak). It is, as a rule, distributed to the enterprise's reserve fund, collective consumption fund, and housing fund; the joint reserve funds; the Yugoslav and foreign joint venture partner's profit shares (if it is a joint venture); and, finally, the business fund.

YUGOSLAV JOINT VENTURES IN PRACTICE

Partners' Contributions

Nature, Amount of Capital Contributions

Kinds of Assets Contributed. The law does not prescribe what kinds of assets may be contributed to the "equity" of joint ventures. Typically, cash will be part of each partner's contribution, with the foreign partner contributing foreign exchange. The Yugoslav partner will in many cases contribute cash out of the earnings it generates while the joint venture's new productive facilities are being constructed and brought on stream. Frequently the joint venture unit will be an existing component of the Yugoslav partner, and in such cases, the Yugoslav partner will contribute this unit, with all of its existing tangible and intangible assets and liabilities. Correspondingly, the foreign partner may contribute new productive assets. Often the foreign partner will contribute patent rights, trademark rights, or other kinds of intangible industrial property such as technical know-how.

There are certain constraints on the parties' freedom in this matter. First, the aggregate value of the assets contributed by foreign parties must be less than the aggregate value of the Yugoslav

parties' contributions (the 49/51 percent rule). Second, the foreign
partner's contribution must not be less than 1,500,000 dinars[27] (except
in special cases approved by the Federal Secretariat for the Economy).[28]

Valuation of assets contributed. Valuation of the partners' contributions is a vexing problem in many joint ventures. The greatest difficulties may arise in the process of reaching agreement upon the
value of an existing unit contributed by the local party. When setting
up a joint venture, the parties should take care in specifying the date
when these assets and liabilities are to be contributed and evaluated.

Note should also be taken of the statutory requirement that the
foreign partner's contributions of nonfinancial assets not be "unreal-
istically valued."[29]

Juridical Status of Partnership Assets. Once the foreign partner's
assets have been contributed to the joint venture enterprise, they
become "social property," subject to all the Yugoslav laws and regulations applicable generally to social property.[30] However, the law does
provide that the joint venture agreement may include a pactum re-
servati dominii whereby the foreign investor may reclaim his assets
upon termination of the joint venture.[31] This device, however, will
be of no practical interest to most foreign investors.[32]

The Partnership Account

The joint venturers' respective "equity interests," as calculated
pursuant to Yugoslav accounting principles, will normally be reflected
fully in the balance sheet prepared by the enterprise pursuant to Yugoslav legal requirements. Frequently the partners will also keep a
separate partnership account, outside of the balance sheet and denominated in a foreign currency, for the purpose of determining the parties'
respective shares of distributable profits and of capital payable upon
termination of the joint venture.

This special partnership account, frequently called the "Nominal
Capital Account," is usually denominated in the principal currency
contributed by the foreign partner, not in dinars. By maintaining the
account in the foreign currency, the partners maintain the value of
foreign investment against devaluations of the dinar during the life
of the agreement. The chronic inflationary tendencies and frequent
devaluations experienced in Yugoslavia over the years have made this
a worthwhile precaution in the past, although the relative strength of
the dinar now calls for careful consideration of the matter.

The Nominal Capital Account consists of all capital contributions
made by the partners, minus any returns of capital to them. Contributions (such as the local partner's contribution of dinars) valued in

currencies other than the currency in which the account is denominated should be converted into the currency of the account at the exchange rate prevailing on the date of contribution.

Future Additional Investments

Since profits will usually be divided on the basis of the parties' respective shares of the Nominal Capital Account, the joint venture agreement should clearly state what additions may be made to that account. For instance, if the foreign partner agrees to contribute to the reserve fund of the joint venture unit (rather than requiring the Yugoslav partner to fund this account out of its share of distributed profits), this should constitute an additional capital contribution, increasing the foreign partner's share of the Nominal Capital Account. Similar treatment may be accorded various other payments made by the local partner.

Types of Investments and Risk-Sharing Permitted

A foreign investor may enter into a joint venture agreement with one or more Yugoslav enterprises, or with one or more units (BOALs). Similarly, the investment may be in one or more enterprises or their component units.[33] Under the present law, the investment may even be made in an organization (called a "community of basic organizations of associated labor") composed of "organizations of associated labor" that are part of one or more enterprises, or in a "complex organization of associated labor," which is an organization composed of two or more enterprises.[34] However, such exotic arrangements as these are likely to be proposed only from the Yugoslav side.

The joint venture agreement will specify whether the foreign investment will be made in the Yugoslav contracting party itself, in one or more of its component units, or in a new entity.

Allocation and Limitation of Liabilities

A major consideration in working out the form and structure of a joint venture is the allocation and limitation of liabilities. This matter should be covered in detail in the joint venture agreement and take into account the relevant provisions of Yugoslav law and the contents of the Yugoslav partner's self-management agreement.

The extent of a foreign investor's liability is limited to the amount of his invested capital, in accordance with the terms of the joint venture agreement. The source of the obligations to which his capital might be subject may depend on whether his investment is made in an enterprise as a whole or in one or more of its component parts, that is, the BOALs.

If the foreigner invests in the enterprise as a whole, he is entitled to share in the profits of the enterprise as a whole but is also responsible, up to the amount of his contribution, for its losses and liabilities arising out of all of its activities. On the other hand, unless the self-management agreement of the enterprise provides otherwise, the assets of each of the enterprise's BOALs are also liable for the obligations arising out of the joint venture's activities.[35]

By investing in only a part of an enterprise (that is, in one or more BOALs), the foreigner can insulate his investment from risks arising out of operations of the rest of the enterprise.[36] However, he may not in that case be entitled to share in the profits of the enterprise as a whole, and the other BOALs of the enterprise will not be responsible for the joint venture's liabilities or losses, unless the joint venture agreement provides otherwise.[37]

Provisions allocating and limiting the liability of the joint venture, the foreign investor, the enterprise as a whole, and its BOALs, become effective when they are recorded in the court register at the seat of the enterprise.[38]

Bankruptcy, Secession, Merger of Working Units

The 1971-73 amendments to the Yugoslav constitution and related laws stress the workers' right of self-determination. In particular, they authorize any group of workers meeting certain statutory tests to declare their unit's independence from the rest of their enterprise or to annex it to another working organization. This rule has both favorable and unfavorable implications for foreign investors. The disadvantage is that after the business becomes successful, parts of the joint venture unit may try to secede from the joint venture unit or the joint venture unit itself may try to secede from the original enterprise. There are two kinds of protection against this. First, the law itself forbids any secession that would have "any damaging effect upon the rights of workers in other sections of the working organization" or upon "the interests and rights of the working organization as a whole which proceed from interdependence in work or common work with joint means," or would "change [their] mutual obligations unilaterally."[39] Secondly, the joint venture agreement may forbid secessions or mergers and may make the violation of such prohibition a ground for termination of the joint venture and restitution of the foreign investment, although the foreign investor must handle this matter with great care and diplomacy, since it involves some deep-felt politicoeconomic feelings about the workers' right of "self-determination."

The separability of working units does, however, provide foreign investors a compensating benefit in the rule that if the investment is made in a separate unit, rather than in the whole enterprise, and the joint venture agreement provides that the joint venture unit is not liable for debts of the larger organization, the joint venture unit will escape a bankruptcy of the larger organization and be free to become an independent enterprise or join another enterprise.[40]

Financing Joint Ventures in Yugoslavia

International joint ventures in Yugoslavia are financed by substantially the same sources of finance as elsewhere. Typical financial plans for joint ventures in Yugoslavia have included long-, medium-, and short-term loans from Yugoslav banks, medium- and long-term loans from foreign banks (including national import-export banks), equipment suppliers' credits, capital contributions from the Yugoslav and foreign partners, cash generated by preexisting operations of the joint venture enterprise, and loan and equity financing by the International Finance Corporation (IFC) or the International Investment Corporation for Yugoslavia (IICY).*

In recent years, there have been a number of loans to Yugoslav industrial projects by syndicates of private foreign banks or other financial institutions. These and most other foreign bank loans and suppliers' credits to Yugoslav enterprises have been guaranteed by

---

*The IFC is an affiliate of the International Bank for Reconstruction and Development (World Bank), formed in 1956 to foster economic development through private enterprise in its less developed member countries. Unlike the World Bank, it can make equity investments as well as loans and accepts no governmental guarantees for repayment of its loans. Having concluded that Yugoslav enterprises are "private," not "governmental" or "public," IFC was one of the first and most frequent non-Yugoslav institutions to make investments pursuant to the 1967 foreign investment legislation.

The IICY was founded in 1969 by IFC and a number of Yugoslav and foreign banks to help foreign industrialists utilize the investment opportunities available under the 1967 joint venture legislation. In addition to providing direct financial assistance, IICY has, for a fee, helped draft and negotiate many joint venture agreements, helped the promoters obtain financing from other financial institutions, and assisted them in dealing with the responsible Yugoslav governmental authorities.

Yugoslav commercial banks.* Recently the Yugoslav bankers' association has begun to set limits on the interest rates they will guarantee. This ceiling varies from time to time and is not well publicized. Prospective foreign investors and lenders should search out up-to-date information on the current ceiling and, in general, the latest trends in the thinking in banking and governmental circles before getting deeply into planning the financing of a project.

Control and Management of Joint Ventures

The Foreign Investment Act allows considerable scope for arrangements whereby the foreign investor's need to share control and management of the joint venture is reconciled with the principles of workers' self-management. In a sense, the difficulties encountered by foreign investors in Yugoslav joint ventures are hardly different or more difficult than the problems involved in the allocation of control in a joint venture anywhere else. In Yugoslavia, the foreign investor's main difficulty will be in understanding the local management principles and institutions. Chapter 14 discusses these in some detail, but a brief synopsis here may make the following discussion of control and management of Yugoslav joint ventures more intelligible.

Management and Executive Organs in an Ordinary Yugoslav Enterprise

Under present law, enterprises are largely free to establish their own internal management structure.[41] Accordingly, there may be collective management organs (workers' council and specialized commissions and other bodies created by the council), on the one hand, and individual executive organs (managing director) and collective executive organs, on the other. The control of the enterprise itself and its most important policy decisions are the responsibility of the workers' council and managing director, while the actual execution of these policies is carried out under the direction of the managing director and other directors. The working community, which consists

---

*Unlike the so-called foreign exchange guarantees which some foreign investors of equity capital have obtained for remittance of profits and repatriation of capital, bank guarantees of foreign loans do not depend upon the adequacy of the borrowers' own foreign exchange allowances. However, the Yugoslav banks can be expected to take into account the amounts of such allowances before determining whether to give their guarantees.

of the whole work force, elects the workers' council and delegates most of its self-management authority to the council, although the working community's views on certain fundamental matters ("matters of status"), such as adoption of self-management agreements and approval of secessions of BOALs or mergers into other organizations, may be expressed directly through referenda.[42]

As a general rule, each BOAL in an enterprise will have its own workers' council in addition to the workers' council of the over-all enterprise. The enterprise's self-management agreement prescribes the division of authority between the respective councils.

The chief individual executive organ, responsible for the day-to-day operations of the enterprise and representation of the enterprise in its dealings with third parties, is called the general director, managing director, or general manager. He is usually appointed for a fixed term (subject to removal for reasons prescribed in the self-management agreement) by the workers' council from a slate of candidates selected after public advertisement on the basis of conditions prescribed in the self-management agreement and statutes.

Workers' Council and Business Committee in a Joint Venture Unit

All other considerations being equal, the foreign investor will, to maximize his control over his investment, want to have the joint venture carried out by a separate "basic organization of associated labor" rather than to invest in the whole of the Yugoslav coventurer.

The Foreign Investment Act authorizes the joint venture agreement to establish a joint business committee whereby the foreign and Yugoslav partners will jointly control the joint venture unit in conjunction with the workers' council of the unit. The act lets the partners settle the jurisdiction and powers of the business committee and the procedures for establishing and running it.[43] Typically, the Yugoslav and foreign partners will elect an equal number of committee members (even though the foreign partner's share of the capital will be less than 50 percent). The investment agreements often provide that the chairman of the business committee will be nominated by one partner and the alternate or vice chairman by the other, with the nominating roles being reversed at the end of each term of office.

The respective jurisdictions and powers of the business committee and the unit's workers' council should be carefully spelled out in the joint venture agreement. The partners can go very far to assure the foreign partner a strong management role, provided the foreign partner is not given substantially greater rights than the Yugoslav partner and the fundamental elements of workers' self-management are not disturbed.

514

Typically, the business committee will be given exclusive jurisdiction over certain matters, whereas for other matters the committee will submit proposals to the workers' council for final approval (for example, annual financial, manufacturing, marketing and investment plans, profit and loss statements, the annual balance sheet, workers' bonuses, and appointments of top managerial and technical personnel). Areas of decision-making assigned to the business committee may include such matters as basic production techniques and strategy; marketing policy; financial policy, including borrowing and lending; reinvestment of profits and allocations to reserve funds; expansion of the business; and general accounting and cost controls.

The workers' council will always have exclusive jurisdiction over certain fundamental aspects of workers' self-management, such as adoption of the joint venture unit's self-management agreement and statutes, appointment of the managing director and his deputy, and general labor relations, including hiring and firing of workers. In these and other areas of the council's jurisdiction, as well as those mentioned above, the foreign partner may of course express his views through the joint business committee or otherwise.

The joint venture agreement should prescribe the procedures to be followed in case of deadlocks between the joint business committee and the workers' council or within the business committee itself. (Dispute settlement is discussed in greater detail in a separate section below.)

Managing Director

Except as the joint venture agreement may otherwise provide, the managing director of a joint venture unit fulfills the same role as in a purely Yugoslav enterprise. He is thus responsible for managing the operation of the plant under the guidelines laid down by the workers' council and the joint business committee. The managing director and his deputy are appointed by the joint venture unit's workers' council in accordance with normal Yugoslav practices, but it is permissible for the joint venture agreement to provide that the deputy managing director will be proposed to the workers' council by the business committee from a slate of nominees presented by the foreign partner. Although the law[44] does not expressly require that either the managing director or his deputy be Yugoslav citizens, practical and indirect legal requirements make it essential that they be Yugoslav. The joint venture agreement may, however, provide for appointment of an assistant general manager, in charge of specific departments, such as production, marketing and financial controls, and reporting to the managing director (or to the joint business committee for certain matters, if so provided in the agreement). The joint venture agreement may also specify qualifications for the office of managing director in addition to those prescribed by law[45]—for instance, fluency in the foreign partner's tongue and a specific technical degree or practical experience.

The joint venture agreement should usually contain specific provision for the appointment of other high-level staff. These key employees, who may be foreigners proposed by the foreign partner, should be nominated by the business committee for final approval by the workers' council. The agreement may give them such important positions as director or deputy director of production, technical matters, and accounting and cost controls.

Although in the last analysis, only the workers' council may control and, if necessary, remove the managing director, the foreign partner may exercise its rights through the business committee and, in the event of a deadlock or dispute, through the dispute settlement machinery prescribed in the agreement. The foreign partner may and in many cases should, require the agreement to give its chief technical representative or the business committee the final authority with respect to production techniques, or at least should delineate with care the degree of freedom the managing director is permitted in this connection.

Labor Relations; Specialized Commissions

Responsibility for labor relations should be left largely to the workers' council and the specialized commissions that operate under its general guidance.* Under general Yugoslav legal principles, the workers' council must retain jurisdiction over such matters as hiring, firing, and individual workers' grievances. Nonetheless, the foreign partner may, and should, help formulate general policies and may even recommend specific action such as the transfer of incompetent personnel from particular posts.

Determination, Distribution, Taxation of Profits

Determination and Distribution

One of the rights specifically accorded to a foreign investor by the Foreign Investment Act is the right to share in the profits of the

---

*Joint venture units may have the same kinds of commissions as are constituted by the workers' councils of other Yugoslav enterprises such as commissions dealing with workers' housing and working conditions.

joint venture so long as it has capital invested in the venture.[46] The terms of such participation are prescribed by the joint venture agreement.[47]

The process of determining how to distribute profits is intertwined with the process of defining distributable profits. It is therefore essential for the foreign investor to get a solid understanding of various unusual Yugoslav accounting concepts and the classification of various items in an ordinary Yugoslav enterprise's "profit and loss" statement. It is also essential for the foreign investor to realize that the law does not require the joint venture's "distributable profits" to be exactly the same as "profit" (dobitak) according to ordinary Yugoslav accounting principles, since the foreign partner need not agree to recognize some of the deductions used to determine dobitak as deductible expenses in calculating the joint venture's "distributable profits." Several mandatory or voluntary contributions and other legal obligations of the joint venture unit may, at the option of the parties, be paid by the Yugoslav partner out of its share of the profits instead of being paid by the joint venture unit itself.[48] The treatment of such payments in any given case will depend, among other things, upon the relative bargaining posture of the two parties, public relations considerations, profitability expectations, and the nature of the various payments. These payments include the contributions of the unit's reserve fund and to the joint reserve funds of the commune and republic, contributions for loans for the underdeveloped regions of Yugoslavia, allocations to the collective consumption fund of the enterprise, supplementary year-end payments (bonuses) to the workers, and allocations to a reserve for expansion.

Some of these payments and allocations do not involve a depletion of the enterprise's assets, but, rather, an allocation of profits to various reserves and restricted-use assets, such as the enterprise's reserve fund and the contributions for loans to the underdeveloped regions. Since these assets may give the enterprise a higher value at the termination of the joint venture, a foreign investor whose agreement provides for him to receive a certain percentage of the enterprise's value upon termination of the venture may be willing to have all such allocations treated as deductions from gross revenues in the calculation of the profits distributable annually to the partners during the life of the joint venture. On the other hand, an investor who wishes to have a high annual pay-out of profits and no capital appreciation (accepting, instead, eventual repatriation of his capital investment at the original principal amount) would probably prefer to have the Yugoslav partner make these payments and allocations out of its own share of the profits. In the latter case, the partners might agree that such payments and allocations would constitute additional investments in the joint venture by the local partner (for example, the local partner's contributions to the unit's reserve fund).

The subject of depreciation charges deserves special mention. To guard against the workers' temptation to maximize the distribution of profits for their personal enjoyment at the expense of maintaining and replacing their capital assets, the laws have required them to depreciate their assets at certain minimum rates that vary according to the kinds of assets concerned.[49] Over the years, probably most enterprises have depreciated their assets faster than the pertinent federal and local laws have required. The laws have until now imposed no ceiling on depreciation charges, which is due primarily to the absence of any income taxes on enterprise income until very recently.[50] If a foreign investor wishes to impose any restraints on a joint venture's depreciation charges, he should say so in the joint venture agreement. If he wishes to maximize his current return by a full cash pay-out of profits, rather than to allow the net worth of the joint venture unit and the value of his investment to keep growing until the joint venture terminates, he will want to impose some limitation on the depreciation charges. On the other hand, he may wish to have a high depreciation rate so that he may repatriate his investment during the life of the joint venture by using the foreign exchange available by virtue of the special "depreciation quota" referred to hereinafter.

The Foreign Investment Act, like the original 1967 law, says the foreign investor can participate in the profits only as long as he participates with his own resources in the joint venture.[51] This rule has been interpreted by some observers as meaning that, as the assets contributed or financed by the foreign investor are depreciated, his right to share in the profits must inevitably diminish. In practice, however, this has not proven to be the case. The Secretariat of the Economy has registered numerous agreements in which the foreign investor's right to profit participations continues undiminished until the venture terminates in accordance with its terms.

The law requires Yugoslav enterprises receiving foreign investments to keep separate books showing the profits realized by the joint ventures.[52] The foreign investors have a statutory right to examine these books.[53] They should, however, require much more. Experience has shown that it is essential for the investment agreement to give the foreign partner an important role in the supervision and operation of the joint venture's accounting department, not only for the purpose of determining profits, but also to work out modern, efficient cost controls and financial reporting machinery during the construction of the project facilities. The Yugoslav authorities and many Yugoslav enterprises will welcome the infusion of up-to-date "Western" expertise into these operations. The joint venture agreement should also provide for possible auditing by independent auditors.[54]

Taxation of Foreign Partner's Profits

Under the original 1967 laws permitting foreign investment, there was a federal withholding tax on the foreign investor's share of joint venture profits.[55] The basic rate was a flat 35 percent of the distributable profits, but this could be reduced by reinvestment of profits. The greater the percentage of profits reinvested, the greater the reduction in the tax rate.

In the years 1969 through 1973, the federal tax was replaced by withholding taxes enacted by the republics and autonomous provinces themselves.[56] The 35 percent rate of the former federal law is still maintained in Serbia, Croatia, and Slovenia but has been reduced to 20 percent in Bosnia and Hercegovina, and to 14 percent in Macedonia, Montenegro, and Kosovo. Incentives to reinvest are still provided.

Transferring Foreign Investors' Profits

The Foreign Investment Act provides that after deduction of any income taxes required by law, foreign investors may transfer abroad their joint venture earnings, subject to the terms and conditions of the joint investment agreement and Yugoslav foreign exchange regulations.[57] Until now, these regulations have allowed transfer of profits only out of foreign exchange earnings from exports and other activities, such as tourism and overseas investments—primarily from the joint venture's earnings from its own exports, but occasionally from earnings of related parties. To overcome the reluctance of potential foreign investors who may have felt that the original foreign exchange allowances were, or might be, insufficient to permit them to remit all of their profits, the Yugoslav Government has progressively increased these allowances since 1967 but has refused to remove entirely the requirement that joint ventures contribute directly or indirectly to Yugoslavia's exports.

At present, the two sources of foreign exchange for remitting profits to a hard currency investor are the profit allowance, which is an amount equal to one-third of the project's export earnings,[58] and the "retention quota."[59]

The retention quota is the portion of a firm's foreign exchange earnings from exports of goods and services that may be "retained" (that is, repurchased from the banking system) for a broad range of purposes, including transfer of profits and repayment of capital to foreign joint venture partners.[60] In recent years, the regulations concerning the retention quota have been simplified and the size of the quota has been increased for most industries. The most recent regulations have allowed retention at rates ranging from 20 percent (for most foreign exchange earnings) up to 100 percent (for earnings from direct investment outside Yugoslavia, and from engineering, civil construction, and scientific research and services performed abroad).

Any unutilized amount of the profit allowance or the retention quota may be carried forward for use in future years.[61]

In addition to the foreign exchange earnings from exports of the joint venture's own products or services, the foreign currency earnings of certain related Yugoslav parties may under certain circumstances generate retention quota funds available for remitting the joint venture's profits. One of these additional sources of foreign exchange is the foreign exchange allowance that the Yugoslav partner in the joint venture may have from its exportation of other goods and services. Also, the Foreign Exchange Law specifically authorizes pooling of retention quotas by parties to agreements on "long-term cooperation in production" or "long-term business technical cooperation."[62]

Reflecting the Yugoslavs' desire to promote only export-oriented joint ventures, neither the laws nor the National Bank has ever provided any official guarantee that foreign exchange would be available to repatriate capital or remit profits. (It is understood that the Yugoslav authorities may be reevaluating the desirability of providing convertibility guarantees for the purpose of attracting more foreign investment.) Commercial banks may undertake to sell foreign exchange for these purposes, but only up to the amount of the enterprise's own foreign exchange quotas.[63] Thus, these so-called foreign exchange guarantees cannot be used to supplement the enterprise's foreign exchange quotas.

The new foreign exchange market instituted in 1973, whereby authorized banks buy and sell foreign exchange for their own account and for the account of their customers, reflects the recent growth in Yugoslavia's foreign exchange reserves and the authorities' confidence that they can continue to move toward free convertibility of the dinar. To the extent these hopes are realized, the question of availability of official or commercial bank guarantees of convertibility of profits will be less important.

Reinvestment of Profits

Article 18(3) of the Foreign Investment Act says that a foreign investor's profits from a joint venture may be reinvested in the same joint venture or in another joint venture, or may be used in Yugoslavia for other purposes authorized by the laws and regulations.

The joint venture agreement should contain well-thought-out provisions regarding the partners' rights or obligations to reinvest profits or make additional investments in the joint venture.

Repatriation, Sale of Foreign Investments

Repatriation of Investments

The Foreign Investment Act says the foreign investor may trans-fer his invested capital under three circumstances: if the joint venture agreement expires at its normal term, upon attainment of the parties' business objectives; if the agreement terminates prematurely in accordance with the Foreign Investment Act; and if the agreement provides that the foreign partner can make partial withdrawals of his capital while the agreement is in effect.[64]

As in the case of profit remittances, the right to repatriate capital is subject to the foreign exchange laws and regulations in effect at the time.[65] Under the present regulations, capital may be repatriated only in amounts not exceeding the aggregate amount of the retention quota, profit allowances, and "depreciation quota" that has not been used up for other purposes.

Every enterprise is entitled to purchase foreign exchange to repatriate foreign capital and repay foreign loans in an amount equal to a specified percentage (the "depreciation quota") of the enterprise's declared annual depreciation charge.[66] Unlike the retention quota and profits allowance, the depreciation quota is not dependent upon export earnings. The amount of the quota is specified in circulars issued by the National Bank. Prior to April 1973, the percentage allowed was 10 percent, of which 5 percent was available in "hard currencies" and 5 percent in "soft" or "bilateral" currencies (such as those of Eastern Europe). In April 1973, the quota was liberalized for various industries that the authorities wished to encourage. The new rates for favored industries ranged from 25 percent for civil engineering firms to 67 percent for copper producers.[67] These amounts are cumulative—that is, any depreciation quota rights not utilized in one year may be carried forward for use in later years.[68] Although the law is ambiguous, it is understood that the pertinent depreciation base is the enterprise's total depreciable fixed assets, whether imported or not. An enterprise's depreciation quota may be pooled with, or sold to, parties with whom it has entered into long-term cooperation arrangements[69] or to other parts of the same enterprise. Like bank "guarantees" for profit remittance, "guarantees" to provide foreign exchange for repatriation of capital are valid only up to the amount of the enterprise's own foreign exchange quotas.

It is conceivable that, in a given case, the depreciation allowance would be sufficient to repatriate the entire foreign capital contribution. However, since the depreciation allowance may not be used to remit profits, it is unlikely that a foreign business would be interested in investing in a joint venture that would generate no foreign currency earnings (even if, as is unlikely, the Secretariat of the Economy would approve such a joint venture). Also, the depreciation allowance may be exhausted by foreign debt servicing, so that none will be available for repatriation of "equity."

The law gives the parties considerable freedom to determine how to measure the amount of the foreign partner's capital interest at the termination of the joint venture. As previously indicated, some investors prefer the division to be made on the basis of the value of the enterprise at that time, with the foreign partner getting a share equivalent to his share of the Nominal Capital Account described earlier. Others prefer to withdraw all of their annual profits during the course of the joint venture and to allow their capital interest to remain unchanged (denominated in the foreign currency in which originally contributed) and to withdraw that amount at the termination of the joint venture. In either case, if the venture suffered unrecovered losses, the foreign partner's capital interest would be reduced in absolute terms, although not in terms of its percentage of "ownership" of the joint venture unit.

Consideration should be given to the difficulty the joint venture enterprise or the Yugoslav partner may have in paying off the foreign investor immediately upon the termination of the venture. In a number of cases this has been handled by providing that the foreigner's "equity" investment will be converted into a loan repayable over a period of several years.

Finally, it should be noted that the law does allow a foreign investor to retain title to assets it contributes to the venture and to reclaim them at the end of the joint venture.[70] Only in very rare cases would either partner be interested in such an arrangement although it might be one way of ensuring that the foreign investor could repatriate his capital investment notwithstanding a shortfall in the joint venture's foreign exchange resources or financial losses from operations.

Transfer of Foreign Partner's Investment
to Others

The Foreign Investment Act says that a foreign investor may, with the consent of the enterprise in which he has invested, transfer his "contractual rights and obligations" to another foreign juristic or physical person or to another Yugoslav organization of associated labor, "unless otherwise provided by the investment agreement."[71] In every case of a proposed sale, the foreign investor must first offer in writing his investment to the Yugoslav enterprise in which he has invested his capital,[72] and the offeree must reply within 60 days unless the joint venture agreement provides otherwise.[73] If the Yugoslav

party refuses the offer, the foreign investor may transfer his investment to another party.[74] All transfers must be promptly registered
in the register maintained by the Federal Secretariat of the Economy.[75]

Dispute Settlement

As explained in Chapter 14, arbitration of economic disputes
involving foreigners is a common practice in Yugoslavia, and the Foreign Investment Act encourages it for joint ventures. The act provides
that disputes arising out of joint ventures will be settled by the competent Yugoslav commercial court unless the parties have agreed to
submit disputes to a special arbitral tribunal within the Chamber of
the Commerce of Yugoslavia, an External Trade Arbitration Tribunal
within the Chamber of Commerce, a separate tribunal set up by the
parties, or a foreign arbitral tribunal.[76] Many joint venture agreements have provided for arbitration by one or another of these methods.

The joint venture agreement should provide internal machinery
and procedures for settling disputes and should also specify what action will be taken in the event of deadlocks of various kinds. In addition, a carefully thought-out provision should specify what law (Yugoslav or foreign) would govern the various substantive and procedural
issues that might arise in implementing the agreement. In practice,
most important questions, except general principles of law regarding
contractual and delictual obligations of private parties, will, as a matter of Yugoslav imperative law, have to be regulated by the laws of
Yugoslavia, such as the laws regarding self-management and the Foreign Investment Act itself.

Termination of Joint Ventures

According to the law, foreign investments in Yugoslav enterprises must be "long-term."[77] This condition is not defined in the
law, except by the requirement that if the agreement specifies a termination date, duration of the venture may not be shorter than the
time necessary for the realization of the joint venture's objectives.[78]

The joint venture may not be terminated before the scheduled
expiration date except pursuant to provisions of the joint venture
agreement giving a party the right of termination "if the joint venture
resulted in losses over two consecutive years, or if business results
are substantially below the envisaged results" or "if the other side
fails to fulfill obligations which it assumed under the agreement."[79]

A permissible variation of the latter clause is a provision permitting the foreign party to terminate the joint venture if the tax laws

or regulations of Yugoslavia are amended to the detriment of the foreigner's investment. Perhaps other mutations would also be permissible.[80] In addition, it is quite usual for joint venture agreements to contain force majeure clauses excusing the parties for involuntary nonperformance of their obligations.

A Final Tip on Yugoslav Joint
Venture Agreements

Draftsmen of Yugoslav joint venture agreements should keep in mind that the Foreign Investment Act is intended to provide merely a framework for investing. Many of the rules and regulations that might be found in positive legislation in other countries (such as the internal procedures of a corporation) are left by Yugoslav law for the joint venture agreements to settle. Such agreements should, accordingly, be quite comprehensive.

The points to be considered for coverage in the agreement should at least include the following: The foreigner's right to share in profits and recover his capital; provision for full financing of the project; partners' initial contributions (kind and value); policy on additional investments by the initial partners or others; complete management and operational structure, with the clearest possible jurisdictional lines between the joint business committee and workers' council, the managing director, and foreign personnel; interrelationships between the joint venture agreement and self-management agreement; responsibility for technical direction of the plant; selection and training of technical and managerial personnel, with specific references to foreign experts needed; allocation of responsibilities for basic production and marketing policies; provision for earning sufficient export revenues to permit transfer of profits and repatriation of the capital investment to the foreign investor in convertible currency; provision for adequate cost controls and accounting systems; precise rules for calculating profits and losses (including wage policies) and dividing them among the partners; rules for building up reserves; rules for depreciating and revaluing assets (within the limits permitted by law); limitations on liability of the parties for debts of the joint venture unit and vice versa; transferability of the foreign partner's investment to third parties; dispute settlement machinery; normal duration of the venture; and bases for premature termination.

Coverage of all these points in a joint venture agreement will not alone ensure a successful cooperative endeavor. The success of a joint venture, like that of any form of business association anywhere, depends upon the parties' continued good will, respect for each other's individual interests, and good faith efforts to attain common objectives.

SECTION II: JOINT VENTURES IN OTHER
EAST EUROPEAN COUNTRIES

COMPARISON WITH YUGOSLAV
LAW AND PRACTICE

As noted at the outset of this chapter, two other East European countries, Romania and Hungary, have enacted laws permitting equity-type participation in domestic enterprises by foreign investors. In addition, a third country, Poland, is reported to be putting the finishing touches on joint venture legislation[81] and, in fact, may be allowing some joint ventures under the framework of existing law.[82]

Romania's enabling legislation,[83] enacted in 1971, was followed by two decrees[84] providing fairly detailed guidelines concerning the constitution and taxation of "joint companies." Hungary's enabling law,[85] enacted in 1970, was also amplified recently[86] but as yet has not progressed much beyond the minimum provisions necessary to authorize the establishment of joint "economic associations"* and provide for their taxation.

Because of their recent enactment and the limited operating experience thus far under the joint venture laws of Romania and Hungary,†many of the details concerning how they will function in practice are as yet unknown. However, certain broad comparisons with Yugoslav law and practice can be made from an analysis of the newer laws and the economic and political structure in which they will operate. Through such comparison, which follows below, potential investors in Eastern Europe should obtain a clearer picture of the fundamental principles that underly each of the three joint venture laws, as well as a better idea of, and the reasons for, their distinguishing features.

---

*Differences in terminology in the joint venture laws of Yugoslavia, Romania, and Hungary often reflect substantive distinctions in the legal frameworks for foreign investment in the three countries and will, therefore, be preserved herein where relevant. For example, the use of the terms "joint company" in the Romanian law, "economic association" in the Hungarian law, and "joint venture" in the Yugoslav law reflects, among other things, the mode by which foreign investment is made in the three countries. In Romania and Hungary, the coventurers form a new company, which is structured much like a Western corporation. In Yugoslavia, on the other hand, the foreigner is not involved in setting up the enterprise that receives the investment but instead pools his resources with his coventurer for engaging in a joint project or "joint venture" in the traditional sense.

† By mid-1974 only 6 joint ventures has been approved in Romania and only 1 in Hungary.

A more complete exposition of the Romanian and Hungarian laws is contained in the respective chapters of Part II of this book.

Similarities

Importance of Joint Venture Agreement

For the foreign investor and his East European coventurer, the most important lesson from the experience thus far with joint ventures in Eastern Europe is the critical nature of the basic agreement establishing the rights and obligations of the parties. The importance of the agreement, which in Yugoslavia is referred to as a Joint Venture Agreement and in Romania and Hungary as a Contract of Association, derives from the fact that the laws permitting or relating to joint ventures in Eastern Europe do not, and were not intended to, regulate all matters that might arise in the course of the formation and operation of a joint venture. Therefore, one of the principal tasks facing coventurers is to draft as comprehensive an agreement as possible in order to fill the gaps left by incomplete legislation. This is particularly true in Romania and Hungary because of the absence of local law regulating autonomous business organizations. Coventurers in these countries, and to a more limited extent those in Yugoslavia, must in effect create a separate "companies act," governing the creation, operation, and dissolution of their joint venture.

Approval of Agreement

The basic agreement between coventurers in Yugoslavia, Romania, and Hungary, including, in the latter two countries, the statutes of the joint venture company, must be approved by state authorities.[87] In Hungary and Yugoslavia, approval is given by a single ministry (Finance and Economy, respectively), although there is coordination with other government entities. In Romania, initial approval of the draft documents is obtained from the State Planning Committee, the Ministry of Finance, the Ministry of Labor, the Romanian Bank for Foreign Trade, and other Romanian banks. After they are signed, the documents are deposited with the Ministry of Foreign Trade, which, upon verifying their legality, submits them to the Council of Ministers for final approval by decree of the State Council.

The decree of the Romanian State Council elevates the Contract of Association and statutes of the joint venture company to the status of Romanian law.[88] Although Hungarian law does not so provide, government approval of joint ventures in that country would appear to have a similar effect. However, government approval in Yugoslavia is not believed to have this broad an impact.

526

Limitation on Share of Equity

Romania and Hungary have followed Yugoslavia's lead of permitting foreign investors to contribute only a minority of the equity capital of the joint venture company.[89] Although the Yugoslav law permits the Federal Assembly to grant an exception to the above rule and the Hungarian law states that the rule will apply "in general," the Romanian law does not by its terms permit a deviation from the 49 percent limitation.

Kinds of Assets Invested

By its silence, Yugoslav law does not restrict the kinds of assets that can be contributed to the "equity" of joint ventures, and this is presumably true in Hungary as well, although the limitation on the fields in which joint ventures may operate in Hungary (see below) will itself restrict the type of property invested by foreigners. Romanian law deals expressly with this question by providing that contributions may consist of cash, assets required for carrying out the joint venture, industrial property, and of other rights.[90]

Restrictions on Fields of Investment

As in Yugoslavia,[91] joint ventures in Romania and Hungary are limited to specified fields. In Romania, these are broadly described as "industry, agriculture, building, tourism, transport, scientific and technological research work,"[92] while in Hungary, joint ventures are limited to research and development, commercial, and service activities[93] and may not engage in production unless express approval is obtained from the Council of Ministers. Joint ventures in Hungary may, however, contract with Hungarian producing enterprises, which in many cases will be the foreign investor's local partner.[94]

Emphasis on Exports

One of the principal objectives of East European countries in allowing joint ventures between domestic and foreign firms is to stimulate increased earnings of hard currency through exports or receipts from tourism. In Yugoslavia, hard currency earnings are both a condition to approval of a joint venture and the principal means by which foreign profits and capital are repatriated. Although the Romanian law does not expressly limit joint ventures to projects that earn hard currency, the law states that joint ventures are formed to "achieve economic objectives whose production is particularly intended for export,"[95] and the economic and political considerations underlying the law's enactment will presumably, as a general rule, limit joint ventures to those projects that "pay their own way" through hard currency earnings. This presumption is reinforced by a provision of Romanian law that requires domestic, as well as foreign, sales by joint ventures to be made in hard currency.[96] Since the Government of Romania must, therefore, provide all hard currency for domestic sales, it will undoubtedly press for hard currency earnings by joint ventures in order to prevent net foreign exchange losses from their activities. Unlike those in Yugoslavia, however, authorities in Romania appear to have the legal discretion to approve joint ventures producing solely for the domestic market, and some may be possible in high-priority industries, particularly if they produce vital products that are presently imported.

The Hungarian law does not deal with these subjects, but the same emphasis on exports and hard currency earnings can be expected.[97]

Voice in Management

Both the Yugoslav and Romanian laws permit foreign investors to be represented on the principal management unit that oversees the operation of the joint venture.[98] Hungarian law is silent on the subject, but coventurers can presumably provide for such representation in the contract of association.

The principal management organ of joint ventures in Yugoslavia, the joint business committee, must share decision-making with the workers' council of the Yugoslav enterprise that carries out the joint venture's activities. Although no similar decision-sharing with employee groups is required in Romania, representatives of the "general meetings of the working people" are to be placed on the joint company's "board of directors," or managing committee, as part of the representation of the Romanian coventurer.[99]

Neither Yugoslav nor Romanian law requires that representation on the principal management unit be in proportion to equity ownership, and in fact, many foreign investors in Yugoslavia have negotiated equal representation on joint business committees even where their interest in the equity was considerably less than 49 percent. Whether this will also be possible in Romania is unclear, although it is noted that the board of directors in the Control Data joint venture in Romania is split according to equity ownership.[100] In that venture, however, the parties have agreed, as expressly permitted by Romanian law,[101] that unanimous votes will be required on important decisions. Provisions requiring unanimity are also common in Yugoslav joint venture agreements, as the law, by its silence, leaves such matters to the discretion of the coventurers.

The nationality of the managing director of a joint venture company is not specified in the foreign investment laws of Yugoslavia, Romania, or Hungary. However, the presumption is that he must be a citizen of the country in which the joint venture is formed, and this has been the practice thus far. This also appears to be the rule for the deputy managing director, but the position of assistant manager may be held by a foreigner.[102] Thus far there is no precedent in Hungary, and the foreign investment law does not deal with this subject.

Government Guarantees

In order to attract foreign investment, the governments of Yugoslavia, Romania, and Hungary have provided for state guarantees of certain rights of foreign investors. The guarantees vary considerably in the three countries, and all need further clarification before their full scope can be known. In Yugoslavia, the guarantee consists of constitutional and legal provisions to the effect that laws, other than tax laws, will not be applied retroactively to existing joint ventures unless the contracting parties elect application of the new laws. In Romania, the government guarantees the transfer, through the Romanian Bank for Foreign Trade or other authorized institutions, of the foreign investor's profits and capital, share on liquidation, and other rights provided for under the contract of association and the statutes of the joint venture company.[103] The Hungarian law provides that the National Bank will transfer abroad "to the extent of the sum paid up to the Bank" the foreign investor's profits and capital in the currency stipulated in the contract of association.[104] In addition, the bank, upon request of the foreign investor, can also guarantee against damages caused by the Hungarian government or coventurer, up to the amount of the foreign investor's contribution to the joint venture.[105] In need of clarification under the Hungarian law is the extent to which the transfer of the foreign investor's profits is guaranteed. The law can be read as limiting such guarantee to the amount of the original investment—that is, "the sum paid up to the Bank"—a limitation that would, of course, be unsatisfactory to most investors.

Arbitration of Disputes

Both the Yugoslav and Romanian laws expressly authorize the parties to agree to settle disputes through arbitration.[106] Foreign arbitration is specifically permitted by the Yugoslavian law and, although not mentioned in the Romanian law, has been approved in practice.[107] The Hungarian law does not deal with the subject of dispute settlement.

529

Tax on Profits of Foreign Investor

Profits of foreign investors in joint ventures in Yugoslavia, Romania, and Hungary are subject to tax. However, the rate and application of the tax vary considerably in the three countries. In Yugoslavia, taxing authority has recently been transferred to the republics, and the rates vary according to the republic where the joint venture is located.[108] The Yugoslav tax is computed on the foreign investor's share of distributable profits, and, except in certain republics, a tax is not presently applied at the enterprise level. The Yugoslav tax laws, however, are in a state of flux, and this rule may be changed at any time. In Romania, the taxing authority is the central government, although the tax statement, together with the joint company's balance sheet, is originally filed for verification with the Financial Department of the Executive Committee of the People's Council of the district (of the city of Bucharest) where the joint company has its registered office.[109] The Romanian tax is applied in two stages. The profits of the joint company are first taxed at a rate of 30 percent before distribution to the coventurers, and the foreign investor's after-tax profits are then taxed at a rate of 10 percent if transferred from the country.[110] In Hungary, the profits tax is applied only at the enterprise level—that is, on profits of the joint "economic association" before distribution to the coventurers. The rate is 40 percent on profits not exceeding 20 percent of the value of the association's capital, and 60 percent on all profits above that level.[111] As in Yugoslavia, the tax on reinvested profits of foreign investors in Romania and Hungary is subject to reduction.[112] In Romania, the tax on profits reinvested for a period of at least five years in the same or another joint company is reduced by 20 percent. In Hungary, the tax on profits reinvested in the same company "may be refunded upon special application, submitted to the Ministry of Finance."

Distinctions

The State as Coventurer

In Yugoslavia, joint ventures with foreign participation are formed between foreign investors and workers' enterprises that are autonomous from the state. In Romania and Hungary, the foreign investor's coventurer is a state-owned enterprise. For the foreign investor, this distinction has a number of ramifications, some of which will only be known after additional experience with joint ventures in the more controlled economies of Eastern Europe. However, several important implications are readily apparent.

Relationships During the Negotiating Stage. Potential coventurers of foreign investors in Yugoslavia will, as a general rule, already be conducting profit-oriented business activities, and their representatives will, therefore, bring to the negotiations a knowledge of many of the commercial and financial concepts that guide negotiators establishing business partnerships in the West.

On the other hand, negotiations in Romania and Hungary are conducted by government officials and/or representatives of state-owned enterprises who, for the most part, have not conducted business operations within the strictures of a market economy and, therefore, may not have the same working knowledge of business concepts that has developed thus far in Yugoslavia.

(It can be expected, however, that negotiators from Romania and Hungary will be well-schooled in the theory, if not the practice, of establishing a business partnership, and many will have negotiated other forms of commercial transactions with Western firms, including, perhaps, joint ventures in third countries.)

The relative disadvantages of conducting negotiations with state officials may be offset by the certainty that comes from the existence of an immediate and constant relationship with persons responsible for recommending the joint venture's approval to their superiors within the government. In Yugoslavia, the authorities charged with approving a joint venture agreement are normally unfamiliar with its terms until it has been submitted for approval. There may, therefore, be greater potential for delay or failure in obtaining government approval of negotiated agreements in Yugoslavia than in Romania and Hungary, where state officials themselves participate in or are intimately familiar with the negotiations. Coventurers in Yugoslavia can, however, mitigate potential problems of this type by informal discussions with government officials prior to finalizing the agreement.

Relationships During the Operating Stage. Relationships between coventurers during the operating stage of joint ventures will also be different in the more centralized economies of Romania and Hungary than in Yugoslavia. In the latter country, coventurers will function in essentially the same manner, under similar financial and commercial strictures, and with the same goals as business partners in Western countries. Although the Romanian Government emphasizes the relative autonomy and profit objectives of joint ventures, it is too early to assess the degree of independence joint venture companies in Romania will have in practice. This is also true of joint ventures in Hungary.

One of the clear differences between joint ventures in Yugoslavia and those in Romania and Hungary arises in connection with domestic marketing of the joint venture's products. In Yugoslavia, domestic sales are made primarily to other autonomous business organizations, under substantially the same contractual arrangements and competitive conditions as exist in Western countries. On the other hand, domestic sales by joint ventures in Romania, and presumably in Hungary, will be made to state-owned enterprises, including in many cases the East European coventurer. Moreover, it can be expected that domestic sales in Romania and Hungary will be made under long-term agreements extending over the life of the joint venture and constituting an essential part of the over-all joint venture agreement.

Another distinction that will arise during the operating stage of joint ventures is the degree of state influence that might be adduced through representatives on the joint venture's management units. The Yugoslav members of the joint business committee will not be state employees, and, as noted previously, the foreign investor normally obtains equal representation on the committee. In Romania and Hungary, however, the East European coventurer will normally be represented on the joint venture's principal management unit by either state officials or officers of state-owned enterprises, and it remains to be seen whether foreign investors in these latter two countries will be permitted equal representation on the joint board.

Structure of Joint Venture Companies

Interestingly, Western investors may feel more at home with the structure of companies that conduct joint venture activities in Romania and Hungary than they do with those in Yugoslavia. In the latter country, foreign investments are made in workers' enterprises, which operate under the same laws, and with essentially the same structure, as enterprises without foreign participation. Although, as noted above, the external activities of these enterprises are similar to those of Western companies, their internal structure is still somewhat mystifying to outsiders.

In Romania and Hungary, on the other hand, the governments have attempted to anticipate such problems by providing that joint ventures will be conducted by newly formed enterprises, which may be structured as joint stock or limited liability companies, governed by articles of incorporation (contracts of association) and by-laws (statutes), managed by a board of directors, and authorized to issue shares to coventurers.

The terminology of the Romanian and Hungarian laws has more than psychological importance. As noted previously, there are few, if any, Romanian and Hungarian laws governing the formation, operation, and dissolution of autonomous business organizations. Therefore, coventurers in these countries have a good deal of flexibility in establishing the structure and governing rules of their joint venture.

Coventurers in Yugoslavia, however, must function under laws generally applicable to workers' enterprises, including, among others, those protecting the right of self-management of Yugoslav workers.

Property Rights

Another distinction that has both psychological and substantive implications for foreign investors is the question of the status of property invested in or acquired by the joint venture company. In Yugoslavia, such property, even that invested by a foreign coventurer, is "social property," and although a right of restitution of specific items of property by a foreign investor can be specified in a joint venture agreement,[113] the ambiguities of the social property concept remain a deterrent to many investors.

The Hungarian law is silent on the subject of property rights, However, the Romanians have again attempted to anticipate the concerns of Western investors by providing that "assets initially contributed by the coventurers as well as those subsequently acquired by the joint company shall be included within its patrimony with the title and effects laid down in the company's contract and statutes."[114] Although the meaning of the term "patrimony" is not totally clear in the Romanian context, the language authorizing the partners to fix the title to assets by contract would seem to permit a type of property right not generally recognized in Eastern Europe.

Remittance of Profits; Repatriation of Capital

In Yugoslavia, workers' enterprises conducting joint ventures with foreign participation are, like other Yugoslav enterprises, entitled to keep only a percentage of their hard currency earnings, and foreign investors are, as a general rule, entitled to remit profits and repatriate capital in hard currency only to the extent that the enterprise in which they have invested has sufficient currency for such purposes within the amounts allowed. In Romania, on the other hand, all sales, including those on the domestic market, are made in hard currency, and joint venture companies are entitled, after payment of taxes, to use such currency for, among other things, remission of the foreign investor's profits and repatriation of his capital. In addition, the government has guaranteed such transfers through the Romanian Bank for Foreign Trade and other authorized institutions. Similar guarantees are also provided under the Hungarian law, although other details concerning the treatment of hard currency receipts and expenditures by joint ventures are not specified, and the full scope of the Hungarian guarantees is somewhat unclear.[115]

Accounting; Determination of Profits

Because Yugoslav workers' enterprises have for a number of years operated for profit in a market economy, accounting regulations and practices have been developed for determination of enterprise profits, and most of these will be applied in some degree in determining the profits of foreign investors. No such precedent exists, however, in Romania and Hungary. Hence, coventurers will be able to specify the accounting procedures applicable to their venture, including those relating to profit determination.

Romanian law expressly provides that profits will be distributed in proportion to equity.[116] Yugoslav and Hungarian law is silent on this subject; however, it is understood that in Yugoslavia there have been cases where other factors have been taken into account in dividing profits.

Duration of Joint Venture

Yugoslav law provides that joint ventures must be long-term and the parties may terminate their venture only under prescribed conditions. No such provisions are contained in the Romanian or Hungarian laws, thus giving the coventurers absolute discretion in establishing the duration and the conditions for termination of their joint ventures.

Right of First Refusal

In Yugoslavia, foreign investors may sell their interests in joint ventures, including to purchasers outside Yugoslavia. By law, however, they must first offer their interest to the enterprise in which they have invested their capital, and penalties are prescribed for violation of this provision.[117] Romanian law leaves such matters to the coventurers, although both sides can be expected to insist on restrictions being placed on transfers of equity interests. Hungarian law does not cover this subject.

NOTES

1. Eastern Europe Report, Business International, S.A., Vol. 2, No. 18, September 7, 1973, p. 259; Journal of Commerce, November 20, 1973, p. 1.
2. Journal of Commerce, January 11, 1974, p. 1.
3. See, generally, Analytical Report on Industrial Cooperation among ECE Countries, E/ECE/844 and Addenda 1 and 2, U.N. Economic Commission for Europe (1973).

4. The 1967 legislation consisted of amendments to the Basic Law of Enterprises (BLE), the Basic Law on Assets of Economic Organizations (LAEO), the Basic Law on Unified Chambers of Commerce and Business Cooperation in the Economy (BALAW), the Basic Law on Contributions and Taxes of Citizens, the Law on Institution of Interest Payments on Funds in the Economy, and a new law, the Law on the Profits Tax of Foreign Persons Investing in a Domestic Economic Organization for the Purpose of Joint Operations: Official Gazette of the Socialist Federal Republic of Yugoslavia (O.G.), No. 31 of 1967 (31/67) and 9/68. Since 1967, there has been a steady stream of amendments to these laws, the Federal Constitution, and other major laws affecting joint ventures. The BLE, LAOE, and BALAW were recently replaced by various new laws, notably the Law on Establishment and Entry into Court Register of Organizations of Associated Labor (LEECR) (O.G. 22/73), the Law on Transfer of Social Assets of the Basic Organizations of Associated Labor (LTSA) (O.G. 22/73); and the Law on Business Associations (O.G. 23/72).

In April 1973, most of the statutory provisions directly regulating joint ventures with foreign participation were codified in the Law on Investments of Resources of Foreign Persons in Domestic Organizations of Associated Labor (herein referred to as the Foreign Investment Act or FIA) (O.G. 22/73). The most important of the other current laws specifically relating to joint ventures are the Law on Foreign Exchange Operations (Foreign Exchange Law or FEL) (O.G. 36/72) and the laws enacted beginning in 1969 by the individual republics to replace the abovementioned federal Law on Profits Tax on Foreign Persons Investing in a Domestic Economic Organization for the Purpose of Joint Operations. See note 56 infra.

5. Constitutional Amendments XXI, XXII (1971); LEECR, Art. 33.

6. See, generally, LEECR.

7. O.G. 22/73.

8. FIA, Art. 2.

9. LTSA, Art. 5; see also FIA, Art. 14(2).

10. FIA, Art. 12.

11. Id.

12. Id.

13. FIA, Art. 4.

14. FIA, Art. 3.

15. FIA, Art. 12.

16. Id.

17. Id.

18. Id.

19. Constitutional Amendment No. XXII, para. 4.

20. O.G. 34/71.

21. It should also be noted that the Yugoslav Constitution provides that the property of a Yugoslav enterprise may not be taken for public use without adequate compensation (Art. 15).

22. FIA, Art. 20(2).

23. Compare FIA, Art. 11.

24. O.G. 71/72.

25. For example, Law on Taxes of Citizens, O.G. of the Socialist Republic of Croatia, Feb. 9, 1973; Law on Orientation of Assets of the Socialist Republic Slovenia for Investment in the Economy for the Years from 1971 to 1976, O.G. of the Socialist Republic of Slovenia (8/73). Formerly, there was also a form of property tax called the "interest on the business fund," which represented a sort of rental charge for the "social property" that the nation had entrusted to the custody and use of the particular working organization. This tax was abolished when the compulsory contribution for loans to the under-developed regions of Yugoslavia was instituted.

26. See Chapter 14 for an exposition of the Chambers of Commerce (sometimes translated into English as "Chambers of Economy").

27. FIA, Art. 12(7).

28. FIA, Art. 12 at last para.

29. FIA, Art. 12(6).

30. See Chapter 14.

31. FIA, Art. 10.

32. Compare note 70 and accompanying text, infra.

33. FIA, Art. 1(2).

34. Id.

35. FIA, Art. 14(1).

36. FIA, Art. 14(3).

37. FIA, Art. 14(2).

38. FIA, Art. 14(4).

39. LEECR, Art. 64(1).

40. Compare LEECR, Arts. 62-64.

41. See LEECR, Arts. 42 et seq.

42. LEECR, Arts. 43, 46, 68 et seq.

43. FIA, Art. 9.

44. LEECR, Art. 134.

45. See id.

46. FIA, Art. 7.

47. Id.

48. Compare FIA, Art. 8.

49. The federal law that regulated this until recently has been replaced by laws of the various republics. For example, Law on the Depreciation of Basic Assets and Collective Consumption Assets of the Organizations of Associated Work, O.G. of the Socialist Republic of Croatia, December 28, 1972.

50. Compare note 25.

51. FIA, Art. 7.

52. FIA, Art. 13(1).

53. FIA, Art. 13(2).

54. See footnote on page 505.

55. FIA, Art. 17, says only that the foreign partner's tax is prescribed by a separate law.

56. Official Gazettes of Croatia (5/73), Bosnia and Hercegovina (36/72), Slovenia (3/73), Serbia (22/73), Montenegro (23/69), Macedonia (45/72 and 15/73), and Kosovo (11/73).

57. FIA, Arts. 18, 19. The currently applicable laws are the Law on Foreign Exchange Operations (FEL) (O.G. 36/72) and Law on Foreign Credit Transactions (O.G. 36/72). Yugoslav enterprises have seven possible sources for meeting their various foreign exchange needs: (1) the so-called retention quota out of their export earnings, (2) depreciation allowances, (3) the profit allowance (for remitting profits and repatriating capital to foreign joint venture partners), (4) quotas for imports of raw material, (5) credits from foreign suppliers and financial institutions, (6) capital contributions from foreign joint venture partners, and (7) certain special quotas.

58. FEL, Art. 51(1).

59. FEL, Arts. 36 and 39(6).

60. FEL, Art. 39.

61. FEL, Arts. 40(2), 51(3).

62. FEL, Art. 39.

63. FEL, Art. 40(1) and (2).

64. FIA, Art. 19(1).

65. FIA, Art. 19(2).

66. FEL, Art. 41.

67. O.G. 18/73.

68. FEL, Art. 51(3).

69. FEL, Art. 41.

70. FIA, Art. 10.

71. FIA, Art. 15.

72. FIA, Art. 16(1).

73. FIA, Art. 16(2).

74. FIA, Art. 16(3).

75. FIA, Arts. 12, 16(5).

76. FIA, Art. 21.

77. FIA, Art. 6(1).

78. FIA, Art. 6(2).

79. FIA, Art. 11.

80. Compare FIA, Art. 11.

81. Eastern Europe Report, Vol. 2, No. 18, September 7, 1973, p. 259; Journal of Commerce, November 20, 1973, p. 1.

82. John B. Holt, "New Roles for Western Multinationals in Eastern Europe," Columbia Journal of World Business, Fall 1973, pp. 131-139.

83. Law No. 1, Official Bulletin of the Socialist Republic of Romania, No. 33, March 17, 1971; 11 Int'l Legal Materials 161 (1972).

84. Decrees 424 and 425, Official Bulletin of the Socialist Republic of Romania, No. 121, November 2, 1972 (herein cited as R-424 and R-425, respectively); 12 Int'l Legal Materials 651 (1972).

85. Hungarian Law Decree No. 19, para. 31 (1970).

86. Minister of Finance Decree No. 28, Magyar Kozlony, No. 76. October 3, 1972 (herein cited as H-28); 12 Int'l Legal Materials 989 (1973).

87. FIA, Art. 12; R-424, Arts. 16-18; H-28, Art. 3.

88. R-424, Art. 17; remarks of Napoleon Fodor, Economic Counselor, Romanian Embassy, at seminar sponsored by the Overseas Private Investment Corporation in Washington, D.C., April 30, 1973.

89. FIA, Art. 4; R-424, Art. 4; H-28, Art. 4.

90. R-424, Art. 14.

91. FIA, Art. 3; see note 14 and accompanying text, supra.

92. R-424, Art. 1.

93. H-28, Art. 2(1).

94. H-28, Art. 2(2).

95. R-424, Art. 20.

96. R-424, Art. 23.

97. Eastern Europe Report, Vol. 1, No. 8, October 20, 1972, p. 106.

98. FIA, Art. 9; R-424, Art. 10.

99. R-424, Art. 34.

100. D. Morse and S. Goekjian, "Joint Investment Opportunities with the Socialist Republic of Romania," 29 Business Lawyer 133, 145, November 1973.

101. R-424, Art. 11.

102. Morse and Goekjian, supra note 100, report at p. 145, that an American employee of Control Data is to serve as the assistant manager of the Control Data joint venture in Romania for the first two years. For the rule in Yugoslavia, see note 44 and accompanying text, supra.

103. R-424, Art. 7.

104. H-28, Art. 11(1).

105. H-28, Art. 11(2).

106. FIA, Art. 21; R-424, Art. 38.

107. Morse and Goekjian, supra note 100 at p. 146.

108. See notes 55 and 56 and accompanying text, supra.

109. R-425, Art. 6.

110. R-425, Art. 1, Art. 13.

111. H-28, Art. 7.
112. See R-425, Art. 4; H-28, Art 7(4).
113. See note 70 and accompanying text; supra.
114. R-424, Art. 12.
115. See text at notes 104 and 105, supra.
116. R-424, Art. 26.
117. See note 72 and accompanying text, supra.

BIBLIOGRAPHIC NOTE

In addition to the references cited in the Bibliographic Note to Chapter 14 and which relate to Yugoslavia's foreign investment legislation, the following works may be noted:

Federal Chamber of Economy (Council for Economic Relations with Foreign Countries), Joint Investment and Production--Technical Cooperation of Yugoslav Economic Organizations and Foreign Firms (Belgrade, 1967); text of original joint venture legislation; introduction by Dr. Nikola Balog, president, Federal Legal Council.

Maggs and Smiljanic, "Investment in Yugoslavia and Eastern Europe," 6 Journal of Law and Economic Development 1 (1969).

McMillan, C. H. and D. P. St. Charles, Joint Ventures in Eastern Europe: A Three-Country Comparison (Montreal: C. D. Howe Research Institute, 1974).

Organization for Economic Cooperation and Development (OECD), Foreign Investment in Yugoslavia (Paris, 1970; out of print).

Overseas Private Investment Corporation, James R. Offutt, ed., Investing in Yugoslavia with OPIC Assistance (Washington, 1973).

20

SETTLEMENT OF DISPUTES:
THE ROLE OF ARBITRATION
IN EAST-WEST TRADE
Howard M. Holtzmann

ACCEPTABILITY OF ARBITRATION

Arbitration clauses are now standard practice in virtually all contracts between Western corporations and Eastern European foreign trade organizations. Parties on both sides routinely express a strong preference to submit future disputes to final decision by arbitrators rather than resorting to litigation in national courts of law.[1]

Arbitration, as used in this discussion, may be defined as a voluntary agreement made by both parties to a contract that any controversies or claims arising out of the contract, or in connection with or relating to the contract, or any breach of it, will be settled by one or more arbitrators, rather than by litigation in the courts. Each party to such an agreement typically expects that the other party will comply with the decision of the arbitrator and that, if it does not, the arbitration decision will be enforced in national courts having jurisdiction.

Western businessmen and lawyers have traditionally preferred arbitration in international trade disputes in order to avoid the uncertainties and complications associated with appearance in foreign courts. In the Western countries, long-established institutions exist that have extensive experience in conducting arbitrations arising out of international trade. Such institutions include, for example, the International Chamber of Commerce (ICC), the American Arbitration

---

Although the author has had the benefit of consultations with colleagues at the American Arbitration Association during the course of preparing this article, the views expressed herein are his own and not official views of that organization.

Association (AAA), the Inter-American Arbitration Commission, the Italian Arbitration Association, the London Court of Arbitration, the French Arbitration Association, the Japan Commercial Arbitration Association, and other arbitration organizations in various countries and specialized trades.[2]

Similarly, trade executives and legal specialists in East European countries have an established tradition of utilizing arbitration for resolving international trade disputes. This is true not only in dealings between socialist and capitalist countries but is equally the practice in transactions between foreign trade organizations of the various socialist countries themselves. Also, as in the West, institutions exist that are broadly experienced in conducting foreign trade arbitrations. The Foreign Trade Arbitration Commission (FTAC) at the USSR Chamber of Commerce is typical of such institutions, and similar arbitration organizations are connected with the central chambers of commerce in each of the East European countries.

This general acceptance of arbitration is raised to the level of government policy in a number of international treaties and agreements. A recent example is the U.S.-USSR Trade Agreement of 1972, which provides that

> Both governments encourage the adoption of arbitration for the settlement of disputes arising out of international commercial transactions concluded between natural and legal persons of the United States of America and foreign trade organizations of the Union of Soviet Socialist Republics. . . .[3]

Similar expressions of policy are included in the U.S.-Polish Trade Agreements of 1972.[4]

As a result, Western businessmen and lawyers will find that their counterparts in the socialist countries accept the concept of arbitration, expect to include an arbitration clause in virtually every trade contract, and are quite familiar with the processes of utilizing arbitration when disputes arise that the parties cannot themselves resolve. Any differences that may arise relate not to the acceptability of arbitration generally but rather to particular questions such as the locale of the arbitration, the nationality and method of choosing the arbitrator, and the rules, if any, to be applied in conducting the arbitration.

EFFECTIVENESS OF ARBITRATION

The effectiveness of arbitration as a means of providing a final and binding resolution of international commercial disputes depends on two principal factors: First, the willingness of the parties voluntarily to abide by the decision of arbitrators; and, second, the existence of a legal mechanism for court enforcement if a party fails to arbitrate or refuses to comply with an arbitration decision. Both of these factors exist in East-West trade and contribute to a healthy climate in which arbitration may reasonably be expected to be effective. First, the long-standing acceptance of arbitration in both East and West has created an atmosphere in which the parties are used to arbitration, recognize it as an indispensable element of international trade, and expect to participate in arbitration when a dispute arises and to abide by the decisions of arbitrators. Second, in those cases in which a party refuses to participate in arbitration or to comply with an arbitration award, local legal practices and international treaties exist for enforcement in the courts of both Western and Eastern countries. These legal sanctions have strong roots in virtually all of the nations involved in East-West trade. Thus, for example, in the United States the law strongly favors recognition and enforcement of domestic arbitration awards.[5] This policy has been extended to foreign arbitration awards by application of the doctrine of comity and, in some situations, through bilateral treaties of Friendship, Navigation, and Commerce.[6]

A similar development of basic legal principles favoring arbitration has taken place in the socialist countries. Thus, for example, a Soviet legal scholar describes Soviet policy favoring arbitration as follows:

> unilateral repudiation of an arbitration agreement . . . bars the disobedient party from having such disputes determined by an ordinary court. In affirming the binding effect of arbitration agreements the Fundaments of Civil Procedure of the USSR and the Union Republics provide that "if the parties have entered into an agreement for submitting their dispute for settlement by an arbitral court," the judge of an ordinary court "shall refuse to accept the statement of claim" (art. 31) and the court itself (should the judge have accepted the statement of claim, without knowing, for example, of the existing arbitration agreement or when such agreement is made subsequent to filing the statement etc.) "shall terminate the proceedings" (art. 41).[7]

The individual national policies favoring recognition and enforcement of arbitration coalesced and found further expression in the United Nations Convention on the Recognition and Enforcement of Foreign Arbitral Awards concluded in New York in 1958.[8] The United States and most West European nations, other than Great Britain, are signatories to the UN Convention of 1958. Socialist states that are parties include not only the Soviet Union but also Bulgaria, Czechoslovakia, Hungary, Poland, and Romania.9 (For GDR see pages 411-412.)

The UN Convention requires each contracting country "to recognize an agreement in writing under which the parties undertake to submit to arbitration all or any differences which have arisen or which may arise between them in respect of a defined legal relationship whether contractual or not, concerning a subject matter capable of settlement by arbitration."10 The Convention provides that a signatory country may refuse to recognize or enforce a foreign arbitral award only if the party against whom the award is rendered bears the burden of proving such things as (1) the agreement to arbitrate was not valid under the law applicable to the contract, (2) notice of the arbitration proceedings was not given or the party was otherwise prevented from presenting his case, (3) the award falls outside the terms of the agreement to arbitrate, (4) the arbitrators were not appointed in accordance with the agreement, or (5) the award has not yet become binding on the parties or has been set aside or suspended.11 None of these grounds for refusal are likely to provide serious problems concerning the enforceability of foreign arbitral awards in Eastern or Western European countries, provided contracts are properly written and arbitration procedures are carefully conducted.

In addition to the grounds for refusal to enforce a foreign award noted above, the UN Convention also provides that enforcement of an arbitral award may be refused in a signatory country if the courts of that country find that "(a) the subject matter of the difference is not capable of settlement by arbitration under the law of that country; or (b) the recognition or enforcement of the award would be contrary to the public policy of that country."12 The first of these grounds is unlikely to cause any major problems in enforcing awards in socialist countries because the decisions of such institutions show that socialist practice recognizes that differences capable of settlement by arbitration include virtually all of the types of disputes that could be expected to arise under contracts between Western companies and socialist foreign trade organizations.13 On the other hand, the ground for refusal to enforce an arbitration award because the enforcing country considers that to do so would be contrary to its public policy is a factor that must, at least at this time, be a basis for some concern by contracting parties in view of the differences in perception of proper public policy that exist on some matters between capitalist and socialist countries. However, this area of uncertainty as to public policy, which one commentator has called "unavoidable,"14 is inherent in any dispute settlement mechanism, be it judicial or arbitral. One can only hope that conflicting concepts of public policy will not intrude into the enforcement of arbitral decisions on commercial matters and that if such problems arise the courts of the country involved will recognize that the overriding public policy to be served is one that favors enforcement of commercial arbitration awards as a necessary element in maintaining vital international trade.

AVAILABLE FORMS OF ARBITRATION

Parties to contracts in East-West trade have a fairly broad, and sometimes quite bewildering, spectrum of choices in determining the form of arbitration to be used. Among the forms of arbitration that are available and being used as of January 1974 are the following:

● Arbitration under the rules of the foreign trade arbitration commission at the central chamber of commerce of the socialist country involved.
● Arbitration in the country of the defendant, using the rules of the local foreign trade arbitration commission if the socialist party is defendant, and when the capitalist party is defendant using the rules of an arbitration institution in the defendant's country.
● Arbitration in a third country, under the Rules of Arbitration of the United Nations Economic Commission for Europe (ECE),[15] as recommended in the U.S.-USSR[16] and the U.S.-Polish Trade Agreements.[17]
● Arbitration in a third country under the rules of the International Chamber of Commerce (ICC) or other rules. ICC rules are not acceptable to Soviet foreign trade organizations but have been agreed to by trading organizations of some other Comecon countries.
● Arbitration in a third country with no specification of any rules at all.

In choosing from among those alternatives, there are a number of factors that should be weighed. These include the following: Where will be the locale of the arbitration proceeding? Who will be the arbitrators and how will they be appointed? What will be the rules, if any, that will govern the arbitration?

Factors in Choosing Locale

In choosing locale, a principal factor is convenience in conducting an eventual arbitration proceeding. In this connection, one should consider the whereabouts of likely future witnesses and of machinery or products that arbitrators might wish to inspect. On the other hand, and quite significantly in cases involving East-West trade, the parties should also analyze existing facilities for conducting an arbitration proceeding, including availability of hearing rooms, interpreters, and bilingual stenographic assistance. Also to be studied are any possible problems that might be encountered in trying to communicate freely and rapidly by mail or telephone with home headquarters; the relative speed, ease, and assurance of securing visas for entrance of counsel, witnesses, arbitrators, and others involved in a case; and any potential difficulties in carrying exhibits or confidential business documents across borders. These conditions, which vary from country to country and which may change from time to time, should be borne in mind when drafting the arbitration clause. The U.S.-USSR trade pact recommends that contracts provide that arbitrations take place in a country other than the Soviet Union or the United States.[18]

Another factor to be remembered when determining locale is that arbitrators will typically apply the law of the locale in deciding procedural questions that may arise in conducting the arbitration proceeding. Such procedural questions are likely to arise even when the parties specify that arbitration is to be conducted under particular rules, such as the ECE rules or the ICC rules, for there are often elements of procedure that are not fully covered by such rules. In cases where the parties specify no rules at all, the range of procedural questions to be answered is, of course, far more extensive. It is also to be noted that, in the absence of specific contrary provisions in the contract, arbitrators in international practice will usually apply the procedural law of the locale even when the contract provides that the substantive law of another country is to govern the transaction. Accordingly, when choosing locale, parties should either be familiar and satisfied with the procedural law of the locale or should specify that some other procedural law is to govern. In the event that the procedural law of a country other than the locale is designated in the contract, it would be wise to check to be sure that the law of the locale so permits.

A further legal factor to be considered in determining locale is the applicability of the United Nations Convention on the Recognition and Enforcement of Foreign Arbitral Awards of 1958. That Convention includes a provision that any country, in ratifying the Convention, may declare that "it will apply the Convention to the recognition and enforcement of awards made only in the territory of another Contracting State."[19] The United States, the Soviet Union, and other Comecon countries that have ratified the Convention have done so subject to such a declaration of reciprocity. Since the UN Convention clause refers to awards made "in the territory of another Contracting State," it is necessary that the locale of an arbitration be in a contracting state in order to ensure applicability of the UN Convention in the various countries that ratified subject to a declaration of reciprocity. It is for this reason that the U.S.-USSR trade pact recommends that

545

the parties specify as the place of arbitration a country that is a party to the UN Convention.[20] Sweden, Switzerland, and France, which are often locales specified for East-West trade arbitrations, all meet this requirement, as they have all ratified the UN Convention. Inasmuch as Article 37 of the ECE Rules permits arbitration awards to be rendered in a country other than the locale of the proceedings, parties operating under those rules should also be sure that the award is actually rendered in a country that is a party to the UN Convention.

In choosing between various possible locales for the arbitration, one should not confuse the geography of the place of hearing and the nationality of the arbitrator, for the locale can, if mutually desired, be in the country of one of the parties while the arbitrator can at the same time be a national of a third country. This, in fact, is typical of international arbitrations conducted in the United States under the rules of the American Arbitration Association, which provide that in such cases "The neutral arbitrator shall, upon the request of either of the parties be appointed from among the nationals of a country other than that of any of the parties."[21] A similar provision is found in the ICC Rules.[22]

Factors in Choosing Arbitrators

The first factor that most parties consider in choosing arbitrators in international trade cases is the nationality of the arbitrators. Western parties typically prefer that the sole or third arbitrator (sometimes called the "umpire") be a national of a country other than the countries of the parties. As noted above, this preference finds traditional expression in both the ICC and the AAA rules.[23] In contrast, most socialist countries prefer a system of arbitration in which the arbitrators are all members of the roster of their own country's foreign trade arbitration institution, which in the USSR and many other Comecon countries is, as a result of rule or practice, usually composed of nationals of the country involved.

While the socialist countries prefer arbitration before their own arbitration institutions as a matter of first choice, all will accept contracts calling for third-country arbitration. Professor S. Bratus, the distinguished chairman of the USSR Foreign Trade Arbitration Commission, writing even before the signing of the 1972 U.S.-USSR Trade Agreement, confirmed the practice that "in most contracts signed by Soviet organizations with corporations and firms in capitalist countries provision is made for the settlement of disputes by neutral arbitration in a third country."[24] Such provisions are recommended in both the U.S.-USSR and the U.S.-Polish Trade Agreements.[25]

Arbitration clauses in contracts in East-West trade typically call either for the parties to agree on one arbitrator or for each party to appoint an arbitrator, and for those two to attempt to agree upon the third arbitrator. It therefore becomes necessary to provide for an appointing authority to name the sole arbitrator or the third arbitrator in the event that the parties or the two-party appointed arbitrators are unable to reach agreement. Appointing authorities are usually arbitration institutions, chambers of commerce, or distinguished individuals in third countries, such as presidents of chambers of commerce or high court judges.

In choosing an appointing authority, it is important to know the practices the authority follows in making appointments and whether the authority is guided by rules or regular procedures. Thus, for example, under rules of the Soviet Foreign Trade Arbitration Commission, arbitrators can be named only from among the 15 members of the commission, all of whom are Soviet citizens.26 Under ICC rules, third-country arbitrators are appointed by an international group, based on nominations of the ICC national committee of the country from which the arbitrator comes.27 The AAA, under its rules, names third-country neutrals from the extensive, open-ended lists of arbitrators it maintains.28 Arbitration institutions make it their business to identify potential arbitrators long before cases arise and thus have ample time to consider each individual's qualifications and areas of specialization. In contrast, when the parties have the president of a chamber of commerce or other distinguished individual as the appointing authority, there are typically no rules to govern the method by which that individual will make the choice of arbitrator, no formal panels, little staff support, and no readily available past record to which parties can refer. Instead, the choice of arbitrator will largely be made based on the personal circle of acquaintances of the individual appointing authority, with whatever staff support his institution may be able to provide.

In drafting arbitration clauses, it should be borne in mind that a clause designating an appointing authority does just that and nothing more. Thus, for example, a clause designating the president of the Stockholm Chamber of Commerce simply provides power for that individual to name a third arbitrator. Such a clause does not bring into play the arbitration rules of the Stockholm Chamber of Commerce nor does it provide for the rendering of any administrative services by the chamber. In contrast, reference in a contract to arbitration under the rules of such an institution as the ICC, the AAA, or the Soviet FTAC not only provides an appointing authority but also establishes the rules that will govern the appointment of the arbitrator as well as other aspects of the arbitration proceeding and calls into operation the administrative facilities of the arbitration institution.

When considering arbitration provisions, a choice must be made between having a single arbitrator or having a panel of three. Some

Western lawyers argue strongly for a single arbitrator in most international cases, largely on the ground that the difficulties of coordinating the available time of three prominent men often result in extended delays and that one arbitrator can more effectively and quickly conduct and complete the arbitration. Those who favor three arbitrators follow the old adage that "there is safety in numbers" and also point out that party-appointed arbitrators are usually fellow nationals of the parties and can bring differing cultural perspectives to bear on the problem. Reflecting the existence of these varied viewpoints, most rules, whether they be those of the USSR FTAC, the ICC, or the ECE, provide the opportunity for parties to choose to have either one arbitrator or three. The difference between the Eastern and Western practice is that under the Soviet FTAC rules, for example, one arbitrator is permitted only in "exceptional cases,"[29] whereas under ICC rules, if the parties fail to agree on the number of arbitrators, one is the usual number and three are appointed only if the dispute "appears important enough to warrant the appointment of three arbitrators."[30] A similar situation exists under the AAA rules.[31] The present author generally favors three arbitrators in all but very small East-West trade disputes because the party-appointed arbitrators can bring to the arbitral deliberations insights into local viewpoints and customs that may be most helpful to the neutral arbitrator in properly resolving disputes growing out of widely different social, economic, and legal systems.

A final point should be noted in connection with the choice of arbitrators. Whereas many Western lawyers, particularly Americans, are used to accepting engineers and other technical specialists as arbitrators in disputes that are primarily technical,[32] Soviet and other Comecon practice favors appointing only lawyers as arbitrators in virtually all cases. Describing the Soviet viewpoint, Professor Bratus has said,

> The main consideration in favor of this attitude, which
> was expressed in the report of the Soviet representative
> and supported by several speakers from socialist and
> capitalist countries, was as follows: Any technical con-
> clusions and calculations in support or refutation of
> proper or improper carrying-out of work undertaken
> should be given a legal assessment, because they deal
> with facts confirming, altering or waiving the rights and
> obligations of the parties.[33]

Accordingly, Western parties should expect that their socialist counterparts will urge that arbitration tribunals consist only of legally trained arbitrators.

Factors Concerning Rules

The first issue to be considered by parties in connection with the choice of rules to govern arbitration proceedings is whether they feel the need for any rules at all. On the one hand there is the combined experience of established arbitration institutions in both the East and West that procedural rules not only facilitate the conduct of an arbitration but also help ensure fairness and remove from the area of controversy a variety of potential conflicts that could otherwise exacerbate the relations of the parties. On the other hand, there continue to be optimists who feel that somehow, without rules, the parties to an international case can manage to meet in a hotel room with one or more arbitrators and conduct their arbitration simply and effectively.

In situations in which the agreement to arbitrate makes no reference to rules, arbitrators will normally apply the procedural law of the locale, which may be found in an arbitration law, in procedural legislation, or in both. However, such laws are typically quite general and do not contain many of the specific procedural guidelines found in the rules of most arbitration institutions.

Whether an arbitration can proceed smoothly without rules, once the locale has been specified and the arbitrators appointed, depends in large part on the procedural skills of the particular arbitrators, the extent to which the parties are prepared to cooperate on resolving procedural points as contrasted with the extent to which one party might desire to delay or frustrate the proceeding, and a certain amount of luck as to whether or not difficult procedural problems arise. If all goes well, "homemade," "hotel room" arbitration may be quite satisfactory. But when difficulties arise, experience indicates that parties are well-served by the existence of sound procedural rules to guide themselves and the arbitrators.

It is in recognition of these practical considerations that the central chambers of commerce of the Comecon countries, as well as various arbitration institutions in the West, have all developed quite detailed procedural rules. Those rules typically cover such areas as institution of proceedings; presentation of answers and counterclaims; appointment of arbitrators, challenges to arbitrators, and substitution of arbitrators in event of death or incapacity; provisions for ex parte hearings and decisions if one party fails to appear after notice; provisions as to the right to be represented by counsel; guides as to transcripts, oaths, costs, fees, language, and experts; general procedures at hearings, including questions of who may be present and of representation by counsel; and rules relating to awards, including whether or not arbitrators must state reasons in detail and whether or not awards will be published or kept confidential. Although differences exist between the rules of Eastern and Western arbitration institutions with respect to locale and nationality of arbitrators, there are large areas of similarity as to most other basic procedures. Donald B. Straus, president of the Research Institute of the AAA, and a recognized authority on rules, has said that "An impartial reading of all these rules of procedure, with few exceptions, reveals that they differ very little in any essential qualities."[34] The mere listing of the topics covered by typical abritration rules should give pause to any lawyer about to embark on a complex international contract in East-West trade without benefit of recourse to established institutional arbitration rules in the event a dispute arises.

A further advantage afforded by the rules of most arbitration institutions is that they provide for various administrative services to be performed for the parties by the institution. Such services include secretariat and other facilitating functions that experience demonstrates are often helpful to the parties. The availability of such administrative services assures fairness and provides a buffer between contesting parties in handling necessary "housekeeping" details of the arbitration. This is particularly valuable in conducting arbitrations in East-West trade in view of the fact that the parties often approach even simple procedural details with different cultural perspectives and the experienced staffs of arbitration institutions fulfill an important function in explaining and expediting the procedures. Few arbitrators have the time, experience, or desire to cope with such administrative details themselves.

CHOOSING THE FORM OF ARBITRATION

In choosing the particular form of arbitration to be included in a contract, parties will wish to consider the various factors relating to locale, choice of arbitrator, and rules discussed above. In this connection it may also be helpful to review the practices followed by parties who have been negotiating contracts.

No central source of information exists concerning the content of arbitration clauses in various East-West commercial contracts. However, an effort to collect arbitration clauses in East-West contracts entered into by American corporations since the signing of the U.S.-USSR Trade Agreement has been undertaken by the American Arbitration Association, in cooperation with the Bureau of East-West Trade of the U.S. Department of Commerce and with the aid of a number of lawyers who have been engaged in negotiating such contracts. While the experience of Americans may not be entirely similar to that of other Western traders and while this compilation may not be complete, it is the best source of data available and is believed to be representative of practices during the period October 1972 to January 1974.35

A total of 14 agreements between U.S. corporations and Soviet foreign trade organizations have been analyzed by the AAA Research Institute. Of these, 10 provide for arbitration in Stockholm, with the president of the Stockholm Chamber of Commerce designated as the appointing authority and with no rules of procedure specified. Three of the 14 agreements provide for arbitration in Moscow, with the arbitrators to be appointed and the proceeding conducted under FTAC Rules. One of the agreements calls for arbitration in Paris, with the arbitrators to be appointed by the Board of the Assembly of the Presidents of the Chamber of Commerce and Industry in Paris and the proceedings to be conducted under the ECE Rules.

A somewhat different pattern has developed for arbitration arrangements between U.S. corporations and trading organizations in other Comecon countries. The AAA Research Institute reports on eight arbitration clauses in recent contracts involving Poland. Of these, five specify arbitration under ECE Rules, with the locale of two in Zurich, and one each in London, Basle, and Geneva; one provides for ICC Rules in Zurich; and two call for arbitration in Zurich under the "laws of Switzerland." Two recent contracts involving Romania provide for arbitration under ICC Rules in Paris. One recent contract with a Hungarian trading organization specifies ICC Rules in Zurich.

In considering the various forms of arbitration available to parties in East-West trade, it must be emphasized that there are a number of developing changes in international arrangements that may affect arbitration in this area. Accordingly, parties would be well advised to check for the latest available information before considering the actual drafting of arbitration clauses.36

Arbitration Commissions in Comecon
Countries

Historically, foreign trade organizations of the Soviet Union and other Comecon countries in negotiating contracts with Western corporations have proposed arbitration under the rules of the foreign trade arbitration institution established at the central chamber of commerce of the socialist country. The Soviet Foreign Trade Arbitration Commission and the Soviet Maritime Arbitration Commission, both at the USSR Chamber of Commerce, are generally representative of such institutions.

In arbitrations conducted by the Soviet FTAC, for example, the proceedings take place in the USSR, the arbitrators must be chosen from a panel of 15 members, all of whom are Soviet citizens, and the rules of the FTAC are applied. Aside from the provision relating to locale and choice of arbitrators, the rules are along lines similar to those of Western arbitration organizations and afford the basic requisites for procedural due process.37

The individuals who head the arbitration institutions in the Soviet Union and other Comecon countries and those who are members of their panels of arbitrators are, typically, distinguished lawyers with substantial expertise in international trade law.

The reaction of Western corporations to accepting contract clauses providing for arbitration before the foreign trade arbitration commissions of Comecon countries is summed up by an experienced U.S. lawyer, who has said, "Although most knowledgeable observers give the FTAC high marks for its overall record of accomplishment, foreign companies are often reluctant to have their trade disputes with Soviet foreign trading organizations resolved by the FTAC."38 The reason for this reluctance is probably not due to dislike of the procedural rules of the socialist arbitration institutions or to distrust of the individuals who comprise their panels of arbitrators. Rather, the preference is based on factors relating to convenience of locale described above and also to the strong Western tradition that in all international trade cases the neutral arbitrators should be nationals of countries other than those of the parties.

Arbitration in the Country of the Defendant

In a move toward establishing a more balanced mechanism for international commercial arbitration, the socialist countries often advocate contract clauses that provide for arbitration in the country of the defendant under the rules of an arbitration institution in the defendant's country. This mechanism is regularly followed in transactions between the foreign trading organizations of the Comecon countries themselves. It has also been adopted in some East-West transactions and, notably, is the form established for USSR-Japan trade in an agreement made between the USSR Chamber of Commerce and the Japanese Commercial Arbitration Association in 1956.

Bratus has commented on this arbitration mechanism from his vantage point as a leading Soviet arbitration expert:

Both sides [in agreeing to arbitrate in the country of the defendant] act in the spirit of mutual trust and base themselves on the principle of equality and equal interest in a just settlement of disputes. Here mutual trust is expressed in the fact that both sides rule out the possibility of calling on so-called neutral arbitration, feeling that since each of the sides could be either the respondent or the plaintiff the settlement of a dispute by local arbitration would be unbiased and founded on an accurate interpretation of the contract and on the norms of the applicable law.[39]

One reason often cited by Western lawyers in opposition to arbitration in the country of the defendant is that, if the socialist trading organization fails to perform, it would be necessary to arbitrate under the rules of the socialist country, a procedure that, as noted above, is not generally favored by capitalist corporations. Moreover, many Western lawyers fear that this arrangement would lead to situations in which parties would maneuver artifically in an attempt to be in the position of defendant when proceedings commenced.

Another point to be noted is that, despite an apparent balance, there is actually a lack of equal reciprocity in arrangements that provide for arbitration under the rules of the socialist arbitration institutions when the socialist trade organization is defendant and under the rules of the ICC or the AAA when the Western corporation is defendant.[40] This is because, as discussed above, many socialist arbitration institutions appoint only arbitrators of their own nationality, whereas the ICC and AAA Rules provide for third-country arbitrators in international cases.[41]

Arbitration in a Third Country
Under ECE Rules

The United Nations Economic Commission for Europe adopted its Rules of Arbitration in 1966.[42] The rules were in large measure designed in order to facilitate arbitration of disputes arising from commercial transactions between trading entities in Eastern and Western Europe. Creation of the rules followed and was pursuant to the European Convention on International Commercial Arbitration of 1961.[43] The rules are, however, basically independent of the Convention. The fact that a country is a signatory to the Convention does not obligate businesses of that country to use the ECE Rules. Also, the fact that a country is not a signatory to the Convention does not bar traders of that country from using the rules. The ECE Rules, like the ICC Rules and other institutional rules, are available for any parties anywhere who may desire to include reference to them in their commercial contracts.

An unfavorable characteristic of the ECE Rules is that they are more general in language and less comprehensive in scope than the rules of many arbitration institutions. A recent informal study by the Research Institute of the AAA done in consultation with about 50 lawyers for corporations engaged in East-West trade indicates that almost half of the ECE Rules could benefit from supplementary language in order to amplify or clarify them or to eliminate ambiguities. Moreover, the ECE Rules have a further disadvantage in that they do not include a structure for administration and, except for functions of the appointing authority in selecting the arbitrator, all other secretariat and "housekeeping" functions are left to be performed by the arbitrators or the parties.

A final point should be noted by parties who desire to refer in contracts to ECE Rules. It is important to designate an appointing authority in the contract. The mechanisms of the ECE Rules that come into play when the parties refer to the rules but fail to designate an appointing authority are cumbersome, generally untested, and may prove unsuitable in actual practice. In this connection it is noteworthy that the U.S.-USSR and the U.S.-Polish Trade Agreements both recommend that parties who elect to use the ECE Rules should in their contracts name an appointing authority in a country other than the countries of the parties.[44]

Arbitration in a Third Country
Under ICC Rules or Other Rules

The International Chamber of Commerce with headquarters in Paris has for many years maintained rules and administered commercial arbitration proceedings in many parts of the world. Its rules are comprehensive, its procedures are highly developed, and its administrative staff is broadly experienced.[45] As noted above, ICC rules provide for appointment of third-country arbitrators.[46]

The foreign trading organizations of the Soviet Union have not generally agreed to arbitration under ICC Rules. However, a number of other Comecon countries, particularly those with closer historic and cultural ties to France, do regularly agree to ICC arbitration. Notably, the U.S.-Polish Trade Agreement recommends ICC arbitration as an alternate to the ECE Rules.[47]

There is also the possibility of arbitration in a third country using institutional rules other than the ICC Rules, such as rules of the Stockholm Chamber of Commerce. However, there is little current evidence of parties electing to include such provisions in East-West trade agreements. For example, from 1962 through 1972 the Stockholm Chamber administered only 13 cases under its rules, and of those only two involved Comecon countries—the USSR and Poland. The predominant practice in East-West trade relating to Sweden appears to be to designate that country as the locale and to provide for the president of the Stockholm Chamber to be appointing authority, but not to include reference to the Stockholm Chamber Rules. Similar practices seem to be followed when Switzerland is designated as the locale and when a Swiss appointing is designated.

Further alternatives for arbitration in a third country under established rules would become possible if success is achieved in developing new rules through the efforts of the UN Commission on International Trade Law and as a result of discussions between U.S. and Soviet arbitration institutions. These projects, which hold great promise for the future, are described below under the subheading "Possible Future Developments."

Arbitration in a Third Country
With No Rules Specified

A substantial number of contracts in East-West trade provide for arbitration in a third country without any reference to institutional rules. Thus, for example, the largest number of reported recent contracts between U.S. firms and Soviet foreign trading organizations provide for arbitration in Stockholm, with the president of the Chamber of Commerce of Stockholm to appoint the arbitrators if the parties fail to do so by mutual agreement. Typically, such contracts include provisions for initiating arbitration by registered mail notice in which the initiating party names his arbitrator. The opposite party then has a specified period, ranging in various contracts from 14 to 60 days, in which to reply and name an arbitrator. If the respondent does not reply, then an arbitrator is to be appointed for him by the president of the Stockholm Chamber. The two arbitrators must then mutually agree on a third arbitrator, and, if they fail to do so within contractually·established time limits, the third arbitrator is to be appointed by the president of the Stockholm Chamber. However, there is no reference to the method by which, or the source from which, the president of the Stockholm Chamber of Commerce will choose the third arbitrator. Although the intent is apparent, the language of some typical contracts does not even clearly require that the third arbitrator be a national of a third country.[48] In practice, the president of the Stockholm Chamber has, when called upon, named a Swedish lawyer as the third arbitrator in almost all cases. Such contracts specify that the arbitrators' award shall be decided by majority vote.

It is to be noted that such contracts do not bring into play the arbitration rules of the Stockholm Chamber. Whatever procedural guidelines are to be applied must be found in the quite broad provisions of the Swedish Act on Arbitrators. Moreover, such contracts do not provide for any administration services to be rendered by the Stockholm Chamber of Commerce, other than the services of its president in appointing arbitrators.

The recent contracts providing for arbitration in Stockholm represent a substantial step forward in extending the principle of third-country arbitration in East-West trade. However, lacking rules and administration, they fall short of providing the best possible mechanism for arbitration.

Possible Future Developments

Recent informal discussions between Soviet and U.S. arbitration experts led to a consensus that it would be helpful for arbitration experts of the USSR Chamber of Commerce to confer with representatives of the AAA with a view toward developing augmented rules and model arbitration clauses that might be made available on an optional basis to parties engaged in U.S.-Soviet trade. It was also the consensus that it would be helpful to try to develop mutually agreeable lists of arbitrators to guide appointing authorities in third countries when cases arise.[49] Such efforts would be consistent with the provisions of the U.S.-USSR Trade Agreement that invite parties to develop "forms of arbitration which they mutually prefer and agree best suits their particular needs."[50] It is, of course, premature to predict whether such joint efforts will be fruitful, or when they might be concluded. However, if they are successful, they would not only improve arbitration in U.S.-Soviet trade but would also provide a valuable model for other international trade.

A second development on the horizon is a UN project that the United Nations Commission on International Trade and Law (UNCITRAL) has recently undertaken to develop a new set of suggested arbitration rules.[51] This project, now in the early drafting stages, is being undertaken in collaboration with the new worldwide network of international arbitration organizations, originally known as the International Organizing Committee and now known as the International Committee for Commercial Arbitration.[52] Representatives of the Comecon countries are closely engaged in this project as are Western arbitration institutions and representatives of other regions. It is reasonable to expect that the results of this project will be applicable and helpful to East-West trade.

GOVERNING LAW

Arbitration provisions in international commercial contracts typically contain clauses designating the particular law that the arbitrators are to follow in interpreting the contract. In East-West transactions that provide for third-country arbitration, the parties have usually agreed to apply either internationally accepted principles of conflict of laws or third-country governing law. In the event the parties fail to specify a governing law in their contract, it is hard to predict whether arbitrators will apply the substantive law of the locale or the conflicts law of the locale or some other law they decide to be the proper law under the rule of conflicts that they consider appropriate.

The survey made by the AAA Research Institute of recent contracts in U.S.-USSR trade provides an interesting cross-section of current practice.[53] The governing law provisions seen in a number of such recent contracts include clauses referring to "the laws of Sweden"; "principles of conflict of laws of the country where the arbitration is to be held and additionally the arbitrators have the right to utilize the customs of world trade"; "Swedish Material Law"; "Principles of Conflict of Laws"; "conflict laws of Sweden"; and "Substantive Contract Law of Sweden." In addition some clauses have been seen in East-West contracts that refer to the Swiss Federal Code of Obligations.

Parties who are considering specifying governing law in an arbitration clause would do well to distinguish between contract law and conflicts law. Failure to note that distinction could lead to unanticipated results. Thus, for example, the conflicts law of Sweden may in certain cases provide that the law of the place where a contract is made shall govern the interpretation of the contract. A Western party signing a contract in Moscow with a Soviet party might provide for arbitration "under the law of Sweden," intending that Swedish contract law would apply to interpretation of the contract. However, arbitrators might well interpret the phrase "under the law of Sweden" to mean the conflicts law of Sweden, in which event Soviet contract law would be applied to interpret the contract because it was signed in the Soviet Union. To avoid such an unintended result, some lawyers provide specifically that "Swedish contract law" will govern. Similarly, in order to avoid application of a variety of different Swiss federal and cantonal laws, including laws of conflicts, some lawyers find it appropriate to refer in the arbitration clause specifically to the "Swiss Federal Code of Obligations."

Also, it is advisable to distinguish between procedural and substantive law in any case in which the parties wish to avoid application of the procedural law of the locale of the arbitration. For, unless this is done, arbitrators will typically interpret a clause providing that the law of a named country other than the locale will govern the contract to mean only that the substantive law of the named country will govern. Accordingly, in such a case, the arbitrators may apply the procedural law of the locale in cases in which no arbitration rules are specified in the contract or if procedural questions arise that are not covered in the rules specified in the contract.[54]

Another point to consider in drafting the governing law clause is whether the parties desire to restrict the powers of the arbitrators to the narrow confines of applicable law, or whether they prefer to authorize the arbitrators to have powers to act equitably _ex aequo et_

bono, or as <u>amiables compositeurs</u>. Such broader powers to act in
equity do not authorize the arbitrators to "rewrite" the parties' contracts but rather provide leeway to render forms of justice that might
otherwise not be permitted within the narrow confines of law, particularly under civil law systems that often stress doctrines of strict
code interpretation. In some East-West trade transactions, it has
been considered helpful to empower the arbitrators to act as <u>amiables</u>
<u>compositeurs</u>.55 In order to avoid ambiguities that might otherwise
arise under European practice, parties who desire to authorize arbitrators to act <u>ex aequo et bono</u>, or as <u>amiables compositeurs</u>, should
specifically include such a provision in their contracts and should
also be sure that the law of the locale permits that type of arbitration.

NEW USES FOR ARBITRATION IN CONTRACTS
FOR INDUSTRIAL, SCIENTIFIC, AND
TECHNICAL DEVELOPMENT

In recent years trade between the Comecon countries and the
West has become increasingly concerned with new types of business
arrangements that are quite different from the relatively simply import-export transactions that traditionally constituted the major part
of international trade. These newer transactions involve many more
complex legal and engineering aspects than traditional import-export
dealings and often require long periods of time to complete. For example, some of these transactions require a contractor to design and
build an entire factory on a "turnkey" basis. Other arrangements
may require the party that is acquiring the factory to perform part
of the work, such as erecting the building in which the factory will be
installed or supplying certain materials and components. A number
of the more complex arrangements contemplate even greater cooperation and provide for joint research, and for the exchange of goods,
services, and know-how between the parties on a continuing, long-
term basis. As Bratus has pointed out, the contractual arrangements
relating to such projects have "outgrown the framework of traditional
sales transactions."56
    There are a number of new uses for arbitration that are uniquely
helpful in these newer forms of contractual arrangements and that
are not generally applicable to traditional forms of sales contracts.
For unlike most import-export transactions in which arbitration is
generally involved only after goods are delivered or the time for
performance is passed, in contracts involving industrial, scientific,
and technical development, arbitration is valuable at a number of
earlier stages.

Arbitration to Solve Unpredictable Problems

In long-term arrangements for industrial or technological collaboration, arbitration is a valuable way to resolve disputes that may arise during the performance of the contract due to changes in technological, economic, or political conditions that the parties could not predict when the contract was initially entered into. The very essence of many such contracts is that the two parties to the contract are agreeing to embark together on a journey into the unknown. The parties to such contracts have a general idea of what they hope to accomplish, but they cannot be sure how long the task will take, precisely how much it will cost, and exactly what unexpected problems or changes in conditions may occur in the future.

The problem is further complicated by the fact that industrial and technical projects generally require many years of effort and the parties to such contracts must therefore consider not only the uncertainties in their own program but also many types of unpredictable external changes that may occur during the long life of their contract. For example, technical advances made by others may cause the project on which the parties are working to become obsolete even before it is finished. Other unpredictable events that may occur include changing political or economic climate and shifts in competitive conditions. Such events may require changes in prices, royalty rates, or other contractual terms.

Often even the most imaginative lawyer and the most far-sighted executive cannot predict all of the things that may happen during the long life of an industrial, scientific, or technical contract. It is at this point that a knowledge of the usefulness of arbitration is of vital importance, because arbitration, and only arbitration, can bridge the gap between the precise statement of contractual rights and responsibilities required in a legal contract and the unpredictability that is an inescapable element in much industrial, scientific, and technical development. A properly written arbitration clause can provide that when unpredictable changes arise during the life of a contract, the parties will attempt first to agree on fair ways to solve the problem and, if they are unable to do so, the matter will then be submitted to arbitration.[57]

In the event parties desire to use arbitration for such broad purposes, they should include specific contract provisions to that effect, including indication that the arbitrators are authorized to exercise powers acting ex aequo et bono, or as amiables compositeurs. Otherwise, arbitrators who are used to dealing in more legalistic terms may decline to decide the issue.

Finally, the provision for arbitration in such situations is important not only because it supplies an indispensable mechanism for solving future deadlocks but, just as importantly, because the existence of arbitration is a strong incentive to the parties to avoid deadlock by reaching mutual agreement when problems arise.

Arbitration in Technical or Engineering Disputes

The disputes that arise under industrial and technical contracts in many cases result from engineering or technological difficulties. Typically, such disputes involve first the question of whether or not there has been a failure to comply with the technological or engineering requirements of the contract, and, if so, who is to blame for it and what action must be taken to correct it.[58]

Clearly, the resolution of such disputes requires answers to technical or engineering questions that can only be given by qualified experts. Moreover, when disputes occur, there are many advantages in having the technical or engineering questions answered by qualified experts as soon as possible. For example, it may be necessary to resolve a dispute at a preliminary stage of construction before work can proceed on later stages of the project.[59]

For these reasons, some contracts for engineering and construction work in East-West trade provide for experts to decide technical disputes while work under the contract is still in progress. Such early intervention by technical experts raises a number of important questions for lawyers who write contracts and arbitrators who rule upon them. These questions result from the fact that contracts that provide for early intervention of experts to decide technical disputes also typically contain an arbitration clause. In such circumstances, the primary questions that arise concerning the relationship between technical experts and arbitrators include (1) What disputes should be referred to technical experts and what should be referred only to the arbitrators? and (2) Are decisions of technical experts final, or are they subject to review and revision by the arbitrators?

As to the first question, lawyers who write contracts for early intervention of technical experts to decide technological or engineering disputes should define as precisely as possible the disputes in which there is to be recourse to technical experts and the disputes to be referred only to arbitrators. Many contracts now being written fail to make that distinction adequately.

As to the second question, whenever parties provide in their contract for intervention by an expert to decide certain technical disputes, the contract should also state whether the decisions of the technical expert are to be final or whether a party who objects to the decision will have the right of appeal under the arbitration clause of the contract. A contract provision that the decision of the expert will be final has the advantage of resolving technical disputes most quickly and economically. On the other hand, when very important issues are at stake some parties may prefer to have the right of appeal to arbitration, which typically ensures greater procedural safeguards and a more juridical approach than are customary in the relatively informal atmosphere in which decisions are made by technical experts. The parties to each contract must weigh these relative advantages and disadvantages and determine the matter in the light of the particular circumstances of their transaction. It appears that Soviet and other Comecon country arbitration experts strongly favor contracts that provide that the decisions of technical experts will be subject to appeal to arbitration, with the arbitrators having unlimited power to review the decision of the experts, often in the light of testimony of counterexperts.

CONCLUSION

Businessmen and lawyers engaged in East-West trade will find that arbitration is the generally accepted method for resolving disputes that may arise under contracts between socialist foreign trade organizations and capitalist companies. They will find, too, that arbitration decisions may reasonably be expected to be effective because, in both East and West, there is a long history of willingness to comply with arbitration decisions and because legal practice and international treaties favor recognition and enforcement of arbitration decisions.

Parties engaged in East-West trade have a fairly broad spectrum of choices among various available arbitration mechanisms. Most Western companies prefer, and socialist trading organizations will usually agree to, neutral arbitration in which the arbitration proceeding is conducted in a third country, before an arbitrator from a third country, and applying law of a third country to govern the rights of the parties.

Arbitration is of value not only for resolving disputes in traditional import-export transactions but also for providing unique advantages in the newer types of long-term business arrangements involving industrial, technical, and scientific development.

Arbitration is well-established as a helpful adjunct to East-West trade. There are hopeful indications that it will become even stronger and more helpful as efforts for further improvement of procedural mechanisms move forward.

NOTES

1. As used herein, the word East refers to the Soviet Union and the East European countries joined with it in the Council for Mutual

Economic Assistance (herein called the Comecon countries); the word West refers primarily to the United States and the countries of Western Europe and also generally includes Japan and other capitalist countries. While China is not within the scope of this chapter, many of the factors discussed herein relating to arbitration between trade entities of countries having different economic systems are also applicable to it.

2. For full listing, see "International and National Institutions Acting in the Field of Arbitration" (Italian Arbitration Association, Rome, 1970).

3. Agreement Between the Government of the USA and the Government of the USSR Regarding Trade (October 18, 1972), Article 7. Text appears at 67 U.S. Department of State Bulletin, No. 1743, pp. 595-597.

4. The U.S.-Polish agreements on arbitration are set forth in two letters exchanged between the U.S. secretary of Commerce and the Polish minister of Trade, both dated November 8, 1972. Text appears in "Fact Sheet, Joint American-Polish Trade Commission, November 4-8, 1972," issued by the office of the U.S. Secretary of Commerce, Washington, D.C.

5. See Prima Paint v. Flood and Conklin, 388 U.S. 395 (1967); see also Aksen, "American Arbitration Accession Arrives in the Age of Aquarius: United States Implements U.N. Convention on the Recognition and Enforcement of Foreign Arbitrators Awards," in American Arbitration Association, ed., New Strategies for Peaceful Resolution of International Business Disputes (New York, 1971) (herein cited as New Strategies); originally published in Southwestern University Law Review, Vol. 3, No. 1.

6. See Aksen, supra note 5. For citation of bilateral commercial treaties of the United States that contain provisions on arbitration, see New Strategies, supra note 5, Appendix B, pp. 196-197.

7. Lebedev, "Maritime Arbitration Commission—Organization and Procedure," (Moscow: USSR Chamber of Commerce and Industry, 1972), p 14.

8. U.N. Doc. No. E/CONF. 26/9 Rev. 1, 6/10 (1958); U.N. Treaty Series, Vol. 330, No. 4739, p. 38 (1959); also reprinted in New Strategies, supra note 5, pp. 8-16.

9. Status of Multinational Treaties (1971) U.N. Doc. SER. D/5, p. 393; see also Register of Texts of Conventions and Other Instruments Concerning International Trade Law, Volume II (1973) U.N. E.73.V.3.; also New Strategies, supra note 5, p. 195.

10. U.N. Convention, supra note 8, Art. II, sec. 1.

11. Id., Art. V, sec. 1.

12. Id., Art. V, sec. 2.

13. See, for example, "Collected Arbitration Cases—Awards of the Foreign Trade Arbitration Commission at the USSR Chamber of Commerce," Part I, 1934-51; Part II, 1951-58; Part III, 1959-62; Part IV, 1963-65 (Moscow, 1972 and 1973).

14. Haight, "Convention on the Recognition and Enforcement of Foreign Awards," U.S. Delegation Report, p. 68.

15. E/ECE/625/Rev. 1; E/ECE/Trade/81/Rev. 1; UN Sales No. E. 70. II. E./Mim. 14.

16. Supra note 3.

17. Supra note 4.

18. Supra note 3, Art. 7, sec. 1(b).

19. U.N. Convention, supra note 8, Art. I, sec. 3.

20. Supra note 3, Art. 7, sec. 1(b).

21. Commercial Arbitration Rules of the American Arbitration Association (as amended November 1, 1973), sec. 15.

22. Rules of Conciliation and Arbitration of the International Chamber of Commerce (June 1, 1965), Art. 7, para. 3.

23. Supra notes 21 and 22.

24. Bratus, "Arbitration and International Economic Cooperation Towards Industrial, Scientific and Technical Development," report to Fourth International Congress on Arbitration in Moscow, October 1972 (herein called Moscow Congress); reprinted in 27 Arb. J. 239 (1972).

25. Supra notes 3 and 4.

26. The 15-member commission was created by Decree of the Central Executive Committee and the Council of the People's Commissars of the USSR on the Foreign Trade Arbitration Commission at the USSR Chamber of Commerce, June 17, 1932 (Collection of Laws of the USSR, 1932, No. 48, sec. 281). The requirement that arbitrators be appointed from among members of the commission appears in Rules of Procedure of the Foreign Trade Arbitration Commission at the USSR Chamber of Commerce, as amended August 12, 1967, secs. 6-10.

27. ICC Rules, supra note 22, Arts. 6 and 7.

28. AAA Rules, supra note 21, secs. 5, 12 and 14.

29. FTAC Rules, supra note 26, sec. 10.

30. ICC Rules, supra note 22, Art. 7, sec. 2.

31. AAA Rules, supra note 21, sec. 16.

32. See, for example, Coulson, "The Architect-Engineer Goes to Arbitration" (American Arbitration Association, 1970), p. 6. See also Stern, "Arbitrating Disputes in Major Construction Projects," p. 5, report to Moscow Congress, supra note 24.

33. Bratus, "The Fourth International Congress on Arbitration," Foreign Trade, No. 4 (Moscow, 1973), p. 48.

34. Straus, "Interim Observations on Arbitration Arrangements in Soviet-American Trade," 28 Arb. J. 108 (1973).

35. Id.; see also D. B. Straus, "Additional Remarks," paper presented at Conference on Legal Problems of Soviet-USA Trade, sponsored by Carnegie Endowment for Peace and American Society for International Law in New York, January 1974 (herein called Carnegie-ASIL Conference). The papers presented at the conference are expected to be published by the ASIL.

36. For example, the U.S. Department of Commerce recommends the American Arbitration Association "as a source of information and assistance regarding alternative arbitration provisions which the negotiating parties may select for their contracts," East-West Trade (U.S. Department of Commerce, April 1973).

37. FTAC Rules, supra note 26. For description of FTAC procedures, see Leff, "The Foreign Trade Arbitration Commission of the USSR and the USA," in New Strategies, supra note 5, pp. 143 et seq.; originally published in Arbitration Journal, Vol. 24, No. 1, (1969); also, New Strategies, Appendix C, pp. 246-252.

38. Starr, "A New Legal Framework for Trade Between the United States and the Soviet Union: The 1972 US-USSR Trade Agreement," 67 Am. J. Int'l L. 196 (1973). Pisar notes in Coexistence and Commerce (1970), that "those nominated by the various communist Chambers of Commerce to serve as arbitrators are in general persons of considerable achievement and high professional and social standing. One cannot lightly assume that such individuals are devoid of intuitive feelings for justice and fair play. . . . To foster contractual discipline at home and confidence abroad, the tribunals may indeed be leaning backward to be harsh with their own" (p. 408). See also, Coulson, "Arbitration in US-USSR Trade Disputes," New York Law Journal, November 13, 1972, p. 1.

39. Bratus, supra note 24, p. 236.

40. See, for example, alternate Rider to General Condition of Order of Amtorg Trading Corporation, which acts as agent in the United States for various Soviet foreign trade organizations.

41. Supra notes 21 and 22.

42. Supra note 15. The ECE rules are described and analyzed in Cohn, "The Rules of Arbitration of the United Nations Economic Commission for Europe," 16 Int'l and Comp. L. Q. 946 (1967).

43. E/ECE/423; E/ECE Trade 48; UN Treaty Series, Vol. 484, No. 7041 (1963-64), p. 364. For description and reprint of text of Convention, see Sarre, "European Commercial Arbitration," (1961) J. Bus. L. 352.

44. Supra note 3, Art. 7, sec. 1(a); supra note 4, para. 1(b).

45. Supra note 22. See Eisemann, "Arbitration Under the ICC Rules," 15 Int'l and Comp. L. Q. 726 (1966). See, also, Cohn, "The Rules of Arbitration of the ICC," 14 Int'l and Comp. L. Q. 132 (1965).

46. Supra note 22.

47. Supra note 4, para. 1(a).

48. For example, see supra note 40.

49. See papers presented by Lebedev (USSR) and Straus (U.S.) at Carnegie-ASIL Conference, supra note 35.

50. Supra note 3, Art. 7, Sec. 1(b).

51. This project is described in report of UNCITRAL on the work at its sixth session, April 1973, in General Assembly Official Records: Twenty-eighth Session, Supplement No. 17 (A/9017), para. 85.

52. For description of organization and activities of the new worldwide network of arbitration organizations, see Holtzmann, "Achievements of the Fourth International Congress on Arbitration: A Report From Moscow," 27 Arb. J. 214-218 (1972); see also, in same issue, the text of Resolutions of Moscow Congress, pp. 225-229.

53. Supra notes 34 and 35.

54. See also discussion in section of this chapter entitled "Factors in Choosing Locale," supra.

55. For example, the General Conditions for supplying plants and machinery developed by the UN Economic Commission for Europe permit granting arbitrators the power to act as amiables compositeurs, as described by I. Rucareanu (Romania) in "Arbitration and Contracts Concerning Projects of Industrial Installations, Supply and Mountings," pp. 7-8, report to Moscow Congress, supra note 24. It is understood that arbitrators are also granted power to act as amiables compositeurs in disputes arising under the arrangements for Soviet-French scientific and technical cooperation, which are described in report by M. Boguslavsky (USSR) on "Inventive Activities and Scientific, Technical and Economic Cooperation of the USSR with other Countries," presented at symposium on "Inventive Activities and Scientific and Technical Progress" (Moscow, July 1969).

56. Supra note 24, at p. 230.

57. Minoli, in his "Report on General Theme" to the Moscow Congress, supra note 24, wrote that arbitration "may be used to settle in the future certain points in the contract where the information in possession of the parties at a given time is insufficient to make a precise agreement . . . [and] arbitration is sometimes the only way of breaking a deadlock when it is practically impossible to lay down precise and detailed contractual rules" (p. 8). See also Holtzmann, "Arbitration and Contracts Concerned with Scientific Research and Technical Work," paper presented at Moscow Congress. Three papers on this subject were included in symposium presented at the Annual Meeting of the American Bar Association in San Francisco in 1972 on the topic of "Arbitration Clauses—Valuable Methods for Solving Business Problems Arising in Long-Term Business Arrangements."

These papers, which appear in 28 Bus. L. (1973) 585 et seq. are Holtz-mann, "An Overview"; Angel, "The Use of Arbitration Clauses as a Means for the Resolution of Impasses Arising in the Negotiation of, and During the Life of, Long-Term Contractual Relationships"; Aksen, "Legal Considerations in Using Arbitration Clauses to Resolve Future Problems."

58. L. Kopelmanas in a report to the Moscow Congress, supra note 24, on "Arbitration and the Technical Verification of Satisfactory Performance of International Contracts in Industry," observed, "It is probably not an exaggeration to say that the technical aspect pre-dominates in all differences which can arise between the parties on the subject of proper performance of the contract" (p. 3). For this reason Section II of the Resolutions adopted at the Moscow Congress expressly recognized "the increasingly important role of persons possessing specialized scientific and technical experience in connection with problems which may arise at various stages of projects for industrial, scientific and technical cooperation": supra note 52.

59. The importance of early intervention by technically qualified experts was emphasized in several reports by representatives of both capitalist and socialist countries to the Moscow Congress, supra note 24, including Pearson (Great Britain), "Role of Arbitrators and Consulting Engineers with Regards to Contracts on Civil Construction Works"; Stern (U.S.), supra note 32; Rucareanu (Romania), supra note 55; and Kopelmanas (Switzerland), supra note 58. See also, Holtzmann, "Use of Impartial Technical Experts to Resolve Engineering and Other Technological Disputes Before Arbitration," Report to 24th Congress of the ICC, Rio de Janeiro (May 1973).

Coproduction agreements, 490 (see also cooperation agreements)

Council for Mutual Economic Assistance (see Comecon)

Czechoslovkia (see Czechoslovak Socialist Republic)

Czechoslovak Socialist Republic, advertising, publicity, and exhibitions, 171, 173; assets of foreign trade organizations, 170; banking, 171, 173-174, 179-180; Chamber of Commerce, 171; codes, 176-177; companies register, 170; constitution, 169, 171; customs and tariffs, 170, 173; foreign exchange regulations, 174; foreign trade arbitration, 181-183; foreign trade contracts, 175-177; foreign trade institutions, 169-171; foreign trade management and planning, 170, 171-172; importing and exporting, 172; industrial cooperation, 172, 180-181; industrial property, 172, 177-179, 467-469; insurance, 171; international agreements, 173, 174, 178, 179, 182; licensing, 172, 180; representation of foreign companies, 172, 175; surveillance of goods and control services, 171; taxation, 179-180; transport, 171

East Germany (see German Democratic Republic)

East-West contracts, after-sales servicing, 459; cancellation, 453-454, 459; choice of law, 451-453, 459; custom, 459-460; export and import licences, 453; export financing, 458; force majeure, 453-454; guarantees, 455; inspection and testing, 455-456; nonperformance, 453-454; payment, 457-458, penalties, 455, 456-457, 458; socialist foreign trade contract practices, 450-451; translation, 458, 459-460 (see also individual country listings)

EEC (see European Community)

England (see United Kingdom)

European Community, agreements with third countries, 62-63; agricultural products, 68-69; changes and restrictions on imports and exports, 60-61; coal and steel, 69-70; common agricultural policy, 262; common commercial policy, 53 et seq; common customs tariff, 54 et seq; cooperation agreements, 65; customs duties, 54-55; customs legislation, 56-57; englargement of the community, 67; export promotion, 60-63; free circulation of goods, 65-67; legal remedies, 74-75; most-favored-nation treatment, 53; national bilateral agreements, 63-64; nuclear energy, 70-72; oil products and natural gas, 72; protocol on German internal trade, 68, 86; quotas and liberalization measures, 56-59; safeguard measures, 58-60; sensitive industrial products, 72 (see also Comecon)

Federal Republic of Germany, Eastern trade, 79-80; export credit programs, 90-91; regulation of imports and exports, 88-90; trade with German Democratic Republic, 79-87; treaty with German Democratic Republic, 86, 187

France, 251-252, 339, 545, 551, 554

GATT (see General Agreement on Tariffs and Trade)

General Agreement on Tariffs and Trade, 26-27, 31, 54-55, 59-62,

568

70, 73, 85, 106, 107, 174, 226-227, 251, 278, 363

German Democratic Republic, advertising, 196-197; Chamber of Foreign Trade, 187-188, 192, 210; codes, 197-199; constitution, 202; cooperation agreement with Montedison, 189; financial, banking, and credit, 189, 192-193, 195-196; foreign trade arbitration, 210-212; foreign trade contracts, 197-200; foreign trade institutions and agencies, 190-193; foreign trade planning, 190, 197; importing and exporting, 193-195; intellectual and industrial property, 200, 201-208, 208-209, 469-471; Leipzig fair, 196; international agreements, 187, 188-190, 194, 199-200, 201, 204, 209-210, 211; joint ventures, 189, licensing, 190, 200-201; local agents, 195-196; new economic policy, 188-189; production enterprises, 190-192; representation offices, 195-196; taxation, 201; trade representatives, 191; trade with Federal Republic of Germany, 187-188

Germany (see Federal Republic of Germany, German Democratic Republic)

Great Britain (see United Kingdom)

Hungarian People's Republic, accession to GATT, 226; access to Hungarian market, 228; agency companies, 223-224; authority to engage in foreign trade, 220-222; Chamber of Commerce, 224, 235, 241; cooperation agreements, 231-232; constitution, 219-221; control of foreign trade, 221-223; copyright, 235; credit, banking, and foreign exchange system,

227-228; customs and tariffs, 225-228; financial institutions, 220-221, 223-224, 227-228; foreign trade arbitration, 241-242; foreign trade contracts, 220-221, 229-231; foreign trade licensing system, 226-228; foreign trade organizations, 221-222, 222-223; industrial property, 235-237, 471-473; insurance, 224; international agreements, 225-226, 235, 241-242; joint ventures, 223-224, 232-233, 525-534; licensing, 236-241; national economic planning, 219-220, 224-225; quality control, 224; shipping services, 224; unfair competition, 235

Hungary (see Hungarian People's Republic)

Industrial cooperation (see Cooperation agreements and individual country listings)

Industrial property, 462-486 (see also individual country listings)

International Chamber of Commerce, 199, 227-228, 262, 303, 540-541, 544, 545-546, 547-548, 550, 552, 554-555

International Coordinating Committee on Trade with Communist Countries (see Cocom)

Japan, export of goods, 34-37; export of technology, 34; foreign exchange law, 33 et seq; import of goods, 38-41; import of technology, 37-38; outward direct equity investment, 33; trade with China, Eastern Europe, and USSR, 31-32, 41-42 (see also Arbitration)

Joint Research and Development, 492

279, 287, 290, 302-303, 303-304, joint ventures, 290-301, 525-534; licensing, 289-290; member of GATT, IBRD, and IMF, 278-279; most-favored-nation treatment, 281, 303; national economic planning and foreign trade, 273, 277-280, 283, 286; representation of foreign companies, 283-284; taxation, 284, 299-301, 303-304; Western access to local market, 283-285

Soviet Union (see USSR)

Specialization agreements, 490

Subcontracting, 491

Union of Soviet Socialist Republics (see USSR)

United Kingdom, arbitration, 108-111; bilateral agreements, 106-108; Department of Trade and Industry, 97-98; export controls, 99-101; Export Credit Guarantees Department, 98, 101-104; export insurance and guarantees, 101-104; import controls, 104-106

United Nations Economic Commission for Europe, general conditions, 199, 449-450, 454; rules of arbitration, 544, 545-546, 549, 551, 552-554

United States, agreement with USSR on financing procedures, 318; agricultural and shipping programs, 10-11; aid and investment programs, 12; Antidumping Act of 1921, 13; credit controls, 8-9, 17; Export-Import Bank, 4, 8-10, 13-14, 16; export licensing, 4-8, 16-17; Johnson Act, 8-9; lend lease settlement with USSR, 13-14; maritime agreement with USSR, 11, 13; most-favored-nation treatment 12-13, 14-17; Overseas Private Investment Corporation, 12;

tariffs, 12-13; trade accords with Poland, 16, 541, 544, 546-547, 554-555; trade agreement with USSR, 13-17; 315-316, 541, 544, 545, 546, 554-555; trade embargo, 4; Trade Reform Act of 1973, 15; trade with China, 3-4, 17

USSR, advertising, 319-320; banking and financial, 313, 316-318, 318-319, 329-330; certificates of authorship, 334-336, 477-478; Chamber of Commerce and Industry, 312, 333, 335; constitution, 311, 314, 320; cooperation agreement, 317; 338-339; copyright, 330-333, customs, and tariffs, 317; discoveries, 477; domestic contracts, 320-321, 324, 325-327; effects of State plan, 326-327; foreign trade arbitration, 313; 322, 323, 325-326, 328, 330, 339, 340-342, 540-541, 542, 547-548, 549, 551-552, 554-555, 556; foreign trade contracts, 320-330; foreign trade monopoly, 311-312, 314, 315; foreign trade organizations, 313, 320-323; foreign trade policy, 312; industrial designs, 336; industrial reform, 321; insurance, 314; intellectual and industrial property, 330-336, 477-479; international agreements, 311, 314, 315-316, 317-319, 330, 332, 333, 334, 338, 339-340, 342; inventions, 334-336, 477-479; joint ventures, 338, 339-340; legal status of foreign trade organizations, 327; licensing, 336; limitation of actions, 328; local agents, 320-321; Ministry of Foreign Trade, 312-313; most-favored-nation treatment, 317; New Economic Policy, 311; notarial acts, 323; patents, 334-336, 337-338; planning, 312, 316-317, 324;

ROBERT STARR is an American lawyer regularly involved in East-West business transactions and has lectured and written widely on this subject. Mr. Starr was formerly special assistant to the U. S. State Department's legal adviser, legal adviser to the U. S. Embassy in Saigon, and counsel to the President's Task Force on Communications Policy. He holds Doctor of Law degrees from the University of Chicago and the University of Aix-Marseilles, and a Master of Comparative Law degree from Chicago. Mr. Starr is a member of the Illinois and U. S. Supreme Court Bars and serves as Counsel to the Law Office Frank Boas in London. He is the representative of the U. S. National Association of Manufacturers on the International Chamber of Commerce's Liaison Committee with socialist countries. Mr. Starr is editor of an American Bar Association study, Business Transactions with the USSR, to be published in 1974.

Professor IVAN APOSTOLOV received his Law Degree at the University of Sofia and studied further in Switzerland, Germany, and Italy. From 1938 to 1950 he was professor at the University of Sofia, lecturing in Civil Law. Since 1950 he has been a member of the bar in Sofia. He is a member of the Law Council at the Ministry of Foreign Trade, an arbitrator at the Arbitration Court at the Bulgarian Chamber of Commerce, and the author of several works on contract law, comparative law, and commercial law.

JAY A. BURGESS—A.B., Brown University; M.A., University of Durham (England); J.D., University of Illinois—is a former Fulbright scholar to Bucharest (1969-70). He is a member of the State Bar of Michigan and the U.S. National Commission for UNESCO (executive committee) and currently of the Office of General Counsel, Agency for International Development, Washington, D.C.

PAUL A. CABLE, a partner in Whitman & Ransom, New York, is a graduate of Harvard Law School. He has lectured on private international law at Harvard Law School's East Asian Legal Center and at Practicing Law Institute, Hawaii State Bar Association, and Federal Publication Inc. seminars.

JAMES C. CONNER is presently senior counsel, International Finance Corporation, Washington, D.C. He was previously in private practice in Washington, D.C., and Philadelphia, specializing in international investment and trade matters. Mr. Conner was awarded an

LL.B. degree with specialization in International Affairs from Cornell University in 1958 and a Master of Comparative Law degree from the University of Chicago in 1961.

ANTHONY RICHARD DICKS has been a Lecturer in the Law Department of the School of Oriental and African Studies, University of London, since 1970 and is a member of the bars of England and Hong Kong. He was a Fellow in Chinese Law of the Institute of Current World Affairs, in New York, 1962-68, and visited China in 1965. From 1968 to 1970, he was a Fellow of Trinity Hall, Cambridge.

R. C. FISCHER received his LL.M. Degree from the University of Groningen, Netherlands, in 1954. From 1956 to 1958 he was a member of the bar in Amsterdam and since then has served as Legal Adviser to the Commission of the European Community.

KAZIMIERZ GRZYBOWSKI—LL.M. 1931, LL.D. 1934, University of Lwow (Poland); S.J.D. 1933, Harvard University—is professor of Law and senior research associate, Rule of Law Research Center, Duke University. He has written a number of studies on East-West legal questions.

Dr. KARL HEŘMAN is a graduate of the Prague School of Commerce (1949), postgraduate of the Prague School of Economics CSc. (1965), and lecturer of foreign trade economics (Doc. 1966). From 1945 to 1960 he was with foreign trade enterprises; from 1960 to 1971 in scientific research on foreign trade planning; from 1968 to 1969 UNIDO expert in Tunisia; and at present is with the Institute UTRIN in Prague.

HOWARD M. HOLTZMANN received a Doctor of Law Degree from Yale Law School in 1947 and is a member of the New York bar. He has lectured and written widely, particularly in the field of arbitration. Mr. Holtzmann is chairman of the board of the American Arbitration Association.

THOMAS W. HOYA has written and spoken widely on East-West trade. His articles have appeared in several legal periodicals including the Columbia Law Review, and he participated recently in the 1973 meeting of the American Society of International Law. Dr. Hoya spent a year in Moscow on the U.S.-USSR Academic Exchange, holds a J.S.D. from Columbia Law School, and is currently acting deputy chief counsel of the U.S. Office of Foreign Direct Investments.

Dr. E. M. JUCKER is a member of the Board of Management of Sandoz Ltd., Basle, and is in charge of the Patent Division.

Professor ALBERT KIRALFY—Ph.D., LL.M.—is Professor of Law at King's College, London University. He was a Visiting Exchange scholar in 1964 at the University of Leningrad and in 1970 at the University of Moscow. His publications include translations of the Russian Civil and Civil Procedure Codes and numerous articles on Soviet law in legal journals, encyclopedias, and composite works.

YORDAN LASKOV graduated from the Faculty of Law, Sofia University, "Kliment Ohridski," in 1952. In 1972 he was awarded a degree by the Institut Prumyslove Pravni Ochrany in Prague. He has practiced as a lawyer for more than 22 years. Mr. Laskov is author or co-author of many books and articles on international commercial law, foreign law, and industrial property.

AXEL LEBAHN studed at the Universities of Göttingen, Freiburg, and Tübingen (where he received a Doctor of Laws) and did postgraduate study in European law at Strasbourg. He was at the cabinet of the vice president of the Commission of the European Communities in Brussels, has done research work on Soviet international economic law in Moscow, and is scientific collaborator at the Institute for International Law, Göttingen.

JULIAN D. M. LEW graduated with an LL.B. (hons.) from the University of London in 1969 and was called to the bar by the Middle Temple in 1970, where he is a practicing barrister-at-law. He is the lecturer in private international and international commercial law at the City of London Polytechnic and academic member of the Centre Charles De Vischer pour le Droit International, Université Catholique de Louvain, Belgium.

JOHN R. LIEBMAN—A.B. Dartmouth College, J.D. University of California—is a member of the California and New York bars. He specialized in international trade matters with the Los Angeles law firm of Diamond, Tilem, Colden & Emery and was associated previously with the Agency for International Development, U.S. Department of State.

DRAGO MAROLT was with the Yugoslav Federal Trade Commissioner in Los Angeles until October 1973. He now resides in Ljubljana. Mr. Marolt holds degrees in law and economics from the University of Ljubljana and was formerly Executive Vice President, United Paper Mills in Ljubljana.

JAMES R. OFFUTT is presently attorney and Counsel to the Board of Directors, Overseas Private Investment Corporation, Washington, D.C. He was previously in private practice in Washington, D.C., specializing in tax, corporate, and legislative matters. He received the J.D. from Georgetown University in 1967.

CLIFFORD A. RATHKOPF, Jr., practices law in the London Office of Donovan Leisure Newton & Irvine of New York and is a member of the New York bar. He graduated cum laude from Columbia Law School and received his LL.M. from Georgetown Law Center and the Institut für auslandisches und internationales Wirtschaftsrecht at the Goethe Universität, Frankfurt am Main.

Professor LOTHAR J. SCHULTZ, Dr. jur., Dr. phil., Universities of Riga, Prague, and Paris, has previously been Assistant Professor, Faculty of Law, University of Riga; Associate Professor holding the Professorial chair, University of Riga; and Reader, University of Göttingen. Since 1964 he has been Professor of East European Law at Göttingen.

Dr. H. STREITZIG studied in Vienna and Graz (Austria) and obtained his doctorate of philosophy in 1957. In 1960 he joined the Insitut International des Brevets in the Hague, and since 1964 he has been with Sandoz Ltd., Basle.

Dr. JOSEPH VARRÓ, LL.D., studied at the Faculty of Law of Budapest University, and in 1935 was awarded his doctorate of law. He has been a legal practitioner-solicitor. From 1950 to 1968 he was a leading legal adviser of state-owned foreign trade companies, and since 1968 he has been the Head of the Office for International Business Law of the Hungarian Chamber of Commerce.

RELATED TITLES
Published by
Praeger Special Studies

CRISIS IN SOCIALIST PLANNING:
Eastern Europe and the USSR
                    Jan Marczewski

EAST AND WEST GERMANY:
A Comparative Economic Analysis
                    Martin Schnitzer

INDUSTRIAL MANAGEMENT: EAST AND WEST:
Papers from the International Economic Association Conference on Labor Productivity 1971
                    edited by Aubrey Silbertson
                    and Francis Seton

THE POTENTIAL FOR JOINT VENTURES
IN EASTERN EUROPE
                    Robert S. Kretschmar, Jr.
                    and Robin Foor

THE SOVIET ECONOMY IN REGIONAL
PERSPECTIVE
                    edited by V. N. Bandera
                    and Z. L. Melnyk

SOVIET FOREIGN TRADE: Organization,
Operations, and Policy, 1918-1971
                    Glen Alden Smith

TRADE WITH CHINA: Assessments by
Leading Businessmen and Scholars
                    Patrick M. Boarman and
                    Jayson Mugar

U.S. AGRICULTURE IN A WORLD CONTEXT:
Policies and Approaches for the Next Decade
                    edited by D. Gale Johnson
                    and John A. Schnittker

YUGOSLAVIA'S FOREIGN TRADE: A Study
of State Trade Discrimination
                    Ryan C. Amacher